In memory of Thomas James Morrison

ACKNOWLEDGEMENTS

All texts share in contingency and the desires of their writers, stimulated by various interactions and experiences. This text is no exception.

The field work on Juvenile Justice teams which began this project was funded by a small grant from the External System Legal Research Fund administered by the Institute of Advanced Legal Studies, London. Ann Marie Gayle served as temporary research assistant. During the course of preparing this text I have been aided by the unstinting support of Terence Kelly, whose close reading of drafts of this text saved me from many mistakes and inspired improvements, and in other forms by Juliana Georgiadis. I thank Julie Herd at QMW for typing tapes and other sections when my word-processing fingers threatened to give out, and Kate Nicol of Cavendish for making copious last minute changes to the manuscript. The longest standing personal debt is owed to Eryl Hall Williams who has been a constant source of encouragement since I was a Phd student several years ago. A number of people, but particularly Nils Christie, Monika Plateck and Tonia Tzannetakis have helped fashion my opinions. I have been moved by the writings of James K Baxter and the new forms of urban poetry exampled by Snakes and Apples. Finally, this text would not have taken on much of its ambitions if not for a certain interaction with Parosha Chandran. Her own post-modernism seeps into many of its pages.

Ultimately, however, while the stimulations which inform this text's creation owe much to others, responsibility for the faults of its reality must rest with me.

Wayne Morrison

March 1995

THEORETICAL CRIMINOLOGY:
from modernity
to post-modernism

Wayne Morrison, LLB, LLM, PhD,
Barrister and Solicitor (New Zealand)
Senior Lecturer in Law
Queen Mary & Westfield College

Cavendish
Publishing
Limited

London • Sydney

First published in Great Britain 1995 by Cavendish Publishing Limited,
The Glass House, Wharton Street, London WC1X 9PX

Telephone: 0171-278 8000   Facsimile: 0171-278 8080

British Library Cataloguing in Publication Data

Morrison, W
Theoretical Criminology: from modernity to post-modernism
I Title II.
344.205

ISBN 1-85941-220-3

PREFACE

This is not a textbook in the traditional sense. Once criminological textbooks could be written in good conscience – they were a rather tedious lot made possible by a diverse set of assumptions (many of which are explored in this text, such as eurocentricity, positivism, a belief in progress, and the mirror of nature thesis). As criminology became more theoretically sophisticated and reflexive in the 1960s and 1970s, those assumptions became questioned and the discipline lost its pretence of coherence, splitting into a range of perspectives.

Criminology has no need to recreate or experience a longing for textbooks which present writings without any attempt to integrate various schemes or contextualise the act of writing. Such a text is either a babble of discourse or a sleeping pill. However, as the concept of a textbook has rightly vanished, so to, it seems, has the idea of grand theorising. Conversely this text is an attempt to lay out a framework for theorising in criminology – it sets out a narrative of the development of criminological theory in terms of central themes in the rise and intensification of modernity.

The text has several interacting layers

- It can be read as a lengthy response to the thesis of Gottfredson and Hirschi (1990) that the secret to explaining crime lies in defining criminality in terms of the varying amounts of self-control individuals possess. Self-control is indeed central, but the position is much more complicated that Gottfredson and Hirschi envisage. To explain this the current text takes up those writers own, albeit undeveloped, proposition that any theory of crime must be a theory of the social order. To this end it has a second function.

- To position criminological theorising within a narrative of the changing themes and social structures of modernity – criminological theorising is both a reflection of, and an attempt to understand, features of the changing forms of modernity. This reading not only allows us to see criminological theory in a different light but also allows us to develop a particular theory of crime; a theory inspired by existentialism in which we seek out the criminogenic processes involved in modernity and post-modernism. This theory provides the third layer.

- The theory holds that a dominant focal point of the social structural changes of modernity and its cultural messages is the creation of self-controlling and self-directing individuals. Individuals who are called upon to relate to the world as an environment to control and fashion to their own ends. Modernity creates an ideal type of self-possessive individuality which is able to cope with a de-naturalised modern life and the multiple expectations demanded by an increasingly complex and differentiated social structure. Not all can live up to this ideal. Reduced to a caricature of itself, the theory presents a similar structure to Merton's (1938, 1957) classic strain theory, that of the tension between the dominate cultural demands and the uneven social-structural position of individuals. Whereas, however, Merton proposed the dominant messages of monetary success and class mobility, this text proposes cultural images of self-possession, self-creation, self-esteem, and self-motivation, which are held out as the driving force behind the various life-projects individuals are encouraged to pursue, while the social structure unevenly distributes the kinds of capital (economic, social and human) which are involved in the creation of this ideal modern person. However, the theory is not a simple redevelopment of strain, since it re-reads control theory in terms of enabling bonds; the freedom at stake in modernity always exists in a dialectic with discipline. Much of the research traditionally conducted under the positivist umbrella of searching for the constitutional features of the offender can be read as indicating processes and events which can reduce or increase the various forms of capital the late-modern individual can trade with in the games of contemporary life. Those with high degrees of capital will find success – those who are keyed into the system have little need to resort to crime and much to lose (in Bauman's words they are seduced) – while those who are phased out (and we use the concept of the underclass and changing forms of economic production to describe this feature) are increasingly subjected to surveillance and repression.

To become self-defining is the fate that the social structure of late-modernity imposes upon its socially created individuality. The individual is called into action; actions which are meant to express his/her self and enable the individual's destiny to be created out of the contingencies of his/her past. But to paraphrase Marx, while individuals make their own choices they do not do so in conditions of their own choosing. The settings of late-modernity emphasize the contingency of the resources informing the mechanisms of choice in the vast market-place of goods, ideas, styles, opportunities, and representations the individual is surrounded by. And while resources differ, all are subjected to variations of a similar pressure as modernity moves into post-modernism, namely that of the overburdening of the self as the self becomes the ultimate source of security. The tasks asked of the late-modern person require high degrees of social and technical skills. To control the self and guide it through the disequilibrium of the journeys of late modernity is the task imposed upon the late-modern person, but what if the life experiences of the individual have not fitted him/her with this power? This text proposes that much crime is an attempt of the self to create sacred moments of control, to find ways in which the self can exercise control and power in situations where power and control are all too clearly lodged outside the self.

A note on the terminology of modernity, post-modernism and post-modernity. A debate concerning post-modernism has been raging for some time in the literature of the social sciences; criminology has been slow to catch on. The questions raised are not mere terminological issues. Has modernity given way to post-modernity? If so what is it? While it is apparent that we have experienced vast changes in recent decades it is not the case that we have entered into a new domain. In particular post-modernity could be defined as the time when we lost confidence in the projects of modernity, but doubts were always part of being modern. Instead of a radical break it is more apt to define post-modernism as the intensification and multiplication of trends and features of modernism occurring simultaneously within modernity while denoting the problematising and ambivalence of modernity. Thus while I contend that we live in processes we can call post-modernism there has not been some grand transformation into a post-modernity. We live within modernity but at a distance from the assumptions which gave it security, which made modernity appear 'natural'. It is therefore possible to talk of ourselves as living in late-modernity, or the post-modern condition, or post-modernism, but not to talk of our inhabiting post-modernity.

Talk of post-modernity or post-modernism has often appeared abstract. Conversely, this text argues it is the lived reality of our being. The text was energised by field research conducted on various Social Service Juvenile Justice teams carrying out community sanctions with young people. Various projects were visited and a number of staff and young offenders interviewed: while I have only reproduced sections of the interviews, two themes stood out: (i) the concentration by Juvenile Justice team members upon what we might call everyday technologies (as opposed to the client-orientated therapy deriving from Rogers (1951)) of the self – their routine tasks were aimed at deriving boundaries around the everyday activities of the offenders, at building the self-esteem of offenders and enabling the offender to cope with the pressures of everyday life without resort to crime (although the staff were conscious of success – the reality of a developing underclass, of client families known for decades to social services, the staff only retained a professional task through a 'principle of methodological optimism'); (ii) the degree to which the discourse of the young offenders mirrored not a reference to stability or equilibrium, but the confusing and pulsating world so central to the images of radical differentiation in post-modernist descriptions of social structure.

While self-control and self-expression have always been a minor concern of criminological theory, its centrality in recent conservative criminology is not accidental. The radical differentiation of social spheres (predicted in the classical sociology of Durkheim as the fate of modernity) so apparent in the social theory of Niklas Luhman (1986), positions the individual as the site of multiple messages, as the intersection of various codes and communicative technologies. Messages and codes which stimulate and faciliate the dialectics of desire and action. The accounts of the young offenders indicate the impossibility of satisfying the melange of desires experienced. The world depicted is one of perpetual entrapment in conditions of stimulated desire and images of an abundance of material goods, with a scarcity of the means of obtaining them. However, while relative poverty and a feeling of absence (of deprivation) shine through their accounts – we are apt to lose sight of Marx and Engels' 19th century message that man must be in a position to live in order to make history, and that life involves, before everything else, eating and drinking, a habitation, clothing and many other things – it is also clear that resentment at exclusion from sites of obvious consumption, so clearly packaged in the communications media but also apparent in the significations of class visible throughout the city (buildings expressing power, BMWs etc), is a motivating factor. While Eysenck would present us with the image of hoards of cortically under-aroused individuals roaming our streets looking for excitement, accounts by young offenders indicate the radical distance involved in the contemporary city between groups geographically close but distant in terms of meaning (for a published series of accounts by young offenders see Graef, 1992). At stake are dilemmas involved in fashion, display, spectacle and the illusion that the self controls the practices and interests operative in the demands for self-definition.

The post-modernist talk of the world becoming 'a plurality of heterogeneous spaces and temporalities' (Heller and Feher, 1988: 1) may appear strange to some, but young offenders are clear: 'You don't live in my world'. And it is implicit in their accounts; as, for example, when one matter-of-factly states:

> 'when you [referring to the author] go down a street you only see cars and houses ... I see opportunity ... Within five minutes I can tell you how many cars have their boots unlocked and windows unbolted ... just by looking ... I look behind what's there.' (Morrison: Fieldnotes)

But this is a special kind of look. When a young offender claims (with reference to stealing from cars and joy-riding): 'I don't hurt people I only deal with things', he does not simply speak the language of Sykes and Matza's (1961) techniques of neutralisation, but offers a comment on the degree to which objects (such as cars, wallets, bikes, goods in shops) can circulate without connection to their human 'owners'.

Multiple realities, attention to the surface, interaction with a world which takes on the semblance of the imaginary – but behind which lurks the cold reality of victimisation – is simply the way contemporary life is lived. While academics may debate the meaning of post-modernism, and wonder if it actually has arrived, young offenders live it out.

If the offender is helped into crime by this non-identification of the victim behind the goods, the same processes inform the growing displacement of the underclass into another world. The homeless on the streets of London or New York, the depiction of the drug trafficker as the new evil menace, and the abstraction of the criminal into sentencing tables, mean a crimin-o-logy can be constructed as if no real persons were involved, since this highlighting of the other in no way requires that we notice what the 'other' is actually like. To paraphrase Durkheim and John Stuart Mill, tolerence is the virtue of a liberal society which knows interdependency, but what happens to tolerence when the society has no need for sections of its population?

Both the victim and the criminal (the underclass) are effectively denied a face (one strand of post-modern ethical concern is founded on the concern with the face found in the writing of Emmanuel Levinas, 1988), since in late-modernity we have no need to meet and interact with the 'other' beyond the routinised methodologies of (non)communication. As post-modern cities develop, even public space is in danger of becoming privatised.

It is difficult to make sense of much of the contemporary world, thus we come to the dangerous ambiguity involved in the post-modern movement. Some have referred to post-modernism as the disappearance of meaning, as the impossibility of attributing labels and qualities correctly in the face of the reflexive questions of our times. We have so much history and so much information that no innocence is possible. This is true but no reason for cynical despair, nor for abandonning the hopes for rational discourse in favour of a privatised universe of speech in which only the loudest or the best backed get a hearing. While post-modernism announces potential liberation in the destruction (deconstrunction) of the modernist structures of binary oppositions (reason-unreason, male-female, white-black, normal-deviant) it confronts us all with the risks of a splintering of the world into competing domains at a time of immense powers and little criteria of how to use and relate to them. While this text cannot provide the answers it can at least offer a narative of how we have come to be, and highlight various features of, 'how we find ourselves'.

CONTENTS

Contents

Contents

Contents

Contents

Contents

Contents

Contents

Contents

CHAPTER ONE

NARRATING THE MOOD OF THE TIMES: CONFUSION, SELF-DOUBT, AND AMBIVALENCE?

'So hard to focus the ball of the human eye
On our terrible Mother, that stone Medusa
Sitting on her hill of skulls – suicides, abortions,
Gang-splashes, bloodstained mattresses, a ton of empty pill
bottles,
And whatever else the wind may blow in the doorway,
including, one may hope, the tired dove
Of the human spirit, raped again and again in the skyway
By the mechanical hawk. So hard for us to praise
The century of Kali – since a poem has to celebrate
Its moment of origin. As yet I am only able
To smile a little, and say, 'Not yet, not yet, Mother!
You must wait till I have bought the right kind of sawblade
'To turn the top of my skull into a drinking cup, –
Then begin! Things have to be done in the right order.'
(James K Baxter, extract from *Letter to Peter Olds*, 1980: 578)

Finding places, finding time, finding beginnings ...

This book should start in a sensible fashion; but where? In what sort of mood should it commence? What is the time and where is the place that we begin from?

We could begin in a mood of contentment, perhaps even joy. Things, on the whole, appear finc for those of us who live in the west. In fact we have never enjoyed so many goods and opportunities. There are some problems with the world ... but domestically progress seems stable if only wages for labour can be cut to ensure a competitive product, etc. John Kenneth Galbraith has recently analysed the mood of the influential groups in the US and Europe in terms of a *Culture of Contentment* (1992), warning that such a culture is short sighted, and is detrimental to long term social stability and health. In particular he argues that the economically fortunate and those aspiring-to-be have a strong electoral position (since those who are not gaining from the system tend not to vote), and control large portions of the media; they oppose public expenditure except where they personally stand to gain; they attack attempts to regulate corporate raiders, property speculators or junk bond dealers, yet if disaster strikes, as when a bank fails, they demand immediate action. The contented seem to believe that others in society only fail for lack of effort, or for deficiencies of their constitution such as low IQ, and thus argue that payments for welfare and public infrastructure should be reduced in real terms. This contentment places future social harmony horribly at risk. It involves a collective refusal to look seriously at the problems of the discontented.

Or, we could begin in melancholy. This appears to be the mood of many intellectuals, particularly those who speak of the coming of a post-modern society. It is a hard mood to describe. Elsewhere I have tried to locate the current mood of criminology within such a post-modern and melancholia frame (Morrison, 1994). The feeling is best summed up by a conception that something has been lost from human endeavour, that the great social projects – liberalism, socialism, communism, radical democracy, nationalism in the third world – have lost their energy as the hopes held out for them in earlier times have been compromised by reality.

Or, we could begin with depression. Things are bad, very bad world wide with social chaos threatening and bad for a lot of people in the west. There are record numbers under psychiatric counselling, drug abuse aids in the wrecking of many people's lives, unemployment climbs and climbs (kept in check only by various changes in the way statistics are compiled); the only growth industry appears to be in prison building and private security.

And our recent history? Two world wars, a third which would have been totally destructive prevented by weapons of such power that using them would have been MAD (mutual assured destruction). Instead we have fought numerous wars by proxy ... and we remember the holocaust.

There are so many books, and articles, and TV shows, and films, we are threatened with drowning in this sea of communication. Images, messages, and interconnections ... Naomi Campbell's image everywhere, and where she isn't there are books which remind us that the beauty of the architecture we are surrounded by in Bristol and London was built in significant part on the basis of the slave trade in Africans ... books which tell us that the contentment of the west is built upon the exploitation of the third world ... articles which tell us that while we may be afraid of street crime, we are really being ripped off by the vast world of unreported and unpunished corporate and white collar crime ... The impossibility of escaping from images ... TV... where does the real world begin and spectacle end? ... what's real and what is imaginary?

What does it all add up to? We need criteria ... big criteria ... big enough to differentiate between kinds of information, between kinds of knowledge, between varying perceptions ... Big enough to escape an inhuman emotivism. Big enough to tell us what are real crimes and what are not, who are the criminals and who are not.

Journeys, snippets ... modernisations

This text takes up the theme of a journey ... Where are we? Over 200 years ago with all the flush of 18th century optimism Saint-Simon declared:

> 'The Golden Age of the human race is not behind us but before us; it lies in the perfection of the social order. Our ancestors never saw it; our children will one day arrive there, it is for us to clear the way.' (1952: 68)

We are those children – are we at the place foreseen? That is one question of this text ... also the attempt to ask, what does it mean to think like this ... what words should we use? One key word that will infuse this text will be *modernity*. What does it mean? By its nature the term is vague, Chapter two shall attempt to define it, but for now we can see it as denoting a grand construction project – the attempt to build the good society; post-modernity is the realisation that the construction has fallen apart.

Our part in this? Crime is read as the most obvious sign of this disintegration. Why study crime? Crime is both an example and a result of immediate and pressing concerns. The first motivation which drives criminology is the feeling that crime is a serious social problem and this reflects for some a feeling that our modern societies are 'out of control' in certain key respects. The existence of such a social problem is also problematic in an important second respect, in that it offends against certain cultural assumptions of modern western societies. Put another way, the cultural underpinning of the confidence of the modern west relies upon certain cultural assumptions, such as 'progress', prosperity and the power of social engineering; mushrooming official crime rates taunts these, showing their falseness, exposing the weakness of modernity.

In the US the Final report of the President's Task Force on Victims of Crime in 1982 stated:

> 'Something insidious has happened in America: crime has made victims of us all. Awareness of its danger affects the way we think, where we live, where we go, what we buy, how we raise our children, and the quality of our lives as we age. The spectre of violent crime and the knowledge that, without warning, any person can be attacked or crippled, robbed, or killed, lurks at the fringes of consciousness. Every citizen of this country is more impoverished, less free, more fearful, and less safe, because of the ever present threat of the criminal. Rather than alter a system that has proven itself incapable of dealing with crime, society has altered itself.' (1982: vi)

The presence of so much desperation and social unrest complicates the notion that modernity would create 'good' or 'grand' societies of peaceful co-existence and economic plenty, in which the conditions for harmonious social co-existence would be achieved. But the present ... How can we characterise the present? In the mid 1970s Bell was clear:

> 'If the natural world is ruled by fate and chance, and the technical world by rationality and entropy, the social world can only be characterised as existing in fear and trembling.'

While the leading Australian criminologist, John Braithwaite, was ambivalent about the prospects for criminology:

> '[Contemporary] Criminologists are pessimists and cynics. There seem good reasons for this. Our science has largely failed to deliver criminal justice policies that will prevent crime. The grand 19th century utilitarian doctrines – deterrence, incapacitation, rehabilitation – are manifest failures. The return to classicism in criminology – the just deserts movement – has been worse than a failure. It has been a disastrous step backwards.' (1992: 1)

Should we be in a good mood or bad, has modern society progressed? It's getting hard to tell. Bauman (1991) has defined *post-modernity as modernity taking a long look at itself* and being confused at what it sees. What has it all amounted to? What has this task of becoming modern been all about? Thus we face a crisis of confidence ... a lack of direction ... a demand for directions ... a crisis of law and order.

Although crisis may have always been a term used by those deeply embedded in the complex flows of social ordering of their contemporary society, the driving force for the post-modern condition seems a sense of bewilderment and ambivalence. It has become difficult even to define the nature of the problem.

The problem of the modern world

The German social theorist Friedrich Nietzsche best expressed the problem of the modern world as our growing perception of the death of God. God's death left a huge void. As Morse Peckham put it: 'in Medieval European thought, the epistemological authority was the word of God as revealed through the teachings of the Roman Church' (1962: 8). Writing towards the end of the 19th century Nietzsche was perplexed. Surely the whole scheme of rational and critical intellectual enquiries which Europe had thrown up in the 17th and 18th centuries had removed any rational basis for belief in God? The foundations of modern thought needed to be thought anew. But while this period had seen important thinkers – Hobbes, Hegel, Marx, Montesquieu, Rousseau, Saint-Simon, Comte, David Hume, Adam Smith, Jeremy Bentham, to name a few – Europe appeared not to have succeeded in the radical revaluation of values, the wholesale redevelopment of its institutions, beliefs and aspirations which Nietzsche believed were necessary to avoid a forthcoming social disaster.

Without such a revaluation Nietzsche feared that nihilism or meaninglessness would overtake the world. For without God how could there be ultimate answers to the fundamental questions of existence? If we really face up to the fact that God was dead what will become of man? Indeed ... what is man? Where did he come from? What gives his existence meaning? What will make him happy? What should structure his relationships with his fellow humans? What is the aim of social life? What is the point to his desires? What gives his life purpose? What ensures frustration? What is the basis of concepts such as guilt, tolerance, good and evil? What is the phenomological reality of his behaviour? What, for example, is a crime? What or who is a criminal? Is the criminal to be loved as a strong man or feared? Is he a social rebel actually to be encouraged, or despised as a socially retarded individual?

We are 100 years on from Nietzsche's bitter discussion of God's death. In the 1990s, for most westerners, God is a memory from more certain times or something to tell the children to believe in to aid socialisation. Occasionally the odd Conservative politician will argue that the fact that we no longer fear suffering in Hell is the cause of the rise in crime, but, by and large, God has been replaced by science, hedonism and the 'care of the self'. Modern westerners live, not so that someday they can gain entrance into heaven and exist in God's grace, but to make a success of their own lives – so that they achieve things for themselves. Science, technology, research institutes, the welfare state, human rights, the United Nations, McDonalds, the world cup, mortgages, holidays in the sun, exercise regimes and cosmetic surgery, all are more important than religion.

Whom do we obey in our daily lives? We do not obey God's will, God's commands – and while we may obey or follow the commands of others, parents, friends, bosses, throughout modern life it is the law that we are principally called upon to obey; the law and the state. It is the state that organises, the state that we appeal to for change ... for legislation ... And of the masses of legal regulation which constitutes our modern socio-political framework, it is the criminal law which appears to cut closest to our interests in personal security and the protection of our property. Those who do not obey the criminal law are criminals. And we have a science, criminology, which investigates why crimes are committed and what to do with those individuals who commit crimes. It is tempting to claim that belief in God has been replaced by faith in reason and science. Criminology claims the status of the rational and scientific attempt to study the phenomena of crime. It was born with the death of God. It was meant to aid in the journey, the construction of a secure modernity, its presence offered confidence and its discourse solace:

> 'The surest sign that a society has entered into the secure possession of a new concept is that a new vocabulary will be developed, in terms of which the new concept can then be publicly articulated and discussed.' (Skinner, Quentin, 1978: vol 1 xii–xiii)

Thus a different definition can be given: criminology is the attempt to produce a coherent and productive vocabulary to delineate and comprehend certain aspects of the social world loosely grouped around the concept of crime.

What is criminology currently? The simple answer is to look at the word: crim-o-logos – the logos, or rational speech, concerning crime. What makes human society possible is language, discourse. Criminology is the discourse concerning crime and the methods by which society deals with crime. Given such a topic it is not surprising that criminology is a blanket label covering a large set of discourses and diversity of material; material which may at times verge on the political, the sociological and philosophical, the rhetorical and the technical. But can this material be read as having a central core, a coherent domain? Or is it totally unstable, a mass of perspectives which tease the reader of an article into thinking that the discourse encountered has sense but negates this as soon as various other articles are read? There is another tension between treating criminology as a special discipline in its own right with its own topic, that is the analysis of crime, and regarding criminology as a synthesis of social sciences (such as jurisprudence, sociology, anthropology, psychology) which themselves may be uncertain as to their own constitution. (After all what is sociology? does it contain politics and economics? Where does social geography fit?)

Reflexivity, and the principle of the recognisability of the world

Modern western societies are reflexive. They constantly ask themselves questions. People are paid, in government think-tanks, in universities, in the media, to ask questions and to reflect upon social processes. Their questions and the attempts to answer them, are recorded in language – but since language is a social cultural product it is a socially constructed grid of understanding. The various attempts to understand the modern world are part of the social process which constitute modernity. For a long time the search for knowledge presupposed that the world was easily recognisable to man's intellectual tools, reason and observation. But recently we understand that the social sciences constantly move in what is termed an hermeneutical circle. The human sciences are human cultural enterprises attempting to understand human cultural enterprises – they cannot produce absolute certainty since that would require some place outside the circle from which to judge pure truth.

Because we are locked into society, because our journey of knowledge occurs within the journey of our societies, we cannot know things about society with absolute certainty – the 'truths' of the social sciences are interpretative. But we need concepts, we need to clarify and analyse our linguistic products. They define the objects we bump into, they lay out the meaning of the courses of action we undertake. As the contemporary Scottish social theorist Alasdair MacIntyre put it:

> '... the limits of action are the limits of description, the delineation of a society's concepts is therefore the crucial step in the delineation of its life.' (1962, 62-3)

It is no wonder then, that in the 200 or so years that some form of criminology has been in existence controversy has raged over the *meaning* of its basic concepts.

The subject matter of criminology is inherently contestable

It may appear strange to begin a book with an admission of confusion but criminology is a subject with a complicated history and a set of polemic arguments about its fundamental subject-matter. Traditionally, the simplest definition has been to define criminology as 'the scientific study of crime and offenders'. As Hermann Mannheim defined it:

> '... criminology means the study of crime ... Provisionally, we may define crime in legal terms as human behaviour which is punishable by the criminal law.' (1965: 3)

This legalistic perspective has been the accepted definition of crime since at least Blackstone in the 1760s:

'A crime ... is an act committed, or omitted, in violation of a public law, either forbidding or commanding it.' (Jones, G ed, 1973: 189)

Law creates its own ontology. But if a crime is something which is solely the creation of law, how can a thorough going social science study it? Surely a social science should control its own basic central core?

Thus, such a definition which, we may note, has basically survived as the foundation of criminology, soon becomes subjected to a whole set of qualifications. There has been and still exists a debate whether the subject–matter of criminology should be restricted to conventional legal definitions of crime, adopt a sociological lens focusing upon 'deviance', or some form of moral-political conception of socially injurious conduct. Since the advent of the Labelling theory perspective in criminology in the 1960s, the issues of linkages and interconnections between the role of the state and the definition of crime, between attaining knowledge about the causes of crime, policy applications, and the punishment question, are hotly debated and complex in their nature.

Reflexivity has meant that criminologists spend a great deal of time and effort pulling apart the apparent simplicity of the definition of criminology as 'the scientific study of crime'. The definition opens up a range of questions concerning issues:

- of motivation, ie why study crime?
- of definition, ie what is a crime?
- of the relationship between crime and offenders, in other words, to what extent can the problem of crime be reduced to the problem of criminals?
- of identification, ie who, or what, is actually the criminal?
- of methodology, ie what is the scientific method?
- of application, ie is criminology a disinterested subject, or one tied to quite specific policy concerns?
- of boundaries, ie is there a clearly defined limit to criminology, or are all questions relating to the creation of criminal labels, of the response to such categories and the understanding of human behaviour, acceptable as part of the field?
- of meaning, ie does explaining crime necessarily mean entering into a general social theory?

How is criminology presented? How are criminological texts structured?

Most criminological texts are organised so as to present a history of criminology, and organised as if criminology had a coherent history which progressed, step by step, improving upon the simpler theories of the past. Until the 1970s this history was written with the assumptions of humanitarianism, progress and efficiency. The past was being overcome, the future was being constructed –

criminology was providing knowledge to build the good society. If history is progressive then greater weight must be placed on what comes later in time; the past is the repository of myths and mistakes. Moreover, all effort is cooperatively proceeding towards an end, the realisation of a rational programme of improvement, production of knowledge, education and emancipation. Criminology was playing its part in the civilising of man, in the production of a new, more advanced way of social life.

This comfortable image fell into despair in the 1970s and 1980s. Things which had been relegated to the past, such as the classical approach to crime (or, indeed, pure constitutional theories) were back on the agenda. Here criminology could not be divided from general trends in the social sciences and culture. This is part of the crisis of modernity. In one definition, modernity ends when it is no longer possible to believe that history is moving in a progressive uni-linear fashion. Then things appear to repeat themselves, and we are assailed with growing support for patterns of belief modernity thought of as traditional, tribal, or irrational. Thus, human events cannot be simply read as making up a uni-linear continuum; social organisation cannot be read as proceeding towards a goal. Instead it is realised that these ideas only made sense when certain fundamental assumptions were in place, when a central ideal of man and society was placed as the criterion of value. Inherently this was the ideal of the civilised, liberal European-American.

Instead of a progressive history we can better present several periods of criminology.

Classicism

The first set of writings we consider as criminology are labelled classical criminology and date from the later 18th century. These had depicted the lawyer as the important person on this planet. It was not, as the later Italian school was to claim, that classical criminology was unscientific, far from it. Classical criminology adopted a certain reading of the sciences of man but simply left the ultimate questions unanswered. It did not matter what was the ultimate cause of human behaviour, the task was to find ways to control and direct it via affecting rational motivation. The underlying social conditions of crime were less important, what was important was administration. The task was to free society from arbitrary authority, to open up the society so that basic true forms of the human condition could be visible. Crime was a concept of demarcation; an inevitable fact of the social condition; law would be an instrument of rational government.

Positivism in the 19th century

In the late 19th century the medical doctor Cesare Lombroso claimed that the answers to crime were to be found in a particular scientific approach called positivism. In particular Lombroso laid claim to found a new science – the science of criminology. Lombroso's answer to the problems of human behaviour lay specifically in biology; but in wider terms we can see it as arguing that all things which occur on earth can be explained by a naturalist paradigm. Man was a well developed animal and the processes of the natural selection of individuals for survival in a complex world threw up variations which were simply predestined to crime. Henceforth the priest and the lawyer/judge were to be replaced by the scientific expert. The mysteries of life had become mere problems for the scientist to remedy.

In the early development of positivism, crime was viewed as a natural problem to be cured, similar to a disease

Consider the language and the implications of the concepts used in the following extract. It is from a 1935 introduction to criminology written by the marxist writer Willem Bonger.

'We have to deal, indeed, with an extensive and deeply-rooted social disease, which has dug itself into the very body of society like a kind of ulcer; at times even threatening its very existence, but always harmful in the highest degree. Countless crimes are committed, and millions of criminals condemned, every year. Economically, the disadvantages to society are very great ... I think it is undeniable that crime is a source of stupendous waste of money to society. Next to the economic, we have, moreover, the still more important moral disadvantages. If criminality is closely bound up with the moral standards of a people, in return it sends out demoralising influences towards the normal sections of the population. And when one adds to all this the damage and grief suffered by the victims of the crime, and also the constant menace which criminality constitutes to society, the total obtained is already a formidable one. Neither ought we to forget the suffering on the part of the criminal himself, who – in whatever way one may wish to judge him, is after all, a part of humanity too.

The reasons for the study of criminology should therefore be clear. Admittedly it is a science which is widely studied for its own sake, just like other sciences; crime and criminals are not a bit less interesting than stars or microbes. The element of *la science pour la science* should be present in every scientist, otherwise he will be no good in his profession; and this applies to the criminologist too. But this point of view is secondary as compared with the practical aspect, just as in the case of medical science. Indeed, comparison with the latter repeatedly suggests itself. Criminology ought before anything to show humanity the way to combat, and especially, prevent, crime. What is required more than anything is sound knowledge, whereas up to the present we have had far too much of dogma and dilettantism.' (1936: 5-7).

The confidence espoused by positivist criminology to solve the problem of crime waned with the advent of labelling theory, and the increases in crime of the late 1960s. There are various reasons. One was a reassessment of the nature of criminological discourse which came about with the labelling perspective in the 1960s. We came to ask can we trust criminology? Is the principle of the recognisability of the world correct? Is there any firm relationship between the word and the world? This became a key question. Is the scientific status, and our acceptance of the ontological entities criminology deals with, warranted? For example are its sources of knowledge truthful, what is the accuracy level of criminal statistics – can theories be based upon these sources of knowledge?

A crucial area of conflict has been, to what does the concept of crime refer?

For much of its history criminology has accepted the legalistic definition of crime as human behaviour which is punishable by sanctions specified by the criminal law. This automatic linkage between crime, the criminal law and liability for punishment has not been universally accepted by criminologists (in part because what can be defined as a crime by the powerful agencies of the state varies over time and place). The struggle to find a method by which the criminologist could scientifically define an object of study (crime, deviance), has been an ongoing feature of criminology since its modern formulations.

- In the late 19th century, and early 20th century, members of the Italian positivist school rejected a legal definition because they considered this as unscientific. They tried to find some underlying natural order to social relations which demonstrated that deviance was unnatural or pathological.

- In the 1930s and 1940s the argument continued but Michael and Adler argued that a scientific criminology could only be developed around a precise and unambiguous definition of crime, which was, in their view, behaviour prohibited by the criminal code.

- Conversely Sellin (1938) decided that acceptance of a legal definition violated a basic criterion for a scientific discipline which should define its fundamental entities itself. He wished to look for conduct norms of social interaction which would provide a universal foundation, irrespective of political and cultural boundaries.

- From the 1940s Sutherland advocated close attention to the notion of social harm, and encouraged criminologists to study a wider range of behaviours than those which the process of criminalisation and prosecution had brought to their attention.

- Tappan (1947) criticised the influence of Sellin and Sutherland, arguing that vague, non-legalistic, definitions of crime were a blight on a sociology which sought to be objective. Instead sociology was to assume that the laws were a reflection of underlying social consensus as to fundamental norms of behaviour.

- In the 1970s the Schwendingers argued that actions which violated human rights should attract sanctions, and should be regarded as the central topic for criminologists. The Schwendingers, however, were not content with legally specified human rights, but claimed that we should label as crimes many of the activities of governments, and agents of national governments. Their critics argued this was to turn criminology into politics, bringing a hopeless relativism to the discipline.

- Clinard (1968) argued that deviance consists of those acts which do not follow the norms and values of a particular social group, crime consisted of behaviours and actions which exceed the limits of tolerance of any particular social group. This approach appeared to leave us with relativism; the criminologist could only study deviance as any particular social group defined it.

- In 1994 Sumner took this approach further, announcing the 'death' of any scientific confidence in the sociology of deviance, or liberal ideas on the rule of law. If criminology was to be scientific it would have to study a 'sociology of moral censure'.

How are we to understand this constant to-ing and fro-ing? This constant search for something to orientate intellectual inquiry? We should be clear about a subsidiary thesis of this work: criminology has been obsessed about the accumulation of information and knowledge, it has not been as consciously concerned to ask 'what is the meaning of all of this information and knowledge?' Nicholas Maxwell (1984) argued that the orientation of modern scientific inquiries was based on the accumulation of knowledge and technological power at the expense of wisdom. A dull specialisation and proliferation of disciplines flourishes with little idea of what if anything it all adds up to. Perhaps criminology is a prime example (in a recent textbook the author, Williams, (1994) could only conclude criminology was a Tower of Babel of discourses).

A period of contextualising of criminology occurred in the 1960s and 1970s

Dissatisfaction with the naive forms of traditional criminology surfaced in the 1960s, and it was felt that criminology ought to be more self consciously aware of its value positions, more socially concerned, committed, and critical of its relationship to power and how it conceived of the social structure. If the world was not a simple place, and crime was something far more complex than a simple matter of anti-social deviance, then the whole status of what it meant to be engaged in criminology needed to be investigated. So-called radical writers claimed that criminology was concerned with providing knowledge to control the lower classes of society, and Becker even asked 'Whose side are we on?' The deviant was, for a time, viewed through a romantic haze: the deviant was the one who fought back against the dominating capitalist structure. But then who did the deviant fight? His (and it was predominately a he according to criminal statistics and victim surveys) victims were overwhelmingly working class. There was little scope for conceiving of crime as inter-class warfare. Intellectually, the issue concerned not only the earlier question, namely, what sort of scientific variable was the concept of crime, but from what view of the social world does the concept derive? How should the criminologist locate him (and increasingly her) self within the overall social order and social history?

In the 1980s criminology quietly began a process of reflexivity. There cannot be an enterprise of intellectual study, of analysis of an object without some prior act of synthesis or conferring acceptance for the place of that object into something more fundamental. Logos, our language, must meet the world in some form, and we are always making some assumptions. Of course, the normal way we encounter the world is through stories. Most trials, for example, are a specialised and particularised modality of narration. What, after all, are the rules of evidence if not guidelines as to what may be included in the story told in court? Our earliest experiences of understanding life come through our role as the audience for others to recount life. We recount life to ourselves. When we analyse an object, or accept a concept, we take for granted some broader recounting. What are the limits to the stories criminology should tell?

An obvious problem arises. If the basic subject matter, ie the definition of crime, is laid down by the political apparatus of the state, how can criminology simply accept crime as some form of natural phenomena? Is not the subject hopelessly compromised without always consciously investigating the creation of crime, or without analysing the connection between the state, social processes and social structures?

This issue has perplexed criminologists. Various ways of avoiding the issue have been engaged in. On the one hand there has been a tendency to treat crime as a formal category, to recognise that it owes its life to the state, but then to conduct sociological or psychological study of offenders while virtually ignoring the fact that this is a problematic issue. This is to assume that the subject matter of criminology can be treated as a matter of analysis without the need for some overall synthesis. However, all criminological work presupposes an image of law and society. This is simply inescapable. After all, ask what is presupposed when we trust the semantics of a label, the ascription of an event as being actually a crime? In other words, the fundamental question of the relationship between the criminal law and society is assumed as answered. Simplifying somewhat, three models have dominated: a consensus or functionalist, a pluralist or interactionist, and a conflict model. Each model brings out certain organising principles and expresses differing suppositions regarding human nature, the operation of everyday thought patterns, and the construction of society and social structure. Each appeals to differing political philosophies. The consensus may appear to be the most conservative politically with the pluralist being a mixture of liberal, conservative and radical positions, whereas the conflict position is normally regarded as left, radical, or possibly Marxist. Perhaps they reflect certain forms of social development: namely the three processes of accumulation which have made up western culture – industrialisation, the statecraft of organising plurality, and capitalism.

The consensus or functionalist model

The consensus model incorporates certain features; (i) society is a relatively persistent stable structure; (ii) society shows a high degree of integration; (iii) the social structure is based on a relative consensus of values, and different positions within it are functionally ascribed; (iv) legal regulation is functionally the most efficient mode of management in modern society. The law may embody coercion, but law reflects the collective will of the people. There is a basic agreement on what is right and wrong in any given society, and formal law is the embodiment of this underlying collective agreement. The law serves all people equally, under the ideology of the rule of law the legal framework is a coherent and consistent body of principles and rules which neither serves nor presses the interests of any particular group of people. Those who violate the law represent some form of subgroup, their behaviour stems from some form of deviant or pathological conception. The normal position for individuals in the society is to agree with the definitions of right and wrong, and the small group who violate the law in this way evidence a maladjustment, or a pathology, or a distinguishing feature which makes them different from the law abiding majority. Society is relatively well integrated, and the consensus model may well claim that law comes out of the customs or the mutually agreed, shared ways for conducting social interaction. It is unusual to find the consensus perspective explicitly stated within criminological writings, but a great deal of what was called traditional criminology simply seems to assume consensus. Much of the work which went under the name of traditional criminology may be seen as deeply imbued with this consensus pre-supposition. It equates modern western society as a liberal democratic society where the legal system, and structure of crime control is based upon the assumption that laws and their enforcement represent what the people want, it is a reflection of their collective will(s).

The pluralist model

The pluralist model reflects an interactive view of social organisation; while consensus models seem to assume the existence of general agreement upon basic values and interests; and the pluralist model recognises a diversity in beliefs and a multiplicity of social groups and social interests. For the pluralist model, law exists not because individuals come to agree upon certain substantive claims, but precisely because they do not agree. It is in the absence of such agreements that law therefore lays down the minimum conditions of the social game. It lays out conditions for conflict resolution; individuals agree that no matter how much they disagree on certain features they will agree to abide by the rule of law. While society may be conceived as made up of different interest groups with divergent goals and divergent values, it is in everybody's interests to maintain a political legal framework which permits these conflicts to be resolved through peaceful bargaining and through the adjudication of an impartial referee, ie a legal judge. We can say that the social structural principles of a pluralist perspective are five. First, society is composed of diverse social groups, this diversity results from the presence of complex division of labour, variations in economic, religious, gender, age, and ethnic variations in the population. Second, there exists among these groups differing and often conflicting definitions of value positions, even concerning the nature of right and wrong. Third, there is, nevertheless, collective agreement on the mechanisms for resolving such disputes, namely a legal system in which these conflicts can be adjudicated. Fourth, the legal system is therefore neutral, it is independent of the conflicts in society. The legal system is a coherent and relatively consistent framework or structure in which the social disputes can be adjudicated. Fifth, the legal system is concerned with the best interests of society. It is concerned, not so much with siding with particular interests, but with the general well-being of a social body.

The conflict model

The third major model was the conflict model. While many of its adherents come out of the Marxist tradition this is not specifically a socialist or Marxist orientation. While the consensus model tends to emphasise the stability and continuity of society, with diversity coming out of the advanced division of labour which industrialisation encourages, the conflict model emphasises change and the division of society which industrial-capitalism relies upon. It has several presuppositions. First, that every society is subject to radical change. Second, that underlying apparent consensus is possible conflict and contradiction. Third, every element in the underlying conflict or contradiction contributes to change, and that social stability is always based to some extent on the coercion of some members of the social organisation by other members.

The meaning of the central concepts of criminology varies according to your scientific perspective

These models do not guarantee semantic adequacy. They are rather frameworks or spectacles to make sense of a complex and multi-layered social reality which escapes our gaze as we search for its totality. Wearing the consensus pair of spectacles one sees stability, one sees agreement; one instinctively therefore sees deviancy and crime in many ways as pathological. Wearing the conflict pair of spectacles one sees more clearly the coercive and repressive nature of the legal system, and the conception of violence which comes to mind is not so much that of the criminal against the social structure, but of the structure against the people. The legal system is not seen as some impartial tool for dispute resolution but rather a mechanism or instrument permitting those with the greatest amount of political power to advance their own interests over the others. Law is therefore neither a reflection of general consensus about values nor a neutral, impartially agreed upon mechanism for the settlement of disputes. It reflects more the methodology and the interests of those who have political power to make and enforce structures which correspond to their own interests throughout the society. The legal structure, although appearing impartial, although in its categories seemingly subjected to principle and consisting of a systematic application of rules, is, in effect, masking an underlying structure clearly aimed at the maintenance of power. The apparent neutrality of law maintains the interests of the elite in two ways; to some extent it may do so openly by advancing their specific interests, but it also does it in a more general way helping constitute a social structure in which particular groups are advantaged in the gaining, usage and maintenance of power. One can say the organising assumptions are therefore five. First, society is composed of diverse social groups. Second, there are differing conceptions of right and wrong – there are diverse values, goals, interests and these conflict with one another. Third, the conflict between social groups is also one of political power; there is always an imbalance of political power, parties who have it struggling to maintain it and subjects who do not struggling to obtain it. Fourth, law works to advance the interests of those with the power to make it, the law is not a value neutral mechanism but a dispute settlement, it is an instrument of those with the power to make law to advance their own interests. Fifth, a key interest of those who have the power to make and enforce the law is to maintain their elite social position; much of the operation of the legal structure is concerned with keeping those with interests different from those in power from gaining political power in conditions where they could radically change the system.

Contemporary criminology has different perspectives on central issues

This perspectivism is not anti-scientific. Note: these different models of social organisation between law and society do not contradict the requirement to speak in scientific terms. They represent more the pre-supposition within which the scientific study takes analytical form. Analysis is orientated towards perceiving differently the objects of investigation, depending on which of these models one is operating in. The conflict position for instance would lead one more to analyse the socio-political and economic relationships within a society and the influence that these have on the rationality of particular individual actions. One would not be led into a presupposition of the irrationality of conflict positions, one would be assuming more the rationality of conflict.

Post-modernism and the acceptance of language games as the reality of social life

What, however, is the impact upon 'reality' of all these perspectives? Surely only one perspective is correct and the others false?

Various responses are possible:

(i)   each perspective captures some truth of the social condition while neglecting others;

(ii) the world is not knowable in its totality hence we must work through perspectives which take us upon different routes;

(iii) since the world is unknowable in its totality the foundations of thought become myths or narratives.

Social theorists have come to accept that there is no 'natural' mode of language. There are only different practices, or to use a term which the Austrian philosopher Wittgenstein coined in the 1950s, there are only different language games, by which he meant different sets of practices of using words and ascribing meaning. This, of course, implies there is no such thing as a 'natural crime'. The ascription of something as a crime is a cultural procedure. In criminology the theoretical perspective which stresses this is called the labelling school and it came to prominence in the 1960s. We can read it as the appreciation of the language-bound nature of human existence at long last coming to criminology. Once you accept this, however, sceptical doubts flare up as to the very basis of the discipline. Since no 'truth conditions', no non-linguistic array of facts can be adduced as pre-existing from the 'non-social' world so as to determine and stabilise linguistic significations from the outside. But if the proliferation of images of the world, if the various histories of our practices and institutions reduces our naive confidence in their embeddedness in a progressive development, they also deaden our sense of reality. To some post-modernist writers this is liberating, it is supposed to usher in a host of previously discarded knowledges and practices, but its effect is also disorientation, a lack of bite by knowledge. One response is, therefore:

(iv) the resort to common sense and the 'back to basics movement'. If the intellectuals come up with so many perspectives then why bother with them? Why not trust to the 'emotive feelings which are stirred in the breast of the decent man' or the rock of basic common sense?

Living, and making sense of life, within multiple perspectives is the problem of the post-modern condition

At the beginning of this chapter an ambivalence of moods, of directions, of gaining orientation was hinted at. This is regarded as the key theme of the post-modern condition – if we live in a world of multiple perspectives, where everything could be regarded from another direction, where one's argument is automatically subjected to the reply 'on the other hand', then the stability of the world becomes a matter of mere perspective. But a world of mere perspectives ushers in relativity in values and ethics and makes it difficult to state any position with certainty (at least rationally). This leads to a loss of direction which in turn results in pessimism, disenchantment and melancholia and the demand for simplistic solutions (is it mere coincidence that the present is characterised both by a drug-ridden culture and a war on drugs?).

But if there is not any natural crime how can criminology have a basic phenomena to investigate?

Some commentators have become sceptical of the whole enterprise of criminology. One, increasingly popular, intellectual tactic is called deconstruction. It means breaking down the comfortable 'normal' reading of a concept, or piece of writing, and exposing the sets of assumptions beneath. In this way we can show that what looked like quite a solid piece of everyday social reality is actually a pragmatic construction over a set of (contestable) attitudes and assumptions. As Carol Smart sees it, the challenge to criminology is so severe as to rob it of all confidence:

> 'The problem which faces criminology is not insignificant, however, and arguably, its dilemma is even more fundamental than that facing sociology. The whole *raison d'etre* of criminology is that it addresses crime. It categorises a vast range of activities and treats them as if they were all subject to the same laws – whether laws of human behaviour, genetic inheritance, economic rationality, development or the like. The argument within criminology has always been between those who give primacy to one form of explanation rather than another. The thing that criminology cannot do is deconstruct crime. It cannot locate rape or child sexual abuse in the domain of sexuality or theft in the domain of economic activity or drug use in the domain of health. To do so would be to abandon criminology to sociology; but more importantly it would involve abandoning the idea of a unified problem which requires a unified response – at least, at the theoretical level.' (Smart, 1990: 77)

This is both true and unnecessarily reductionist – why should sociology be the master discourse? The message of deconstruction runs something like this: if God is actually dead then there ultimately is no 'absolute' or 'real' presence in language. A text cannot guarantee its own meaning. Therefore all texts, all intellectual projects, are mere reflections of the wills to power in some form or other of the authors, or of the groups which engage in them.

Why is this misguided? Certainly, it is true that accepting the death of God means accepting her abstention, of accepting her absence as the fundamental coordinator of existence. And any presence which we substitute will be an expression of our desire to interpret human history, society and culture in some way. But this does not mean that we are doomed to a state of non-presence. There is an ontological status to being, to crime, to the criminal. An ontological status which is, however, pragmatic. In other words it is a function of social processes and we define it, we know of it, through the epistemology of other processes. In other words – social processes are social processes, social reality is social reality. The trick is to realise that this is no mere tautology. To know a social process is to engage on a social process, to try to understand social reality is to construct social reality. Crimes must be located in social processes, this does not destroy criminology but adds to it. We must then come up with some criteria for judging social processes; and for developing an idea for how to proceed.

Because we are trapped in the circles of social processes does not condemn criminology to mindless relativism, nor should it amount to a surrender of modernity to the forces of the pre-modern masquerading in the guise of a return to basics

Crimes do not have a self-sustaining ontology, and thus there can be no one solution to the causation of crime for criminology to find. But there is another presence which gives meaning to the events of the social world. The ultimate presence to social reality is the act of creation of the social; if criminology has an ultimate presence it lies in the interpretation of an aspect of this. Perhaps in the attempt to transform the inhospitality of human society into the conditions of social and personal hospitality. Put another way, God was replaced by human endeavour. Modern society, not just in the west but throughout this planet, is the result of our attempts to master and transform the world. There are many processes, many layers of interaction, many contingencies and unintended consequences – but it is a human creation and thus the burden for understanding it falls upon us alone.

The current position: etiological scepticism and conservative responses

One way of handling the difficulty of life in the midst of multiple perspectives is to concentrate upon the task at hand, to become a mere technicality. Technical power is, of course, one of the features which marks out modernity from the pre-modern, but for most of modernity technical power was regarded as one mode of building better societies, of enabling greater happiness through enabling people to possess a greater variety of social goods and attain greater mobility etc. Criminology took as its task the understanding and control of crime: but in recent years the ambivalence of the late-modern or post-modern condition has resulted in a new orientation. The task of developing a society without crime has been quietly replaced by the ideas of mere containment or management of crime and offenders. Target hardening, opportunity theory, humane confinement, just deserts, the allocation of scarce resources as between police areas, differential policing (ie community policing for safe areas, military policing for tough inner-city areas) are reflective of a narrowing of concerns for criminology. It is as if the possibility of gaining secure knowledge as to the causal process of crime has been surrendered as too difficult.

But criminology only makes sense when it is joined to a task: criminology always has had a conservative task – unthinking control – but it also has had a liberating and utopian orientation, in which the task for criminology was to peruse the emancipatory dreams of the enlightenment.

In British criminology this was most clearly articulated in the now classic modern text of 'radical criminology', *The New Criminology* (Taylor, Walton and Young, 1973). This text called for:

'... a criminology which is ... normatively committed to the abolition of inequalities of wealth and power, and in particular of inequalities in property and life-chances.' (Ibid: 281)

The text warned that if criminology was not so normatively committed, it was bound to fall into correctionalism, or the simplistic attempts to merely reform individual offenders without looking up from the task and considering the nature of the social order. Specifically, the text argued that criminology had to face up to 'the total interconnectedness of these problems and others', which was only possible if criminology turned what was previously regarded as 'a discussion of what were previously technical issues' into a 'need to deal with society as a totality' (Ibid: 278).

The New Criminology took the Marxist understanding of the social structure to attempt this. Specifically, their notion of the type of 'social formation' in which crime existed in the west, was basically the structure determined by the economic foundations of the capitalist mode of production; thus the text could end with a romantic anti-capitalist flourish:

> 'For us, as for Marx and the other new criminologists, deviance is normal – in the sense that men are now consciously involved (in the prisons that are contemporary society and the real prisons) in asserting their human diversity. The task is not merely to 'penetrate' those problems, not merely question the stereotypes, or to act as carriers of 'alternative phenomenological realities'. The task is to create a society, in which the facts of human diversity, whether personal, organic or social, are not subject to the power to criminalise.' (Ibid: 282)

This soon looked terribly naive and possibly anarchistic. The causes of crime were not really at issue, they were the inevitable by-product of the radical poverty, social inequality and disorganisation of capitalism; instead the real issue was criminalisation. Freedom and happiness were a matter of throwing away the confining and dominating institutions. Such Marxist-inspired faith has vanished: but if the utopian appeal of socialism was thrown out, then is criminology doomed to little imagination and mindless technicism?

The advent of post-modernity has thrown all of this into a grand state of confusion – not only does it seem strange to talk of utopias but is any form of utopian thinking possible? Criminology appears to have become dominated by a refusal to think of the big picture and a piecemeal reaction to the pressing demands of the political right. It has become easy for some commentators to talk of the paradox of an increase of crime at the same time as we witness an increase in social wealth. Why do they see this as a paradox? It is argued that if poverty and social deprivation or exploitation cause crime then we would expect crime to decrease in the west as the welfare state, the increase in living standards and the increase in workers rights and so forth took place. Instead the opposite has occurred. Crime has increased at the same time as western societies appear to have become much richer. This has caused several conservative writers, for example, James Q Wilson (1985) to refer to the 'paradox' of 'crime amidst plenty'. For Wilson the 'ethos of self-expression' has taken precedence over 'self-control'.

The final (conservative?) position: the concept of the self and self-control as the bed-rock for founding a general theory of crime

This conservative position reached its most eminent expression in the recent work of Gottfredson and Hirschi, *A General Theory of Crime* (1990). This text has received widespread attention, particularly in the US. It asserts two things:

- the possibility of creating a general theory of crime;
- that the key to this lies in controlling the independent variable, that is, the concept which serves as a common ground, which will enable the various works undertaken in the name of criminology to be reconciled. The concept they propose for this is *self-control*.

According to social control theory, as previously developed by Hirschi (1969), people commit criminal acts when they are not prevented from doing so by their bonding to conventional society. Motivation to crime is assumed as part of human nature, and any crime is capable from those unrestrained by fear of the social consequences of detection, whether seen in terms of the formal, or state sanctioned responses to crime, or informal. The social control paradigm does not in principle differentiate between types of crime; there are not types of criminals, people merely differ in their propensity to engage in certain activities.

Building upon the control perspective, Hirschi and Gottfredson seek to combine control and the emphasis which positivism has shown upon differentiation and typologising individuals, to create a positivistic general control theory for criminology. First, they differentiate *criminality*, as stable differences among individuals in the propensity to engage in criminal acts, and *crimes*, as criminal events which may be occasioned by a variety of factors, for example, opportunity. Second, they conclude that 'self-control' is the constant which ties together the various theories which have previously accounted for criminality. For Gottfredson and Hirschi, crime is a mundane and little paying occupation, criminals are losers, yet they keep on, relatively speaking, at it. Why? Different levels of self-control provide the answer.

Of central importance to their work is the demand that any criminology actually be clear as to the concept of crime used as the foundational core. Gottfredson and Hirschi analyse the formal properties of crime to argue that certain general features can be taken from any crime, no matter its seriousness or type. In doing this they draw upon earlier attempts at constructing analytical structures, such as that which Hindelang, Gottfredson and Garofalo created for victimisation:

> 'For a personal victimisation to occur, several conditions must be met. First, the prime actors – the offender and the victim – must have occasion to intersect in time and space. Second, some source of dispute or claim must arise between the actors in which the victim is perceived by the offender as an appropriate object of the victimisation. Third, the offender must be willing and able to threaten or use force (or stealth) in order to achieve the desired end. Fourth, the

circumstances must be such that the offender views it as advantageous to use or threaten force (or stealth) to achieve the desired end.' (1978: 250)

Hirschi and Gottfredson differentiate between crime and criminality. Crime is an event for which various circumstances are required, while criminality is a relatively constant propensity of individuals:

'Crimes are short term, circumscribed events that presuppose a peculiar set of necessary conditions (e.g., activity, opportunity, adversaries, victims, goods). Criminality, in contrast, refers to stable differences across individuals in the propensity to commit criminal or theoretically equivalent acts.' (Gottfredson and Hirschi, 1988: 4)

The independent variable – criminality – is the key to the criminological task. The concept of self-control provides the explanatory foundation. Their analysis is a refined positivism: we are offered a theory which sticks close to the proximate and the observable. There is no attempt to place on the agenda the broader context of these events and acts. Moreover, a reduction occurs in the nature of crime which is presented as unplanned, trivial, and mundane activity carried out by persons who are lacking in self-control. These authors state they are concerned with the characteristics of 'ordinary crime', and claim that we can see a common core in white-collar offences, homicides, burglaries, thefts and various other offences. These all share similar features and the people who engage in these activities share similar characteristics"

'Crime involves the pursuit of immediate pleasure. It follows that people lacking self-control will also tend to pursue immediate pleasures that are not criminal: they will tend to smoke, drink, use drugs, gamble, have children out of wedlock, and engage in illicit sex.' (Ibid: 90)

We can read Gottfredson and Hirschi as demanding that criminology reorient itself away from a mindless production of information and knowledge. In other words that criminology develops an intellectual rigour based around an understanding of the nature of crime. This is an essential point and moves us away from the obsession with information and knowledge onto at least a weak form of wisdom. Gottfredson and Hirschi, however, draw their net extremely narrowly The theory produced is classical positivism in the true sense, ie it is faithful to the data. Indeed it is a comprehensive reassessment of the data and a sophisticated embodiment of it. It also suffers in true positivist fashion, ie its limits are the limits of its data.

Self-control is talked about as if it were an entity, as if it were an ontological substance, as if one could have a certain quantity of self-control. By contrast we may conceive that the ontological reality of self-control is relationality. Quantities can thus be seen as related to power; the study of self-control as being fundamentally a study of power forms, the mediation, representation and articulation of power flows and strategies through human forms. Nowhere within *A General Theory of Crime* is a critical reading of the social creation of self-control entered into. Strangely in their conclusion they note:

'A general theory of crime must be a general theory of the social order.' (p 274)

But this is left undeveloped, something to be engaged in 'had we unlimited time, space, and imagination'.

Interactionism as a theme for a general theory

Let us take Gottfredson and Hirschi at their word: a general theory must be a theory of the social order. But how is such a theory to be constructed outside of the certainties that the perspectives of the consensus, conflict and pluralist models of law and society provided?

One way is to work outwards from the routine interactions of everyday life. Based on a reading of the crime as routine activity Robert Reiner (personal communication) suggests a broader four-fold analytical structure to understand the factors of crime. For crime to occur there needs to be:

- A *legal category* which specifies that the action or omission which the person or group has engaged in or failed to perform is to be called a crime. This is the reality of the labelling perspective as this labelling process varies across time and cultures/societies. To understand this aspect we need to study the labelling process and the socio-political factors behind the creation of criminal categories and the de-criminalisation of others.

- The *motive* to engage or refrain from the action so labelled. Criminology has sought to study this through both individualist and sociological approaches.

- The *opportunity*. There has to be the possibility of engaging in the activity or refraining from the required activity. In other words there has to be:

    (i)   a target, something which provides the material for the crime, the situational aspect; and

    (ii) vulnerability. The target must be soft enough for the act to be successful. In recent years a lot of activity has been focused on crime prevention techniques and target hardening.

- The *absence of control*. This can be either:

    (i)   external or situational. This is where the classical emphasis upon the fear of punishment and the impact of deterrence impacts. Under the image of the offender as a rational actor crime is a rational choice, a calculation able to be changed by an efficient system of criminal justice; or

    (ii) internalised control or conscience which is the result of proper socialisation.

If we wish to think towards a general theory which faces up to the dilemmas of the late-modern, or post-modern social order, then our understanding of the nature of crime and self-control must not be created in such a way that it is separated from a meta theory of modern life and its problems – we must locate the domain of study within modern life and its problems. That is, it must place on the agenda questions which it may not be able to answer, but which it must recognise. Questions about the form and development of what is of value for human life, actually (ie positively) and potentially. It must offer ways of better interpreting and understanding the problems of living, proposing and analysing possible programmes, suggesting and activating possible forms of human action and interaction. The problem of crime is a problem of victimisation and of suffering, of power and abuse, of action and reaction – the problem of criminology is thus to help understand the conditions and factors which influence these, and, thereby, help to discover activities and modes of living which develop and strengthen human interaction and solidarity. Maxwell suggested:

'... the basic task of rational inquiry is to help us develop wiser ways of living, wiser institutions, customs and social relations, a wiser world.' (1984: 66)

Put briefly, if the problems of criminology are to be properly understood, criminology requires an understanding of modernity. It is modernity which breaths life into the criminological enterprise and which provides the context for its material, in other words we need *a criminology of modernity*.

The possibility of a criminology of modernity?

The attempt to phrase the project in this way, is a recognition that many of the competing perspectives (of which the most central was between consensus, in its varying forms, and conflict or Marxist) were differing ways of fighting for the progressive imagination *within modernity*. The collapse of communism throughout the late 1980s and early 1990s has resulted in a re-reading of Marx and we can now see the similarities in humanitarian desire between central themes of liberalism and socialism.

The critical task is to try to find ways in which modernity can be challenged, humanised, developed and understood. To call for a movement into post-modernism may be ill-conceived, after all modernism may be more complex than many claim. It may offer many ways of development which have yet to be expressed ... we may not know the resources and extent of the task until we attempt to bring modernity even more to wholesale fruition.

Our bias is therefore clear – before we join the post-modernist bandwagon and lose ourselves in the dialectic of hope and despair let us try and see through what modernity was about and what it has to offer. To see in what ways both crime and the study of criminology are located in its networks.

CHAPTER TWO

THE PROBLEM OF MODERNITY

There is a mode of vital experience – experience of space and time, of the self and others, of life's possibilities and perils – that is shared by men and women all over the world today. I will call this experience 'modernity'. To be modern is to find ourselves in an environment that promises us adventure, power, joy, growth, transformation of the ourselves and the world – and, at the same time, that threatens to destroy everything we have, everything we know, everything we are. Modern environments and experiences cut across all boundaries of geography and ethnicity, of class and nationality, of religion and ideology: in this sense, modernity can be said to unite all mankind. But it is a paradoxical unity, a unity of disunity: it pours us into a maelstrom of perpetual disintegration and renewal, of struggle and contradiction, of ambiguity and anguish. To be modern is to be part of a universe in which, as Marx said, 'all that is solid melts into air' (Marshall Berman, 1983: 15):

'There is merit in the "modernity" of a society, apart from any other virtues it may have. Being modern is being 'advanced' and being advanced means being rich, free of the encumbrances of familial authority, religious authority, and deferentiality. It means being rational and being "rationalised" ... If such rationalisation were achieved, all traditions except the traditions of secularity, scientism, and hedonism would be overpowered.' (Shils, 1981: 288)

The concept of modernity

Recently the concept of modernity has come into wide use complementing the rather simple-looking but not unambiguous term of 'modern society'. We rather naively labelled the social formations of Europe and North America during the last few centuries 'modern society', and relied upon a basic distinction between these social formations and so called primitive or traditional societies. The concept of modernity denotes more a sort of condition or an experience, an existential interpretation of modern society. The concept is used to try to analyse what it is about social existence in modern society that renders it fundamentally different from what has gone before.

The birth of modernity is roughly placed at around three centuries ago in the period that has come to be called the Enlightenment. The Enlightenment is most commonly described as a strange sort of 'coming out' party. A party where there is a great deal of behind the scenes preparation, confusion on the night, but, once over, its subject 'man' has 'come of age', and is free to go out into the real (the true) world, a free man to make his own destiny.

In a sense stories of the Enlightenment and its resultant 'freedoms' appear inescapably linked to certain spatial metaphors also found in earlier writings. The orthodox narrative of our progress portrays the crucial transformation of the

Enlightenment as follows: Plato had depicted men as living in a cave, prisoners of their inability to use reason, governed by ignorance and myth; Plato, aided by Aristotle, had formulated an awareness of the glorious potentiality of reason, but this, in its turn, was surrendered to the forces of organised religion and subjected to the politics of absolutist authority. Without the proper use of reason, man looked out into the world and saw strange and complex things, and, afraid of mystery, constructed new and even more elaborate mythologies to make the events of the world appear meaningful. In the Enlightenment, man thrust free of the hold of those mythologies and the domination of that authority, to bring light to the cave – alternatively, he left the cave to construct a home outside in the light of the continuing knowledge he obtained of the real causes and springs of nature – he was no longer subjected to the illusions and personifications of the realm of mystery but became possessed of the capabilities of scientific reason. From then on, his continuing battle was to separate opinion from knowledge, politics from engineering.

Requiring a place to inhabit, man set out to develop social theory and to use this to construct a citadel in which co-habitation would be possible. The enemies of successful co-habitation were strongly identified with politics and metaphysics. It was felt that social and individual freedom would flow from proper social arrangements, and man could only discover these when the logos of discussion was freed from the illusions of metaphysics and the arbitrariness of politics.

We summarise thus: the aim of social theory was to create a building of objective knowledge that would not be at the mercy of metaphysical speculation or of political storms. Modernity was a constructivist project.

Whether guided by the empiricist or the rationalist approach, concomitant with man coming out of the cave into the light of true knowledge, he also slowly comes out of the social relations which the German theorist Tönnies was later to label as the *Gemeinschaft* and into the *Gesellschaft* – this transformation replaces the legitimations and ideologies of the *Gemeinschaft,* incorporating domination-submission as the habitual acceptance of tradition or the authoritarian stipulation of the significant relations of the world, and the centrality of the exercise of parental responsibility with its accompanying submission to parental will. The growth of *Gesellschaft* law and rationality is inimical to set relationships of dependence and status and the transference of supposed hierarchies from nature requiring a new way of relating to the world – a way in which the hold of tradition and authoritarian stipulation over practice gives way to a new style; of openness to truth and to 'problem' as the drive of practice.

Modernity breaks from the grip of the past via an act of self-definition wherein it conceives itself as a 'problem': a complexity which determines both the nature of the structure of being – the problem of the 'what is it?', and the methodology of action, 'how is it/the other to be done?'. Modernity becomes a series of problematics, and the achievement of this status is itself the harbinger of modernity. The symptoms of modernity, are thus the very things which bring it about.

The problematics of modernity stand linked and indicative of the constructivist project. The 'solution' of the one impacts and interacts with the nature of the other and the framing of the construction of the future. The life of the cave of the *gemeinschaft* rested on the 'social space/terrain' of a perceived harmony constructed out of the ties of friendship, tradition and the habitual/common acceptance of religious ordering and a telos of nature; the destruction of that 'natural harmony' throws open the 'nature' of modernity's 'nature' as a problem to be resolved. The problem of modernity consists, among others, as the problems of:

- how is one to conceive of society – the methodology of vision and understanding?;
- how is one to organise society?;
- how is one to control power?;
- how is one to achieve social control?;
- how is one to understand oneself?

where the solution of each relates to the others.

Modernity demands reasons for action as opposed to following custom and tradition. Do you consider yourself an emancipated modern individual? Do you consider that you are responsible for mapping out the course of your life? That in living your life you are going to follow your own chosen thoughts and life plans and not merely follow on expected paths which others, say family or social group, have mapped out for you? If you claim to be a true modern it appears central to our modern self-image as freed, truly modern, self-directing individuals, that we moderns do not live in the customary and tradition-bound ways that people have inhabited for thousands of years. We do not follow traditions as if they were showing us the natural form of life. We take ourselves away at a distance from the traditions and follow courses of action depending upon our choices – we map out paths, choose rationally. We ask what are the ends we want to achieve – what are the appropriate means? Action becomes rational, efficient, anti-traditional.

The processes that give shape and form to modern society are normally defined as urbanisation, industrialisation, capitalisation, secularisation, democraticisation, and a more empirical and analytical approach to knowledge. Perhaps, above all, modern society exhibits rationalisation: modern life is a rationalised existence emphasising planning and control. And we hold out modern society as a valuable and progressive creation. Of course, these processes extend over a long period of time and do not necessarily lead into each other. Modernity is a complex structure with interacting processes which have different effects creating a range of conflicts, implications and legacies. Spatially, different regions, and different precise historical locations experience and develop different features.

Modernity and control

Central to modernity is an emphasis upon control and the reduction of the world to a collection of phenomena to be analysed and mastered. Mankind takes charge of building the future society rather than seeing social formulations as being in the hands of someone other than man, for instance God. Politically, the American and French Revolutions seemed to epitomise the notion of humans breaking out of the old feudal hierarchical 'natural social structures' and attempting to build new social structures on rational foundations. Such freedom became linked to technological power with the intensification in the growth of industrial society, the whole productive take-off in the mid 19th century of a number of European countries and the US; a world of limitless possibilities appeared open.

Important areas are culture and knowledge. The French scholar Michel Foucault, for example, analyses modernity in terms of a crucial development in the late 18th, early 19th centuries, whereby new discursive formations emerged, namely the humanities, or sets of discourses of biology, political economy and linguistics. These discourses, or human sciences, claimed to set out the nature of modern man. Other scholars define modernity in terms of the development of key philosophical and political ideas, the work of Immanuel Kant, Frederick Hegel, Rousseau, and David Hume, for example, create legacies setting out the contours of the modern imagination. Modernity is partly constituted by philosophical discourse filtering into, and helping to constitute, the intellectual structure of modern society. According to Jurgen Habermas the modern imagination is a self-reflective attitude towards our whole life conditions; to be modern is to see a new horizon unimaginable to the pre-modern. It is to see the world as a site for progress, for productive and co-operative labour, and as a location for the self to become happy. The modern reorganises time and space so that the present and the future, rather than the past, are our focal concerns. For the modern interaction is a process of constructing the future, of making the future better than the present. It therefore becomes possible to talk of modernity as a construction project: the project of building the future good society.

Modernity and civilisation

The modern person is advanced, in control, skillful, in short civilised; in modernity the civilised man replaces the natural man; he who was located in tradition and custom, whose life chances were dependent upon his locality and environment. Put another way, modern society can be seen as the end of natural history, a period in which mankind in some way transcends his natural features, in terms of the abilities of the body and his environmental dependency, and becomes more a product of culture, a product of history, a product of the contingent interactions of diverse social processes. For some time it was common to assume progress and talk of modern man as civilised, as transcending his primitive state where he was presumed to be ruled by basic needs and instincts. This civilised man is a product of culture rather than being merely a natural entity, and is automatically seen as superior to the primitive or savage predecessor. By contrast, Freud and Nietzsche talked of civilisation as the suppression and sublimation of the natural, rather than the replacement.

Modernity as the product of a transformation

Common to the talk of modern society and modernity is the idea of a transition, a transformation beginning in the enlightenment, and intensifying in the 18th and early 19th centuries, which brought into focus the outline of our contemporary existence. Of course, it is not a question of simple clear ruptures or transitions, there are many diverse developments and features in the economic, social, political and cultural practices which occur over a long time. Capitalism, for example, did not just spring into action in a particular way but developed slowly over centuries.

Modern social life as a normative project

Moreover, since the project of modernity relates to the idea of control, the idea of progress, the idea of betterment, the idea that through co-operative and interactive situations, one can construct a new social environment, social life becomes a normative project. Of course to talk in terms of modern social life as a project does not mean that there are neat pure institutions which automatically reflect our normative aspirations. Contemporary social structure is the result of a whole complex of determinants and contingencies, of ambiguous results and unintended effects. Even at the level of the normative discourses (ie the philosophy of ethics and politics and related disciplines such as jurisprudence) and working with the idea that there is a discursive rupture which brings about the establishment of modern ideas as new imaginary locations, significations, descriptions and attempts at analysing both individuals and society modernity is not dominated by one set of discourses — there are always competing domains and multitudinous sites

The twin stages of modernity

It is a mistake to talk as if modernity is some easily understood social formation brought into existence by the social processes released by the enlightenment. For much of the last 200 years, social theory was imbued with ideas of progress, social evolution and the functional coherence of the social order. Social theorists tried to paint the big picture — they needed to. If the death of God defined the modern then all the questions were unanswered. Two main methodologies for gaining the answers were utilised, dominating at different stages:

- through philosophy — this is what is meant by the normative project. Men, such as Descartes, use their powers of reason to find (supposed) certainties (such as a pure, stable, reasoning self) and principles of organisation;

29

- through scientific observation – by subjecting the observable entities of the world to scrutiny, and depicting the human condition as a series of socio-technological problems solvable with the right application of knowledge and technical power.

These methodologies helped constitute two historical stages:

- the philosophical destruction of the old feudal order and its replacement by the principles and universal pretensions of liberalism aimed at the creation of rationally governed nation states – philosophy and law provided the tools to construct a new structure, and in this social structure legitimation largely relied upon narratives, such as the idea of the social contract, and legalistic notions, such as rights, developed into the idea of the rule of law – this stage takes place throughout the 18th century and into the 19th. Individuals are understood through philosophy, thus we have ideas of universal human nature, and differentiation is largely a case of their possession of some legally recognised criteria (such as property), or citizenship;

- the construction of an organised and regulated social structure loosely based on the demands of industrial manufacturing, the legitimation of which was loosely based upon sociological ideas which saw society as a coherent whole, with a relatively stable and developing structure within which people and institutions (such as the family) had understandable functions to perform – this stage takes place in the late 19th century and throughout most of this century. Individuals could be recognised and located in this structure by exhibiting some observable criteria which indicated their role (such as sexuality which was thought to demarcate the respective functions of male and female), and whether they were normal or deviant (we can call this positivism – the belief that the surface characteristics of entities can be understood as reflecting their true, inner nature).

Post-modernism, or late-modernity (the two terms may be used rather co-extensively) occurs from the mid 1970s with increasing complexity, ambiguity, and self-doubts as to the reality of social progress. These processes intensified with the increase in communication, the tremendous increase in quantity and diversity of information and information technologies (ie mass communication technologies such as TV's, computers), the internationalisation of mass culture and, the growing inability of the nation state to control its economies, with the development of international credit flows etc.

We have referred to large scale social processes, what about the individual? In a very real sense the individual is the object or creation of modernity. Simply put, the individual as we conceive it, the thing we moderns take for granted we are, is the product of the social conditions of modernity. Of course individuals existed in pre-modern society, but the constructive feature of modernity is located around the ideas of freedom, emancipation and autonomy. We can call this the discourse of liberation or progressive differentiation. But the process is not one way. Although the individual is the subject of modernity, the individual is also the agent. Modernity demands self-analysis, it demands reflexivity. Historically, although such self-analysis appears as a desire of certain intellectuals, for example, Socrates, from earliest writings, the effectual modern beginnings of this may well have been in the quest for autonomy in the area of scientific research. This demand for autonomy was linked to purity, the ability to pursue science as and for itself, the ability to pursue pure knowledge, the ability to escape from the dilemma which Galileo was in, wherein if the findings of your science conflict with the decrees of religion, the science must be declared wrong. Instead of such dependency, and submission of one sphere to another, modernity allows differentiation: we say that science can be autonomous. Science can pursue its own criteria of validity. It can be a self-determining structure.

Once the idea of self-determination is allowed to one sphere, the intellectual concept can be universalised. It can be carried over from the scientific into the political. This is obvious in the demands of the self-determination of nations, but it impacts more imperceptibly into the constitution of the personal – it creates the discourse of self-determination of the individual. Self-determination involves the liberation of the individual from the supervision and regulation of other determining spheres, the dominant structuring of submission either to an absolute ruler or a settled hierarchy of feudal categories. Ambiguity cannot help but be present with self-definition, since the proceeds must involve resources and the finding of goals. How could the self be determining if the self has no idea of what to be, images of becoming, or the means of achieving this? Hence the determining of the self depends upon the constitution of the social.

At any point in an historical process it is only too easy to accept the present as if it was some natural determination forgetting its contingent nature. Thus we have become familiar with talk of freedom as a basic, or inalienable, self evident human right. But there are no self-evident or inalienable human entities, only human artifacts. The sociological imagination demands that we ask what the processes at work are, and what is the collective outcome of such ideals? What are the consequences, and what are the preconditions for this freedom of the individual, this granting in our modern imagination, as we do in the legal mind, of a right to be free, a right to be an individual? Sociology thus points us to the notion that for the individual to find freedom there must be a political structure and a society in which there are rules which contribute to the creation of such freedoms and indeed protect such freedoms. For example, keeping violence, fraud and theft at bay enables a space for a new individuality to develop. The establishment of individual rights, the establishment of a legal order giving primacy to individuality and setting out a collective justification necessary to these rights, namely the establishment of a jurisprudence (legal positivism) or a political philosophy (utilitarianism; natural rights) and a sociology which implicitly constructs a discourse of liberation of the individual, was, and is, of fundamental importance as a means of understanding and constructing modern society.

It may appear that I am defining modernity as if the end product of modernity is the process of individuality and individualisation and that truly modern discourse is that which promotes and strengthens such a process of individualisation. Am I claiming that the true discourse of modernity is the discourse which sets in motion the processes of individuation? From the vantage point of Britain in the mid 1990s, the creation of a radical individualism appears the historical purpose of the main discourses of modern society, but individualisation has not been without valid critiques. Perhaps the greatest critic of seeing modernity as a process of emancipation of the individual was Karl Marx. He would have described the range of discourses feeding individualisation as incoherent, as ideology. For Marx, as we shall see, the alleged universalist, scientific theories of 18th and 19th century political economy and liberalism were masks, or shadows, for the interests of the emerging bourgeoisie. But let us bear in mind that Marx was not discarding the process of individuality and emancipation, rather he was attempting to identify the real insights and the real benefits from such processes, and to demarcate these real benefits from delusions. It is essential to look beyond the mere superficiality of discourse to try and find what are the underlying social structures. We need not follow Marx into the task of reducing the complexity of social structures into some master framework which is determinate, such as the workings of the economy. Although it may not offer the illusion of control, we can settle for social complexity.

Most writers do not deny the idea of liberation, nor decry the idea of the individual, but rather disagree about the form of the social context in which these discourses occur and the consequences, in other words they disagreed about what exactly is this project of modernity.

Is modernity exhausted? Has it lost its force?

For Marx the individuality and freedom of western 19th century liberal society was a radically incomplete project. His contemporary heirs, such as Jurgen Habermas (1985), would agree. But can it be completed or is the social structure developing in such a complex and multi-layered form that it is no longer possible to think in 'modern' ways? Currently there is a debate about whether modernity, or modern society, has become radically transformed to something new, and the terms post-modernity or late-modernity have surfaced. For many commentators we are currently in the early stage of a whole new structure and are experiencing a transformation out of modernity. Our current problems are viewed as radically new and we can no longer talk of ourselves as moderns or of the need to carry out the projects of modernity.

Post-modernity, or the realisation of the impossibility of fulfilling modernity?

Modernity was that mode of organising experience so that constructing a grand future on this world was the goal. This future society would be the place where the Enlightenment project would be realised; its foundations were to be the scientific knowledge gained from analysis of the physical and human worlds, its methodology the commitment to following the knowledge project through instead of non-rational forms of calculation. Progress was assured if one only kept to the task. Modernity is destruction and construction, scepticism and commitment to knowledge – everything must be subjected to the scrutiny of critical thought – all forms of social life examined and replaced if necessary. The good will survive and new forms of social existence will be allowed to rise up into permanence. In the midst of this the true will stand out:

'Constant revolutionising of production, uninterrupted disturbance of all social conditions, everlasting uncertainty and agitation distinguish the bourgeois epoch from all earlier ones. All fixed, fast-frozen relations, with their train of ancient and venerable prejudices and opinions are swept away, all that is solid melts into air, all that is holy is profaned, and man is at last compelled to face with sober senses, his real conditions of life, and his relations with his kind.' (Marx, quoted in Callinicos, 1989: 30)

But we have not found certainties, only the continual production of perspectives. For Alisdair MacIntyre (1981) the great projects stand exhausted: socialism, communism and liberalism, all are intellectually discredited. To Lyotard *The Postmodern Condition* is characterised by an incredulity towards meta-narratives, that whole spectra of understandings which lay outside science but which legitimated not only science but all forms of social co-operation and purposive activity.

'The idea of progress as possible, probable or necessary was rooted in the certainty that the development of the arts, technology, knowledge and liberty would be profitable to mankind as a whole.

After two centuries, we are more sensitive to signs that signify the contrary. Neither economic nor political liberalism, nor the various Marxisms, emerge from the sanguinary last two centuries free from the suspicion of crimes against mankind.' (1984: xxiii-iv)

Later he asks: What kind of thought is able to include Auschwitz in a general process towards a universal emancipation? The question is simply left: 'Where after the meta-narratives, can legitimacy reside'? What can give legitimacy to social life? Where can any co-operative or normative inspiration reside? If we killed God in the name of science and science ends in chaos, what is to prevent us from becoming a society committed to crime?

Some appear to see this as the consequence of the post-modernist denial of the possibility of knowing total truth. There appears a fun or gaming element to post-modernist discourse, an anti-epistemological thesis where we must learn to free ourselves from a concern with truth and enjoy the present. What has been said of the relativism of Feyerabend can be read as a general fear:

'... life will only be worthwhile when we stop taking it too seriously, and free ourselves from a puritanical and dedicated search for 'truth' and 'justice' ... Reasoning is simply a game which the Dadaist plays preferably with those who are naive enough to believe that we can get closer to the truth by attending to the content of arguments and by discussion.' (Krige 1980: 109)

This aspect of post-modernism becomes labelled as part of a retreat to irrationality, a consequence of failing to find secure overreaching perspectives; it seems no wisdom is possible.

For Zygmunt Bauman (1993) we face a paradox. The post-modern condition provides a form of wisdom, but this is a wisdom which recognises the difficulties of coherent action. Our concern to understand the nature of the human condition, and the changes which have occurred over the last 200 years, and our description of a project of the post-enlightenment offers a form of wisdom about our human condition (after all is not Lyotard's talk of the collapse of meta-narrative itself a large meta-narrative?). However, the social conditions we live in make acting on this awareness problematic. The post-modern crisis is the paradox of post-modern wisdom, and post-modern impotence:

'What the post-modern mind is aware of is that there are problems in human and social life with no good solutions, twisted trajectories that cannot be straightened up, ambivalences that are more than linguistic blunders yelling to be corrected, doubts which cannot be legislated out of existence, moral agonies which no reason-dictated recipes can soothe, let alone cure. The post-modern mind does not expect any more to find the all-embracing, total and ultimate formula of life without ambiguity, risk, danger and error, and is deeply suspicious of any voice that promises otherwise. The post-modern mind is aware that each local, specialised and focused treatment, effective or not when measured by its ostensive target, spoils as much as, if not more than it repairs. The post-modern mind is reconciled to the idea that the messiness of the human predicament is here to stay. This is, in the broadest of outlines, what can be called post-modern wisdom.' (1993: 245)

We live in a time of strain; of contradictions and uncertainties. However, for writers such as Habermas, to welcome this talk of a post-modern society or indeed embrace it as something to be played within is a mistake. The problems that we face in contemporary society are the problems of not having carried out the project, not having taken the key themes of the modern imagination far enough. For the heirs of Marx, modern society is a contradictory society. On the one hand we may have universalistic rhetoric, talk of human rights and talk of the right to self-determination, while, on the other hand, we have strong barriers and boundaries between social groups which prevent the enjoyment of these liberties, and stifle the reality of self-determination. The opportunities and resources available to groups and individuals vary, while the rhetoric of emancipation and the rhetoric of liberty carries across the social orders. Therefore the opportunities of expressing oneself, the opportunities of developing one's interests, the opportunities of becoming thoroughly modern, are structurally limited.

The strains of modernity contained within the discourse of emancipation

What are the strains of modernity? The process of individuality has burdens and opportunities. If one sees the personal project of modernity in terms of a dramatic increase in individuality, the social context displays an increased performance level throughout the economy, politics, science, and philosophy. There is a dramatic increase in opportunities, what we may call life-chances. However, if it is true that modern society has an increased level of operationality which sets the individual free from many of the concerns of traditional societies, we must be aware that the new arrangements also put tremendous strains on these individuals who are required to perform at a higher level. Today's individuals, for example, have to cope with multiple role expectations according to their status in different spheres of society, and according to the idea that the question of who they are is not to be reduced to one particular status (or a mere two statuses). For example, the notion of individuality and equality places on a similar level the young black woman and the young white male. The modern identity for both is as individuals possessing legal rights. Their traditional status of blackness or whiteness, male or female are, ideally, in the Utopia of modernity, irrelevant. The strains on the individuals, however, can be clearly identified by contrasting the notions of their ideal role performance with social reality. The empirical analysis of social structure reveals the gap between the idea and the actual.

The reality of social stratification compromises the discourse of liberation and authenticity. The discourse of modernity postulates 'ideal' universalisible characteristics, but the socio-political conditions of life are localised and contradictory. The outer skin of the black woman is not meant to matter in modernity, this is the normative project of the discourse of liberation. But the living world may locate her in the inner city, the subject of a familiarity with racism, subjectification and degradation.

The need for empirical analysis of the reality of the socio-political location of individuals and groups

In other words we can contrast the discourse of the ideal project in modernity with what Habermas (1979) has come to call 'a life world' in which individuals are located on their everyday levels. Moreover, if we accept the Durkheimian model of modern development in terms of increasing division of labour, differentiation of spheres, and the creation of multiple roles, we can expect even more strains placed on the individual in carrying out everyday life amidst the radical pluralisation and, perhaps, contingency or disintegration of any idea of fixed institution arrangements or preplanned social lifestyle. Having characterised the discourse of modernity as setting out modern society as a construction project within which the individual life becomes also a project – we realise both are difficult. If the early discourse of modernity as liberation has succeeded in creating the primacy of individuality, then the new discourse we are currently surrounded by may trap the self in a situation where it is impossible to satisfy the demand that one creates oneself into a coherent whole. If one constantly strives, one constantly also, therefore, works in a dialectic of desire and satisfaction or achievement; one creates but has no time to relax, the new self instantly becomes compromised by alternative conceptions of value and this stimulates further desire – coherence is rendered problematic.

The discourse of liberation and authenticity impact upon the modern self

The discourse of liberation and authenticity pose problems for the formation of the modern self – instead of the joy of free self-creation and self-control an existential void may be the result. Consider, first, the ideal discourse of individuality. In the following extract the writers contrast the identity of a person in a pre-modern or honour bound social network with the modern or dignity bound situation:

'The concept of honour implies that identity is essentially, or at least importantly, linked to institutional roles. The modern concept of dignity, by contrast, implies that identity is essentially independent of institutional roles ... In a world of honour the individual is the social symbols emblazoned on his escutcheon. The true self of the knight is revealed as he rides out to do battle in the full regalia of his role; by comparison, the naked man in bed with a woman represents a lesser reality of the self. In a world of dignity, in the modern sense, the social symbolism governing the interaction of men is a disguise. The escutcheons hid the true self. It is precisely the naked man, and even more specifically the naked man expressing his sexuality, who represents himself more truthfully. Consequently, the understanding of self-discovery and self-mystification is reversed as between these two worlds. In a world of honour the individual discovers his true identity in his roles, and to turn away from the roles is to turn away from himself – in "false consciousness", one is tempted to add. In a world of dignity, the individual can only discover his true identity by emancipating himself from his socially imposed roles – the latter are only masks, entangling him in illusion, "alienation", and "bad faith". It follows that the two worlds have a different relation to history. It is through the performance of institutional roles that the individual participates in history, not only the history of the particular institution but that of his society as a whole. It is precisely for this reason that modern consciousness, in its conception of the self, tends toward a curious a historicity. In a world of honour, identity is firmly linked to the past through the reiterated performance of proto-typical acts. In a world of dignity, history is the succession of mystifications from which the individual must free himself to attain "authenticity".' (Berger, Berger and Kellner, 1974: 90-91).

Modernity tells the person to break free of the structured status of his or her birth, these are mere contingencies for her, or his, authentic self, which is her/his responsibility to create and safeguard. For the modern individual personal development and struggle is a battle against fate and social ascription of his/her worth and appropriate role.

However, the potential cost is high, the reality may be to discover an existential void. Who is the individual if he/she cannot rely upon the certainty of the traditional institutional roles? Claude Lefort (1988) reads the contemporary individual as a burdened site.

Thus when he is defined as independent, the individual does not acquire a new certainty in place of the old. Rather he is doomed to be tormented by a secret uncertainty while the emergence of the individual implies he is to control his own destiny; he also has been dispossessed of his assurance as to his identity – of the assurance that he once appeared to derive from his situation, from his social situation, or from the possibility of attaching himself to a legitimate authority.

Having created the self which is to be authentic and free, self-controlling and self-directing, modernity risks becoming a site of radical insecurity for the self.

Criminology and the social structure of modernity

We have identified the increase of individualisation and individuality as central to modernity but we can ask 'how universal was the reality of resources and conditions for authentic individuality to come about?'

If we define modernity as being the last 200 years, in the early period a few benefitted at the expense of many. Latterly, increasing differentiation and democratisation occurred with a greater openness and plurality. The variety of individual life styles and life projects available to the majority of the population has expanded. This has various consequences.

First, there has always been a process of inclusion and exclusion. There have always been winners and losers. We do not need to talk solely in terms of a Marxist class analysis; instead we can talk in terms of those central to modernity, who have access to the resources, who share in the increase of life opportunities, life chances, and those who for some reason are excluded. We have also highlighted another problem at the level of the individual. Socially, the increase in individualisation, individuality, may be a reflection of the increase in division of labour, the increase in differentiation of social spheres highlighted and perceived by writers, such as Emile Durkheim, may have allowed the liberation of individuals through the development of a range of different groups and different role activity. The project has intensified; the current splitting of the self.

Thus individuals no longer need socialisation into one of a variety of social roles, but need rather a high level of socialisation into an ability to construct, safeguard, and control the self, in the face of multiple expectations and multiple demands. Pluralisation and disintegration of institutional arrangements may reflect in the pluralisation and disintegration of steady life styles, and the emphasis upon liberation may take over from the emphasis on stability or order. The praise of individualisation may intensify to such an extent that it is very difficult to ascertain what exactly is this individual, self-racked by plurality.

Second, the discourse of liberation is always in tandem with what we might call a discourse of disciplinisation or control. Liberation requires control – this is a paradox of modernity, and the paradox of criminology. Much of criminology is itself able to be viewed as a discourse about social control. Much of its practical concern is to provide ideas and material for the powerful to govern the social body. Writers such as Norbert Elias (1939, 1991) highlight the point that for the individual to become the core entity of modernity, for the individual to become the basis of the civilising process, a certain predictability of the self as well as the institutions of the social is required. The state must be rational and predictable for the self to be secure enough to experiment, experience and grow. But the individual must also become predictable and self-governing to allow the state to keep to its legitimate areas.

What is the state? The state may be identified (using the definition provided by the German social theorist Max Weber) as that institution which has a monopoly upon violence and the raising of taxes; the state is a container of modernity, an instrument which restricts practices, which lays out methodologies for the discipline of individuals, which lays down rules by which the games of the modern are to be played. The state enables as it controls, frees as it disciplines. Discipline is not always obvious. It is not a question of law alone, but also of education and training. These disciplinary tentacles cannot as easily be seen as coming from the state, whereas the criminal law appears a more open exercise of power. But we may note a fact that any student who goes through a liberal law course finds; we are offered a jurisprudence which does not speak of law openly in terms of coercive rules. The idea that the criminal law is the will of the powerful backed up by the threat of violence, institutionally reinforced by policing and sentencing, by public execution etc, has become hidden in our jurisprudence. Discipline also comes quietly and slowly through the emphasis upon self-government, self-limitation and self-control. Much of the discourse which surrounds the everyday operationality of modern law assumes an internal, or acceptant, view of law as the norm. It assumes that law is rational and that the rules of the social game are acceptable to all. Thus to break them is to take an unfair advantage, in a sense to deny oneself the status of being modern. It is therefore easy to see why in *A General Theory of Crime*, Michael Gottfredson and Travis Hirschi (1990) argue crime is caused by the absence or failure of self-control within the individual. In a way we can see this text as the culmination for criminology of key themes of modernity. A reflection of the discourse of individuality and the paradoxical discourse of discipline; at the level of the self, the failure of self-discipline or self-control is defined as the cause of crime; the level of self-control constitutes criminality.

The role of liberalism in the constitution of modernity

One critic may ask: 'Your picture of modernity reads as if philosophical and political liberalism is the discourse of modernity. Is not the ontological core of liberalism the irreducible naturalness of the individual? And the primacy of the individual the end state of social development? Your picture of modernity is therefore reducible to the history of liberalism – are you suggesting that the history of criminology is the history of liberalism?'

Let us be clear – the discourse of liberalism has dominated the West. Many defenders of modernity hold out the concept of the open society, the liberal-democratic West with human rights and the rule of law, as the great achievement of the last 200 years. The liberal is proud to claim that his creed separates economics, politics and religion, thus allowing the differentiation of spheres which ensures growth and freedom. Some sociologists, such as Ralf Dahrendorf (1979), may even confidently proclaim that the liberal rarely needs to be ashamed of the realities created in his name as the socialist has to be much of the time.

Liberals are sympathetic – even if they wish to distance themselves from its purity – to Friedman's statement in *Capitalism and Freedom* (1962) that the country is the collection of the individuals who compose it. The pure liberal appears unable to recognise society blinded by the array of individuals. By contrast, the position outlined in this text is that individualism is a product of social structure, the individual cannot exist outside of the social and that neither freedom nor non-freedom is natural. Our position cannot agree with liberalism that the individual is the irreducible natural core of social ontology – there is no natural core. With humanity there can be no recourse to some secure, objective, naturalist paradigm which determines social development and social structure, there is only, at any one time, the determinants of a context, of a situation. Instead of constructing or deconstructing the tangled paths of criminology and liberalism we shall, in the next chapter, look at the implications of four of the central social theorists of modernity writing towards the end of the 19th century: Max Weber, Karl Marx, Emile Durkheim, and Friedrich Nietzsche.

CHAPTER THREE

THE THEORISTS OF MODERNITY: AN INTRODUCTION TO MAX WEBER, KARL MARX, EMILE DURKHEIM AND FRIEDRICH NIETZSCHE

Max Weber and the rationalisation of the world

Max Weber's (1864-1920) most famous theme is that modernity is crucially constituted by a growing rationalisation of the social world.

Central to modernity is the use of reason and the desire to assert control over the process and forms of the world. If we are to become the masters and possessors of the earth, as the French philosopher Descartes had earlier claimed, then subjecting the processes of the world to rational (scientific) investigation and employing reason to organise ourselves, and our institutions, appears to be the enlightened mode of operation.

Although this seems to be the only route to success, rationality has a price. For if modernisation takes place through increasing rationalisation, what happens to those aspects of social life that cannot be thought of as truly rational? Do they become downgraded; cast away?

Weber thought rationality would dominate in three ways:

- the *control of the world through calculation* (resulting from the growth of the technological attitude, the world becomes the site of problems to be solved with the correct technology);
- the *systematisation of meaning and value* into an overall consistent scheme;
- the methodological living of daily life according to rules. Rationality means following a rule, or an abstract moral principle, rather than acting on impulse, randomness or emotionality. Rationality means building up a logically consistent pattern linking our thoughts and actions, and following this pattern to its conclusion. It means consistency in linking our words and actions, our aims and like activities, creating an efficient ordering of means to ends.

As a consequence, Weber thought, we faced an inevitable systematisation of belief, the elimination of logical inconsistencies, the disarming of the magical and mystical, and a movement away from particular or local forms of thinking to the more abstract or general. This entailed the reduction of all individual instances of experience and of thought, whatever their diversity, to the status of general classes. Moreover, rationalisation demanded that we purge from our ways of thinking and acting, forms that could not be justified on the basis of their anticipated consequences, themselves rationally justified by more generally defined ends and rendered predictable by generally valid empirical laws. Rationalisation is the systematisation of belief and action. But it is also the destruction and stifling of a great deal of the richness of human life. What happens to the non-rational aspects of humanity? Does the resonance go out of life? The tragedy? Are we doomed to live out formally effective lives with little magic or warm human contact?

Although his belief patterns are being destroyed, the tribal person who believed in demons and Gods, who followed customs and traditions, may have been consistent in his thoughts, actions and beliefs. If we imagine ourselves inside the pattern and structures of his beliefs then he is behaving in a rationally consistent fashion; this rationality Weber calls *substantive*. Under substantive rationality there are certain things, values which are simply accepted as true and fit a picture of the cosmos (world) so accepted. But we 'moderns' argue that everything has to be subjected to the test of sceptical reason, and if something cannot survive rational testing then we reject these beliefs while committing ourselves to the methodology of reason itself. The commitment to reason as the mode of organising life constitutes a pattern in which the methodology outweighs any specific commitment to a particular view of the world – this Weber calls *formal* rationality. Rationality comes to dominate life. It does not matter what beliefs we hold substantially, we must be rational – we must calculate, analyse, reduce.

The nation state and the rise of capitalism

The rise of modern rationality is closely linked to the development of capitalism as a mode of economic and social life and the rise of the nation state. One of the determining contexts for modern law is the growth in importance (and now possible decline) of the nation state. Like the English Jurisprudent John Austin (1832), Weber saw the state as a particular form of political association and was clear on the necessary linkage between the ability of the modern state to govern and law. In his famous lecture *Politics as a Vocation* Weber poses the question: 'but what is a political association from a sociological point of view?'

His answer:

'Ultimately one can define the modern state sociologically only in terms of the specific means peculiar to it as to every political association, namely, the use of physical force. Every state is founded on force said Trotsky. That is indeed right. If no social institution existed which knew the use of violence, then the concept of state would be eliminated, and a condition would emerge that could be described as anarchy in the specific sense of this word. Of course, force is certainly not the normal or the only means of the state – nobody says that – but force is a means specific to the state. Today the relation between the state and violence is an especially intimate one. In the past the most varied institutions have known the use of physical force as quite normal. Today, however, we have to say that a state is a human community that (successfully) claims the monopoly of the legitimate use of physical force within a given territory. Note that 'territory' is one of the characteristics of the state. Specifically, at the present time, the right to use physical force is ascribed to other institutions or to individuals only to the extent to which the state permits it. The state is considered the sole source of the 'right' to use violence. Hence, 'politics' for us means striving to share power or striving to influence the distribution of power, either among states or among groups within a state.' (1984: 32–33)

To give more of the flavour of Weber:

'Like the political institutions historically preceding it, the state is a relation of men dominating men. A relation supported by means of legitimate (considered to be legitimate) violence. If the state is to exist, the dominated must obey the authority claim by the powers that be.' (1984: 33)

For Weber more interesting questions were the issues of when, and why, do men obey, and upon what inner justifications, and upon what external means does this *domination* rest?

Let us consider for a moment the social context of Weber. He witnessed the unification of Germany under Bismark, and the emergence of the modern German state founded, in part at least, upon the strength of Prussian hegemony. In his later life he saw the phenomenal growth of industrialisation in Germany; the failed attempt to create a German empire, and the culmination of great power rivalry in the catastrophe of World War I. He stood at a site where many of the processes of modernity intersected. Weber asked how government, the maintenance of political authority, operates within capitalism. To maintain political authority, power based purely on physical force is unstable and ineffective. It is important to achieve legitimate domination 'ie the probability that a command with a given specific content will be obeyed by a given group of persons'. How does such obedience come about? Weber proposes a model of three 'ideal types' of *authority:*

- *Traditional authority* – which rests on an established belief in the sanctity of immemorial traditions and the legitimacy of the status of those exercising authority under them. This form of authority had been most widespread in the history of the world.

- *Charismatic authority* – which rests on devotion to the specific and exceptional sanctity, heroism or exemplary character of an individual person, and of the normative patters or order revealed or ordained by him. This form was unstable and unpredictable.

- *Rational-legal authority* – which rests upon rational grounds and a belief in the 'legality' of patterns of normative rules, and the right of those elevated to authority under such rules to issue commands. This form was coming to dominate modern western societies.

Weber considered the growth of rational-legal authority as the predominant aspect in the process he called the *rationalisation of the modern world*. Whereas for most of human existence the legitimacy of social systems had rested on traditional, magical or religious elements, modern society appeared to be founded on an authority which had itself became rational, that is, it was understood as a calculated form of social structuring, enabling the functional integrity of a society or social organisation. This in turn, Weber thought, depends upon:

- A legal code which consists of legal norms, established by agreement or by imposition, but which are accepted on grounds of expediency or rational values or both. This has a claim to obedience of at least the crucial members of the corporate body, and usually claims the obedience of all members of the society or organisation.

- A logically consistent system of abstract rules which are applied to particular cases. Thus social order exists within the limits laid down by legal precepts and follows principles which are capable of generalised formulation.

- The typical person in authority occupies an 'office', which defines his or her responsibilities. This person, who is an official, even the elected president of the state, is also subject to the impersonal regulation of the law.

- The person obeying authority does so only by virtue of his or her membership of the corporate group (that is, not on any personal basis) and what is obeyed is the law (rather than the person in authority).

- Obedience is given to officials, not as individuals but to the impersonal order they represent. An administrative staff (that is, a bureaucracy) is formally charged with looking after the interests of the corporate body within the limits of the law.

The power of the state officials resides in their legal office not themselves.

Thus it is law, its precise demand and its administration, which encapsulates the element of calculation in rational legal authority.

Weber considered that the emergence of the Western form of capitalism had given an immense stimulus to rational legal authority and the calculative attitude. The predictability of relationships and outcomes, required for capitalist interaction, was enabled by the formally rational structure of legal domination.

The mood of Weber

In the enlightenment (Europe in the late 17th and 18th centuries), the appeal to reason was on behalf of the desire to be free. Freed from the bondage of false belief and the hierarchies of feudal society, humanity would enter into an age of progress. Modernity should bring freedom – the liberation from the restraints of substantive rationality; freedom from the necessity to believe X because that is what your social group or society socialised you into. Freed from illusion we can choose our values, develop new ones in the interaction with other individuals, cultures, ways of life in the variation of the world. This freedom of culture could mean the potentiality for a more varied and exciting world than any previously in history. But Weber was pessimistic. Modernity was more likely to become a gloomy, bureaucratic state, where administered uniformity severely limited freedom. He talked of the iron cage of bureaucracy and rationality. Individuals were not likely to have the capacity to choose among the possible array of life chances, of values; instead a vast administered state would dominate. What would individuals do? Weber thought that their life would be determined by their functional role, their public space outlined by social rationality, and the only happiness would be in the anti-rational spaces. The individual would find solace in personal relationships, romantic love and escapist music, the experience of art, the cultivation of a limited private sphere, as this-world escapes from institutional routines. The only hope was that we might sustain a will not to be ruled like sheep – but this was doubtful.

The problem of discipline

Nowhere was Weber's gloom more evident than in his concept of disciplinisation. The control of individuals in modern society was increasingly a matter of discipline, an adherence to the norm, and an internal attitude of restraint and foresight. Two institutional orders, the monastery and the army, had provided the original sites for the development of discipline which had spread throughout the social order.

The monastic orders of medieval Europe had provided a life lived under the command of rigorous diets and timetabled regularities which subordinated passion to the will and which separated the desires of the soul from those of the flesh. Goffman (1961) recognised the monastery gave a total environment of control and a culture of restraint devoted to the regularisation of human sexual emotion. Weber argued the ideas of the protestant spirit transferred this culture to the wider society.

Weber argued the army was the original focus of this social discipline whereby large bodies of men were moulded into a disciplined unit by personal discipline and bureaucratic demand systems. Modernity saw a spread of this disciplinary focus throughout the social order.

Karl Marx

Whereas Weber pointed to the trap of rationality and discipline, Marx saw the main limitation of modern society in the alienation (or distancing of modern man from his real nature and products of his labour) of man under capitalistic economics. Alienation means that man is unable to recognise his true state and build the required conditions for real social progress.

Marx declared that capitalism values men primarily through their differing abilities to produce commodities. The rich and diverse productive activity of mankind is reduced into a process of producing commodities for exchange. Any social relationship man has with the items he produces is lost; while the worker puts his labour value into a product, this labour value is ignored and the only value which is considered of importance is the quantity of money for which the commodity produced can be exchanged. The productive features of human life are further dehumanised when this exchange value is thought of as something which inheres in the commodity itself, rather than relating to the activity of the worker. Man's basic productive activity is thereby obscured by the process of exchange, and the productive role and capacity of the individual is not recognised. Instead, an abstract thing, Capital, is seen as the primary productive entity. Capital is seen as producing a surplus value, and buying labour power (the employment of the worker) is merely a lesser unit in the means of production. The individualist orientation of the contractual form of relationships which dominate modern capitalist life disguises the social character of man's existence and labour. In a more subtle process than the openness of the master-slave relationship, capitalism turns men into items for the market; man is reduced to one more commodity and the very basis of social life becomes unrecognisable. What can people trust? What process can rank values, offer rewards, distinguish between an important role and an unimportant one? Where is certainty? The market becomes the only trusted source of values and the social character of man's existence becomes classified according to the social activity of the market; that is the exchange relationship between commodities and human deeds. By some strange slight of the intellect, the market is perceived as self-regulating, and the role of law is merely to protect against abuse. Ideally, there would be no laws for the capitalist except the laws of exchange – those which protect property, enable and enforce contracts, or prevent fraud and abuse.

But what of the normative content of customs, of morality? The social relationships between men become merely ideological formations. Although law and morality may appear to be self-sustaining and independent spheres of meaning, their real meaning is found in terms of their relationship with the underlying demands of the economic structure of the social order. Instead of capitalism being controlled by men, it is ultimately the demands of capitalist commodity production which controls men's productive activity and the form of their social interaction.

Ultimately, the basic form of the economic structure delineates the social structure. Society is dominated by the formation of a structure of class relations. The bourgeoisie control and exploit the workers, taking away the proletariat's products and regulating their productive activity. In turn the bourgeoisie is locked into, and controlled by, the demands of the process of exchange and the fluctuations of the world market.

Above all, man comes to view the world, its components and social relationships, in terms of commodities; life loses its coherence and the sociality of modern man is radically devalued. How can modern life have real meaning? As life is reduced to an exchange of commodities the magic of life turns into absurdity.

How is this made possible? Why does man not see the reality of his social situation? Man is blinded by the dictates of the so-called science of liberal political economy. This liberal science depicts the socio-economical conditions as actually reflecting underlying natural processes. The emerging liberal social sciences were an attempt to present production as encased in eternal natural laws independent of history, at which opportunity bourgeoisie relations were then quietly smuggled in as the inviolable natural laws on which society and the particular relationships of people are founded (1975: 45).

Instead of accepting the laws of political economy as truths, as proof of the correctness of political economy, Marx claimed dominant economic interests were the underlying origins of modern social relations. These interests create and perpetuate the modern capitalist social structure. Modern capitalism is the most powerful productive system yet evolved, and it brings out, as never before, some of the range of man's creative abilities, but it also frustrates other aspects of man's creative potential. This is the contradiction at the core of modern society.

Man's alienation under political economy, and its super structural forms, implicates the state and the law in a crisis of contradiction. Whereas real politics would involve the pursuit of communal ends, under liberal bourgeoisie capitalism the question of political legitimacy is visualised, not in terms of communal ends, but in terms of the interests of liberal political economy. Concepts of justice and morality are but elements of the super structure of particular societies and are, by definition, ideological; they are both necessary concepts for the system to operate, but they are also false to man's true nature and real needs. It is not that society under capitalism necessarily fails to live up to the principles of morality, or standards of justice, which are thrown up by its philosophies, they may well do that, it is rather that such standards and principles are themselves incoherent and contradictory in their nature when one considers the potentiality of the social structure and the philosophical ideal. Moreover, when we come to understand the genesis, the operation and the prognosis for such philosophical ideas of justice, morality and emancipation, we realise it is inherently impossible to realise their emancipatory consequences under the structure of capitalist economic norms.

The essential element of modern law under capitalism is its intimate relationship with the state. Liberal bourgeois accounts have drawn upon notions of independent juristic relations, or an independent rational jurisprudence and the thesis of separation of powers, to build an impractical ideology of the 'Rule of Law'. By contrast, Marx emphasises the relationship between law and the state apparatus of a class society. For Marx the state is both a political body and a reflection of social organisational power.

In a primitive society there was no political state to dominate; instead life was characterised by a primitive, but simple, equality and groups which communally owned and controlled the production of a relatively limited range of social goods. The development of a complex division of labour, and the corresponding development of class divisions shattered this primitive communal unity. Conflict arose between individual interests and between individual and social interests. This process created individuals who began to interact with one another by exchanging units of private property, and to interact within a new social structure by exchanging individual freedom for social protection. The state arose from these exchange relations and was implicated in their regulation, and itself became a power seemingly above them. As Engels stated:

> '... in order that these antagonisms, classes with conflicting economic interests, shall not consume themselves and society in a fruitless struggle, a power, apparently standing above society, has become necessary to moderate the conflict and keep it within the bounds of "order"; this power, arisen out of society but placing itself above it and increasingly alienate itself from it, is the state.' (1973 [1884]: 229)

The state has the role of regulating the process of exchange through the framework of law. Law renders social interaction and the market predictable. Thus the state preserves society, but it does so at the same time as there is a growing fragmentation of individual and social life. Whereas it appears to do so as an independent, ie a non-specific, political power and is visualised in the developing jurisprudence as a universal phenomenon, in fact the state is an expression of the interests of the dominant economic class.

Jurisprudence is not to be trusted

Liberal jurisprudence expresses the liberal democratic state as if it were a community, but this is an illusion. Marx draws attention to the deeply embedded forms of social life in the ancient and feudal states which preceded the modern liberal democratic state associated with capitalism. In these ancient and feudal states, a 'substantive unity between people and the state' existed. In the modern state, however, this becomes embodied only into the abstract form of the legal constitution which develops a particular ideological reality alongside the real life of the people. Thus citizens of modern liberal democracies lead double lives; one, in the political community as an abstract species being possessed of rights and whose communal nature is expressed in the constitution, and the other in the civil society as concrete egotistical individuals. For Marx:

> '... where the political state has attained its full degree of development man leads a double life, a life in heaven and a life on earth, not only in his mind, in his consciousness, but in reality. He lives in the political community, where he regards himself as a communal being, and a civil society, where he is active as a private individual. The relationship with a political state to civil society is just as spiritual as the relationship of heaven to earth.' (1975: 220).

The political ideology of the state and jurisprudence gives an increasingly illusory identity to individual and social life. Capitalist modernity dissolves the natural unity of man's social existence and the fruits of production, and increases the distance between rulers and the ruled. Modern social existence becomes mediated through institutions which is understood only through the writings of political economy and the discourses of liberal philosophers. This philosophical discourse speaks in terms of universal human interests but social reality distorts this. The contrast between, for example, the ideas of democratic representative democracy, and the reality of social life in civil society, means that social order is full of contradictions. Bourgeois jurisprudence presents modern life as the greatest freedom ever attained for mankind. In its philosophy modern society is based on the ontological core of the fully developed independence of the individual. However, these individuals occupy radically different places in a stratified social order. Moreover, whereas individuals appear to be more independent in liberal democracy, the state increasingly dominates and masters society. The state is far from being a servant of society.

Such domination is achieved by the hidden hand of the market. Liberal bourgeois philosophy has torn apart the motley feudal ties that bind man to his supposedly natural superiors, it has left no other nexus between man and man than naked self interest 'in callous cash payment'. This domination was clear in the appalling conditions of the working classes in the 19th century; there capitalism had substituted an exploitation which was legitimated by religious and political illusion, with a naked, shameless brutal exploitation so apparent in the slums of Manchester and Liverpool. But the full extent of domination in the apparently free liberal democratic state is not so obvious – whereas the domination by man over man was more open, and economic exchange less developed, in previous examples. In the modern liberal democratic state, domination is more hidden, while exchange processes are more obvious. Public life has become an arena for private individuals, and the seemingly universal and natural claims of the rights of man are but a social expression of particular historical interests. Political emancipation, the break down of traditions and hierarchical status of feudal society, represents not real freedom but rather economic oppression of the proletariat by the bourgeoisie.

What is the real basis of the law?

Marx identifies the liberal jurisprudential theories of Hobbes, and other command theorists, as clearly founding the basis of right, the basis of law, in power; but Marx goes further to demand that this basis should itself be investigated. What gives rise to political power? Ultimately he finds this not in the expression of specific individuals or groups, not in their will, as the imperative theories may have told us, but in the real basis of economic conditions which structure the state's interest. Thus the new demands for freedom are claims made for some 'right' to freedom, and are an expression of power which must be traced through a series of economic processes. In class terms we see the power of the bourgeoisie over the proletariat. In *The Communist Manifesto*, Marx and Engels were explicit:

'... by freedom is meant, under the present bourgeoisie traditions and production, free trade, free selling and buying.' (1978: 486)

The supposed freedom of modernity is only a formal freedom; in reality peasants were driven from the land to become the 'free labourers' of the modern city. Certainly man is freed from the old relationships, from feudal service, but he is also free from his relationship with the land, his existential confidence in the ways of a life which appeared natural and from the forms of existence which rendered life into a whole. What is to replace this destroyed existential security?

Freed from all dependency on natural forms, or natural property, the modern individual is freed from his means of production, and is forced to sell his labour power to live. Capitalism is also freed to exploit this labour power to extract surplus value. Although this may be expressed in terms of the supposed free contractual agreement, the relationship between the bourgeoisie and the proletariat in reality is a position of forced labour and exploitation. What of rights? Does not liberal democratic freedom throw up an equality of rights? In *On The Jewish Question,* Marx agrees but states that:

> '... equality simply means equal access to liberty, namely that each man is equally considered to a self sufficient nomad.' (1975 [1843]: 230)

Policing becomes a core concern of capitalist social structure

The idea of rights, and the idea of society being increasingly an site of free equal individuals brings to the fore notions of security and violence. We demand a right to security:

> '... security is the supreme social concept of civil society, the concept of police, the concept that the whole of society is there only to guarantee each of its members the conservation of his person, his rights and his property.' (1975: 230).

The right to security protects egoism, it protects the possessive individualism of modern civil society; security is the guarantee of this egoism, or driving force of commodity exchange. Security preserves the capitalists right to extract surplus value, and the proletariats' right to sell their labour power. It preserves class relations, which makes society a mere means to man's physical existence, and not his true social end.

What is required to escape? To achieve true emancipation?

Ultimately we must transform the class structure of modernity into a post-modernity of communism:

> 'When, in the course of development, class distinctions have disappeared, and all production has been concentrated in the hands of a vast association of the whole nation, the public power will lose its political character ... in place of the old bourgeois society, with its classes and class antagonisms, we shall have an association, in which the free development of each is the condition for the free development of all.' (1978: 490-491)

What happened? What was the effect of Marx's writings?

This text is written in 1995; five years on from the collapse of the Berlin Wall and the collapse of those political systems which claimed to be founded upon Marxism. The historical period which began in 1917 has now come to an end. The combination of Marxist-Leninism not only has no future as a political project but its history has been rewritten as a horrific failure – we know it was inhuman; we know it extracted a terrible cost from the environment.

What can we learn from the experience and what is left of the great counter-tradition to liberalism after this political collapse? This is a question which has vast repercussions, for it is not just in the societies where it officially took power that Marxist and Leninist doctrine had real effects, but also in the West. The growth of the Liberal West has owed a huge amount to a continual debate and learning process with the critical tradition of Marxism. What, if anything, is to replace this tradition?

Many of the thoughts of Marx, which made an impact beyond his immediate political following, have been absorbed into the critical conversations which have energised social-democratic and liberal thought. Among these was a uniquely powerful image of the global energy and unrelenting expansiveness of capitalism, an unforgettable focus upon the authority relations of modern industry, and a dramatisation of the structural antagonism generated by this productive process. At the most general level, Marx's work has entered our language, transforming our questions about the world. We can separate three themes:

- A critical methodology, we can call this a *hermeneutic of suspicion*. Thus we must subject laws, and other forms of organisation in society, to a rigorous testing. Who wins, who loses? This question can be our constant companion.

- *A moral intuition*, a demand that we must strive to build the good life. For Ernest Gellner a simple moral intuition underlay the idea of socialism:

    '... greed, acquisitiveness, competitive ownership, possession as the main symbol of human achievement and status – all of this is bad. It is not merely bad, it is also perfectly avoidable. Ownership and economic competitiveness are not inscribed into the nature of things or rooted in human character. On the contrary, they are incompatible with the true essence of mankind: men who endorse individual acquisitiveness and possession are alienated from their own true nature. The absolutisation of greed is a law of False Consciousness imposed by a temporary and pathological social order, which tries to protect and fortify itself by such falsehood, by generalising and treating as inherent its own distorted, historically specific visions of man: but the truth of humanity lies in spontaneous work and co-operation.' (1994: 150)

    This is more than any scientific creed; it is a commitment to an idea of what it means to be truly human.

- The organisation of these aims into a scientific approach which can be applied into areas such as criminology. Two examples:

(i) Marxism inspired a flourishing of 'radical' marxist orientated theorising during the 1970s in the US of which Richard Quinney was, perhaps, the most prolific theorist. In Quinney's (1974) analysis, the law was structurally bound with conflict and oppression, due to an economic determination in which the basic demands of the capitalist mode of economic production determined, ultimately, the form of everything else in the social structure. Thus:

(a) American society is based on an advanced capitalist economy.

(b) The state is organised to serve the interests of the dominant economic class, the capitalist ruling class.

(c) Criminal law is an instrument of the state and the ruling class to maintain and perpetuate the existing social and economic order.

(d) Crime control in capitalistic society is accomplished through a variety of institutions and agencies established and administered by a governmental elite, representing ruling class interests, for the purpose of establishing a domestic order.

(e) The contradictions of advanced capitalism – the disjunction between essence and existence – require that the subordinate classes remain oppressed by whatever means necessary, especially through the coercion and violence of the legal system.

(f) Only with the collapse of capitalist society and the creation of a new society, based on socialist principles, will there be a solution to the crime problem. (1974: 16)

(ii) In the UK the major text was *The New Criminology* (1973).

Three young sociologists, Ian Taylor, Paul Walton and Jock Young published one of the modern classics of criminology in 1973. It was a socialist-orientated critique of previous 'traditional' criminology, and a passionate appeal for a society in which the power to punish was not used to control deviance; instead they felt the freedom and non-oppressive nature of a socialist social order would enable a society of non-aggressive diversity to flourish. The book was extremely hard hitting in its criticisms of earlier theories, and rather patchy in its optimism. Its utopian aspect has been shattered with the coming of post-modernism. One of its leading authors, Ian Taylor (1994), remains a committed and extremely sophisticated commentator on the linkage between the political economy and crime; while Jock Young (1986, 1987, 1992; Lea and Young, 1984) has adopted a *left realist* approach wherein the hopes for a fundamental socialist transformation of the social order has turned into a concern with dealing with crime and social disadvantage at a local level.

While we may wish to hold to some of the deeply humanist leanings of Marxist thought, the organisation of Marx's ideas into what came to be called 'a science of Marxism' is problematic, for we can now fully recognise that the predictive power of Marxism dealt in articles of faith rather than inescapable truths. Marx was far more successful in warning of the power of capitalism than in demonstrating in any conclusive fashion why it had to come to an end. It was eloquence, rather than science, which established the association between the end of capitalism and the destiny of the working class. Moreover, he never succeeded in establishing a coherent theory of the connections between property relations, legal regulation and political forms. As a result, his refusal to accept that capitalism might be controlled by political reform and collective pressure was ultimately a dogmatic assertion. Crime was always loosely fitted into the scheme: one did not really know whether the criminal was the proto-typical revolutionary, waiting to grow into the committed statesman of a new order, or a true social parasite.

Post-modernism is linked to the demise of Marxism, both as the inspiration for real political orders and as the source of the great counter-political culture in the west. Marxism, in the sense of a set of sociological and political claims, cannot stand aside from the political events of the last few years. While Marx was no more responsible for the Gulag than Nietzsche was for Auschwitz, it is the case that the legitimacy claimed by Lenin and Stalin was that bequeathed by Marx, and the sad fact is that after allowance has been made for 'backwardness' and 'underdevelopment', the one social and political alternative to capitalism constructed on the basis of Marx's ideas, although arguably more egalitarian, has also proved itself to be more authoritarian, less efficient and less desirable than the system it was supposed to replace. For all these reasons, we need to understand what was missing in communist societies which so-called liberal democratic societies have. What gave the West the flexibility and the ability to survive crisis, such as the depressions of the post Second World War, and retain of social cohesion in the face of a plurality of populations and ideas?

But the west cannot be complacent: the need for critical thinking is as pressing as ever. For the gulf between the world's rich and poor is growing wider; inhuman forms of labour exploitation, indebtedness and intimidation are still to be combatted. New conflicts have emerged while old ones persist. Presently, in the West there are huge arguments over the future of the welfare state (long a case of debate for Marxists – was the welfare state a victory over the capitalist or does it serve to keep capitalism flourishing by diminishing the harshness of capitalist exploitation?). Moreover, the welfare state leaves the question of justice unanswered. There has not been an acceptable answer to the search for the true principles of justice that would guide modern western societies – they have broadly accepted utilitarianism with various constraints (see, for example, the constraints that the philosophy of John Stuart Mill in the late 19th century placed on utilitarianism). But the search for set principles for social organisation has not been answered. Philosophical arguments over justice have led not to settled positions, but to a range of unsettled arguments which are vulnerable to counter arguments. This self-created predicament has sometimes been referred to as the post-modern political condition. It denotes the position where we accept that there are no fixed and settled cannons for organising the just society. We have seen recently a move from creating new theories of justice to spending time on discussing procedures. What procedural consensus (eg law) is possible? If this is the case we are indeed in a radically different situation from that which has characterised much of modernity, but let us not forget that conditions of exploitation do exist. An example from a not-too-distant place is the Bhopal incident in India in the early 1980s where a large multi-national company clearly ignored safety questions in the egoistic pursuit of profit resulting in the poisoning of thousands of working-class people (Pearce and Tombs, 1989). Is it really the case that underdeveloped countries can only develop by allowing the exploitation of their workers? In the west, exploitation in real hard conditions is actually returning. In reply the influence of Marx lives on in three areas at least:

- An *idealist* commitment to Marxism which claims that it is only by remaining faithful to Marx that we can fully understand the nature of the state and its regulation of society.

- A *left realist* approach which keeps the moral intuition and some of the critical approach but works within the structures of liberal democratic society. This is committed to a grass-roots democraticising of the institutions and taking seriously issues such as the victimisation effects of crime.

- Many Marxists have become fashionable *post-modern scholars*; particularly fond of deconstructive strategies.

The humanist sentiment and the critique of exploitation lives on ... but the methodology varies.

Emile Durkheim (1858–1917)

Durkheim and modernity

The work of Emile Durkheim has left a large legacy for criminological writings. There are a number of themes in Durkheim's work which we shall bring out:

- the idea of sociological positivism, and the argument that sociology could provide a master-discourse as well as have its own special province;

- social solidarity as the glue to society, and the division between *mechanical* and *organic* solidarity;

- the use of law as an index of social solidarity;

- the normalcy of crime in any society which has power centres;

- the openness of human nature and the vast range of human desire;

- the ever present possibility of *anomie* or a state of normlessness overtaking social life;

- the necessity to construct a moral individualism to counter utilitarianism as the basis of social solidarity in modern societies.

Sociological positivism

Durkheim specified that sociology should use the methods of observation and hypothesis testing with which the natural sciences operate. However social phenomenon are very different entities to observe than natural phenomenon. How, for example, do we identify social class? For Durkheim the fundamental subject matter for sociology was moral phenomenon. Moral phenomenon cannot be directly observed, but must be observed through the use of indexes; through other phenomenon which express a presence of the underlying moral conditions. In *The Division of Labour and Society* Durkheim argued that law provided an index of social solidarity. By observing the law and legal institutions we could identify different forms of underlying social solidarities. Moreover, whilst the forms of social solidarity were difficult to get at, the form and content of law can be easily observed from the written record of legal history and the actual operation of institutions such as the criminal justice system. Durkheim's positivism is a methodology of using indices or easily observable entities as expressions or reflections of underlying moral phenomenon. Through the registration and calculation of movements and trends in such observable indices, we can come to understand trends and changes in the underlying moral phenomenon. This method was clearly visible in Durkheim's work in *Suicide,* where he used the official suicide statistics as indices of social cohesion and social isolation. In using such positivist methodologies Durkheim argues that there are no crucial distinctions between the natural sciences and the social sciences. The subject matter of the social sciences is social facts not visible to crude observation, but these social facts are to be treated as natural things. Moreover, as is clear from Durkheim's *Rules of Sociological Methods*, social science can be value free. The sociologist or criminologist is to be detached and objective in his analysis. Society and social phenomenon are actual entities existing 'out there', and it is possible for the observer to come to describe and explain them using various other indices.

Social solidarity

In *The Division of Labour and Society* Durkheim argues that there are two types of social solidarity which characterise societies. Durkheim uses these types, or models, in a similar way to a methodology that Weber had used in looking at the vast variations in human society, namely we need to develop ideal types or models which guide us in our understanding. Neither kind of social solidarity will exist in pure form. In modern societies, organic solidarity predominates. While in pre-modern, more simple societies, mechanical solidarity dominates.

In Durkheim's work there is always a duality of processes and functions in operation. For example, the very concept of society involves an almost positive notion of solidarity (ie the achievement of cohesiveness or integration) and regulation (ie restraints upon the pursuit of self-interest of people).

In pre-modern societies mechanical solidarity is based on likeness and uniformity, on shared values, ideas and beliefs among the social body. These shared ideas, values and beliefs constitute what Durkheim calls the 'conscience collective'. The life situation in pre-modern societies is a clear response to the homogeneity of groups which demonstrate similarities between individuals and the strength of the common moral symptoms. We may say that there is very little emphasis upon individuality or individual personal identity, on the contrary, the emphasis is on integration into the group and group identity.

In modern society, exemplified by a complex division of labour, an organic solidarity develops. As roles and occupational tasks become more and more specialised, individuals occupy different occupational roles, with a concomitant difference in life experiences and social knowledge. These different experiences and lifestyles lead to different outlooks and beliefs. Accordingly, the conscience collective must become more fluid and decline in its intensity of hold over individuals. For Durkheim the conscience collective of modern societies was increasingly tied up with the moral affirmation of the dignity of the individual. Organic solidarity was based not on likeness, homogeneity and uniformity of belief but on heterogeneity and interdependency of social roles.

The use of law as an index of social solidarity

Mechanical solidarity found its legal effect in penal or repressive law. To Durkheim the function of such law was to express and protect the collective conscience, to affirm the shared belief by quickly condemning and punishing those who denied, or went against, the shared expectations about behaviour. When a crime occurred in conditions of mechanical solidarity the crime was not an event against individual, but an attack on the entire social fabric and therefore likely to be dealt with harshly. In organic solidarity the law comes to be more responsive to individualism, for example, the criminal law moves more to protect the rights of individual persons and their ownership of property. The law becomes more concerned with restitution rather than punishment. Durkheim argued the growth of restitutive civil law represented the most easily observable indices of the development of organic solidarity. Empirical research on this point, however, appears to show that Durkheim's argument on legal evolution is historically incorrect. Many would argue that it is modern society which makes use of repressive law, and that the methodologies of simple or so-called primitive societies were actually much more restitutive. Although the empirical evidence weakens Durkheim's analysis in terms of the empirical substance of his models, this does not affect the theoretical validity, or insights to be gained from his arguments on the forms of social solidarity.

Crime is normal in a society

Durkheim argued that crime is normal in society because there is actually no extra social, or natural, dividing line between criminal activity and other more acceptable activities. The dividing line is a process of demarcation and labelling, which serves to distinguish the acceptable and the unacceptable conduct. The use of the concept of crime is merely the strongest labelling procedure or processes which work to maintain social solidarity. Its effectiveness actually comes from the process of punishment and social emotions which are engendered. For by observing the punishment of people, and participating in the feeling of moral and social outrage at the offence, individuals become bound to the common perception of the justified and unjustified, of the right and wrong. The process of punishment is inescapable, as Durkheim points out in a famous example:

> 'Imagine a society of saints, a perfect cloister of exemplary individuals. Crimes, properly so called, will there be unknown; but faults which appear venial to the layman will create there the same scandal that the ordinary offence does in ordinary consciousness. If, then, this society has the power to judge and punish, it will define these acts as criminal and will treat them as such. For the same reason, the perfect and upright man judges his smallest failings with a severity that the majority reserve for acts more truly in the nature of an offence.' (1965: 68-69)

Even if the behaviours that are labelled criminal at time X in a society, were to be discontinued at time X2, new behaviours would be considered as crime. Crime therefore is an inevitable concept of organised society to respond to the inescapable diversity of behaviour within society. Durkheim calls upon us to consider that crime is actually a factor in public health, an integral part of social organisation. That does not mean to say that there are not abnormal or pathological levels of crime, but that both the absence of crime and a surplus of crime is pathological. A society in which there is no crime would be a rigidly over-policed oppressive society. But a society which is experiencing too high a rate of crime is a society in which the balance between regulation and individuality has broken down.

Crime is the flip side of modern individual freedom. As Durkheim claimed:

> 'To make progress, individual originality must be able to express itself. In order that the originality of the idealist whose dreams transcend his century may find expression, it is necessary that the originality of the criminal, who is below the level of his time, shall also be possible. One does not occur without the other.' (1965: 71)

Durkheim and the openness of human nature

Durkheim built upon the philosophical tradition that human beings are ultimately social animals. For Durkheim there is a difference between the regulation of physical or instinctive needs, and social needs. For example, when we eat to satisfy the cravings of physical hunger at a certain point the body itself will resist additional food but our social needs for example, those for wealth, prestige or power are regulated externally through the constraining forces of society. At root, our desires were 'an insatiable and bottomless abyss'. Without regulation, without a structuring of understanding and interpretation of the meaning of being a human being, all expectations are meaningless, all potentialities are both possible, and yet void. Without regulation the desire for absolute freedom becomes self-destructive:

> '... it is not true, then, that human activities can be released from all restraint ... its nature and method of manifestation ... dependent only on itself, but on other beings, who consequently restrain and regulate it.' ([1897] 1951: 252)

Society installs a subjective understanding of the legitimacy of the state of affairs of the social body. The smooth functioning of the system is founded on the subjective understanding that a certain order of positions and rewards is natural.

> 'As a matter of fact, at every moment of history there is a perception, in the moral consciousness of societies, of the respective value of different social services, the relative reward due to each, and the consequent degree of comfort appropriate, on average, to workers in each occupation. The different functions are graded in public opinion, and a certain coefficient of well-being assigned to each, according to its place in the hierarchy. According to accepted ideas, for example, a certain way of living is considered the upper limit to which a workman may aspire in his efforts to improve his existence, then there is another limit below which he is not willingly permitted to fall unless he has seriously demeaned himself.' ([1897] 1966: 249).

But this complex set of beliefs can come apart. Such was the case in the breakup of the ancient civilisations and Durkheim believed a similar process was at work. Discontent, frustration, meaninglessness, in short ... anomie was growing.

The notion of anomie

Durkheim's concept of anomie has spawned a vast literature. As with the Marxist notion of alienation, it has symbolised one of the characteristic problems of modernity, and the self-identity of modern individuals. Again there are two aspects at work. One is the absence of regulations or rules so that one's understanding of social order is insufficiently co-ordinated. This sense of anomie is a social structural problem, not a psychological condition. However, the second effect is that this state of affairs produces in the individual a sense of isolation and of the meaninglessness of life and work. Note that here the psychological factor reflects a condition of the social organisation as a whole. Durkheim argued that the economic structure of *laissez faire* society, with its strong emphasis upon self-interested behaviour was itself a major source of anomie. Another cause, however, was the forced division of labour where individuals are located in a structure of specialisation and economic hierarchies where their position was not freely chosen but thrust upon each person by the accident of birth, by the custom and rituals of their socialisation, and by operation of law. Perhaps if all the rituals of primary ordering were operating to make the individuals content with their position, anomie would not be a danger. However a primary motivating force for modern society is the drive for self-interest and the arguments that the self is responsible for his or her destiny. In reality many individuals find themselves estranged, resentful and aspiring to social positions which are in fact arbitrarily closed off to them. Durkheim argues that this is most clear when we note that individuals enjoy special advantages because of their possession of inherited wealth, or where, because of prejudice in society, a distinction is attached to individuals independent of their merits because of contingent facts (such as gender, race and class). Robert Merton (1938) was to call the reaction to this an 'anomie of injustice'.

Durkheim illustrated the concept of anomie through his analysis of the social causes of suicide. Although it may appear that suicide is the ultimate individual act, Durkheim attempted to show that this behaviour was, in fact, the result of networks of social processes. His methodology has become the standard bearer of sociological positivism, and consisted of an analysis of variations in rates of suicide in different nations and different sub-groupings within French society. By analysing the rates Durkheim sought to show that it was sociology, not psychology, that could provide us with the real information for the understanding of the nature of suicide. This reliance upon official statistics has also provided us with a case study of the dangers in relying naively upon official statistics in constructing theories, or ascertaining trends in phenomenon. Durkheim hypothesises that there were two main 'suicidogenetic' social currents. These are the dimensions of (i) integration (the extent to which individuals experience belonging to the collective), and (ii) regulation (the extent to which actions and desires of individuals are bound by moral values). Again with Durkheim it is all a question of the mean. There can be too much integration and too little integration; over-regulation and under-regulation. However, the empirical assertions of the specific theory are called into question when the validity of the statistics he used is doubted.

Durkheim's analysis of suicide as the paradigm example of positivism and statistics

Durkheim developed an analysis of suicide which has become a motif for constructing positivist theories upon statistical data. To demonstrate his argument that suicide, which was considered a personal act of the will of an actor, was actually highly dependent upon a range of social factors, he measured the rates of suicide for various groups and correlated these with indices of social factors: this would lead us to the social laws of suicide. The individual will of a person heavily constrained by a set of laws which flow through him and these 'real laws are discoverable'. The subject is constrained by 'real, living, active forces which, because of the way they determine the individual, prove their independence of him.' There are types of suicide determined by their own configurations of 'social facts' (eg, the 'egoistic').

Durkheim built up his distinctions on the basis of treating the official rates as given. The criticisms of Durkheim mirror those which positivist approaches to criminal statistics suffered generally.

First, the positivist self-criticism: the data Durkheim analysed was official statistics from the 1840s to the 1870s, and this information is subject to error. Errors of collection and reportage thus prejudice the analysis, through data fault. Similarly, much of subsequent criminological investigation can be seen as an attempt to explain the official crime statistics – if these are suspect, then so is the whole analysis. The positivists' message is to correct such errors by providing real, actual data as 'true facts' upon which to join correlations of 'observable occurrences'. Such alternative measures as self-report, or victim studies, are relied upon to correct the picture the official statistics give.

Second, the interactionist approach. The statistics are never capable of conversion into 'real facts' or 'actual empirical data' at all, since the original or basic data, involve a process of interpretation and symbolic construction of meaning which is unable to be analysed, other than spuriously, by positivist methodology.

The interactionist approach to suicide can be seen in Atkinson's concentration upon the 'process' of categorising deaths as 'suicide'. He rejects the objectivity of a real rate of suicide which would provide the material for analysis. Instead coroners interact with the situations surrounding death, and their courts interpret events, producing suicide rates as a result of the interaction of their 'common sense' theories of suicide with the material presented to them. Coroners bring sets of narrative expectations, or patterns of cultural history, which, if the material fits, mean that a suicide will most likely be registered. If not further investigation will be conducted, or no suicide is found (see JM Atkinson, 1971; Douglas, 1967).

Friedrich Nietzsche (1844–1900)

Whereas Marx saw modern man as trapped within the capitalist mode of production and suffering under commodity fetishism, for Nietzsche culture and ascetic ideals constrained man. Mankind cannot exist without intellectual frameworks; horizons which give meaning to the world and existence. Man needs imaginative leaps to give purpose to social life and to create new projects.

Man's intellectual frameworks were not modern enough

The structures of belief and meaning that modern man found were not yet truly modern, they were still in the shadow of certain beliefs, such as the belief in God, the belief in some foundation or point to being, and belief in a certain limitation of truth. Modernity was one-sided in that it constructed technologies and forms of knowledge which were the result of man's desire to dominate nature by reason and science, but they did not provide mankind with thorough-going structures of meaning. Man had power without direction; knowledge without wisdom.

The paradox of the whole and the parts

Modern man would come to live in a paradoxical position where he was surrounded by petty truths without the big truth. He would inhabit a structure of understanding which would force men to keep searching for truth and for meaning, even though that structure of understanding constantly reveals to mankind that ultimate truth is not to be found. Nietzsche feared that the outcome would be a form of social paralysis, or weariness, as man sees flux and chaos, change and difference everywhere, and accumulated masses upon masses of meaningless data.

The danger of nihilism

In modern society the will for truth, the will for science, the will for power, the will to master, results in the inability of man, the esteeming animal, to actually fully appreciate the value of existence. Thus, whereas Marx sees capitalism as the problem to be overcome, Nietzsche defined the major problem as nihilism. Nihilism involves man's pursuit of goals, commodities and truths, in such a way that he cannot fulfil himself. Again Nietzsche asks us to question the basic premises upon which modern society has developed. Structurally, Nietzsche calls into question any identification of positivist functionalism. We are not to accept that the structures of modern society are in any way a natural or inevitable product of some form of evolution for the better. Instead of any form of consensus about our institutions and our networks of social control we must understand that behind them all have been diverse programmes, sets of projects, and desires responding to different stimulations and fears.

The structures of contemporary social life are the result of a combination of what Nietzsche would call wills to power. Thus we must keep on asking, not what things are for, but how do they come about, what are their historical origins? How did the Enlightenment, or the structures of liberal bourgeois thought, come into play and what and whose interests do they serve? What do their origins reveal about the scope, the limits and the contradictions, of modern thought? The givens of our society are historical products, nothing can be accepted as unquestionable, and we must even at times suspect our very questions, for there is no virginal pursuit of truth and knowledge. Knowledge is never pure; we do not seek knowledge for itself, but always as useful for some project.

Is Nietzsche concerned with politics? Consider the notion of the state and the choice of communal ends, and the fact that these ends are imposed and defended by potentially violent political means. Weber demanded political legitimacy be understood in terms of domination, not merely impartial principles of morality or justice; the rule of law is one tactic, one conception of domination. Surely then Nietzsche's relevance is undoubtable, for, by denying the possibility of any functionalist positivism, indeed any possibility of a pure regime of truth, Nietzsche makes the question of any principles of social justice or of legality as one amongst a range of objects for political and social analysis.

The supposed truths of political and social science, or of moral philosophy, are not the truth of what we might call theoretical rationality, pure in, and of, itself, but are rather products of thought in the realm of practical wisdom. There are truths which are only an advanced form of the customary morality created by a people to sustain particular forms of communal life. In *The Genealogy of Morals,* Nietzsche traces the historical origins of the moral world of modern man to sets of psychological conditions and desires surrounding social existence. Nietzsche understands the creation of all social values, indeed of the very structure of society, in terms of political domination which is most powerfully achieved by agreement as to the nature of things – ie by getting people to agree on the nature of the problem. Who controls the modes of thought of a society has the keys to domination. When we co-operate in a set of policies because that is the rational course of action, we are placing ourselves in the supposed neutral grip of knowledge, but can we trust that knowledge? Can we really be sure that the knowledge is actually holding out the real image of society? As Nietzsche puts it in his series of notes which were to be made into a text of reconstruction of social values, and published after his death as *The Will To Power.*

> '... all unity, is unity only as organisation and co-operation – just as a human community is a unity – as opposed to an optimistic anarchy, as a pattern of domination that signifies a unity, but is not a unity.' (1968: Aphorism - 561)

Domination is necessary for the creation and imposition of communal ends; domination is the secret of politics. Therefore there are no apolitical positions. In the complex psychological origins of all social values including, one might argue, the principles of modern law, there is a struggle, an imposition by domination of one set over another. All forms of reason, whether these are the reasoning forms of political rationality, of moral rationality, or of legal rationality, cannot escape their political nature. It then follows that there is no totally predeterminate result to any form of social, moral, political or legal deliberation. It is not that the structures of thought themselves can ever determine an outcome.

Outcomes can possibly be determined by the political or moral assumptions which one section, or one political position has adopted in the past, since if one is to be faithful to these assumptions this may lead you onto certain outcomes. But even this commitment is itself a political stance.

To many critics today this analysis of deliberation smacks of radical indetermination of all decision making and therefore points to nihilism. But Nietzsche's argument is not that nihilism is the inevitable consequence of modernity, but that nihilism is the result of the processes of modernity if we do not develop a coherent position against it. It is necessary to be fully aware about what one is doing even when one believes that one is being led by determinate rationality.

The legacy of Weber and Nietzsche in the work of Foucault

As we shall see one of the most popular recent writers from France, Michel Foucault (1973, 1977, 1979, 1980, 1988), creates a body of writing concerning the concept of disciplinisation, a relation between discipline, constitutionalism and power which is located in legacies of Nietzsche and Weber. Foucault identifies power working:

> 'perpetually to reinscribe this relation through a form of unspoken warfare; to reinscribe it in social institutions, in economic inequalities, in language, in the bodies themselves of each and everyone of us.' (1980: 90)

Foucault develops the power and domination which Nietzsche highlights as not the easily identified power of the sovereign, of direct political institutionalisation of the state (which it would seem that Weber and indeed classical criminology will point us to). Instead, Foucault implicitly draws upon Nietzsche and Weber to highlight another form of power, a form he calls disciplinisation. In Foucault's analysis, we moderns are not free self-determining creatures, but are rather subjected to a set of demands to be properly functioning, to be normal, to be the best we can be. How do we know what this is? Only through the various knowledges of normalcy, the knowledges of the self – thus we are subjects of these knowledges. But are these knowledges actually true? We inhabit a multiple form of subjugation which surrounds us, and indeed operates through our understanding of the necessary functionality of roles and plays within the modern social organisation.

Culture and knowledge largely constitute the conditions of the modern

One consequence of this, of course, is that we are led into an understanding of culture as not being merely expressive, but also as constituting modern identity while repressing potential elements. This is a crucial area of focus in the modern array of cultural studies which seek to understand and to investigate the operations of what has come to be called the culture industry. Culture is often understood as if it was the manifestation of the expressive needs of modern society but culture may well sublimate on repress other needs even as it created further needs, in turn creating forms of subtle domination.

What are the implications for criminology? One obviously concerns the conception of crime and the various knowledges which criminology throws up. Nietzsche in a way would be arguing that to think of any such thing as an essence to crime, an essential nature to crime and therefore to search for the essential nature of criminality or of the criminal is to create an illusion. It is to transform a mere set of contingent facts, ie legislation, behaviour which goes against the legislation, into some form of slippage of essentialism. One must constantly investigate in the historical form how the facts of particular crimes came about and how these serve particular interests.

Another central theme of Nietzsche is that of the modern administered world. Nietzsche's work espouses a radical individualism that strives to overcome the constraints and repressions of such administration. We might argue, however, that whilst Nietzsche highlights this concern, and points to the necessity for the individual to undercut presuppositions and assumptions that structure this administration, we cannot provide the individual with a radical new philosophy and conceptions of existence which enables the individual to, if you like, float free. Social structure binds. Nietzsche takes the drive of modernity towards radical individuality, radical freedom to its rhetorical extremes; ... the consequence is a void when the free man searches for humane foundations.

The void underlying modern existence

Nietzsche's radical individual is so free that the world, and the certainties of the world, disappear into a metaphysical abyss. How can a truly modern individual achieve stability? How can modern individuals create structures which give life coherence without recourse to pre-modern formations, such as religion? Two figures deeply inscribed in Nietzsche's work are that of Apollo and Dionysus: the Appollonian attitude desires stability, order, attachment, commitment, security, while the Dionysian attitude involves:

'... the affirmation or passing away and destroying ... of saying yes to opposition and war; becoming, along with a radical repudiation of the very concept of being.' (Ecce Homo [1888], in 1966: 729)

What is it to be modern? Again with Marx, Nietzsche would agree that modern life, the essential aspect of modern life, is not the pursuit of self-preservation, or even of material comfort, but is a richer creative process. This creative process must be viewed against a backdrop of striving to destroy what has gone before. Creation is not merely a question of expanding life chances that are to be proclaimed as a goal for modernity. What drives the creative process of modernity is the very phenomenon of willing, of desiring to better ourselves, as individuals and society; through this process modern man realises his destiny and also understands the pathos of his condition. For, to will, to desire, if unorganised, is to encounter chaos, a void of continual destruction, creation and deconstruction. Mankind is trapped in the constant movement between scepticism and deconstruction and the need for some certainty to give coherence to action. We recognise that mankind has a metaphysical need for certainty, for a stable world with fixed boundaries in which to act, otherwise man will become paralysed by the chaos of his experience, and, in seeing the possibilities of becoming everywhere, will be unable to progress at all.

'This is a universal law, a living thing can only be healthy, strong, and productive with a certain horizon; if it is incapable of drawing one around itself ... it will come to an untimely end. Cheerfulness, a good conscience, belief in a future, the joyful deed – all depend, on the individual as well as the nation, on there being a line which divides the invisible and clear from the vague and shadowy (*Use and Abuse of History*, 1957: 7-8).

Man must, of necessity, create philosophical, moral, and political systems expressed in language. These, however, are interpretations created by man and imposed on the fluctuating chaos of reality to meet his needs for certainty. These interpretations are the highest manifestations of the will to power:

'... to impose upon becoming the character of being – that is the supreme will to power.' (1968: Aphorism, 617)

The created nature of modern man

Man's destiny, man's own being, is tied up with the process of knowing the world, for, in the search to master the world, man must also constitute and master himself. The role of intellectual endeavour is to give images, ideals, to structure our will to power. As Nietzsche says of the philosopher:

'... in the philosopher there is nothing whatever that is in person; above all his morality be of decided and decisive to who he is – that is to what order of rank the innermost drive of his nature, stands his relations to each other.' (*Beyond Good and Evil*, in 1966: Aph, 6)

In seeking to understand the world, in creating structures of social theory, politics and moral philosophy, man gives form to the world, he changes it and in a sense changes himself. Whilst man is to some extent therefore, mastering nature, even exploiting it, subjecting nature to his will, he is also creating and mastering the chaos which is the openness of human nature. In knowing and striving, man creates not only an understanding of the world, but also an understanding and interpretation of himself. When man masters nature he also masters himself, and man comes to obey the philosophical and moral systems he creates. All life is a form of exploitation and domination:

'... life itself is essentially appropriation, injury, overpowering of what is alien and weaker; suppression, hardness, imposition of one's own form, incorporation and at the least at its mildest exploitation.' (Beyond Good and Evil, in 1966: Aph, 259)

Commanding and obeying oneself and others is the nature of life, as Nietzsche's great literary character, Zarathustra, expresses it:

'... wherever I found the living, there I heard also the speech of obedience. Whatever lives obeys. And this is the second point; He who cannot obey himself is commanded. That is the nature of the living. This, however, is the third point that I heard; that commanding is harder than obeying; not only because he who commands must carry the burden of all who obey, and because the burden may usually crush him. An experiment and hazard appeared to me to be in all commanding, and where ever the living command it hazards itself. Indeed even when it commands itself, it must still pay for its commanding. It must become the judge the avenger and the victim of its own law'. (Thus Spoke Zarathustra: in 1968: 226)

Nietzsche would agree with Marx that our modern consciousness is founded upon the historical conditions and forces in which we live. However Nietzsche does not agree that those forces can be reduced for some master model, for example, a thesis of economic structuring, for even that particular interpretation of reality would be an historical contention. Marx's social theory is a reflection of his desire to locate the source, or the essence, of man's problematic condition in a particular structure; in Marx's case, the capitalist mode of production, etc. But Nietzsche claims all the interpretations which make up social theory are attempts to shape social consciousness and to impose particular interpretations upon the openness of social reality. All interpretations, all knowledge, are creations of the will to power, and serve to change man's conception of reality. In so doing they change man's internal relationships to his drives, his ambitions, his desires; they structure his relations to the external world and they create, thereby, the conditions for his future activities. What is history? History is the ongoing set of projects, some successful, some mere attempts. It is a set of frustrations of man in his attempts to understand and master nature, himself, and his fellow human beings.

Man is differentiated from animal existence by a huge differentiation in power. This power is cultural and imaginative; it gives man greater freedom and scope for creative development than the animal, modernity creates social power by releasing the processes of individualisation. The sovereign individual is the great creation of modernity.

'... this emancipated individual with the actual right to make promises, this master of a free will, this sovereign man – how should he not be aware of his superiority over all those who lack the right to make promises and stand as their own guarantors, of how much trust, how much ear, how much reverence he arouses ... and of how this mastery over himself also necessarily gives him mastery over conditions and over circumstances over nature and over more short willed and unreliable creatures.' (Genealogy of Morals, Second essay, Section 2)

Modern man exerts more power than the pre-modern, because he has distanced himself from static routines, from being embedded into stable sets of traditions, structures and rituals, he can direct his willing, his desire, his imaginative grasp of the possible, to a broader range. This freedom means modern man can create formal structures of rationality, abstract cultural and creative. Modern man steps out of the locality through the power of writing and developing systems of information storage. Mankind forces itself from the bonds of immediate experience so that abstract thought and national planning is possible.

This new social/cultural understanding, the new social consciousness of progress, of predictability and of the engagement in social projects, demands a certain predictability and progressive being to individual man.

> To ordain the future in advance man must first have learned to distinguish necessary events from chance ones, to think causally, to see and anticipate distant eventualities, as if they belong to the present, to decide with certainty what is a goal and what it means to it, and in general be able to calculate and compute. Man himself must first of all become calculable, regular, necessary. (*The Genealogy of Morals*, second essay, section 1).

This self-consciousness is a result of the modern conditions of existence, only as a social animal can man become conscious of himself as an 'individual' self, and the conditions of modern society are furthering this process via the reflexivity, or creation of knowledge, about the social and the human. Modern man is creating a new structure of intellectual and social consciousness; upon this his sensibilities, his very civilisation is built. Modern man exists under the rule of language, under the sovereign of words and naming processes. Man is trapped within the possibilities and weaknesses of the structures of communication. As compared to many of the animals, man is an extremely weak and vulnerable animal. Nietzsche calls man the most endangered animal, he uniquely needs the protection of his peers. Man is forced to communicate his distress and this requires the human species to develop his consciousness to a higher level:

> 'Consciousness is really only a net of communication between human beings; it is only as such that it had to develop; a solitary human being who lives like a beast of prey would not have needed it. That our actions, thoughts, feelings, and movements enter our own consciousness at least part of it, that is a result of a must that for a terribly long time lauded it over man. As the most endangered animal he needed help and protection, he needed his peers, he had to learn to express his distress, and to make himself understood; and for all of this he needed consciousness first of all.' (*The Gay Science*, 1968: Aph 354)

Is modern liberal society necessarily progressive? In *Beyond Good and Evil* Nietzsche scornfully talked of the tendency for people to demand new conditions of society in which exploitative aspects would be removed. Nietzsche thought this was impossibly utopian: 'It is as if they promised to invent a way of life that would dispense with all organic functions'. There would be no ultimate escape from the necessity of exploitation and politics. It may well be that the modern state is a political mode of organisation which holds itself out as functional, as carrying out necessary and natural tasks, but the society shaped and created under this form will in a real sense, be an illusory community. The modern state is a political organisation much greater in power than previous forms of social organisation; it's bedrock is ultimately its cultural forms, its ways of thinking. Whereas for Marx the modern state responded to the need to organise social and political life, so that particular economic relations centred around capitalist formations of credit, debt, buying, and exchange, were effectual for Nietzsche the processes of buying and selling and exchange are vitally important not so much for their economic consequences, but for their psychological consequences. The organisational instrument of the modern state is law, and underlying the legal framework, are forms of knowledge, ie jurisprudence, structures of modes of discourse centred around political legitimacy and which portray law in an acceptable mode. These underlying forms of discourse enable the institution of law to gain psychological acceptance by the populace.

This acceptance is blinded to the reality of coercion which still lurks behind law – jurisprudence created concepts of justice and rights, but these are special artefacts and ought not to blind us to the organic struggle beneath such civilised discursive forms. Law remains

'... the most decisive act of a modern supreme power ... Just and unjust exist, accordingly, only after the institution of the law ... to speak of just or unjust in itself is quite senseless; in itself of course no injury, assault, exploitation, destruction, can be unjust since life operates essentially through injury assault, exploitation, destruction.' (*The Genealogy of Morals*, second essay, section 12)

One cannot step outside of the processes of political or jurisprudential or moral discourse, to come up with some method by which one can say whether, for instance, modern liberal democracy was truly or absolutely just or unjust. The very terminology, the very ability to speak in terms of the just or the unjust, can only be done through a particular form of language, which we might call a language game. These language games come about as a result of a the work of jurisprudence or political–social discourses. It is impossible to speak outside of a language which itself is already deeply embedded in a relationship with the very institution which one is trying to understand. What is the ultimate aim of legal regulation? The state may claim that it is an organ operating so as to look after the common interest. However, this is becoming difficult since the regime of legal regulation is increasingly pluralistic, and deciphering its forms is increasingly difficult. What constitutes the unity of the people? Political freedom must not be seen as human freedom, while for Marx political freedom masks social inequality, for Nietzsche it hides the psychological repression of individuals. Modern Europe was being subjected to two distinct impulses. One was the drive to individuality, associated with the need for individual freedom, and the creation of individual projects; the other was a tendency towards equalitarianism. The discourse of rights, political equality and the role of jurisprudential knowledge was to attain equivocation between these processes. Justice would be a method of translating different claims so that they could be rendered commensurable; although no two individuals or things are ever fully equal, the desire for justice is to some extent an expression of good will amongst the parties:

> 'Justice on an elementary level is the goodwill amongst parties of approximately equal power to come to terms with one another, to reach an understanding by means of a settlement – and to compel parties of lesser power to reach a settlement amongst themselves.' (*The Genealogy of Morals*, second essay, section 8).

The discourse of liberal democratic life, the aims of the modern society, claimed that it had found truths of political economy to guide the society. It claimed there was a set of foundational structures which could be studied and understood which explained how social processes worked. Writers who claimed utility provided the key to social progress, moreover, made a false claim to reconcile differences and oppositions. Nietzsche, however, asks what is to happen if in reality not all individuals are actually incorporated? As Nietzsche expresses it:

> '... refraining mutually from injury, violence and exploitation and placing one's will on a par with that of someone else – this may become in a certain rough sense, good manners among individuals if the appropriate conditions are present (namely, if these men are actually similar in strength and value standards and belong together in one body). But as soon as this principle is extended and possibly even accepted as the fundamental principle of society, it immediately proves to be what it really is – a will to the denial of life, a principle of disintegration and decay.' (*Beyond Good and Evil*, Aph: 259)

If substantial sections are denied the will to life; if they cannot exercise their will to power, why will they refrain from violence? From fraud? From expropriation? Both liberal democracy and socialist equality could suffer. It is a strong criticism of administrative social equality:

> '... equality of rights could all too easily be changed into equality violating rights – namely into a common war of all that is rare, strange, privileged, the higher man, the higher soul, the higher duty, the higher responsibility and the abundance of creative power and masterfulness.' (*Beyond Good and Evil*, Aph: 212)

Behind the desire for equality, Nietzsche finds a herd morality, ultimately epitomised in the rhetorical demands for a socialist structure. The pursuit of individuality, rather than equality should be the goal of social relations. But in the liberal democratic structure the demand for equal respect for individuals put down and defended in law, criminal law and penality, may itself only make sense if all the appropriate conditions are present. That is, if the social structure systematically excludes individuals, then the conditions of the fundamental principle of individual respect are not working to the advantage of all – the reality of law in this situation is both oppressive and creative. In the conditions of modernity it is law, rather than tradition or status, which formulates the conditions necessary to constitute and preserve a community. Modern social life involves the creation of social structures which intensify social power and enable the preserving of power – those who do not fit in will feel the down-side of this power. The weak will become criminals, and become subjects for the exercise of the power to punish; but others will be labelled criminals because they wish to defy the herd. Criminal acts may be either the result of weakness or of the will to power; criminality becomes the site of multiple flows and effects. Social explanation is unavoidably multi-faceted, but power, and the call to power, is at the centre.

CHAPTER FOUR

THE PROBLEM OF CLASSICAL CRIMINOLOGY: STABILISING DISORDER THROUGH LAW; OR HOW TO ACHIEVE THE RULE OF LAW AND HIDE THE CHAOS OF EARLY MODERNITY

'Julius stopped in front of his friend. "Listen, Rupert. If there were a perfectly just judge I would kiss his feet and accept his judgments upon my knees. But these are merely words and feelings. There is no such being and even the concept of one is empty and senseless. I tell you, Rupert, it's an illusion, an illusion."

"I don't believe in a judge," said Rupert, "but I believe in justice. And I suspect you do too, or you wouldn't be getting so excited."

"No, no, if there is no judge there is no justice, and there is no one, I tell you, no one." ' (I Murdoch, *A Fairly Honourable Defeat*, 1970)

Introduction to classical criminology

The 18th century was dominated by two opposite psychological states: fear and hope. Classical criminology was born in the dialectic of fear and optimism. Fear of the breakdown of society, fear that the cosmos appeared one huge void, fear of the absence of secure foundations to existence. Fear ... of the mob, the ragged poverty-stricken mass of humanity which the movement out of the tradition-bound localities of the pre-modern had created.

God was slowly dying; the cosmos appeared unhinged. If there was no God to centre things around, then there was only the mass of individuals and their capacities (reason, experience, their ability to interact with nature). How could these be put into productive form? What would secure order? By what device could practical answers be given, what mechanism of control could be devised?

The 16th and 17th centuries grappled with the transition to the modern, the English social theorist Thomas Hobbes (*Man and Citizen: De Homine and De Cive; Leviathan*) stood above all in linking fear and knowledge to construct a new imperative of human endeavour. The demand was clear: give us real knowledge, knowledge of the human condition so that we can create a device to provide social stability. Hobbes understood clearly that every human society is, at its most basic form, men bonded together in the face of death. To brood on the inevitability of death leads to despair. Hobbes arranged a bargain with the cosmic forces – natural human politics is freedom and power structured only by the madness we face when our reason encounters the mystery of the human condition – we resign our search for ultimate grounding to organisation; we grant a sovereign the right, and ability, to brood for us. Hobbes gave the legacy of sovereignty and law as the instrument of command. He bequeathed a powerful intellectual device which still provides guidance; we create governments of strength through the guiding idea of contract, that fundamental jurisprudential imagination of the modern. The content and shape of modern law is founded not upon God's will, but on the will and desires of man as he grapples with the problems of the human condition.

God's death demands new legitimation strategies

God's death left man alone on the world. True, there were a lot of men – if God did not control the law then who did? If the will of the law was not God's, then whose? Two opposing answers: it must be the will of one of us, the strongest – or it must be the will of all of us. The law must be the instrument of one, or all must be made into one. Authority versus radical democracy; totalitarianism versus radical democracy; the command of the sovereign versus law as the expression of the will of the people (the general will as in Rousseau; law as the progressive uncovering of right, as in Hegel; law as the peoples' bible book of freedom, as it appeared to the early Marx).

What does classical criminology comprise? Classical criminology is a label used to make sense of a period of writings in the late 18th and early 19th century, which reformed the system of investigation and punishing of criminal offences. A reasonably coherent, rational intellectual structure was developed which legitimated the creation of a system of criminal justice which predominates today.

We can give a narrow or wide reading of classical criminology. Most texts give a narrow reading, they see it as concerned with setting up a rational framework for a modern system of criminal justice, but it is also part of the attempt to provide answers to the question of structuring government when we are in a social situation devoid of a foundational touchstone such as God. We shall use the writings of Beccaria, Bentham and John Austin as representative of this enterprise.

Beccaria (1738-1794)

Cesare Becarria is usually depicted as a humane reformer reacting to a time when the criminal law, and its enforcement, was barbarous and arbitrary. Certainly Becarria's social context was one of secret accusations, brutal executions, torture, arbitrary and inconsistent investigations and findings of guilt, and class-linked disparities in punishments. However, we simplify the development in depicting Beccaria as an humanitarian; the context is the rationalisation of the criminal justice system. Rationalisation is no unitary process. There are many layers of cultural and political implications and effects at work. For example, we can place classical criminology within the history of ideas, in particular the development of philosophical radicalism; in terms of constitutionalism and governmentability it is part of the developing notion of 'the rule of law'; politically it is part of the changing political struggles where a growing middle class sought political power to accompany their economic power and break down the political monopoly enjoyed for instance, in England, by the landowning class; culturally it is an effect of the hopes of progressive social engineering, epitomised here by the Italian Caesar Beccaria and the Englishman Jeremy Bentham.

In *On Crimes and Punishment* Beccaria considered crime an injury to society. It was this injury to society, rather than to the immediate individual(s) who experienced it or the abstract sovereign, that was to direct and determine the degree of punishment. At one level Beccaria's text exemplifies Weber's analysis of the link between legal rationality and capitalism – Beccaria claims that the fundamental principle of the criminal law should rest upon positive sanction. Every member of the society is to have the perfect right to do anything not expressly prohibited by the law. Thus the law is to simply lay out minimum rules of social life and within those rules the populace can experiment, diversify and grow in knowledge, experiences and life forms. The law would bind the society and guide society by laying out clear, rational rules. The rules are laid down by a Sovereign body guided by a new science of decision making, namely utilitarianism (or the assumption that all social action should be guided by the goal of achieving the greatest happiness for the greatest number). From this viewpoint, the punishment of an individual for a crime was justified, and justifiable only, for its contribution to the prevention of future infringements on the happiness and well-being of others. Beccaria reasoned that certain and quick, rather than severe, punishments would best accomplish the above goals:

'... in order for punishment not to be ... an act of violence of one or many against a private citizen, it must be ... public, prompt, ... the least possible in the given circumstances, proportionate to the crimes, [and] dictated by the laws.' ([1764] 1963: 99)

Torture, execution, and other 'irrational' activity must be abolished. In their place, there were to be quick and certain trials and, in the case of convictions, carefully calculated punishments. Beccaria proposed that accused persons be treated humanely before trial, with every right and facility extended to enable them to bring evidence on their own behalf. In Beccaria's time accused and convicted persons were detained in the same institutions, and subjected to the same punishments and conditions. In place of this, Beccaria argued for swift and sure punishments, to be imposed only upon those found guilty, with the punishments determined strictly in accordance with the damage to society caused by the crime.

It is often said that classical criminology ignores the causes of crime, but Beccaria certainly held that economic conditions, and bad laws, could cause crime. Additionally, he was clear that property crimes were committed primarily by the poor, and mainly out of necessity. Moreover, he was aware of what has come to be called opportunity transfer; that is, that imposing a severe punishment on a particular crime could deter someone from committing it, but at the same time make another crime attractive by comparison. Beccaria was also aware of the cultural power of severe punishments to add to the desperation of the populace and encourage them to indulge in violence. As he put it, laws could promote crime by diminishing the human spirit. A careful matching of the crime and its punishment, in keeping with the general interests of society, could make punishment a rational instrument of government. Jeremy Bentham extended this with his notion of a 'calculus' for realising these interests.

Jeremy Bentham (1748–1832)

A radical utilitarian, Bentham applied Beccaria's ideas to British conditions. Modernity was to be guided by the fundamental reference point of a science of ethics founded upon nature's command: 'the greatest happiness of the greatest number', a criteria Bentham attributed to the Scottish philosopher David Hume. Bentham gave precision to this idea, in part, through a pseudo-mathematical concept he called the 'felicity calculus'. This 'calculus' was intended as a means of estimating the goodness or badness of acts, the only 'measure of right or wrong'. Thus Bentham declared that notions of indefeasible rights, or contractual limitations on the power of government, were either meaningless or else confused references to the principle of utility. The basis of government was not contract but human need, and the satisfaction of human need is its sole justification. However, Bentham had a rather limited notion of need.

Bentham meant to make the law an efficient and economical means of preventing crime. Like Beccaria, Bentham insisted that prevention was the only justifiable purpose of punishment, and, furthermore, that punishment was too 'expensive' when it produced more evil than good, or when the same good could be obtained at the 'price' of less suffering. He recommended penalties be fixed so as to impose an amount of pain in excess of the pleasure that might be derived from the criminal act. It was this calculation of pain compared to pleasure that Bentham believed would deter crime. These ideas were formulated most clearly in his *Introduction to the Principles of Morals and Legislation*, first published in 1789, where the foundation of progress appears to lie in fully understanding the key principles and functionality of nature:

> 'Nature has placed mankind under the governance of two sovereign masters, pain and pleasure. It is for them alone to point out what we ought to do, as well as to determine what we shall do. On the one hand, the standard of right and wrong, on the other the chain of causes and effects, are fastened to their throne.' (Chapter 1 Section 1)

We can read 'nature' and find not only a description of how we operate, but, properly understood, the key to how we should operate. Moreover, this provides the key to progressive rationality. We can quantify our pleasures and pains, we can create a mathematics of happiness. With Bentham calculation overwhelms the humane approach – humanism is always a quantifiable conception. While Beccaria kept to some Kantian notions as to the dignity of man, Bentham would have none of these limitations upon the scientific reorganisation which the principle of utility appeared to make possible. For example, Bentham argued that capital punishment should be restricted to offences 'which in the highest degree shock the public feeling'. He went on to argue that if the hanging of a man's effigy could produce the same preventive effect as the hanging of the man himself, it would be a folly and a cruelty not to do so (Radzinowicz, 1948: 381-382). He also suggested how capital punishments might nonetheless be used to maximum effect:

'A scaffold painted black, the livery of grief – the officers of justice dressed in crepe – the executioner covered with a mask, which would serve at once to augment the terror of his appearance, and to shield him from ill-founded indignation – emblems of his crime placed above the head of the criminal, to the end that the witnesses of his sufferings may know for what crimes he undergoes them; these might form a part of the principal decorations of these legal tragedies ... Whilst all the actors in this terrible drama might move in solemn procession – serious and religious music preparing the hearts of the spectators for the important lesson they were about to receive ... The judges need not consider it beneath their dignity to preside over this public scene.' (quoted in Radzinowicz, 1948: 383-384)

Bentham also attempted to radicalise imprisonment, an institution then used merely to hold persons awaiting trial or debtors. He spent much of his life trying to convince authorities that an institution of his design, called a 'Panopticon,' would solve the problems of correction, of poverty, of idleness and mental instability.

There were three features to the panopticon. First, the architectural dimension; the panopticon was to be a circular building with a glass roof and containing cells on every story of the circumference. It was to be so arranged that every cell could be visible from a central point providing a hierarchy of continuous surveillance. The omniscient prison inspector would be kept from the sight of the prisoners by a system of 'blinds unless ... he thinks fit to show himself'. Second, management by contract; the manager would employ the inmates in contract labour and he was to receive a share of the money earned by the inmates, but he was to be financially liable if inmates who were later released re-offended, or if an excessive number of inmates died during imprisonment. Third, the panopticon was to open to the inspection of the world, an all-encompassing supervisor, which would control the manager. The idea was not fully acted upon although two prisons along this design were built in France (Petite-Roguette, 1836; Rennes, 1877) and one in the US (Stateville, 1926-1935). The panopticon keeps its importance not for the institutions actually constructed, rather for the type of disciplinary rationality the scheme displays.

Bentham was a source of many modern ideas. He argued strongly for the establishment of the office of public prosecutor, and he furthered the notion that crimes are committed against society rather than against individuals. Beyond this, he argued that many victimless crimes were imaginary rather than real offences, and he argued for the development of official crime statistics or 'bills ... indicating the moral health of the country'.

In reality, Bentham placed the civil law as the most important facility for modern social life – the criminal law, ideally, would protect the workings of a social body organised around the centrality of exchange relations. In his work on the penal code more than a quarter of the total concerns schemes of compensation; just under one half deals with indirect means of preventing offences; less than one eighth is devoted to punishments. He argues for sure and direct punishment but warns that the criminal law can be counterproductive; the civil law ought to be doing the majority of work for a modern society. Bentham asked for a system which will rid the world of 'criminal consciousness' and of the penal emotionality epitomised by the executioner. Among the ideas he suggested: the tattooing of all men; each person should have a unique name; vegetable gardening to be encouraged; tea and coffee to be subsidised at the expense of alcoholic liquor; music, drama and card games to be encouraged (not because he liked them, he apparently detested the opera, but to keep people occupied and their attentions turned to harmless pursuits). Time was to be filled up; marriages contracted for a limited period should be permitted to use up the sexual passions of those men who could not afford to maintain a family; prostitution should be permitted to prevent private vengeance for adultery; symbolic measures should serve to minimise real punishments. To his critics, this was to be the all-supervised society; the price of the happy society was domination by the gaze of utility.

Understanding classical criminology and its continuing appeal

Many of the individual proposals have particular themes influencing them. For example, the replacement of torture to gain confessions is clearly part of the movement towards forms of evidence involving human judgment. What constituted 'proof' was changing in the sciences, and in the law circumstantial evidence was beginning to be accepted.

The development of imprisonment has been much debated. (See Stanley Cohen, *Visions of Social Control*, 1985) One point is surveillance. In the pre-modern village and town strangers were not common. Visibility and understandability of action was so much part of the reality of life that it went uncommented upon, but the new cities were full of the dispossessed and homeless, the wanderers (vagrants) who, by definition, had no neighbours, were not known. Confinement was one answer as was the attempt to gain predictability in the behaviour of strangers through techniques of disciplinary behaviour.

Part of the appeal of classicism is its self-image of rational administrator, but there is a deep, epistemological basis for the success of classicism. It lies in the type of knowledge, or the limits of knowledge, which can provide an adequate foundation for legal regulation and reasoning. Note that we have defined modernity as a radically reflexive terrain and seen modernity as a form of social organisation which steps out of the local, out of tradition, embraces rationality and calculation, seeks emancipation and autonomy, above all knowledge. It seeks information about its practices and subjects them to analysis. Against this backdrop how is it that law has become the pre-eminent device for providing frameworks for modernity? How can law be so successful? What forms of knowledge and studies of organisation are involved with legality?

This is a topical issue of no mere academic importance. Currently there are fears that the authority of the legal order, in particular obedience to the criminal law, is being undercut. In response we have seen a return to formal frameworks for sentencing, and the demand for a strict adherence to clear-cut principles for punishing offenders proportionate to the ranked seriousness of the crime they have committed.

The rule of law as an expression of current features of modernity

Some questions appear and reoccur in every era – what are the contours of modern life? What are its boundaries, what are its foundations? Is modernity founded on a secure bedrock or on shifting sands?

Sociologists, and social geographers, tend to think they run the show of answering these questions, but lawyers think differently. Lawyers understand that whatever else we are in modernity, we are legal subjects. This is not just our prejudice. Above the confusion of the modern urban locality certain signs of permanence arise. Life is stabilised by the fixed points of symbolic reference, or monuments that incorporate and preserve a sense of collective identity (think of the role of the Statue of Liberty, the Eiffel Tower, Nelson's Column in Trafalgar Square or the hope for Canary Wharf in London). One non-physical but vitally important monument is the legal order. The countries of the modern west are proud to be considered *Rule of Law* societies.

The contemporary liberal legal philosopher Ronald Dworkin may overstate somewhat, but consider this opening statement from *Law's Empire*:

'We live in and by the law. It makes us what we are: citizens and employees and doctors and spouses and people who own things. It is sword, shield, and menace: we insist on our wage, or refuse to pay our rent, or are forced to forfeit penalties, or are closed up in jail, all in the name of what our abstract and ethereal sovereign, the law, has decreed. And we argue about what it has decreed, even when the books that are supposed to record its command and directions are silent; we act then as if law had muttered its doom, too low to be heard distinctly. We are subjects of law's empire, liegemen to its methods and ideals, bound in spirit while we debate what we must therefore do.' (1986: vii)

Consider the imagery Dworkin uses. It is not powerful groups which yield the sword and order punishment, but law itself. It is not the decrees of humans that are announced in the law, but the law itself that speaks. Dworkin tells us that we are the products in part of one of the great ideas of modernity – the rule of law. The law has a constitutive or productive capability. As moderns we ask the right to reject the identities provided us by our locality, our gender, our ethnic origin, our religion, our class, our physical appearance, in favour of something abstract yet concrete – our legal identity as free and equal rights-bearing citizens of the legal order. Before the law we ask to be considered as equals, irrespective of all our empirical differences. And when our rights are breached we ask that the law hold to account those who have breached our rights – the law it seems does the punishing – society is governed by rules and principles and when the rules are broken other rules determine the consequences. But what sense does this make? And what is at stake in this area? What is the connection between legal order and social order? Does law reflect sociological truths or can law create its own regimes of truth? On whose terms is the discussion held? The legacy of Hobbes is usually referred to as the image of *sovereign and subject* (Cotterrell, 1989: Ch 3); and while Hobbes leads on to Bentham and Austin with the theory of law as the instrument of political power (utility) the more basic feature of Hobbes' scheme is not the repression of anti-social desires and passions from without, but the dissolving of them from within. Hobbes achieves pacification through control on language. The destructive passions are constrained by depriving them of an appropriate vocabulary and site of utterance. The courtroom under legal positivism (the theoretical perspective bequeathed by Hobbes and developed by Bentham and Austin) speaks of law, and law only; morality has no conceptual or necessary niche in the ontology of law. If a vocabulary of ethics, law, and politics, entirely rational and neutral in tone can be developed as the mode of speech, it might quieten the murderous and violent passions within us all. In combining to form organised society, Hobbes declares, we have also agreed to communicate upon the terms of the sovereign. This may appear a well struck bargain. But the price is that henceforth *important* discussions upon the human condition will be in terms of reason and science, rather than the passions or myth, or theology. To authority we yield up our judgment, to the scientist our understanding; the bargain may be worth it, but we have paid a high price (the holocaust is but one example) and may pay more – even, ultimately perhaps, environmental destruction.

The period of classical criminology is often down-played in criminological books written by sociologists or relegated to mere historical significance in others (such as Vold's 1958, 1978, 1986 *Theoretical Criminology*). This is wrong. We have never moved on from the dilemmas which Classicism contains – the advent of just deserts and the return to legalism of the last two decades is only one indication of this. The deeper concern is actually about understanding and organising human existence.

A basic question: how is legitimacy of criminal justice established?

Whatever the socio-cultural context, the concept of criminal justice combines the idea of crime with the idea of justice. But what is a just judgment in criminal justice? In other words, how do we actually know that the decisions made in the name of criminal justice are correct? How do we know that the structure is legitimate and the actions done are just?

The reflexivity of modernity places this constantly on the agenda. And we ask it daily. We complain about unjust decisions, about miscarriages of justice. What are we doing when we complain? Are we not demanding that criminal justice create and preserve a structure of legitimacy? For Weber modernity relies upon a particular form of legitimacy, we accept the social order and the commands of political superiors, because of the combination of legality and rationality. It may be that we desire a substantially just society, but what if we disagree on what that means? Does this destroy legitimacy? It does not appear so; instead the quest for legitimacy can become purely formal. Thus, whatever is done according to the due process of law is a legitimate and correct outcome. In this way law creates its own system of conferring legitimacy, it becomes an autopoietic structure which does not need answers to the fundamental questions of existence to continue. We can become creatures of the law and subjects of legal regulation whatever our beliefs about the ontology of life. A Moslem, a Jew, a Catholic and someone who just enjoys football and a cold beer, can disagree on everything about the meaning of life and yet agree to abide by the legal system. We can call this the solution of *ambivalence through division*. Of course, dialectics are in play – the legal system cannot dictate the meaning of life otherwise disagreement about the meaning of life, would become a problem for legality. What law regulates must be thought out, law cannot behave irrationally. But it can determine the conditions of its own rationality through its supposed autonomy. For the contemporary Harvard Law Professor Roberto Unger the law achieves autonomy when:

'... the rules formulated and enforced by government cannot be persuasively analysed as a mere restatement of any identifiable set of non-legal beliefs or norms, be they economic, political, or religious ...

An autonomous legal system does not codify a particular theology. As a body of profane rules, it stands apart from the precepts that govern man's relationship to God and from any single religion's view of social relations ... Legal reasoning has a method or style to differentiate it from scientific explanation and from moral, political, and economic discourse ... A special group, the legal profession ... manipulates the rules, staffs the legal institutions, and engages in the practice of legal argument.' (1976: 53)

The themes of classical criminology help constitute the rule of law and remain essential to contemporary life. How this came about, and in what ways this reflects fundamental issues of the human condition, is a difficult and complex story some aspects of which shall be sketched as follows.

Classical criminology destroys the magical irrationality of the pre-modern

Our narrative has portrayed modernity as born with the destruction of the intellectual synthesis of medieval Europe relying upon the belief in God. Theology provided a power base to legitimate a political domination of church and sovereign throughout Christendom – a domination torn asunder in the changes of the Enlightenment.

The conventional accounts of criminological development, ie Vold (1958, Vold and Barnard 1978, 1986), Leon Radzinowicz, *Ideology and Crime*, 1966), Taylor, Walton and Young, *The New Criminology* (1973), see the change in Weberian terms of criminal law as surmounting its 'irrational' roots, and discern its development and differentiation in terms of the process of the rationalisation of societies in general, and of the law in particular. Weber's typology of legal conflict is carried out in the dimensions of rationality, versus irrationality and formal versus substantive.

Vold (1958, Vold and Bernard, 1978, 1986) starts his narrative with the freeing of intellectual thought on crime from the domination of semi-religious demonological explanations. Demonological explanations make use of the principle of other-worldly power to account for events, the rejection of demonism turns man's attention on to this world and the inherent structures of the world. The enlightenment attitude is openly scathing of popular fallacies, and is also a criticism of the current legitimative conceptions for authority. These popular beliefs tied to the practices of wergild, a contest of sin and crime, trial by battle, trial by ordeal, compurgation, and the use of miraculous signs or omens to indicate guilt or innocence, in a ritualisation of life. Behind such popular attitudes were also, however, sophisticated intellectual systems which drew out the remaining traits of what David Jones (1986), in his selective overview of criminology, calls 'classical realism'.

The legitimation of decisions in the theological system depended on an overall synthesis

What is characteristic of these systems is the interdependence of each part in an overall conception; an interdependence which involves the aesthetic. In the scholastic system of Thomas Aquinas, for instance, the emphasis is on a synthesis of classical philosophy, Christian theology, and the concerns of politics. The duty of civil participation, natural political action, must be viewed in relation to citizenship in the Kingdom of God. The state is a natural institution, deriving from the nature of man, and is orientated towards satisfying and encouraging man's natural potentiality. The entire scheme of society and its laws are evaluated by a notion of the whole. A notion which, in its heritage, draws upon a sympathetic dialectic with the legacy of Aristotle where the choice of, and respect for, a common measure is what gives the polity a sense of balance and harmony. The identity of the elements of justice, and what designates their place in the right order of that society, the rule of justice at the foundation of the socio-political association, is the centrality of the notion of the common good. The common good allows the positioning of individuals since:

> '... the goodness of any part is considered in comparison with the whole ... Since then any man is a part of the state, it is impossible that a man be good unless he be well proportioned to the common good. [Law is] a rational ordering of things which concern the common good, promulgated by whoever is charged with the care of the community.' (Aquinas: *Selected Political Writings*, p 57)

Penal activity is not merely to reflect the power and authority of the sovereign, but to be aligned by reason and aimed at benefiting the common good. The penal practices affecting the body share both in the rationality of obvious power but also represent an intellectual acknowledgement that the defilement which sin brings is close to the symbolism of the physical. It is a touching, a contagion of the social world which demands a cleansing. This is a cleansing for which soap and water will not suffice but demands a ritual purification, a prescribed and sanctioned ceremony. Crime is a privation which comes about by a deterioration, or misuse, of man's reason by deference to the force of passion, or a training in vice not virtue. Evil is the possibility of wrong choice which accompanies man's freedom, but choice is not something radically free, springing out of an existential void, but part of the practice of life – the development of man's practical rationality. Moral evil is the product of the will, whereby the essentially good element in the willed act lacks its true end. The privation may be righted by Divine grace; as Alisdair MacIntyre (1988) brings out in his *Whose Justice? Which Rationality?*, for medieval thought the human condition is incomplete in itself, it simply does not possess powers of governing itself – it is created and ultimately dependant.

The critical philosophy of the enlightenment opposed such a state of dependency and denied confidence in revealed knowledge. Knowledge must face a sceptical challenge, and the progressive construction project was to be based on the security of man's epistemological properties.

One result was to frame foundational knowledge claims in a negative fashion – thus for Thomas Hobbes in the 17th century, and David Hume in the 18th, dominant social institutions arise not so much from knowledge of the good but from the fear of the consequences of unrestrained natural inclinations. The path to institutional reform is via knowledge of the facts of the human condition. But these are isolated facts – it is no longer, for Hume, possible for one man ever to claim that he can know the human condition in its entirety, all he can know is some or other facts of the human condition. This change is slowly apparent in the projects of writers who change both the nature of their concerns (their ambitions as to their coverage of humanity) and the facts they report. The writers who make up classical criminology use a new science of human nature. Although criminological positivism was later to claim that the writers of the classical school, who presented law as the only mechanism that could govern society, were unscientific, and too wrapped in the metaphysics of philosophy to understand humanity scientifically, the classical school writers used a growing science of man that was laid out in the work of Thomas Hobbes, John Locke, Francis Hutcheson and David Hume in particular.

What is central is the belief that law must reflect the rationality of existence. The search for the truth of the human condition replaces the search for the revealed truths of religion. For example, the first step Beccaria takes is the critique of religion as the legitimation of law. For Beccaria the problem with God is that he knew too much; instead the human judge must only act in accordance to human guidelines.

If the human soul is unknowable to humans then a particular system laying out 'a truthful account of the totality of the basic intentions of the soul, evil and wickedness' cannot be legitimate foundations for judgments in the criminal law. The source of judgments for punishments carried out under the criminal law must be the law itself, and this law is to be created, or posited, by humans in political society acting in accordance with their human sciences offering 'truths' of the human condition.

Let us jump ahead of our story. How does the post-modern perspective impact? The current attack on truth, and the realisation of the pragmatic contingency of science, means that the judgments of this new rule of positive law (law, that is, which is laid down by humans for the guidance of other humans) encounters a realm of mystery as the absolute ontological foundation. Although classical criminology argued it found its truth in utility as the reasoning of nature, we now see that ultimately the full workings of the mind, of the soul are not knowable to man. Law can only work at a different level, a level of practical rationality. Law can work on its own species of intentionality; legal intention. This is the intention to commit an illegal act as it is laid down in the definition of the crime. It is not that real subjects do not have motives, desires, real human needs, it is simply that these are irrelevant to the legal investigation.

What does this foundation of mystery entail?

Suppose that, once we reject God, life becomes unknowable in its totality. Suppose that the relationship between human bodies (the organic material from which we modern humans are formed) and external nature (the world of earth and material things, gravity, strains, events and social things) is constructed in a way which is inherently opaque to human analysis. What if human knowledge can never encompass reality? What if reality ultimately remains a mystery? How can a legitimate social order be constructed? On what basis can 'society', conceived as created by humans, be built?

The legal methodology is to 'legislate', to lay down ... to command. In *Legislators and Interpreters: On Modernity, Post-Modernity and Intellectuals*, Zygmunt Bauman (1987) argues that while the enlightenment has entrenched itself upon our collective memory as a powerful drive to bring knowledge to the people, to restore clear sight to those blinded by superstition, to give wisdom to the ignorant, to pave the way for progress, in reality the substance amounted to the drive to legislate, organise, and regulate, rather than disseminate knowledge. The 17th century threw up a crisis of government both on a issue of epistemological foundations (of the legitimacy of government), and the practical problems of what to do with the growing concentrations of masterless men in the expanding urban centres. The philosophies preached solved this in the rationalisation of the state power, and the socialisation of the subjects, in accordance with the idea of reasonableness and the advancement of truth and knowledge.

Since this process of legislation took place over variable sets of truths and knowledges the result was, however, that society must always be unstable, social existence ambivalent, its categories never fixed and the full force of social effects untraceable (Thus Bauman's analysis of Modernity can lead to texts such as *Modernity and Ambivalence*, 1991). Even if normative projects and knowledge guide social construction and the fashioning of ourselves, society will always be more than the effect of human projects – 'ourselves' and our relations – too mobile for incorporation into a stable modern social structure that will be a full reflection of our ambitions. If the ontology of existence is a mystery, each structure of knowledge, each theory, each perspective, each project or design based thereon, will capture only some formation, only some characteristic while consequently releasing others, will encounter new resistances while thereon overcoming previous ones – will engender new contingencies while subduing old ones.

How is modern society made if not as a reflection of underlying natural laws of social evolution?

Partly social order is imagined. We dream or construct ideas which are then acted upon and consequences follow. Real things are constructed out of imaginary ones. However, while our ideas of how society is formed include the notion that society is made by men – through interpretation of man's hopes, fears and aspirations – and thus not reducible to determinate natural laws – this notion co-exists with the idea that we can come to know the basic underlying social structures, and social laws of social evolution and define, thereby, the guiding principles of social development in a series of law-like generalisations which we can then align ourselves to (the naturalist paradigm). Reflexively, we realise that society is made by us, but we cannot face up to the responsibility, and therefore dream that we are following some master blue print laid down by nature (perhaps the writings of Karl Marx provides the example *par excellence*).

This sets up an inescapable tension in writing: on the one hand, a critique of existing forms of knowledge occurs which creates scepticism and a void of mystery suitable for the writer to put forward new proposals, while, on the other hand, the writer usually demands that the proposals he puts forward and couches in scientific terms should gain acceptance. He claims to bring truth ... while sometimes denying that truth can be easily found.

In *The Legitimacy of the Modern Age,* Hans Blumenberg (1983) depicts legitimacy problems as a consequence of the claim to carry out a radical break with tradition, and the incongruity between this claim and the reality of history, which must always rely upon the past. For Blumenberg the key principle of the modern age is that of self-assertion, but this principle always operates within a context. All schemes operate against earlier attempts, and set out an intellectual field for other theories to operate in.

These tensions run through the writings of Beccaria, Bentham and Austin. Their writings are concerned to lift the burden of rigid hierarchy and settled traditions that defied and constrained the practical and passionate relations of people. The new science of utilitarianism, for which Thomas Hobbes and David Hume provide the foundations, is put forward with the claim that this can tie together the otherwise disparate elements of social life. Their texts offer a two-fold process of dissolution and construction – the very weapons turned against the old intellectual structures also provide the materials and methods for their substitution.

Consider our description of the basic problem of modernity as defined by Nietzsche: the central dilemma is how to structure social existence after God's death. What was religion? Religion was a framework of thought which gave an other-worldliness to the existential dilemma, it provided a body of proposition answering the question of what reality was and a set of doctrines about how people ought to live (existential questions concern not only the security of self-identity but also how to relate to other human beings – 'who am I?' is a similar question to 'who are they?'). That is, religion reconciled the personal within the framework of the whole. People were called upon to live in a certain way as a direct result of a structure of knowledge about the world being shaped in a particular way. In other words the argument of how people ought to behave, or what we now might call morality, was based on an ontology. It has become popular to argue that this breaches a fundamental rule of modern logic, that is, that we cannot infer an ought from an is. But this is somewhat misguided, since, when we actually look at the religious structures of medieval Europe we find an intermingling of descriptive and prescriptive ideas; we find that, in many ways, what was at stake were ideas or concepts about the relationship of humans and the world; and how humans ought to strive or build a coherent life. This striving was intimately tied up with particular visions of reality and imperatives for action (MacIntyre, 1988).

A well-developed vision of the social and the personal must be a descriptive, as well as a prescriptive, view of the people in society who will form the social life. The central prescriptions of how people ought to be cannot be disentangled from our understandings of social reality; our understandings of reality in turn give energy to our desires to transform reality and change our contexts. To become a fully articulated person in an existentially contented human society (surely the central eschatological feature of the utopian project of modernity, and the redemptive project of religious conceptions) we must achieve two goals. We may refer to one as the harmony of social life, sometimes called community, and the other we may call the satisfaction of our intellectual drives, sometimes called objectivity. By community is here meant human association, where it would be is here meant complete in and of itself, wanted for its own sake, as well as any conception of it merely satisfying the personal wants of the individuals that make it up. Such a utopian settlement would provide the foundation for a full understanding of the value of association, and perhaps involve a heightened appreciation of the very vulnerability of the human condition. Objectivity, in our context, represents the understanding that the social order is, in a way, satisfactory; it satisfies our intellectual digging into legitimacy and sources of foundations. It is satisfactory in that it is not a fraud, or the result of the arbitrary imposition of interests or ideals. It is not reducible to an image of violence, subjugation, superstition or oppression.

Let us ask again 'what was the pre-modern naturalistic premise?' Society was perceived to have an eminent order of hierarchy and division and the maintenance of this order was taken to satisfy the deepest practical and spiritual needs of the collective and its individual members, the whole guaranteed by a particular structure of power and rights or duties. Interpreted through philosophy and theory, the desire of association underlying this resulting social order is put forward as a true face of social community. What happens when this synthesis, this relationship between community and objectivity, is rejected? When one denies the existence of a natural structure of division and hierarchy? Surely it is no longer possible to distinguish clearly between the two situations, and say, over here lies a social order cleansed of force and fraud, over there the world of superstition, treachery and violence. Both have the use of power, both have violence, both have suffering, both can be criticised and justified ... What is required? A new jurisprudence – a new objectivity. What is the nature of this? Is it simply a different structure of justification, a different structure of legitimation, a different structure of what Foucault would call power? Objectivity is the goal, but all justifications are likely to be controversial, precisely because there is no natural foundational background picture to society on which to rely in formulating them. Thus, the escape from the 'unnatural' pre-modern naturalist paradise must itself require a new form of narrative, a new form of structuring, and a new position whereby a narrative depicting a new 'natural form of order' is put forward. Moreover, each new justification once accepted will itself exhibit a pressure towards extensionality or universality.

The modernist struggle against arbitrariness, against violence, against deception, requires people to build a society that is less of a hostage to itself. A central intellectual weapon is scepticism; a thoroughgoing sceptical methodology whereby no central element of its arrangements must be left invisible, or immune to the challenge of critical rationality. Scepticism and constructivism. How can the tension be reconciled? How can a framework for social life be constructed if it is built in the ruins of that which did not survive the sceptical challenge, remnants which we know may not long survive further challenges? How can the void beneath human existence be rendered as if it were of no consequence?

In the liberal tradition objectivity is achieved, not by holding fast to a given substantive content and resolutely defending this in the face of all objections of fraud or illusion, but, in a sense, by rendering the structure insubstantial, by turning it increasingly into a structure of no contextual substance. This is a realistic methodology insofar as it recognises that all hierarchies and visions have self-destructed in modernity insofar as they demand a substantive content. In the liberal vision of the structure of modern science, for example, that of Karl Popper, we get a paradox: with modern science it is not that the foundations are ultimately true, it is that the foundations are methodologically open to revision, ie the test of falsification. Modern science does not rely upon a substantive content which is absolutely true; it relies upon a methodology of testing, and a methodology of building upon the experienced results of testing. The substantive content is constantly revisable; it is the best we can do at this time. Similarly with the constructed society. To the liberal the open society is preferable to any settled ontology of justice. To say what the content of the just society would be, is to close off the conversation, it would end liberal history.

Classical criminology talks the language of a 'true' science of man and society, but actually creates a structure separate from nature; it founds the social upon myth and politics

The writers of classicism reject tradition and religion in the name of science. Beccaria (1963:96-97) claims to bring absolute truth. But ultimately their science is not as powerful and truthful as they claimed, therefore their real foundations are myths, stories, narratives which serve to give a foundation to replace the pre-modern concepts of nature. But if a naturalist premise is rejected what happens to the idea of community? Community becomes not a natural phenomena, but political in character.

In his lectures delivered between 1828-30, John Austin (1832, 1873) the first professor of law at London University, was specific. With modernity, social life moves out of what he terms a 'natural community' to a 'political community' or a 'political society'. At stake is a new form of objectivity for law and the justification of government. Specifically we have a background image of social development (the necessity for strong government to guide social development) and a social science which will guide this government (ie utilitarianism). We deny any unjustifiable or non-revisable relationship and structuring of power; we now premise power on certain instrumental and other forms of legitimation. Certainly power is still at stake, and this power will not exist in a vacuum devoid of social interests. But in this context Austin is proposing a new ideal of objectivity – that of guidance by truth rather than by social interests – to serve as the ideal for a positive jurisprudence of political community. Of course, this attempt to make the power and context of its exercise visible, and vulnerable, to knowledge claims cannot escape the weakness of the political context. When one reads the detail of the work of Caesar Beccaria, Jeremy Bentham and John Austin, we can see the way in which the social theory of classical criminology over-turned a particular form of naturalistic structuring. This sceptical and deconstructive work did not adopt an empty naturalist position, on the contrary it strove to put forward a new form of objectivity, and a new set of determinate social laws. The modernity of classical criminology was to be knowledge-led and utilitarian. It was to turn its back upon irrational emotionality and non-purposeful ritual. All factors of social life were to become calculable, rule bound, and efficient.

The need for objectivity and professionalism

What was the reality of criminal justice procedure that classicism faced? In *Inventing Criminology: essays on the rise of 'Homo Criminalis'*, Piers Beirne (1993) opens his chapter on Beccaria's work with the events surrounding the execution of Jean Calas. Jean's son, Mark Anthony, the eldest son of a reasonably prosperous cloth merchant, had been found dead on the 13 October 1761 at his father's shop. He had died of strangulation, the only suspects were those members of the household present at the time of his death. It included his father, his English mother, a younger brother, a servant woman and a guest who happened to be the son of a prominent protestant lawyer. Each was arrested, imprisoned and charged with the murder. At first the Calas family claimed that Mark Anthony had been murdered, probably because they wished to escape the public humiliation that would have befallen the kin of a successful suicide when the body was dragged naked through the streets before being hanged by the neck. Soon, however, the family admitted that he had committed suicide as he had often threatened to do. The judges of the Toulouse Parliament disregarded this and convicted Jean Calas of the murder of his son, the motivation was presumed to be the anguish of the son's conversion to Catholicism. The criminal procedure had involved gruesome torture during which he had however, maintained his innocence, and he was executed on 18 March 1762. The sentence of execution required that he be dressed:

> '... in a chemise with head and feet bare, would be taken in a cart from the palace prison to the Cathedral, there kneeling in front of the main door, holding in his hands a torch of yellow wax weighing two pounds, he must make an *amende honorable* asking pardon of God of the King and of justice. Then the executioner to take him in the cart to the palace of St Georges where upon a scaffold his arms legs thighs and loins are to be broken and crushed. Finally the prisoner should be placed upon a wheel with a space turned to the sky alive and in pain and repent for his said crimes and misdeeds, all the while imploring God for his life, thereby to serve as an example and to instil terror in the wicked.' (Beirne 1993: 11-12)

Beirne concentrates upon the reaction of Voltaire who wrote on 29 March 1762 to a friend distraught at the way the fanatical city of Toulouse had glorified Mark Anthony as the martyr, and a catholic one at that:

> 'For the love of God, render as horrible as you can the fanaticism which would have it that the son had been hanged by his father, or which has caused an innocent man to be placed on a wheel by 8 of the King's counsellors.' (Ibid: 12)

It was clear to Voltaire that Jean Calas had been the victim of religious persecution. No witnesses had been called to the trial or orally examined, no advocate was provided for the accused, the evidence of guilt was purely circumstantial, the proceedings, although lawful, were a mockery and gruesome and he was convicted by eight judges with five dissenting. Voltaire urged his friend to complain loudly about the horrible events in Toulouse, and began a campaign for the reversal of the conviction giving one of the most famous battle cries of the French enlightenment, *Ecrasez l'infame!* In a short book published in 1763 Voltaire protests a strong belief in the executed man's innocence. He argued that it was impossible for Jean Callas, an old man of 68, suffering from illness, to have strangled and hanged his young and very powerful 28 year old son. Moreover, the whole procedure of the case was deemed unjust; Calas had been condemned by eight votes with five abstaining, but the extreme gravity of the crime, infanticide with its horrible punishment, should demand a unanimous verdict. Furthermore, with such an extraordinary crime, the evidence should be obvious and clearly perceptible to everyone, since a guilty verdict leads to death. If there is doubt it ought to mean that the death sentence is not carried out. The first copies of Beccaria's work *On Crimes and Punishment* appeared in Italy two years after the execution in 1764.

This work occupies a hallowed place in the history of criminology. Beirne is undoubtedly correct in arguing that it has been grossly misunderstood and misrepresented, whilst *On Crimes and Punishment* is usually read as a treatise for a metaphysics of a free willed rationally acting individual, who can be punished for a mistake in his rational calculations, for breaching his rational obligations, Beirne identifies the scientific approach of Beccaria in *On Crimes and Punishment* as heavily influenced by the early 'sciences of man' of the Scottish enlightenment, in particular by Hutcheson and Hume. This emerging science of man provides the background synthesis for the texts of classical criminology, for Beccaria, and for those who applied him, such as Bentham and Austin. It is this science which provides the touchstone of utilitarianism and certain narratives of social evolution. Law is the tool of the sovereign; the image of law Austin gave was of 'the command of the sovereign backed by threats and habitually obeyed' (John Austin, *The Province of Jurisprudence*, 1832). But we unnecessarily reduce this concept if we mistake it for a mere empirical reflection of the fact of hierarchical social power, instead the ethos of the writing is to position power within a 'legal-rational' framework. Specifically, law was to be the instrument of rational government.

What is rational government?

We are still searching and this is the name of the modern game. In the hands of the classicists there were two themes. One concerned the need to stabilise society, the other the need to create a template which would allow real progress to occur.

The need to stabilise potential chaos

In the classical criminology of Beccaria, Bentham and Austin we give up power to a strong sovereign to rule over society. The father figure for this is the intellectual work of Thomas Hobbes. Hobbes understood the problem as one of building over the void of a world in perpetual flux. Order must be created to 'restrain what was natural.' The issue was how to frame a template so that the commands would become accepted by the populace.

Certainly criminal justice was in dire need of rationalisation. In Britain the period 1688 to 1820 saw a rise in capital statutes from 50 to 200 and the enforcement of the criminal law attracted an ambiguous response – an irrational law invited resistance. Britain was the hanging country of Europe. Although it had one of the lowest rates of violent crime in Europe, and with Russia and Sweden having reduced their public executions to about a dozen a year by 1786, in 1788 London saw 15 executions on a single day! The average length of the criminal trial took eight and a half minutes (Gatrell, 1994). Although sometimes a festive occasion, often the execution was simply bungled (the condemned urinated and defecated, the hangman was sometimes drunk, the victim's neck usually didn't break, and the offender strangled slowly to death). The populace were sickening of the sight. Further, most of the crimes were property offences. The penal operation of law need legitimising. As society became more urbanised and industrialised, less ruled by custom and locality, class warfare threatened to break out. As Douglas Hay (1975) put it in *Albion's Fatal Tree*:

> '... the ideology of the ruling oligarchy, which places a supreme value on property, finds its visible and material embodiment above all in the ideology and practice of the law. Tyburn Tree, as William Blake well understood, stood at the heart of this ideology; and its ceremonies were at the heart of popular culture also.'

Change was slow. In 1869, Nicholas Ogarev, a Russian exile who had come to England seeking a more enlightened and rational society, wrote a letter to his mistress, Mary Sutherland, about the execution of a would-be suicide in London.

> 'A man was hanged who had cut his throat, but who had been brought back to life. The doctor had warned them that it was impossible to hang him as the throat would burst open and he would breathe through his aperture. They did not listen to his advice and hanged their man. The wound in the neck immediately opened and the man came back to life again although he was hanged. It took time to convene the aldermen to decide the question of what was to be done. At length the aldermen assembled and bound up the neck below the wound until he died. Oh my Mary, what a crazy society and what a stupid civilisation.' (Quoted in Jacoby; 1985:134)

Scholars as far apart as Radzinowicz and Foucault have catalogued 'the end of the spectacle', wherein the power which displayed itself via the ceremony of public punishment was replaced by the prison (M Foucault,1979, *Discipline and Punish*, and Leon Radzinowicz and Roger Hood,1986, *A history ..., Vol 4,*

'*Grappling for Control*', pp 343-353). It appears safer to accept a thesis of gradual development rather than a sudden transformation. Pieter Spierenburg, in *The Spectacle of Suffering: Executions and the evolution of repression: from a pre-industrial metropolis to the European experience*, sets out to demonstrate that:

'Foucault's picture of one system quickly replacing another is actually far from historical reality. The infliction of pain and the public character of punishments did not disappear overnight. Both elements slowly retreated in a long, drawn-out process over several centuries.' (1984: viii.)

This change undermined 'theatrical' penality which had 'echoed a long tradition of public punishment', and which Bentham described as 'an imposing commentary – a sensible and speaking image of the law', wherein the power of the sovereign was expressly tied to the truth of law and the truth behind law (the right to rule).

The normal criticisms of classicism which commentators concentrate upon are that it set out an unworkable code, and that it ignored social inequalities and diverse environmental backgrounds in operating an 'ideal' philosophic justice at odds with social reality. Vold implicitly uses Weber's formal/substantive topology in echoing the positivist response:

'... puzzling questions about the reasons for or causes of behaviour, the uncertainties of motives and intentions ... were ignored for the sake of administrative uniformity. This was the classical conception of justice – an exact scale of punishments for equal acts without reference to the individual involved or the special circumstances in which the crime was committed.' (1978: 26)

Radzinowicz, aligns himself with a sophisticated version of the narrative of humanitarian progress:

'... the rigidity of the classical school on the Continent of Europe made it almost impossible to develop constructive and imaginative penal measures ... because they would have conflicted with the principle that punishment must be clearly defined in advance and strictly proportionate to the offence.' (1966: 123)

By contrast the authors of *The New Criminology* point out the contradictory tensions within Beccaria's work in both proposing the notion of equality and also defending the possession of property. The democratic stress of early utilitarianism is seen as nothing more than the ideology of the rising bourgeoisie, and social contract theory as ideologically part of their protection against feudal interference; ideology which bore little relation to middle class practice:

'... a system of classical justice of this order could only operate in a society where property was distributed equally ... Such distribution was never contemplated.' (Taylor, Walton and Young, 1973: 6)

But the critics have been outflanked by history. They wrote in a time when positivism was thought to have replaced classicism. Classicism has not only survived, it has strengthened in recent years. We need a deeper understanding, to acknowledge that modernity has many layers, many differing forces.

In their texts the writers declared their modernism: Beccaria determines his text as the rhetorical break between theology, politics, and the application of punishment – a move from practical action as political service to administrative action as obedience to rational performance. My subsidiary thesis here is simple: Matza overstates the case when he argues that 'positive criminology achieved the almost impossible, the study of crime separate from the contemplation of the state', and sees the positive criminologist as the technician of the state (in *Delinquency and Drift*, 1963, and *Becoming Deviant*, 1969) for the break was already present in Beccaria. Henceforth, the subject of criminal justice will be the objects of 'the legal system', and discussion conducted within the boundary of 'legal doctrine' and developments of that discourse. Additionally, the opinion that classical criminology is concerned with the mediation of power between the state and the individual criminal, while positive criminology neglects the question of power, overlooks the degree to which Beccaria consciously designs an instrument of crime control. Thus the distinction future analysers draw, for example in juvenile justice between welfare and justice or the use made of Packer's (1968) two models of criminal justice, the crime control and the due process, are overstated and misconceptions. A detailed reading of Beccaria, only done in outline here, leaves no doubt that *due process is part of crime control*. The elements of 'due process' help to secure the legitimacy and authority of the criminal justice system. Due process considerations are not created merely for crime control, since they are themselves reflections of moral and political values in the wider social order, but their appearance in criminal justice is not contradictory to the control function. They enable the discourse of justice to be confined within the procedural confines.

The results of the constructionist project: the creation of hybrids such as 'rights'

The view of law as a crucial instrument of the rational creation of modernity is central to the authors we identify as representing classical criminology. Bentham is clear as to the fruits of government:

'We know what it is for men to live without government, for we see instances of such a way of life – we see it in many savage nations, or rather races of mankind; for instance, among the savages of New South Wales, whose way of living is so well known to us; no habit of obedience, and thence no government – no government, and thence no laws – no laws, and thence no such things as rights – no security – no property; – liberty, as against regular control, the control of laws and government – perfect; but as against all irregular control, the mandates of stronger individuals, none. In this state, at a time earlier than the commencement of history – in this same state, judging from analogy, we, the inhabitants of the part of the globe we call Europe, were; – no government, consequently no rights: no rights, consequently no property – no legal security – no legal liberty: security not more than belongs to beasts – forecast and sense of insecurity keener – consequently in point of happiness below the level of the brutal race.' (*Fragment on Government*)

But while the writers of classical criminology declared that they were merely being truthful to a new science of human nature and the underlying structure of the world, we can now see that rights, obligations, duties, property, liberty, and the predictability of social interactions are not natural things. They depend upon certain understandings, certain narratives, certain discursive structures (such as Bills of Rights or accepted interpretations of the constitution), and they cannot exist outside of society (as Hobbes knew so well, they are internal to 'civil society'). But they are not entirely social, or a mere issue of discourse. They are real, but they refuse to be simply objective entities residing in nature, instead they cry out their social existence; they are formed and impacted via discourse but exist outside of it; they are created by the collective, but used against the collective. Such entities are constructed, but they cannot be reduced to a pure social dimension because this dimension is actually populated by objects brought about in its construction.

People get terribly confused by the ability of positive law to create social objects. Sometimes bizarre statements are made such as talk of 'natural rights'. Of course there is no such thing as a natural right. As Bentham observed, concerned as he was to talk correctly, to claim such an ontology is sheer 'nonsense on stilts'. But that does not mean that to claim such rights is mere rhetoric. It is rhetoric, it is to enter into a discursive battle, but results follow. A social arrangement may be constructed – reliances created, patterns of behaviour follow and expectations are aroused. The creations of law are real, but not natural in the traditional sense. No wonder people get confused. After all, is it our fault that the networks spanning and interweaving the nature – society/culture complex are simultaneously real (and thus we have a tendency to think of this ontology as if it were like nature), narrated (and thus we have a tendency to perceive them as entities of discourse, of culture), and collective (such as truly social entities ought to be)? Modernity is full of hybrids. Entities which span the natural and the social world. Entities which exist, to some degree, independently of both the non-human existence and security of nature, and also the political epistemology of society. And intellectuals, philosophers, sociologists, lawyers (at least in their jurisprudential forms) work on translating the meaning of these hybrids, and purifying the variety of claims made about them. But we live with these hybrids, they make us modern.

CHAPTER FIVE

READING THE TEXTS OF CLASSICAL CRIMINOLOGY: BEYOND MERE COMMAND INTO SYSTEMATIC LEGITIMATION?

'The autonomy an individual can enjoy does not ... consist in rebelling against nature – such a revolt being futile and fruitless, whether attempted against the forces of the material world or those of the social world. To be autonomous means, for the human being, to understand the necessities he has to bow to and accept them with full knowledge of the facts. Nothing that we do can make the laws of things other than what they are, but we free ourselves of them in thinking them; that is, in making them ours by thought. This is what gives democracy a moral superiority. Because it is a system based on reflection, it allows the citizen to accept the laws of the country with more intelligence and thus less passively. Because there is a constant flow of communication between themselves and the state, the state is for individuals no longer like an exterior force that imparts a wholly mechanic impetus to them ... The role of the state, in fact, is not to express and sum up the unreflective thought of the mass of the people but to superimpose on this unreflective thought a more considered thought, which therefore cannot be other then different.' (Emile Durkheim, [1898] 1900: 91-2)

In the above passage Durkheim emphasises the democratic force of the legal order relies on the implicit acceptance by the populace that the legal order reflects the natural order of things. Social cohesion cannot be founded on the impersonal rationality of law alone: it needs a 'mystical' support of legitimation; it needs a social psychology in which the state is imbued with a force over and above any mere show of violence. This is a dilemma for a pure theory of modern law: legal positivism, the belief that law is simply the law, and that the concept of law has no necessary connection with morality, is logical but inhuman; it cannot offer an imagination of law that would bind us together in any way. Hence the legal order needs to imbue itself with a cultural force. But does this cultural force need to be consistent? Need it amount to some overall coherent world view; some regime of virtue as Alisdair MacIntyre (1981) believes we need – while he argues our current situation is incoherent? Do we require a range of philosophers to interpret our legal system so that it is seen to be a coherent and morally principled universe of reason?

Why should a workable legal order require principled consistency?

Note the liberal idea of legal regulation: legal regulation can lay down certain rules of the social game leaving you free to get on with the self-interested tasks of being the producer and consumer of goods, contracting for gain etc. The legal order works to provide a measure of predictability and consistency: it provides the form of contract, property relations and so forth. But it is only the framework: within it forms civil society with all its contradictions, its compromises and its human selves (divided between roles – father, insurance salesman, captain of the village cricket team, creditor, debtor, keen collector of ...). The liberal civil society can operate with a different range of pressures and rewards than would be allowed if a unified structure existed wherein the legal order was one aspect of fully penetrating and coherent social morality; moreover, civil society allows the legal order to form into a *legal system*.

What is the nature of the criminal justice system?

Law books frequently use the word 'system' and are nearly always imprecise with it. There is a very vague reference in legal studies to a variety of subject headings such as 'The English Legal System' or the 'Criminal Justice System' or 'The Penal System'. But the vocabulary is sadly lacking in precision. It is rare to find any analysis of the notions of system or legal or criminal, instead, in referring to the Criminal Justice System they appear to merely accept some form of common sense understanding of what counts as the elements constituting such a 'system'. Recently, legal theory has begun to take on board systems theory in the notion of law as an autopoietic system (a self-regulating system, see the work of Gunther Teubner, 1987, 1989, 1993). Such systems analysis appears apt for the post-modern condition: it defuses the debate between conflict/Marxist/radical approaches to law, and the consensus model. Instead law is studied as one of the general sub-systems of the social system, with particular system requirements and effects; we can then investigate whether it is fully autonomous or relatively autonomous of the overall social system, without the seeming messiness of political ideology (thus we may see this development in conservative or enlightening terms, depending on one's political ideology!). What happens when we look at criminal justice as a system? We identify certain things:

- That the criminal justice system is not a system, but a sub-system of the legal system and the overall social system.

  The conditions required for the existence of social sub-systems are:

  (i)   a distinct, specific and specialised social activity; objectives corresponding to this activity, specific and classifiable that can be labelled; situations determined by the relation between activity (social agents or subjects; groups and individuals) and objectives, so as to constitute an indissoluble whole;

  (ii) organisations and institutions justifying one another at state level, or at the level of another state-sponsored institution; the institutions make use of the organisations to shape social activity, and the development of a competent bureaucracy which is hierarchically structured;

  (iii) texts (forming a corpus) that ensure the communication of activity, the participation of its organising actions, the sway and authority of the corresponding institutions; these texts may be organised into codes, or they may consist in the reports of binding decisions to structure hierarchy (ie in which legal techniques of interpretation serve to identify and uncover such entities as *ratio decidendi, obiter dictum*, the rules of statutory interpretation), documents, treatises, manuals, guides, or the illustrations and literature of publicity, from which the explicit corpus and code may be analytically deduced; such analyses, when successful, reveal and define the appropriate terms by which the system communicates and refers back to itself it's success.

• That the system can take on board a range of activities depending upon the success of its textual identification; ie the systematic acceptance of the entity being correctly described as a crime, the acceptance of policy directives (for example, policing priorities).

• For successful system functioning, the social activity, the institutional configuration, and the internal communication, need to be in a series of feedback loops. The autopoietic nature of system development lies in the relations between self-observation, self-constitution, and self-reproduction. Once legal communication on the fundamental distinctions (the illegal - legal, crime – non-crime, process of guilt finding – sentencing) has been differentiated from general social communication, they can become self-referential and be discussed in terms of legal categories. Norms for its own operation, structures, processes, boundaries, attitudes and activities are established. When these norms are broken (as, for example, under prohibition when the laws against alcohol were not correctly enforced and a vast underworld was thereby encouraged into existence) the system may understand that either corrective measures (the rooting out of 'corruption') or withdrawal (the ceasing of the prohibitive policy on alcohol), are required.

Legal practice is a formalised, specialised activity, the object of manuals and codes of practice – it is also a body of social rituals, a site of tensions.

Sub-systems are the result of a sort of nucleus of significance favouring a certain sphere of social space, so that it acquires powers of attraction and repulsion. The legal sub-system gains autopoieticity in denying its political nature. Strictly speaking, it is not political: the trick is that while its creation is political, its operationality depends upon the continual self-understanding that what it is doing is specifically legal. However, of course, the flow of legal communication (courts, writing, commentaries, preparation of manuals, decisions on the creation of new laws) depends upon a range of tactics (hermeneutics, rhetoric, symbolism, signification, irony, metaphor, syllogisms) which are in a sense, necessarily political in that they cannot be reduced to a strictly closed formalism.

It matters to the operation of the Criminal Justice System that it can achieve a high degree of autopoieticity; this demarcates it from the political sphere – its decision-making processes are not deemed as political. In the political sphere is found those matters that can properly be debated and about which we can form and test our opinions; matters that require judgment; and about which it is correct to say that we seek to persuade each other through public argument. We avoid the political by various suppositions. One important effect is that:

'... we do not, for example, debate about matters where there are clear decision procedures for determining whether they are true or false, for example, mathematical truths or even empirical claims which can be settled by the appeal to facts.' (Richard J Bernstein, 1986: 252)

The criminal justice system can operate safely in a society full of conflict and social contradictions and retain the attributes of formal rationality through defining the types of argument that can take place in the legal court room. It achieves a 'cognitive transparency', or clear identification of the discursive objects which can be allowed into discussion. One key success of the classical reforms was the creation of a 'tariff system', where a table of sentences matched to offences by length and severity were in turn linked to the gravity of the offence. Logically, this also required a defining and ranking of offences in strict order, and this, preferably, required the creation of a comprehensive criminal code. A discourse which serves the purpose of system effectivity, and system legality, can then be established: the correct judgment is that made by a properly authorised official operating within an institutional framework, applying the organisational power in accordance with the correct norms (Hans Kelsen 1967, was perhaps the greatest jurisprudential writer to bring out this essential feature of autopoietic development) and orientating him/herself by the communicative process of correct language and textual reference.

This is the nature of our present situation: our criminal justice systems operate a rationality bequeathed by the success of the classical writers to found the legal dogmatics of a self-referential structure. We can see this better in investigating more fully the texts of Beccaria and John Austin.

Reading classicism I: The construction of Beccaria's text

Beccaria's text is built upon the work of others; its methodology is to grasp the narratives already accepted as images of the human condition, and to inter-play them to create the new social space of a 'rational penology'. Beccaria joined in the train of the new, more modest, sciences of man.

First he provides a narrative history to position the present. Beccaria utilises the 'fiction' of a social contract which he claims as an historical act (whereby independent and isolated men, weary of living in a continual state of war, sacrificed a part of their liberty so they might enjoy the rest of it in peace and safety). This is in turn linked to an ontological doctrine (namely, that man's rampant individualist nature ensured that every man was willing to put in the public fund only the least possible proportion, 'no more than suffices to induce the others to defend it. The aggregate of these least possible portions constitutes the right to punish; all that exceeds this is abuse and not justice; it is fact but by no means right'). The necessity of punishment is presented as empirically based on the nature of man's position, and governed by man's reason for its legitimation. Punishment was in the class of 'tangible motives' required 'to prevent the despotic spirit, which is in every man, from plunging the laws of society into its original chaos' (1963: 11-13). In a universe which was not moral neither could the multitude be naturally moral; men could not be left to socially co-exist. The paradox of crime was that it was both rational and irrational. It was rational for an individual to choose to commit a crime – he may well have his reasons, which Beccaria acknowledged were possibly political – and yet crime was a social irrationality. The irrationality of crime stems from its contravening the rationality of the social contract. Man's selfish rationality has identified subjection to the power which the social contract grants as the most beneficial mode of social existence, and the rational choice of an individual to choose criminal behaviour, ie behaviour outside the terms of the contract, is to choose the irrationality of behaviour beyond the social contract. It is an irrationality to be constrained by a fully rational crime control mechanism.

The criminal justice system could pacify the arbitrary and disruptive influences of social life, and provide the social engineering required for progress. It is a systematisation of penology rather than some simple humanisation we are offered. As Thorsten Sellin (1977) labelled it, Beccaria's replacement of capital punishment with penal servitude was a punishment worse than death: a living death. Penal servitude, and the associated repeated public sighting of the prisoner, is a rational advance, since with regard to the deterrent effect of punishment Beccaria argued that it is not the intensity of punishment that has the greatest effect on the human spirit, but its duration; for our sensibility is more easily, and more permanently, affected by slight but repeated impressions than by a powerful, but momentary, action. The death penalty can only create an impression which, for all its immediate force, men soon forget, but:

> '... in a free and peaceful government the impressions should be frequent rather than strong ... The death penalty becomes for the majority a spectacle and for others an object of compassion mixed with disdain: these two sentiments rather than the salutary fear which the laws pretend to inspire occupy the spirits of the spectators.' (1963:47)

Furthermore, this right to control is fundamental to orderly political structure and its continuance is a crucial social task. It is, of course, also a political task – but we are not led to see it as such. Instead the operation of the penal machine is depicted as a technology of the social – something to be discussed as a matter of efficiency; and on its own terms, not those of politics.

The neo-classical revival of just-desserts, and rational choice theory, have relied upon the technique of deterrence laid down in classicism. Beccaria espouses his version of the penal spectacle as able to deter any potential justification the populace may have in breaking a law they consider creates or reinforces an unjustifiable situation. The penal equation reinforces the economic and social structure under which the majority live, and which the offender views as 'fatal to the majority'. Beccaria uses a materialist early science of human nature in discussing the idea of 'motive', and thereby considers the rationality of thieves or assassins as calculable: the offender(s) are those individuals 'who find no motive weighty enough to keep them from violating the laws, except the gallows or the wheel'. Although they cannot give a clear account of their motives this 'does not make them any the less operative'. It is not that Beccaria refuses to understand the predicament of the offender, but the social discourse of politics and desire are not legally recognised terms of communication. Beccaria recognises that the offender may have an understandable set of motives for his crime, but this is of no legal consequence. Beccaria presents the thought process of an offender as asking:

'What are these laws that I am supposed to respect, that place such a great distance between me and the rich man? He refuses me the penny I ask of him and, as an excuse, tells me to sweat at work he knows nothing about. Who made these laws? Rich and powerful men who have never deigned to visit the squalid huts of the poor, who have never had to share a crust of mouldy bread amid the innocent cries of hungry children and the tears of a wife. Let us break these bonds, fatal to the majority and only useful to a few indolent tyrants; let us attack the injustice at its source. I will return to my natural state of independence; I shall at least for a little time live free and happy with the fruits of my courage and industry. The day will perhaps come for my sorrow and repentance, but it will be brief, and for a single day of suffering I shall have many years of liberty and of pleasures. As King over a few, I will correct the mistakes of fortune and will see these tyrants grow pale and tremble in the presence of one whom with an insulting flourish of pride they used to dismiss to a lower level than their horses and dogs.'

Moreover, there are narratives of the common life which help the offender deny the certain pain he or she will suffer.

Then religion presents itself to the mind of the abusive wretch and, promising him an easy repentance and an almost certain eternity of happiness, does much to diminish for him the horrors of the ultimate tragedy.

Therefore it is vital to create narratives and images which will present themselves to the mind of the potential offender so that the urge to crime will be controlled.

But he who foresees a great number of years, or even a whole lifetime to be spent in servitude and pain, in sight of his fellow citizens with whom he lives in freedom and friendship, slave of the laws which once afforded him protection, makes a useful comparison of all this with the uncertainty of the result of his crimes, and the brevity of the time in which he would enjoy their fruits. The perpetual example of those whom he actually sees the victims of their own carelessness makes a much stronger impression upon him than the spectacle of a punishment that hardens more than it corrects him. (1963: 49-50).

For Beccaria it is important to separate the administration of law from the political question of the content or style of law. The narrative participation of individuals in an ongoing social contract united men under the authority of the sovereign. In the substantive institutions which took the name of justice, neither the people nor the judges were empowered to interfere by continually making, or altering law; or have discretionary power to choose penal measures. Judges were not to be allowed discretion: only the sovereign was so entitled as he was 'the legitimate depository of the actual wills of all'.

It is vital to set out a clear cut and easily understood discourse on the criminal code and the respective roles and duties of each legal officer. Beccaria argues that:

> 'there is nothing more dangerous than the popular axiom that it is necessary to consult the spirit of the laws ... Our understandings and all our ideas have a reciprocal connection; the more complicated they are, the more numerous must be the ways that lead to them, and depart from them. Each man has his own point of view, and, at each different time, a different one. Thus the 'spirit' of the law would be the product of a judge's good or bad logic, of his good or bad digestion; it would depend on the violence of his passions, on the weakness of the accused, on the judge's connections with him, and on all those minute factors that alter the appearances of an object in the fluctuating mind of man.' (1963: 14-16)

Subjectivism is acknowledged and constrained. The identification of the harm of crime also needs to be developed into a systematic form:

> '... the measure of punishments is not the sensibility of the criminal, but the public injury ... equality of punishments can only be extrinsic, since in reality the effect on each individual is diverse ... And who does not know that external formalities take the place of reason for the credulous and admiring populace?' (Ibid: 70)

Henceforth the self-understanding of the system is to occur only through a language beknown to the system: 'legal dogmatics'.

We are told of the chaos that not accepting the Criminal Justice System would result in. Beccaria follows the lead of Hobbes and places individual men in the state of nature in a chaotic state - man needs a common reference point to orientate himself and his relations with his fellows but can find none in his understanding of nature. His need for survival, his need to escape death as long as possible, demands a rational organisation and the construction of a minimum society (For Hobbes, whose discussion Beccaria follows, see *Leviathan*, Penguin Edition, Part 1, particularly Chapter 13). For Hobbes, certain qualities lead man to form society, namely:

> 'The passions that incline men to Peace, are Feare [sic] of Death; Desire of such things as are necessary to commodious living, and a hope by their industry to obtain them.' (p.188)

Man has a desperate need to escape from the chaos of the natural condition, and the result is the political *Leviathan*. The naked irrational flow of power is incorporated and rationalised in the creation of a nexus of political power, sovereign power - the overcoming of natural terror by submission to legitimate power:

> 'Where there is no common Power, there is no Law: where there is no Law there is no Injustice.' (Ibid: 188)

These background conditions (or assumptions) concerning key 'facts' of social existence demonstrate the need for, and legitimate, a mechanism of control. The operation of this mechanism can become an organisational concern taking a set of operative conditions and debates as its own. The social is safe within the confines of that regime of law, safe within a containment, a subjection to that political creation. Key principles which structure the criminal justice organisation, notably the need for a direct linkage of penality to offence, flow from empirical observation on the nature of the human condition. Specifically, no man will give other than what is the minimum to sustain co-existence. Hobbes sums up his deductions of the laws of nature in the maxim 'do not do that to another, which thou wouldest not have done to thyself' (Ibid: 21).

Once accepted the system can display a formal rationality, and set out its principles of decision-making, which ensure that when these are followed we believe the decision was just. The system does not have to offer any social justice, only the stylised form of reciprocity which gives rise to stable expectations. Man does not need any idea of the 'good' society to constitute civil society out of the state of nature. Beccaria holds that man does not need to come out of himself and participate substantively in a common realm. He may rest in essentially solitary existence - but, if imposed upon he can impose back. Paradoxically, although the sovereign is to embody the 'common will' the principle does not draw the substantive thoughts of the individual into the common will - on the contrary it specifies that man will regard himself as the stranger to/of all others and they to/of him. And in such strangeness all are equal. Each is thus the abstract equal of all others; and in that abstraction equality reigns over any 'fact' of their difference.

The legitimacy of the rule of law is posited as the necessary creation of, or rational reflection on; the empirical operation of the world. Empirically, Hobbes states, all men are equal in the face of death, and the power of any is not sufficient to disallow the potentiality of death at the hands of any other. Additionally, the empirical result of individualism is that men must judge themselves as equal, not because of a natural ordering of telos made visible to all, but because in the absence of such, none will accept being unequal to others. Thus, because of the absence of a common point of reference, an equality (abstract) in law must be accepted; moreover, it is recognised that it must be contrary to the facts but the facts also determine that we must act as if it was not! Leo Strauss (1953) analyses at length this transition. For Strauss the dilemma was clear:

> 'Reason is impotent because reason or humanity have no cosmic support: the universe is unintelligible, and nature 'dissociates' men. But the very fact that the universe is unintelligible permits reason to rest satisfied with its free constructs, to establish through its constructs an Archimedean basis of operations, and to anticipate an unlimited progress in its conquest of nature.' (1953: 201)

Consider the context for this control. We have stressed the breakdown of the surveillance of the pre-modern. Bauman (1987) asks where Hobbes got the ideas and imagery for his dreaded state of nature thesis? He suggests Hobbes found them in the social reality he saw around him. Beccaria is specific:

'What man of any sensibility can keep from shuddering when he sees thousands of poor wretches driven by a misery either intended or tolerated by laws (which have always favoured the few and outraged the many) to a desperate return to the original state of nature – when he sees them accused of impossible crimes, fabricated by timid ignorance, or found guilty of nothing other than being true to their own principles, and sees them lacerated with meditated formality and slow torture by men gifted with the same senses, and consequently the same passions?' (1963: 43)

The state of nature was caused by man's irrational and unjustified social structures, it was up to man to develop a new and rational social ordering. Modernity can be built on systematic structures.

Beccaria's thesis, finally, is a rhetorical testament to progress. It is a vindication of the progressive potentiality of modernity, and a celebration of the decision to peruse truth. The first epoch was the formation of the great societies of men organised around the 'false divinities' of 'primitive errors'. Now is the second epoch:

'... where truth, after progressing slowly at first and then rapidly, sits at last as a companion to monarchs on their thrones and enjoys a cult and altar in the parliaments of republics.' (1963: 96–7)

Under the influence of Beccaria's pen we shall move beyond those present laws which contain 'the dregs of utterly barbarous centuries', we 'directors of the public welfare', and we shall create a sight that will lie before our eyes illuminated in the peaceful splendour of progress. This transfer of a whole structural scheme of aesthetic, theoretical, technical, and moral progress within a collective idea of unified history, presupposes that man sets himself as the only one in charge of this totality, that he supposes himself to be the one that 'makes history'; but he makes history progressively under the guidance of 'proper knowledges'. It is only then that he finds it possible to deduce the movement of history from a proper self-understanding of the rational subject. The future can become the consequence of our actions in this present, and these are moved by our present understanding of reality. Thus the 'plea' of Beccaria, 'not to demonstrate what the law is, but rather to incite men to make it what the author thinks it ought to be' (1963: xviii), is to use the law to constitute a new society.

With both Hobbes, Beccaria, Bentham and Austin, we avoid the question of the actual substantive content to equality in the social – that question, the social critique of the liberal equality of modernity, can but come later – reaching a particularly critical conception with Marx and his own modern measure of commonalty, namely, 'the complete social theory'. But in Hobbes and Beccaria, it is the absence of any reference, except the philosophic 'experience' of the state of nature, which drives us to see posited law as 'the order of things' and to achieve a new regime of 'objectivity'. Equality (of Being, of Rights), is thus posited as an unreflexive axiom of judgment.

The criminal justice system can take on the characteristics of an autopoietic system – the law must be internally ordered by reason, since it is such reason and logical form which ensure laws operation, its objectivity. Law is rational and formal, to be applied in the social, its policy aspects discussed and changed in the political. The role of the judge is to reflect what the law is. The inheritors of the criminal law can look back upon Beccaria – and the 'rights' approach, which through its Kantian forms later develops into the 'due process' defence of the institutions of criminal justice – and thus blind themselves to what Beccaria achieved; an instrument designed for control, which legitimatises itself to mediate between the open power of the sovereign and the latent power of the subject; above all, a criminal justice system.

The success of classicism enables 'crime' to spread

Let us be clear about the complexity of the 'functions' achieved by this part of the philosophical birth of modernity. The emphasis upon control, explicit in classical criminology, should not blind us to the constructivist aspects. The rule of law allows diversity and progress; it creates 'crime' as a central foundational conception for that modernity. Crime, as a concept and the implicit range of responses of dealing with crime, for example, 'philosophies of punishment', are then notions to be utilised in the constructionist project of modernity. One hidden curriculum of classicism is not so much to devise a mechanism to control and, in time, eradicate crime, but to assert that 'crime' and its associated conceptual apparatus are central to modernity. The implications of this are clear:

Firstly, crime overwhelms 'non-crime'. As modernity spreads, aspects of social interaction which involve 'harm' become questioned in the form – 'can this be fitted into the rational scheme of criminal jurisprudence?'

Secondly, crime becomes the technique of 'formal social control', displacing alternative mechanisms – the result is a concentration of functional power in the hands of professional criminal justice personnel. A power which is legitimated according to conceptions of specific role performance. Modern criminal justice organisations are, thus, not only a technique of ensuring formal social control but also products of the type of social control being aimed at in modernity.

By contrast Donald Black outlines how much 'crime' is actually not an affront to societies' morality but:

'... quite the opposite. Far from being an intentional violation of a prohibition, much crime is moralistic and involves the pursuit of justice. It is a mode of conflict management, possibly a form of punishment, even capital punishment. Viewed in relation to law, it is self-help. To the degree that it defines or responds to the conduct of someone else – the victim – as deviant, crime is social control.' (1984: 1)

The impact of state control over 'crime' thus robs 'traditional self help' of its meaning and makes problematic 'modern self help'; the ability of individuals or groups to respond in certain social participatory ways is taken away by the state. Modern legality is 'governmental social control'. Black leads to the conclusion that the reality of much crime, for instance, inner city 'drug wars', and self help actions, is that:

'... in modern society the state has only theoretically achieved a monopoly over the legitimate use of violence. In reality, violence flourishes (particularly in modern America), and most of it involves ordinary citizens who seemingly view their conduct as a perfectly legitimate exercise of social control.' (Ibid: 13)

Thirdly, the 'freedom' of crime, ie the metaphysics of rational choice, and the imposition of key elements of social judgment on the constitution of the social self of individuals after the act (and thus the encouragement to think in a criminal fashion) spreads. When modernity declares its 'right' to autonomy, to the 'liberal' freedom of individualism, it also declares the right to crime', that its citizens have a 'right' to be criminal and thus a 'right' to be punished.

Fourthly, to ensure the freedom of crime as a concept, punishments are required to become 'modern' − too harsh a punishment interferes with the acceptability of 'crime' as the natural form of modernity. That is to say, that as well as any 'functional' fit between the demands of social structure and the type of penality experienced in punishment (see Rusche and Kirchheimer, 1968 etc) the practical experiencing of the system must not be incongruous with the cultural and narrative sensibilities of that social structure.

Reading classicism II: John Austin and the role of knowledge

Our question here is simple: *What guides the Law?* Classical Criminology saw the science of utility as providing the engine of rational social change. John Austin is popular in jurisprudence courses where he is inevitably read in a simple form. A neglected aspect of Austin is his complete faith in the role of secure knowledge of social reality and the underlying 'natural' laws of the world. This is not so much natural law in the religious sense, although he has carefully turned God's will into the principle of utility, but confidence in the ability of the new scientific approach to uncover the real features of the operating and determining structures of the world.

Austin is clearly of the view that modern societies are constructions of human endeavour, they are the instruments of politics. The relationships which exist between individuals in modernity are essentially both political and individualistic; thus politics is to be a matter of technique. Austin certainly sides with technology and control against emancipation. The goal of society is the happiness of the individuals who make it up:

'When I speak of the public good, or of the general good, I mean the aggregate enjoyments of the single or individual persons who compose the public or general ... the good of mankind, is the aggregate of the pleasures which are respectively enjoyed by the individuals who constitute the human race ...' (1862: 161).

This is to be guided by knowledge of the truths of the human condition: 'the neglect of plain and palpable truths is the source of most of the errors with which the world is infested' (Ibid: 161).

Having established positive law as the proper province of jurisprudence Austin in Lectures III and IV sets out a defence of the principle of utility (the proximate test of law and the technique for policy making in social administration) and on understanding of the goal of political organisation, the common good.

His first claim is that men are fallible, human beings simply cannot alone master the truth of the human condition; submission to authority, testimony, and trust are inescapable. Even in an ideal system of law and morality, exactly attuned to the principle of utility, although the rules may be known, the rationale behind them could not be known in its entirety. Moreover, while we accept that in science the role of experts is to investigate, analyse and disseminate their findings, and we, the public should 'commonly trust the conclusions which we take upon authority', and this trust, this deference to authority is 'perfectly rational', no such structure exists within ethics. The sciences related to ethics (legislation, politics, and political economy) are in a state of confusion, in large part because those who have investigated ethics have not adopted the scientific attitude of impartiality, and 'therefore have differed in their results'. This dooms the multitude, who have not the time nor the resources to adopt a fully critical and inquiring attitude to the evidence, to the mercy of opinion. Concomitantly, much of the legal and moral structures currently in place 'rest upon brute custom and not manly reason', and there are many obstacles to the diffusion and advancement of ethical truth. At the time of his jurisprudential writings Austin was, however, optimistic that a proper science of ethics could establish itself and overcome these obstacles. In time, while profound knowledge would be confined to the few who were experts, the multiple could grasp the leading principles, and 'if imbued with these principles, and were practised in the art of applying them, they would be docile to the voice of reason, and armed against sophistry and error'. The consequences of such a diffusion of ethical truth would be a drastic reduction in social strife, and a proper understanding of the nature of social co-operation. Austin gives the example of the institution of private property, demanded by utility, but about which many 'pernicious prejudices' exist.

> 'To the ignorant poor, the inequality which inevitably follows the beneficent institution of property is necessarily invidious. That they who toil and produce should fare scantily, whilst others, who "delve not nor spin" batten on the fruits of labour, seems, to the jaundiced eyes of the poor and the ignorant, a monstrous state of things: an arrangement upheld by the few at the cost of the many, and flatly inconsistent with the benevolent purposes of Providence.' (All quotes, Ibid: 131–2)

This prejudice has many effects. It creates many of the crimes which have poverty as their immediate cause, but which really come out of a misunderstanding of what is socially possible. Crucially it blinds the people to the real cause of their sufferings, and the only real remedies available. 'Want and labour spring from the niggardliness of nature, and not from the inequality which is consequent on the institution of property.' Austin claims the condition of man on earth demands the institution of private property, and the crucial mechanism of capital is a direct consequence of property. Although the poor are used by capital, necessarily parting with their labour and presently 'condemned' to 'incessant drudgery', Austin recognises the co-dependency which the process engenders: 'In effect, though not in law, the labourers are co-proprietors with the capitalists who hire their labour'.

Austin then makes a remarkable claim: in effect, he states, that if the poor come to understand the principles of political economy they can change the nature of their position and bargaining strength, and thereby force a dramatic betterment of their condition. Again it is Austin's absolute certainty in the force of a truth which allows this: 'In the true principle of population, detected by the sagacity of Mr Malthus, they must look for the cause and the remedy of their penury and excessive toil.' Using their knowledge they would break their 'sordid subjection to the arbitrary rule of a few', they would understand that attacks on property are actually attacks on the institutions which create accumulation, they would see they are actually deeply interested in the security of property, and 'if they adjusted their numbers to the demand for their labour, they would share abundantly, with their employers, in the blessings of that useful institution'.

Austin is certain 'that there is no particular uncertainty in the subject or matter of those sciences'; the difficulties are external, in the attitudes of those who have studied them, progress is assured if they would pursue truth 'with obstinate application and with due indifference' (quotes, Ibid: 131-33).

What of today? We can see that much of the point of the writings of post-modernism, and legal scholars, such as those of the Critical Legal Studies movement, lie in the rather banal fact that things have not worked out as Austin expected or hoped. The disinterested pursuit of knowledge has not resulted in a structure of coherent and settled truths. Instead, perspectivism, relativism, and subjectivism reign. The confidence in underlying natural laws of social and human development has long since vanished. Law cannot claim its legitimacy as simply bringing out the underlying functionalities and structures of social interaction. Note: Critical Legal Studies writers, such as Roberto Unger (1987), have a concept for the Austin style confidence in an underlying natural order which the law is to reflect – they call this 'objectivism'.

Austin's confidence in the *Truth* of *An Essay on the Principle of Population*, which Malthus placed as the foundation of political economy is instructive. Partly as a response to the optimistic reading of the necessity for human progress which Condorcet and Godwin had put forward, Malthus injected the pessimistic contention that population, if unchecked, increases geometrically, while food supplies increase arithmetically, with predictably disastrous consequences. Malthus' 'scientific' achievement in uncovering one of the basic laws that govern human society was not seen as theory, but a truth which necessarily must guide policy. As Malthus put it: 'I see no way by which man can escape from the weight of this law which pervades all animated nature'. Malthus attacked by use of this principle all utopian, radical and grand, social engineering projects; limited and piecemeal reform was the only realistic course. Furthermore, the law must align itself with the underlying law of social development; nothing must be in place which would encourage the poor to breed. If the legal structure contained any provisions which improved the condition of the poor it would simply result in their producing more children, and a corresponding reduction in wealth creation. Legal enactments were not to be prohibitive of choice, but designed to make clear the negative consequences of certain choices. To discourage the poor from producing children in conditions where they could not guarantee their support, a law should be made declaring that no child born from future marriages would be eligible for poor relief. Thus: if any man chose to marry, without a prospect of being able to support a family, while he should have the most perfect liberty to do so, to the resulting consequences of poverty they must, however, be left. 'To the punishment therefore of nature he should be left, the punishment of want ... He should be taught that the laws of nature, which are the laws of God, had doomed him and his family to suffer for disobeying their repeated admonitions.' This is presented as not the punishment of the politically powerful, but of the operation of natural social laws, the positive law enacted by the political state is only the mediatory instrument. Moreover, no provision can be made for abandoned or illegitimate children: 'If the parents desert their child, they ought to be made answerable for the crime. The infant is, comparatively speaking, of little value to society, as others will immediately supply its place.' Malthus is equally hostile to any notion of inherent rights, even, as the following passage suggests, any talk of a right to a social existence.

> 'A man who is born into a world already possessed, if he cannot get subsistence from his parents on whom he has a just demand, and if the society do not want his labour, has no claim of right to the smallest portion of food, and, in fact, has no business to be where he is. At nature's mighty feast there is no vacant cover for him. She tells him to be gone, and will execute her own orders' (quotes from Malthus in Arblaster, 1984: 246).

Strict adherence to the principles of political economy soon lead to British liberalism's greatest 'massacre' – the condemning of one and a half million Irish to starvation in the late 1840s, when the British government refused to intervene in the famine caused by the failure of the potato harvest, although Ireland was actually exporting food while the poor starved. It also led to the cruelty of the new poor law (Arblaster, 1984: 254-259). The plight of the poor was determined by the laws of political economy – it was nothing to do with the law, said the 'liberals', and the taking of food by the starving was simple theft. Observing this, Marx was unimpressed – the state, that body which Austin so clearly thought could use the law as the instrument of rational government, was nothing but a committee to manage the affairs of the capitalist class.

After the destruction of the classicist faith in utility what guides the law?

There are two lines of enquiry in answering this. One is to trace the development of law as autonomous, to understand the systems effect and the autopoietic ability of legal sub-systems. Another, is to trace how utilitarianism developed under the influence of John Stuart Mill (1962 [1861]) who offered a reconciliation of utilitarianism as a general framework for the rationality of legal engineering, with a liberty or harm principle, whereby strict limits were placed on the scope of the law to interfere with individual activities. Mill moved utilitarianism away from the simple mathematics of units of pleasure, onto the idea of maximising social happiness by extending the ability of the population to follow their individual preferences. This preference utilitarianism would mean that the aim of the society should be to maximise the number of options available to the individual. From this point of view as long as liberty and diversity is being promoted then legal regulation is progressive.

Jurists hold that legal regulation, by its nature, seems to imply obedience; why?

Sociologists have tended to be sceptical of a fundamental concern of liberal jurisprudence, namely, that the idea of the rule of law involves the normative acceptance that a degree of obligation is inherent in the idea of rule-bound activity. In the early part of this century the great Austrian jurist Hans Kelsen (1967) saw legality in terms of a structure of oughts; law was one particular kind of normative bind. Within the Anglo-American tradition the high point of this view was found in the work of the Oxford liberal jurisprudent H L A Hart (1961).

H L A Hart: the critique of classicism in Austin and the response of the civilised man

In a modern classic *The Concept of Law* (1961), H L A Hart talked of the concept of law as a system of primary and secondary rules which could not be reduced to ideas of power or commands. Hart constructed his text upon a critique of Austin's theory of law as an instrument of command, power and obedience. Hart actually constructs a model which is not faithful to Austin, but is remarkably like a model of pure classicism; in fact remarkably like the conservative neo-classical response to crime of recent years.

Specifically, Hart denies that one can see law in terms of threats alone. The legal (normative) structure of a society is said to be distinguished by a 'critical reflective attitude'. Legal phenomena can only be adequately understood through the attitudes human beings take towards their behaviour. The internal point of view, characteristic of rule bound practices, is manifested in demands for conformity, criticism of deviation, acceptance of the legitimacy of criticism, and distinctive kinds of justification for action expressed in 'ought' language.

This is radically different from the control emphasis of classicism. Although we accept that using the law in some sense makes certain behaviour obligatory, we are asked not to see law as an instrument of control and thus capable of analysis in terms of certain probabilities, patterns and predictions of behaviour; nor to weigh up the impact of legal prohibition on the motives of the potential offender. Instead we are to give primacy to an internal attitude of critical reflective acceptance. Hart rejects the imperative conception of law: modern law is a matter of rules not imperatives. Modern law is not a system wherein the will of the politically powerful is expressed and backed up by threats, but it is a interacting structure of rules, in which the attitude of critical acceptance grants a feeling of obligation to play by the rules of the social practices thus organised.

Hart is clear that rules contain an internal and external perspective. Some people do not share the internal attitude, thus Hart points to an irreducible tension:

> 'At any given moment the life of any society which lives by rules, legal or not, is likely to consist in a tension between those who, on the one hand, accept and voluntarily cooperate in maintaining the rules, and those who, on the other hand, reject the rules and attend to them only from the external point of view as a sign of possible punishment. One of the difficulties facing any legal theory anxious to do justice to the complexity of the facts is to remember the presence of both these points of view and not to define one of them out of existence. Perhaps all our criticisms of the predictive theory of obligation may be best summarised as the accusation that this is what it does to the internal aspect of obligatory rules.' (1961: 88)

We are a long way from the climate of classical criminology. We appear to have undergone the social journey that Kant desired when he declared that a man who obeyed the law out of fear or calculation was a mere animal. Kant looked forward to the day when social order and personal attitudes would coincide, when the law would be purely self-applicable. Hart seems to declare that we have become these civilised men. His theory declares that the power and sanction-based image – where a man only behaves as he does for fear of the consequences imposed by some commander - is unacceptable. The command theory fails to allow for the finer feelings of the modern individual, the internal aspect. Modern civilised people act out of acceptance, their voluntary acceptance of the rules of the game, of the institutional framework of society. No coercion is needed, there is no need for threats or force. Law is the internalised acceptance of rules by civilised people. Hart indicates that there will always be a minority of others, those who do not possess this internal point of view - outsiders who 'reject the rules and attend to them only from the external point of view as a sign of possible punishment'. Society is torn by the tension between the two. But, Hart explains, one need not fear:

> 'Though such a society may exhibit the tension, already described, between those who accept the rules and those who reject the rules except where fear of social pressure induces them to conform, it is plain that the latter cannot be more than a minority, if so loosely organised a society of persons, approximately

equal in physical strength, is to endure: for otherwise those who reject the rules would have too little social pressure to fear (especially lawyers and officials) – or, as Austin would have it – obedience through threats, enforced by the sovereign. Or, as others would have it, through a minority class enforcing their will on the majority.' (1961: 89)

Hart is not alone, most liberal writers appear to assume an obligation to obey the law. As Ted Honderich put it in an article entitled 'Violence for Equality' in *Enquiries in Political Philosophy*.

'All of us save some true anarchists have the conviction that the members of a society have some obligation if the society is at all tolerable which is to say that it has risen above barbarism, ancient or modern. Many things are not to be done for a reason having to do with the fact that they are illegal as distinct from other reasons which might also exist. It is thought by some that this obligation to keep to the laws is at its strongest with respect to the laws prohibiting violence.' (104)

Further on he states:

'Political obligation is obviously a kind of moral obligation although not the most familiar kind. The idea is that the subjects of governments, or some governments, are under some moral obligation to give up all courses of action which are made illegal. There is a moral restraint or prohibition on subjects with respect to these courses of action which are prohibited by the law of the state.' (106)

On arguments for a sort of natural, intuitive understanding of obligation to obey law, Iredell Jenkins writes:

'Why should, and do we, have an obligation to obey the law? I believe that the only answer is that we just do. As in the case above we are simply made that way; we are social creatures so we are responsive to our fellow creatures; we accept the terms of social life. We accommodate ourselves to the provisions that are necessary to preserve the social fabric.' (*Social Order and the Limits of Law*: 196)

Modern writers are ambivalent about using the metaphor of a social contract but for David Lyons:

'This argument maintains that each and every one of us is party to an agreement either of the rest of us or with those who rule. We have pledged ourselves to obey the law and our pledge binds us. Moreover, it binds us unconditionally: nothing done by the law or by those in power can possibly nullify our agreement. For if the contract can be nullified by, say, outrageously unjust requirements or prohibitions then the contract does not necessarily bind us.' (1984: 211)

But David Lyons does not even find this argument of obligation through contract convincing from the point of view of those who have taken part in the elections. For Lyons:

'[such an idea] is incredible, not just because the contract must be constructed as unconditional but more simply because few of us have ever been parties to such an agreement. We have never literally pledged ourselves to obey the law. If we had not done so then we cannot we bound by such a pledge.' (Ibid: 211)

Iredell Jenkins highlights the more organic, or living relationship that exists between the state and subjects, seeing society as a political community:

'I think that it is this lived relationship that we have with our fellow creatures and hence with our society and hence again with the government that is the agent of our society and hence finally with the legal system that is the instrument of the government; that is the real source of the obligations that we feel and acknowledge to obey law. We should, and do, feel this obligation because we have lived on certain terms with our society and so with its governments and its legal system.' (*Social Order and the Limits of Law*: 199)

For conservative philosophers such as Ted Honderich: 'We have a natural duty to support and advance the institutions in our societies. We have a natural duty to obey the law and to refrain from violence' (*Inquires into Philosophy*: 137).

Yet philosophy cannot explain why we should expect obedience to the law. It has no thesis on how Hart's internal attitude is created. Nor can it guide us in processes to ensure that the numbers with the external attitude remain small. Modern philosophers, such as Simmonds (1979) and Lyons (1984), have argued that individuals should approach the law pragmatically rather than working on the basis of any automatic presumption that they should obey. Lyons seems to give us a picture of legal systems as being full of moral problems, fallible, and, for Lyons, law must earn respect.

Without faith in utilitarianism, and devoid of a natural law system, how can the positive law earn respect?

Much of the debate in this area has been conducted in the terrain of abstract political philosophy, or moral philosophy and many people feel frustrated with this. Smith (1990) for instance, argued that the whole debate was so ensconced in sterile academia that we should move any emphasis away from philosophical questions of why people ought to obey the law to the questions of:

'... when they ought to obey, when not, and what sort of government they should be expected to tolerate, or not.' (1990: 867)

Perhaps a simple answer is that criminological writings have never really addressed this question. Traditional criminology appeared to assume that obedience was normal. But what is at stake here? Is it some sort of voluntary commitment to act in accordance with the law, on condition that the society provide social goods and measures of success? Most citizens of contemporary societies have never entered into any explicit promise. It is only infrequently that oaths of obedience have been taken, normally by immigrants or certain ranks of civil servants.

What are these tacit or implied promises to obey? It once was popular – for example, in the work of John Lock in the 16th century – to imply a promise to obey from the continued residence of the individual in a society. That has been replaced today by a more popular version in a promise to abide in the democratic process and keying into the law-making process via voting. Certain modern philosophers, such as Singer (1973), argue with an analogy of the law of estoppel; in voting one's voluntary behaviour encourages others to believe that one consents to the decision which will come out of this process and that one will abide by the outcomes. Having voted, the citizen is estopped from arguing that he has not given his consent when the government embarks upon any particular policy which he does not agree with. To vote, and yet refuse to be bound by the result, is not only unfair upon those who participate in good faith, it can also lead to the breakdown of democracy as the whole decision making procedure falls apart. But this version of consent theory seems to rely upon the empirical reality of promissorial obligation. What happens to those who do not vote?

Fishkin pointed out in his work, *Democracy & Deliberation* (1991) that the crisis of legitimacy facing contemporary liberal democratic regimes is precisely linked to the whole position of non-participation. Non-participation occurs in various forms; in its most obvious form there is simple non-voting, but even the amount of participation which voting engenders is small. Fishkin finds very problematic the whole idea of informed majorities participating and consenting to the structure of legal regulation. John Kenneth Galbraith's (1992) argument in *The Culture of Contentment* is premised upon the notion that half the population of the US does not vote in presidential elections, fewer still in congressional elections – implying that the whole philosophical notion of participatory consent is simply empirically invalid. Moreover, even if the philosophical concept of consent could be rendered meaningful, to vote does not imply a pledge of obedience to the regulative and distributive structure of the law. The content of the promise could vary immensely. It could amount to a stance of justified disobedience, or that the participant's consent not to break the law is merely for selfish reasons, or personal convenience, indeed for motives such as we impute to a crime. The normal distinction between a civil disobedient and a criminal is that the criminal acts out of selfishness, whereas the civil disobedient is disobeying the law in a principled stance on behalf of the society or his or her idea of society.

But if we were to hold, as has sometimes been argued (Robert Dahl for instance, in the 1960s, popularised the notion of a supermarket theory of democracy), an individualist utilitarian theory of democracy, where participation in the democratic process is linked with the understanding that certain social goods are flowing to the individual, what gives coherence to the totality? Why, if the goods do not come back to an individual, is the individual obligated to play his or her part at all? Could not even the act of voting, upon this analogy, be said to imply that if the structure does not give the individual the goods he/she wants then he/she can feel him/herself free to simply take them, even if that is a selfish act, because the very process of voting is itself selfish? Why should the citizen who feels himself or herself systematically excluded feel any sense of gratitude or respect towards the government and the legal order or his fellow citizens, who appear to be gaining from the order of things? Why should he or she feel any sense of fair play towards his or her fellow citizens?

The combination of utilitarianism and liberalism appears to offer an argument that where a legal structure is simply morally neutral, or neutral between particular social groups, and sets out the rules of the social game, the obligation to play the game relies upon the notion that the whole structure benefits us; and that when this structure benefits everyone there is a moral obligation to obey in order to preserve common security, or you are bound to express your gratitude for the structure by obeying the rules. In recent years Soper (1985) has argued that since government and law-making are necessary to human well-being, people should respect the good faith efforts of those in authority in their bid to rule, and the most important way of showing this respect is by accepting the *prima facie* obligation to obey the laws. This is a form of fair play argument; the obligation to obey seems to rely upon the notion that the procedures for the distribution of the benefits and burdens of the structure of social co-operation are reasonably fair. But must this fair play apply on both the general, or abstract, and particular levels? As H L A Hart argued:

'... when a number of persons conduct any joint enterprise according to rules and thus restrict their liberty, those who have submitted to these restrictions when required, have a right to a similar submission from those who have benefitted by their submission.' (1955: 185)

But do not all these arguments seem to hark back to the image of small scale locality? Consider these conceptions of fair play, gratitude and respect. Do they not ring true when we consider social life as a matter of reciprocity, or as a matter of what you might call, communities? But do they fit the abstract conception of the modern nation? What exactly is it that people are obliged to obey out of their abstract identity as a citizen in radically divided societies? What happens if we can argue that in our late-modern, or post-modern times, there are many citizens who receive comparatively few benefits; what happens to this idea of fair play as being the basis of the sweeping obligation to obey? Santos (1977) in looking at the disaffected citizens of the Brazilian shanty towns, points to the fact that they have little obligation to obey the official, what they call, asphalt laws of the Brazilian state. Indeed, the whole of his article relates to how, according to the state, the entire residency was illegal and they had simply devised their own unofficial legal system. In Galbraith's *The Culture of Contentment,* the complacency of the majority class in late-modern society is reflected in a growing underclass which is being systematically excluded and ignored by the complacent, contented majority. What is it that the underclass can be said to owe gratitude and moral obligation towards? How is the system in substance fair towards them? If fair play does not apply to them how can any general obligation to obey the law bind them?

Another argument may, however, be simply pragmatic necessity. Society needs certain rules to exist. Without these rules being enforced the whole structure would collapse. Tonore (1981) argues that duty arises out of necessity.

In the same way as the duties of care and responsibilities arise because of proximity to those in need, citizenship entails that the state counts upon one to obey. The state is in a non-voluntary position of having to care for its citizens out of necessity, but in order to perform this duty the state needs a reciprocal obedience. Furthermore, if the state is committed to extract promises of obedience from alien residents it chooses to associate with, or allow into its domain, it must have at least as much right to the co-operation of natural citizens it is forced to associate with. And there are certain variations which hark back to the Aristotelian notion. For example, the jurisprudential writings of John Finnis (1980) seem to advocate a natural duty to obey. According to Finnis, individuals have a duty to promote 'the common good' and 'human flourishing', which, in turn, generates a duty to obey state laws, since these are the natural means of promoting universal human goods such as knowledge and play. Similar, to the argument from fair play, reciprocity is ensured, the state has its obligations while the subjects have theirs. But what if the state denies responsibility? What if it radically 'privatises' social space?

Conclusion: the dialectic of systems and selves

The dialectic which extends from the basis of the writings of Beccaria, Bentham and Austin onwards is simple: coercion is necessary to stabilise the chaos of the early modern social order but in the normative project of modernity coercion is not the secret of the relationship of law and society. As Austin put it, an educated populace is of greater benefit to the enlightened legislator than an army of policemen. And the construction of civil society? The 18th century empiricist approach of Edmund Burke was clear:

> 'Manners are more important than laws. Upon them, in a great measure, the laws depend. The law touches us but here and there, and now and then. Manners are what vex and soothe, corrupt or purify, exalt or debase, barbarise or refine us ... They give their whole form and colour to our lives. According to their quality, they add morals, they supply them, or they totally destroy them.' (Quoted in Eagleton, 1990: 42)

What creates the living constitution of civil society in modern societies? We will go on to describe the influence of locality, of urbanity in later chapters, we have argued that the stability of the legal order is one aspect, but a crucial factor lies in attitude, in behaviour. It is not just that (as Spinoza put it) human nature will not submit to unlimited coercion, but rather, there needs to be an interactive balance between the structures of power as visualised through the judicial apparatus of the state and the expectations and behaviour of the subjects/citizens. Call it hegemony (in keeping with the Marxist tradition), call it legitimacy (Weber), call it consent (communicative theory), call it the internal normative attitude (Kelsen and H L A Hart), all may point to various procedures, the social order needs more than a criminal justice system which obeys its own autopoietic structure, it needs more than a rational, clear-cut code capable of easy administration: it needs a combination of external rules and a population whose modes of behaviour and expectations are compatible with the rules. To be effective, to operate without stifling society, law must combine with the aesthetics of social conduct (what we call 'culture'). The rule of law requires *moral subjects*; it requires *socialised subjects* – a civilised society requires a particular form of social self. The person of Hart's *Concept of Law*, the ideal subject of late-modernity, is not the calculating subject of the neo-classical rational man, but a civilised individual. We must ask how did this individual come about and what of our present? Does the return of 'the need to fear punishment' rhetoric; does the return to a war on crime mentality; does the return to a mind-set harking back to the early modern classical emphasis on calculation and control through the manipulation of the external aspect of rules, reflect a situation where the onset of post-modernism has created a decivilising movement which renders necessary an uncivilised response? Or is this understanding of the need for civilised selves existing in a humane civil society a theme that the onset of the neo-classical movement appears to overlook – perhaps at our expense? Is the present rush to Law and Order politics actually a reversal of modernity? A rush to justice that may destroy justice?

CHAPTER SIX

CRIMINOLOGICAL POSITIVISM I: THE SEARCH FOR THE CRIMINAL MAN, OR THE PROBLEM OF THE DUCK

If it looks like a duck and walks like a duck and quacks like a duck ... then it is a duck. (Traditional proverb)

'[Criminals are characterised by] human deformities and monstrosities, physically illshapen, weak and sickly with irregular features, they bear a sinister, ignoble, and furtive expression. They have an unbalanced and distorted cranium, and are of a low level of intelligence, apparently devoid of the nobler sentiments; with a depraved if not utter absence of moral sense or conscience.' (Boies, 1893, quoted in Garland, 1985: 194)

Introduction to criminological positivism

Until interest in classical criminology revived recently, scientific criminology was assumed to have begun with a series of late 19th century writings inspired by an Italian Doctor, Lombroso. Today, he is widely credited with having drawn up the scientific manifesto reorientating criminology away from its connection with crime and the rational administration of a judicial mechanism, towards studying the criminal and the conditions which created the criminal. Lombroso was not alone – there has been, and still is, a vast network of scholars and research projects dedicated to reducing the problem of crime to the problem of the criminal. Although an individualist orientation has been a major tendency in positivism, its desire to escape legal categories is epistemological: how does one create a science which avoids taking as its object of analysis something that another discipline, ie the criminal law, has been responsible for defining? Moreover, the ideology of the criminal law appeared to institutionalise a purely abstract or formal self, rather than deal with real people exhibiting real characteristics. Criminological positivism wanted to define the limits of its intellectual horizons for itself, and thus argued at its inception that the solution to understanding the problem of crime was to study the criminal and the factors which constitute him... but who or what or where is the criminal? A widely accepted solution has been the methodology our opening proverb outlines.

Thus positivism has sought to identify the criminal by the externally observable characteristics of those individuals who are found where the criminal lives, ie to analyse the individuals found in prisons, in probation departments, on community service, in geographical localities of high crime rates. Thus positivism accepted the result of a series of labelling processes: it took for granted the fact that because a person had been labelled a criminal by a series of processes, and had contributed in a major way to being so labelled by some action or omission (again perhaps because of a variety of motives), then either investigating his constitution, or the forces that pushed him into the situation, would reveal the secret to the nature of the criminal.

From the vantage point of the 1990s to read the work of the late 19th century writers we call positivists is to encounter an array of strange assertations and bizzare characters, one often wonders how they could have thought what they wrote. The story is sometimes told of the students of a famous entomology professor who glued the head of one bug onto the body of a second bug and added the wings of a third, took their creation to the professor and asked him what it was. He looked puzzled for a time, then brightened considerably. 'Yes,' he said, 'I believe I have seen one of these before. Tell me, did it hum when you found it?' 'Oh yes,' the students replied, 'it hummed quite loudly.' 'Well then,' their professor replied, 'it must be a humbug.'

Criminological positivism has taken a lot of humbugs seriously, but in a sense it has not taken them seriously enough. For a criminal is in a real sense a hybrid. The criminal cannot exist in non-social nature – criminality an existential condition only known to human society. One cannot be born a criminal, it is an achieved status.

Crime is a social entity. Our account of classical criminology and the rule of law, outlined how law creates a structure of rules and clear cut demarcations which can fit (efficiently or not) over a diverse social body. We argued that the notion of crime is a fundamental feature of modernity. Crime is neither natural, in the sense that there is simply some objective phenomena out there which will always be a crime irrespective of culture, nor is it fully relativist, since if we accept crime as a harm; it is a reality like the objects of the natural world. However, in the 19th century a range of writers came to argue that law was irrelevant, redundant, that it did not offer real social guidance and social protection, and that progress was to be achieved by a thoroughgoing naturalist premise. All activities were to be treated as events occurring in the material world and were to be understood and dealt with in the same way as the natural scientist dealt with physical substances. A new spirit, or mode, of relating to the problems of the social world was offered; it was named 'positivism' early in the 19th century by the French social thinker, August Comte:

> 'The true positive spirit consists in substituting the study of invariable laws of phenomena for that of their so-called causes whether proximate or primary.' (*A General View of Positivism*, 1848)

For Comte (1974) human history revealed a *Law of Three Stages* of intellectual development:

- the *theological* or *fictive* stage – characterised by religion;
- the *metaphysical* or *abstract* – characterised by the products of philosophy and law;
- the *scientific* or *positive* stage – this was currently developing and was characterised by a clear cut distinction between science and morals, of visualised 'moral' or social problems as capable of being understood and

solved by applying the methodologies used in the physical (or natural) sciences. Observation, experimentation, and the quantification of data, would reveal the structures causing the entities or behaviour we wished to explain. The question to be asked was 'how did this come about?', rather than 'why did it come about?' This knowledge would give us a whole new dimension of power and provide the foundation for social progress.

Intellectual revolution or a narrowing of concerns?

For most of criminology's history Comte's view of progress was accepted; it was common to speak of an intellectual revolution occurring from Beccaria to Lombroso (this is the sort of phrase used in such texts as Vold and Bernard's *Theoretical Criminology* (1958, 1978, 1986) wherein a scientific approach was held to replace the perspectives of religion, philosophy and metaphysics. Although this is how the early positivists saw it themselves, if is a gross simplification. We have seen that classical criminology was actually a reflection of the new sciences of man put forward by Thomas Hobbes and David Hume among others. A full account of the epistemology of criminology and criminal justice is outside the province of this text, suffice to claim that there has been a problem of the foundation or the limits of study[1].

The growing empiricist science of man provided a critique of the social contract theory which Beccaria assumed as the basis of social order, and re-orientated the focus of study away from questions depicting a hypothetical origin to society and the ideal social order, onto an empirically orientated inquiry. The question of social order was viewed as something knowable and reducible to laws of social evolution. Man could take charge of social development by combining a sociological interest in social-cultural development, with an anthropological interest in the structure of human nature.

The essential presupposition for positivism is the belief that ultimately science can disclose the objective reality of the social and natural world. As Michael Gottfredson and Travis Hirschi state in a recent work *Positive Criminology*:

> '... certainly one feature of positive criminology has always been its belief in an objective external reality capable of measurement. Public disclosure of the understood reality, the procedures used for its measurement, and frequent independent replication are essential tenets of this perspective.' (1987: 19)

Rephrased in terms of the representational ability of language, positivism seems to insist that language consists of humanly created symbols which reference, symbolise or name (and so may communicate reality, more or less

---

1 Even while enagaging in empirical observation the question of how the entities observed came to be in the condition in which they were found must implicitly, at least, be part of a general theory.

complicatedly, and be capable of correct and clear usage) the things that humans wish to talk about. Furthermore, that there exists some natural, non-contingent, structure and hierarchy of these things which exist independent of human cognition, thereby providing an immanent natural order or picture of reality which science is uncovering. Positivism finds truth when science uncovers the natural structures of division and hierarchy which underpin the good, the normal, the 'natural' order of things.

The current pragmatic philosopher Richard Rorty (1979) has referred to this belief as 'the mirror of nature' premise. Science aims to provide verifiably accurate (albeit through some complicated structure of methodology and abstractions) representations of the reality out there which we come to understand through a mirror effect.

The mirror of nature idea assumes that since we have specific words and concepts these refer to natural entities, or things, which fit into a certain place in the rightful, or natural, order of social life. Thus, the word 'crime' implies a crime is an empirically verifiable event; the word 'criminal', leads us to assume there is a category of people who can be positively identified through some procedure as naturally criminal; the word criminality leads us to assume there is some stable propensity of individuals. An early positivist trap: since we use the word criminals to refer to those adjudged guilty of crimes, in order to investigate the characteristics of criminals the early positivists simply went to the prisons and other segregative facilities, and sought to measure the bodies and brains of the inmates as if this would give scientific data. The positivist approach does not seem to ask how the state of affairs they are using as the basis of their data comes into being. Gottfredson and Hirschi put this problem slightly differently: early positivism did not create a reflexive awareness of the nature of crime as part of a general theory, instead it was:

'... a "science" much concerned with allocating "findings" to its constituent disciplines and not so much concerned with understanding nature ...

The biological positivists did not have a conception of crime derived from a general theory of behaviour. They were therefore forced to accept the criminals provided them by the state: 'A criminal is a man who violates laws decreed by the State to regulate the relations between its citizens' (Ferraro 1972 [1911]: 3). Crimes were then merely acts in violation of the law. The biological positivist's problem seemed simple enough. All one had to do was locate the differences among people that produce differences in their tendencies to commit acts in violation of the law.

Absent a conception of crime, the positivist has no choice but to elaborate types of offenders. These typologies may be based on the frequency of offending, the seriousness of the offence, the object of the offense, the characteristics of the offender, or the nature of the prior and subsequent offences, but whatever their dimensions, they lead to complication rather than simplicity, to confusion rather than clarity ... Absent a concept of crime, the positivist method leads ineluctably to typologising without end.' (1990: 49-50)

A great deal of effort and research time went into the construction of typologies and correlated information. Positivism ensured a fetish for classification, typologising, and counting. A M Guerry, for example, devoted abundant energy to statistics on crime and suicide. By 1832 he had amassed 85,564 individual case reports on suicides, each with a guess at motives, and between 1832 and 1864 he analysed 21,132 cases of persons accused of attempted or successful murder, while constructing a typology of 4,478 classes of motives. Although the classification systems were in part a necessary attempt to deal with the sheer weight of numbers of the entities which could be included in the developing, rather open-ended field of study, it is a mysterious exercise reading these works entering what appears a dream-world. One can be easily reminded of a typology which Foucault read in a work of Borges, and which served as the instigating event to his writing *The Order of Things*. The typology was from 'a certain Chinese encyclopedia' in which it is written that:

'... animals are divided into: (a) belonging to the Emperor, (b) embalmed, (c) tame, (d) suckling pigs, (e) sirens, (f) fabulous, (g) stray dogs, (h) included in the present classification, (i) frenzied, (j) innumerable, (k) drawn with a very fine camelhair brush, (l) et cetera, (m) having just broken the water pitcher, (n) that from a long way off look like flies.' (Quoted in Foucault, 1970: xv)

Foucault asked both, how could they think that? and why is it that we could not think that?

Even with current studies one sometimes shares Foucault's bewilderment at typologies. Take Wille (1974) for example, who grouped murderers into ten types: (1) depressives, (2) psychotics, (3) murderers with organic brain dysfunction, (4) psychopaths, (5) passive-aggressive individuals, (6) alcoholics, (7) hysterical personalities, (8) child killers, (9) mentally retarded murderers, and (10) murderers who kill for sexual satisfaction.

In contrast, Guttmacher (1973) suggests six categories of murderers: (1) 'average' murderers free from prominent psychopathology but lacking societal values, (2) sociopaths desiring revenge on the population at large for maltreatment during childhood, (3) alcoholics who kill their wives over fear of losing them, (4) murderers avenging a lover's loss of interest, (5) schizophrenics responding to hallucinations and delusions, and (6) sadists who kill to achieve sexual pleasure.

The positive approach has come up with numerous classification systems. They come out of descriptions of offenders' backgrounds and description of the form their acts of murder took. It is as if the analyist is expecting the world to reveal its structures and messages without the need for meaningful interpretation.

The scientific status of the vast works done under the positive spirit is deeply questioned by a naive approach to the dependent variable, namely, that the criminal law produces the label crime which is then applied to the individuals positivists have studied. The dominant assumption of positivism has been that of some underlying process of natural cause which a science can uncover. Breakthroughs were constantly being announced requiring new research – but it is difficult to see how the research and the hybrid nature of crime were actually connected. For example, during this century some have placed great hopes in endocrinology as the science which could tell us the influence of the ductless glands and hormones; an abnormally low or high concentration of hormones was thought to affect the personality through effecting the brain. Podolsky relates that several psychiatrists at Sing Sing Prison analysed the blood samples of the inmates attempting to see whether specific crimes were related to specific hormonal imbalances.

'It was found that in cases of robbery and burglary the prisoners usually lacked pituitrin and parathyrin in their bodily chemistry. In criminal actions involving grand larceny there was lack of parathyrin and pituitrin, but there was an increase in thyroxin and thymus hormones. In petty larceny there was a lack of parathyrin and pituitrin but an increase in thymus secretion. Murderers usually had a decrease in the amount of parathyrin, but there was an abnormal increase in thymus, adrenalin, and thyroxin.

Further studies revealed that in fraud there was an increase in thyroxin but a decrease in pituitrin and parathyrin. In forgery there was too much thyroxin and thymus and too little parathyrin. Rapists were found to have an overwhelming supply of thyroxin and estrogens and too little pituitrin. Those prisoners who had been sentenced for assault and battery were found to have too much adrenalin, too much thyroxin and too little pituitrin and the estragon.' (1955: 678)

While classical criminology appeared to accept that all people could commit crime depending upon the circumstances, positivist criminology tried to *categorise*, *differentiate*, and *typologise*. What would this information provide? Note two early points:

• The distinction between causal factors and correlations

Even if crime was some sort of unitary phenomenon capable of being thought of similar to a disease (the basic metaphor which a great deal of positivism appeared to use), it does not follow that the conditions, factors, 'facts', discovered cause the event; they may be merely accidental or themselves the result of other factors, such as class position, access to resources, etc.

• The strength of the positivist enterprise depends upon the truth of the original suppositions.

Alasdair MacIntyre (1981: 92) recalls that Charles II once invited members of the Royal Society to explain to him why a dead fish weighs more than the same fish alive; a number of subtle explanations were offered to him. He then pointed out that it did not. As John Tuky once put it: 'You can always get a precise answer to the wrong question.'

In the late 19th century Nietzsche was already calling positivism a superficial approach to knowledge. What happens is that 'man' as a moral entity ceases to be a unit of study: instead it is some naturalist combination, such as the chemicals of the brain, or the electric conductibility of the body, which provides the foundation. A gap appears between man as a moral unit capable of being held responsible for his/her actions, and man as a mere genetic/chemical/behavioural entity, or man as the weak object of social structure, for which the language of responsibility is inappropriate. As Podolsky (1955: 675) put it: 'Life, in the final analysis is a series of chemical reactions'. What this form of empirical analysis appears to offer however, is the possibility of making law-like generalisations which can give those who can use the knowledge the power to predict and therefore control future events. This is clear from the structure of texts; in reading older criminology textbooks the next chapters after the various chapters on positivism, are normally on prediction studies (or, indeed, whole books, eg S and E Glueck, 1959).

A caveat for understanding the term positivism in criminology. The term positivism does not simply denote individualist approaches. It also has a wide sociological use as is apparent in looking at criminal statistics. However, the individualist version of positive criminology is characterised by the search to discover, within the composition of the individual, the causes of criminal and delinquent behaviour. The scientific method is used to differentiate offenders from non-offenders on a variety of characteristics. The method of positive criminology assumes that there are identifiable factors that make people act as they do (*determinism*) and that the variability to be explained is associated with the variability in the causal agents (*differentiation*).

In ideal form positivism side-steps the issue of criminal justice ... it substitutes concerns for social justice, social protection and social management. It does not need a crime for its power to operate since crime is only a symptom, an outward sign of a *pathology*. You do not need a trial and representation by lawyers, due process is not involved: instead you require a hearing by a committee of social scientific experts.

Modernity, construction and the social control perspective

Positivism offers another form of social control to that of the criminal law. Scholars are divided as to whether the 19th century, when positivism gathered in strength, was facing a social control crisis or not. Certainly, the 19th century saw a huge emphasis upon developing control, with commentators becoming confused by the apparent rise in crime figures and the development of police forces. By the end of the century, however, ambivalence reigned. To some, Britain appeared to be a more peaceful and controlled society than at any time since the enlightenment. This may have contributed to a change in emphasis from seeing the offender as an individual being held responsible for mistakes in rational calculation or control, to seeing the offender as someone subjected to forces beyond his or her control, either stemming from individual or constitutional factors, or social forces which determined his or her conduct. This is a duality: if we can understand the forces which cause criminality we can build a secure social order by removing these causes, if we can locate the causes of crime then the good society can be built that does not have these factors. This is to be a controlled process. If we have imposed order over the wilderness we can set it free.

To Radzinowicz and Hood (1986), the Victorian Britain in the late 1890s had become relatively successful in containing crime; the transition to an industrialised urban existence had been brought under control, and the structure of modern policing and criminal statistics were largely in place. Other commentators, such as David Garland in *Punishment and Welfare* (1985), have depicted Britain as experiencing a crisis of penality. For Garland, the pretensions of the Victorian social control strategy, based on the liberal notion of the minimal use of the state, and a framework of the rule of law with its presupposition of the responsible individual, were breaking down. For Garland:

> '... the Victorian penal system was constructed around the categories of a strict legalism (individual responsibility, the free and equal subject, legalism, a classical criminality of reason, etc) and directed at a particular social class ... Penality was ... one element within a generalised disciplinary strategy involving a number of institutions, ideologies and diverse practices ... the tenets of this strategy ... were grounded in an individualistic and hierarchical form of social organisation dominated by the property-owning classes.' (1985: 53)

The cost was the political alienation of a considerable sector of the population. The strategy relied upon the underlying epistemological belief in the ideology of laissez-faire individualism and the free market, with the social reality of a disorganised and powerless repressed class. However, both of these tenets were subjected to revision in the 1890s. Capitalist economic forms moved into a larger scale of semi-monopoly capital, and the working class became organised around unions and other forms of struggle. The organisation of society became a 'social question', with ideas on the enlarged role and functions for the state, and the idea of conscious planning and organisation of the society. For Garland penality needed a new form of legitimation; it found it in the critique of classicism and the setting up of a 'mission for criminology'. Garland quotes Wilson in 1908:

> 'When a criminal is caught ... his case should be sifted from before the time when he saw daylight. The questions to settle are:
>
> Who are you?
>
> How are you?
>
> Why are you?
>
> What are you?'

(Quoted Garland, 1985: 88)

The variability of crime was turned into a *practicable* object, namely criminality, which could be the subject of a positivist study and the object of a practical policy. As a social problem criminality could possibly be reformed, extinguished, or prevented.

There was, however, no one master-logic to the interconnection between the development of criminological ideology, penality and the changing form of modernity. From the constructive point of view the idea of the welfare-state provision was to engage the state in order to create for the ordinary people (who only had an abstract freedom but no real positive freedom) the conditions for greater advance and freedom. But this was done at the same time as normalising procedures were installed, conditions of supervision and identification of the norms of proper behaviour. Moreover the image of the delinquent and the criminal was functional in dividing the working class from itself. Criminology began the search for the typologies and differentiations of individuals, the search for the objectivity of criminality that portrayed the criminal as other than the normal. Furthermore, there developed in the late 19th century a specific relationship of the development of the new forms of criminological knowledge and the institutions of punishment, particularly the prison. Garland argued that the emergence of the individualistically orientated positivist criminology owed much of its emergence to the institution of the prison. Hence there became a specific link between future analysis of the prison and knowledge(s) which sought to answer the question of what the offender was. The development of a specific body of knowledge on the institution of punishment was, thereby, compromised. As Ruggles-Brise put it: '... *la science penitentiary* develops gradually into the science of the discovery of the causes of crime – the science of criminology' (1925, quoted in Garland, 1985: 82).

The developing penology was limited in the questions and theoretical frameworks it could pose for the institutions of punishment. It simply could not pose the issue of criminalisation (as Durkheim had hinted) in terms of culturally specific patterns of labelling. Instead of seeing the processed offender (the person in prison) as the end result of an interactive process of labelling and behaviour, of a process wherein the power to punish was central, of a process wherein the institutional arrangements were partly responsible for the end product, the offender was treated as if his own constitution (or the constitution of his immediate environment) was deviant. For Garland the study of the institutions was constrained by the two concepts of criminology, those of *individualism* and *differentiation*; traditional penology's understanding of penal institutions was thus how best to put these concepts into institutional reality.

To some extent Garland's position in *Punishment and Welfare* neglects the rationalisation of government inherent in the writings of Bentham and Austin, overstates the feeling of crisis, and neglects the complementary nature of legality and the creation of normalcy. The argument here is simple, it is not that positivism represents an advance over legality – as the writers of criminological positivism themselves claimed at the time – or that positivism is required because a system of legality which is fully in place is breaking down, but that legality needs positivism in a complementary fashion for it to develop. Moreover, as it functioned, positivism was inconceivable without legality. A rational legality means that the investigator can turn his attention to the subjects of this legality as if legality did not impose itself. He can expect the normalcy of law abiding behaviour, and become surprised by illegal activity. It is only in this way that the law of Austin (the command of political superiors to political inferiors – the law of command and subjection) can become the rules of Hart (the law of normative expectation – the feeling of the citizen of being under an obligation). But if the knowledges of positivism became knowledges which served to civilise man, they began with the assumption that the criminal was less than human.

Cesare Lombroso (1835-1909)

Lombroso, who graduated from the same university as Beccaria exactly 100 years later, once referred to himself as 'a slave to facts'. Most commentators read Lombroso as applying the biological ideas of the immediate post-Darwin era to the study of the criminal; specifically applying the concept of atavism and the principles of evolution to depict criminals as biological 'throwbacks' to a primitive, or 'atavistic,' stage of evolution. For Lombroso (1911) criminals could be distinguished from non-criminals by the presence of physical anomalies that represented a reversion to a primitive or subhuman type of person.

Between 1859-1863, while serving as an army physician, Lombroso examined approximately 3,000 soldiers in a search to locate the causes of several diseases in mental and physical deficiencies. He was to apply this methodology to search for the causes of crime, ie an investigation of the physical constitution of the offender. This is, perhaps, empiricist epistemology at its purest: by observation and careful measurement the physical features which constitute the criminal will become known. In a famous passage Lombroso relates a moment of enlightenment when, as a prison Doctor, he was conducting a post-mortem examination of a particularly famous inmate by the name of Vilella. He observed a depression in the interior back part of his skull that he called the 'median occipital fossa', and which he recognised as a characteristic found in inferior animals.

> 'This was not merely an idea, but a revelation. At the sight of that skull, I seemed to see all of a sudden, lighted up as a vast plain under a flaming sky, the problem of the nature of the criminal – an atavistic being who reproduces in his person the ferocious instincts of primitive humanity and the inferior animals. Thus were explained anatomically the enormous jaws, high cheek-bones, prominent superciliary arches, solitary lines in the palms, extreme size of the orbits, handle-shaped or sessile ears found in criminals, savages, and apes, insensibility to pain, extremely acute sight, tattooing, excessive idleness, love of orgies, and the irresistible craving for evil for its own sake, the desire not only to extinguish life in the victim, but to mutilate the corpse, tear its flesh, and drink its blood.' (Quoted, Wolfgang, 1960: 184)

Consequently, Lombroso conducted thousands of post-mortem examinations and anthropometric studies of prison inmates and non-criminals. He concluded that the criminal existed, in the natural order of things, as a lower form of human evolution than the average man, with very distinct physical and mental characteristics (see editions of *L'Uomo delinquente*, first published in 1876). Lombroso constructed a four-fold classification:

- born criminals, those with true atavistic features;
- insane criminals, including idiots, imbeciles, and paranoiacs as well as epileptics and alcoholics;
- occasional criminals or criminaloids, whose crimes were explained largely by opportunity; and
- criminals of passion who commit crime because of honour, love or anger. They were propelled by a (temporary) irresistible force.

Later, additional categories gave some allowance for the influence of social factors and he speculated somewhat as to the interaction of genetic and environmental influences (thus providing, to some extent, a precursor to modern socio-biological schemes). Although he went some way to developing a multiple factor approach, he never seems to have moved from the foundation that the true or born criminal was responsible for a large amount of criminal behaviour.

Shortly after his death, Lombroso's work was subjected to intensive scrutiny by Charles Goring who published *The English Convict* (1913). Goring had employed an expert statistician to administer the computations concerning the physical differences between criminals and non-criminals, but after eight years of research and comparing some 3,000 English convicts with various control groups, Goring concluded that there was no absolute differences between criminals and non-criminals except for stature and body weight. Goring concluded 'that there is no such thing as an anthropological type of criminal', but added:

'... it appears to be an equally indisputable fact that there is a physical, mental, and moral type of normal person who tends to be convicted of crime.' (1913: 173)

Thus, while Goring concluded that this was no evidence that criminals were biologically inferior, he found differences in rates of alcoholism, epilepsy, and sexual behaviour as well as inferior intelligence. While he heavily criticised the specificity of Lombroso's work he called for more detailed research. We have, therefore, a refutation of the specificality of Lombroso's theory, but an acceptance of the direction of research. This is the search for knowledge which desperately needs a highly articulated general theory to tie the information together, or to distinguish important variables from the unimportant, but this does not normally happen. Instead, the criminal – like the duck – is simply assumed to be a product of some underlying natural order of things.

Raffaele Garofalo (1852–1934)

Adopting an early sociological perspective, Baron Raffaele Garofalo attempted a definition of crime in positivistic terms which distinguished between 'natural crimes', to which Garofalo attached great importance, and 'police crimes', a residual category of lesser importance. 'Natural crimes' are those which violate two basic 'altruistic sentiments', pity (revulsion against the voluntary infliction of suffering on others) and probity (respect for the property rights of others). 'Police offences' are behaviours which do not offend these altruistic sentiments but are nonetheless called 'criminal' by law. Natural crimes were important both for being more serious, and because the category itself provided a unifying principle, connecting the criminal law and natural social processes.

In *Criminology* (1885: English translation 1914) Garofalo criticised Lombroso's theories as inadequate as an explanation for the 'natural crimes' of 'true criminals'; although he concluded that criminals have 'regressive characteristics' indicating a 'lower degree of advancement'. True criminals lacked the basic altruistic sentiments and were thus ill-suited for society. They were, in short, an evolutionary mismatch, and the solution to this evolutionary problem is elimination:

> 'In this way, the social power will effect an artificial selection similar to that which nature effects by the death of individuals inassimilable to the particular conditions of the environment in which they are born or to which they have been removed. Herein the state will be simply following the example of nature.' (1914: 219–220)

While the classical theorists saw the symbolic value of punishments as offering a means of deterring crime in the general population, Garofalo's emphasis on Darwinian reasoning saw society as a natural body that must adapt to the environment and be protected against crime. Social protection was crucial, and adopting a positivist perspective meant that classical ideas, such as the ideology of moral responsibility and the proportionality of the punishment to the crime, were redundant. The actions of the true criminals indicted their inability to live according to the basic human sentiments necessary in the society, and their elimination served to protect society; for the lesser criminal, incapacitation – by life imprisonment or transportation – would suffice. The society ruled over the individual, and the individual represented just a cell of the social body which could be removed without much loss.

Enrico Ferri (1856–1929)

Ferri's work always emphasised the interaction of social, economic and political factors which contributed to crime, but all of which worked at an individual level, on the predispositions of the person. In Ferri's *Criminal Sociology* crime was 'the effect of multiple causes' that include anthropological, physical, and social factors. Such factors produced criminals who were classified as:

- born or instinctive;
- insane;
- passional;
- occasional;
- habitual.

The positive 'science of criminality and of social defence against it' was easy to distinguish from the classical tradition.

> 'The science of crimes and punishments was formerly a doctrinal exposition of the syllogisms brought forth by the sole force of logical fantasy. Our School has made it a science of positive observation, which, based on anthropology, psychology, and criminal statistics as well as on criminal law and studies relative to imprisonment, becomes the synthetic science to which I myself gave the name "criminal sociology" '.

Positivism displays an ambiguous relationship between knowledge and politics. Positivism should, epistemologically, be the weakest form of knowledge claim. Positivist knowledge is only as good as the methodology which gives rise to it, and it does not claim some overriding general theory; but while positivism claims to be value free and apolitical, we often see in application, as with Ferri (or Marxism), a structure whereby it is claimed that this knowledge is the 'truth' which must therefore be applied and the strength of this claim silences moral-political debate. After all if one is committed to truth how can one can argue with the truth that Le Bon, for example, demonstrates, that men's brains are larger than women's, and civilised brains are larger than those of savages? At root is a dispute about the epistemological criteria which should demarcate good science from poor or pseudo-science. The 19th century still awaited Karl Popper's (1968) replacement of the criteria of verification for distinguishing good scientific methodology (held in the 19th century), by the criteria of openness to falsification. For early positivism it was thought that to be scientific was to be in possession of the truth, or at least part of the truth. Although contemporary positivism is, or should be, more modest, the link between 'facts' and politics can prove particularly ambivalent. For most of his life Ferri was a committed Marxist and was a member of Parliament for many years; he actually lost a professorship because of his Marxist leanings. But if Lombroso was a slave to facts, Ferri was in awe of the principle of determinism and attempted to merge Marxian and Darwinian principles into conclusions that today seem highly dubious:

> 'The Marxian doctrine of historical materialism ... according to which the economic conditions ... determine ... both the moral sentiments and the political and legal institutions of the same group, is profoundly true. It is the fundamental law of positivist sociology. Yet I think that this theory should be supplemented by admitting in the first place that the economic conditions of each people are in turn the natural resultant of its racial energies.' (1917: 118)

Throughout his life Ferri attempted to integrate his positive science with political change – he believed wholly in modernity as a constructivist project. The various attempts to change the penal code were rejected because they constituted too great a change from classical legal reasoning. Disappointed in socialism Ferri turned to fascism as the system most likely to implement the type of reforms he thought necessary. Thorsten Sellin once said that fascism appealed to Ferri because it affirmed the primacy of the state's authority over the individual, and constrained the excessive individualism he had often criticised.

Early criminological positivism and the rule of law

In the eyes of the early positivists, the classical approach assumed the equality of mankind. But this was contrary to the facts.

As W Douglas Morrison (1895) put it in the introduction to the English version of *The Female Offender* by Caesar Lombroso:

'The laws assume that the criminal is living under the same set of conditions as the ordinary man. They are framed and administered on this hypothesis; and they fail in their operation because this hypothesis is fundamentally false.

It may safely be accepted that the ordinary man – that is to say, the man who habitually lives under ordinary social and biological conditions – is on certain occasions deterred from entertaining certain kinds of anti-social ideas by an apprehension that the practice of them will be followed by public indignation and public punishment ... But is it a fact that the criminal population is composed of ordinary men?

On the contrary, there is every reason to believe that vast numbers of the criminal population do not live under ordinary social or biological conditions. It is indeed a certainty that a high percentage of them live under anomalous biological or social conditions. And it is these anomalous conditions acting upon the offender either independently or, as is more often the case, in combination which make him what he is ... (vii - ix)

A patient suffering from an attack of typhoid fever cannot be subjected to the same regimen, to the same dietary, to the same exercise as another person in the enjoyment of ordinary health. The regimen to which the patient is subjected must be suited to the anomalous condition in which he happens to be placed. Criminal codes to be effective must act upon precisely the same principle.' (ix)

Consider the crime rate of women, which was considerably lower than that of men. Why was there not an abundance of the criminal type among women? According to Lombroso:

'[a] very potent factor has been sexual selection. [Early] man not only refused to marry a deformed female but ate her, while, on the other hand, preserving for his enjoyment the handsome woman who gratified his peculiar instincts. In those days he was the stronger, and choice rested with him.' (Ibid: 109)

Most women offenders fell into the occasional offender category. The hope for reform stems from recognising, typologising and differentiating the respective individuals and groups. For example, while Durkheim may search for the causes of suicide in sociological fluctuations, for Lombroso:

'Suicide for love has certainly a physiological root, being the effect of an elective affinity strengthened by the reproductive organs and the peculiar repugnance to separation induced by these molecules of the organism.' (p 180)

'Of course it is almost always the woman who conceives the suicide and carries it out with most resolution.' (p 281)

The constant intersection of biology, politics and history (or at least images of each) which characterised late 19th century writing have not disappeared. In this century it produced somewhat extreme examples in the work of Hooton and Sheldon and was clearly influential upon the Gleucks.

A E Hooton

In the late 1930s A E Hooton, a physical anthropologist at Harvard, drew uncritically upon the Lombrosian theory of biological premonitions to combine biological and psychological variables. Hooton was precise:

'... whatever the crime may be, it ordinarily arises from a deteriorated organism.'

Hooton simply brought the theory to a set of data (again persons already selected out by the system and labelled as criminals) with little critical appraisal, and attempted to find as much information to strengthen it, rather than attempt to find weaknesses on falsification points. Hooton took physical measurements of 4,212 white prisoners from correctional institutions in Massachusetts and seven other states and compared these to measurements from 313 civilians from Massachusetts and Tennessee. His work stands as a prime example of bad science. Not only can we address a range of usual positivist qualifiers to it, for example, inadequate and non-comparable control groups, assuming causation rather than mere correlation for the factors observed, inferring biological inferiority from features which may just as well have demonstrated biological superiority (nowhere does he specify what inferiority or superiority amounts to!), but the connections between his assumptions, his methodologies, his data and his solutions all appear to be thought out before his work was undertaken. He believed in biological inferiority and set out to demonstrate it:

'Criminals as a group represent an aggregate of sociologically and biologically inferior individuals ... Marked deficiency in gross bodily dimensions and in head and face diameters are unequivocal assertions of undergrowth and poor physical development.

Low foreheads, high perched nasal roots, nasal bridges and tips varying to extremes of breadth and narrowness, excesses of nasal deflection, compressed faces and narrow jaws fit well into the general picture of constitutional inferiority. The very small ears with submedium roll of helix, prominent antihelix and frequent Darwin's point, hint at degeneracy ...

... smaller size, inferior weight and poorer body build, his smaller head, straighter hair, absolutely shorter and relatively broader face, with prominent but short and often snubbed nose, narrow jaws, small and relatively broad ears.

There can be no doubt of the inferior status of the criminal both in physical and sociological characteristics. The poorer and weaker specimens tend to be selected for antisocial careers and for ultimate incarceration. The dregs of every population mixed and pure are poured into the prison sink.

Criminals are organically inferior. Crime is the resultant of the impact of environment upon low grade organisms.. It follows that the elimination of the crime can be effected only by the extirpation of the physically, mentally and morally unfit or by their complete segregation in a socially aseptic environment.'

Since the processes of inferiority and selection caused the development of crime, the solution Hooton proposed was the segregation of the criminal population into a self-contained area with closed inbreeding. He believed this could set into motion processes of selective struggle which may raise the level of the person above that of criminal inferiority. Purity of contacts must, however, be maintained! No politicians, criminologists or uplifters allowed near!

'[Governments] should expropriate some very considerable tract of desirable land and establish a reservation for permanent occupation by paroled delinquents. Such a reservation should have its frontiers closed under supervision ... Emigrants from prison into such a reservation should be kept there permanently. I am rather inclined to believe that in a generation or two some of these penal reservations might develop into such prosperous and progressive areas that the inhabitants would be unwilling to receive more colonists from the jails. If natural selection were allowed to operate in such a society, it might work out its own salvation. It would, however, be quite essential to keep out extraneous politicians, criminologists and uplifters.' (E A Hooton, *The American Criminal, An Anthropological Study*, 1939; *Crime and the Man*, 1939, quotes in Tappan, 1960, 87–88)

Ironically, Hooton's lack of a criterion of 'biological inferiority', or a systematic general theory connecting this condition to crime, meant that even contemporary commentators could reverse his findings. Ashley Montagu applied biological standards used in physical anthropology for defining advanced, primitive, and indifferent human characteristics, to claim that Hooton's criminal series showed:

'... only 4 per cent of primitive, 15.8 of indifferent and the astonishing amount of 49.5 per cent of advanced characters, more frequently than the noncriminal population. Therefore we can see that Hooton's findings actually make his criminal series a considerably more advanced group biologically than his non-criminal series.' (1941: 51)

W H Sheldon

Sheldon's (1942) theory linked body–build and personality. Sheldon (1940, 1942) described three basic body types, or somatotypes, based upon in-depth study of five regions of the body:

- head, face, neck;
- arms, shoulder, hands;
- thoracic trunk;
- abdominal trunk;
- thigh, calf, and feet.

Nude photographs are taken front and back and we can distinguish (or at least Sheldon could, few other scholars appeared able to understand exactly how!):

- the broad and muscular mesomorph;
- the thin and bony ectomorph; and
- the large and heavy endomorph.

Some individuals are 'pure' types, while others are hybrids incorporating elements from two, or even three, builds in their physique. Sheldon further suggested that each body-build is characterised by a particular type of personality: the mesomorph is an adventurous, aggressive person; the ectomorph a restrained, introverted individual; the endomorph a sociable, outgoing character. Each individual will display a mixture of these personality traits according to his or her own particular somatotype. Moreover, Sheldon even managed to make three temperamental patterns corresponding to the three models:

> 'Viscerotonia or Oral type: displays a tendency towards relaxation, conviviality, and gluttony for food, company, and affection or social support;
>
> Somatotonia or Urethral type: displays tendency for assertiveness, physical adventurousness, energetic, love of domination and power, courage, aggressiveness;
>
> Cerebretonia or Anal type: displays a tendency towards restraint, love of privacy, overintensity, apprehensiveness, secretiveness, emotional restraint, hypersensitivity.'

Tables are constructed, graphs are drawn – life becomes reducible to quantities. In an amazing text Sheldon (*Varieties of Delinquent Youth*, 1949) sets out the photographs and somatotypes of a sample of almost 200 males from a private treatment unit, and gives a humorous and sometimes irreverent prognosis for each one. He is so scathing of one that he predicts that only two possibilities are open for his life-direction: serious criminality or to become the President of the United States! Sheldon argued that delinquents were characterised by a preponderance of mesomorphs, some indication of endomorphy, and a marked lack of ectomorphs. Sheldon concluded this pattern differed from that found in non-criminal populations, demonstrating that there were differences in the physiques of delinquent and non–delinquent males. Sheldon also drew attention to a significant delinquent type he termed 'Dionysian', individuals characterised by exuberant, extravertive, non–inhibited and predatory qualities. Sheldon was impressed by the amount of time and effort the boys often put into predation, ie the pursuit of sex and petty crimes. He argued that the persistently criminal boy was expressing a Dionysian reaction which was almost as much part of his constitutional design as the way he walks. For Sheldon the level of persistent predation displayed could not have been achieved without a strong temperamental predisposition toward predation. The vast variety of crime is twisted and fitted into various typologies, and dubious connections are drawn from a variety of sources. For example, tensions from the sona and gut cause the type of antidisciplinary religious outlooks which characterised the later stages of the Roman Empire and present day Freudian psychoanalysts! Both the boys in the sample and the then current crop of American Businessmen were predominantly Dionysian!

While Sheldon translated the complexity of individuality into a mathematical formula (he came to refer to his subjects by their somatotype scores, for example, 7-1-7, or 2-7-1), his text also reveals an empathic understanding at odds with such mathematical fetishism. This is clear from his discussion of two groups of boys:

'These boys were on the whole having a good time ... The youngsters must be judged against their own standards and criteria, if they are to be judged at all. They were doing pretty well at finding a way of life that served their own purposes, and they had fun, probably more fun than average or ordinary people have. They were more interesting than ordinary people are. If they are to be compared, individual for individual, with the social work profession that with manifest bewilderment was trying to ride herd on them, I think the boys had the better of it ...

The youngsters seemed to be more realistically aware of the essentially predatory philosophy underlying the social structure than were those who had been – and still are – attempting to re-educate these youngsters away from such a philosophy. I many times had the feeling, in talking with the boys, that I was in a false position. I felt sometimes like the envoy of a dishonestly predatory enterprise sent to decoy and trap into a kind of slavery those free spirits who had thus far managed to elude the snare ...

They saw human society in a truer light and were more truly engaged with life than were most of their elders who were professedly engaged in dealing with 'delinquency' but in fact were concerned mainly with their own security and righteousness.' (1949: 827-828)

The Gluecks (1950; 1956) matched 500 officially labelled offenders and 500 controls by age, IQ, race and area of residence. They found twice as many mesomorphs and less then half as many ectomorphs among the offenders. Cortes and Gatti (1972) also appeared to support Sheldon in finding that officially defined delinquent populations have more mesomorphs than would be expected. However, other studies, such as McCandless *et al* (1972), which failed to find any correlation between either convicted or self-reported offending and body build in 177 adolescent males randomly selected from 500 boys aged 15-17 at a training school, are less supportive. In reviewing the literature, Rees (1973) argued that while some studies had found a correlation, the overall conclusion was that no link between body-build and crime had been established. But, even today, this does not deter those who are desperate to reinstate constitutional factors. In their huge survey, Wilson and Herrnstein (1985) devote several pages to reproducing diagrams and photography used by Sheldon, and conclude that 'wherever it has been examined, criminals on the average differ in physique from the population at large. They tend to be more mesomorphic (muscular) and less ectomorphic (linear)'. They add that where it has been assessed the 'masculine' configuration called andromorphy also characterises the average criminal (1985: 89).

The whole enterprise smacks of a preference for tasty ducks.

The legacy of positivism: disentangling the mess

Constitutional positivism has resulted in much crass criminology. Consider genetic transmission and the issue of eugenics. In pure form, a theory of crime based solely upon genetic transmission would hold that crime is a direct product of heredity – a criminal is born not made. We have seen that Lombroso originally argued that criminals were the product of a genetic constitution unlike that found in the non-criminal population. However, Lombroso gradually broadened the range of causal factors, first through the notion of 'indirect heredity', whereby criminality could be acquired through contact with other 'degenerates', such as insane people or alcoholics, and later with environmental conditions, such as poor education. Lombroso came to argue that about one-third of offenders were born criminals but the remainder had to be accounted for by some other means of explanation.

The recent approach of sociobiology has tried to link social behaviour with genetic transmission and some proponents have looked towards a 'criminal gene' which sets into play the propensity for criminal activity. In *Born to Crime: the genetic causes of criminal behaviour* (1984) Lawrence Taylor argues that in the future we will routinely use genetic screening and genetic surgery, and that a 'bit of cut-and-sew work' could be employed to correct 'genetic abnormality that is likely to manifest itself in future violent conduct' (1984: 154). It is, however, difficult to prove any genetic propensity to violence, let alone explain how this causes crime. As Gottfredson and Hirschi state, biological positivism cannot trace the complicated line from genes to the range of complex behaviour which can fall under the label of crime. Such positivism seems to impliedly equate aggression or violence with criminality, but this may only be one factor involved in some situations.

The attempt to locate proof of genetic transmission for criminality has focused on three populations – the family, twins, and adoptees.

Family studies

The family has been treated as if it was a stable entity and studied to examine whether the processes within a criminal family differ in functioning from non-criminal families, and to estimate the degree of similarity between the behaviour of the offender and their biological relatives. Longitudinal research has gathered much data concerning the family backgrounds of offenders (Farrington *et al* (1986); West (1982); Offord (1982)). Family studies rely upon the position that since biological relatives share varying degrees of genetic constitution (the closer the biological relationship, the greater the genetic similarity), if criminality is inherited, criminal families will reproduce criminality in their children. From Lombroso onwards a common theme has been the idea that offenders come from families with a criminal history (Dugdale (1910); Estabrook (1916)). Recent studies, for instance Osborn and West (1979), found that about 40% of the sons of criminal fathers were criminal themselves, compared with a figure of 13% for sons of non-criminal fathers. In reviewing this evidence Hurwitz and Christianson (1983) distance themselves from the claim that crime is inherited; instead of causal proof, all we can discuss are correlations.

Note: the finding of an empirical correlation, for example, between two variables – family criminality and offspring criminality, does not prove that a causal relationship exists between those two variables. Instead a third variable, perhaps environmental rather than genetic, may be an important factor in the offending of both parents and their children. The shared genes do not cause the high correlations in the offending records of family members, but the fact that all the family members had poor schooling, or inadequate diets, or were unemployed, or lived in the same city area, or were of the same social class. The 'under-the-roof' culture, that is the range of social and psychological factors within the family environment map influences the adoption of criminal values, behaviour, and so on. From the positivist perspective, greater control of variables is required which would allow the effects of either heredity or environment to be controlled, so that the effect of the other can be accurately assessed. The study of twins is a traditional methodology, which goes some way in this direction.

Twin studies

There are two different types of twins. Identical, or Monozygotic (MZ), twins develop from the splitting of a single egg at the time of conception and so share exactly the same genetic constitution. Fraternal, or Disygotic (DZ), twins develop from two different fertilised eggs and are therefore no more alike than any other pair of siblings, sharing about 50% of their genetic constitution. The key point of demonstration is a rather large assumption namely that if the two members of a twin pair experience the same environment, then any major differences between members of a pair may be due to genetic variation. As MZ twins have identical genes then it would be predicted that their behaviour would show greater concordance than that of DZ twins. (Concordance can be seen as the degree to which related pairs of subjects within a study population display the same behaviour. Expressed as a percentage, a 50% concordance would indicate that in half of the total sample each member of a twin pair showed the same target behaviour, a 75% rate that three-quarters of the twin pairs showed the same behaviour, and so on.) The twin study method has been widely used in seeking to determine the influence of heredity in, for example, intelligence, and also in disturbances such as alcoholism, depression, and schizophrenia.

From the clearly titled *Crime as Destiny* by the Austrian physician Johannes Lange (1929) there was little doubt of the aims of these studies. Indeed, MZ twins generally showed a much higher degree of concordance than DZ twins for criminal behaviour; the seven studies in Table 1 up to and including 1941 show a mean concordance rate of 75% for MZ twins compared to a mean 24% for DZ twins. However, extremely small sample sizes, dubious methodologies of samples, and the suspect determination of whether the paring is really D2 or M2 make the process questionable.

Technological advances, such as fingerprints, blood typing, and serum protein analysis increased the certitude of, at least, the type of twins studied. The result was a decrease in concordance, the five studies in Table 1 reported from 1961 onwards show a mean concordance of 48% for MZ twins, compared to 20% for DZ twins.

	MZ Twins		DZ Twins	
	No of pairs	% concordant	No of pairs	% concordant
Lange (1929)	13	77	17	12
Legras (1932)	4	100	5	0
Rosanoff et al (1934)	37	68	60	10
Kranz (1936)	31	65	43	53
Stumpfl (1936)	18	61	19	37
Borgstrom (1939)	4	75	5	40
Rosanoff et al (1941)	45	78	27	18
Yoshimasu (1961)	28	61	18	11
Yoshimasu (1965)	28	50	26	0
Hayashi (1967)	15	73	5	60
Dalgaard and Kringlen (1976)	31	26	54	15
Christianson (1977)	85	32	147	12

Table 1 Summary of twin study data

For sympathetic commentators, the results are impressive Taylor (1984 25–49) concludes that 'nature's own laboratory teaches us that much of human behaviour – including criminal behaviour is caused by genetic factors'. However, it is extremely difficult to distinguish the effect of social environment from how genetics 'causes' the complex phenomenon of a social hybrid.

Adoptees

An alternative strategy to the use of twins is to study children separated from their parents and raised in another family. The study of adopted children offers a means to do this, and several large scale studies have been carried out. Mednick, Gabrielli, and Hutchings (1984), for example, analysed 14,427 male and female adoptees and their biological parents (all the non-familial adoptions in Denmark between 1924 and 1947). Certain interesting correlations were produced, but considering all the social variables, and the effects of the Second World War, it is difficult to see the value of the information. Trasler, in addition, warns of the impossibility of the methodology to cover social and political factors in the process: 'this area is a methodological minefield because of the complex and unexplicit policies of adoption and fostering agencies' (1987: 190).

Other constitutional studies

Other studies have examined dietary factors such as levels of protein, carbohydrate, and sugar in relation to criminal behaviour (Schoenthaler and Doraz 1983). Yet further studies have focused upon the effects of hormonal influences (Rada (1983)), allergic reactions (Mawson and Jacobs (1978)), food additives (Hawley and Buckley (1974)), and lead pollution (David et al (1976)).

Another line of research has concentrated upon neurophysiological correlates of criminal behaviour. The typical strategy in this research is to compare the neurophysiological functioning of so-called criminal and non-criminal groups. The measure of functioning is usually made via the electroencephalogram (EEG), an instrument which records the electrical activity of the cortex. The EEG can be used to detect unusual patterns of activity, or to search for some type of neurological dysfunction. Historically, abnormal EEG has been associated with unusual crimes such as murder by the insane (D Hill and Pond (1952)). A number of studies, however, have failed to show any long-term correlation between abnormal EEG and future behaviour (Loomis et al (1967)). Similarly, while some studies have linked EEG abnormality with violence (D Williams (1969)), others have failed to replicate this finding (Moyer (1976)) or, indeed, to show any relationship at all between EEG and delinquency (Hsu et al (1985)).

While some of the more unusual conditions, such as brain lesions, may explain why, in some extreme individual cases, the individual came to be in trouble with social control agencies, the case for a general biological theory of crime is intellectually suspect. This does not deter its practitioners, who claim the problem can be rectified with a better data base, and note that serious biochemical research has only been undertaken in this field for about a decade, and improvements in statistical sampling or the technologies of measurement, for example, precise neurological measurement or the use of the EEG; which is acknowledged to be problematic in terms of providing objective information.

By contrast, Gottfredson and Hirschi are scathing:

'... improvements in statistics, measurement, and sampling by themselves cannot overcome problems inherent in biological positivism. More than 100 years after Lombroso initiated this line of inquiry, the major contribution of biological research would appear to be that data suggesting that biological variables may be correlated with crime. Unfortunately, this evidence is often so suspect that scholars friendly to the idea of biological causation are left wondering why this discipline has so much trouble contributing 'acceptable' facts to the field of criminology.

The reasons for the absence of influence from biology are not hard to find. The discipline proceeds without a concept of crime and without a concept of criminality ... the history of XYY chromosome research tells a similar story: extraordinary effort expended to document the possible existence of a small effect, the significance of which is unclear even to those pursuing it.' (1990: 62)

There are, however, several scholars who still pursue this work, and constitutional theories of crime have not been totally rejected. At one level they influence the common sense perceptions of criminal justice personnel. Feldman (1977) suggests that certain aspects of physical appearance, including body-build, can be instrumental in attracting police attention or influencing sentencing decisions. With certain stereotypical images of criminals in use (Bull (1982); Box, S (1983); A G Goldstein et al (1984)), then those individuals who match the stereotype may be being over-selected from the criminal population. As well as this 'selection effect', Feldman suggests various other ways in which body-build might be related to crime: the muscular individual may be more likely to be invited by peers to participate in criminal acts; or certain body-builds may be more likely to be successful at crime.

Humans are a mind-body-environment complex, thus genetic potential may contribute to difficulties with learning, education, and socialisation, and so be a factor in the processes which create social and individual resources. This influences life chances and decision-making, and affects the various pathways of life. The arrogant mistake of constitutional theories is to stress the role of inherent biological factors of body-build and, as we shall see, the psychological construct of personality, at the expense of social factors, in the claim that these inquiries can force nature to reveal the 'cause'. But nature is neither so simple, nor so blatant.

CHAPTER SEVEN

CRIMINOLOGICAL POSITIVISM II: PSYCHOLOGY AND THE POSITIVISATION OF THE SOUL

'It would be wrong to say that the soul is an illusion, or an ideological effect. On the contrary, it exists, it has a reality, it is produced permanently around, on, within the body by the functioning of a power ... on those one supervises, trains and corrects, over madmen, children at home and at school, the colonized, over those who are stuck at a machine and supervised for the rest of their lives.' (Michel Foucault, quoted in Rose, 1990: v)

Positivism, learning and psychology

Once it was common to talk of humans possessing a soul; the positivist approach reduced this to a matter of mental hygiene. In this chapter we shall look at three influential theories which focused on the psychology of the subject, and his/her learning ability; those of Bowlby, Eysenck, and Sutherland. Each theory concentrates on what may be seen as different sites in a chain of processes; the journey through the pathways of everyday life. The chapter concludes by looking at the notion of the psychopath.

A note of warning: psychological studies, like the search for constitutional factors, appear to presume that law abiding behaviour is the normal state of affairs. A lot of the early studies simply assume a consensus by all normal people that the law reflects their interests; therefore to breach the law is abnormal behaviour. Contemporary studies attempt to escape from this naivete by drawing a distinction between crime and criminality. For contemporary positivist scholars such as Wilson and Herrnstein (1985), or Gottfredson and Hirschi (1990), the key to modern criminology is to explain criminality. The presumption is that properly socialised individuals, or properly controlled individuals (individuals who exercise proper levels of self-control), would not commit crime. Throughout their work the search is for the flaw in the person, in his constitution or genetic inheritance, that makes socialisation more difficult. The lack of socialisation creates a condition of criminality, or propensity to commit crime.

One example is intelligence. It is argued by positivist psychologists that there is a direct link between low intelligence and crime. How is this?

Typical IQ tests consist of two sub-groups of tests, one involving verbal skills, such as word knowledge, verbally coded information, and verbal reasoning, and the other non-verbal, for example, assembling objects and completing pictures. There is little doubt that IQ tests measure something substantial; demonstrating a high cognitive ability to score at a series of tests. There is little doubt that high IQ scores predict high academic capability and the capacity to learn tasks and skills. Some tests have been absurd (for example, one test used on South African Blacks in the 1920s, asked candidates to complete certain pictures, one of which was of a missing net in a tennis match. It was little wonder that individuals who had never witnessed a tennis match in their life failed to score highly!) Relating IQ scores to criminality is a project laden with pit falls.

The first studies seeking to locate any relationship between IQ scores and criminal involvement were conducted in the early part of this century (for example, Goddard (1914, 1921)) and argued for a strong relationship between criminal activity and low intelligence. Over time a disparity in testing between convicted offenders and 'normal' citizens of around 8 IQ points has remained stable (Hirschi and Hindelang (1977)). It may be that this disparity is partly a result of various factors, notably:

- Officially designated offenders come largely from the least well-off socio and economic groups and members of these groups - perhaps for a variety of environmental conditions early in life - have lower than average tested IQ; hence class needs to be controlled to gain better accuracy. To avoid arguments that the social conditions of early child development may be causal of low IQ scores, Murray and Herrnstein (1994), in *The Bell Curve*, imply that low IQ may be the reason for both their membership of the lower classes and criminal involvement.

- Some commentators have suggested that the less intelligent may be more likely to be caught. Low intelligence may affect both the selection of the type of offence and the methodology. However, West and Farrington (1977) found the relationship between intelligence and crime remained when crime was measured by self-report studies.

- It has been suggested that low intelligence may result in the accused agreeing with police suggestions and thus easier to convict. Gath (1972) found that juveniles with IQ scores over 115 were less likely to be caught, and if convicted, less likely to be sent to institutions thereby avoiding their labelling and criminogenic effects.

How is it suggested that low IQ can lead to greater criminal involvement? Hirschi and Hindelang (1977), writing from a social control theory perspective (see Chapter Eight), suggest that low verbal IQ results in poor school performance leading to negative attitudes to school and to success through legal channels. The individual then drops out of school and does not attain reasonable employment. Delinquent activity then results. Other constitutionally minded commentators suggest that anti-social behaviour preceded school problems, and that similar background factors may be responsible for both conditions: ie low IQ and anti-social behaviour. Labelling theorists (see Chapter Fourteen) infer that original problems may lead to the individual perceiving him or herself as stupid, and therefore not trying fully at the tests. Conversely, teachers may respond to the results of IQ scores, and encourage high scorers while downgrading low scorers. All of these suggestions are controversial.

Quay suggests that low IQ can interact with child rearing practices:

'In the early years lower IQ makes a child vulnerable to poor parenting and even makes poor parenting more likely. The probability of this increases if the IQ deficit is accompanied by a fussy or a difficult temperament, motor over-reactivity and poor inhibitory control. All of these combine in the early onset of troublesome behaviour. The affected child is now at a double disadvantage when he enters school. He has both less intellectual ability, particularly in the verbal spheres, to cope with academic problems and he has oppositional and aggressive behavioural problems alienating to teachers and peers ... both are likely to lead to school failure ... which reinforces more conduct-disordered behaviour ... All of these factors and others (eg, deviant parental and peer models) interact to produce behaviour which is legally prescribed.' (1987: 114)

Quay's argument is *interactional*, ie it postulates that low IQ can have a role in a complex series of interactions and feed-back processes. Many of the earlier (and still influential) approaches are not so subtle. For example, Wilson and Herrnstein (1985), who place discussion of IQ in their chapter on constitutional approaches suggesting it is largely inherited (most biologists believe that IQ differences are almost entirely environmental and the result of training, stimulation and possibly diet), imply that low IQ causes difficulties in socialisation. For them an undersocialised individual has a criminal propensity since he or she has less internal prohibitions against committing a crime. In a remarkable assertion they use this as a partial explanation for the low crime rates of Japan. Wilson and Herrnstein state simply:

'The average Japanese score is about 110, well above that for any country for which data are available [they footnote a study by Lynn]. It is certainly above the American average, which is set at 100 for the test on which the Japanese score 110. Japan therefore has a smaller fraction of its population in the range of scores between 60 and 100, the range at highest risk for criminal behaviour ... a society's willingness to rely on internalised values depends, inversely, on how large a segment of the population will fail to learn them. The segment in Japan is much smaller than that in America.' (1985: 456)

This turns a whole set of highly contestable contentions into what looks like accepted wisdom. Conversely:

- The study referred to by Lynn appeared in *Nature* in 1982 and was subjected to withering attack by Stevenson and Azuma in the same journal in 1983. Lynn had used a small sample of the children of well-off Japanese and compared this with a much larger and scientifically representative sample of American children. There is actually little methodologically sound evidence of a substantial difference between Japanese children and American.

- To assert that a lower section of the Japanese population have low IQ's and this means that the Japanese are more easily socialised into internal prohibitions against lawbreaking, assumes that the law has a similar role in the socio-cultural environment of both countries.

When we observe the social world what we see is partially created, provided by structure, by human conceptual thought. Crime is a creation of conceptual thought. To assert a direct link between psychological profiles and criminality needs explaining in some general theory. Instead Wilson and Herrnstein offer little in the way of a general theory and repeat the mistake of positivism in attributing the causes of crime from the study of those officially designated as 'criminals' or, as they state at the beginning of their chapter: 'people who break the law are often psychologically atypical' (1985: 173). This is a common methodology: take a sample of individuals who have come to your attention for delinquency, or having been convicted for crime, and analyse their background and mind-set. We see a direct link between the clinic, an institution designed to deal with troublesome people, and the creation of positivist knowledges purporting to explain the psychological functioning of these persons.

Bowlby's theory of maternal deprivation and crime

The creation of Bowlby's thesis is a good example of the close linkage between positivism and the clinic. His thesis arose from his experience with 44 juvenile thieves referred to his child guidance clinic from 1936 to 1939 (Bowlby 1944; 1946). After comparing this group of children with a matched group of non-delinquent children, also referred to the clinic, Bowlby grew convinced of a demonstrable link between early separation from the mother and juvenile theft. Thirty nine per cent of the delinquent children had experienced complete separation from their mothers for six months or more in the first five years of their life; but only 5% of the non-delinquent group had a similar experience. While later studies failed to provide such clear evidence (Bowlby et al (1956)), Bowldy was already convinced (1951) that early maternal deprivation was causally related to anti-social behaviour. Two ideas provided the foundation: (i) a warm, close, and unbroken relationship between child and mother (or permanent mother substitute) is essential for mental health; (ii) separation and rejection from and by the mother accounts for most of the more intractable cases of delinquency (Bowlby (1949, 1951); Bowlby and Salter-Ainsworth (1965)). As Bowlby put it:

'Essential for mental health is that a child should experience a warm, intimate, and continuous relationship with his mother (or permanent mother substitute) in which both find satisfaction and enjoyment ...

Maternal separateness and parental rejection are believed together to account for a majority of the more intractable cases [of delinquency].' (1949: 37)

Bowlby's theory appeared to offer dramatic new possibilities for establishing mental hygiene. Instead of focusing upon evidencing psychoses and incarceration in a segregative institution, preventative action in the community could be undertaken. If the precise nature of troubles in childhood and their later effects could be established, then techniques for early intervention could be developed.

Bowlby was given an international stage for his ideas when asked to prepare the report for the WHO on the needs of homeless children. Bowlby (1951) not only restated his views on maternal deprivation but developed these in a package of ideas on the connection between mental health, childhood, the social consequences of maternal deprivation, the tasks of government and the role of specialist expertise. In short, the task of creating a good population meant it should be the responsibility of government to supervise and regulate the relations between mother and child.

There have been many criticisms of Bowlby's theory. One line concerns the experimental methodology operating in the two major empirical studies. Both Patricia Morgan (1975) and Feldman (1977) highlight serious flaws, including the unrepresentative nature of the samples, poor control group matching, and unreliable methods of assessment. The theory itself has also been criticised (see Hall Williams (1981)). Wootton (1959) specifically pointed out the absence of evidence that the damage from separation is irreversible, and that in any event the type of delinquent with which Bowlby was concerned forms only a small minority of the total delinquent population. In his defence sympathetic commentators caution that Bowlby never made the more extravagant claims for his results that some of this critics have suggested he did.

Bowlby's theories gave rise to a body of research which investigated the effects of maternal deprivation on childhood development. The basic idea was extended to account for a range of childhood disorders; to generate policies for the treatment of the effects of deprivation, and to reinforce government policies designed to strengthen the role of the nuclear family, or support the solo mother (Bowlby (1979); Rutter (1972, 1981); Sluckin et al (1983)). A provocative and emotive concept - the broken home - had been created and there were many parties interested in writing its effects (Grygier et al (1970); Little (1965)). Certain findings indicated that a broken home played some part in the development of delinquent behaviour; other factors, such as family tension and levels of violence within an 'unbroken' family may have even greater effect. Longitudinal studies have shown that the important family influences are much more complex than simply maternal deprivation alone (West (1982)). A Clarke and A Clarke (1976) place the broken home idea into one of the 'myths' surrounding early childhood experience, arguing that the real issue is the quality of upbringing. In the US the Gluecks preferred the idea of 'under-the-roof culture', specifying that the moral and emotional conditions of the youth's home had more effect upon behaviour and attitudes than maternal deprivation. The broken home concept operates as a very strong popular or 'lay' explanation of criminal involvement (Furnham and Henderson (1983); Hollin and Howells (1987)). Perhaps what is at stake is both more simple and yet deeper than the idea of material deprivation: namely that family experiences and the quality of life enjoyed during a person's early years create strong social and personal resources for the individual to use in his/her future life paths. While the right's view of the family appears to focus almost exclusively upon control - hence the broken home reduces the family's traditional capacity to discipline and punish children - the experience of family life is a contributing process in the creation of an active and positive self-hood. If crime is essentially an intersubjective phenomenon - a relationship between offender and victim - the quality of intersubjective experiences in early life can be expected to impact upon later perceptions of social relationships. Further, those children whose socialisation has imparted them with a range of social skills will be better able to negotiate the complicated pathways of late-modern life than those with low social skills; those with a confident and secure sense of self-worth better able to withstand the stresses and disorientating effects of late-modern urban culture. (For an overview of families and children see Currie (1985:ch 6).)

What is a problem family? What is the well adjusted family? In reading the literature on family studies one is tempted to argue that perhaps it is not a static conception but an attitude. An attitude in which the 'family' accepts responsibility for managing the relationships within it and forms a consensual partnership with social expertise. The modern family accepts the responsibility for managing itself according to the norms of proper conduct; the ideal modern family produces individuals of high self-control. But can individuals vary in constitutional propensity or ability to learn self-control? The ability of the individual to control his/her own stimuli was a latent theme of the best known of the British positivist psychological theories, that of Hans Eysenck.

Eysenck's theory of crime

Eysenck's control-orientated theory incorporates biological, social, and individual factors into a master language which is inscribable, calculable, easily understandable and offers treatment potential. Through genetic endowment individuals are born with slightly different cortical and autonomic nervous systems which affect their ability to learn from, or, more properly, to condition to, environmental stimuli. An individual's personality is defined by the individual's behaviour, which is influenced by both biological and social factors.

Eysenck's theory derives from his work conducted during World War II on soldiers referred to the Mill Hill Emergency Hospital. Eysenck claimed the neuroses exhibited were not so much illnesses as a simple failure to adapt to army routine and discipline. Eysenck went beyond the parameters of medicine and gained his data from combining the techniques of questionnaires and drafting scales, with small scale studies into humour, levels of aspiration, irritability and the rigidity with which his patients held views.

Eysenck conceptualised personality in terms of a two-dimensional space along two axes, introversion-extraversion (E) and neuroticism (N); later work (HJ Eysenck and SBG Eysenck (1968)) described a third dimension, psychoticism (P). Each of these dimensions is conceived as a continuum, with individuals located through their test scores. Extraversion runs from high (extravert) to low (introvert); similarly neuroticism runs from high (neurotic) to low (stable); as also does psychoticism.

The extravert is cortically under-aroused and therefore is continually seeking stimulation to maintain cortical arousal at an optimal level: thus the extravert is impulsive and seeks excitement. The introvert is cortically over-aroused and therefore tries to avoid stimulation to keep arousal levels down to a comfortable, optimal level: introverts are therefore characterised by a quiet, reserved demeanour. A key idea is that of learning via conditioning: using the behavioural learning by Pavlovian conditioning or association rather than operant conditioning leads us to expect extraverts to condition less efficiently than introverts. Neuroticism, sometimes called emotionality, is argued to be related to the functioning of the autonomic nervous system (ANS). Individuals at the high extreme of this continuum are characterised by a very labile ANS, which causes strong reactions to any unpleasant or painful stimuli: High N individuals display moody, anxious behaviour. Low N individuals have a very stable ANS and so display calm, even-tempered behaviour even when under stress. As with E, N is also linked with conditionability: High N leads to poor conditioning because of the vitiating effects of anxiety; Low N leads to efficient conditioning. As assessed by psychometric tests, each individual scores on both E and N; therefore their position on these two dimensions of personality can be plotted.

Tables can be constructed which locate various individuals according to their cortical capabilities. We can, ideally, plot an individual's learning ease and socialisation potential. As conditionability is related to levels of E and N, stable introverts (Low N – Low E) will condition best; stable extraverts (Low N – High E) and neurotic introverts (High N – Low E) will be at some mid-point; while neurotic extraverts (High N – High E) will condition least well.

Not all features of the thoughts, attitudes, and sentiments of people can be so easily reduced. Eysench has difficulty in specifying what exactly the third personality dimension, psychoticism (P), refers to. Although he claims a genetic basis for P, he has been unable to describe any biological basis in detail (HJ Eysenck and SBG Eysenck (1968; 1976)). The target seems obvious: the psychopath (SBG Eysenck and HJ Eysenck (1972)). Operationally, the P scale attempts to assess attributes such as preference for solitude, a lack of feeling for others, sensation-seeking, tough-mindedness, and aggression. However often he refines and revises it (SBG Eysenck et al (1985)), it is still difficult to see what exactly, if anything, the P scale is measuring (Howarth (1986)).

Eysenck has published widely on his theory of the relationship between personality and crime laying out the basic theme that criminality and antisocial conduct are positively and causally related to high psychoticism, high extraversion, and high neuroticism. Extraverts and possibly persons high on the psychoticism scale, have biologically determined low degrees of arousal and arousability and seek behaviours (risk taking, sensation seeking, impulsivity and so forth) that increase the cortical level of arousal to a more acceptable amount. This behaviour is not necessarily anti-social, it may occur through participation in sports, adventures and other arousal-producing activities. But neuroticism-anxiety acts as a drive that combines with learned behaviour patterns based on the biological foundation in such a way as to increase the anti-social behaviour produced by the P and E personality traits.

From this perspective the conscience is a biologically influenced phenomena. Pro-social conduct has to be *learned* by the growing child, and this learning is accomplished through a process of Pavlovian conditioning. Pro-social conduct is praised, anti-social conduct is punished by peers, parents, teachers and others. Through a constant repetition of such reinforcements, the 'conscience' becomes established as a conditioned response, leading to pro-social and altruistic behaviour. As introverts form conditioned responses of this type more readily than extraverts, they are more easily socialised through Pavlovian conditioning and hence are less likely to indulge in anti-social activities.

We can see how the theory ties together biological material and the environment through the medium of the individual. Each individual develops a particular conscience and this is the result of a set of conditioned emotional responses to environmental events associated with anti-social behaviour. For example, the child who misbehaves incurs parental wrath; the fear and pain this brings is associated with the antisocial act, and through this conditioning process the child becomes socialised. The speed and efficiency of social conditioning will mainly depend upon the individual's inherited biological personality in terms of E and N. As the High E-High N combination leads to poor conditionability then such individuals will be least likely to learn social control and therefore, it is predicted, will be over-represented in offender populations. Conversely Low E-Low N would lead to effective socialisation, so that these individuals would be predicted to be under represented in offender groups. The remaining two combinations, High E-Low N and Low E-High N, fall at some intermediate level and so would be expected in both offender and non-offender groups. The third personality dimension, P, is also argued to be strongly related to offending, particularly with crimes which involve hostility towards other people. Eysenck suggests that persons with strong anti-social inclinations will have high P, high E, and high N scores. Eysenck controls for the heterogeneity of crime, there are politically motivated crimes, impulsive crimes, crimes committed by the intellectually disadvantaged, and so on, by his notion of anti-socialness.

In spite of the fact, or perhaps because of it, he wrote at a time of increasing dissatisfaction with ideas of rehabilitation and the growth of labelling theory, Eysenck's theory of crime attracted considerable attention and led to a great deal of empirical research (for example, Bartol (1980); H J Eysenck (1977); Feldman (1977); Powell (1977)). In effect Eysenck had laid claim to found an independent profession of clinical psychology and there were many to seize the possibility. Using the terms of investigation that Eysenck laid down, investigators support the contention that offenders will score highly on P, and the majority of studies show that offender samples score highly on N. The data is mixed for E: some studies reported high E scores as predicted in offender samples, others found no difference between offender and non-offender samples, and a small number of studies reported lower scores in offender groups. The general pattern for P, E, and N is similar with both young and adult offender groups. In seeking to account for the discrepant findings for E, SBG Eysenck and HJ Eysenck (1971) suggested that E might be split into two subscales, sociability and impulsiveness, with only the latter related to offending. A study by SBG Eysenck and McGurk (1980) confirmed that an offender sample scored higher than a non-offender sample on impulsiveness, with no difference between the two samples on a measure of sociability.

These investigations essentially replicated Eysenck's work, with the majority of studies examining the so-called personality traits singly, rather than in combination; few studies attempted to control for the type of crime. Crime was treated as a single naturalist phenomena. Even on the conditions laid down by Eysenck, the methodology was often suspect, since Eysenck's argument concerned the combined effects of different personality traits and the concept of 'antisocial crimes'.

Eysenck himself finds fault with many of the early studies:

'Many of the studies were carried out before the hypothesis was put forward and used questionnaires and inventories less than ideally suited for the purpose and sometimes only tangentially relevant. Control groups were not always carefully selected; some investigators, for instance, have used the ubiquitous student groups as controls which is inadmissible. There was often failure to control for dissimulation through the use of lie scales. Where lie scales were introduced, sometimes very high levels of dissimulation were recorded, but this information was used in the interpretation of the data. The fact that criminals are not a homogeneous group was disregarded; different investigators have studied different populations, specialising in different types of crime.' (Eysenck and Gudjonsson, 1989: 57)

Some studies which appeared to live up to Eysenck's criteria, such as two studies by Allsopp and Feldman (1975; 1976), suggested that the key lay in the combination of P, E, and N.

Hindelang and Weiss (1972) roughly supported a relationship between personality type and nature of offence; the High E-High N cluster was associated with general deviancy (behaviour such as petty theft and vandalism), but not with major theft and aggression. SBG Eysenck et al (1977) asserted that 'con men' showed lower P scores than other groups, with property and violent offender groups displaying lower N scores; no variation was found on the E scale. McEwan and Knowles (1984) however, could not find any large relationship between the types of offences committed and personality clusters in their study. McEwan (1983) created various subgroups finding the highest conviction records were among the subgroup with a high score. Eysenck constructed an entire conceptual scheme and frame of reference. To test his theory scholars had to work within his definitions, including that of crime. Hopes were, for a time at least, high.

Sympathetic commentators, such as Feldman (1977), predicted that the Eysenckian personality dimensions were likely to be influential in building a scientific explanation of criminal behaviour. Some of the interest appears to have decreased, and, although Eysenck has remained convinced of the potential to create a fully scientific criminology, he has become more modest regarding his theory. He has become more conscious of the nature of crime as a process and acknowledges that the theory cannot predict criminal involvement for all offenders. Further, some critics argue that the foundational base of the theory, the link between classical conditioning and socialisation, simply could not be established satisfactorily (Raine and Venables (1981)). Others have contended that there are an array of personality traits other than those defined by Eysenck, for example, McGurk (1978); McGurk et al (1981); McGurk and McGurk (1979). Furthermore, why accept a trait theory of personality? Is this not only one of a number of ways of conceptualising 'personality'? (Phares (1984)). And one which has come under fierce attack and is almost discredited. Rose summarises the enterprise in the following terms.

> 'Eysenck's theory is an attempt to depict a psychological activity in such a way that biological, environmental, and psychological factors are reduced into a form suitable for integrating the theory into mainstream criminology. It also afforded the promise of treatment. Eysenck produced ... a way of understanding and treating conduct that did not require reference to the hidden depths of the soul. It remained at the level of the problem itself – the discrepancy between the behaviour produced and the behaviour desired. But as important, it was an analysis that did not require reference to organic malfunction, for we were not dealing with illness but with the contingent mis-shaping of a psychology that was not sick, by means of process that were themselves normal. Hence psychologists could make a claim to clinical expertise that was apparently neither a threat to nor subordinate to medicine ... Behavioural therapy would allow psychologists themselves to have a say in the questions, and to claim exclusive capacities to carry out treatment.' (Rose, 1990: 234)

Doubts can be placed on the ethics and humanity of behavioural 'treatment' techniques (see the classic film *Clockwork Orange*). In general critics claim this line of reasoning offers a psychology of social adaptation concerned with the overt conduct of individuals, rather than with their subjective experiences and motivations. Furthermore, the treatment offered is criticised as actually the shaping of conduct towards ends required by the dominant power structure.

This functionalist and consensual identification of the legal structure of society as deserving of obligation is clear in Eysenck's latest and most general pronouncements on crime and society. While asking for a more behaviourist, and individually focused, system of punishment/treatment, Eysenck argues that a sea-change in attitudes, and child-rearing practices is called for to combat crime:

'Crime ... is essentially a function of the ethos of the society in which we live; it reflects the practices of positive and negative reinforcement, of reward and punishment, of teaching and conditioning, which are prevalent, and these in turn are mirrored and reflected by the types of films we see, television programs we watch, books and newspapers we read, and teaching and example we receive at school.

If parents do not insist on decent and moral behaviour in their children; if schools do not maintain discipline, and even preach rebellion and resistance to authority; if criminals and vice generally are constantly portrayed in a positive fashion in films and on television; and if even the representatives of organised religion fail to speak up for obedience to the law and fail to condemn terrorism – then clearly the task of enforcing law and order will be the more difficult, and will possibly become impossible. Add to this the leniency of punishment so often preached by those who erroneously assume that it is society rather than the individual who is guilty of criminal conduct, and we have a situation where anything that can be done directly to improve the rule of law can only be a palliative. The permissive society is earning the rewards it deserves ...' (Eysenck and Gudjonsson, 1989: 255)

Eysenck's theory appears to demand a fully integrated sociological, biological and environmental thesis on crime. Let us be clear, however, of the role that Eysenck sees for the interaction of psychological, genetic and constitutional factors:

'Psychological factors in criminality relate to genetic and constitutional causes and to personality and other sources of individual differences. This does not mean that some people are destined to commit crimes. Criminal behaviour as such is not innate. What is inherited are certain peculiarities of the brain and nervous system that interact with certain environmental factors and thereby increase the likelihood that a given person will act in a particular antisocial manner in a given situation.' (Ibid: 247)

Although, therefore, he acknowledges that criminal behaviour is at the end of a long process, his image of the process is rather individualist and positivist.

'Much criminal behaviour can be construed as the end product of a chain of process. The first stage consists of the desire for certain goods or outlets. Most commonly, this involves a desire for material goods, status among peers, excitement, sexual gratification, and the relief of anger and hostility. Second, illegal and socially disapproved methods are chosen as acceptable means for satisfying these needs and desires. The reasons for this may be manyfold. They may involve faulty learning and inadequate moral development, the tendency to respond to stress in a particular way, and distorted attitudes and attributions. The third and final stage involves a number of situational and opportunity factors, where the criminal is the outcome of a decision-making process involving perceptions of benefits and costs at any one point of time.' (Ibid: 248)

The work of Edwin Sutherland suggested a sociological method in which otherwise socially disapproved methods for achieving desires are chosen; in a particular learning theory he called differential association.

Edwin Sutherland and the theory of differential association

At the end of the 19th century the French scholar Gabriel Tarde (1912) proposed that patterns of delinquency and crime are learned in much the same manner as any occupation, primarily through imitation of, and association with, others. Bad company was a central theme of 19th century accounts. Edwin H Sutherland (1939) whose work can be loosely placed in the tradition of the Chicago-school along with W I Thomas, Robert Park, Clifford Shaw and Henry McKay, was to offer a more sophisticated version, arguing that criminal behaviour is learned through associations established with those who violate society's norms. The cultural learning process involves not only the actual techniques of crime, but also the motives, drive, attitudes, and rationalisations favourable to the commission of anti-social acts (Sutherland and Cressey (1978)). Sutherland argues that there is no possibility of a person deterministically participating in criminal behaviour by inheritance, since all patterns of behaviour for humans only make sense in a cultural environment. All behaviour is assimilated from the surrounding culture. Criminal behaviour is learned behaviour, as is so-called normal law-abiding behaviour. It is learned through interaction with other persons, usually within intimate personal groups. A process approach is evident. A criminal identity and career results from a long series of experiences, but a single experience may cause a dramatic change in life. We are given the picture of life courses and vital turning points:

> 'A boy who is arrested and convicted is thereby publicly defined as a criminal. Thereafter his associations with lawful people are restricted and he is thrown into association with other delinquents. On the other hand, a person who is consistently criminal is not defined as law-abiding by a single lawful act. Every person is expected to be law-abiding, and lawful behaviour is taken for granted because the lawful culture is dominant, more extensive and more pervasive than the criminal culture.' (Criminology, 3rd ed, 1939: 6)

The theory of differential association was postulated in positivist terms: a person becomes delinquent because of the presence of an excess of definitions favourable to violations of the law, over definitions unfavourable to violations of the law. However, differential association emphasised the variable character of each person's exposure to definitions favourable and unfavourable to conduct in violation of the law. At the time, Sutherland had a fierce antipathy for psychiatry and was determined to espouse the ability of sociology to explain human action (Gaylord and Galliher (1988)). The theory is expressly sociological and the learning process is seen in determinist terms coming from social conditions and contacts outside the individual.

Most textbooks on criminology use Sutherland's 1947 formulation of differential association, but his original version is in some ways more interesting. In his textbook (1939) 3rd ed, first edition published in 1924, Sutherland's theory asserts that:

- The processes which result in systematic criminal behaviour are fundamentally the same in form as the processes which result in systematic lawful behaviour.

- Systematic criminal behaviour is learned in intimate association with those who commit crimes.

- Differentiation association is the specific causal process in the development of systematic criminal behaviour.

- The chance that a person will participate in systematic criminal behaviour is determined roughly by the frequency and consistency (duration and intensity) of his contacts with patterns of criminal behaviour.

- Individual differences among people in respect to personal characteristics or social situations cause crime only in so far as they affect differential association or frequency and consistency of contacts with criminal patterns.

- Cultural conflict is the underlying cause of differential association and therefore of systematic criminal behaviour.

- Social disorganisation is the basic cause of systematic criminal behaviour.

There are elements which overlap and which are almost tautological in the above propositions (for example, Sutherland amplified on the second point by saying: 'since criminal behaviour is thus developed in association with criminals it means that crime is the cause of crime'). The important considerations which are in this original formulation, and which have been rather neglected in the subsequent interpretation of Sutherland's theory, is the presence of cultural conflict and social disorganisation. Influenced by his friendship with Thorsten Sellin, Sutherland considered cultural conflict as the most visible symptom of the social disorganisation which characterised modern society. His theory was originally concerned with how an individual was to experience this and how certain courses of action flowed from the dominant forms of communication.

Sutherland sought to construct a purely sociological theory, but others have seen his theory as able to be incorporated into psychological paradigms. Ronald Akers (1977) highjacked the learning process of differential association theory by integrating it with Skinner's (1953) operant theory of behaviour thus making the theory compatible with behavioural and social learning formulations. This version was even more deterministic and positivist than Sutherland's own sociology. It was, however, the deterministic trend in Sutherland's formulation which allowed this appropriation.

The theory has been most influential. Many american commentators, for example James F Short (1957), conducted studies that were generally supportive. Short, however argued that delinquency was more strongly linked to the intensity, than either frequency, duration, or priority, of the association. In a subsequent replication study, Harwin Voss (1964) built on this arguing that individuals who associated with delinquent friends engaged in significantly more delinquent behaviour than individuals whose contact with delinquent peers was minimal. Enyon and Reckless (1961) argued companionship with anti-social peers often preceded the onset of both self-reported and officially recorded delinquency.

Taken literally, and positivistically, Sutherland's formulations on differential association predict specialisation in criminal and delinquent behaviour based on the associations one makes. But both longitudinal analyses of criminal violence (for example, Farrington (1982); Wolfgang *et al* (1972)) and research on 'delinquent career-lines (for example, Smith, Smith and Noma (1984)) have not found specialisation in general, thus indicating a more common underlying process.

Differential association theory has been one of the top three theories of American criminology (with strain and social control). It has stimulated much research on the issue of peer groups.

In their analysis of juvenile delinquency rates across the social classes Reiss and Rhodes (1964) sought to identify the role of differential association. The boys in their sample selected friends who were as delinquent or law-abiding as they were; However, this varied according to social class, with working-class male youths demonstrating a clear differential association effect for both serious and less serious offences, with middle-class youths displaying a differential association effect for less serious crimes but not for more serious ones. Reiss and Rhodes were unable to demonstrate that delinquents learn specific criminal techniques within the context of peer relationships.

Robins, West, and Herjanic (1975) linked delinquency to sibling delinquency, and Johnson (1979) reports that boys who claim delinquent friends are more likely to engage in criminality than boys who claim no delinquent companions. In their longitudinal study West and Farrington (1977) demonstrated that the antisocial activities of friends and associates predicted delinquent behaviour on the part of a group of young Londoners. Clinard and Abbott (1973), conducting trans-national research, found data largely congruent with Sutherland's ideas on differential association in the experiences of developing countries.

Sutherland saw differential association as a process, rather than a static phenomena – this has spawned different models attempting to explain exactly how the process of differential association operates. Charles R Tittle, Mary Jean Burke, and Ellen F Jackson (1986) argued that differential association worked indirectly by way of a learned symbolic context (ie the motivation to engage in crime) rather than directly through imitation or modelling. In a second study they argued that the importance of peer associations mainly stemmed from the fact that they elevated criminal motivation and not because they taught attitudes and rationalisations consistent with deviance.

Some scholars have attempted to develop predictive indices. Combining elements from Sutherland's differential association theory with Becker's (1963) early work on marijuana use, James D Orcutt (1987) sought to predict marijuana use in college students, given certain motivational and associational conditions.

Students with positive, neutral, and negative definitions of marijuana usage were asked to estimate how many of their four closest friends smoked marijuana at least once a month. The results indicated that students with negative definitions of marijuana usage tended to avoid marijuana, regardless of how many friends were semi-regular users, while those with positive definitions of marijuana usage were liable to smoke marijuana themselves if at least one of their four closest friends was also a semi-regular user. In the group with neutral attitudes toward marijuana usage, personal usage was virtually zero if none of the four closest friends were users of this substance, but rose to one in four in cases in which one friend was a semi-regular, and one in two if two or more friends were semi-regular users. This is roughly in line with Sutherland's contention that a person will engage in an illegal act if he, or she, is exposed to an excess of definitions favourable to violating that particular law or social rule.

Differential association has proved extremely stimulating to American criminology. Its critics have referred to a rather loose formulation, and its positivist emphasis. Common arguments against it include:

- It cannot explain why delinquents and criminals take advice from delinquent peers and associates, rather than from non-criminal family members and classmates (Wilson & Herrnstein (1985)).

- It seems blind to the problem of the loner, and the fact that many serious, recidivistic offenders have never integrated well into groups, delinquent or otherwise, and so have had less of an opportunity for differential association than better adjusted adolescents (Hirschi (1969)).

- Researchers have often overlooked the possibility that delinquent associations may be a result, rather than cause, of an early delinquent life orientation.

- Cressey (1960) believed that critical aspects of the theory were untestable, although the results of several recent studies appear to hint that the theory is much more amenable to examination than was once thought (compare Orcutt (1987); Tittle et al (1986)).

- The theory assumes a consensus as to what lawful and deviant behaviour and values are. Sutherland certainly never deeply questioned the dominant value structure of American society. Although he saw cultural conflict and social disorganisation as important, he believed in the social structure as largely progressive. The issues of differential rewards and punishments did not feature strongly in his work. Even in his most famous work, *White Collar Crime* (1949), which set out the abuses of professional businessmen, no criticism of the American capitalist system was evidenced.

A rather neglected theme of Sutherland's was communication. Sutherland had said that learning, interaction and communication were the processes around which a theory of criminal behaviour should be developed. This could take us into the terrain of culture and the subjective meaning of actions, techniques for avoiding others interpretation of one's actions and the consequences. Remember Sutherland's original formulation included the themes of culture conflict and social disorganisation. We have already mentioned that he was clearly influenced at the time by his friendship, and working relationship with Thorsten Sellin who wrote *Culture Conflict and Crime* in 1938. The genesis of that text was as follows: in the late 1930s Sutherland and Sellin had been appointed members of a committee of the Social Sciences research Council to organise a report on a central problem in criminology. Culture conflict was their theme and although the final report was written by Sellin, Sutherland was influential. Sellin writes that Sutherland's theory of differential association may even have been Sutherland's attempt to tell him where he had gone wrong! Whatever the truth, Sutherland wrote to Sellin shortly before *Culture Conflict and Crime* was published giving the following discussion:

> 'It seems to me that the relatively low rate [of crime] of the large [immigrant] colonies is due to "isolation" from conflicting patterns. They live their own life in the midst of an American city almost as in their home community. Consequently, they have few conflicts. Conflicts must grow out of cultural contacts. Moreover, the family and the neighbourhood in such situations work together consistently in the direction of control of the individual member, while in the smaller [immigrant] groups, there may be no such harmony between the patterns of these two primary groups, and consequently there may be a high delinquency rate. In other words, it seems to me that the cultural conflict should be regarded as taking the form of such divergences between the smaller groups as well as in the larger national groups. The probable conflict of cultures does not consist merely in the fact that the law of one group says thus-and-this, while the law of the other group says so-and-so. Rather more important I believe is the fact that the informal codes differ on hundreds of other things, thus undermining the legal codes of both groups.' (Quoted in Gaylord and Galliher, 1988: 129)

In recent years John Braithwaite has tried to develop a communication based theory of punishment in *Crime, Shame and Reintegration* (1989). Braithwaith suggests that the key to crime control is a process of shaming the offender within a cultural commitment to reintegration.

Braithwaite focuses on White Collar crime as an area where this would have great effect, but asserts that there is a general process applicable to all crime. Sutherland had been the pioneer:

> 'The data which are at hand suggests that white collar crime has its genesis in the same general processes as other criminal behaviour, namely, differential association ... Businessmen are not only in contact with definitions which are favourable to white collar crime but they are also isolated from and protected against definitions which are unfavourable to such crime ... As a part of the process of learning practical business, a young man with idealism and thoughtfulness for others is inducted into white collar crime ... He learns specific techniques for violating the law, together with definition of situations in which these techniques may be used. Also, he develops a general ideology ... "we are

not in business for our health", "business is business", or "no business was ever built on the beatitudes".' (1949: 239-140)

The prevalence of white collar crime demonstrated the normalcy of crime

Neither biology, economic deprivation, psychological imbalance or the broken home appealed as the likely starting point for the explanation of crime perpetrated by the economically powerful. Differential association, however, gained strength as a general explanation by its ability to look at this area far removed from the usual subject matter for criminology in the same way as with crimes of the economically powerless. Yet, here there may have been a bias, for Sutherland, as the majority of criminologists have done, offered the most 'normal of the theories' as the explanation of crime committed by the most normal of people, the capitalists themselves. By contrast, the idea of the psychopath appeared to provide an opposite location: the site of the pure criminal. For Eysenck:

> '... the psychopath presents the riddle of delinquency in a particularly pure form, and if we could solve this riddle in relation to the psychopath, we might have a very powerful weapon to use on the problem of delinquency in general.' (1977: 55)

The extreme criminal: the idea of the psychopath

The psychopath is the supreme image of the dangerous criminal – a figure of such coldness and inhuman modes of thought that he defies normal learning processes and social bonds. The popular film *Silence of the Lambs* contained both an anti-hero psychopath (acted by Anthony Hopkins), and an evil psychopath. The concept of psychopathy is both open-ended and ambiguous. Currently it is used interchangeably with anti-social personality disorders, to refer to a severe disorder of personality, of emotional adjustment, or maturation, whereby a person behaves in an extreme manner, either violently or in a bizarre, heterodox, way, and has gross inability to relate to others in what is regarded as the normal fashion. In particular he or she has great difficulties in initiating, developing and sustaining a non-destructive and rewarding social and emotional relationship. The condition is regarded as persistent and intractable to classic forms of medical and psychiatric treatment; for instance analytical or supportive psychotherapy, behaviour therapy and physical methods.

In a recent review, Dolan and Coid (1993) argue that the 'untreatability of psychopaths' may, in part, result from the professionals' inadequate assessment in the first place, followed by an inability to develop, describe, research and adequately demonstrate, the efficacy of treatment strategies (1993: 267).

It has been argued that while psychopathy may exist in a setting of subnormality and mental illness, it also exists as a clinical entity apart from these conditions and without organic brain lesion. Herschel Prins distinguishes pseudo-psychopathy (due to established brain damage, etc) from essential psychopathy.

Psychopathy is seen in people who have not learned to relate, and in whom persistent attempts to relate have led to a worsening, a destruction of any ability to relate in accepted emotional and social terms. Reactions of others – anger, disgust, over-sympathy, over-mothering – perpetuate and worsen the condition; as the person develops from childhood into adolescence and adulthood the condition becomes fixed and eventually obdurate to treatment.

The concept is highly controversial, almost everyone agrees that the term psychopath, or psychopathy, is unsatisfactory. It is imprecise as a medical diagnosis; it has variable legal significance, and it expresses more the emotional state of the user, namely exasperated hopelessness, tinctured with anger and even contempt than an entity precisely captured by the 'science'. Barbara Wootton claimed that the concept of the psychopath was, in fact, *par excellence*, and without shame or qualification, the model of the circular process by which mental abnormality is inferred from anti-social behaviour while anti-social behaviour is explained by mental abnormality (1959: 250).

On the other hand, many practitioners argue that the term refers to some phenomena, although what exactly it is, and what the limits are, is not easily ascertainable. In American the term sociopath is used, which is free from many of the emotional connotations attached to psychopath, but is no more precise. In its 1975 review the Butler Committee accepted the practice whereby clinicians use a diagnostic term 'personality disorder', followed by a description of the predominant features in the individual comprising the 'disorder'.

Special provision currently exists in the UK for detaining patients in secure hospitals under the 1983 Mental Health Act because of their 'persistent disorder or disability of mind (whether or not including significant impairment of intelligence) which results in abnormally aggressive or severely irresponsible conduct' (MHA, s 1(2)). Hamilton (1985; 1990) estimates that this form of legal categorisation is responsible for around 25% of the patients in the English maximum-security hospitals. However, when diagnostic tests were given to patients, a large discrepancy was found between the clinician-led characteristics which are looked for in defining the psychopath.

The clinician-led form of definition appears to the critics to be circular; psychopathology becomes defined by the characteristics which clinicians in practice use in cases of doubt. Cleckley listed various characteristics of the psychopath derived from practice. The World Health Organisation depicts the condition as coming to attention, because of a gross disparity between the behaviour and prevailing social norms, and characterises the condition by:

- callous unconcern for the feelings of others and lack of capacity for empathy;
- gross and persistent attitude of irresponsibility and disregard for social norms, rules and obligations;

- incapacity to maintain enduring relationships;
- very low tolerance to frustration, and a low threshold for discharge of aggression, including violence;
- incapacity to experience guilt, and to profit from experience, particularly punishment;
- marked proneness to blame others, or to offer plausible rationalisations for the behaviour bringing the subject into conflict with society;
- persistent irritability. (Quoted in Dolan and Coid, 1990: 14.)

We face a paradox: the term is not popular and the condition, if it exists, is not a well defined phenomena. But, pragmatically, it seems to refer to a condition or problem of the mental functioning of the individual which is accepted as real. The terminology seems to cover a severe personality disorder which shows itself in a variety of attitudinal, emotional, and inter-personal behavioural problems. As a matter of empirical differentiation certain factors are often relied upon which may or may not be present in individual cases:

- Periods of emotional and social deprivation in infancy and childhood. Here Bowlby has been relied upon, while McCord and McCord (1964) suggested lack of affection and severe parental rejection were primary factors. The longitudinal study of Robins (1966) correlated a series of early experiences: early referral to a child guidance clinic for theft or aggression, a history of truancy, lying, non-compliance, no signs of guilt or remorse, general irresponsibility regarding school and family routines. Other factors included little or no parental discipline and anti-social behaviour by the father which also is present in a wider range of later problems.
- Long periods spent in institutions, resulting perhaps from the need to control a difficult or unmanageable child or adolescent, leading to ambiguity in the forming and development of relationships.
- A highly exaggerated need for reassurance of identity, sexuality, sanity and existence ('I don't feel me').
- A misdirection of aggressive drives seen in offences of arson, burglary and assault.
- A misdirection of sexual drives, seen in offences of rape, sexual assaults, deviancy and exposure.
- A marked feeling of unworthiness, uselessness, lacking in value as a person underlies the extreme behaviour.
- An appearance of coldness and lack of feeling. A dissociation at the time of committing extreme violence, murder or rape.
- A dehumanisation and, at times, feelings of internal elation during the process of hostage holding, wounding, feelings of all-powerfulness, with lack of ability to relate to the victim or to the police.

- Almost total lack of judgment in behaviour, even though the person is of normal intelligence and is not suffering from any psychotic or organic illness. This lack of judgment is the result of inability to perceive his own needs and the needs and responses of others, and is interpreted as a lack of conscience.

- A low level of anxiety which is uncovered in treatment. It is apparent that the person prevents the anxiety coming into consciousness by more and more repetitive acting out. A typical sequence of events is taking and driving away a car, a police chase, accident, arrest, court case and subsequent imprisonment, fight, wrist slashing, drugs, drink and unawareness of the social pressure of his peers, the police, his parents, his wife.

- Impulsivity. He reacts to inappropriate social stimuli by impulsive behaviour which he rationalises from his own primitive needs. It is in this phase that, when examined either by the judiciary, the police or psychiatrists, he is observed to have no remorse.

- Lack of response to ordinary learning methods, to early childhood punishments, and to the isolation, confinement and deprivation of over-exaggerated bodily needs, that may be necessary for his management and containment, but which reinforce his feelings of unworthiness and isolation. Cleckley (1976), in *The Mask of Sanity*, argued that the psychopath is unable to learn from experience.

- Lack of trust in extreme cases is almost complete, but particularly during periods of crisis leading to, or during the commission of a crime.

- Lack of social skills. Inability to use the telephone; to apply for a job; deficiencies in social relationships; inability to organise and enter into an outing or a social evening. These people cover up this deficiency by taking drugs, becoming drunk and prevent themselves facing their social deficiencies by causing a diversion, such as picking a fight.

The aetiology of psychopathology?

The term psychopath developed from an 18th and 19th century idea of moral imbeciles suffering from an 'illness of morality'. In this century, many practitioners have sought constitutional and environmental components in the definitive conditions, but exploration of heredity pre-disposition, chromosomes, organic underlying causes, lesions in the temporal or frontal lobe, have yielded little help in diagnosis, prevention or treatment. In most cases no definite hereditary predisposition or organic lesion is seen. An 'immature' electro-encephalogram shows a variable and ill defined pattern, but there is no correlation between presence or degree of violent behaviour and EEG patterns. Perhaps this is part of the fascination of the psychopath; a figure who will not, or cannot, play the games of normal social interaction and experience fellow feeling towards humans, but for whom no organic cause can be found.

If this is not a 'moral disorder' then there must be a treatment?

The psychopath defies conventional therapeutic treatment, since this relies on an implicit commitment between physician and the patient based on trust and good faith, but this person cannot enter into such a commitment because of a lack of ability to trust. Impulsiveness and lack of judgment prevent his attending clinics, taking medicines (the effects of which are dubious), or entering into a classic psychotherapeutic relationship. Supervising the person during treatment is also a problem since his impulsive acting out behaviour will be accentuated during any process of change in treatment. This person is intractable to treatment by psychoanalysis, supportive psychotherapy, and physical methods; in conventional hospital treatment regimes he disrupts the treatment of other patients and staff management and has to be expelled. These settings appear to offer him the opportunity to act out his distorted methods of relating, and actually intensify his pattern of behaviour. The therapeutic community directly designed for the treatment of personality behaviour disorders attempts to allow him to grow; experiment with emotional and social relationships and so develop an awareness of himself and his behaviour in relation to others. In Britain a therapeutic community system for the treatment of behaviour disorders was set up by Maxwell Jones at the Henderson Hospital in the 1950s, and developed in England at HMP Grendon Underwood and HMP Wormwood Scrubs Annex, and in Scotland at the (recently closed) Barlinnie Special Unit.

The original idea was to place emphasis on the individual's responsibility for his behaviour, while providing a milieu to allow him to examine his emotional needs, the emotional needs of others, his effect on the feelings and behaviour of others, and their effect upon him; to allow him to form and reform, thus readjust to others and explore and correct his faulty mechanisms of relating. He thus tests out the boundaries of both the institutional structure and others in relationship to his own emotional needs and behaviour. Permissiveness, accompanied by boundary drawing, enable him to grow and establish a less faulty and destructive method of operating.

Such 'communities', as they have evolved in the various locations, have taken on special characterises and changing clients. Attempts have been made to evaluate the treatment regime at Grendon in terms of change, growth and reduction of destructive behaviour. The goals of the regime have been: the prevention of repetitive, escalating, extremely violent behaviour patterns; improvement in social and emotional methods of operating; ability to form satisfactory, deeper relationships in a domestic setting; understanding and directing of sexual and aggressive drives in a non-destructive manner; growth and development in the patient's feeling of his own worth; finding and developing aspects of his personality that are of value to himself and others. In coming to an appreciation of the needs of others he is able to reinforce a poorly developed conscience, a sense of his own responsibility, to develop social and emotional skills, an appreciation of regret and remorse in a caring environment.

At the same time, he is protected from his own destructive impulses but contained predominantly by pressure from his peers.

What sort of regimes do the penal systems of England, Wales and Scotland use?

The best example is the Grendon Treatment Regime. Grendon is made up of six therapeutic communities, and an Assessment Unit. Each of these communities consist of inmates, prison officers, psychiatrists, a psychologist and a probation officer or social worker. The underlying philosophy is that a person is considered to be responsible for his behaviour. He must have some degree of self-motivation for change. His aim is to become aware of his behaviour, and how this is regulated by his emotions/feelings, and how these two affect his relationships: this is seen as a combination of *behaviour* and *feelings* leading to *relationships*.

Therefore the task is to develop and correct social skills by involvement in the community, and to self-consciously examine and bring about an alteration in life style. Importantly, the ideology is that the person is in treatment in the community. He is not sick, being treated by a doctor and nurses, but, a person allowing himself to share in the support, examination, confrontation by his peers of his whole life situation. The orientation is positive, aiming to develop and enhance those positive qualities he may possess and so produce some feeling of self-worth.

Ideally, psychopharmacology is not used in the treatment methods no psychotropic drugs nor night sedation. (Drugs for medical conditions are of course prescribed as required, eg penicillin.)

There are two main operating assumptions:

- A person is considered responsible for his behaviour and he and the community have resources to control this behaviour without the protection of medication.

- In the intensive treatment he must be aware of his feelings relating to his behaviour and how this affects his interpersonal relationships. This perception is dulled or altered by medication. There are (a) group meetings involving staff and men with community meetings, small group meetings, encounter groups, role-playing groups, psychodrama – with audio visual aids, work groups, discharge groups, operatic groups, family groups, committee meetings, transactional analysis, areas of decision making, management and control groups using therapeutic community principles such as democratisation, boundaries and limit drawing, role mobility, communication. The community or wing meeting is the central point of the treatment.

Evaluation of the treatment effects of Grendon

There have been various studies concerning the recidivism rates after treatment at Grendon. George (1971) following 263 subjects for two years found 59% have committed a crime in that period, but of those who had stayed in the Institution for more than one year the figure was 40%; Newton (1971) following 377 for two years found 58% for those who had stayed less than one year, and 50% for those who had stayed more than one year; Gunn et al (1978) following 61 for two years found 70%; Robertson and Gunn following the same 61 for 10 years found 92%; Cullen (1992) following 214 for two years found those who had stayed less than 18 months 40%, but only 20% for those who had stayed more then 18 months, Genders and Player noted that the population of Grendon had changed. Gunn's subjects were younger and were on shorter sentences, whereas Cullen's subjects had more often committed crimes related to violence and sexual victimisation. Recidivism rates were in general lower for those who had stayed longer in treatment.

Gunn et al (1978) argued that evaluation of treatment regimes in terms of reconviction rate was not valid, since reconviction depended upon a myriad of personal, environmental and situational factors, many of which the prison psychiatrist cannot be expected to influence. In all the main areas that were measured – psychiatric state, symptomatology, personality, attitudes to authority figures and self – large changes were recorded between the first and subsequent assessments. They also showed significant reduction in neurotic symptoms, anxiety, tension and depression. Using methods involving semantic differentials, several areas of therapeutic significance emerged.

There was a rise in the esteem or 'myself element' and a fall in the unrealistically high estimation of psychiatrists. Changes show the men gained, increased in self-confidence and worth. It was found that the results reflected the orientation of the Grendon therapeutic regime with its primary emphasis laid on the people's own ability to help themselves.

What is to be made of the psychopath concept? It too often seems to be used as a catch-all concept to incorporate those individuals who appear extremely anti-social and for whom no appropriate medical terminology can be found. But why should anti-social behaviour, even of an extreme nature, presuppose psychopathy or a psychopathic personality?

The Mental Health Act which includes the concept of psychopathic disorders as a mental disorder and which still keeps this in amended form, has been mainly unsatisfactory in providing treatment for this group of people.

There is a conflict between the needs of treatment, the rights of the individual and the safety of the public. The individuals concerned are not invariably dangerous. They may be potentially dangerous, but other factors play a very important part such as social situation, marriage, housing and drinking habits. Careful evaluation is required in each case and at regular short intervals.

Doctors refute the criticism by some sociologists that they are neither curing nor caring but simply acting as agents, sometimes repressively, of social control.

Psychosurgery, or the destruction of brain tissues, can reduce aggressive drives and violent behaviour, although these techniques are very imprecise and are irreversible. They have been used in the past for treatment of impulsive aggression, but are not in use today in most countries. The film *One Flew Over the Cuckoo's Nest* demonstrated popular revulsion against the possibility of turning a 'normal' person into a human cabbage. Because of their irreversible nature such techniques pose serious ethical problems and patients must be aware of the direct and side effects of the treatment, and enter into it voluntarily.

Numerous sociologists, philosophers, and writers have expressed the fear that if the authorities or the medical profession take away a person's aggressive drives they leave him unable to protect himself from the aggression of society or his peers in the open situation (see Burgess' *Clockwork Orange*). We have, perhaps, a dispute between the pretensions of experts to control from the outside by behavioural modification, or by providing internalised knowledges and skills for the individual to learn self-knowledge and self-control. Whereas constitutional theories appeared to trace a direct line from a supposed genetic inheritance of aggressive tendencies and crime, the aim of psychotherapy is not to defuse aggression, but to enable a patient to use his drives in a non-violent non-impulsive manner. Steps should be taken in each case to enable the patient to understand his new situation and be aware of areas of vulnerability to be avoided.

Psychopathology and interactive communication

An interesting avenue for investigation came accidentally out of a study conducted by Widom (1976) to gauge the ability of individuals labelled as psychopaths to perform certain cognitive tasks. Playing a Prisoner's Dilemma game, primary psychopaths functioned just as well as the male nurses used as controls. When a person also judged a primary psychopath played with another person judged a primary psychopath they cooperated well. Teams of persons judged to be secondary psychopaths preformed less well. None of the psychopaths were, however, playing with a person adjudged to be normal; when this occurred cooperation lessened. This study reinforces the issue that the psychopath may be acting on the basis of his perception of the 'other'. Howells (1983) specifically argues that persons adjudged to be psychopathic, attribute negative intentions to other people. They interact with others on the presumption that others are the source of negative actions rather than positive occurrences, and, instead of waiting for the inevitable, they get the blow in first.

In actual social interactions this becomes a self-fulfilling prediction. As Rime, Bonvy, and Rouillon (1978) describe those individuals labelled psychopaths they observed, the psychopath displays an 'over-intrusive social presentation'. By comparison with the controls they observed, those labelled as psychopaths leaned forward more, and looked more at the person they were interacting with in conversation, while smiling less. Their intense self-presentation resulted in a 'spontaneous attitude of retreat' by the others, who drew back from the interaction. Thus, the others actually appeared to the psychopath to be hostile.

The knowledges of psychology: tools of control in modernity?

Psychology presents a variety of tools and knowledges: methods of awareness (which strive to make a self visible to the person), algorithms of interaction (whose work is to make human relations calculable), narratives of feeling (which instruct us how to understand the mechanisms we have for identifying and valuing the things which stimulate our emotions) to direct the awareness which is itself aroused. The aim of these knowledges and methodologies is to visualise the healthy, and get rid of pathological aspects. The task is to change anxiety into excitement through techniques of self-reflection and self-examination, and thereby to ensure that we become a reflexive self, more able to redirect our forces. Thus we can learn processes of control over ourselves which the behavioural manipulators claim they can exercise from without.

What is at stake with this interaction of knowledge, psychotherapy (of various kinds) and social life? Perhaps Rose sums it up:

'In each of these fields, and others that could be identified, what is at stake is a reciprocal relationship between elaboration of a body of knowledge and practice and the production of the self itself, as the terrain upon which our relationship with one another and with our bodies, habits, propensities, and pleasures is to be understood. No doubt one would be wise not to overstate the constitutive powers of psychotherapeutic discourse and practice. Their potency derives from their confluence with a whole political rationality and governmental technology of the self. But none the less it is important to recognise that what is at issue in these therapeutic technologies of knowledge and power – no longer sex, not even pathology, but our autonomous selves.' (Rose, 1990: 245)

We can be highly suspicious of positivist psychology, after all are humans really reducible to behavioural complexes? From one point of view, of course, we are, we are the thinking animal ... but we are more ... we are the animal that uses logos, language, and cultural weapons. Psychology can provide another array of tools. These tools can control us, render us powerless if we wish, but they can also be tools whereby we can learn to recognise and simulate the mental technologies of creative adjustment. Psychology offers us instruction in an additional vocabulary for describing and accounting for the pains of our lives, and for dealing with others in the social interaction that life inescapably is about. It provides a range of discourses which are both authoritarian disciplines, justified in modernity by reference to scientific methodology, but can also become popular, available, recognisable to each of us. These knowledges can translate our complexes and fears into less threatening shapes, and enable us to articulate forms of being that we come to recognise as part of our ontology. They also offer us hints of the forces impinging upon ourselves. We learn a language and a technique, a process which makes us governable, and yet offers us the possibilities of governing ourselves. This reflects the dialectics of modernity: control and autonomy, responsibility and inclusivity, civilisation and citizenship.

CHAPTER EIGHT

CRIMINOLOGICAL POSITIVISM III: STATISTICS, QUANTIFYING THE MORAL HEALTH OF SOCIETY AND CALCULATING NATURE'S LAWS

'In following attentively the regular march of nature in the development of plants and animals we are compelled to believe in the analogue that the influence of laws should be extended to the human species.' (Quetelet, 1826).

'We can assess how perfected a science has become by how much or how little it is based on calculation.' (Quetelet, 1828)

'I cannot repeat too often, to all men who sincerely desire the well-being and honour of their kind, and who would blush to consider a few francs more or less paid to the treasury as equivalent to a few heads more or less submitted to the axe of the executioner, that there is a budget which we pay with a frightful regularity – it is that of prisons, chains, and the scaffold: it is that which, above all, we ought to endeavour to abate.' (Quetelet, 1842)

The positivist approach has strong connections with statistical analysis. As outlined in the writings of its originators, such as August Comte in the 1830s positivism was to be a form of social mechanics or social physics. For Comte, positivism denoted not just a methodology, but a whole new and progressive frame of reference to relate to the world; a framework which would bring progressive government and serve as the foundation for a modern social order. We have already noted how Comte gave a narrative history of the world in three stages, but we may ask: Is this positivism actually a radical advance over the assumptions of the classical school?

The resolution of chance and the chaos of the natural state

Hobbes' *Leviathan* is not simply a text of political philosophy, but a text of the foundations of modern social theory. Hobbes offers a simple ontological message: beneath the appearance of order, nature is actually disorientating; nature is full of contingencies; nature is a state of flux, a constant process of becoming and appropriation. When Hobbes tells us that civil society is what we formed by our creation of, and submission to, political power, he is also telling us that what we are today is what we have made ourselves. The foundations of our nature, the core of our 'self', the foundation of social order, is not stability, but process.

If this sounds familiar it is because this is announced as the radical post-modern message thought to mean the end of social theory. Today we no longer believe in some prince (Machiavelli), or some general will (Rousseau), or some all powerful Sovereign (Hobbes), who will impart meaning to our social life and enforce solidarity. The post-modern age wonders at what there is in common that might serve as the touch stone to grant unity to social life, and ensure progress. The thesis advanced in the present text is that there is actually nothing radically new in the post-modern message about nature; early modernity faced this issue. Except, early modernity did not learn to live without God, it tended to transfer God's will into a belief in a natural order, and the image of society as a functioning whole – this was as much a dream, a solace, as our earlier creation of God. Post-modernism is the refusal to continue with that dream. We are too much aware of our history to keep up the dream ... or are we?

How did early modernity create the dream of natural order and functionality? We have already investigated the writings of the classical school in Beccaria, Bentham and John Austin and how they used ideas of a new science of man, narratives of progress and faith in utilitarianism to ensure an overall synthesis of social life and history to position their analytical projects. Theirs was not a theoretical project without solace.

For example, consider John Austin's rule bound utilitarianism.

Austin (1832: Lecture III) argues that the world operates according to the will of God. We moderns wish to be happy; happiness is the goal of individual and social life. We can understand how to organise the happy society through observing the functional operations of the natural world, made visible by the science of positivism, and calculable through the moral science of utilitarianism. In effect God becomes a geometer, or more specifically, the enlightenment has persuaded Austin that the reason underlying the world's operation is fundamentally mathematical; hence, human welfare and security depend upon our obedience to the rule-like, or axiomatic nature, of mathematical thinking. For Austin, God has bequeathed an understandable nature, and the combination of positivism and utilitarianism tells us what is the nature of things, and how they ought to be organised. If we wish to avoid unnecessary suffering we do not have a choice. In Lecture XXIII Austin (1873) specifies the coercion involved in truth, political philosophy and the prison. While we may have a choice as to whether or not we will obey, certain consequences follow. The underlying truths of the world, political power, prison walls – which all are general contexts we find ourselves in – require involuntary participation.

In this system the happiness of human society will depend upon uncovering the rules, or laws, of the underlying natural order. The happiness of the individual rests upon the connection between his moral being and his rewards, as guaranteed to the Christian pre-modern by God and now to the modern by the fruits of rational government. For the early utilitarian, human judgment (the rightness or wrongness of individual acts and decisions) is possible because nature is purposive. The fact that nature is accessible in terms of functions, rules and laws, gives us our faith in progress, enables us to understand the necessity for our social duty, and ensures we put up with the inequalities of the social order; inequalities, which Austin impresses upon us, are functionally required.

The battle for sociology: a moral science or a statistical science?

Although Durkheim held the first Chair in Sociology anywhere in the world, Auguste Comte is usually credited with founding the discipline of sociology. In his recent book, *Inventing Criminology: essays on the rise of 'Hone Criminalis'*, Piers Beirne (1993), claims, however, that the real foundation was laid by the analyses which the Belgian astronomer Adolphe Quetelet made in the name of a statistical science of mankind.

Comte resisted such a statistical orientation and, having seen his original suggestions of 'social mechanics' or 'social physics' used by Quetelet, he coined the name 'sociology' to avoid being restricted into seeking regularities and probabilities. Quetelet was, however, the better politician. He organised a world statistical congress and was influential in starting various statistical societies. Quetelet triumphed over Comte: sociology became obsessed with statistics, and to this day perhaps the dominant theme of sociological theory takes it as axiomatic that sociology is searching for social laws, and that these will be cast in a statistical form.

Durkheim took this up, in part at least. Sociology was to be a science investigating social facts (or *moral phenomenon*), based on the sheer regularity and stability of quantitative social facts which could be ascertained by correlating statistics of social events, such as economic production, with statistics for activities, such as crime or suicide, which otherwise may have been thought of as psychological in cause. Thus:

'... social phenomena could no longer be deemed to be the product of fortuitous combinations, arbitrary acts of will, or local and chance circumstances. Their generality attests to their essential dependence on general causes which, everywhere that they are present, produce their effects ... Where for a long time there has been perceived only isolated actions, lacking any links, there was found to be a system of definite laws. This was already expressed in the title of the book in which Quetelet expounded the basic principles of the statistics of morality. '(Durkheim and Fauconnet, 1903, quoted in Beirne, 1993: 97)

At the centre of Quetelet's legacy was the idea of the 'average man' (*homme moyen*). 'If the average man were ascertained for one nation, he would represent the type of that nation. If he could be ascertained according to the mass of men, he would present the type of the human species' (1831, quoted, Beirne, 1993: 77-78); Crime was, he thought, a factor of derivations from the normal, possibly derived from biological defects: 'a pestilential germ ... contagious ... (sometimes) hereditary'; on a factor 'of the milieu in which man finds himself' (both quotes, Beirne, 1993: 90).

Quetelet implicitly identifies the average man as the person who (although he may have propensities to deviate keeps them under control) is law abiding, in good physical and psychological health. A man who exhibits:

'... rational and temperate habits, more regulated passions ... foresight, as manifested by investment in savings' banks, assurance societies and the different institutions which encourage foresight.' (1842: quoted, Beirne, 1993: 89)

The average man stood for the mainstream of the civilising process, the proper citizen of modernity. The deviant was his opponent and both the deviant and the social and constitutional forces which caused deviancy ought to be removed:

'... the practical outcome of Quetelet's criminology was the application of his binary opposition of normality and deviance to the domain of penality ... Quetelet urged that governments identify the causes of crime in order to reduce or, if possible, eliminate the frequency of crime. Since the number (of crimes) cannot diminish without the causes which induce them undergoing previous modification, it is the province of legislators to ascertain these causes, and to remove them as far as possible.' (Bairne 1993: 90-1)

Crime is not a function of activity and censure, but a natural phenomenon. It has a place in the natural order of things only because we have not succeeded in organising social forces in harmony. Our aim should be to remove deviations:

'The more do "deviations from the average disappear ... the more, consequently, do we tend to approach that which is beautiful, that which is good".' (Beirne, 1993: 92)

We need a full cataloguing of 'moral statistics' to observe normal behaviour and to gauge the moral health of our society. The present official statistics stem from this attempt.

Criminal statistics

One of the main reasons for the concern with crime today is the dramatic increase in recorded crime over the last 30 years. Our primary measure of this is the official criminal statistics, and we should not lose sight of the fact that concern with crime has a long history with both Plato (in ancient Athens) and Beccaria commenting on increases. Paul Wiles (1971) points out that writers such as Petty and Gaunt hoped, as early as the 17th century, that proper statistics would be crucial in the making of policy decisions and in judging the moral health of the nation. Beccaria and Bentham advocated that criminal statistics be centrally correlated and used as a political barometer 'furnishing data for the legislator to work on'. Quite what they measure is problematic. Downes and Rock (1988) reflect a strong current in modern criminological thinking when they state that the official statistics are a better reflection of social attitudes towards crime and criminals, than they are a measure of actual criminal behaviour.

The problem of criminal statistics

Official statistics are a social construction which we cannot treat as truly reflective of the type or level of crime that occurs in society. We can speak of 'the dark figure of crime', or use the analogy of the official statistics as an iceberg, where what is revealed is a fraction of the actual events capable of being called crime. The actual proportion of crime the dark figure represents is difficult to calculate, but it is the majority for many crimes. The official statistics are the product of a long social process, with a series of gates both into and out of the process, and various decision making opportunities.

Problems in the compilation of official statistics

- They record a socially constructed concept, ie crime.

  We must first acknowledge that crime is itself a socially constructed concept, and that the definition of crime as behaviour punishable by the criminal law, is fraught with difficulties. For example:

  (i)   Criminal laws are not fixed in all societies. The substantive activity covered by the criminal law varies across time, and between different cultures.

  (ii) Research shows that the criminalisation of conduct and activities has been influenced by power, class conflicts, and moral enterprenuership.

  (iii) The pace of modern social and technological change leads to an increase in criminalisation as part of legal regulation. New technology gives cars, televisions, computers, designer drugs, etc. all of which have sets of regulations passed to govern their use.

  Therefore, although the official criminal statistics are expected to reflect the level of crime in the society the very definition of what constitutes a crime is variable. Crimes do not have an ontological necessity but a construction that changes across time and place.

- Crimes need reporting. A large number of crimes are not reported to the police for a variety of reasons.

  (i)   The victim may be unaware that a crime has been committed, for example if the victim is a large corporation or where there are a number of victims, none of whom have been affected in an immediately visible way. The victim may participate in the illegal activity consensually for example drug use or prostitution.

  (ii) The victim may be unable to report the crime for a variety of reasons. For instance a threat has been received.

  (iii) The victim may consider that the offence is too trivial to report. The British Crime Survey consistently reveals that a majority of victims feel this way about many events capable of being reported.

  (iv) The victim may not want to get involved in the time consuming activity of reporting.

  (v)   The victim may be unsure of the consequences of reporting, and fear that the consequences outweigh the harm caused; for example, in sexual crime the victim may be afraid of the stigma, and the ordeal of court appearances.

(vi)   The victim may know the offender and may not want to see him or her punished.

(vii)   The victim may have no faith in the criminal justice system.

(viii) The victim may be afraid of publicity surrounding the crime, and may not wish attention drawn to him or herself.

(ix)   The victim may wish to deal with the matter himself.

(x)   The victim may find his or her property returned before he reports it as stolen.

- Some crimes are more likely to be reported than others. Murder is a good example; the victims are normally reported as missing, and discovered bodies appear always to be reported. Property crimes show an increasing tendency to be reported, as this is a prerequisite for insurance claims. The British Crime Survey estimates that in 1972, 78% of burglary was reported, whereas in 1987, 90% was reported. Thus we can see that whilst the actual number of offences may increase by x percentage, the reported percentage may increase by a factor of x.

- Police practices in recording crime. The police have a statutory obligation to record crime on the following conditions:

(i)   where sufficient evidence exists that a crime has actually been committed;

(ii)   the case is sufficiently serious to warrant police attention and be recorded.

These criteria allow much discretion between police areas and police forces. The procedural rules for recording crimes are governed by internal regulations, and these can lead to discrepancies between forces. Different police forces may have different techniques for logging phone calls onto crime complaint forms, and this may affect their respective crime figures.

Home Office compiling can also be open to different interpretations. In some circumstances this may result in several offences being counted as only one event. Alternatively, when an offender is known as a hard case for example, some police officers may well load-on offences.

Another problem is that once an offence has been classified, then it may not be altered every-time it transpires that the offender is only convicted of a lesser offence.

Studies reveal that individual police officers use their discretion in deciding which crimes to record. As Cicourel (1968) observed with juvenile justice many offences are a 'matter of negotiation'; the recording of burglary or robbery could be flexibly negotiated. Other commentators have noted that the police record large numbers of crimes, many of which are not recorded in the criminal statistics, unless they are brought to court; additionally the police are not the only agency exercising supervision over areas which may be classified as crimes. Tax evasion is often policed by Inland Revenue, and smuggling is the province of Customs and Excise.

• The uses of criminal statistics. Hall Williams (1981) argues the benefits of official statistics for the following reasons:

(i) They are freely available.

(ii) They have already been processed in an accessible fashion.

(iii) They are published relatively soon after the period to which they relate.

(iv) They may be a useful starting point for further work, for example the official statistics are at least an indication of the size, nature and locality of the crime problem.

(v) Wallace suggests that the official statistics can provide a useful insight into crime and criminologists can use them if they accept safeguards, and interpret them in the light of their knowledge as to their creation.

(vi) They can highlight patterns and trends.

In summary: although as a whole the official statistics are unreliable as a measure of absolute trends and patterns, if seen as an indication, and properly interpreted, they may be used profitably by criminologists and they may have a range of potential uses which may not yet have been fully explored. However, it is possible to draw many false conclusions from the official statistics and many myths about the extent and nature of crime have begun in this way. Historically, the reliance upon the official criminal statistics in constructing positivist sociological theories has led criminologists to concentrate almost solely upon street crimes, and the activities of working class males, partly because these are the activities and offenders traditionally represented in the criminal statistics.

Attempts to mitigate the failings of the official statistics

Self report studies

In these studies the subjects are asked whether they have committed any particular kind of offence, and they record a different level of activity to that of the official figures. However, they have a number of problems such as those documented by Williams (1994).

Problems of validity

How sure can we be that the subjects are telling the truth?

• Subjects may forget crimes they have committed, or rationalise their activities.

- The sample may not be representative of the population as a whole. Many of the early self-report studies were carried out on adolescents in particular students. Thus, even from this limited group, the individuals who had dropped out of 'the course, who were not present on the day, may have had an important contribution to make that was missed'.
- It is difficult to compare the studies, as many used rather individualistic methodologies.

Victim or crime surveys

Victim or crime surveys are not new, however, they became popular in the 1960s in the US as a result of growing concern with the reliability of the official statistics. It has been suggested that the victimisation studies shed a great deal of light on matters not reported and on discrepancies between the reports of crime, and the figures recorded by the police. These surveys may also ask questions about police behaviour, and the attitude of the respondents to police practices. They can also provide information as to why victims have not reported crime, and highlight which offences are more likely to be reported. Crime surveys have therefore become a very valuable tool.

Problems of crime surveys

- They cannot give a true picture of crimes which do not have any clearly identifiable victims, such as pollution.
- They have limited information concerning serious offences.
- Corporate crimes are difficult to cover.
- Feminists have been critical of the survey of methodology noting that the assaults which women receive are underestimated, since they are often unprepared to report them to the interviewer as their assailant may be in the same room at the time of the interview.
- Victims forget about crime.
- Victims may not know that they have been victimised.
- They may invent offences to impress the interviewer.
- They omit offences to speed up the process.
- Evidence has revealed that many respondents are quite ready to define certain events as not crime which could actually be called crimes.

Therefore inaccuracies are inevitable. There are several additional methods of gaining information and competing perspectives in the field of criminology. Among them are:

- Anthropological methods

  Originally used for the study of other 'ethnic groups', this is now applied to the investigation of life styles and attitudes in modern city life. These include joining a group, or watching their behaviour, and making observations about it over a period of time.

- Snowballing

- Case study of deviant biography

  The deviant biography offers an in-depth detailed biography. It yields information from a course of interviews, or personal knowledge, which can be considered in a leisurely manner. It is useful information for trying to understand the development of individual life styles and important decision opportunities; but can be self-serving and biased.

- Participant observation

  This involves the active collaboration of the sociologist. It involves the sociologist moving in person amidst the social group and environment to be understood. It has a long tradition, in particular with the University of Chicago, stemming from the 1920s where the head of the sociological department, Robert Park, stated that there was a difference between knowledge about, and acquaintance with, phenomenon. Participant observation attempts to reach into the experience and empathise with the subjects being viewed. The problems with participant observation involve:

  (i)   maintaining the balance between being a member of the group, and yet being able to objectively comment on it.

  (ii) not everyone can gain entry into the 'deviant world', it is often difficult to arrange.

The contemporary problem of reflexivity and criminal statistics – do we need a science of interpretation?

Official statistics in Criminal Justice provide a wealth of valuable information, including data on punishment systems, and the individuals who undergo punishment. However, contrary to the hopes of their originators, we cannot work out from the official statistics whether our contemporary societies are in the grip of a crisis threatening their very survival, or whether the increase in social goods, the spread of opportunity, a decrease of tolerance towards violence, and the increasing use of formal agencies (ie the police) to deal with troublesome situations, gives us record high rates of crime in the midst of personal security. Politicians seize upon the official statistics to declare the need for a war on crime, and argue that crime is threatening the very fabric of modern society. In an effort to achieve this, legislation is provided which aims to deter the image of the rational calculator. In the US the 'three strikes and you're out' (whereby life sentences without possibility of parole are imposed on offenders convicted of a third violent crime) legislation, if enforced, would halt all non-criminal court cases (due to the increase in contested trials) and create a record number of individuals in prison. As Diana Gordon (1991) defines it, we witness a *Justice Juggernaut: fighting street crime, controlling citizens* gaining in momentum to deal with a situation the reality of which we do not truly know. Furthermore, criminological research on penology specifies that the measures taken are most likely to be counter-productive and result in greater rates of criminal involvement. Ironically we now find our security threatened as much by the fear of crime and reaction to the perceived crisis, caused in part by the media reporting of the official statistics, than actual crime. Individuals who have the least rate of victimisation fear crime the most. We have so many figures, we turn from collecting them to asking what does it all mean? Our pursuit of a moral barometer produces an ambiguous instrument. What was meant to be an instrument of security ends up causing insecurity. (For qualifications on the present official statistics see *The Economist*, 15 October 1994.)

How did we get to the point where statistics dominate criminological discourse?

Historically, this dramatic increase in our use of numbers results, at least in part, from industrialisation and the influx of people from the country into the town; it was aided by the advance in sophistication of the government armies of the Napoleonic era. These vast armies entailed an echelon of quartermasters keeping track of how much was needed to feed, arm and equip units scattered throughout Europe, Egypt and the East. Accurate information proved as valuable as the weapons of war.

What sense can be made of the proliferation of numbers? To what extent do we need a computer to determine the meaning of social life? Do statistical forms of information provide appropriate images for theorising? The statistic is a quantification of social life. Such quantification is permissible on the basis of the identification of a domain of objects by way of their properties. Queletet, but not Durkheim, appears to have believed that crime was a deviation from the average state of *being*. In other words crime was a natural phenomenon, an ontology which was pre-methodologically given, and able to be quantified, rendered into figures by the simple act of observation and cataloguing. Whereas for Durkheim, crime was an act of censure, and thus crime was still natural, a truly moral or social interactive phenomena, ie act of man's reactions to events. What is the effect upon quantification? If the naturalness of crime is not some natural essentialist ontological state, but only a relational state of being, in other words, if recorded crime is not a reflection of some external reality oblivious to human action, but a reflection of process, then our attempts to make something meaningful out of these figures depend, not on the figures, but our capacity to see how the elements fit together. The question 'how much crime is there?' is reconstructed into 'what does it mean for these figures to be produced?' Or 'What does it mean for these figures to exist?'

Charles Lindblom (1990) argues that one result of this dominant approach in the social sciences is that human beings have been robbed of their capacity to understand their situation. This 'professional impairment' has occurred as a result of the translation of social life into the language of the calculable, the rigorous; the coherence of mathematical formula is produced at the expense of insight into the contexts of action, and the meaning or characteristics of social situations as the actors perceive them.

Perhaps two key examples are the reduction by criminological positivism of two of the most fertile bodies of American criminological theorising, anomie (or strain theory) and control theory, into a mass of sterile theorising. In both cases positivism has picked up these theoretical outlooks and applied them in the hope of finding quantifiable social laws which impel actors, in other words, flows of social forces which cause crime. The idea that we may be setting out interpretative ideas for social conditions which provide contexts and conditions, to which actors *respond* in variable and partially unique ways, is under-developed in the mainstream criminological approaches.

Strain theory

Durkheim sought to create a sociology capable of understanding the processes and effects of the transition from tradition-bound societies to modernity. In conditions of dramatic transformation a state of normlessness or anomie was engendered, a term that serves as the foundation for Robert Merton's (1938; 1957) strain theory of criminal behaviour. Merton's theory is one of the disjuncture between the goals, or desires, the dominant culture of a society instills in its members, and the socially accepted means of attaining them.

It is reasoned that if a person is thwarted in his or her efforts to realise these goals legitimately, he or she may attempt to achieve them via a variety of illegal manoeuvres. Lower social class individuals, frustrated by their inability to participate in the economic rewards of the wider society, are said to redirect their energies into criminal activity as a way of obtaining these rewards (Merton, 1938; 1968: 185ff).

- Success, measured by the amount of money and material possessions, is a strong value in American culture.
- Everyone is encouraged to believe that, like every other person, he has a right to be successful, and that by trying his best he will certainly achieve his goals.
- Nevertheless, because of social conditions and economic realities, not everyone, or every group, possesses the required means to succeed; hence, anomie and crime.

For Merton the dominant theme of American culture was the emphasis on monetary success, but this placed strains on individuals differentially located in the social structure. The American dream emphasis two images – one of monetary success, and the second of the possibility of social ascent for all members – while the social structure only allows the image to be a reality for a few. Different individuals experience strain differently depending on their location in the social structure; these different pressures typically produce various sorts of outcome.

The key term used was *anomie*, taken from Durkheim but with changes:

'Anomie is ... conceived as a breakdown in the cultural structure, occurring particularly when there is an acute disjunction between the cultural norms and goals and the socially structured capabilities of members of the group to act in accord with them. In this conception, cultural values may help to produce behaviour which is at odds with the mandates of the values themselves.

On this view, the social structure strains the cultural values, making action to accord with them readily possible for those occupying certain statuses within the society, and difficult or impossible for others. The social structure acts either as a barrier, or as an open door, to the acting out of cultural mandates. When the cultural and the social structure are mal-integrated, the first calling for behaviour and attitudes which the second precludes, there is a strain toward the breakdown of the norms; towards "normlessness" ' (1968: 216-17).

Merton proposed a typology of adaptation which is often represented in one of the most famous tables in criminology:

Mode of adaptation	Culture goals	Institutional means
I. Conformity	+	+
II. Innovation	+	-
III. Ritualism	-	+
IV. Retreatism	-	-
V. Rebellion	+/-	+/-

The last four of these are seen as deviant adaptations. Most of the activity labelled crime in America comes from the innovation response. American culture stresses the goal of material success for everyone, but the actual social structure does not provide legitimate means to achieve this. As a consequence individuals feel strain and resort to illegitimate means, ie crime, to achieve the cultural goal. Individuals who cannot achieve the cultural goal, but have been so strongly socialised into following only legitimate methods that they cling to these in a ritualistic way and sublimate the original aims, adopt the response of ritualism. For Merton this is a typically lower middle class adaptation, and was the result of a coincidence of strict socialisation and opportunities. It is the perspective of the frightened employee, the zealously conformist bureaucrat in the teller's cage of the private banking enterprise, or in the front office of the public works enterprise. Retreatism, by contrast, involves rejection of both goals and means–withdrawal from the social race altogether. The retreatist is in the society, but not of it. He has so strictly internalised notions of the legitimacy of certain means that he cannot innovate, but, lacking the opportunity to use legitimate means, he escapes from moral conflict by renouncing both means and goals. Into this category Merton places psychotics, aurists, pariahs, outcasts, vagrants, vagabonds, tramps, chronic drunkards and drug addicts. Rebellion involved not merely the negative rejection of social goals and means by the retreatist, but a positive attempt to replace them with another set seen as morally superior. Rebels endeavour to introduce a social structure in which the cultural standards of success would be sharply modified, and provision made for a closer correspondence between merit, effort and reward. For Merton, as for Durkheim, those labelled a rebel, revolutionary, non-conformist, heretic or renegade in an earlier time may become the cultural hero of today.

Strain theory has been read to hold a stable and optimistic view of human nature; man is basically a conforming being who only violates society's laws, norms, and rules after the disjunction between goals and means becomes so great, that he finds the only way he can achieve these goals is through illegal channels. Man is basically good, but the arrangements of the social structure create stress, strain, and eventually crime is engaged in to alleviate this tension. Since it is the fact that legitimate opportunities are unevenly distributed throughout a society which explains the presence of a strong link between crime and social class (Merton [1938] 1957), changing the opportunity structure should reduce crime. In discussing the foundations of strain theory, Merton maintains that a greater emphasis on goals than the means used in attaining them and a restriction of legitimate opportunities available to portions of the population are necessary conditions in the development of a sense of anomie and strain, which in turn contributes to society's crime problems.

The ideas of strain and anomie appear of fundamental importance. However, the sociology which took up these themes largely constructed tests of a barren and sterile positivism in the name of empirical investigations. The search was for statistical laws, or correlations, between class position and delinquent activity. Many of these studies have yielded results which were seen as largely inconsistent with Merton's original hypothesis. Generalisations were made, predictions attempted with data sets which assumed generality. Research used general indices – on social class, inequality, and the effect of dropping out of school, for instance – which were not sub-divided enough to get micro pictures, and too general to avoid ambiguity. The results obtained largely called into question many of the tenets supposedly espoused by strain theorists. The results of many of the earlier research studies on social class and crime were consistent with the supposition that more persons from lower than higher socioeconomic backgrounds engaged in various forms of illegal activity (see Reiss and Rhodes,

1961). More recently conducted investigations, however, particularly those in which self-report data have been utilised, show the relationship between social class and crime to be slight, if not insignificant (see Tittle, Villemez, and Smith, 1978), although controversy continues to surround the proposed association between social class and crime (see Braithwaite, 1981). It is argued that research on income inequality, while ultimately inconclusive, is surprising in light of Merton's structural expectations (see Messner, 1982; Stack, 1983). In addition, studies on school and crime suggest that dropping out of school normally leads to increased rather than decreased (as it was thought strain theory would predict) levels of antisocial conduct (see Shavit and Rattner, 1988; Thornberry, Moore and Christenson, 1985).

Some positivist studies have resulted in support of Merton's theory, Brennan and Huizinga (1975), for example, found that youth perceptions of limited opportunity, anomie, peer pressure, and negative labelling, accounted for 31% of the variance in the frequency of self-reported acts of delinquency in 730 adolescents. Cernkovich and Giordano (1979) argued that while male and female delinquents expressed a greater sense of blocked opportunity than male and female non-delinquents, this variable explained only 10% of the variance in delinquent behaviour. In an effort to examine the primary tenets of strain theory directly, Stack (1983) compared the reported rates of homicide and property crime, with the Paglin-Gini index of income inequality for all 50 US states. A multiple regression analysis of these data revealed that income inequality was associated with homicide, but not property crime. Stack reports further that a preliminary analysis of data collected on 29 nations yielded similar results. Some commentators argue that this finding presents problems for strain theory since Merton appears to argue that income inequality should lead to increased levels of economically oriented crime. But all this seems to work with a rather static model of society and of the communication effects of culture. We shall look at culture in Chapters Twelve and Thirteen, but here we can ask why is it thought that class or income can be measured in such a way that the effect of cultural messages are the same for all the members of a grouping? We know in life it simply is not the case. Even if we can group together a substantial body of persons into a category, the amount of contingency and diversity in life (in the receipt of cultural messages), means that any prediction which does not account for various sub-groupings and is loosely formulated is dubious.

Consider the way in which Merton phrased his scheme:

'It will be remembered that we have considered the emphasis on monetary success as one dominant theme in American culture ... The theory holds that any extreme emphasis upon achievement ... will attenuate conformity to the institutional norms governing behaviour designed to achieve the particular form of 'success' ... It is the conflict between the cultural goals and the availability of using institutional means – whatever the character of the goals – which produces a strain toward anomie.' (1968: 220)

Theorists and researchers critical of strain theory argue that this model suffers from redundancy to the extent that goal commitment, in the absence of differential means to goal attainment, may account for a person's involvement in criminal activity (Johnson, 1979; Kornhauser, 1978). Hirschi (1969) claimed to demonstrate that commitment to conventional aims was sufficient to explain criminal involvement, and that additional factors, such as those adhered to by strain theorists, were largely superfluous to the crime-goal relationship.

Listen to some of the criticisms:

- problems with its empirical validity;
- it is regarded as too general and imprecise (Bahr, 1979);
- it does not account for the criminality of persons growing up in middle-class homes (Elliott & Voss, 1974), this appears to be in contradiction to the second complaint and is simply not sustainable. As Box (1983) has demonstrated, anomie is a good theory to use to analyse white collar crime! (What was Micheal Milken, the founder of Junk Bonds, if not a great criminal innovator?);
- it overlooks important individual differences in behaviour (Wilson and Herrnstein, 1985);
- the original formulation placed individuals into box-like slots on a pin-ball machine;
- it is claimed to be unsuccessful in explaining why most working-class youth never resort to crime, or why many delinquents abandon the criminal way of life by the time they enter adulthood (Hirschi, 1969);
- contrary to the predictions of strain theory, high aspirations in working-class youth tend to correlate inversely with later delinquency (Elliott & Voss, 1974; Hirschi, 1969);
- while there is some support for Merton's contention that most Americans share middle-class goals (Erlanger, 1980), there is other research that disputes this basic premise of strain theory (Kitsuse and Dietrick, 1959; Lemert, 1972).

What has been the usual form of response? To try to integrate it with other models of criminal behaviour. This is to be expected, and welcomed, and has spawned a tradition specifically addressing particular forms of sub-cultural effects (see Chapter Twelve). Cloward and Ohlin (1960) tried to integrate strain theory with Sutherland's differential association approach, by arguing that the effects of strain will not operate unless one also has the opportunity to learn from delinquent peers. Later Elliott and Voss (1974) argued their support for the differential association component of the model, but rejected the strain/anomie aspect. Using a vast data base on youth behaviour, Elliott, Ageton, and Canter (1979) tried to combine strain theory with Hirschi's (1969) social control theory, a move many thought was combining polar opposites. The results were inconclusive.

What can we make of this?

Commentators have argued that because these large scale statistical investigations do not come up with specific correlations capable of generalisation then the theory has no creditability! In other words positivist scholars claim we cannot use the theory as a form of hermeneutics – we can only speak in terms of anomie if we can create some gigantic mathematical formula out of it.

Let us ask what we want from a theory. If the answer is an aid in understanding aspects of our predicament, to understanding features of modernity, then the judgment that a theory is enlightening is not to be judged on the condition that we can create arithmetical or quasi-mathematical measuring of all the steps involved in the understanding. What is the project criminology? Is it to try to play a part in the construction process? If so why should the desire to make theories count in that process be limited to theories that involve counting?

But there is another set of criticism aimed at Merton (and at Sutherland and the work of the Chicago School). It comes from writers on the right, for example Wilson and Herrnstein (1985), who assert that these 'perspectives were the product of sociological thought that tends to draw attention away from individual differences toward social categories'. Additionally, the right criticises these theories because the authors experienced 'reformist impulses that led them, implicitly or explicitly, to explain social problems by reference to those factors that are, or appear to be, susceptible to planned change'. But perhaps the greatest sin was mixing categories. Merton, it appears, has made the sin of believing that evil may flow from good.

> 'Whereas an older generation of criminologists, of which the Gluecks were very much a part, thought that evil causes evil (for example, bad families produce bad children), many members of the new generation were attracted to the idea that 'good' often causes evil (for example, that the desire for achievement, or the decisions of police and judges, will cause people to break the law). This view was most clearly suggested by Merton: a cardinal American virtue, "ambition", promotes a cardinal American vice, "deviant behaviour".' (all quotes, Wilson and Herrnstein, 1985: 215)

Each objection requires interpretation:

- Any theory must have a starting point, a set of presumptions upon which a logical structure is built. Theories seek truth, but must operate through conceptual schemes. Each conceptual scheme must be founded on a set of assumptions. (This is why it is very difficult to integrate social theories, since successful integration can only be achieved if the founding assumptions are translatable). Whereas sociology presumes that large scale social forces are crucial, Wilson and Herrnstein start from the assumption of methodological individualism. However, every act of analysis must be from a prior synthesis (albeit unarticulated) – is it the case that Wilson and Herrnstein prefer some underlying natural order with individuals constitutionally genetically endowed, rather than asking the question: by what social processes are individuals constituted?

- The argument regarding social reform is an argument concerned with the concept of modernity. Is modern society a normative project? A result of man's conscious and unconscious efforts, of planned consequences and unintended consequences, of a mixture of planning and chance, but for which man must take responsibility? Or is some underlying structural-functional development in play, and man should not attempt to take charge?

  Should man absolve himself from social responsibility for the social?

- Note the interconnection of these two issues. A policy of locating responsibility on to the subject and the near institutions (for example, the family) will appeal, when we fail to recognise the ontology of social forces over which we ought to take some control, if we specify the primacy of methodological individualism.

- The mixing of good and evil is exactly the point which stems from Durkheim, not only in the idea of unintended consequences, but additionally, though the idea of irony. It is not just that, for Merton, ambition may have the consequence of being a criminogenic factor, that innovating may lead to either Jesus Christ or Micheal Melkin – the founder of 'Junk Bonds' and convicted of massive white collar crime – (in his original article Merton specifically addressed the question of White Collar crime), but that a process of ironic consequences and contingencies may be involved. Thus, the same ontological subject (an American) may become a criminal, or a successful businessman, depending on where the accident of birth had located him in the social structure, and the set of contingent factors which may determine which adaption he adopts. There is nothing predetermined, there is nothing of a natural constitution which will a priori determine this outcome before social process are negotiated through. This seems to offend constitutional theorists like Wilson and Herrnstein. Their, sometimes not-so-subtle, agenda is to refute the possibility of social projects.

For most of this century the societies of the modern west, the societies of middle modernity, appeared relatively peaceful. Externally there were wars which badly affected the second decade, and whose impact led onto the Second World War. Capitalism nearly collapsed – first in Britain after the First World War, then in the US in the 1930s, it was saved by massive government intervention into the economy and the market (ie capitalism was saved by what appeared its enemy, aspects of socialist economics). It seemed a social structure, that following Lefebvre ([1971]; 1984), we can call the bureaucratic society of controlled consumption (and increasingly monopoly controlled production), was being set in place. It appeared to many that the good society was being formed; a place where human beings could become *satisfied*. Intellectuals today are notoriously difficult to appease, but for most of this century society was deemed to have a functional coherence (both the Marxist and the liberal agreed on this). Books were written stressing the functions of the nuclear family, the functions of this and that ... everything was functional, even those things that were not, which were dysfunctional and so proved the point even more! Of course we now can see – using Popper's analysis of science – that functionalism was the worst form of crass theorising (it is impossible to logically disprove if you accept its tenets!). But if you believe it, then it imposes a secular religion upon you (seen clearly in Marxism but also with its liberal adherents). The function of production was to provide those goods which would satisfy human needs. This was very clear in Marxist social policy, but was also fundamental to the liberal – except that the liberal could not specify through collective-decision making what the appropriate needs were – this had to be left to the market to sort out on the basis of responding to aggregations of individual preferences.

All this makes sense if human beings have ascertainable needs and these are apparent from the nature of humans as a generic species. But what is the case if humans do not have a basic fundamental nature with a set of natural needs, but instead consist of embodied interactional sites of desires and aspirations? What happens if the coherence of human nature depends upon the interaction of body and culture?

Merton's theory offers a specific interpretation of a particular set of public images of the social. We can understand the desire for money as a desire for the medium of exchange through which a more varied set of existential desires can be satisfied (or at least played with). Reflexively, we can understand the state of society in which the desire for material success is the dominant cultural goal as an indication of a crucial steering mechanism of social development. Merton's theory occupies a particular level of generality. It is not specifically located as a sub-section of some total social theory such as Marxism, but rather asked questions at a level some called 'middle range' theory. Ian Taylor (1994) includes Merton's theory in his discussion of 'the political economy' of crime; reading Merton as intending to offer a critique of the effects of the major cultural message of American society – a message which ranges across all the class structure. Most of the studies that have (mis)applied Merton have been empirical studies with limited theoretical ambitions.

What has happened to Merton? What can we take from him? It can be argued that the bureaucratic society of controlled consumption, and the placement of class via location *vis à vis* production, has grown into, and largely been supplemented by, a much greater fluidity of social status based on consumption power. No only has desire been unleashed in late-modernity as never before, but social stratification is complex and based increasingly on social resources and consumption power. The existential nature of late modern life (the multiple flows of images and communications passing through the self) has rendered the static nature of the Mertonian choices unbelievable. But this does not mean that the basic idea is false – indeed it appears to have even more power when we return to aspects of the original Durkheimean formulation.

Consider Nietzsche's attempt to probe beneath the desire for money: Nietzsche argues that when the value of an item is determined by its market exchange rate, in other words what the person who will consume it is willing to pay, then the ability to consume is the public display of one's power. Thus the desire for money is only the superficial signification of the will for power:

> 'The means employed by the lust for power have changed, but the same volcano continues to glow, the impatience and the immoderate love to demand their sacrifice: and what one formerly did "for the sake of God" one now does for the sake of money, that is to say, for the sake of that which now gives the highest feeling of power and good conscience' (*Daybreak*: Aph: 204).

Power is not a simple need, it is a deeply interpretative want.

Social control theory

American sociology, largely through the work of Travis Hirschi (1969), took up a reading of Durkheim's ideas combined with the assumption of classical criminology that a tendency to crime is normal in any human being, to argue that criminal behaviour results from a failure of conventional social groups (family, school, pro-social peers) to bind or bond with the individual. To maintain social order society must teach the individual not to offend. We are born with a natural proclivity to violate the rules of society, thus delinquency is a logical consequence of one's failure to develop internalised prohibitions against lawbreaking behaviour.

> 'Delinquency is not caused by beliefs that require delinquency but is rather made possible by the absence of (effective) beliefs that forbid delinquency.' (Hirschi, 1969: 198)

Hirschi's theory focuses on how conformity is achieved; his is not a theory of motivation but of constraint. While it culminates in the thesis of self-control which we have been working to understand, from his original 1969 work, we can see that although allowing for external sources of social control, Hirschi stresses the role of internal controls in directing social behaviour.

Hirschi's (1969) social control theory of criminal behaviour was developed around four key concepts and several important institutions. The concepts are those of *attachment, commitment, involvement,* and *belief,* while the institutions are those of the *family,* the *school* and the *peer* group. They combine in that:

> 'Positive feelings toward controlling institutions and persons in authority are the first line of social control. Withdrawal of favourable sentiments toward such institutions and persons at the same time neutralises their moral force.' (1969: 127)

Attachment denotes the strength of any ties that may exist between the individual and primary agents of socialisation, such as parents, teachers, and community leaders. Thus, it is a measure of the degree to which law-abiding persons serve as a source of positive reinforcement for the individual.

Commitment involves an investment in conformity or conventional behaviour, and a consideration of future goals that are incompatible with a delinquent lifestyle. *Involvement* is a measure of one's propensity to participate in conventional activities, and directs the individual toward socially valued success. The more time one spends in conventional activities, the less opportunity one will have to engage in illegal behaviour. *Belief* denotes acceptance of the moral validity of societal norms, and reflects the strength of one's conventional attitude. Hirschi's work is positivist in that each of these elements is meant to be capable of empirical measurement and quantification. In his original formulation he did not specify how these four elements might interact, but was content to hypothesise a relationship between attachment and commitment, attachment and belief, and commitment and involvement. Delinquency was associated with weak attachments to conventional institutions and modes of conduct.

Hirschi (1969) tested his social control theory by administering a questionnaire to a group of 4,000 high school students. He found a meaningful connection between self-reported delinquency and poor attachment to one's parents, and support for the validity of each of the four key elements (ie attachment, commitment, involvement, belief). He has provided fertile ground for many other studies. For example, Michael Hindelang (1973) observed a negative correlation between delinquency and each of Hirschi's key elements, only differing from Hirschi in that, while Hirschi found a negative relationship between peer attachment and delinquency, Hindelang recorded a positive association. Hindelang argued that Hirschi's theory requires a greater elaboration in terms of peer attachment since divergent outcomes will likely result from attachment to conventional rather than unconventional peers.

Hirschi's social control theory spanned a vast literature on juvenile offenders, mostly supportive (see Austin, 1977; Bahr, 1979; Jensen and Eve, 1976; Johnson, 1979; Poole and Regoli, 1979; Rankin, 1977). There has been less specification for how the theory accounted for adult offences.

These studies appear to make a good effort at reducing family attachment into a calculable entity. An example is Wiatrowski, Griswold, and Roberts (1981) who performed a multivariate path analysis of longitudinal data collected on 2,213 Michigan high school students. After controlling for ability, social class, and school performance, Wiatrowski et al, found general support for social control theory, although they redesigned key elements of the theory of social control to help mathematical operationality. Whereas attachment to parents, involvement with conventional activities, and belief in moral validity of the existing social structure were all part of the multivariate solution, commitment tended to drop out of the analysis (possibly because of redundancy or low reliability), and several factors overlooked by Hirschi (eg dating, school attachment) worked their way into the equation. This is fairly typical: the basic idea of the social control model receives general empirical support, but the theoretical entities behind the data get somewhat modified and refined.

The desire to typologise and analyse particular variables, and link these with specific types of crime is also strong. For instance, Jill Rosenbaum (1987) used self-report data from the Seattle Youth Study (Hindelang, Hirschi & Weiss, 1981) to group subjects by offence category (violent behaviour, property crimes, drug offences) and correlate to offence type. She argued that social control theory successfully accounted for drug offences, but did only a fair job in accounting for property crimes and a poor job in accounting for violent behaviour. We then have to fit the nature of violence into positivism.

There have been numerous attempts to integrate social control with other theoretical perspectives. Hence, several recent research studies show that dropping out of school is normally accompanied by increased, rather than decreased, levels of subsequent criminality (Bachman and O'Malley, 1978; Polk, Adler, Bazemore, Blake, Cordray, Coventry, Galvin and Temple, 1981; Shavit and Rattner, 1988; Thornberry et al, 1985), a relationship that falls more in line with social control theory than the strain model. But why should they be seen as mutually exclusive? Stephen Cernkovich (1978) found support for both the strain and social control models in a self-report study of 412 male high school students and noted that the combined effect of these two theories accounted for more variance than did either model separately.

We can go around in circles weaving a merry dance. In an analysis of data from the Richmond Youth Project, Gary Jensen (1972) concluded that control theory was supported, over differential association as an explanation of delinquent patterns of behaviour, but when Matsueda (1982) reanalysed the same data he came to an opposite conclusion! While Thompson, Mitchell, and Dodder (1984) report that their findings, on family attachment, peer associations, and delinquency are also more congruent with differential association than social control conceptualisations, Amdur (1989) finds fault with how the variables in this study were measured. With a study with greater attention to the concepts of investigation, John Hepburn (1976) discerned greater support for social control theory, than Sutherland's differential association perspective in a sample of 139 mid-Western males ages 14 to 17. Using a series of partial correlations to test these two theories, Hepburn determined that delinquent definitions (eg level of personal restraint, and willingness to engage in law-breaking behaviour) preceded delinquent associations. Poole and Regoli (1979) also ascertained support for the social control formulation on peer influence and crime: Adolescents with weak parental support were more susceptible to negative peer influence, while strong parental support served to insulate adolescents from the effects of anti-social peers.

Social control theory draws upon the insights of classicism while trying to create a positivist language. It is one sided, in that it does not address the issue of socio-cultural and socio-structural sources of motivations to offend. It works with an image of human nature that implies that crime is the inevitable result of lack of proper controls. Hirschi is guilty of adopting a manipulative view of family relationships (for example, the young person who has a part-time job is less able to be controlled by his or her parents, since they no longer have sole control of the purse strings). How can bonds be captured in positivist language? Again it appears to over-predict: a substantial proportion of poorly bonded persons do not develop delinquent patterns of adjustment (Elliott *et al*, 1979). Hirschi has also been criticised for not specifying how bonds are severed, broken, or fail to form in the first place (Colvin and Pauly, 1983). Additionally, Colvin and Pauly take Hirschi to task for adopting a largely dichotomous approach (strong-weak) to an issue (bonding) that seems to vary along several dimensions, qualitative as well as quantitative, and for minimising the significance of the socialising agent in the actual bonding process. At least, in his attempts to bring in individualist features – unlike Wilson and Herrnstein (1985) who argue that some individual differences exert a direct influence on crime and delinquency – Hirschi considers the impact of individual differences (eg intelligence, temperament), to have an indirect effect (via bonding).

The interaction of socialisation and control, or restraint, is a vital aspect of the dialectics of modernity. But, as Hirschi's formulation has been taken up by American sociology, the information being created is so capable of correction and methodological qualification, that we are in danger of being lost in mindless information games. Some criminologists, who apparently always wanted to be professors in mathematics departments, find social control theory difficult to use; while it is generalisable, suggestive of ideas and reasonably well substantiated from an empirical standpoint, they see it as lacking in precision and operationality in terms of reducing its suppositions to clear mathematical quantities.

But a workable control theory can be achieved that does not surrender to the numbers fetish. Friday and Hade's (1976) explanation of delinquency in industrialised societies, for example, combines theories of modernisation, urbanity and social integration.

They argue that conformity will be greatest among youth drawn into intermeshed role relationships across five institutional spheres: kin, neighbourhood or community, school, work and peers. The more that activities and time are dispersed across the five spheres, the more likely a youth is to avoid delinquent behaviour; and the greater the proportion of youth in a society are so immersed, the lower the rate of youth crime. Youth who are involved in one or other sphere to the exclusion of the others, are more likely to deviate than integrated youth, because intimacy in many spheres promotes commitment to societal values and norms by exposing the youth to larger numbers of conforming definitions, and by imbuing him or her with a sense of being part of the whole. No one sphere, can become too important, because the other spheres counterbalance.

Further, Friday and Hage contend that the degree of social integration so conceived is affected by the level of modernisation and urbanisation. The more modernised and urbanised a society, the more are youth isolated from active participation excluded from at least some of the five institutional spheres, due to extension of the period of training for adult roles. Most modern youth spend no time and have no involvement in the institutional sphere of work; partly as a result of that, they are limited to kin and community relationships. Since youth must rely upon role relationships in school and among peers, they are inherently less constrained by overlapping role relationships, and they are more subject to peer pressures for fun and status seeking, which often involve deviant or criminal behaviour. Hence, the greater the modernisation and urbanisation, the less the overall integration of youth, and the freer they are to commit criminal acts.

What are we to make of these 'control theories'?

The first thing that strikes one located in Europe and not in America reading this tradition of work is how American and narrowly focused all this is. When a European criminologist thinks of control, his or her thoughts are located at the level of the nation state, or the depiction of gender, or the construction of a power/knowledge spiral. Today it is virtually impossible to talk of control in Europe without immersing oneself in the traditions of Nietzsche and Weber, via their modern interpreter Michel Foucault, the demands of the social structure, via a reading of Marx or Durkheim, or the whole structuralism debate occasioned by structural anthropology.

The big problem European intellectuals have tried to cope with, is how to relate the actions of individuals and groups to the level of state–societies, in such a way that the nature of nationwide organised practices and restrictions become apparent. The problems of the individual *vis-à-vis* control are the generalisable forms of control of the capitalist nation state, or the socialist state, the liberal state, the utilitarian (panoptician) state, and so forth. They may not have been able successfully to make the connections but that was how the question was framed (see *The New Criminology*, Taylor, Walton and Young, 1973 for example).

American intellectuals, on the other hand, do not conceive of control on the level of the nation state, but as a function of the relation between the individual and his immediate surroundings, the urban district, the family, the peer group, the school. To the European, American writing in this area has seemed micro-sociological, while to the American, the European writings have appeared to be really politics. The reason perhaps is that the writings of the European scholar are always a process of arguing against an earlier form of social structure and control, so that a new form can be constructed, while the American counterpart is writing in the context of the image of constructing over the frontier. So much as the European is afraid of the *ancien regime,* and the revival of a totalitarian state, the American is disputing the merits of radical liberalism and civic republicanism. The American sociology which operated at a higher level, such as Robert Merton's middle range theories, and Talcott Parsons (arrived at a theory of modern societies as functional systems, themselves differentiated into functionally related structures of sub-systems), substituted some other conception for the state.

What is the impact of post-modernism? Surprisingly, we have to adopt a lot of American theorising, since the post-modern condition is one that demands theorising beyond the level of the nation state. If we have to take from a large basket of different perspectives, this is not a measure of failure, but a reflection of the diverse and conflicting ways it is possible to interpret social existence. In doing so, however, we need to face up to the conditions of late-modernity. We do not need to simply discard positivism, but to create a form of rationality sufficiently powerful to do justice to the human constitution, and sufficiently precise to enable us to engage in our projects, without destroying its objects of analysis. The aim of positivism was to come to a secure knowledge of what is, but with humanity the purpose of knowing what we are, cannot be distinguished from the task of knowing how to be. That is to say, that the social sciences cannot shuffle off the task of being moral sciences by adopting the guise of mathematics. For, in the rush to busy ourselves counting, we must always be in the business of working out what counts. Accepting, of course, we do not want to lose ourselves to the impersonal power of bureaucracy.

CHAPTER NINE

POSITIVISM AND THE DREAM OF ORGANISED MODERNITY

'Another consequence of the development of bio-power was the growing importance assumed by the action of the norm, at the expense of the juridical system of the law. Law cannot help but be armed, and its arm, *par excellence,* is death; to those who transgress it, it replies, at least as a last resort, with that absolute menace. The law always refers to the sword. But a power whose task is to take charge of life needs continuous regulatory and corrective mechanisms ... Such a power has to qualify, measure, appraise, and hierarchise, rather than display itself in its murderous splendour; it does not have to draw the line that separates the enemies of the sovereign from its obedient subjects; it effects distributions around the norm. I do not mean to say that the law fades into the background or that the institutions of justice tend to disappear, but rather that the law operates more and more as a norm, and that the judicial institution is increasingly incorporated into a continuum of apparatuses (medical, administrative, and so on) whose functions are for the most part regulatory. A normalising society is the historical outcomes of a technology of power centred on life.' (Michel Foucault, 1980: 144)

Criminology and the dream of organised modernity

Positive criminology surrounded itself with a meta-narrative of reason, progress, and humanitarian reform. From the late 19th century until the advent of labelling theory in the 1970s, major text books claimed modern criminal justice institutions were an orderly, functional and rational evolutionary advance over the pre-modern (for example Barnes and Teeters, 1951). While the pre-modern person was viewed as born into a locality of status and custom, constrained by ritual and barbaric punishments, the modern individual inhabited the practices of a rationalised and knowledge-led, bureaucratic modernity.

As late-modernity took stock of itself, writers declared this was not only bad anthropology (full of the eurocentric emphasis and false in its depicting of the pre-modern), but bad sociology (in that the assumption of orderly laws of social development cannot be sustained), self-defeating in terms of social control (in that it down-played all methods of settling disputes by compensation, restitution, mediation, and ritual symbolism), and possibly anti-communitarian (in that it took important process of social control and organisation out of the hands of the locality) – bureaucracy and positivism became subjected to a variety of attacks.

Instead of the development of modernity being a unilinear development of reason, progress, humanitarianism and civilisation, modernity was seen to be a complicated structure of various forms of social control. Several themes are worth mentioning:

- the development of social distance;
- the development of bureaucracy and its linkage with knowledges of disciplinisation;
- the dialectical processes of civilisation.

Social distance

The pre-modern person was embedded into locality. Socialised by ritual and custom, he could recognise friend from foe in the identities of neighbour and stranger, or in the uniforms of status. The central feature of modernity, without which the whole system of a common body of laws and criminal labels could not be possible, is the development of the modern state and organised bureaucracy. As opposed to small scale societies, which are sometimes referred to as stateless or Acephalus, modern society sees a transformation in the process and rituals for dealing with troublesome situations and mechanisms of socialisation within the social body. It is this development which organisationally creates the structures involving the labelling of certain persons and activities as 'criminal'. Michalowski (1981) identifies stateless societies as characterised more by order and cooperation than by chaos and competition. They display little stratification in terms of differential access to material goods and political power and are small economically cooperative and relatively equalitarian societies with simple technology and divisions of labour based mainly upon age and sex. These societies lack rulers or governments with the power to command, direct and correct the behaviour of others.

Such anthropological accounts describe the pre-modern state of nature in opposing terms to the narratives which Liberal writers of the Enlightenment, such as Thomas Hobbes, relied upon. Against Hobbes' assumption that humans are essentially autonomous, self-interested creatures, whose egoistic pursuits need to be formally restrained to avoid chaos and anarchy, the anthropological picture of acephalus societies suggests that the tribal forms of life achieved the opposite outcome through effective forms of interaction and socialisation.

We have seen how in defining the spirit of positivism, August Comte presented modernity as the age where power was led by positive knowledge. Modernity was to be the rule of scientific expertise. In large part, the image of bureaucratic managerial expertise has become a deeply embedded cultural icon of modernity. It offered a new form of social control – control based not on embedment but social *distance*.

This theme was central to Nietzsche, who argued that modern values and intellectual horizons were formed under *a pathos of distance* whereby modern man, the individual, begins his ascent into an open world; as an individual or member of a group he demands a modernity capable of embodying his own plans and projects in the natural and social world. He disdains the techniques and values of the past in favour of those he calls modern. However, modernity is not without its rituals of social control. Although dressed up in terms of rational advance, formal social control in modernity appears to be characterised by a history of ritualistic exclusion. The offender is not reconciled with victim or the victim's kin. Such a structure of reconciliation would place a great deal of power over crime and deviance at a local level. However modernity is characterised by such power being given to the state and criminal justice operating as a function of state bureaucracies.

As modernity advanced, criminal justice and welfare systems developed concrete institutions and their staff to deal with crime, offenders and deviants – but what comes first? Are mad and criminal individuals simply thrown up and correctly recognised and then sent to a special institution, an asylum or a prison? Or do prisons and asylums come into existence and demand clients?

The major commentators, for example, Scull (1976, 1979) Rotham (1971, 1980) and Foucault (1965, 1973, 1976) are divided on many issues, but all agree that with the processes of industrialisation and division of labour:

> 'The community acquired an ethical power of segregation which permitted it to eject, as into another world, all forms of social uselessness.' (Foucault, 1965: 58)

Foucault argues that institutions demand clients, and as the control and subsequent elimination of leprosy began emptying the royally endowed charity leprosariums in Europe in the 14th and 17th centuries, by the 17th and 18th centuries these institutions were being filled with an assortment of socially unwanted people: the poor, the insane, the criminal, the destitute through physical impairments, and the orphaned. The institutions took in the various populations and only with the 19th century came the classifying and segregation of the unwanted into different and specialised institutions as we know it today.

Foucault highlights one aspect of a complicated process, however, this isolation and exclusion of the deviant came to be conducted under the legitimacy of legal rational forms of discourse. Authorised legal exclusion of individuals is a fundamental feature of formal modern law. Administered by fulltime agents of the state, legal regulation and specialised diagnosis by recognised social scientific experts has come to be the enforcing mechanism of the power of centralised authority.

The advanced division of labour means that decisions made about the members of the lowest classes, the labouring working class, the social residue (the classes of people from which most of the traditional offenders come from), are made by professionals (lawyers, judges, probation officers, doctors, psychiatrists, prison governors, parole boards) using specialised techniques. The behaviour of the person becomes institutionally criminalised or pathologised (medicalised). The criminal became the subject of generalisable knowledge and rules, rather than local knowledge about his or her particular environment and conditions. This process has intensified in recent years with the introduction of sentencing guidelines and tables which indicate the disposition that particular crimes should receive: the result? The individual is not looked at as a spatially located social network. As the Norwegian criminologist Nils Christie has recently put it:

'A political decision to eliminate concern for the social background of the defendant involves much more than making these characteristics inappropriate for decision on pain. By the same token, the offender is to a large extent excluded as a person. There is no point in exposing a social background, childhood dreams, defeats – perhaps mixed with some glimmer from happy days – social life, all those small things which are essential to a perception of the other as a full human being. With the Sentencing Manual and its prime outcome, the Sentencing Table, crime is standardised as Offence Levels, a person's life as Criminal History Points, and decisions on the delivery of pain are reduced to finding the points where two lines merge.' (1993: 138)

These rituals of reordering declare they are non-rituals – thus the rituals of dealing with troublesome situations are limited in their flexibility and lose any prospect for the reconciliation of the conflicting parties. The advent of the sentencing manual is the logical conclusion of a procedure that cannot involve diversity unless diversity is written into the rules of the game. Formal legal rationality implies usually predictability, certainty and uniformity of outcome. Furthermore, in dealing with the trouble maker the legal institution strips the conflicting parties of the power to manage the conflict and converts each group into a labelled entity, ie an offender and a victim, and the system operates according to the meanings invested with these labels. Nils Christie (1977) has termed this the theft of conflicts from the people by the state.

Howard Becker (1963) argued that under the criminal justice methodologies of modern societies, the troublesome individual becomes defined as an offender or criminal, and is symbolically forced outside the normal life of the social group. In these processes he is singled out rather than reconciled to the social body; he is ritualistically converted into an 'outsider'. Problems and troublesome situations become labelled as offences, and opened to management not as human indices of trouble inside the social body, but as criminal acts which are outside the normal. The discourse of crime symbolically reflects the notion that crimes are invasions of the social body rather than eventualities from within. One effect is that the modern structures of formal social control actually prevent members giving attention to troublesome situations which require social measures, but draws attention onto those individuals who have committed offences and who can be excluded. Such individuals become labelled as criminals and are seen as the trouble. Whereas the reordering rituals of pre-modern societies attend to situations of trouble and attempt to reconcile the parties involved, modern societies may give less attention to the situations of trouble, attending instead to the troublemaker, thus burdening that individual with blame and becomes, drawn into the necessity to exclude or incapacitate him or her. Usage of the whole criminal offender mentality may thereby lessen our ability to face up to and deal with the very troublesome situations out of which the people we so label emerge.

The effect of the criminal label and procedure of treatment/punishment may reduce the binds of the social networks in which the individual was located and which constrained and sheltered him (thus informally controlling and preventing crime); thus increasing the likelihood of offending in the future. The growth of formal systems of control may reduce informal or localised control.

Moreover, the continuation of troublesome situations in the face of the failure of the rituals to successfully control such behaviour may lead to a progressive weakening of confidence in institutions and rituals. This in turn may lead to demands for greater methods of exclusion focused on the criminal. Crime thus demands more criminal justice and crime control measures, which creates more criminal labels which feeds back into more criminal acts, which in turn stimulates a demand for more criminal justice and crime control measures.

Some commentators, such as Malcolm Specter (1981) and Luke Hulseman (1986), argue that the concept of crime has become too foundational in our modern methods of thinking about troublesome people. Spector reminds us that there are a number of other methods of social disapproval and control such as concepts of tort, sin, disease and the development of streamlined civil procedures.

In early modernity a crucial 'job' of law was to ensure predictability in social relations, the positive spirit sought to render the foundations of a now-unpredictable social world largely understandable and thus controllable. The task was to create an edifice of knowledge bases and scientific laws to control the conditions wherein man found himself; however, as Weber warned, the danger was that man may himself soon become only one item in the overall package to be controlled, or exterminated if he remained opaque to analysis. If man was only to be known by the methodologies of science and placed in the categories of bureaucracy, a new form of tyranny may be formed – we tend to associate the mention of the horrors of mass tyranny with the names of Hitler or Stalin, but Weber was pointing to a feature intimate to modernity itself.

The development of bureaucracy and the knowledges of disciplinisation

Under the influence of Weber and Nietzsche, criminologists in the 1970s came to look for power in other forms than as expressed through law. Sociology had been stressing the reality of bureaucratic power, and criminology came to realise that positivism was implicated in the disciplining of the human subject. The French social theorist Michel Foucault defined positivism as part of a new kind of power which emerged in the 19th century which he called biopolitics, based around the idea of the norm. *The law of the classical* criminologist, the 'juridical system of law', becomes complemented by a power which provides the structure and organises, administers, and constitutes activities and forms of social life, an essential regulatory mechanism:

There are two modes or sites for techniques of regulation.

'First, the disciplines offer a "anatomo-politics of the human body" and centre on the body as a machine: its disciplining, the optimisation of its capabilities, the extortion of its forces, the parallel increase of its usefulness and its docility, its integration into systems of efficient and economic controls.' (Foucault, 1980: 144)

'Second, regulation occurs at a more general level of a "bio-politics of the population" and centres on the species body, the body imbued with the mechanics of life and serving as the basis of the biological process: propagation, births and mortality, the level of health, life expectancy and longevity, with all the conditions that can cause these to vary.' (Ibid: 139-140)

Foucault thereby asks us to reflexively consider the status of the positivist discourses on the body and the depiction of the other as dangerous or degenerate. Naturalist views of the body are implicated in the repeated attempts made by the dominant in society to justify their position with reference to the supposed inferior biological make-up of the dominated. Consider who have been the outsiders of modernity, the others who have not shared in its rewards: there are three major groups, the mob, women and the ethnically other.

Some commentators have traced the growing fear of the body's irrationality to the protestant reformation which stressed personal piety, individual judgments, self-control and self-scrutiny. Winthrop Jordan notes that contacts with others from overseas were useful to Englishmen in the 18th and 19th centuries as social mirrors wherein by observing 'savages' the Englishmen could see attributes which they suspected in themselves but of which they could not speak. As the body became one among the other entities in the world as a site for observation, instead of openly confronting and talking about the fears and concerns of the flesh, the dominant white male dealt with his collective anxiety by projecting them onto the bodies of women and blacks. Women's bodies were thus inherently unstable, a source of temptation which threatened to corrupt the rationality of the white male existence. Their legitimate role was to reproduce a healthy race fit for domestic and colonial rule. The uncivilised bodies of blacks represented unsuppressed urges and irrational powers constituting physically powerful but uncontrolled sexual beings which represented a threat to the moral order of Western civilisation. This was most visible in greatly exaggerated reports of the sexual appetites of black men and the size of the African penis. The early evolutionary ideas postulated a close evolutionary relationship between the African and the ape. James Walvin (1982) relates how for much of the 17th and 18th centuries it was commonly believed that sexual intercourse took place between Africans and apes.

Some of the ideas concerning black bodies may come out of the need for ideologies to legitimate the experience of imperialist domination and slavery but it is quite likely that ideas of 'white' and 'black' predated imperial domination and were fitted onto the experience of contact. For Jordan:

'White and black connoted purity and filthiness, virginity and sin, virtue and baseness, beauty and ugliness, beneficence and evil, God and the devil.' (1982: 44)

Clearly such distinctions aided the legitimation of colonisation and slavery. From its beginnings, the European slave trade produced a discourse which portrayed African men and women as savages who were ugly, violent and lascivious. When attacked in the 18th century the slave trade was defended partly through defining the African in terms of their otherness from European culture – whereas the European male was civilised and rational, Africa was a pre-social locality, exhibiting a state of nature which was inherently incapable of self-government, in large part due to the unrestrained biological drives of its primitive peoples. The growing empirical sciences purported to identify the reasons why blacks were constitutionally inferior. As Paul Broca, explained using craniometry:

'A prognathous [forward jutting] face, more or less black colour of the skin, woolly hair and intellectual and social inferiority are often associated, while more or less white skin, straight hair and an orthognathous [straight] face are the ordinary equipment of the highest groups in the human species ... A group with black skin ... has never been able to raise itself spontaneously to civilisation.' (Quoted in Gould, 1981: 83-4)

The condition of the black body and its potential for physical labour and breeding defined its worth in exchange in slave trading. It also justified many of the para-judicial punishments which post-dated emancipation. In the lynching of blacks between 1885 and 1900 (which was mostly done in public with high prices being paid for choice seats and often special trains being laid on to transport white families from some distance away) rape was only asserted in one third of all cases, however, the justification used in all cases included protecting white women from the bestial black male (Carby, 1987). In many lynchings the final act was castration, for which a member of the public often paid a special price to perform.

It is tempting to believe that we have escaped from these beliefs – but consider what roles are offered to black actors or the presentation of the black body in magazines and soft-porn (as well as hard porn). In mostly white pornography the occasional black is both allowed and reduced to his or her extreme sexuality.

In contemporary America while 50% of men convicted of murder involving rape in the Southern states are white, over 90% of men executed for this offence are black. Most of these were accused of the rape of white women, while Staples (1982) maintained that as of the early 1980s no white male had ever been executed for raping a black woman.

The imagery of the black body varies between races. In Mrinalini Sinha's (1987) analysis of the ideology of British imperialism in late 19th century Bengal, Bengali men were defined as effeminate. This questioned masculinity made them unfit to share political and administrative power. Early or child marriage was evidence of unrestrained sexual desire, and these early sexual experiences corrupted the moral fibre making Bengali's incapable of exercising rational restraint in other areas.

The negative construction of black bodies has made them targets for various forms of moral panics. Restrictive health criteria were introduced as part of immigration controls in 1905 legitimated on the basis of fears of degeneration of the British race.

Various groups have been so associated. In the 1870s and 1880s Jewish refugees from mainland Europe were considered less civilised, unclean and immoral while in the 1950s blacks took on labels the Irish and Jews had taken in the 19th century. West indians, in particular, were seen as carefree, low-living, immoral, disorderly colonial peoples. Whereas in the 1850s Irish immigrants were considered as particularly dangerous, in the 1950s their arrival was officially hardly noticed despite the fact that they outnumbered immigrants from the New Commonwealth.

The visualisation of the body provided a way out of one of the great practical problems for early liberal modernity. The implications of liberal philosophy appeared to be for universality and inclusivity. For example, liberal modernity espoused universal, inalienable and equal rights. How then could the real world of male domination over women be maintained?

The simple answer, as Laqueur (1987: 19) puts it was to postulate 'a biology of incommensurability'. A naturalist interpretation of women's bodies justified the inequalities in gender relations in the 18th and 19th centuries. Thus by investigating the body we could see the very basis for the division in human identity and social demarcation of role and rewards. Specifically science demonstrated their unstable bodies and fragile minds. To be a woman was to possess a mind and a body unable to withstand the rigours of mental work, and unsuitable for major calculations. The lesson to be drawn from the investigation of women's bodies was that they were fitted by nature for the production and care of children and thus should be restricted to the important task of socialising and moralising the children.

Arguments by women to be included in the mainstream of modernity could be easily disposed of through science. Gustave Le Bon after measuring the huge total of 13 skulls felt able to conclude that women:

'... represent the most inferior forms of human evolution and that they are closer to children and savages than to an adult, civilised man ... A desire to give them the same education, and, as a consequence to propose the same goals for them, is a dangerous chimera.' (Quoted in Gould, 1981: 104-5)

Furthermore, overtaxing the brain of women would interfere with their reproductive ability. Moreover, the periodic disturbances which menstruation imposed on women meant they were unsuited for any role which required consistency of orientation.

Positivism thus helped determine the meaning of the liberal constitution; it gave substance to the transformation of early, or liberal modernity, into middle or organised modernity. It helped demarcate those fit to be insiders and those who, by 'nature', must be outsiders. Michel Foucault linked the rise of positivism to the concept of governmentality, which covers a new form of political rationality which sees the task of ruling as the calculated supervision and maximisation of the forces of society, the dynamics of the population; the guidance and regulation of the health and performance of the population, its wealth, health, longevity, its capacity to wage wars and to engage in labour and so forth. As an object of rule, population requires knowledge of the numbers of subjects, their ages, their longevity, their sicknesses and types of death, their pleasures, their desires, their habits and vices, their rates of reproduction.

As modernity develops the authorities have new tasks for which the law is unsuitable, these are tasks of maximising the forces of the population and the individuals within it. The questions become how to minimise their troubles, how to organise them in the most efficacious manner. Law does not need to know fully about subjects in order to prohibit activities, but to govern rationally the concerns of subjects it is necessary to know them; to understand their state, to recognise their preferences – to recognise who the subjects of your government are. To govern rationally a territory, a population requires that you know this territory, this population. A certain social geography is required:

> 'To govern a population one needs to isolate it as a sector of reality, to identify certain characteristics and processes proper to it, to make its features notable, speakable, writable, to account for them according to certain explanatory schemes. Government thus depends upon the production, circulation, organisation, and authoritisation of truths that incarnate what is to be governed, which make it thinkable, calculable, and practicable.' (Rose, 1990: 6)

Such knowledges need to be transcribable. The phenomenon to be investigated needs to be translated into information which can be recorded, transcribed onto paper, computer disks, made into diagrams, tables, and, above all else, recorded in numbers.

Governing the population came to mean creating a bourgeois citizenship

In *Legislators and Interpreters* (1987) Bauman's thesis of development in modernity was two-fold. The project of the enlightenment was simultaneously geared to reorganising the state around the function of planning, designing and managing the reproduction of social order and towards creating an entirely new, and consciously designed, social mechanism of disciplining action, aimed at regulating and regularising the socially relevant life of the subjects of the teaching and managing state.

Two themes shine through Bauman's work:

* the destruction of localised forms of life which are then reconstructed in light of the new disciplines – a process which inevitably involves the intellectual constructing images of normalcy etc;
* the social structural aspect where the construction of the modern state and civil society requires a form of subject (citizen) to be (un)consciously created.

Bauman describes the ferocity of the fear and assault on popular customs and local cultures in the name of the domestication of *les classes dangereuses*. For

Bauman, as for Nietzsche, the modern subject, the citizen of the new state and its intellectual discourse of law and rationality, was secured through a brutal violence (the punishments of the ancient regime and their transformation into the reasoning of the reformatory prison). The intellectuals applied supposedly neutral scientific knowledge to reshape the ideas of the proper functioning of social objects and the relations between social orders and behaviour.

Positivism depicted the illiterate and unwashed masses as uncivilised. This continued a tendency clearly apparent in Beccaria's text (1764) where he identified the past with ignorance and barbarism. Local customs, for example, the weight given to the concept of honour with its duels and the violence of the penalties openly and publicly celebrated, were to be overcome. The masses seemed to epitomise all that was regressive, uneducated, irrational. Urbanisation and an increasing division of labour created a splitting of social worlds, the powerful and wealthy were withdrawing from participation in the festivals and activities of popular culture. For Pick:

'The lowest stratum was both a recognisable sector of the population and simultaneously the destination of all individuals when forced into crowds. Between culture and anarchy, safety and activist violence, there was only "a very thin and precarious partition". To enter the crowd was to regress, to return, to be thrown back upon a certain non-individuality, the lowest common denominator of a crowd of ancestors – a world of dangerous instincts and primitive memories.' (1989: 223)

The contrast with the upper middle class appeared to be between *us* and *them*, between a *man civilised and perfected* and a *brute and savage man*. Lombroso was clear 'Why does the criminality of the rich take the form of cunning and that of the poor violence? ... The upper classes represent what is truly modern, while the lower still belong in thought and feeling to a relatively distant past' (quoted in Morris, 1976: 84). Progress denoted the civilising of mankind. It required the investigation of the man, knowledge and treatment. In part it was a struggle for authority; the authority to determine knowledge, or the meaning of what was going on in social life. The learned turned their backs upon their own participation in the practices and manners of drunkenness, of petty crimes and festival orgies declaring such actions deviant. For Bauman:

'... the concept of civilisation entered learned discourse in the West as the name of a conscious proselytising crusade waged by men of knowledge and aimed at extirpating the vestiges of wild cultures – local, tradition-bound ways of life and patterns of cohabitation. It denoted above all else a novel, activist stance taken toward social processes previously left to their own resources, and a presence of concentrated social powers sufficient to translate such a stance into effective practical measures. In its specific form, the concept of civilisation also conveyed a choice of strategy for the centralised management of social processes: it was to be a knowledge-led management, and management aimed above all at the administration of individual minds and bodies.' (1987: 93)

Bauman sees the process of civilising of the subject as part of a choice of strategy for the centralised management of social processes; it was also a consequence of power, of domination. In the 18th century, Bagehot, for example, supports the idea of 'veritable progress' by pointing to the 'undeniable' differences 'by which a village of English colonists is superior to a tribe of Austrialian native who roam about them.' The most marked difference, and therein proof of civilisation, progress and superiority, is that the English 'can beat the Australians in war when they like; they can take from them anything they like, and kill any of them they choose' (1956: 151). By contrast Norbert Elias depicted the civilising process in a more abstract social-structural and functional way; a dialectic of self and social order.

The dialectics of the civilising process

In a comprehensive set of work ranging over most of this century, Norbert Elias (1939, 1991) has advanced a thesis that a 'civilising process' underlays modern, capitalist-bourgeois society which is characterised by two interrelated processes of unification.

The first of these involved the formation of a political centre. Following a long struggle with resistant forces, primarily those protecting estate interests, the political centre, which we call the (modern) state, succeeded in securing a monopoly on the physical use of violence, the levying of taxes, and the generally valid promulgation and implementation of norms. This process of monopolisation, borne, advanced, and shaped by an expanding bureaucracy, subordinated all local and regional authorities to a central authority. From autonomy sprang dependence. The internal civilising of society was achieved, as Hobbes had already made clear, at the price of a statist monopoly on violence and its demands.

Second, the macro-societal nationalisation of social violence was accompanied by a micro-societal process that produced new patterns of psychic behaviour. Corresponding to the large-scale process of monopolisation, a transformation occurred within the logic of the individual psyche. An internal process of regulation emerged, which can be described as a psychic form of structuralisation and monopolisation. Traditional forms of spontaneity and immediacy were abolished; a *superego* representing social norms and a disciplined and disciplining *ego* were ceded a priority and placed above the *id* of drives. The individual now possessed within himself a model of state monopoly, an ever-present psychic ruler.

In this view, the civilising process is an interlocking of processes, with the two poles of the forceful construction of a statist monopoly on violence, and the emergence of an apparatus for psychic discipline coordinated with it. Both of these forms of unification are fundamentally ambivalent. Granting the nation-state the monopoly on violence risks creating a super-powerful *Leviathan* demanding constant demonstrations of respect in both word and deed; democracy does not reduce this danger since it becomes a monopoly of those active enough to be considered the majority. The monopoly on violence may permit the implementation of one-sided interests, as long as they coincide with those of the monopoly. The psychic self-disciplining of the individual, while resulting in a disciplining of behaviour commensurate with the requirements of the external monopoly may constantly demand sublimations and repressions.

This was recognised in a lesser tradition of the writings of the late 19th century. There is a strong streak, for example, in the writings of Nietzsche and Freud, or in the philosophy of John Stuart Mill, that cried out that man needed to be not more controlled, but that he was pathologically over-controlled. This line of thought cried out for discourses and methodologies of liberation, which enabled individuals to grow beyond the levelling and standardising tendencies that much in the structure of everyday life was imposing. Freudian analysis, for example, is a technique of freedom which comes after freedom from tradition, from unchosen ties with others, to demand a freedom from the contradictions within oneself. The knowledge of the 'self' offers techniques of becoming free, of becoming the new self which will enjoy modernity, namely the normal, well behaved citizen. As political subjection gave way to political citizenship, the selves of the previously excluded, namely the property-less, the working class, had to be constructed so as to fit the functionality of the places on offer.

Thus the modern individual must be constructed to take his or her place in the social order; but is this a process of civilisation or disciplinisation?

The civilised human being, a man possessed of a civilised mind-body complex, which Norbert Elias refers to, must be distinguished from the positivist naturalised forms or the disciplined self which Foucault feared the bureaucratic society demanded. Elias tends to give a picture of function dependency; the emerging modern personality is developed not as a consequence of some imposed pattern, but as a consequence of the increasing differentiation of social patterns and functions. The growing need for self-control is part of the self-steering mechanism of individuals involving reflexivity, or self-scrutiny, and foresight. By contrast those writers who adopt a perspective through the ideas of Nietzsche, Weber and Foucault seek to identify the way in which the political power centre not only lays out prohibitions for openly anti-social conduct, but quietly regulates the minutiae of emotional states, ethics, and the management of personal conduct. They ask 'how is the integration, sequencing, and co-operation of subjects in networks of command achieved?' The answer appears as the complex of discipline and knowledge – if the self is to be self-regulating then the conditions under which the self comes to recognise his or her problems, understand the nature of its behaviour, and accept certain solutions, is clearly a determining factor in the outcome. The pessimistic legacy of Weber causes a suspicion of discipline behind the supposed welfare tendencies of the late-modern state. Policing can be a subtle process; law enforcement only the most prominent aspect.

In his lectures, Beccaria placed policing as a task of political economy understanding the connection between the task of good government and the production of industrious, able, obedient and disciplined subjects. Thomas Hobbes had claimed that man was not fitted for society by nature, but by discipline. This tradition places discipline as the central concept spanning political rule and the arts of self-government. Discipline provides a way of organising social life according to rational thought, exactitude, and supervision. It schooled a mode of personal existence accepting the processes of self-scrutiny, self-evaluation and self-regulation – but what criteria should be used and how narrow should this process be? At one extreme we have John Stuart Mill desiring we become all as Socrates, while Bentham was content for us to become happy chess pawns.[1] Foucault warns of images of the Brave New World, of being constantly watched, inspected, spied upon, dressed in directions from above, indoctrinated, surveyed, taxed, controlled in every action and every movement.

---

1   Bentham hoped for discipline, routinisation and predictability as the outcome of his grandest reform proposal of all: his Panopticon or Inspection House. This life-long project protected his jurisprudence, integrating that jurisprudence with utility theory and making it a practical possibility. This prison is based on the idea of panoptic gaze, ie continuous and concealed surveillance. Bentham believed he had found the 'Columbus Egg' of politics (*Panopticon*: 66) and argued it provided a technique with a multitude of purposes.

> 'Morals reformed, health preserved, industry invigorated, instruction diffused, public burdens lightened, economy seated as it were upon a rock, the guardian rock of the poor-laws not cut but untied – all by a simple idea in architecture ...
> No matter how different, or even opposite the purpose: whether it be that of punishing the incorrigible, guarding the insane, reforming the vicious, confining the suspected, employing the idle, maintaining the helpless, curing the sick, instructing the willing in any branch of industry, or training the rising race in the path of education; in a word, whether it be applied to the purposes of perpetual prisons in the room of death, or prisons for confinement before trial, or penitentiary-houses, or houses of corrections, or work-houses, or manufactories, or mad-houses, or hospitals, or schools.' (*Panopticon*: 39–40)

All these disciplinary institutions would share the regulated coding of human conduct in a restricted space, continuously controlled by officials; a technology of division of space into separated parts, partition of time into a routine, the detailed coding of human action of the inmates, and the use of the panoptic gaze. The idea reflects the epistemological basis of the growing scientific approach; that of control through transparency or 'seeing without being seen' (Ibid: 44). The Panopticon provides a technology to reinforce the conscious intentions of power. Circular in shape, the cells are located on the outer frame with the inspector's lodge at the very centre of the circle; the area in between is left open and all the inmates' cells face the inspector's lodge. The cell walls facing the inspector's lodge and the ones on the opposite side are made of glass, so that a guard situated in the central lodge can easily control each and every one of the inmates, and by turning around can capture all in his gaze. The inmates cannot see their overseer, since the walls of the Inspector's lodge are darkened with blinds and screens. As well as the cells, the Panopticon accommodates a chapel and a separate hospital department.
The panoptic gaze is ever present, penetrating every part of the cells and corridors of the building; it follows the smallest movements of the inmate who is always within the gaze and understands this. Even if the inspector's lodge were left empty for some time, the inmate would never be able to tell. The guards, additionally, needed to be constantly watched; the inspectors lodge also watched the activities of all staff. Hence we have a hierarchy of continuous surveillance; the institution itself is open to the general public and the inspection of a judge or governor. The panopticon was to have no closed areas, no secrets, it was to be open to the inspection of the world and, thereby, abuse of power was impossible. Is this the model of a hell, or of a perfect organisation? And what of the effects upon the inmate? Bentham himself preempted the critical question

> 'whether the liberal spirit and energy of a free citizen would not be exchanged for the mechanical discipline of a soldier, or the austerity of a monk? – and whether the result of this high-wrought contrivance might not be constructing a set of machines under the similitude of men? ... Call them soldiers, call them monks, call them machines: so that they be happy ones, I should not care.' (*Panopticon*: 64)

After all, asked Bentham: 'To how many hundred thousands of his Majesty's honest subjects is such luxury unknown!' (Postscript: 119). All references to *collected works*.

Modern democracy is dependent upon the existence of certain kinds of subjects who do not require a continual external policing. The external constraint of police was transformed into an internal constraint upon the conduct of the self, the formation of subjects who were prepared to take responsibility for their actions and for whom the ethic of discipline was part of their mental fabric.

There is a subtle dialectics in play: participation in the differentiated roles opening up with modernity results in experiences and forms of self-scrutiny which create the fully modern person, but only the fully modern person is deemed fit to participate in these roles. In *The Subjection of Women*, written in the mid 19th century, John Stuart Mill (1970) argued that we could not say that women were naturally fit only for subordination because we know nothing of what they might become if the principles of freedom and equality were extended to sexual relations and life projects. Mill argued that individuals developed a sense of justice through participation in as wide a range of public institutions as possible; confined to the family – which the law allowed to exist as a sea of despotism – women could never learn the social skills and thought processes participation in a full social and political life required.

But participation, inclusivity, was not the phenomena that the positivist sciences of criminology were engaged in. They were rather legitimating differentiation and exclusivity. For much of the 19th century, and in this century, socialisation of the lower classes was a question of learning one's place in the order of things.[2] In the name of civilisation, of progress, of normalisation, the sciences of numbering, of weighing, of measuring, strove to create the thoroughly naturalised society. It was meant to be utopia, but ... once the holocaust was witnessed, it looked like hell.

The reflexive questioning of civilisation

The holocaust is the crime of the century – it is the great problem for criminology. A problem of such importance that it does not appear in any textbook. It poses an issue of the deepest sensibility and epistemological structure: namely, was the evil of that crime – the holocaust – caused by evil ... or by good? Was the holocaust at odds with modernity, or was it the logical consequence of fundamental features of modernity? Is it an event which was a one-off crime ... or is it latent within the deepest structure of modern social constitutions? I suspect the latter part of these questions. Perhaps the reason why the holocaust cannot find a mention in texts such as *Understanding Deviance* (Downes and Rock, 1988) is because it is not deviance – it is central to the process of modernisation.

---

2   This is Foucault's image in *Discipline and Punish*; on a more everyday level the history of James Walvin (1982) in *A Child's World: a social history of English Childhood* 1800–1914, illustrates how much socialisation was a matter of 'knowing one's place'.

The Jewish social theorist Hannah Arendt believed that the holocaust destroyed the solance of any belief that evil must be motivated by evil and conducted by evil people. Instead:

'The sad truth of the matter is that most evil is done by people who never made up their mind to be either good or bad.' (1971: 438)

The reason was the weakness of individual human judgment in the face of reason, in the face of the claims of organisation, in the face of the claims of the normal, in the face of the claims for progress, in the face of the legitimation of our traditions. Its effect was to destroy our belief in the right of our managerial rulers to think for us. As she put it at the end of her preface to *The Origins of Totalitarianism* in 1951:

'We can no longer afford to take that which was good in the past and simply call it our heritage, to discard the bad and simply think of it as a dead load which by itself time will bury in oblivion. The subterranean stream of Western tradition has finally come to the surface and usurped the dignity of our tradition. This is the reality in which we live. And this is why all efforts to escape from the grimness of the present into the nostalgia for a still intact past, or into the anticipated oblivion of a better future, are vain.' (1951: Preface)

We no longer can take our civilisation for granted. Nor can we accept a unilinear image of progress in human affairs.[3] The criminal (albeit not prosecuted) atrocities of the conflict in the ex-Yugoslavia or Rwanda are but the extreme of a whole series of tribalisms the world experiences as the internal dispute within middle modernity between Organised Capitalist Bureaucracy and Organised Socialist Bureaucracy (a dispute sometimes called the Cold War) ends. Organised modernity finds its sources of authority (particularly the nation-state) questioned, and its knowledge bases subjected to the problem of multiple perspectives; our concern is ambivalent. Against chaos, Hobbes and others laid the foundations for the making of power – reason has spread power throughout modernity – but if we wish to embrace pluralism to protect us from power, then what gives us enough reason, enough *meaning*, to act in the face of late-modern power? Such is the post-modern dilemma but, even before post-modernism became apparent, criminology was implicated in the questioning of organised modernity in two forms: (i) the horror at the crimes of obedience; and (ii) the critique of bureaucracy.

The impact of crimes of obedience and crimes of bureaucracy

The immediate post-Second World War Crime Tribunals felt the need to appeal to pre-modern (pre-positive) images of natural law to undercut the defence of bureaucratic legitimation (the defence of superior orders). The horror at the Holocaust was different from the horror of the quantitatively greater numbers

---

3   Nor have we learnt, perhaps, how to internalise the *concern* to prevent major crimes.

involved in the slavery early modernity took a great deal of its wealth from, in that it was the extreme example of the positivist reduction of social problems to matters of technological calculation. Modernity had congratulated itself on the abolition of slavery – surely the horrors of Nazism were the results of a few evil men? It appears the depth of such crimes could not be so easily washed away. The holocaust was the extreme of a range of positivist discourses which spoke of the need to take scientific action to grapple with the (non)social problems of crime, imbecility, feeblemindedness, the reproduction of the poor and the wretchedness of the lowest strata of society.

The binding force of positivist 'reason'

The holocaust lay at the end of the widespread dream of a purpose-designed world devoid of troublesome deviants; a world where societal perfection was achieved by the elimination of the 'other'. In this solution, the plight of the wretched and the miserable is ameliorated by the removal of the undeserving wretched and miserable. For Zygmunt Bauman (1989, 1991: ch 1) the holocaust is not at odds with the spirit of modernity, rather it is the pure form of the normalising ambitions of the spirit of modernity. Once social order had been reduced to the status of a technical problem, and the desirability of the rulers to administer the necessary means had been granted, then its performance was a matter of cool calculation of costs and benefits. National Socialism (and perhaps the work of Stalin) held itself out as founded upon scientific methodology, and an unflinchingly modern view of the world. In the late 19th century Ernst Hackel declared that:

'... by the indiscriminate destruction of all incorrigible criminals, not only would the struggle for life among the better portions of mankind be made easier, but also an advantageous artificial process of selection would be seen in practice, since the possibility of transmitting the injurious qualities would be taken from those degenerate outcasts.' (Quoted in Bauman, 1991: 31)

Once the quantity of bad genes was lessened due to the scientific policy of physical destruction and reproductive regulation, the nation would benefit from a 'lessening of court costs, prison costs, and expenses on behalf of the poor'. The prospect of scientifically managing and eliminating defective human stock, the science of eugenics (or the science of human heredity and the art of human breeding), was universally debated. The final solution adopted in Germany was merely the end point of ambitions inherent in the consciousness of modernity. As Bauman sees it, it earned its terrifying fame not because of its uniqueness, but because it was actually put into full practice. It was the extension of the fully mobilised organisational resources and political power of the centralised modern state. It was not an uncommon view, shared by many individuals around the world, that the advent of city life, advances in food production and medicine had meant the survival of the unfit. Why should the deviant, and/or the criminally-inclined, be allowed to breed and spread the pool of weakened blood/genes?

In the US several states passed compulsory sterilisation statutes covering young women in certain situations. Several due process objections were in time raised. In 1927, Justice Holmes, speaking for the US Supreme Court in *Buck v Bell*, laid these due process objections to rest and upheld sterilisation as falling within the permissible constitutional dimensions. The case concerned Carrie Buck who had been committed to a Virginia mental institution as mentally deficient. Both her mother and her own illegitimate daughter were similarly feebleminded. Under the state's procedure for effecting sterilisation, it was determined that the best interests of the patient and society would be served if Miss Buck was rendered infertile. The Supreme Court addressed itself to the substantive question of whether the state had the power to order the sterilisation of an individual's power of procreation. Without evaluating the scientific evidence, the court stated that it could not, as a matter of law, override the determination of the legislature that certain conditions are hereditary and inimical to the public welfare, nor could it override the determination of the Virginia Supreme Court of Appeals that the petitioner possessed those inimical characteristics. The rationale was announced by Justice Holmes:

> 'In view of the general declarations of the legislature and the specific findings of the Court, obviously we cannot say as a matter of law that the grounds do not exist, and if they exist they justify the result. We have seen more than once that the public welfare may call upon the best citizens for their lives. It would be strange if it could not call upon those who already sap the strength of the State for these lesser sacrifices, often not felt to be such by those concerned, in order to prevent our being swamped with incompetence. It is better for all the world, if instead of waiting to execute degenerate offspring for crime, or to let them starve for their imbecility, society can prevent those who are manifestly unfit from continuing their kind. The principle that sustains compulsory vaccination is broad enough to cover cutting the Fallopian Tubes ... Three generations of imbeciles are enough.' *Buck v Bell* (1927) 274 US 200, 207

The structural features of crimes of obedience

The following section draws heavily upon the work of Kelman and Hamilton (1989) on the issues of mass murder, highlighted by the holocaust and the 1968 My Lai massacre in Vietnam, which they define as *crimes of obedience*. Their central question is what explains sanctioned massacres?

The question is intensified because of the genocidal or near-genocidal nature of the event and the fact that the activity is directed at a target that did not provoke the violence through its own actions. The authors suggest it is an environment almost totally devoid of the conditions that usually provide at least some degree of moral justification for violence. Neither the reason for the violence nor its purpose is of the kind that is normally considered justifiable.

While it may tell us something about the types of individuals most readily recruited for participation, the search for constitutional factors – specifically psychological dispositions within those who perpetrate these acts – does not yield a satisfactory explanation. For example, to claim that the individuals are giving bent to their strong sadistic impulses goes against the fact of no evidence that the majority of those who participate in such killings are sadistically inclined, in fact Arendt (1964) points out that the Nazis made a systematic effort to weed out all those who derived physical pleasure from what they did. Some individuals can be described as sadists and evil, but their existence does not explain the existence of the concentration camps in which these individuals could give play to their sadistic fantasies. The structure which gave them opportunities was buttressed by the participation of large numbers of individuals to whom the label of sadist could not be applied.

Eric Fromm (1941) had analysed the appeal of Nazism in terms of the prevalence of sadomasochistic strivings, particularly among the German lower middle class. Again such dispositions may present a certain state of readiness to participate in sanctioned massacres when the opportunity arises, but cannot explain the major motivating forces. Similarly, high levels of frustration within a population are probably facilitators, rather than instigators, of sanctioned massacres, since there does not seem to be a clear relationship between the societal level of frustration and the occurrence of such violence.

What of an explanation in terms of an inordinately intense hatred toward those against whom the violence is directed? Bauman (1991) notes how many who laid the foundations were committed to the cool reason of science, and Kelman and Hamilton relate that many of the active participants in the extermination of European Jews, such as Adolf Eichmann (Arendt, 1964), did not feel any passionate hatred of Jews. As for My Lie, they argue there is certainly no reason to believe that those who planned and executed American policy in Vietnam felt a profound hatred of the Vietnamese population, although deeply rooted racist attitudes may conceivably have played a role.

Hatred and rage play a part in sanctioned massacres; perhaps in target selection. There is a long history of profound hatred against such groups as the Jews in Christian Europe, the Chinese in Southeast Asia, and the Ibos in northern Nigeria, which helps establish them as suitable victims. Hostility also plays an important part at the point at which the killings are actually perpetrated (see our late discussion on existentialism), even if the official planning and the bureaucratic preparations that ultimately lead up to this point are carried out in a passionless and businesslike atmosphere.

Hostility toward the target, historically rooted or induced by the situation, contributes heavily toward the violence, but it does so largely by dehumanising the victims rather than by motivating violence against them in the first place.

The authors redirect the question: the issue that really calls for psychological analysis is why so many people are willing to formulate, participate in, and condone policies that call for the mass killings of defenceless civilians. They argue it is more instructive to look not at the motives for violence but at the conditions under which the usual moral inhibitions against violence become weakened, and identify three social processes that tend to create such conditions: *authorisation*, *routinisation*, and *dehumanisation*.

Authorisation, is the process whereby the situation becomes so defined that the individual is absolved of the responsibility to make personal moral choices. *Routinisation*, is the process whereby the action becomes so organised that there is no opportunity for raising moral questions. *Dehumanisation*, is the process whereby the actors' attitudes toward the target and toward themselves become so structured that it is neither necessary nor possible for them to view the relationship in moral terms.

Authorisation

Authorisation creates a situation in which the presence of authority – directly or implicitly – upsets the moral principles that generally govern human relationships. The legitimate authorities explicitly order, implicitly encourage, tacitly approve, or at least permit, violence. The authorisation of such acts seems to convey an automatic justification upon them stripping the individual of the feeling that judgments or choices need to be made by him finally. Particularly when the actions are explicitly ordered, a different kind of morality, linked to the duty to obey superior orders, may take over.

A host of questions arise. Why should the situation strip individuals of the obligation to decide for themselves? Why should the obligation to obey take over? Under what conditions are individuals prepared to challenge the legitimacy of an order on the grounds that the order itself is illegal, or that those giving it have overstepped their authority, or that it stems from a policy that violates fundamental social values? Regardless of the answers in particular instances, Kelman and Hamilton believe the basic structure of a situation of legitimate authority requires subordinates to respond in terms of their role obligations rather than their personal preferences; they can openly disobey only by challenging the legitimacy of the authority. An important corollary of the basic structure of the authority situation is that actors often do not see themselves as personally responsible for the consequences of their actions.

Perhaps another way of putting this is that authorisation prepares the context for the event.

'In the My Lai massacre, it is likely that the structure of the authority situation contributed to the massive violence in both ways – that is, by conveying the message that acts of violence against Vietnamese villagers were required, as well as the message that such acts, even if not ordered, were permitted by the authorities in charge. The actions at My Lai represented, at least in some respects, responses to explicit or implicit orders. Lieutenant Calley indicated, by orders and by example, that he wanted large numbers of villagers killed. Whether Calley himself had been ordered by his superiors to "waste" the whole area, as he claimed, remains a matter of controversy. Even if we assume, however, that he was not explicitly ordered to wipe out the village, he had reason to believe that such actions were expected by his superior officers. Indeed, the very nature of the war conveyed this expectation. The principal measure of military success was the "body count" the number of enemy soldiers killed and any Vietnamese killed by the US military was commonly defined as a "Viet Cong". Thus, it was not totally bizarre for Calley to believe that what he was doing at My Lai was to increase his body count, as any good officer was expected to do.' (1989: 17)

The military authorities implicitly condoned these types of actions by not only failing to punish such acts in most cases, but by devisory strategies and tactics based on the proposition that the civilian population of South Vietnam – whether 'hostile' or 'friendly' – was expendable. The policies of search-and-destroy missions, the establishment of freeshooting zones, the use of antipersonnel weapons, the bombing of entire villages if they were suspected of harbouring guerrillas, the forced migration of masses of the rural population, and the defoliation of vast forest areas helped legitimise acts of massive violence of the kind occurring at My Lai.

Further the tactics of military training instills unquestioning obedience to superior orders, no matter how destructive the actions these orders call for. Kelman and Hamilton go further, conducting empirical research which showed that this orientation of discipline may be rather widespread in the general population. The disciplined subject may be prone too easily to follow authority.

Routinisation

Once the authorisation processes have created a situation in which people become involved in an action without considering its implications and without really making a decision, individuals are in a new psychological and social situation in which the pressures to continue are powerful. Influences which may have caused moral dilemmas now have less effect. Routinisation destroys the processes which differentiate the strange from the normal, thus preventing the individuals involved from confronting the true meaning of the events.

Dehumanisation

If authorisation processes override standard moral considerations, and routinisation processes reduce the likelihood that such considerations will arise, the strong inhibitions against murdering one's fellow human beings are reduced by stripping the victims of their human status. The victims are deprived of both (i) identity, standing as independent, distinctive individuals, capable of making choices and entitled to live their own lives-and community; and (ii) fellow membership in an interconnected network of individuals who care for each other and respect each other's individuality and rights. Establishing a category which defines out a particular group, overcomes certain of the moral restraints against killing them.

Dehumanisation occurs to varying degrees; with sanctioned massacres an extreme degree of dehumanisation is obvious, in so far that the killing is not in response to hostile action, but because of the category to which they happen to belong.

> 'They are the victims of policies that regard their systematic destruction as a desirable end or an acceptable means. Such extreme dehumanisation becomes possible when the target group can readily be identified as a separate category of people who have historically been stigmatised and excluded by the victimisers; often the victims belong to a distinct racial, religious, ethnic, or political group regarded as inferior or sinister. The traditions, the habits, the images, and the vocabularies for dehumanising such groups are already well established and can be drawn upon when the groups are selected for massacre. Labels help deprive the victims of identity and community, as in the epithet "gooks" that was commonly used to refer to Vietnamese and other Indochinese peoples.' (1989: 19)

The dynamics of the massacre event further increase the participants' tendency to dehumanise their victims; the participants in the bureaucratic apparatus increasingly come to see their victims as bodies to be counted and entered into their reports, as faceless figures that will determine their productivity rates and promotions. While those who participate in the massacre directly are reinforced in their perception of the victims as less than human by observing their very victimisation; the conditions of their victimisation serve to justify their victimisation.

Alasdair MacIntyre and the critique of managerial expertise

In *After Virtue*, Alasdair MacIntyre (1981) asked the question: are our bureaucratic rulers justified or not? and gave a resounding no! MacIntyre sees Weber and Nietzsche as providing the two great critiques of modernity. While Marx in a sense, glorifies modernity (espousing an optimism in the power to organise if in accordance with the correct social theory), Nietzsche warns of a herd mentality and a radical splitting of the moral universe, while Weber pessimistically gives the image of the bureaucratically organised world. For MacIntyre, Weber's analysis of legitimacy captures the spirit of organised modernity in the claims to managerial efficiency which aspire to value neutrality and manipulative ability. But while they do manipulate they are not value neutral. We have formal rationality and substantive incoherence. Organisational modernity rests on misconceptions.[4]

Is post-modernism the end of the dream of organised modernity?

MacIntyre wrote against the backdrop of a period which culminated in the 1970s; an era of governmental social engineering. The 1980s were to prove radically different. They were a time when many agreed with MacIntyre in his diagnosis – bureaucracy was assailed from various quarters of the political spectrum – but instead of a return to notions of community and the need to construct an all encompassing image of social totalities and live a life of 'virtue', the official solution was to destroy governmental regulation and dissolve bureaucracy in favour of the market.

---

4   In post-modernism we realise that nature is not so accessible to being set out in a structure of laws offering generalisations and predictive powers as modernity believed. The social cannot be represented in a simple structural-functional framework. How do we present ourselves to ourselves? How do we find ourselves? For Rosen to speak of the human condition is already to grant that human nature is inaccessible:
>   '... our condition today is how we happen to find ourselves, the 'way we live now' rather than the way in which we have deviated from how we ought to be living.' (1980: 221)
Science has dissolved any pretence to 'natural' existence. We require instead a more moral science, a hermeneutics of interpretation of the human condition. As Nietzsche (paraphrasing Kant) said: '... we find in social order only what we have put there – social order is our creation'. When our social sciences reveals the regularity of nature, sets out the location of deviants, the insane, the normal, the well-balanced, within flows of determinism, this is not our science revealing the truths of nature, but our methodologies presenting us with interpretations to make sense of the world. As John Stuart Mill almost said, social life is natural, but at a distance from nature.
Let us be clear: this is not to say that science is wrong, this is the result of our science. Many criminological texts refer to positivism as being the result of a world that Darwin had changed forever; a world now subjected to the laws of natural selection, but Darwinism actually indicated indeterminacy and uncertainty in nature.
It is a measure of the greatness of men that they are misunderstood, Darwin is a classic example. Two points:
•   Darwin did not ever use the image of the survival of the fittest. This Hobbesian imagery was read into him by the Victorian evolutionist Spencer. Darwin rather referred to the struggle for existence.
•   Darwin does not believe that evolution has a design. Rather he claims to refute teleology in organic evolution. His argument involves particular mutations and the subsequent reproduction of these if favourable environmental conditions are present. Genes that confer a reproductive advantage will have their representation in the population increased, whereas:
'... those whose consequences for reproduction are relatively deleterious will be gradually eliminated. Through this mechanism of natural selection, working retroactively on populations of unique individuals, and not through the implementation of a transcendental design, the challenges presented to life by an ever-changing environment have been – and continue to be – met through adaption as divers as they are ingenious.' (Ingold, 1986: 174)
Darwin was troubled by this. Ingold quotes from a letter he wrote shortly after the publication of *The Origin of Species* wherein Darwin confessed of his inability to 'think that world as we see it is the result of chance; and yet I cannot look at each separate thing as the result of design ... I am, and shall ever remain, in a hopeless muddle' (quoted in Ingold, 1986: 175).
We have a problem: how can we grant a creativity and assert the progress of human societies without falling into teleological thinking? Put simply: how can we think of human development as something more than a mere banging together of chemical and physical bits without going to the other extreme of believing in some grand script of the drama of the cosmos that we are called upon to discover and play our part in (as Marx and other appeared to believe)? One aspect is our conception of ourselves: we believe that the successive peeling away of the skins of being human must stop somewhere ... there must be a foundational point where we stop digging and say 'this is it. This is the fundamental building block of being human'; we have yet to fully embrace the existential message that human nature is a function of social-cultural development.

Crime soared, but so, according to the official measurement of societal happiness, ie the amount of consumerable goods, did success. As the market was deemed to be the solution to the problem of organising society, the image of the criminal as a rational calculator, deciding to engage in crime as and when an opportunity presented itself, and seizing up the risks of detection and the possible punishment costs, became official government policy in the US and Britain. Crime was no longer to disappear with the task of organising the good society, but to be managed by deterrent penal sanctions and an effective criminal justice process. The image of the criminal was repositioned away from sociological positivist's search for deterministic social laws into the freedom of the abstract rational self. Of course the self had to come from somewhere, but to escape from a general social theory which implicated political economy or social structure, the self was the product of the family. The criminal self was the self that a pathological (broken)family had (mis)socialised.

The post-modern condition: life within the unorganised structures of organised modernity?

The paradox of the post-modern condition is that we are surrounded by the institutions of modernity, by large organisations, by the bureaucracy of the nation state (and beyond, for example, The United Nations, European Union) but we have lost faith in bureaucracy. We inhabit modernity but have lost faith in its promises. Ideas of coherence become compromised. Writers from the Right, such as James Q Wilson (1975, 1983 and with Herrnstein, 1985) stated their conclusions clearly: it is impossible to think of crime as something which projects of improving social conditions will have any effect upon. They argued that we have now improved the conditions of the vast majority of people in the West beyond the consideration of the elites of the 19th century but we have record levels of crime – therefore we need to return to the precepts of classicism, to law and order and to strict punishment systems. We have to emphasis control and hold the individual responsible for his or her actions. The knowledges of positive criminology, which Foucault had seen implicated in the developing structures of bureaucratic control, were now held to be providing excuses for deviance. As bureaucracy was to be done away with so was the aim enterprise of criminology to find the social causes of crime. Control of crime was to be conducted without the leadership of criminology.

What are we to make of this? The context of late-modern or post-modern control is the affluent society or what, quoting Galbraith, we have called life in the *Culture of Contentment*. The basic needs of all are catered for yet crime advances ... we have created a science to talk of crime and to offer a technology of control yet it seems powerless. Thus law and order returns, the symbolism of the law, the police, target hardening, opportunity theory, life mediated by the institutions of modernity and social distance yet radical communication technologies ...

Concentrating on the historical forms or images of control may miss the real form of social control in late modernity. Classical criminology gives us the route of a state-led criminology. It points us towards a science of government in which the state lays down rules, in which the state organises sanction patterns and specifies certain forms of formal social control. We tend to think that social control has therefore become formalised. The traditional reading of criminological positivism complements and reinforces this – it offers the prospect of knowledge at the service of the bureaucratic professionals. But social control has not become so reduced; it is more a function of the hidden resources of every day life and the narrative forces of the contemporary communication and consumer-orientated international society.

Social control in post-modernism: the seduced and the repressed

In *Legislators and Interpreters*, Bauman (1987) suggests that modernity has failed to construct a thoroughly rationalised society. While early modernity asked for the intellectuals to act as legislators, and middle modernity to provide the knowledge for bureaucracy, the authorities are no longer looking for the counsel of intellectuals and philosophers. There are philosophers desperately trying to offer the discourses necessary to construct communities, but the rulers have turned away from any gardening ambitions and bureaucracy (although paradoxically bureaucracy keeps expanding) to the market. The result is a new dialectic of social control. On the one side we have *those who are tuned into the market who become seduced by its items and messages*; a group of people who are now effectively and efficiently integrated through a new cluster of mechanisms of public relations, advertising, desires and perceived needs, institutional and individual bargaining. Bauman suggests opposed to these are the new poor, who are not really consumers since their consumption does not matter much for the successful reproduction of capital (they often consume low quality produce). They are not the core members of the consumer society. We have two systems of control: *seduction* and *repression*. Seduction is for the core members of the society, while on the other side we have *those who have to be disciplined by the combined action of repression, policing, authority and normative regulation*. Bauman suggests they are not part of the 'cultural game', even 'if, stupidly, they think otherwise', but this is the point, they do think so. We cannot locate the offender in another (asocial)foundational naturalism. The offender is demarcated in the process of action, in the committing of a crime (in victimisation) and in labelling and in reaction to the events and actions which he/she has taken.

The market provides the acid test of eligibility for membership of the late-modern consumer society. The market appears thoroughly democratic – it ranks people according to ability (IQ, for example) – and it reaches out to anyone who would listen, and everybody is encouraged to listen. Which implies that potentially, everybody is encouraged to listen or forced to hear and potentially, everybody is seduced or seducible. But can satisfaction be achieved? Bauman believes the burden falls most on those with lean resources. He quotes Jeremy Seabrook remembering a young woman:

'I think of Michelle. At fifteen her hair was one day red the next blonde, then jet-black, then teased into Afro kinks and after that rattails, then plaited, and then cropped so that it glistened close to the skull. She wore a nose-stud and then her ears were pierced; in the bright feathers, rhinestones or ceramic or silver. Her lips were scarlet, then purple, then black. Her face was ghost-white and then peach-coloured, then bronze as if it were cast in metal. Pursued by dreams of flight, she left home at sixteen to be with her boyfriend, who was twenty-six. If they took her home, she said she would kill herself. "But I have always let you do what you want", her mother protested. "This is what I want". At eighteen she returned to her mother with two children, after she had been badly beaten by her man. She sat in the bedroom which she had fled three years earlier; the faded photos of yesterday's pop stars still stared down from the walls. She said she felt a hundred years old. She felt weary. She'd tried all that life could offer. Nothing else was left.' (Quoted, Bauman, 1987: 181)

We are told that we are all members of consumer society, yet we are not equally located structurally. This is a more complicated set of messages than Merton (1938, 1957) envisaged, and difficult (for reasons we shall indicate) to feel secure within. Bauman suggests that once seduced, Michelle and her ilk soon discover that the goods they covet, apart from being attractive to everybody, bring happiness only to some. Michelle can only guess this, since the only thing she knows for sure is that she herself is not among those 'some'. The consumer society creates a circle of desire and the need to possess a commodity; but gaining the commodity does not cause satisfaction – a continuous process or consumer game is set in motion in which the game itself is the only reward, offering as it does the ever renewed hope of winning. But to reap this kind of a reward, one must be able to go on playing without end, so that hope is never allowed to die and defeat always means losing a battle, not the war. Once you stop playing, the hope disappears, and you know that you have lost, and that there will be no next stage at which you win.

But we must play – how else can the materiality of life be provided in late-modernity? What happens if one was not to play the game? Is seduction or repression the only games in town? and in this context what is the true meaning of crime?

Is crime a concept of universal application which, in empirical reality, is only applied to those who evade seduction? Within such a division does the national operation of criminal justice lose any sense of authenticity? But while we doubt, while we may experience reflexive dilemmas, the power and authority we entrusted to authority and bureaucracy continues to create more crime control. Crime control becomes an industry (Christie, 1993) and a very realistic one.

And, currently, in moving against positivism, against bureaucracy, the dominant strands of contemporary criminology claim we must be realistic. We must acknowledge the reality of the crime we can see and experience, the reality of the criminal self we can capture and punish. In this we are asked to renounce the large scale constructivist aims of modernity, but the aim of criminology should not be to allocate responsibility around a privatised self - it must be to acknowledge the ambiguous relations between the self and the context. To do this we must move therefore to the terrain that realist criminology (both of the Right and the Left) asserts should be our foundation; that is we must analyse within the terrain of the *common life*.

CHAPTER TEN

MORALITY, NORMALCY AND MODERNITY: THE MORAL INTENSITY OF EVERYDAY LIFE

'The woman carrying her own coffin
Got on to the bus at 3.45 pm.
Nobody spoke. The driver punched her ticket
With a sour face. Not all Maoris are cheerful
And it was a wet day. When she sat down
I felt by radar under cape, suit girdle,
A sharp continual trembling of the womb.
Ah, yes – the coffin – it was large and black
Like a violin case. She held it by one handle
Against her knees. I wanted to say,
'Madam, your death is showing' – or else,
'Don't be sad; we're all in this together' –
But it didn't seem right. Not there
With everyone behaving so well;
And she could have thought I was making a pass.
A big-boned woman, fortyish,
With a country look. After all, why shouldn't
She carry her coffin wherever she liked
Democratically?
When she got off
At the Post Office corner, I was relieved
To see her saddle-up her own death and ride it
Like a great black stallion down Featherston Street.'
(James K Baxter, *The Woman in the Bus*, 1980:326)

Analyticism and the problem of contemporary criminology

Contemporary criminology is racked by multiple perspectives and etiological
scepticism – in response conservative scholars, such as James Q Wilson and
Herrenstein (1985), Gottfredson and Hirschi (1990), and in related fields social
theorists, such as Charles Murray (1984, 1994), espouse two tactics: the use of
statistical analysis and the categories of everyday life. The official statistics are
used to determine the scale of the problem, and the analytical categories of
everyday life are taken as starting points to create theories which have intuitive
appeal; we are presented with theories of control and rational deterrence which
the ordinary man (including the ordinary politician asking for advice in the
midst of law and order politics) can relate to.

Conversely, for a public surrounded by the media's constant parading of
criminal statistics and horror stories, the need to espouse a general social theory

of crime smacks of ivory tower irrelevancy or another form of do-gooder 'social liberalism'. *Into this breach has stepped right realism.* Right realism speaks the language of popular dissatisfaction and popular anger, it is not some simple pragmatic managerialism, but an appeal to the world view of the ordinary person who understands that the others have lost the fear of punishment, that the criminal justice system is loaded in favour of the criminal, that liberal lawyers get too many criminals off, that the courts do not pass sufficiently stiff punishments, that offenders do not receive their 'just deserts', and that criminology provides justifications for crime, that the rehabilitative ethos merely provided excuses for offenders (see, for example, Patricia Morgan, *Delinquent Fantasies*, 1978). Alongside right realism we have a dry narrowly focused managerialism, exampled by government bodies which sponsor research into the effect of steering car locks and surveillance cameras.

The mundaneness of ordinary everyday life provides the common focus for the institutional appeal of situational crime prevention, opportunity theory, rational choice, and the move of Gottfredson and Hirschi (1990) to relocate crime as a mundane activity of the everyday life. What is the theoretical effect? Several consequences, for example, follow from Gottfredson and Hirschi's 'general theory':

- Since most offenders share (along with others who are accident prone or liable to addictions) a number of characteristics, of which the dominant one is low self-control, it is pointless to go into analytical reductionism and create special theories for different types of crime; by concentrating upon self-control (a factor which we have agreed is central to our modern understanding of ourselves as moderns), we do not need to go into medium or macro-sociological theories in a search for causal influences – at best these are secondary or minor influences, at worst simply wrong and misleading;

- most criminal activity is 'ordinary crime', consisting of trivial and mundane criminal acts. Throughout the text they compose images of 'the typical or standard burglary', 'the typical or standard robbery', 'the typical or standard homicide', which is drawn from the official criminal statistics. For example: their picture of 'the standard or ordinary embezzlement' which is the core case of white collar crime is 'in the ordinary embezzlement a young man recently hired steals money from his employer's cash register or goods from his store'. Thus they argue that embezzlement of large amounts of money by older employees in positions of trust is a 'rarity'. To someone who has been following the Auditors reports on EU (EEC) fraud and the claims that billions are defrauded in the Common Agriculture Policy and related matters, but virtually no one is prosecuted, this smacks of a simple uncritical acceptance of the official statistical picture. Put another way: their picture of typical embezzlement is the picture of the type of employee who can easily be apprehended and prosecuted. An employee with little power and little ability to cover his or her tracks; in other words, the outcome of easily solvable crimes. By contrast the crimes of the powerful are able to be covered with layers of complications and evidential ambiguity. But most reliable assessments demonstrate there is no comparison in the amount of money and long term social damage involved – in non-official analytical projects calculating the amount of crime we are surrounded by, ordinary crime pales into a lesser breed. In the Bhopal incident, for example, the death toll reached 6,400 plus with more than 100,000 poisoned. But in ordinary, everyday life it is 'ordinary' crime that is feared and rendered the object for right realists and contemporary governmental policy. After all, is not the fact that ordinary everyday life appears so easy to understand the reason it can serve as the foundation for analysis in the midst of this confusing world?

This intellectual endeavour of trust in the ordinary life amounts to an attempt to resolve the ambivalence and ambiguity in the analytical treatment of existence by recourse to our recognition of ourselves by intuition. While we have stressed the special nature of a crime, it is neither a natural phenomenon in the sense that natural crimes exist (before law crime does not exist), nor a object of radical relativism (once enacted law defines certain things as crimes and this is a social reality), the intuitions of everyday life appear to resolve any practical ambiguity. In ordinary life intuitions work to add weight to a theory since we presume that intuitions refer to natural essences rather than conceptual constructions. After all, state realists, ask a victim of violence who or what he has been attacked by and the response is not that 'I was the victim of a conceptual entity, a social hybrid', but rather 'it was a person, a real criminal, and the event was a crime, a real entity'. The more a theory can appeal to the intuitions of the people it appears clear that the theory is saying something meaningful about social life. Of course, Marxists have had a traditional way of dealing with this – to rely upon the intuitions of everyday life to support your theory is (i) to rely upon the classical unity of being and thinking; and (ii) this unity is actually to believe in ideological constructions. The belief patterns of everyday life are themselves the product of larger forces and it is these that ultimately must be investigated if real understanding is to be achieved. But to talk of the need to critique ideology, is understandably out of fashion, and those who believe in basing social theory on the categories of everyday life might reply: but did you yourself not want a human reduced to the status of an automaton? Did you not demand that criminology treat its objects as human beings? And is this not what we believers in the categories of everyday life are doing? But can this turn to everyday life really offer any substantial theoretical understanding? Or are we merely seduced into enjoying the theoretical game of analysis? To answer this we must realise that the turn to ordinary everyday life was the answer many philosophers – who had given up on the traditional task of rationalism and empiricism to tell the essential story of the world – offered as secure understanding.

H L A Hart: everyday life as the site of analysis

The methodological message of H L A Hart's *The Concept of Law* (1961) was simple: to fully appreciate the role of law in social life one should start with the mundane and the ordinary. This work, called by the author 'an essay in descriptive sociology', would never find its way onto any sociological course – whatever Hart does in this text it is not sociology as the discipline is taught in university departments bearing that name. Hart's approach is rather the sociology of a barrister, the sociology of the trained advocate who believes that no brief is beyond him or her.

Hart's sociology makes no reference to Weber (though the whole work presupposes Weber), nor Marx, or Nietzsche, or Durkheim (though the whole work presupposes Durkheim). His position is disarmingly simple yet dynamically radical: radical beyond the dreams perhaps of its author. Basically Hart asserts:

- social order is founded upon everyday life appearing natural to the normal person;

- modern social order cannot survive on coercion from above, whatever the type of social order it needs the acceptance of the populace, ie it must appear legitimate;

- modern social formations are legal orders which use the idea of a rule to structure social activity – social order is a rule bound set of practices; law a specific form of rule;

- the laws that govern everyday behaviour are a set of rules emanating from the state and the state is itself created by rules;

- thus, theories of society that put humans above the law (as Hart reads Austin) are wrong, since the power that these humans exercise is a factor of law.

- law, therefore, is both the product of power, and the creator of power – law is productive; it produces forms of social arrangements that can form the site of power, yet this power also derives from law;

- everyday life is a set of games – we can never know what the overall purpose of these games are;

- there is no way of telling what the purpose of life is – all we can provide with certainty are negative assertions and basic truisms. Specifically, the legal order is not the arrangements of a suicide club, rather survival is paramount. If we were to ask what are the naturally basic things that the legal order has to do we need to look at the basic facts of the human condition and construct laws which fulfil the functional demands of enabling survival having regard to the structure of the human predicament. When we look at the basic facts of the human condition we discover that humans are vulnerable, that they are approximately equal, that humans have limited altruism, that they exist in a world of limited resources. Given these minimal conditions, certain understandings or rules, such as the institution of property, or rules forbidding the taking of another's life, follow.

- to understand the reality of law and order one need only look to how normal people in the practices of everyday life use legal phrases and related concepts, such as the distinction between the phrase *being obliged* (which fits the non-legal demand for something when the person is in fear of his or her life, such as the demand a bank-robber makes of a bank-teller) and *being under an obligation* (which fits a legal and legitimate demand, such as the demand for taxes which a government makes of its citizens).

Hart's work is the most widely read and widely criticised text in modern jurisprudence. It is often dismissed as the product of a brief period of time when the world looked to intellectuals as if it made sense, as if the entire world could be seen as some gigantic structural-functional machine moving forwards in a progressive and civilising fashion. The image of the world as some form of progressive natural order has had as much appeal to certain modern intellectuals as God did to the pre-modern. Both solved the same problems: it is impossible to know the ultimate answers for both (how could a mere man know God's mind?), the secret lay in looking at the flow of everyday life and reading the message of God's will, or the functionality of the natural order revealed in them, and align oneself to those requirements. Hart called this, the basic truth of the talk of natural law.

Hart's jurisprudence suits the liberal idea of the rule of law. For Hart, the key characteristic of law is that some form of behaviour (positive act or omission) is made obligatory: coercion is fundamental to the idea of law, but this is not simply a matter of the threat of violence. Public order cannot rest solely on the threat or application of force by authorities. The coercion of a rule comes from the internal attitude, it is a self-regarding attitude. Social life comprises a series of games: a game is a rule bound practice. It is impossible to participate fully, to play the game as one who wants to play it well, without knowing the rules since the rules give structure to the game. Games are social activities, they require the majority of the participants to play by the rules otherwise the game would collapse. Persons obey the rules of a game only when the group they are playing with approve of those who abide by the rules, and disapprove of those who violate them.

The continuance of the practice rests upon the majority of the participants having an internal attitude, that is to say they wish to participate in the practice (ie they train hard, they play hard, and they seek to be good at that game, hence they do not cheat), it is vitally important for the officials to have the internal attitude (why would the players play by the rules if the referee was open to deciding points by taking bribes?).

The complexity of the mundane: the richness of everyday life

That we 'get through' our daily routines without too many problems is so obvious that it is banal. It is this phenomenon that makes modern urban existence appear 'natural' and appear so 'everyday' it arouses no existential sense of bewilderment or wonder.

But why is it that we consider everyday life natural? Consider everyday life in London: to live in London is to live amidst diversity and plurality unheard of for most of human existence. On an historical scale modern life is totally unnatural. Little in our biological and social evolution up until the last 100 or so years could have prepared us for the existential beingness of modern cities such as New York, Los Angles or London.

Criminology repeatedly has asked the question 'why do people offend?' and some of its quasi-philosophers have replied 'because we are surprised by misbehaviour' (Nigel Walker, *Behaviour and Misbehaviour*). But surely the question should not be why do some people not commit crime but why is there so little? Not why are some people not able to cope with the pressures of modern city life but how is anybody able to cope at all?

The tactic of right realism appears to ignore the macro-scale considerations, the context of the development of modernity, which we have sought to locate criminology within, so let us forget our previous chapters and ask naively 'how does this city existence hang together? Why do we trust the people we mix with? Are they not mostly strangers? Why are we so civilised, so trustworthy, so well behaved, so non-violent?'

Take one of my 'typical or standard journeys': I have various choices – car, bicycle or public transport. When travelling into the city centre during the day I normally do not drive, instead I leave my house and either walk to the tube station, or, if its raining, or I'm feeling exceptionally lazy, I drive to the tube station leaving the car there. I put my car radio in the boot, a safety precaution, but why do I expect the car to be there when I return? Walking down the street I pass a mixture of people of Asian, African and European descent, I might pass a Mosque, a Synagogue, a Hindu Temple, a Catholic Church, perhaps even one of those Church of England buildings that have not as yet been turned into yuppie flats. I wait at the station before entering into a crowded carriage full of total strangers. Sometimes I may come across someone I know but, even then, I don't feel a rush of relief. It doesn't matter to my security that I may not meet a single familiar face of my journey to work; I engage with a *mass of strangers* with what Anthony Giddens has termed *civic indifference*. Even when (as increasingly happens) the tube remains stationary in a tunnel for some time (perhaps even with dimmed lighting) no great overwhelming existential fear arises. Nor, although, I live is an urban area sometimes referred to as a 'mixed inner city area' do I fear walking home late at night from the tube. How is this possible? What are the preconditions and stabilising factors at work in this apparently mundane but, upon examination, evidentially artificial way of living?

You may ask, is not this civil indifference just a phrase describing a non-caring, non-interested relationship to other people? Milligram (1970) argued that urban residents encounter so many different people and so many different sights, that screening mechanisms are psychologically required to prevent 'information overload'. To control the otherwise extreme range of demands which might be made of the individual 'norms of noninvolvement' develop which structure social interaction. Urban residents deal with others in terms of roles, rather than as whole individuals.

Consider the high level of interactive skills and self-control which is required in another scene: an average tutorial/seminar class at the college where I teach may contain individuals from four different continents, a variety of religious affiliations, and be roughly balanced along gender lines. Consider the level of socialisation into the personal skills of tolerance, or non-violence, which is actually required to carry out a university seminar group.

A male fundamentalist Islamic student may have to listen to the opinion of a female Jewish student. He is even expected by the seminar leader to take her opinion seriously ... and vice versa – all permeations are possible. Arguments are expected to be conducted at the level of reasoned discourse – pride and honour are not expected to lead to duels, to physical fights – is this not amazing?

Consider, also the immense problems of getting through the layers of complex rituals and procedures which every day life demands. Take the finding of sexual partners, which takes for the civilised human so much more time and effort than any other species in the animal kingdom. Late modernity places the onus firmly upon the individual. Although friends and family may make introductions, in the modern west the individual is expected to do the finding and choosing for him or herself. Students learn screening techniques and the different approach rituals which the various locations of teaching room, cafe, bar, party and library require. Messages, significations, body language, gossip from other quarters - all must be scrutinised and interpreted – effort undertaken, rejection accepted, alternatives arranged or the quality of interaction uplifted ... Moreover we must learn to tell when sexual desire turns into romantic love, and, if and when this happens, a new set of rituals and interactions with families and the legal system may be engaged in.

And we think we do it ourselves. Modernity tends towards an ideology of the self as the creator of his or her own values and the designer of his or her own destiny. We believe we control the important aspects of our lives. However, complex webs of culture and social structure bind us. Even when we may think we are free in our actions the reflexive knowledge projects of modernity soon turn our freedoms, our self-determinations into illusion. We may think we have fallen in love and rejoice; writing letters full of quotes from our favourite poets. Until we read works such as Niklas Luhmann's *Love as Passion* (which demonstrates how the romantic ideal of togetherness is a functionally determined effect of modern social structure); or Michel Foucault's *History of Sexuality* (which shows how modern sexual freedom is domination in another form – we are free but only to enjoy 'good' sex, taught how to achieve satisfactory orgasms); or Anthony Giddens' *The transformation of Intimacy: sexuality, love and eroticism in modern societies* (in which modern sexuality, which Giddens describes as 'plastic', is a direct function of its technological freedom from reproduction – such technological advancement results in the need for a radical democratisation in sexuality and intimacy). Or we may sit opposite a Professor of Biology at a formal Cambridge University dinner who informs us that we can have sex with a variety of people, but can only successfully marry a person whose body odour is compatible with our own!

What do we do? We go back to our poets.[1] We refuse to believe it. If we really did believe that our bodies, our language, the social structure, our class, our roles, conditioned our thoughts and behaviour so completely that we were reduced to the ontology of mere puppets or ciphers in a code, that we were just objects moved around by social structure ... why would we continue?

But the knowledge commitment of modernity tells us we ignore these discourse which situate us at our peril. Of course, sociology tells us by way of consolation, we can play at the roles. Erving Goffman (1974), a sociologist who specialises in the prisons and little gaps between the big social structures of everyday life, tells us that when we think we are escaping from roles we do not like we are merely playing with other socially provided roles. The linguistic philosopher/social theorist Wittgenstein (whom H L A Hart relies upon) said much the same thing in his work of the 1950s when he said that our routines of everyday life were actually structured language games. It is impossible to escape from language games, but this does not mean we must be reduced to idiotic inactivity – we can keep adding to the games, changing little bits, making new moves, demonstrating the contingency of social life. Even Foucault, in the later volumes of *The History of Sexuality*, relented from his image of the individual as the object of overlapping power forms, holding that we can use the discourses of modernity to create space for self-expression and active, creative, play.

When Marx said that society thought through us he did not mean that we have no room for manoeuvre. What he meant was that there could never be a non-social individual. The individual can only exist inside the social; the dialectic is inescapable and the foundation for all thought, for all liberty. As he put it:

> 'Human beings make their history themselves, but they do not so voluntarily, not under circumstances of their own choosing, rather under immediately found, given and transmitted circumstances.' (Quoted in Wagner, 1994: xiii)

This is the key lesson of the sociological imagination: we, our freedoms, our modern rituals, our ability to trust, the individuality that we pride so much, all are the creations of modernity. They only exist inside a certain sets of social structures. Our socialisation, our awareness of choice, our being, is largely the consequence of the contingency of our locality. But how free are we? How predetermined are we to simply act out a script written by our birth, our parents, their class, their skills at socialisation, the level of love their marriage

---

1   Poets have, classically, been perceived as the enemy of rational scientists. Perhaps poets always laughed at the pretensions of science to 'explain everything'.

contained? How much can we escape from the past? How true is it to say that society is built upon the foundations of common sense attitudes and expectations?

The narratives of civil society

Everyday life is a communicative space – disobeying the rules leaves one open to criticism. Whatever the process it clearly relies upon sets of narratives of life. Let us go back in time to early modernity, to the experiences of the Scottish Writer, David Hume, and the German Philosopher, Immanuel Kant.

David Hume (1711-1776) and the foundation of experience

In *The Treatise of Human Nature* (1978) David Hume set out to found modernity upon the security of the truth of human nature. If we were to understand the basic nature of the human condition we could then build up the good and just society. Ultimately, Hume argued, we need a conception of the self: our true knowledge of the structure of the self will be the touchstone for securing modern society.

Hume is not alone in this desire, for example, if Liberalism is to be seen as beginning with the work of Locke and Hobbes, both roughly labelled as empiricist, its beginning placed great reliance upon a notion of the individual's private consciousness (a conception of the self) as the foundational basis upon which the political entity of the autonomous individual could be fashioned. Thus, the intellectual soul which Descartes discovers, through the introspective voyage of sceptical doubting, as a self-contained ego of reason, is matched by the Hobbesian conception of the self as the seat of desires and volition.

When, however, Hume sought a firm place to secure modernity upon, he was disappointed, for the self was not stable. Hume could not even find a semblance of a stable self through introspection:

> '... when I enter most intimately into what I call myself ... I can never catch myself other than the series of perceptions which are present at that time ... the mind is a kind of theatre, where several perceptions successively make their appearance; pass, re-pass, glide away, and mingle in an infinite variety of postures and situations ... there is properly no simplicity in it at one time, nor identity in difference.' (1978: 252-3)

What is the self? To what do we refer when we speak of a person's self? For Hume the self is only a creation of the facility of memory. A person's memory organises his or her experiences into patterns of beliefs and reactions, into patterns of expectations and sets of trusts or fears. The memory allows the imagination to shape a series of somewhat related perceptions into a unity and creates a *fiction* of the self, by which means order can be made of otherwise chaotic presentations. The fiction of the self is, thereby, a product of the memory, via the faculty of recall and reflection on our past perceptions, which represents them as linked together into a network of relationships. The memory, via this act of recall and fictional creation, transforms a 'bundle or collection of different perceptions' into the fiction which provides us with a notion, an idea, representing diverse perceptions into a patterned entity which is the only possibility of continuous identity that exists. What sort of presence does the self then have?

Although the belief in the self is a 'natural belief', and thus demanded by the functioning of nature, the claim that it amounts to a real personal identity is a 'confusion and mistake' (Ibid: 254). Moreover, Hume states that the fiction of the self has another function. For when we do not utilise this fiction 'we are apt to imagine something unknown and mysterious'. In other words the use of the fiction of the self, and the reflexive acknowledgement that it is a fiction, saves us from the trap of metaphysics; that is, from the enthusiasm of metaphysics. There is no secure self; there is no-extra social self. The self is the product of the everyday life experiences and it is given shape through the narratives of everyday life.

Hume revealed that when we reflexively try to find the self we perceive a site of interaction, a theatre, and not a structure. When we bore into the self, trying to understand and control its aspects, we lose ourselves in an existential crisis – we find no secure place from which to make correct decisions, which to keep as our touchstone – we find ourselves hopelessly lost and despair of all activities and have no criteria to differentiate good thoughts from bad, no criteria to differentiate pleasure from vice. To retain our sanity we must return to the narratives of the common life, to the flows of stories about what we are and should be. We, however, gain a measure of freedom through adopting an attitude of mitigated scepticism towards the various narrative which surround us and offer us directives. We must live by stories; people carry stories which define for them their characteristics and tell them what sort of person they are. But this does not mean we are to return to an uncritical approach to these stories; we must free ourselves yet we recognise that the purity of the naked self cannot exist. All social interaction occurs with people who bring images and understandings to the interaction. Occasions and events have narrative histories. Individuals are not simply pre-programmed computer bites but subjects engaging in the practical activity of making their way through varying life situations.

Immanuel Kant and the need to rely upon pure reason

Kant (who lived between 1724 and 1804) claimed that Hume woke him from his dogmatic slumbers. How could man survive as a moral agent in a truly scientific world? And if the self was a creation of the narratives of everyday life, what happened to morality? Did moral obligations become subjective, or emotive; simply a matter of conventions and reactions to events and scenes? Or worse, a matter of mathematics, of a utilitarian calculation of the costs and benefits?

The developing physical sciences, which were premised upon the assumptions of cause and effect, appeared to have the potential to destroy many of the fundamental ethical and religious beliefs of the time. The physical sciences worked on the assumption that everything that happened had a cause and the cause *determined* the events that happened – therefore, once we knew the antecedent conditions, what happened was the only thing that *could* have happened.

This led Kant to conclude that the physical sciences could completely explain all the events in the natural or physical world; but when we are considering our own conduct, in particular, our moral predicaments and decision making processes, we believe that we (and everybody else) had alternative courses of action in front of us. If we did not have this belief, how was any ascription of responsibility possible? How could we either believe that we were responsible for what we actually do, or that others were responsible for what they did? Thus it seemed to Kant that certain fundamental beliefs and features of our everyday life, of what Kant would call our practical rationality, were contradicted by the basic presuppositions and structures of physical science; or what Kant would call theoretical rationality. Let us put the question in another way. If all the operations of the entities in our universe were governed by scientific laws, is there really any room in such a universe for human beings operating as moral creatures governed by free will? Concomitantly, where, in a universe able to be understood by science and governed by scientific laws, did God fit?; God's existence appeared to be something apart from such a system. Kant believed that previous thinkers who had considered this matter had fudged the issue by downgrading the ambitions of the physical sciences. Traditionally, when it came to a conflict between believing in science or believing in God, science lost out. This position, however, was no longer tenable in the enlightenment context of critical rationality.

Kant basically divided the world into two spheres of existence; crucial to this division was the distinction made between what he called 'things-in-themselves' (or the world as it is 'in itself'), and the world of 'appearances'. The world that we will experience and be able to understand through our sensory apparatus, the world which we can come to observe, is a world of what Kant called 'appearances'. This is the world that science can come to understand. But there is another world which is knowable via the very fact of working through the meaning of our moral convictions. Note here that Kant uses these moral convictions, uses the very fact of our every day intuitions and expectations, as presuppositions for a whole structure, a form of reality which is independent of the empirical world of matter in motion governed by scientific laws. Thus we can have two distinct sciences: the sciences of the *Sein* and those of the *Sollen*. On the one hand, there is the world of appearances which the physical sciences and principles of scientific structure provide the whole truth about (the sciences of the *Sein*). On the other hand, there is the world of things-in-themselves, and in this world we are able to use a whole set of human concepts, such as those of free-will, of rational agency, of good and bad, of the soul; a range of concepts which determine what one '*ought*' morally to do. These series of *ought* propositions and related concepts, do not reside in the world of appearances, but exist outside the world of appearances, and they are unknowable to the sciences of the world of appearances.

Criminology has been tormented by this division; criminal justice administration has seen a great battle in perspectives between the presuppositions of the criminal law, with its notions of free will, responsibility, and ascription of causality to the offender so that we can blame him or her, and the structure of much of positive criminological knowledge, which has sought to explain the offender's actions through his or her background, social position, biological and psychological constitution, etc. We can get to a position where the human sciences, of which criminology is a part, have implicitly said: 'do not blame the offender, he or she was not responsible for his or her actions, do not punish them but treat them, crime is the same as a disease'. While the discourse of the criminal law says: 'no, we have to relate to offenders as independent, self-controlling responsible individuals in charge of their own destiny'.

On which side was Kant? In fact the Kantian division allows us to make sense of this whole debate. On the question of human action, and the types of causality that we could use to explain this, Kant's answer was to create two spheres of knowledge. When the actions and choices of humans are regarded as events in the spacial-temporal world, then they must be subject to the laws of empirical necessity. When we begin, as independent observers, to explain human action, we may trace the commission of crime to factors such as heredity, education and environment. These are, however, so effective in our explanatory scheme as to have made it impossible for the individual not to have acted in this way. We can do no other, since assuming laws of nature we must conclude physical necessity, that is the physical impossibility of doing other – theoretically we assume an inevitability of action – otherwise our science cannot come up with the laws of predictive generalisations we are committed to. If this is so then when we ascribe a range of freedoms to a person's actions, this is only the consequence of our lack of information as to all the conditions, circumstances, factors and degrees of influence that prevent us from a total knowledge of that person's action – and hence from predicting exactly what he or she would do in the circumstances.

However, Kant notes, that even in the light of this potentiality being realised, we persist in holding a person responsible for his or her actions, and we join in the general social practice of attaching an appropriate blame or reward.[2] In our usage of theoretical reason, we adopt a stance which has developed into the various roles of criminologist, sociologist, psychologist and so forth, whilst in

---

2   Conversely, those who are thoroughgoing, such as B F Skinner, cannot speak any language of praise or blame. Skinner acknowledges this, demanding that we move beyond dignity, humans are nothing but conditioned animals.

our role in civil society where we attribute praise and blame, we consider the situation in the light of 'practical reason'. It is in this light that we hold moral feelings and legislate laws, which have as their presupposition that people need not breach them. To pass a law is to assume that people can do the prohibited activity; the law has no reason for existence otherwise. In fact, we are saying that a person should not do certain things, and if a person should not have done an action but actually did, then we are saying that it must have been possible for him or her not to have done it. But, we, as psychologists and so forth, have the potentiality to offer a complete explanation in such a way for there to be simply nothing visible to us that could have enabled the person to have refrained from the action. It is in this quandary that Kant introduces a strange concept peculiar to human action. He calls this 'another causality', that of 'freedom'.

This is one example of what Kant termed 'transcendental objects'. These are objects that transcend experience and sensation based systems of description. The criminologist who bases his or her approach upon the foundations of empiricism will never be able to consider the operation of this 'causality'. However, by the use of transcendental objects, we may regard the offence in question (he uses an example of lying) as completely undermined in relation to the person's previous condition. It is 'as if the offender started off a series of effects completely by himself'. Kant goes on to say that when we are faced with a situation where our theoretical reason tells us empirical conditions have determined a persons actions, we may still legitimately hold that person responsible and blame him or her. Thus we are justified in holding a man responsible for his actions, even as we, as (future) criminologists, can also say that 'before ever they have happened, they are one and all predetermined in the empirical character'. But how are we justified in this? Kant states:

'... this blame is founded on a law of reason by which we regard the reason as the cause which, independently of all the above mentioned empirical conditions, could and should have determined the man's actions in another way. We do not indeed regard the causality of reason as something that merely accompanies the action, but as something complete in itself, even if the sensible motives do not favour but even oppose the action; the action is imputed to the man's intelligible character and he is wholly guilty now, in the very moment when he lies; therefore the reason was wholly free, notwithstanding all the empirical conditions of the act, and the deed has to be wholly imputed to this failure of reason.' (*Critique of Practical Reason*, A.555)

As well as the closed and determined grip that the empirical observer can hope to identify there is always 'another causality' operative which can ensure a different action; and this 'another' is of its nature not able to be located in any spacial-temporal causal series. The ability to partake of this other realm of causalities is, moreover, that aspect of human beings which makes them fit subjects for moral praise and condemnation which accompany participation in the linguistic and practical arrangements of our world. Furthermore, it is upon the supposition of the operation of a person's 'will', and the concepts associated with it, that practical, free and rational life is possible. This rational, free life comes from the interaction of the will with an *a priori* law essential to the operation of morality. Kant held:

> 'These categories of freedom – for we wish to call them this in contrast to the theoretical concepts which are categories of nature – have a manifest advantage over the latter. The latter categories are only forms of thought, which through universal concepts designate, in an indefinite manner, objects in general for every intuition possible to us. The categories of freedom, on the other hand, are elementary practical concepts which determine the free faculty of choice. Though no intuition exactly corresponding to this determination can be given to us, the free faculty of choice has as its foundation a pure practical law *a priori*, and this cannot be said for any of the concepts of the theoretical use of our cognitive faculty.' (*Critique of Practical Reason*)

These concepts are the foundation of practical life – they provide the foundation of our reactions to others in our everyday existence. They present, however, a terrible morass, for they are 'beyond the limits' of scientific reason. The scientific attitude will try to render them nonsensical.

The problematic of being a modern and being moral

Thus we have the great problem for criminology of free will – that cornerstone of the jurisprudence of the criminal law which early positivism found a discredited metaphysical illusion. What is free will? Kant called it autonomy, and appears to have recognised it as the capacity for moral self-direction. For Kant this was linked to man's independence from God, from society and from nature, his ability to act rather than be acted upon, his intrinsic quality as a supremely free agent who, when rid of dependence and oppression is clearly able to see by virtue of his reason where his moral duty lies. But this is a huge problem: specifically (i) what is the ontology of this moral agent?; and (ii) what is the status of morality?

Ultimately, the ontology of the moral agent is beyond ontology. It resides in the mystery of humanity. Kant needed to bring God back in to provide some foundation, some entity which stood outside the coordinates of time and space, beyond those things which science could tell us about.

And if we are not to base morality on some source of God's will, or mere social convention, then we have no other basis than to base morality on the foundation of mystery. Most of modernist discourse on morality is Kant versus Hume in various guises. Either we rely upon the source of morality in the narratives of the society (and here I place both the Aristotelian tradition of reading moral duties from the meanings internal to the set of localised practices of the political community, rather than an appeal to abstract principles and the argument that morality is the observance of the socially prescribed duties, either lawful or in convention, as simply the different ends of the same continuum), or we have the argument for (abstract) universality. Universality attacks all community sources of morality. Communitarianism appears to set relativism against absolutism. From the time when the Greeks feared the worldliness of the Sophists, people have feared that pluralism and diversity must lead to moral confusion and a lack of moral regulation, but is this so?

Perhaps Durkheim can help. One consequence of his analysis of the development of modern forms of solidarity is that to be a modern person, surrounded by complexity and differentiation, one has to be more moral than the pre-modern. It is easy, very easy to believe in God or to live in a stable community when there is only a limited stock of social knowledge: it is very difficult to live, as a moral person, in modernity. A moral individualism requires an increase in moral intensity and self-regard and self-questioning.

This argument is at the crux of the problem of law and order in late modernity. For many commentators appear to believe that we live in amoral times, however, are we not incredibly interested in being moral, in doing the right thing? And can there be anything more moralistic than the concept of the self-sustaining individual? The issue is rather does the demand to be a modern self, a self-controlling, self-directing individual find the necessary resources in the narratives of everyday life ... or is he or she surrounded by a huge amount of moral discourse that does not make sense. Many commentators, for example, Alisdair MacIntrye (1981), argue the latter.

In *After Virtue*, MacIntrye gives a narrative of the fate of moral theory in modernity. His argument is that while we are surrounded by a huge melange of moral discourse it doesn't make sense, there is a lot of moral noise but no coherence. To use our picture from Hume, there are copious narratives telling us what we ought to do, what morality demands, or that, conversely, we should listen to the moral voice within, but it amounts to radical ambivalence. We are told that every attempt to achieve an objective morality has failed, and we are left with our feelings or emotivism. The problem is that we no longer distinguish between manipulative and non-manipulative social arrangements. How can we understand our desires? How can we rank our life projects? Will we not be at the mercy of every advertising strategy, every new image of the good life? Must bureaucracy overwhelm life functions because we can not decide things morally?

In MacIntyre's narrative, we have opened up social life so that the self can choose and enjoy a variety and heterogeneity of human goods, can discover the free path to human flourishing, but our result in the late 20th century is that we doom ourselves to moral impotence. We would like to shape our lives ourselves, to make a glorious story of our existence, but we are denied a coherent moral language by which to do so. We are also denied any notion of the achievement of a political community as a common project. The danger is that the liberal individualist world will lose any semblance of coherence and exhaust itself. A process of civil war and a new Dark Age will ensue. Put into criminological terms: consider the arguments of the right that faulty socialisation is the key to low self-control and criminality, Macintyre asks, how can one educate and civilise human nature into virtue in a culture in which human life is in danger of being torn apart by the conflict of too many messages, so much relativism?

MacIntyre finds our societies have little moral resources to withstand the increase in complexity and incoherence of our positions. For MacIntyre a new dark age is already upon us, the post-modern condition is not one of freedom but radical incoherence and instability. As a consequence of this collapse we inhabit social distance and listen to incoherent appeals to common moral feelings which legitimate using a technical rationality not tied to any overall view of social structure and social purpose. MacIntyre, however, offers an analysis, a diagnosis; we may accept it, but the solution, to retreat into small scale well organised, morally structured communities, amounts to a privatisation of social space which offers no social programme but dooms the others to more of the same. Indeed, as we survey the world, the rise of ethnicity, of tribalism, of fundamental religions, of the demand for moral absolutes, is legitimated on their own terms by the desire for moral stability.

Born again communitarians are disillusioned with modernity, and seek to relocate a post-modern moral self into the stable moral framework of cultural homogeneity. Is this the only recourse? Do we witness a resurgence of medieval conditions? Has modernity moved into a phase of intensified fragmentation and incommensurability? Let us not overlook the scale of the problem which, to use Durkheim's phraseology, establishing a thoroughly modern everyday existence entailed, the task is to create the conditions for a modern moral individualism.

Durkheim's model of modernity restated

Focusing primarily upon the relative differentiation of roles, Durkheim held that in a society characterised by what he termed 'mechanical solidarity', every person does many different types of tasks. This society has only a low level of technology and operates as a subsistence society. Little interchange of goods ensues. In a stratified subsistence economy there is little differentiation in life style between chief and lesser members. Modernity, however, benefits from role-differentiation and specialisation which leads in turn to an increase in the exchange of products – a society characterised by an advanced division of labour. A new form of social cohesion is required, the framework of which Durkheim outlines as 'organic solidarity'.

Societies with marked role-differentiation have many more norms than do societies with smaller amounts of it, for norms create roles, and the greater the number of roles, the greater the number of norms. In such societies, roles become more complicated and sophisticated, and hence the norms become more complicated and sophisticated. Simpler societies have not only fewer norms, but less complicated ones as well.

Durkheim believed that the law would reflect the system forms of integration. He separates criminal juridical rules into 'two great classes, according as they have organised repressive sanction or only restitutive sanctions' (1933: 69). The only common characteristic of all crimes is that they offend the 'collective' or 'common conscience' of the society, which he defined as 'the totality of beliefs and sentiments common to average citizens of the same society', and which formed a 'determinate system which has its own life'. (Ibid: 79) The relative strength of this reaction becomes a function of the solidarity of the collective conscience.

The criminal law stems from the collective conscience:

'... thus we see what type of social solidarity penal law symbolises. Everybody knows that there is a social cohesion whose cause lies in a certain conformity of all particular consciences to a common type which is none other than the psychic type of society ... the nature of the collective sentiments accounts for punishment ... Moreover, we see anew that the power of reaction which is given over to government functionaries, once they have made their appearance, is only an emanation of what has been diffuse in society since its birth [ie the collective conscience].' (Ibid: 104–7)

While this view has been seen to be the basis for a whole tradition of 'consensus' views of law which provide a foundation for the relationship of law and society for a large number of theorists, Durkheim does not suggest that there is some easy consensus of norms and qualitative judgments in modern society. The determinist, positivistic, framework which Durkheim gave in his early work on suicide and the division of labour, where social control was explained largely in terms of external constraints, ie by 'social facts', must be seen in conjunction with his developing notion that social norms far from being mechanically imposed on the individual by the actions of the surrounding society, came to be internalised in the personality of social actors. This process of internalisation is a process whereby society came, so to speak, to reside inside us, and thus became part of the individual's psyche through both informal and formal processes of socialisation. Thus the essence of social control was increasingly the individual's sense of moral obligation to obey the rule – the voluntary acceptance of social duties – rather than in simple conformity to outside pressures.

This process is extremely problematic in modernity since it depends on the nature of the social structure and in particular the state of the division of labour. Thus in societies with a minimum division of labour, ie pre–modernity, essentially a similar process of socialisation is experienced by all. But in societies of advanced division of labour, differential processes of socialisation are experienced. Therefore, the collective conscience becomes more complex and abstract in modernity, and Durkheim argued the sanctity of the individual would become the organising principle of the penal system. Today we understand that law has not changed in its penal element as Durkheim envisaged; ie that punishment has not become marked by compensation, restitution and a leniency of sentencing. Indeed several empirical studies have claimed exactly the opposite result. But let us remember Durkheim is suggesting the law becomes less repressive as participation and interdependency builds, what if sizable sectors of the population are not participating and are not required by the others? For Durkheim modernity would encourage the feeling of interdependence and a growing awareness of the need to respect the individuality of others – forces of social division, the growth of an underclass, clearly render problematic Durkheim's description.

The task of moral socialisation in late-modernity: the example of gender relations

To contemporary criminologists of the Right, faulty socialisation is a primary cause of crime. For Gottfredson and Hirschi (1990) low self-control is a product of bad childbearing practices and the decline of familial institutions. But what is required in late-modern socialisation and how does it differ from the demands made of socialisation previously? Consider a central unit which the Right claim is in decline: the institution of marriage.

Modern marriage is a site of flows and demands operating both as a site for socialisation of offspring and for the personal and emotional fulfilment of its adults. It is held out as the goal of romantic and intimate connection; it is a central site for the operation of self control and maturation into a responsible parental figure. In *The transformation of intimacy, sexuality, love and eroticism in modern society*, Anthony Giddens (1992) provides an account of the modern sexual revolution, which he analyses in terms of change in the generic distribution of sexuality. Late modernity experiences the free floating disembodiment of sexuality, or what Giddens calls plastic sexuality, that is sexuality freed from its intrinsic relation to reproduction. This allows the conditions for a radical democratisation of the personal sphere. The drive for authenticity and emancipation works in this area to construct the notion of the potentiality for a pure relationship, a relationship of sexual and emotional quality, explosive in its potentiality and destructive of pre-existing forms of gender hierarchy.

The notion of romantic love leads into the conception of a pure relationship. Romantic love presupposes that durable emotional ties can be established with the other on the basis of qualities intrinsic to that tie itself; the possibility of romantic love is a necessary presupposition of the concept of a pure relationship. This is aided by the technological changes, better contraceptive methods, which free sexuality from the essential connection with pregnancy and death which characterised the experience of sex for women. Plastic sexuality is de-centred sexuality; a freedom from the needs of reproduction, a freedom which originated in a tendency to limit the family size, but becomes transformed as a result of a spread of modern conception and new reproductive technology which instead of controlling the impact of sexuality emancipates sexuality. This new form of sexuality is available to be used as part of the expression of, and indeed the creation of, personality and becomes intrinsically bound up with the creation and reproduction of the modern self. At the same time, at least in principle, plasticity transforms sexuality from being something almost entirely wrapped up in the expression of male power (what psychoanalysts call the rule of the phallus or the overwhelming importance of the male sexual experience), into something which can be more controlled and possessed by the woman. For Giddens modern society has a covert emotional history, a history of the sexual pursuits of men kept separate from their public selves. The sexual control of woman by men was much more than an incidental feature of the creation of modern social life, but was a basic element of social structure. Plastic sexuality, however, weakens the structural elements of male domination – control declines. A rising tide of male violence towards women may be a consequence since these processes help create a vortex or emotional abyss, in which the demand is for the overcoming of the old structures of domination/passivity, which the creation of new forms of communication between the sexes which has not yet been built. For Giddens the transformation of intimacy has radical possibilities and a range of dangers.

Giddens analyses a novel by Julian Barnes: *Before She Met Me*. This is a story of the everyday life in late-modernity of one Graham Hendrick, an academic historian who leaves his wife, and begins a relationship with another woman. The change has ultimately tragic consequences. At the beginning of the novel, Graham who is in his late 30s, has been married 15 years and fears that he is on the downhill slope. At a relatively boring party, he meets Ann, an ex small-time film actress who has become a fashion buyer. The meeting stirs in him barely remembered feelings of hope and excitement: 'he feels as if some long broken line of communication to a self of 20 years ago had suddenly been restored'. He is 'once more capable of folly and idealism'. Soon a full blown affair is under way, he leaves his wife and children and sets up house with Ann. The real crux of the novel is Graham's progressive and obsessive discovery of the lovers in Ann's life before he entered it. She hides little, but equally, provides no information unless Graham asks for it directly. Graham becomes obsessed to uncover the full sexual details of Ann's past. He watches her cameo parts on the screen to see whether she will give away anything by her glances. Through his research Graham discovers that his best friend Jack, to whom he had even confided his problems with Ann's life before she met him, had been a lover of Ann several years before. Graham arranges to meet his friend as if to continue his discussion but stabs the bewildered Jack, repeatedly 'between the heart and the genitals'. Graham puts a plaster on his finger, settles down in the chair with the remnants of his cup of coffee that Jack had made for him. At the same time Ann grows worried by Graham's absence which is stretched across the whole night, telephones the police and several hospitals and searches through Graham's desk to find any clue of his whereabouts. She unearths evidence of Graham's impulsive enquiries into her past and the fact that he has found out about her relationship with Jack. The only sexual encounter she has actively hidden from him. She goes to Jack's flat and finds Graham there together with Jack's body. Without understanding why, she lets Graham calm her down and tie her arms together with some washing line, Graham calculates that this procedure will give him time enough to kill himself before she can dash to the telephone for help. He then cuts his own throat, Ann, however, dives head-first through the glass window screaming loudly. When the police arrive, Graham is dead and the implication is that Ann also is dying.

What is the novel about? Probably not jealousy since when she reads through the material that Graham has collected Ann concludes that 'jealous was a word she wouldn't use of him' – the important thing is that he could not handle her past. What is the violence of the ending about? Giddens suggests that Graham's violence is a frustrated attempt at mastery. The secrets that Graham sought to discover in Ann's sexual history are bound up within non-conformity to what he expects of a woman. Her past is incompatible to his ideal. The problem is an emotional, and what you might call, resource, one. While he understands that it is absurd to expect Ann to have organised her previous existence in preparation for meeting him, yet her sexual independence, even at a time when he did not exist for her, is unacceptable to such a degree that the end result is violent and destructive. Giddens reads the novel as a mirror of the contemporary fluctuations and tensions engulfing sexuality, equality, emancipation, the desire for romantic love and the desire for pure intimacy. The male entering a true late-modern relationship would take for granted that it is a common place empirical fact for a woman to have various lovers prior to his arrival, perhaps even during a serious sexual involvement. Whilst in the past, such a woman would have been either a prostitute or regarded as loose woman, and the status of a virtuous woman attributed to those women for whom these facts did not apply to. Today such a woman is to be regarded as normal. On the other hand, men had been allowed or regarded as needing sexual variety for their own physical and emotional health. This double standard allowed men to engage in multiple sexual encounters before marriage and perhaps even after marriage. In the history of divorce, a single act of adultery by a woman was an unpardonable breach, adultery on the part of the husband was regrettable but understandable. But as later modernity has thrown up increasing sexual equality, it has called upon both sexes to make fundamental changes in their outlooks on behaviour towards and conceptions of one another. The adjustments or demands on women are considerable, but so too are those made of men, and how can traditional forms of socialisation provide men with the tools to come to understand women? In this novel, Graham neither understood his first wife nor, while feeling a great love for Ann, did his understanding escape caricature. The research he does on her does not enable him to know her as a self at all, instead he cannot escape characterising the behaviour of his first wife and Ann through the traditional metaphors of woman as emotional, physical creatures whose thought processes do not move along rational lines. While he has compassion for them, and although he does not define his new wife as being a loose woman (we note that when she had visited Jack after having married Graham she firmly rejects any advances that Jack made to her), Graham cannot free his mind from the idea, and from the reality of a threat that he feels from activities which occurred before he was 'in control' of her.

In the novel we also see the contrast between the two marriages, the early marriage is in many ways a more naturally given phenomenon based upon the conventional division between housewife and male breadwinner. His first wife

Barbara, saw marriage as a state of affairs which was not a particularly rewarding part of life and similar to a job that one does not particularly appreciate, but faithfully carries out her duties. By contrast the marriage of Ann is a complex series of interactions which have to be constantly negotiated and worked through, thus Graham inhabits an existential position in the second marriage that was only barely emerging at the time of his youth; a world of sexual negotiation, of relationships in which conceptions, commitment and intimacy have come to predominate in a way his own resources, as yet, have not equipped him for. The novel is about male power, male disquiet, and male violence in a world undergoing profound transformation. A world in which women no longer go along with male sexual dominance, and where both sexes must cope with the implications of this change; a world in which the personal life has become an open project creating new demands and anxieties. The terrain of this project is always an interactive site between huge forces. Male sexuality may have appeared unproblematic in the context of the separate and unequal social circumstances concerning the gender structure of early modernity which was the norm until recently. A range of social circumstances concealed and constituted it:

- the domination of men over the public sphere;
- the double standard of sexual behaviour;
- the associated schism of women into pure (marriageable) and impure (prostitutes, harlots, whores, concubines, witches);
- the understanding of gender differences as given by God, nature or biology;
- the problematising of women as opaque or irrational in their desires and actions;
- the sexual division of labour.

With these supports crumbling, we should expect male sexuality to become troubled and often compulsive. Several commentators have referred to this as the late-modern crisis of masculinity. And for men, to some extent welcoming the fact that women have become more sexually available, and at least claiming in the long term they want a partner who is intellectually and economically their equal, there is also the obvious and deep-seated unease when faced with the reality of such considerations. As the articles of our popular magazines narrate it, in reply they may claim that women have lost the capacity for kindness, that women do not know how to compromise any more, that women do not want to be wives any more, that they want to have wives themselves. In article after article, in book after book, come accounts of life situations in which men declare they want equality, but also make statements which indicate that they are not fully aware of the implications of such equality. Everyday requires a high reformability of social skills. Life is a series of games with new rules and structures, games which require new sets of techniques and skills. Late-modernity requires a richer process of socialisation than ever before – a socialisation into a new self. But if the requirements have intensified, the locality of this process has become more fragmented and insecure.

CHAPTER ELEVEN

LOCALITY AND CRIMINOLOGY: FROM THE POLIS TO THE POST-MODERN CITY

'The old European concept of politics as a sphere encompassing state and society was carried on without interruption into the nineteenth century. On this view, the economy of "the entire household", a subsistence economy based on agrarian and handicraft production and expanded through local markets, forms the foundation for a comprehensive political order. Social stratification and differential participation in (or exclusion from) political power go hand in hand – the constitution of political authority integrates the society as a whole. The conceptual framework no longer fits modern societies, in which commodity exchange (organised under civil law) of the capitalist economy has detached itself from the order of political rule. Through the media of exchange value and power, two systems of action that are functionally complementary have been differentiated out. The social system has been separated from the political, a depoliticised economic society has been separated from a bureaucratised state.'
(Jurgen Habermas, *The Philosophical Discourse of Modernity*, 1987: 37)

The paradox of city life: social distance, physical proximity

Cities embody a paradox of social geography in that they are full of strangers: socially distant but physically close. We have left the polis far behind; modern social life is urban and individualist. Modernity up-rooted populations, took them out of their ritualised and 'natural' locality into the city and the nation state.

In our familiarity and our modernity urban life may appear only too natural. But urbanism terrified Rousseau in the 17th century, and this fear was strong in the writers of the 19th century grappling to understand urban life and predict its consequences. Take, for example, the German social theorist Tönnies who constructed two opposing models of Community and Association (*Gemeinschaft und Gesellschaft*). The growing urban life developed its own culture which was radically opposed to the pre-modern one focused on the village and feudalism. The pre-modern, or *Gemeinschaft* society, was founded on the living experiencing of a notion of a settled order of nature which ran through the organisation of kinship, neighbourhood and friendship.

'The idea of a natural distribution, and of a sacred tradition which determines and rests upon this natural distribution, dominate all realities of life and all corresponding ideas of its right and necessary order, and how little significance and influence attach to the concepts of exchange and purchase, of contract and regulations. The relationships between the community and the feudal lords, and more especially that between the community and its members, is based not on contracts, but, like those within the family, upon understanding.' (1955: 67-8).

By comparison, modern life, that of the *Gesellschaft*, knows no underlying natural order but founds itself on the idea of contract.

'The theory of *Gesellschaft* deals with the artificial construction of an aggregate of human beings which superficially resembles the *Gemeinschaft* in so far as the individuals peacefully live and dwell together. However, in the *Gemeinschaft* they remain essentially united in spite of all separating factors, whereas in the *Gesellschaft* they are essentially separated in spite of all uniting factors. In the *Gesellschaft*, as contrasted with the *Gemeinschaft*, we find no actions that can be derived from an a priori and necessarily existing unity; no actions, therefore, which manifest the will and the spirit of the unity even if performed by the individual; no actions which, in so far as they are performed by the individual, take place on behalf of those united with him. In the *Gesellschaft* such actions do not exist. On the contrary, here everybody is by himself and isolated, and there exists a condition of tension against all others. Their spheres of activity and power are sharply separated, so that everybody refuses to everyone else contacts with, and admittance to, his sphere; ie intrusions are regarded as hostile acts. Such a negative attitude towards one another becomes the normal and always underlying relation of these power endowed individuals and it characterises the *Gesellschaft* in the condition of rest; nobody wants to grant and produce anything for another individual, nor will he be inclined to give ungrudgingly to another individual, if it be not in exchange for a gift or labour equivalent that he considers at least equal to what he has given.' (1955: 74).

The focus of attention changes, the community-society contrast specifies that the social order is no longer founded on organic bonds, but on a process of calculation. Whereas in small scale communities one is concerned with the maintenance of all those local ties which strengthen bonds, which provide informal strength, control and security, the modern looks outward into the world for exchange, gain and profit. 'The whole country is nothing but a market in which to purchase and sell' (1955: 90).

Tönnies pin-points two processes: one, the change in physical locality, the other, the change in the types of social relationships. Much of the writing on social control has focused either upon a rural-urban contrast, or a contrast between informal and formal social controls. For example Zarr writing of the development of cities in Africa:

'The effectiveness of tribe and family as agents of social control has always depended upon the cohesiveness of the particular unit. In the urban areas, this cohesiveness increasingly gives way to individualism and the vacuum created by the decline of the family and tribal authority has only been filled by the impersonal sanctions of the law.' (1969: 194)

Urban life involves a whole different set of existential questions (it is no coincidence that the development of the existential philosophy comes about with life in large urban settings). It is a contrast of moods, or perceptions, of the person to the environment.

Georg Simmel applied Tönnies' concepts in an 1903 essay *The metropolis and mental life*. Simmel reflected the Weberian apprehension of modern mass society and saw the individual as resisting becoming a mere clog. But such resistance was itself the cause of numerous social problems; in resisting the power of the large scale 'socio-technological mechanism', various pathologies surfaced. To survive we adopt a disinterested or rational attitude. Urban life robbed the self of familiar images. Images become involved in a rapid telescoping where many unpredictable and unexpected spectacles impact upon us. In this complex and increasingly pulsating world we need to develop rational thought processes, rather than rely upon our habits to cope successfully. Life in the city depends upon exchanging money, hence we reduce social relationships to a medium of exchange. We learn to calculate the terms of social life; we develop a blasé attitude to cope with the many varied experiences and individuals we encounter; if we were to inquire, truthfully, into the concerns of more than a select few, we would be destroyed by information overload – we must keep the others at a mediated distance for the sake of our own self-balance. But this means that meaningful communication becomes difficult; we create a formal reserve which further estranges individuals from other members of urban society. The individual is pushed, in exaggerated form, onto what he believes are his own resources, and engages in a frantic search for the basis of an authentic self-identity. To operate in the modern terrain the individual must be able to understand and recognise its entities, must be able to expect certain outcomes, and rely upon certain undertakings.

While the environment of the pre-modern lures us with its familiarity, it traps us into frozen status and identifies as it locates us within its customs and its status. By contrast modernity is to be the locality of freedom; therefore the environment of the modern cannot appear so threatening that we are trapped into inaction or hide ourselves behind our own fortresses. How does modernity achieve this confidence in disembeddedness? The existential trick is that the locality of modern life will be mastered and controlled, made predictable and rational.

Crime links with fear, trust, and predictability

This is crucial since modernity puts into place a unique set of processes concerning trust: we need to trust strangers since we operate in localities over which we, as individuals, have little control. Modernity creates new forms of risk (cf Giddens 1984) however, the risk, which is an ever present feature of modernity, is rendered predictable, understandable. Crime offends against existential security in that to be defrauded, to be the victim of assault or rape, to buy an item relying upon assurances which then turn out to be lies ... makes the world a more threatening place.

Both the experience of crime, and the reported rates of crime may change our relationship to locality. Consider what existential effect the following incident which was reported to have occurred in the suburb of Briarcliff, New York, may have had on the couple:

'A young couple went to dinner one evening at a local restaurant, and returned to find their car apparently stolen. After reporting it to the local police, they returned to their home and the next morning were surprised to see the car in the driveway, with an envelop on the windowshield.

"There was an emergency and we had to borrow the car", the note read. "Please excuse the inconvenience, but perhaps these two theatre tickets will make up for it." The couple surprised but pleased, told the police that their car had been returned, and the next Saturday used the theatre tickets.

When they returned that night, they found that their house had been completely looted.' (Andelman, 1972: 49)

How have writings, which we can describe as criminological, tackled the urban question?

Telling the story of urban existence: I, the oral-ethnographic efforts

The oral-ethnographic tradition attempts to communicate the human experience and offer an *understanding* based vision of the human consequences of social conditions, poverty and crime. Using direct observations, life histories, unpublished documents and a range of first hand data sources, we are offered commentaries on the effects of socio-economic change on the structure of social relations.

Frederick Engels

In *The Condition of the Working Class in England,* Engels (1845) used his own impressions of Manchester (called by a character in Disraeli's *Coningsby* 'the most wonderful city in Modern times' and 'the city of England' which had come to symbolise the achievement of capitalist industrialisation in all its grandeur and grimness), together with contemporary accounts, pamphlets and newspapers, to compile a radical and sensitive account of working class life. The themes of relative deprivation and of crime as a rational reaction to the visible inequalities produced by the industrial revolution, run through his account:

'The worker lived in poverty and want and saw that other people were better off than he was. The worker was not sufficiently intelligent to appreciate why he, of all people, should be the one to suffer – for after all he contributed more to society than the idle rich, and sheer necessity drove him to steal in spite of his traditional respect for private property.' (1845: 242)

Crime was understandable resistance, often amounting to the desire for justice against the powerful:

'Acts of violence committed by the working classes against the bourgeoisie and their henchmen are merely frank and undisguised retaliation for the thefts and treacheries perpetrated by the middle classes against the workers.' (1854: 242)

Engels saw the growth of criminality not only among the deprived working class, but also in the 'surplus population' of casual workers, what Marx called 'the lowest sediment', and others termed 'the residuum'. Engels saw the problem in terms of a culture which had developed as a response to their social and physical location:

> 'Apart from over-indulgence in intoxicating liquors, the sexual immorality of many English workers is one of their greatest failings. This too follows from the circumstances in which this class of society is placed. The workers have been left to themselves without the moral training necessary for the proper control of their sexual desires. While burdening the workers with numerous hardships the middle classes have left them only the pleasures of drink and sexual intercourse. The result is that the workers, in order to get something out of life, are passionately devoted to these two pleasures and indulge in them to excess and in the grossest fashion. If people are relegated to the position of animals, they are left with the alternatives of revolting and sinking into bestiality. If the demoralisation of the worker passes beyond a certain point then it is just as natural that he will turn into a criminal ... as inevitably as water turns into steam at boiling point.' (1845: 144–5)

This has echoes in recent American writings on the underclass, and the accent placed upon faulty training early in life is representative of the general control perspective. Engels, however, is clearly putting this behaviour into a social context, albeit with a reductionism to environmental determinism, which is missing from much recent conservative writings (and subjected to strong criticism by Elliott Currie (1985)).

Engels is not merely describing conditions but interpreting the plight of the lower classes. In interpreting he brings his own values to the fore; his work is deliberately a treatise against capitalism, and the absence of any concern with the general welfare of society, or of social justice, on the part of the capitalists. The weakness with his writing lies in the possibility that the immediacy and purity of the experience of the subjects being communicated will be distorted and twisted by the interpretation.

The surplus group (lumpen-proletariat or residuum) became of considerable interest to social commentators of different persuasions, for example Charles Booth and Henry Mayhew.

Henry Mayhew

Henry Mayhew's (1812–1887) street biography appears as an early social ecology approach to the study of crime, based on observation and description of the social conditions of the developing urban centres. His four volume *London Labour and the London Poor* offered vivid accounts of the expanding masses which filled the growing cities of Victorian capitalism. Mayhew was ambivalent; while he defined criminals as 'those who will not work' (the title of Vol 4), his descriptions captured much of the reality of social deprivation which characterised his times:

> 'There are thousands of neglected children loitering about the low neighbourhoods of the metropolis, and prowling about the streets, begging and stealing for their daily bread. They are to be found in Westminster,

Whitechapel, Shoreditch, St Giles, New Cut, Lambeth, the Borough and other localities. Hundreds of them may be seen leaving their parents' homes and low lodging-houses every morning sallying forth in search of food and plunder.' (1862: 273)

Beyond the descriptions of degradation that characterised this period, Mayhew saw the weaknesses of the human self. The problem was seen in terms of defective socialisation, or non-conformity 'to civilised habits' (*Criminal Prisons of London*, 1862: 386) and the policy prescription was clear:

'It is far easier to train the young in virtuous and industrious habits, than to reform the grown-up felon who has become callous in crime, and it is besides far more profitable to the state. To neglect them or inadequately to attend to their welfare gives encouragement to the growth of this dangerous class.' (1862: 275)

The demand for reform flows both from fear and self-interest. It is a reaction to the image of what this failure of socialisation could accomplish, but it also reflects an assumption that a healthy individual is a individual capable of exercising self-control and rational calculation. For Mayhew predictability obedience and normal behaviour is more important than the individual thinking about his situation. As with Bentham's idea of the panopticon the task is to make the behaviour of the lower classes conform to expectations. However, we can see also the growth of a new ideal, implicitly at least, is an individual capable of disciplining his impulses and planning his life. However, it was clear to Mayhew that many individuals are by nature incapable of self-control and self-motivation:

'I am anxious that the public should no longer confound the honest, independent working men, with the vagrant beggars and pilferers of the country; and that they should see that the one class is as respectable and worthy, as the other is degraded and vicious.'

Only 5% of these vagrants and pilferers were 'deserving'; they were generally a 'moral pestilence ... a stream of vice and disease ... a vast heap of social refuse' – a 'dangerous class'. Mayhew criticised the authorities for not taking steps to enable them to practice trades, in his *The Criminal Prisons of London* he defined these 'criminal tribes' as 'that portion of society who have not yet conformed to civilised habits'. They did not rationally control the passions of their bodies or condition themselves for the tasks of hard labour:

'Still the question becomes – why do these folk not settle down to industrial pursuits like the rest of the community? ... It is a strange ethnological fact that, though many have passed from the steady and regular habits of civilised life, few of those who have once adopted the savage and nomadic form of existence abandon it, notwithstanding its privations, its dangers, and its hardships. This appears to be due mainly to that love of liberty, and that impatience under control, that is more or less common to all minds. Some are more self-willed than others, and, therefore, more irritable under restraint; and these generally rebel at the least opposition to their desires. It is curiously illustrative of the truth of this point, that the greater number of criminals are found between the ages of 15 and 25; that is to say, at that time of life when the will is newly developed, and has not yet come to be guided and controlled by the dictates of reason. The period, indeed, when human beings begin to assert themselves is the most trying time for every form of government – whether it be parental, political or social; and those indomitable natures who cannot or will not brook ruling, then become heedless of all authority, and respect no law but their own.' (1862: 384)

Poor were of two classes, 'wanderers' and 'settlers'; with 'savagery' inhering in the former. He described them in terms we are familiar with from positivism:

'... there is a greater development of the animal than of the intellectual or moral nature of man, and that they are all more or less distinguished for their high cheek-bones and protruding jaws – for their use of a slang language – for their lax ideas of property – for their general improvidence – their repugnance to continuous labour – their disregard of female honour – their love of cruelty – their pugnacity – and their utter want of religion.' (*The Other Nation*: 69)

Telling the story of urban existence: II, the ecological paradigm and the attempt to develop a science of the city

The most famous tradition for analysing urban life in criminology flows from the work of the University of Chicago department of sociology conducted from the 1920s onwards. Urban sociology developed when American sociologists sought to evolve a scientific approach towards the problems of order in the modern city; the city itself was the laboratory in which the empirical features of life unfolded.

Chicago at the time had the reputation of being the crime capital of the world and professional crime and juvenile delinquency featured as important areas for research alongside homelessness, suicide, drunkenness and vice. The University of Chicago Sociology Department drew upon work being done by bio-ecologists on the structure and development of plant associations and constructed a social ecological approach.

As utilised in biology, the ecological approach highlighted a process whereby vegetation and animal life adapts to the environment by distribution over a localised area in an orderly pattern. This enables both adaptation to the environment, and the attainment of complementary uses of habitat resources.

By analogy a similar process was envisaged in the city. The various sub-populations were viewed as jostling for spatial positions that would provide them with terrain to perform their diverse functions in a developing division of labour. For Robert Park (1916) the city was:

'... a great sorting and sifting mechanism, which, in ways that are not yet wholly understood, infallibly selects out of the population as a whole the individuals best suited to live in a particular region and a particular milieu.' (1952: 79)

The city presented so many images, so many processes ... how could order be constructed? Borrowing the formalism of scholars in the continental tradition, in particular Simmel, the 'Chicago School' developed the earlier ideas of criminal areas, contamination and the 'social physics' of the 19th century

English observers of urbanisation, into an approach where crime rates were seen as a result of variables demonstrated in the physical environment of zones of the city.

A model was constructed wherein cities were portrayed as growing outwards in a series of concentric zones from a centre, with each of the zones exhibiting specialised activities and populations. The centre was a business and industrial zone. Outside this was a zone of transition characterised by a high predominance of substandard housing held for speculation in expectation of commercial and industrial expansion. In this area the housing was undesirable, deteriorating and cheap. It was also in close proximity to industry and business, housing slums of primary immigrant settlements, the poor and dispossessed, and the vice business. Zone three was characterised by secondary immigrant settlement and workingmen's homes, while zone four was the better residential area, and the fifth, and last, the commuter zone. The work of University of Chicago Sociology Department was added to by research conducted at Chicago's Institute for Juvenile Research. There, Shaw and McKay (1931, 1942) mapped out juvenile-court referral rates and found that these correlated closely to the zones. Rates were highest in the inner-city or core areas, and grew less as distance increased from the centre. They attributed causal significance to the concept of 'social disorganisation', or disturbance of 'the biotic balance and social equilibrium'; a condition found particularly in the 'interstitial areas' (areas in between the organised natural areas).

In time the general processes of invasion, dominance and succession, which determined the concentric growth patterns of the city, were complemented by a series of individual case studies portraying the actual conditions in which individuals found themselves.

Four points:

- The ecological approach can become overly naturalistic and positivistic where all the emphasis is placed on observable entities. Was social ecology a metaphor, or did science demand the methodology of a 'natural' science be applied onto the social environment? One practitioner defined it in 1925 as:

'... the study of the spatial and temporal relations of human beings affected by the selective, distributive and accommodative forces of the environment.' (McKenzie, R D 1925).

While Park appeared to go beyond any idea that the city was an artefact of man's making to imply the processes were beyond man's conscious control.

As with most forms of positivism the task is two fold, first to draw up a set of data, in this case the patterns of spacial distribution and movement, and second, to use this to get to the underlying reality which is to be analysed through this data. The data gives the clues as to the underlying processes, but if the data is doubtful – and the Chicago School relied heavily on official police and court statistics to measure delinquency in the differing areas – then so is the whole set of forces which are claimed to underlie it (criticism was quick to surface: for example Sophia Robinson in 1936 highlighted the weakness of relying upon official statistics).

- This approach reduces the significance of social and cultural factors to the geographical. Social ecology reconciled the apparent diversity of Chicago life and deviance via the concept of social disorganisation. However: (i) even the geographical approach was context specific. Various scholars attempted to apply the concentric zone model in other countries but found that the model presupposed the easy availability of land. In various countries cities often developed over land already in heavy demand, thus different patterns were observed; (ii) as the American sociologist David Matza was later to point out, to place the cause of social disorder as social disorganisation, and to locate this in terms of invasion and interstitial zones, has the effect of making social diversity the product of social pathology – it implies that there is some natural and normal formation of city life, and that conflict and strife were a reflection of the competitive principle of ecological progress. This introduces a value position as to what is the desirable form of proper social life and thus contravenes the actual self-image of social ecology's value free empirical, scientific status. To locate delinquency as caused by 'transitional' areas in the city where the normal normative structure and socialisation practices had broken down, indicates a background assumption of value consensus on social life which is problematic.

As critics such as Taylor *et al*, (*The New Criminology*, 1973: iii) have pointed out, the social reality of the modern city cannot be reduced to a series of observations on the spacial and physical level. Environmental determinism down plays the range of institutional, political, cultural and ideological factors involved and the complex interactions of intentional actors involved in city planning.

- One legacy of the early Chicago school's work is the techniques of information gathering it employed. A whole methodological heritage developed. But in lesser hands the linkages often took on moralistic overtones. While it seems to reduce the city to a mechanical inventory for study, the other the lack of comprehensive theory may allow the data to be used to blame particular groups.

- Scholars in Britain tried to apply the Chicago model to British cities. The first major work, by Terence Morris (1957) soon found the counterfactual effect of council estates which were the site of high offending rates but located in the outer rings. Morris indicated the crucial difference was the market freedom of American cities and the effects of local authority housing policies in the different areas of British cities. London grew as the coming together of various sites and was heavily affected by transport decisions made by politically influenced authorities. Perhaps the failure of the Chicago School model to universalise destroys the idea that social processes are able easily to be viewed through methodologies of the hard sciences! The science of the city saw the operation of the city as part of a natural system obeying natural laws of evolution; conversely, we cannot escape the reality that politics, big business, local authorities, the dynamics of particular local factors, all must be considered. Moreover, these interact in ways which often cannot be predicted: for example, corporate decisions to locate and invest may depend upon rumours of the problems of the locality.

The Chicago School used a concept of social disorganisation to explain the ecology of crime

Natural areas were classified by the dominant behaviour of their inhabitants. Local communities were a coming together of diverse individuals (Chicago was experiencing mass immigration), but a process of selection took place amongst these individuals and the environment which produced a 'biotic balance' of communities. Successive waves of immigration caused different types of housing, living and working zones to appear with specific cultural and physical characteristics. Diversity was selected out of the communities with each natural area being symbiotic for particular types of behaviour.

In *Delinquency Areas* (1929), Shaw and McKay demonstrated consistent differences in criminal activity between zones over an extended time, putting the highest rates in the zone of transition. Deviance was a natural response to locational and social factors in these zones.

> 'Delinquency and criminal patterns arise and are transmitted socially just as any other cultural and social pattern is transmitted. In time these delinquent patterns may become dominant and shape the attitudes and behaviour of persons living in the area. Thus the section becomes an area of delinquency.' (Shaw et al, 1929: 206)

The concept of 'disorganisation' provided the connection between types of area and social behaviour. Thus, poor housing, squalid over-crowding, and lack of community provisions in transitional areas were not seen directly as the causal influences of delinquency, but operated through the breakdown of inter-area social control. This notion of disorganisation has had a lasting impact in presenting the constitution of the local urban environment as a criminological factor.

What is a socially disorganised area? Shaw and McKay defined disorganisation by means of certain features and processes. Quantifiable features were rates of truancy, tuberculosis, infant mortality, mental disorder, economic dependency, adult crime and juvenile delinquency. There dominant features and processes were identified: the economic status of the community, the mobility of the community, and its heterogeneity. By implication poverty, high mobility, and heterogeneity lead to weak social control and high delinquency.

Social disorganisation can be criticised for being a class–relative reference point; what is to define the socially organised?. The circularity or tautology of the argument is apparent since deviance is defined in terms of disorganisation and disorganisation is indexed by deviance. Kornhauser (1978: 118-120) locates the problem in the failure of social ecology theorists to be explicit about the causal structure of their theories. She claims they would be on safer ground if they really meant that poverty, heterogeneity and mobility cause social disorganisation, and that crime and delinquency are correlated consequences.

But is social disorganisation quantifiable?

An alternative, more hermeneutical (ie interpretative) approach relies heavily upon descriptive and oral recollections. These studies seek to explain the operation of – 'slum' and 'ghetto' communities in terms of sets of meanings which are internal to them. They seek to suspend the class-reference label of disorganised in favour of drawing out what the forms of organisation internal to these communities are. As we have seen, in early 19th century England Engels correlated various reports in *The Condition of the working class in England* to interpret crime as a rational reaction to relative deprivation. He developed accounts of the deprived working classes, the 'surplus population' of casual workers, street sweepers, beggars, prostitutes and peddlers, arguing that they were provoked by their acute distress to wage an inarticulate form of warfare against the bourgeoisie. While deviance was not, however, organised or effective class activity, it showed the potentiality for developing such activity. Engels' observations are not merely empirical descriptions but are an exercise in normative interpretation; it is obvious that aspects of 19th century city life offended his notions of social justice. His recognition of the spatial dimensions of crime, and his relating this to the process of economic development, also point to the role of economic determinants in shaping the process of urbanism.

Henry Mayhew's 'street biographies' (1882) contain a wealth of description as to the occurrence of everyday deviance and crime – a normal occurrence in the midst of London's impoverished and decrepit living environments. He also relates his fears of the transmission of deviant values between deprived children and the adults who virtually school them in crime. Although the state of the economy, and the lived in environment, appear as causal factors, Mayhew also concentrates upon inadequate parental socialisation and control.

Charles Booth's massive enquiry, which began in 1886, was based on the notion that 'the statistical method was needed to give bearings to the results of personal observations and personal observation to give life to statistics'. His treatise on *Life and Labour of the People in London* (1902-3), which runs to 17 volumes, places crime in a social, environmental and locational context making deviance part of the life and work of both perpetrators and victims. Deviance is seen as socially created rather than simply a pathological condition of individuals alone.

Certain recent writers, such as Phillipson (1971) and Taylor et al, *The New Criminology* (1973), have claimed that socially disorganised areas are actually quite organised; in fact sociology, as a discipline, appears orientated to find an underlying order in what appears diverse and disorientating. The ecological model was criticised as giving a simplistic view of the slum or inner city as a breeding ground for social problems; for depicting certain areas as places of unpredictability, fear, tension and instability of social relations. The city, it is argued, is more than a particular formation of physical environment which is pathological, decaying, poorly serviced, squalid and insanitary. The Chicago School had added to the apparent convergence of official rates of crime, illegitimacy, family instability, mental illness and so forth claiming causal links. Their associations fitted in perfectly with the assumptions of architectural determinism (thus slum clearance projects), which in simple terms held that clearance of physical slums lead to the destruction of social disorganisation. That policy can now be seen as a failure and the culture of poverty theorists, such as Oscar Lewis (1959), who depicted a cultural orientation of those living in poverty as characterised by an absence of social organisation beyond the family, a tendency to authoritarianism, helplessness, dependency and inferiority, can be seen as expressions of the over simplifications of such analyses. Participant observation, conversely, has depicted the high degree of organisation within the slum (eg Thrasher, 1929, and *The Gang*, 1937; Suttles, G *The Social Order of the Slum*, 1968). Studies show that there are sets of social control effective there (Whyte, *Street Corner Society*, 2 ed, 1955; Glazer and Moynihan, 1963). There is little evidence that formal agencies of social control (namely, the police, schools, welfare,) are any more effective on their own in middle class areas in directing behaviour and structuring social organisation, but that in such areas these agencies flow out of middle class cultural forms themselves and complement them. However, the feelings of social or individual satisfaction, or frustration, are problematically present in any area, and it is unfounded to deny their existence in the 'slum'.

This section has stressed the positivist and naturalist tendency of the Chicago School, however, we should not neglect another feature, the attempt to understand the lived reality of urban life. The young Edwin Sutherland, teaching at the neighbouring University of Illinois at Chicago, and preparing the first edition of his Criminology text book in 1924, says this of inner city poverty:

'Poverty in the modern city generally means segregation in low-rent sections, where people are isolated from many of the cultural influences and forced into contact with many of the degrading influences. Poverty generally means a low status, with little to lose, little to respect, little to be proud of, little to sustain efforts to improve. It generally means bad housing conditions, lack of sanitation in the vicinity, and lack of attractive community institutions. It generally means both parents being away from home for long hours, with the fatigue, lack of control of children, and irritation that go with these. It generally means withdrawal of the child from school at an early age and the beginning of mechanical labour, with weakening of the home control, the development of anti-social grudges, and lack of cultural contacts. Poverty, together with the display of wealth in shop-windows, streets, and picture shows, generally means envy and hatred of the rich and the feeling of missing much in life, because of the lack of satisfaction of the fundamental wishes. Poverty seldom forces people to steal or become prostitutes in order to escape starvation. It produces its effects most frequently on the attitudes, rather than on the organism. But it is surprising how many poor people are not made delinquents, rather than how many are made delinquents.' (1924: 169-170).

We should note the final two sentences: one criticism of the attempt to link poverty or unemployment with crime has always been that the majority of the unemployed, or working class, are not convicted for crime. If poverty causes crime, it is argued, then we would expect all poor people to commit crime - this is nonsense, but often said. As Sutherland is indicating, the link between crime and poverty (or unemployment) is not simple, and the causes of crime are not unitary. Perceptions ... attitudes ... bitterness ... the reality of social bonds ... the ability to achieve desires ... there are multiple effects of poverty that interact and produce a range of possible combinations, so that prediction on the individual level is a different project to grasping general tendencies. Sutherland argued that 'the proper method of explaining a process is by describing what is going on in that process rather than by trying to relate something in the process to something outside the process' (1926: 62).

In subsequent years the Chicago School took a pluralist approach to the ecological composition of the city and adopted a sympathetic observation of daily life. The aim was to obtain policy orientated findings relevant to the perceived needs of the local populations which would direct relevant social welfare planning. The work of Howard Becker, such as *Outsiders* (1963), is a case in point. David Matza (1969) was to call this a Neo-Chicagoan approach and labelled it 'appreciation' rather than 'correctional'. However, even then their approach remained largely within the uncontested context of a free market economy and a capitalist-liberal political democracy. The world of everyday deviancy was experienced and communicated; it was set into the wider geographical structure of the city, but the structural flows which were deemed relevant were so tied to ecological modelling, or the lived in context of everyday reality, that questions of economic structure, or of a differential distribution of power in the national political economic context, were never allowed to be raised as factors which constrained or created daily city life. By contrast the study of everyday life should provide a meeting point for various disciplines and aim for a combination of micro-, and macro-, sociological forces. A city is a site of culture and existential concerns, such as a consideration of the rational and the supposed irrational, of the strong and the vulnerable, which permits the formalisation of concrete problems of construction – ie how the social existence of modern human beings is produced, its toing and froing from want to affluence, from appreciation to depreciation, from celebration to crime.

Understanding urbanity: III, beyond the naturalist paradigm

Anthony Giddens (1989) argues that studying the modern city cannot be divorced from considering the general social characteristics of societies, and the social transformations brought about by the formation and development of capitalism. Whereas in pre-capitalist society, the city was the centre of state power it only hosted a limited range of productive and commercial operations; the vast majority of the population were engaged in agrarian occupations. It was capitalism which moved the population into the city, moreover, it did this, in the main, by developing entirely new cities. Manchester, the site Engels observed, for instance, moved from 10,000 inhabitants in 1717, to 300,000 in 1851 when it was a manufacturing centre, and more than 2,400,000 by the end of the 19th century.

With the driving force behind the growth of urbanity being capitalist development, the traits of contemporary urbanism displayed the effects of 'commodification', the process where all entities in the social world come to be perceived as goods, capable of being bought and sold in order to generate profit. We can make sense of modern urbanism and the structuring of daily life within it by seeing how space itself becomes commodified in capitalist societies. Modern urbanity is marked by increasing alienability of land and housing (alienable means that property can be transferred by some mode of payment). For example, the policy of the 1925 English Property Law Legislation is precisely to simplify conveyancing, the state guarantees registered title to increase the alienability of land. This commodification is the mediation which ties together the physical milieu and the productive system of capitalism. Giddens highlights three features:

- Capitalist urbanism becomes a created environment which dissolves previous divisions between the city and countryside, replacing it with a distinction between the 'built environment' and the environment of 'open space'.

- In pre-capitalist societies human beings lived close to nature and many cultures conceived of themselves as participating in the natural world. Capitalist societies radically separate human life and nature, in the first instance in the capitalist workplace, in which the technological factor sever human beings from the influence of the soil, weather, or cycle of the seasons. The situating of the workplace in an urban milieu of commodified space, moreover, strongly reinforces this. The settings of our lives are almost wholly of human manufacture.

- Therefore the very concept of urban sociology is problematic; the urban environment is constituted as a built environment through a process in which capitalist production, class conflict, and the state are intertwined. Perhaps what is needed is a specie of intermediatory concepts, such as theories of housing classes, which complement the ecological heritage with accounts of how city-dwellers strive to influence decision making about the milieu in which they live. The immediate context in which people live is housing markets, connected to industrial and financial capital, on the one hand, and labour markets on the other. Locating the distribution of urban neighbourhoods in the active struggles of groups in housing markets emphasises factors of generalised importance in the capitalist societies. Considering factors such as access to decision making as to allocation of local authority housing, budgets, zoning priorities, political conflict between local authorities and central government, leads us away from any notion that the differentiation of city areas and housing types are a 'natural process'.

Can cities be controlled so that community can be created as a livable urban space?

Many features of cities are the result of attempts to control the processes within them and to create livable space. For example, Macintosh (1975: 22-23) argues that one reason the Concentric-zone effect the Chicago School discovered did not hold for London, was the government sponsored roads through 'rookeries', or urban areas characterised by high rates of offending, in order to disperse offenders throughout the city. In the field of architecture and urban design the modern dream was that planning and development could focus on large-scale, city-wide, technologically rational and efficient urban zones, backed by absolutely no frills architecture. Space is something to be shaped for social purpose.

The physical composition of the city is also a message, a discourse. What is being said to the recipient? What messages impact on the individual as he or she travels around the city? Consider the symbolic poverty of certain areas and the visible richness of others. Thus zones are not indicators of disorganisation and organisation, but are significations of poverty and power, versus wealth and powerlessness, or differential consumption power. The latest model BMW or Jaguar, versus the rusting 10 year old Toyota.

Currently it is fashionable in the US and Britain to decry all that was done to cities in the postwar reconstruction period of high modernism. Jane Jacobs (1961) voiced a withering attack upon the modernist pretensions to rebuild cities in *The death and life of great American cities*:

> 'Low income projects that become worse centres of delinquency, vandalism and general social hopelessness than the slums they were supposed to replace. Middle income housing projects which are truly marvels of dullness and regimentation, sealed against any buoyancy or vitality of city life. Luxury housing projects that mitigate their inanity, or try to, with vapid vulgarity. Cultural centres that are unable to support a good book-store. Civic centres that are avoided by everyone but bums, who have fewer choices of loitering places than others. Commercial centres that are lacklustre imitations of standardised suburban chain-store shopping. Promenades that go from no place to nowhere and have no promenaders. Expressways that eviscerate great cities. This is not the rebuilding of cities. This is the sacking of cities.' (Quoted in Harvey, 1989:71-2)

In England, Alice Coleman furthered this theme (see *Utopia on Trial*, 1985) and applied the ecological approach to the problems of public sector housing (1988). Coleman's thesis was of strong environmental determinism. She appears to mistake a correlation between bad design and anti-social behaviour with causation. Coleman saw crime as a factor of anonymity, lack of surveillance and easy access and exit in housing estates. Design changes could, therefore, radically reduce crime. Specifically, there should be a halt to the building of public sector flats and stabilising features should be incorporated into designs. Oscar Newman's ideas of defensible space should be considered and, for example, overhead walkways abolished; every dwelling or block of flats should have its own enclosed garden area instead of being surrounded by anonymous open space; a large scale programme to modify existing estates should be undertaken.[1]

But we should not give prominence to physical space as if it were an independent determinant factor. The implementation of Coleman's ideas on several estates brought varying results. In London, when walkways were removed from the Lisson Grove estate, crime dropped by 50%; in the Lea View estate, after a range of design modifications crime dropped dramatically; while on the Wigan House estate, there was little change. Is the reduction of crime attributable solely to the change of physical design, or are there a range of more subtle factors at work, including a change in the mood and perceptions of residents on the estate? What is the effect of a changed perception by residents that someone is doing something about the problems of the estate? Can this lead to the residents exerting more restraining pressures?

This tendency to blame physical form for social ills is a kind of simplistic environmental determinism that cannot be accepted in isolation. We should not neglect the wider impact of what the much maligned planners of the large scale estates were attempting to do in the post Second World War era. To a large extent they had tried to create, not recreate, modern communities, and while some housing projects were dismal failures, others were not, particularly when compared with the slum conditions from which many of the people had come.

Locality as a site of social interaction

Modernist planning had sought to perfect the good model, it could not fight the strength of the capitalist market *processes*. Cities are sites for social interaction on a large and small scale and the essence of life is process. The question is how can these processes be humanised, and the conditions for a meaningful social existence be made possible? For a time, those who wrote from a socialist perspective argued only a wholesale replacement of the values underlying the social structure would suffice. As Quinney and Widlerman put it in their 1977 book *The Problem of Crime*:

> 'Urban America as we know it has become outmoded and like the dinosaur, is threatened with extinction unless we radically restructure our urban institutions along truly humanitarian and socialistic lines, free from alienation, competition, hierarchy and exploitation. Such restructuring, for example, would accord priority to decentralised power structures of community control over massive dehumanised and centralised power structures (1979: 149-50).'

---

1   Oscar Newman (1972) created a theory of 'defensible space'. This sought to identify the features of low-crime neighbourhoods and buildings that make them 'defensible'. These include a strong sense of territoriality; natural surveillance of public spaces; a good image and attachment by residents to the locality. Territoriality implied that as people felt attached to a locality they were inclined to defend it against intruders; natural surveillance referred to the ease by which residents could keep watch over places where crime might occur, thus potential offenders are likely to go elsewhere. Neighbourhoods which appeared run-down or vandalised were more likely to become even more so.

The recent post-modernist movement in social geography argues that instead of waging war upon social disorganisation, we should learn from healthy city environments with their subtle systems of organised complexity. The post-modernists argue the energy and vitality of successful social interaction depends upon diversity, intricacy, and the capacity to handle the unexpected in controlled but creative ways. The cry goes up to turn against the limited period of modernism and seek differentiation. The idea is consciously to only plan and think on the small scale – to attempt to construct a whole series of little communities. There are some (for example, Krier 1987) who think we should be seeking to create a city form made up of complete and finite communities, each constituting an independent urban quarter within a larger family of urban centres. Thus, it is hoped, the symbolic richness and purity of ethnic diversity and participation will create a tolerant and vibrant whole. The danger is this in turn would create a new set of problems; specifically a return to pre-modern forms of ethnic solidarity.

Present cities are socially created places. If the concept of community has any force as a goal, then community has to be actively and consciously created anew in defence of a sphere vulnerable to colonisation by the operating dictates of the market. We may not, in the end, want community. We are trapped in the range of processes which modernity has unleashed, we cannot stabilise them without recognising their scale; nor does the idea of insulating ourselves into some small pockets of resistance (as some, such as Alisdair MacIntyre (1981), appear to desire) hold much for humanity. Once the idea of process is to the forefront then we are led to consider the catalysts of these processes. In post-Second World War city planning, urban planners and designers in the period of high modernism made a mistake in waging war on diversity, fearing chaos and complexity because this was identified as disorganised, ugly, and irrational – thus their approach engaged in a reductionist association of processes which were complex with social disorganisation. But the late-modern city has defied this modernist approach – it has responded to processes of capitalism on the global scale, together with the increasing complexity and power of technology, communication, transportation, and the desire for individuality. The result may be a city environment appearing as if it is about to disintegrate, as if the city will soon to be transformed into the terrain of *Blade Runner* or *Escape From New York,* or other cinema representations of the urban future. To survive we must humanise the processes, although the chances of defeating them by negation alone appear slim. Perhaps it is not the inclusivity of community we can strive for, but a modernised structure of *civil society*.

End-Game: the city as a site of communication and the arrival of the post-modern city

Post-modernism indicates a loss of control of the nation state over its affairs. Post-modernist discourse speaks of a world in which social and economic forces cannot be contained within the area of the nation state. Global forces are transforming the economic bases of the city areas. In industrial terms, the West experiences a change from a heavy manufacturing industrial base (displaying the Fordist arrangement of the large scale factory with a set assembly line, employing a large number of semi-skilled males, and using raw materials themselves produced in very labour intensive ways, and transported onwards to markets by rail and sea) to a situation where a considerable amount of production is relocated in Newly Industrialising Countries (NICs). The world has moved into a new logic and geography of production, employment and distribution, which has changed both land-use and the opportunities for social occupation. This has effects on the ordering of the urban hierarchy and has profoundly affected the economic links between geographical locations. Several trends have appeared across the developed capitalist countries: a decline in manufacturing and an increase in service employment; a decline in the status of the industrialist and engineer, with a rapid growth of the producer services sector at the top of the urban status hierarchy; a concentration of economic power in multinational forms and financial institutions; the transnationalisation of information and capital flows; the decentralisation of manufacturing and routine office functions; the demand for a greater flexibility for production technologies and a decline in the role and status of non and semi-skilled labour; the social fragmentation of industry; the need for new forms of cooperation and coordination between economic sectors; and the linking together of spatially distant sites of production and distribution. The financing needs and techniques available for modern corporations, as well as take-over strategies, have become larger and more complex. In short, the whole organisation of social practices across time and space has been radically disorientated from its modernist structures of production, exchange and consumption.

Cities have changed and their layout and functions depend upon their respective niches within the economic and political hierarchy of their nation, and the place of the nation in the world economy. Western cities are capitalist, but are not simply different models on the one capitalist city theme. Some cities, have become premier global cities, while others have suffered the decline into 'rust-belt' status. All cities have been affected by the internationalisation of capital and the rise of new technologies that have caused the outflow of manufacturing from old urban centres to peripheral areas at home and abroad. Some, for example, London, Tokyo, New York, Los Angeles, have gained from the increasing importance of financial and coordinating functions, as well as tourism and cultural production. Above all the fate of cities takes place within a new set of spatial and social circumstances for which we use the terms post-industrialisation, transnationalism, or post-modernism.

Politically, economic activity has to respond to (and has mostly encouraged) a change in the overall technology of production away from hierarchical to market forms of control. Instead of settled concentrations of populations forming hierarchically organised structures (communities) around sites of industry and manufacturing, Scott argues:

'... the net effect will be an intricate labyrinth of externalised transactions linking different producers, many of whom will coalesce in geographical space to form clusters and subclusters of agglomerated economic activity.' (1988: 54)

Perhaps the new urban region will be looser, connected by modern communication and transportation technologies. The process, however, cannot be reduced to some simple economic determination – various subprocesses of local political and organisation forms operate with particular localised effects.

Large cities create various 'technoburbs', or peripheral zones, with concentrations of knowledge and skill intensive functions, while the central areas retain the concentration of finance, advanced services, entertainment, and site of immigrant location. The daily life-world of the citizen reflects the development of communication and transport: the experiences of those of the outer suburbs may be more of communication with other regions than with the core of their city. This new city life promises greater freedom: people live lives that are not limited to their locality or region, they move rapidly across major areas of their country and freely travel to other countries (at least they do if they have the resources, otherwise they watch others do it). The post-modern city is a communication and transportation network, a site where images from all parts of the world are available, where freedom tempts and desire is encouraged.

The onset of new divisions, social polarisation and the development of an underclass

As we shall discuss in Chapter Seventeen, controversy surrounds the changing social structure of major urban areas. Against the development of what is now termed post-industrialisation, or post-modernism, for most of the 1960s and 1970s politicians argued that a return to affluence would soak up the unemployed, and recreate the forms of social interaction and relative economic stability and homogeneity that appeared to characterise the immediate post-Second World War period. Instead more complicated social structures emerged, with a lower class unable to find work within the prevailing occupational hierarchy and drifting into the status of an underclass; a working class employed, perhaps, as clerical personnel in large offices, or as low-level service workers in hospitals, hotels, and retail establishments; a technically trained middle class acting as the support structure for the major firms and government; a disparate group of aspirants seeking fame in the entertainment industry; an astonishingly affluent upper class occupying the top echelons of the big law partnerships, real estate development firms, investment banks, security brokerages and media companies; and in some cities, such as New York, a largely immigrant stratum working in the old manufacturing sector, and frequently also forming its managerial ranks (for example, Asian families revitalising the English textile business). These groups inhabited a city where former manufacturing buildings and dockland sites housed the affluent; recent immigrants imparted life to decayed neighbourhoods; previously sound housing deteriorated as a consequence of low-income occupancy, and inadequate or non-existent government subsidies; while monies for Local Authority housing was restricted, and investment in such accommodation often became a question of *The Colour of Money* (Mullings, 1991), and parks and abandoned buildings became the dormitories of squatters. Increasing land values in the urban core encouraged the dispersal of mobile middle-class residents and back office functions, even as professional and managerial personnel gentrified centrally located housing. Private market forces wrought this physical and social restructuring of major cities, but the state encouraged the process by relaxing planning controls and underwriting development costs. In Britain the 'right to buy' legislation, whereby residents inhabiting local authority accommodation were given the right to buy previously rented property at substantial discounts on market prices, had one effect in 'residualisation', or increasing demarcation of housing estates into upwardly mobile and problem estates. The interaction between macro- and microsociological factors occasionally brought results which were locally unpredictable. Violent urban disturbances, for example, may have served to force investment in particular areas. As one localised study in London argued:

'An assessment of the scheduling of major housing investment programmes in the boroughs studied, suggests a relationship between the approximate dates of approval and the incident of urban unrest. When poorly represented people actually took charge of a situation through riot or threat of riot there appears to have been a greater drive towards investment in the most volatile areas. Since the 1980 urban riots there appears to have been a mushrooming of major projects on run down estates, disproportionately populated by black households.' (Mullings, 1991: 49)

Meanwhile the state reinforced 'private' business concerns by guaranteeing that banking failures would not result in either a crisis of confidence or the sort of economic disaster which occurred in 1929.

The decline of certain cities had disproportionate effects by ethnicity. The population of Detroit in 1950 was nearly 2 million, of which 15% (about 300,000) were black; this had fallen to a little over 1 million in 1990, with a black proportion of over 70% (over 700,000). Thus the white population had declined from 1,700,000 to less than 300,000 in only 40 years. First the white middle classes, and then black professionals, moved in massive numbers from the city to its independently governed suburbs. As its population has fallen, Detroit's murder rate has increased tenfold, from six murders a year per 100,000 people, to about 60 per 100,000 people in 1990 (*The Economist*, 1990).

With intensification of capital flows and concentration of finance in central areas, for cities such as London, New York or Los Angles, areas of the old city were reconquered by a new gentrification. Government allowed big business and real estate speculators to have their head, with the argument that the effects of a new wealth would 'trickle down' to the poorest sections. The 1980s were talked of in terms of an urban renaissance, but many community groups pointed to the persistence of the older characteristics, including high levels of unemployment and poverty, deteriorating housing, declining public and private services. From this perspective, the trickle down effect appeared nonsense, or one sided; all the costs and few of the benefits.

Dualities or pluralities of life worlds may exist in the same city. London, Los Angles, or New York may contain two or more separate economies, occupying increasingly segregated neighbours and social systems. While we may see a zoning of areas in terms of wealth, Los Angles, London or New York may witness a juxtaposition of homogeneously low and high-income areas, the homeless sleeping rough on the streets of the richest areas, the broadening of educational and employment opportunities for some, and the narrowing for others. The new high-skilled labour force occupy a different social geography of the city, to the misery of those on the margins of the market and outside it. While their lives may be in close spatial proximity, they are distant in social and economic expectations, and perceptions of legitimacy.

An environment of communication

Our scenes and ideas are no longer a factor totally of spatial locality. The city is a site of communication dominated by the technologies of imagery and signification (television, advertising hoardings, radios, cars), but situated within themes of the aesthetics of decline and renewal. Everyday life is a routine existing in commodified spaces (the experience of which is clearly influenced by which mode of transport is your usual one: the bus, the tube, the train [and which class], or the car [and which type of car]?). This is the terrain of divisions and tensions: not just public and private, but surveyed and targeted; the predominance of 'urban style' with all its various manifestations; the gleaming towers of the new, status-conscious, post-modern architecture, the development of 'graffiti art'.

The city is a site of the communication of popular culture ... music, noise, beat, the symbolism of fashion ... How do individuals construct their self-identities in these surroundings? What is going on? Is the culture of the modern city a radical democratisation of life forms ... or a bureaucratic society of little noticed, but very real, enforced consumption?

Perhaps the reality contains both aspects. Daniel Bell (1979: 20) talks of the impact of the professional cultural mass (DJ's, advertising, publishers, TV personalities etc), who turn the creative energies of designers and artists into commodities for mass consumption, and who are moved by the constant need for consumption to keep capitalism developing. For Bell, we have lost a sense of hierarchy in cultural authority, which has been replaced by an 'anything goes' levelling (pop-art, pop culture, ephemeral fashion, mass taste – the circular effect of the pop-ratings), where the quality of a product is judged by the number of sales. Thus, culture becomes a qualitatively mindless (replaced by emotivism or whatever sounds or feels good at the time), hedonist consumerism. A top record stays at Number One on the charts for a matter of a few weeks, but then the DJ asks 'Haven't you all become sick of this – I know I have,' and so it plummets.

Chambers (1986, 1987) argues working-class youth in the post-Second World War era have increasingly come to participate in the capitalist consumer culture, where they actively use fashion to construct a sense of their own public identities. A dialectic is in place. On the one side, the impact of a mass fashion and advertising industry, on the other, the desire for individuality and authenticity. Out of this comes increasing flexibility and short-termism. Above all, throughout all, moves the growing importance of image:

> 'Post modernism, whatever form its intellectualising might take, has been fundamentally anticipated in the metropolitan cultures of the last twenty years: among the electronic signifiers of cinema, television and video, in recording studios and record players, in fashion and youth styles, in all those sounds, images and diverse histories that are daily mixed, recycled and 'scratched' together on that giant screen which is the contemporary city.' (Chambers, quoted in Harvey, 1990: 61)

Reality becomes a mobile set of signifiers. Is Madonna really Marilyn Monroe? What does it signify to be 'dressed like a virgin'? Who gains out of 'cherishing you'?

Harvey suggests, that in the era of mass television:

> '... there has emerged an attachment to surfaces rather than roots, to collage rather than in-depth work, to super-imposed images rather than worked surfaces, to a collapsed sense of time and space rather than solidly achieved cultural artefact.' (1990: 61)

What is going on? Who, or what, determines the superimposing of different worlds in the advertisements we are surrounded by? And what is their effect(s) upon desire? Upon *motivation* to crime? Who determines the winners and losers?

The late-modern, or post-modern, city as a mobile site

The depthlessness of the late-modern architecture of the city becomes a cultural manifestation: appearances, surfaces, instant impacts with an ambivalent concern for sustaining identity and power over time (Jameson, 1984; Jencks, 1984).

Does a new sense of dimension or (non)control result from the flows of spectacles and images of the late modern city? Consider the growing preoccupation with instantaneity – 'we dream the same dream, we want the same thing ... oh, oh, heaven is a place on earth' (Belinda Carlisle, 1989). Was it two songs or one? And in *Real* (Album of 1993) in 'Situation Flammable' ... if life is a big scary animal ... who or what are the big scary animals? Consider also the impact of technological advances for transport links and communication, including the international flow of television. What are we to make of Harvey's suggestion that in the age of mass television there has emerged an attachment to surfaces rather than roots, to collage rather than indepth work, to superimposed images rather than solidly achieved cultural artefact? Why should individuals who feel the pressure of urban society, for the everyday world does not pressurise everyone to the same extent, feel bonding to the historically created bonds of civil society? In a world of the mass, of the technologically produced, why should those almost invisible renderings of human endeavour warrant protection?

We are referring to the visualisation of buildings – new technologies for construction mean that urban forms can be more dispersed, decentralised and deconcentrated than ever before. While modernist forms highlight utilitarian functionality, certainly the representational appearance of community can come back in with post-modernist architecture. In the best light, we can see a challenge for the urban designer to communicate with different client groups in personalised ways considering different situations, functions and taste cultures. So called post-modern architects are working with signs of status, history, commerce, comfort, and ethnic domain. They are attempting to create images of neighbourliness catering to the taste of the locality. The danger is that these features are expressed through the process of the market and popularism. Rowe and Koetter, in a recent work entitled *The Collage City*, see the icon of the abstract entity 'the people' coming into play at the expense of real human concerns.

> 'The architectural proponents of populism are all for democracy and all for freedom: but they are characteristically unwilling to speculate as to the necessary conflicts of democracy with law, of the necessary collisions of freedom with justice.' (Quoted in Harvey, 1990: 76)

The image of the people as the source of legitimacy presumes assimilation and hides the fact of real diversity – the problems of minorities and the underprivileged, or the diverse counter-cultures, get forgotten. The hope for community based planning that will cater for the needs of both rich and poor alike tends to presuppose the existence of close-knit, cohesive urban communities as the basic point of reference in an urban world that is in flux and transition.

Different urban cultures and community groups express their desires through differentiated access to political power and market status. For many critics, the development of the city is likely to become even more market driven in post-modernity, since the market is increasingly held out as the only possible universal language of communication. Although in the short run we may get interesting examples of cross-gentrification, a mixture of configurations, market and land-rent potentials will shape urban landscapes into new patterns of conformity. One tendency will be the further division of the city, and the marcation of locality into areas corresponding to the secure and the dangerous, respectively inhabited by the well adjusted citizen and the criminal. While the transport and communication melange will ensure that even these are not hermetically sealed. Again the individual is pushed into the dialectics of control and angst, of the feeling that he ought to know what is going on, and the impossibility of grasping meaning. Almost by necessity, late-modern city life imposes a tension boardering on the radically schizophrenic. The surroundings are all artifacts; they are all creations of modernity and cannot claim any natural stability. They display the symbolism of power, but their contingency is too obvious. If stability is sought in these forms, incongruity results. Urban residents need distractions from the onset of this absurdity of contingency.

In part, the production of needs and wants, the mobilisation of desire and fantasy, depend upon the politics of distraction, as part of the tactics of the market, to sustain consumer demand. Modern politics may require the disorientation of potentially opposing groups to maintain the mirage of technical superiority.

We talk of a shrinking world; communication and transport infuse local space with the events of more distant space, so that it becomes confusing to draw steady time-space lines to preserve a sense of control over the locality. In an unruly world displaying disjointed moral, political and economic systems, with images of stock market crises daily, the architecture of order is one theme which may stand amidst change, decline, power, and transitoriness. But what is the message to the individual of the contemporary city?

'Destruction and demolition, expropriation and rapid changes in use as a result of speculation and obsolescence, are the most recognisable signs of urban dynamics. But beyond all else, the images suggest the interrupted destiny of the individual, of his often sad and difficult participation in the destiny of the collective.' (Rossi, 1982: 22)

Again the concepts of familiarity and distance are in play; they provide a locus of control. Not control of the individual, but the individuals' existential perception of security, the understanding that he or she is in an environment that is not threatening, that the environment is itself under control. Thus it is not some mechanical social disorganisation that should be taken out of the social ecology approach as the relationship of locality to crime, but a human understanding that a locality that does not provide the material and psychological resources for self and group growth, providing instead messages which are disorienting and confusing, will stimulate impulses to do something. On some occasions crime may stem from an absence of control, but that this does not function as usually acknowledged; instead of crime being undertaken when control has lessened, and so crime appears as the negation of control, crime may well be an attempt to seize control of the moment. This theory will be developed in our consideration of culture, the influence of Matza and a reading of existentialism, but here we should also recognise that if crime is, in part, an attempt to seize control in an environment which threatens one with systematic powerlessness, it is a movement which is destructive and adds to the criminogenic condition; it is an action which causes harm to the networks of the locality. But this locality may not be apparent to the offender, to this actor, since it may present itself as fiction, fragmentation, collage, and eclecticism which, if infused with a sense of ephemerality and chaos, impacts upon the sensibilities of orientation and disorientation creating a new mood of life and action. Freedom and frustration: the divisions remain. Perhaps the offender would 'wish the same things, dream the same dreams' ... but if one is alienated, distanced from one's locality, why should one wish to caress it?

Modernity: the desire to construct a home and the differing experiences of post-modernity

Modernity wished to create a home for mankind on this planet. Is our urbanity the place we can call home? If modernity was intended to be a construction project, have we found a home? Or is crime a sign of homelessness. Consider two statements. The first is by Parminder Chadda (1992), a female, Asian poet, born in Kenya, about her relationship to Southhall, that strongly Asian suburb of London. It is an image of home, a home that offered some security, so that the self could move on but still be bound. The second by Strome Webber (1992), an African-American poet, relating her image of New York and the lack of freedom to be herself (a lesbian searching for the personal, and social liberation, modernity promised).

Southall

'Oh dear Southall
didn't we struggle to call you home
But you, alone gave birth to us
and weren't we strong in you once
In your arms we ran and played,
and then,
God, how your streets aroused us
But we came away
We couldn't control you
We couldn't let you control us
And so we struggled, we discovered
We came to find 'our place'
and you are now so culturally accessible
and we are of course, so safe
Oh dear Southall
Coming to you now still bolts the system
and why not? Maybe it should
We have no right to call you ours:
Maybe we should have stayed
Oh, and as the Broadway looms, and
the traffic jams start,
Some part of our naive hearts
still call out to seek refuge
but too much has passed between us
How is it that you rule us?
We fought to leave
We struggle to return
How indeed you fool us'

to be a woman in new york city

'to be a woman in new york city
is to be a warrior
these days
i'm so sick of violence
i'm ready to kill somebody
like every two-footed dog
i heard say bitch this year
& laugh/yes every mother's son
why waste the oxygen?
consider the greenhouse effect
& all this so called expression
of popular culture
that uses me for an asswipe
or a jack off rag
may the poison you disperse
so freely/choke you slowly
while mr. t fucks you up every orifice
(wit no grease)
& i'll play those records LOUD in yr ear
yeah motherfucker i house you
you in MY HUT NOW
little mister man
you who are not my daddy
my brother my son or lover
MIND YR BIZNISS
my hair my ass my tiddies
my girlfriend are MINE
you know you cd be LIVING
instead of barking & scratching
on street corners
whyn't you STAND UP
let go of yr dick
& be a human being'

We search for home, late-modern (or post-modern) urbanity provides it, and dislocates it. For some time criminology shared in the dream of total reconstitution; the image of the total renewal of the society. Realism has now set in.

New left realism

In the UK, new left realism refers to a movement loosely grouped around Middlesex University under the guidance of John Lea and Jock Young. Its founding text is: *What Is To Be Done About Law And Order* (1984). Left realism originated as a political platform – an injunction to the political left to take crime seriously – rather than an academic theory. It is concerned both with the crimes of the powerful (organised crimes, the crimes of powerful corporations, and of the state), and with the problems of street crime, such as mugging, burglary and interpersonal violence. Together, these activities have a real and destructive impact on the poor and working class communities which are least able to cope with them.

Left realism is both an outgrowth of the 'radical' tendencies of the new criminology of the 1970s, and a consequence of the decline of utopian energies. The crime problem is no longer seen as partly created by media myths, moral panics, or false consciousness; crime is acknowledged to be a real problem, and fear of crime has both a rational core and real effects. Crime has anti-social impacts and results in real victims. Crime, however, should cause us to think about the moral bonds of the social order and the idea of disorganisation – crime appears to be implicated in a rather special way. For example, the traditional emphasis upon inter-personal crime, as identified with street or lower class crime has both social causes and social effects. Moreover, while the particular psychological form, or correctionalist perspective, early positivism took was misconceived, the search for finding the causes of crime should not be discarded. As mainstream Criminology has come largely to abandon these etiological questions in favour of a know-nothing managerialism, left realism argues that radicals must return to the obvious contexts in which crime emerges in modern capitalist society (poverty, racism, deprivation, social disorganisation, unemployment, the loss of community) and demonstrate causal links.

Rhetorically, left realism discards earlier idealist notions which elevated the criminal into a 'primitive rebel' or cryptopolitical actor. Marxist concerns and imagery of economic determinism are valuable, but while important for retaining a grasp of the overall social, historical and economic context of crime and social life, criminology cannot afford political marginalisation. It should strive for relevancy by operating on the very same terrain that conservatives and technocrats have appropriated as their own.

Left realism strives to gain touch with the everyday realism of crime. By use of victim surveys and local knowledges, it moves closer to the commonsense public knowledge of what constitutes the crime problem. Only here, it is claimed, in the age beyond grand scale utopian visions, can any credible alternative to mainstream criminology be constructed, and the possibilities for effective participation in policy-making be realised.

A particular focus of attention is the problem of community integration and policing within the locality of inner-city socially deprived areas. Working with tools derived from Merton and American sub-cultural theory (see Chapter Twelve) the experience of relative deprivation and the individuals' perception of unjustified inequality is highlighted. In modern inner-city life, working-class individuals inhabit a locality of immediate surroundings of neglect and deterioration, alongside advertising images of the glittering prizes of capitalist society. Relative deprivation explodes the mythology of equality of opportunity and the easy availability of wealth and affluent lifestyles, it enhances the sense of frustration and failure experienced by marginalised groups. The impact of communication, advertising and transport destroys any insularity of working class communities and renders difficult local solidarity. Left realism also understands much crime as innovative, as rational adaptations by individuals to the situations they find themselves in.

The concept of relative deprivation describes feelings which are not specific to inhabitants of absolute deprivation but can be experienced also by the successful white male in business, who is constantly chasing a new consumption dream. The feelings of relative deprivation demand action, not merely to achieve what are perceived as the necessities of life, but also to attain status. In late-modernity self-worth is often gauged by the power to display status goods, such as particular types of clothing, sports shoes, watches, video recorders and other items which are valued not so much for their functional utility, but for their symbolic messages. Left realism argues that the impact of relative deprivation was made worse in the 1980s by an increasing culture of pure egoism. This culture of egoism appears in the economic and political discourse, characterised by the Thatcherite claims for privatisation strategies, and the actions of large multinational companies, as exampled by the Bhopal incident in India. At the same time large numbers of people were becoming economically marginalised through no fault of their own, thus being cut off from legitimate channels of consumption, while the Company Directors, whose decisions were responsible for their redundancies, enjoyed record pay-outs. The 1980s were, therefore, a period of increasing relative deprivation.

Victimisation and opportunity are other issues. For example, increased affluence has increased the level of car ownership and the amount of time spent outside the home. This leaves more homes unguarded, while also increasing the pool of people vulnerable to crimes of violence committed in public places. Certain cultural values intensify the vulnerability of particular groups by providing offenders with labels to produce twisted justifications. Social groups identified as outsiders are particularly liable to victimisation. On the one hand, they are less likely to get support from the community, for example, by neighbours in cases of racial harassment on housing estates, while, on the other hand, a rapist attacking a lone woman may feel that 'she is asking for it' by being alone in particular social locations, such as bars and clubs.

Crime is located as the particular outcome of a complex set of social structures. It is impossible, analytically, to divorce crime from the whole set of social processes which locate and structurally limit working class localities:

'Crime is the end-point continuum of disorder. It is not separate from other forms of aggravation and breakdown. It is the run-down council estate where music blares out of windows early in the morning; it is the graffiti on the walls; it is aggression in the shops; it is bins that are never emptied; oil stains across the streets; it is kids that show no respect; it is large trucks racing through your roads; it is streets you do not dare walk down at night; it is always being careful; it is a symbol of a world falling apart. It is lack of respect for humanity and for fundamental human decency.

Crime is the tip of the ice-berg. It is a real problem in itself but it is also a symbol of a far greater problem; and the weak suffer most.' (1984: 55)

'Crime impacts upon the public perception, but we are apt to be confused by its nature and limits. We fail to see its wider nature, its linkages, implications and underlying depth. The event which is labelled a "crime" creates an immediate impression upon our mind, and is the most blatant example of anti-social behaviour, but it is only the tip of the iceberg of a whole series of more frequent, supposedly everyday, events which are not deemed as criminal acts. Nor do they readily come to mind as the source of the expressed criminality. Petty vandalism may be regarded as just kids fooling about; larking and hooliganism as mere exuberance, but they are also part of a structure of aggression – thus left realism argues against the commentators who maintain that because most crime is minor, it is unimportant. Consider sexual harassment; rape should not be clearly demarcated from the considerable level of sexual harassment at work and in the streets. Such harassment is often deemed as a minor inconvenience or the woman misinterpreting what are really complimentary behaviour; but rape is the end-point of a continuum of aggressive sexual behaviour. It's comparative rarity does not indicate the absence of anti-social behaviour towards women; on the contrary it is a real threat which also symbolises a massive undercurrent of harassment.' (1984: 58)

Thus, we see a depressing dialectic: crime is not only an effect of structural dislocation and powerlessness, but also reinforces and perpetuates such powerlessness. Crime is an expression of alienation, frustration, and the way in which unfairness is experienced in the world; but its commission propagates itself by involving others and intensifying the powerlessness experienced in that locality. While the harshness of crime is a survival mechanism in an unjust world, the commission of crime continues and develops this experience of harshness among the poor. It feeds upon itself by further brutalising an environment already brutalised. 'Paramount in this context is a feeling of political and social impotence.' (1984: 61). For left realism the differential location of crime, with high rates of crime experienced in particular localities, is an obvious and blatant injustice affecting that locality. Moreover, it is in such localities that the police themselves are apt to act criminally, which further intensifies the feelings of political impotence and social stigmatisation. Bad policing creates crime by destroying community interaction, destroying the flow of information to the police and destroying the perception that real criminals will be apprehended. Discriminatory legal treatment further marginalises vulnerable groups; black youths, for example, economically marginalised to begin with, are forcibly impressed with their political marginalisation and powerlessness by illegal treatment by the police. Left realism attempts to combine perspectives from both strain and control theory. While street crime is caused by the experience of injustice in brutal circumstances, anti-social behaviour is also a function of the degree of social control. Society is not held together by the thin blue line of police, but by the feelings of the public and the everyday bonds of civil society. The police can only operate effectively when civil society is reasonably coherent; for example, the police require a steady flow of information from the public. It is the public which inform the police of a crime, either as victims or witnesses and provide the police with the information, to solve it. The public are both alarm systems, providers of information and witnesses in court. If any one of these functions breaks down, crime would go unsolved. Street crime however, has a paradoxical image, which means it can be easily appropriated by the New Right. The New Right sees in street crime only the interaction of a predator and victim. The narrative and cultural forces tending towards individualisation in modernity, encourage the search for causality to be located within the construction of the offender/criminal. Conversely, for left realism, street crime is the most transparent of all injustices. The act of crime is a breach of justice, in that it is an infringement of the law, but the causality of crime is unjust, in that it offends the structure of social justice. We see a form of divided victimisation: while the offender is a victim of social injustice, his/her own victim becomes a victim twice over. To left realism, street crime is the outward manifestation of the underlying levels of deprivation and the structures of racism, chauvinism, and egoisms running through the social order. By contrast, the concentration of right realism on controlling the offender, omits the real and pressing problems which working class people experience.

Investigating Los Angeles: Mike Davis and the post-modern City of Quartz

For Mike Davis (1990) in his book *City of Quartz*:

> 'The ultimate world historical significance – and oddity – of Los Angeles is that it has come to play the double role of utopia and dystopia for advanced capitalism. The same place, as Brecht noted, symbolises both heaven and hell. Correspondingly, it is an essential destination on the itinerary of any late-twentieth century intellectual, who must eventually come to take a peep and render some opinion on whether 'Los Angeles Brings it All Together' (the city's official slogan) or is, rather, the Nightmare at the terminus of American history .'.(Flysheet)

Los Angeles incorporates many of the features of post-modern concerns. From its beginning Los Angeles was an imagined city - it was a site with few natural reasons for existence, apart from the images of the future held by powerful investors. Its development depended upon a huge artificial harbour, the piping in of water from a long distance, and the mythology of real estate speculators that here was a city in the making. But what was first imagined, became, admittedly in changed forms, a reality. Contemporary Los Angeles portrays immense technological power (it is the site where the space shuttle lands, and in the giant shed of Air Force Plant Forty-two the stealth bombers and other secret weapons of destruction are assembled); it is also the home of gangster rappers, like the former group NWA (Niggers With Attitude) who featured sirens and gun shots as background accompaniment to brutal and super-realistic x-rated tales of drug dealing, gang-banging and police confrontations. The records/discourse of NWA claimed to be merely telling the real story of what it is like living in the ghetto. As the lead singer EZ-E stated '... we are giving reality. We are like reporters. We give them the truth. People where we come from hear so many lies that the truth stands out like a sore thumb'. But this reportage out of Compton was done for a specific purpose: 'We are in this to make money'. Thus the story of the effects of commodification and consumerism, telling the reality of the streets like it is, becomes another commodity. The work of the gangster rapper, telling the exploitation and horrors of the down-side of late-modernity, becomes translated into another consumer unit. The rapper becomes a celebrity, presented by the smiling white record company executives, while the audience looks at their customised assault rifles and listen to the rhythm of recent drug-busts, mega-bangs and funerals of friends. In their own way NWA join with the mainstream Hollywood of *Rambo* and *Robocop* in providing fantasy power trips of violence, sexism and greed.

The physical structure of the city towers over an emerging poly-ethnic and poly-lingual society. Perhaps the two most obvious symbols are the recently rebuilt commercial down town, with its amazing celebrations of accumulation, and the run down bungalows of the ghettoised areas. For Davis contemporary Los Angeles witnesses the destruction of public space. Space becomes either ghettoised and segregated into ethnically strong territories, or privatised. It becomes divided between arenas of non-security and Fortress LA:

> '... the carefully manicured lawns of Los Angeles's Westside sprout forests of ominous little signs warning: "Armed Responses!" Even richer neighbourhoods in the canyons and hillsides isolate themselves behind walls guarded by gun-toting private police and state-of-the-art electronic surveillance. Down-town, a publicly-subsidised "urban renaissance" has raised the nation's largest corporate citadel, segregated from the poor neighbourhoods around it by a monumental architectural glacis. In Hollywood, celebrity architect Frank Gehry, renowned for his "humanism', apotheosises the siege look in a library designed to resemble a foreign-legion fort. In the Westlake district and the San Fernando Valley the Los Angeles police barricade streets and seal off poor neighbourhoods as part of their "war on drugs". In Watts, developer Alexander Hagen demonstrates his strategy for recolonising metal fences and a substation of the LAPD in central surveillance tower. Finally on the horizon of the next millennium, an ex-chief of police crusades for an anti-crime "giant eye" – a geo-synchronous law enforcement satellite – while the other cops discreetly tend versions of "Garden Plo"', a hoary but still viable 1960s plan for a law-and-order armageddon.' (1990: 223)

Davis draws out how Los Angeles has become a post-liberal space, where the overriding concern to defend luxury lifestyles creates a network of repressions of space and movement. A range of electronic technologies survey a post-modern space, clearly demarcated for the inhabitation of the insider at the expense of the others. The images of carceral inner-cities (*Escape from New York, Running Man*), hi-tech police death squads (*Blade Runner, Robocop*), sentient buildings (*Die Hard*), Vietnam like street wars (*Colours*), are not fantasy, but representations of existing trends. Modernity is turned on its head. The ideal of control of space becomes the denial of social integration. The dialectics of modernist social control (that of control and liberation), progress as a balance of repression and reform, is overtaken by a rhetoric of social war which positions the interest of the urban poor and the middle classes as incompatible and irreconcilable. Fortress LA refers to the unprecedented tendency to merge urban design, architecture, and the police apparatus into a single all-encompassing security effort. Security becomes itself a commodity defined by income. It is obtained by membership of an enclosed residential enclave and access to private security forces:

'While the city becomes segregated into zones of crime rates, fear moves beyond them. Statistically crime rates are self-contained within ethnic or class boundaries, kept out of the middle class areas by the boundary of security. But the fear of crime enters the middle class area through the media ceaselessly providing images of a criminal underclass and psychotic stalkers.

Sensationalised accounts of killer youth gangs, high on crack [images] of marauding Willy Houghtons ferment the moral panics that reinforce and justify urban apartheid.' (Ibid: 236)

The contemporary architecture and symbols of surveillance create pseudo-public spaces – shopping malls, office centres, cultural centres – a defended space shouting a rhetoric of keep out to the other. While architects may not be able to read the semiotics, pariah groups, for example, poor latino families, young black men, elderly homeless white females, do not need lessons in decodification.

The consequence of this security is *the destruction of accessible public space*. Predestrian streets become traffic sewers, public parks become waste bins for the homeless and wretched. The interior surveyed is safe; the exterior public space is discarded. The city becomes a collection of forbidden territories. We see a spatial apartheid reinforcing clustered development, the city is pluralised, but into socially homogeneous areas. When middle class individuals necessarily interact with the homeless or working poor, as at places where welfare is distributed, design precautions to ensure a lack of human contact (for example, grills, electronic bars) are incorporated.

Perhaps this control of space is most exampled in what Davis calls the development of the Panopticon Mall. Davis gives as a prime example, the layout of Haagen's Watts centre:

'The King centre site is surrounded by an eight-foot-high, wrought-iron fence comparable to security fences found at the perimeters of private estates and exclusive residential communities. Video cameras equipped with motion detectors are positioned near entrances and throughout the shopping centre. The entire centre, including parking lots, can be bathed in bright four-foot candle lighting at the flip of the switch.

There are six entrances to the centre: three entry points for autos, two service gates and one pedestrian walkway. The pedestrian and auto entries have gates that are opened at 6.30 am and closed at 10.30 pm The service area located at the rear of the property is enclosed with a six-foot-high concrete block wall; both service gates remain closed and are under closed-circuit video surveillance, equipped for two-way voice communications, and operated for deliveries by remote control from a security "observatory". Infra-red beams at the bases of light fixtures detect intruders who might circumvent video cameras by climbing over the wall.' (Ibid: 243).

The LAPD have invested in technological capital over patrol manpower. At the same time they have developed a paranoid *esprit de corps*, becoming a 50 pilot airforce maintaining on average a 19 hour per day vigil over high crime areas. (By way of contrast this exceeds the British Army's aerial surveillance of Belfast, the capital of Northern Ireland.) The LAPD see themselves as engaged on a war with a force as strong as the Viet Cong. This force comprises members of local black gangs divided into several hundred fighting sets while loosely aligned with two hostile super-gangs: the Crips and the Bloods. Officially these gangs are portrayed as urban guerrilla armies organised for the sale of crack, outgunning the police with copious supplies of uzi and mac/10 automatics. With a public campaign over drugs centring around the so-called crack-blizzard, even black leaders have weighed police misconduct as a lesser evil compared to drug dealing gangs. The fight against the drug gangs is often portrayed as handicapped by misguided civil libertarian measures and badly interpreted constitutional protections. Davis depicts the war on drugs as meaning every non-Anglo teenager is now a prisoner of gang paranoia and associated demonology. The authoritarian reach of police control extends into schools with schemes such as school 'Buy', where school visits by the police as friends are replaced by the inducements of undercover police enticing students to sell them drugs. Officially presented as an attempt to prevent the infiltration of drugs into schools, this appears to its critics a cheap source of the felony arrests which make the war on drugs statistically viable; at the same time, new sentencing guidelines and laws with mandatory punishments have been introduced. Davis reports the result as Kafkaesque class justice:

'... in South Central LA, a young black three-time loser, never charged with violent crime, but holding a weapon, was sentenced to life imprisonment without possibility of parole for the possession of 5.5. grams of crack. A 20 year old Chinese man received two life terms (parole in forty years) for being accessory to the murder of federal agents even though he was not at the scene, did not know that the murders would occur, and was described by the judge as playing 'only a minor role'. Meanwhile, a 21 year old Baldwin Park Chicano, high on PCP, who ran into the back of a truck and killed his passenger, was charged with murder because he was a suspected gang member. Finally, an elite LAPD stake-out team that the Times had exposed as a virtual police death squad, ambushed four young Latinos who had just robbed a MacDonalds in Sunland with a pellet gun. Three of the Latinos were killed by the cops, while the forth, seriously wounded, was charged with murder for the deaths of his companions!' (Ibid: 288).

This is a justice which since 1974 has arrested two-thirds of all younger black males in California and provided a mass of prisoners an estimated four-fifths of whom were addicted to some form of drug. As communism recedes, the image of a black criminal underclass takes on the role of *the evil other*. The war on drugs becomes a war on the underclass: a variant of the fallacy which reduces the war on crime to a war on offenders. At the same time it is increasingly difficult to gain empathetic views, given the reality of this new enemy. Statistically, young blacks have been systematically excluded from the growth in suburban service employment. Most of the Californian job creation occurred in areas with a black population of less than 1%. The unemployment rate for black youths in Los Angeles county remained at 45% throughout the late 1980s. In 1985 a public housing survey conducted on various projects in the ghetto stated that there was only 120 employed bread winners out of 1,060 households in Nickerson Gardens, 70 out of 400 at Pueblo Delrio and 100 out of 700 at Jordan Downs. Yet spending on the state school system has fallen sharply, with a drop out rate approaching 50% in many of the inner city high schools. Statistically, black males from South Central are three times more likely to end up in prison than at the University of California. While the problem of drug addiction is simply faced with the criminal penalty there are no schemes of education concerning drug usage, that would be unthinkable, drug education usually consists of exhortation to say no. Whereas prison expenditure rises, drug rehabilitation is starved of funds. Drug treatment programmes are labelled, along with youth employment schemes, or gang counselling, as the weakness of permissive wishy-washy liberals.

Davis suggests that gang members have become the stoic philosophers of a cold new reality. The sub-cultures of the Crips and the Bloods have now an impressive, almost irresistible, force. Gang bonding becomes a family for the forgotten, providing excitement and a localised social solidarity blocking out other empathies, while transforming self-hatred and low self-esteem into tribal pride. Gang membership also provides a model for status. Their consumer power and uniforms include Gucci T-shirts and top of the range Nike trainers. A cycle of youth consumerism, and the fantasy of personal power, dances with self-destruction; moreover the social contradiction of this post modern city is the blocked mobility of the youth, in the midst of a communication and transport world offering total mobility. With the only legitimate employment on offer often being minimum-waged armed security guards for the enclosed spaces of the rebuilt down-town, or the middle class area, where their role is to keep out their own non-uniformed selves. For Davis it is little wonder that entry into the underground economy, with guns blazing, and crack dealing franchises, is highly prized. Writing in 1989 Davis predicts a growth of hatred and of 'Black-lash' against the institutional structure:

> 'These particular contradictions are rising fast, along a curve asymptotic with the mean ethos of the age. In a post-liberal society, with the gangplanks pulled up and compassion strictly rationed by the Federal deficit and the Jarvis

Amendment, where a lynchmob demagogue like William Bennett reigns a drug czar – is it any wonder that poor youths are hallucinating on their own desperado power trips? In Los Angeles there are too many signs of approaching helter-skelter: everywhere in the inner city, even in the forgotten poor-white boondocks with their zombie populations of speed-freaks, gangs are multiplying at a terrifying rate, cops are becoming more arrogant and trigger-happy, and a whole generation is being shunted toward some impossible Armageddon.' (Ibid: 316)

In 1992 Los Angles experienced the worst riots in American history and the world came to talk of the rage of the underclass. A host of questions emerge. Does this post-modern city' point to a generalisable future? If the post-modern city cannot be controlled by a humanised political economy, are we to face patrolling, surveillance and segregation? Is the culture of the rule of law to be divided into a contrast of deterrence and community bonding?

It is difficult to give an answer. However, it may be that the practical range of responses varies according to our conceptual and imaginative grasp of the post-modern city and whether we can find the energy to turn against the processes of division intolerance, and the 'false-necessity' of listening only to the dictates of the market.

CHAPTER TWELVE

CRIMINOLOGY AND THE CULTURE OF MODERNITY

'It all depends on where you are.
It all depends on when you are.
It all depends on what you feel.
It all depends on how you feel.
It all depends on how you're raised.
It all depends on what is praised.
What's right today is wrong tomorrow.
Joy in France, in England sorrow.
It all depends on point of view.
Australia or Timbuctoo,
In Rome do as the Romans do.
If tastes you happen to agree,
Then you have morality.
But where there are conflicting trends,
It all depends, it all depends ...'
(Abraham, 1955 (Quoted in Edell))

'... whether systematic delinquency does or not develop is determined not only by associates that people make with the criminals, but also by the reactions of the rest of society toward systematic criminal behaviour. If the society is organised with references to the values expressed in the law, the crime is eliminated; if it is not organised, crime persists and develops.' (E Sutherland, *Principles of Criminology*, 3rd ed: 8-9)

Social order is a series of complex, interconnected and variable patterns of interaction among people in various social settings – social order is networks of social practices ordered across space and time. If geography represents nature culture is 'second nature'. It provides the medium for human life and human expression – the site of human activity. From birth humans learn and internalise a range of attitudes, norms, values and expectations. The child learns to speak and use a living social language; a language which consists of words and ideas, appropriate emotions, symbols, traditions. Culture shapes and moulds, limits and develops, the plasticity of the human (potential) self. From a functionalist perspective, while the modern self may escape from the bonds of tradition and custom he or she must inhabit culture:

'Culture, as a normative system, is a functional requirement of a human social order. Because of the enormous degrees of biological plasticity and cognitive ingenuity that, together, produce the broad variability characteristic of human behaviour, the absence of this normative dimension would render human social systems impossible. The range of behaviour patterns potential in any individual is much broader than the limited range required for the performance of any custom or set of customs. beyond a certain point, whose limits are still unknown, variability in behaviour precludes the very possibility of custom. In other words, human societies have to set limits (by means of prescriptive and proscriptive norms and of rules) to the range of permitted variability in customary behaviour.' (Melford E Spiro, 1968 vol 3: 560)

Many westerners have been shocked by the strength of the prohibitions a strong cultural network offers. In the midst of famine in India one reported:

'Through all these months the white Brahmin cattle wandered by the hundreds through the streets of Calcutta, as they always have, stepping placidly over the bodies of the dead and near-dead, scratching their plump haunches on taxi fenders, sunning themselves on the steps of the great Clive Street banks. No one ever ate a cow; no one ever dreamed of it. I never heard of a Bengali Hindu who would not perish with all his family rather than taste meat. Nor was there any violence. No grocery stall, no rice warehouse, none of the wealthy clubs or restaurants ever was threatened by a hungry mob. The Bengalis just died with that bottomless docility which, to most Americans, is the most shocking thing about India.' (Fisher, 1945: 439)

Why does the strength of a coherent culture to restrain crime appear so shocking? Where, asks the liberal, is the will to live, the call to action? Why do they not do something? This non-western (perhaps, dare we say it, non-modern) culture appears to overwhelm that injunction to life, to survival at all costs, Hobbes placed as fundamental to human nature.

For Thorsten Sellin (1938) modern crime came out of 'cultural conflict', a situation which modern western society was increasingly experiencing. Sellin defined a well integrated social group as possessing a coherent and strong culture, or sets of conduct-norms, setting out the routines of everyday life. As modernity developed, cultural conflicts arose which meant the individual was subject to competing definitions of the correct or incorrect action in given situations – crime resulted:

'For every person ... there is from the point of view of a given group of which he is a member; a normal (right) and an abnormal (wrong) way of reacting, the norm depending upon the social values of the group which formulate it ...

A conduct-norm in its irreducible form ... is a rule which prohibits, and conversely enjoins, a specific type of person, as defined by his status in (or with reference to) the normative group, from acting in a certain specified way in given circumstances.' (1938: 30, 32-3)

Cultural conflict takes two forms. Primary culture conflict results when the norms and value systems of different cultures clash (for example, when immigrants continue to observe the customs of their country of origin; Sellin relates the case of a Sicilian father who killed the sixteen-year-old seducer of his daughter and was shocked to learn he had committed a crime); secondary cultural conflicts 'grow out of the process of social differentiation which characterises the evolution of our own culture' (Ibid: 105). As social differentiation develops, various groups are created, which create their own sets of interpretations and central values:

'Cultural conflicts are the natural outgrowth of processes of social differentiation, which produce an infinity of social groupings, each with its own definitions of life situations, its own interpretations of social relations, its own ignorance or misunderstanding of the social values of other groups. The transformation of a culture from a homogeneous and well-integrated type to a heterogeneous and disinterested type is therefore accompanied by an increase of conflict situations.' (Ibid: 66)

Sellin reads the central idea of social differentiation, which Durkheim placed so central to the development of modernity, as leading to a splitting of society into various sub-groups. This cultural-conflict theory appeared to imply: (i) that offenders were responding to norms and values at variance with those of the general culture; and (ii) offenders derive from groups which are more or less culturally isolated. Thus criminologists took as their research agenda the key postulate that crime is the product of a value system fundamentally at odds with those of the culture at large. Sellin's formulation is, perhaps, rather unfortunate in that it leads to the argument of sub-cultural identification predominating, rather than the image of any one modern culture having various, competing, even contradictory messages. Merton placed this assumption of the one dominant cultural message, that of materialism, central to his theory of anomie (or strain). We have suggested that this may have reflected a society of controlled bureaucratic consumption, however, times have changed.

In the west, late-modern desire occurs largely in the context of non-systematic cultural surroundings. We have seen MacIntyre's pessimistic prognosis in *After Virtue*. In Durkheim's late 19th century analysis the open-ended possibilities of desire were kept within limits by the social structure:

'The economic ideal assigned each class of citizens is itself confined to certain limits, within which the desires have free range. But it is not infinite. This relative limitation and the moderation it involves make men contented with their lot while stimulating them moderately to improve it; and this average contentment causes the feeling of calm, active happiness, the pleasure in existing and living which characterises health for societies as well as for individuals. Each person is then at least, generally speaking, in harmony with his condition, and desires only what he may legitimately hope for as the normal reward of his activity. Besides, this does not condemn man to a sort of immobility. He may seek to give beauty to this life; but his attempts in this direction may fail without causing him to despair.' (1951 [1897]: 250)

As modernity has intensified the demands of desire have increased – the social order is meant to produce; success is meant to be attainable and this success means the possession of goods. People are meant to desire and to keep on desiring. Is this desire natural? In *The Protestant Ethic and the Spirit of Capitalism* ([1905] 1930) Weber highlighted the importance of culture by arguing that people do not 'by nature' want to earn more and more but simply wish to reproduce the conventional conditions of existence. The social system needs to arouse desire for production: how could a surplus be produced if there was no market or any demand for additional commodities? Weber highlighted two themes underlying the development of capitalism: the separation of the peasantry from the means of production (the land) by the means of various forms of enclosure and the development of an ascetic calling in the world to dominate and master the environment. Human geography and culture interact; culture is part of social geography. Weber sees a progressive distancing of man from an embeddedness in his natural environment (which gave a form of natural community) where man's thoughts were naive compared to today and he only had a limited conception of his needs and desires. As capitalism develops the body is rationalised and needs/desires are amplified. Capitalism requires an expanding process of secular amplification and displays of desire (advertising, marketing). The first law of the market is that desire must be stimulated – but what limits or controls can be legitimately placed on desire? And what happens when they are frustrated? What happens when the items desired are not forthcoming?

Richard Cloward and Lloyd Ohlin argue the result depends on how an individual perceives the legitimacy of the social order and locates failure:

'The most significant step in the withdrawal of sentiments supporting the legitimacy of conventional norms is the attribution of the cause of failure to the social order rather than oneself, for the way in which a person explains his failure largely determines what he will do about it.

'Whether the 'failure' blames the social order or himself is of central importance to the understanding of deviant conduct. When a person ascribes his failure to injustice in the social system, he may criticise that system, bend his efforts toward reforming it, or dissociate himself from it – in other words, he may become alienated from the established set of social norms. He may even be convinced that he is justified in evading these norms in his pursuit of success-goals. The individual who locates the sources of his failure in his own inadequacy, on the other hand, feels pressure to change himself rather than the system ... By implication, then, attributing failure to one's own faults reveals an attitude supporting the legitimacy of the existing norms.' (1960: 111-112)

Perhaps the most basic theme of culture and crime can be summarised as follows: culture can be a strong restraining medium, or it can be a medium through which the solution to frustration or stress takes the form of a criminal act.

Consider the logical oppositions:

- If we accept culture as the medium: the necessary environment for human understanding; then

- culture can be restraining; for example, in the case of Japan.

Conversely:

- culture can be criminogenic; in particular, we should note the idea of modernity as radically individualist and freedom loving; disrespectful of authority.

We may then need to ask whether late-modern or post-modern culture is developing into a super criminogenic form. One theme appears to argue that

Western modernity, as it is currently developing, is inherently criminogenic. In his *Thinking About Crime*, James Q Wilson made 'attitude formation' a crucial variable. Attitudes are shaped and supported by intimate groups, family and close friends and Wilson argues the west is producing a radical individuality amounting to a cult of self gratification, rather than self-control.

Wilson seems to understand that crime is socially located. For example, he sees drug dependence as a feature of that fraction of the population whose lives are in a state of perpetual disarray; however, Wilson espouses a form of right realism, in that whatever the ultimate causes, we must face up to the fact that we have to deal with these disturbed persons:

> 'We have not learned how to reach deeply into the lives of such persons; we can alter prices, change penalties, and provide counselling, but we cannot create character or restore a lost, or perhaps never extant, sense of identity.' (1974: 180)

For Wilson, as indeed for MacIntyre (albeit they consider themselves on opposing sides of the political spectrum), contemporary cultural emphasis is upon an ethos of self-expression rather than self-control. Thus culture affords an important remedy for crime; the solution to crime is to understand culture and change its most criminogenic forms.

Culture as a restraining medium: the case of Japan

Japan has appeared as the odd one out in terms of the growth of crime since the First World War. After the devastation of the end of the Second World War Japan was under foreign occupation and experiencing an extremely high crime rate. As Japan subsequently developed into the second most industrialised and capitalised country in the world, its crime rate has fallen. Both the quantity of crime, and the quality and quantity of fear of crime is low in Japan. In 1990 the major reported crime in Japan (a country of 120 million people) was larcenery – 88%, with fraud and embezzlement at 3% each, indicating that minor offences predominante in officially reported crime. The majority of larceny offenders were juvenile (under 20 years old) and were mainly convicted for bicycle theft, motorbike theft and shop lifting. Few violent crimes were reported in 1990: 1,200 homicides; 1,600 robberies, 23 of which had death as a result and 671 resulted in bodily injuries; only 81 of the burglaries involved rape. When traffic offences are included, traffic negligence comprised 26% of all penal code offences involving 600,000 offenders and the death of 12,000 people. Japan has less than one-twelfth of the number of reported homicides than the US or one-sixth of the US rate per head of population, but has more than 1.2 times the clearance rate. (Figures from Moriyama, 1993)

What factors influence the crime situation? Three direct factors have been mentioned:

- Strict and effective legal control over firearms; since the confiscation of swords by the ruling elite in the 16th century to prevent rebellion, modern

Japan does not have a tradition of weapon carrying. Only 1% of so-called armed robberies are carried out with a gun compared with more than 60% percent in the US. Japan does have organised gangs which carry guns, and there have even been reports of a mortar attack on a police station when a 'disorientated police officer' made the mistake of investigating organised crime.

- Japan has only a small incidence of illicit drug usage.

- Criminal justice agencies are very effective; the relationship between police and public is good and there is a high clearance rate. There is a large flow of information from public to police and most Japanese suspects speak freely.

Various indirect factors have been proposed:

- The homogeneity of Japanese society

It should be noted, however, that while the largest ethnic minority in Japan is 650,000 Koreans, Japan has its own version – *Bura Kumim* – of the untouchables of the Indian Hindu system. There are about 3 million *Bura Kumin* in 6,000 ghettos in Japan.

- Geographical isolation

Nonetheless, there are several other countries which possess one or other of these factors yet still experience a high crime rate. Britain, for example, is an island nation, and Poland and Hungary have similar levels of homogeneity. Tadashi Moriyama (1993) therefore argues that other factors have to be looked at to explain the low crime rate. Specifically, the process of social conditioning to established norms. He argues the following factors are crucially important.

(i)   the absence of an established class system

The Maji-restoration of the mid 19th century ended the policy of isolation and formally abolished the hereditary system through which occupational posts had been filled, replacing this with selection by competitive examination. After the Second World War the aristocracy was abolished and an education policy specifically geared to meritocracy was established. More than 90% of Japanese consider they belong to the middle class. Age represents the primary social distinction between Japanese. The emphasis upon meritocracy results in an extremely competitive attitude, particularly concerning school education. Most Japanese children attend a second private school after their public school is finished, normally studying until 9 pm; many Japanese students also attend school on Saturdays while further private tuition may be provided on Sundays. It is not unusual for Japanese high school students to be in a closely supervised educationally related activity for more than 70 hours a week. They simply do not have free time to commit delinquent acts unless they engage in truancy, thus there is a strong correlation between school truancy and delinquency.

(ii)   Strong family loyalties and duty to the group

The dominant social value in Japanese society which provides the framework for respect and interaction of human relationship is the group rather than the individual. Family cohesion and solidarity is strongly emphasised. The family is called *Uchi* meaning inside as opposed to *Soto* or *Yoso* meaning outside. It is common to refer to companies as *Uchi* designating a special sense of belonging. The dominant demarcation of Japanese social life is between persons inside the group and those outside. The special term for foreigners – *Gaijin* – indicates those unable to truly enter into Japanese groups. Membership of the group involves a tight relationship, with mutual help and a willingness to intervene and support or admonish each other. One of the great fears of the Japanese is ostracism or *Muahachibu*. The first reaction to trouble is to seek to maintain harmony within the group. While individual members of a group owe a duty of mutual help to each other, each owes a responsibility to the group irrespective of any legal standing. A structure of duties pervades the company, the school and even government with senior employees often resigning for minor misdemeanours of lower employees which bring dishonour on the organisation. Parents frequently apologise for the behaviour of their grown up children.

(iii)   A culture of *shame* as opposed to that of *guilt*. This distinction comes from the work of Ruth Benedict (1946), a cultural anthropologist who was asked by the American Government to explain the attitude of Japanese soldiers following orders despite the most adverse circumstances. Benedict argued that the Japanese were dominated by external signs of good behaviour and the need reciprocally to balance obligations. Shame denotes the reaction by a person to the criticism of the others; whereas a guilt society is orientated more towards the achievement of self-regulation. The sense of shame is a strong deterrent to crime in that individuals are deeply concerned with the views and opinions of others. Their own view is of lesser importance and perhaps underdeveloped; thus the behaviour of Japanese people is substantially controlled by others, especially family members, neighbours, relatives, colleagues at the work place or school mates. The Japanese place great emphasis upon keeping what is called a 'clean face'; juveniles do not like to make their parents' faces dirty. To commit a crime is to bring reaction not only upon oneself but upon all the others involved in the group.

(iv)   The family model of social control. The Japanese group enforces collective responsibility, or collectivism, which is reinforced by the culture of shame and the philosophy of confucianism. The family model is involved in social control in three ways:

(a)   The formal criminal justice system uses both the family, and the family model, as much as possible. Police interrogation, which is supervised by the prosecution, is conducted in the guise of the interrogator as a father figure; confessions are obtained in over 85% of all cases. Even the trial takes on the structure of a family investigation, and there are only a few cases in which a defendant does not admit his guilt;

(b)   the family model clearly works as a form of informal control. If an individual deviates family members quickly learn, while the fear of ostracism may prevent much deviance;

(c)   confucianism emphasises obligations and respect to ones parents and implies that people should not bring dishonour on their family.

This homogeneity and family orientation minimises individuality and diversity, moreover, there are signs it is under considerable stress in contemporary Japan. The culture of shame and familisation makes for a society with very predictable and tight relationships, various tensions are apparent, namely:

• Security versus freedom

Self-expression is down played, and Japanese tend to follow others and the group uncritically.

• Rights versus obligations

Japanese social relations are characterised by a sense of obligations rather than rights. To claim rights is viewed as the act of an aggressive person threatening the social harmony or natural order. In criminal justice the emphasis is upon the obligations and duties of offenders rather than their rights. The aim of criminal justice, particularly for minor offences, is to gain an apology from the offender, together with a statement that he or she recognises the duties they have breached and will respect the social harmony in the future.

• The new individual versus the traditional Japanese. There is much talk in Japan that the young are developing a new persona which appears to be adopting the Western approach. These *Shin Jinrui*, or new species of humanity, tend towards individualism and talk in terms of their rights.

• Internalisation versus internationalisation

The traditional vision or horizon of the Japanese person has been inwardly focused, but economic success is demanding that Japan looks outwards. Although the Japanese government has not encouraged foreign visitors or tourism, the number of foreign visitors, as well as foreign persons, or *Gaijin*, residing and working in Japan has increased. An increasing number of Japanese work abroad for a period, and increasing prosperity means that Japanese people can now take more than one foreign trip in their lives. It is therefore more common for Japanese persons to have encountered some diversity and variety of experiences.

The social cost of the low crime rate of Japan is the devaluation of the individual. Individuals who seek to develop projects of free self-expression and the pursuit of individual life plans find barriers and experience great stress; the desire for freedom encounters structures of security and predictability in social relations. Many suicides in Japan appear to be from embarrassment at particular actions or the individual being unable to take the stress of group involvement. Moriyana claims that the development of guilt in Western societies historically comes from the relationship of the person with an abstract God, where ultimately they have to account to God for their actions and thoughts. In Japan condemnation comes from other people on a collective basis.

Culture as criminogenic

A traditional area of concern for criminology has been in the area of culture and youth crime.

The main object of analysis for sociological theories of crime, from the 1930s onwards, involved urban male youths. The 1950s saw work develop on both juvenile delinquency and gang involvement. This area is generally referred to as *sub-cultural theories*, which postulate that delinquent sub-cultures are created within the wider culture of society. There are three areas of explanation:

- The work of Albert Cohen, sometimes referred to as the middle class measuring rod.
- The differential opportunity structure theory, associated with Richard Cloward and Lloyd Ohlin.
- The lower class value system, associated with Walter Miller.

Albert Cohen

In *Delinquent Boys* (1955) Cohen criticised previous theories for not differentiating between the terms *culture* and *sub-culture* sufficiently. Cohen argued that a specific kind of criminal behaviour, a non-purposeful and non-acquisitive crime characterise juvenile delinquencies. For Cohen previous criminology had taken adult crime, as exemplified by theft and robbery, as its paradigm case. Cohen was more interested in delinquency which was primary expressive and appeared purposeless, even nihilistic in character, as exemplified in almost random acts of violence, vandalism and joy riding. Although such crimes had been mentioned in Thrasher's classic study of the *Gang in Chicago* published in 1927, later sociology, under the influence of Merton, had concentrated upon the fundamental purpose of material gain as principally characterising crime. Cohen reasoned that criminological theory should provide both an explanation of the nature of the delinquency to be studied, as well as an account of the characteristics of the people engaged in it. Cohen's account is still very much influenced by the same sociological structure which Durkheim laid down, in that sub-culture is seen as a functional creation enabling individuals to handle many of the problems created for them by the social structure. Culture is made up of traditional ways of solving problems, or learned problem solutions, which are transmitted through the process of childhood socialisation.

Cohen's theory is termed a *strain* theory, in that the criminogenic mechanism lies in the incompatible demands of structure and culture with the consequential creation of sub-cultures to solve the problems thus caused. Again like Merton, Cohen appears to assume a universalistic set of achievement-oriented standards as comprising mainstream society. Instead, however, of Merton's goal of success Cohen argued that delinquent youth were more motivated by gaining status among their peer groups. Much of the competition for status takes place in the setting of school which, for Cohen, is a largely middle class institution. To succeed in that institution a youth is judged according to criteria of ambition, responsibility, achievement, deferred gratification, rationality, courtesy, the ability to control physical aggression, and the constructive use of time in the rational pursuit of property. The lower class youth finds himself being evaluated by the middle class measuring rod. Lower class male youth have little chance however of achieving the standards required because of their structural position. Moreover, lower class youth have little ascribed status by virtue of family position and are typically losers in the competition for achieved status. Such a youth has three options:

- If he is bright he may attempt upward mobility. This 'college boy solution' lays emphasis upon educational achievement.

- The less able may accept becoming what Cohen calls 'stable corner' boys. These youth continue to conform to middle class values without any great success, and accept a low status position amongst their peers.

- The delinquent option or solution. In this case, the lower class youth initially strongly aspired to middle class standards of success, but his repeated failures in the school system, both academically and socially, cause him to reject the school and the system of values it represents. This is made possible by a psychological process which Cohen calls 'reaction formation'; a Freudian term describing the process by which a person openly rejects that which he wants or aspires to, because he can neither obtain or achieve it. By means of this process, the attachment to middle class values of utilitarianism, respectability, deferred gratification, and the avoidance of aggression, is transformed by a powerful rejection. The values are inverted, but the resultant value structure is not a simple opposition, but characterised by ambivalence.

Many lower class youth come to repudiate middle class values and assume a malicious and hostile attitude towards the sets of standard and behavioural patterns symbolising the middle class. A youth searches for a peer group or gang; within this supportive context he nurtures developing feelings of hostility derived from his damaged self-image. These groups are formed by youths in order to validate their choices and reinforce their new values. The delinquent gang becomes to its members a means to acquire status and to hit back at the system that has labelled them as failures. The gang inverts the rules of middle class society and provides a mechanism for attaining status via the sub-culturally legitimate use of aggression and hostility – the delinquent gang is characterised by a sub-culture which allows the use of violence and hostility – in time this becomes a way of life in inner city environments. Much of the delinquency committed in the gang context appears to serve little useful purpose, such as vandalisation and malicious destruction of property, random and unprovoked assaults and gang wars. Cohen noted six characteristics of the delinquent behaviour of the juvenile gangs.

- They are non-utilitarian

  Goods would be stolen merely for kicks and given away, discarded, or destroyed, rather than consumed, or sold for profit.

- A strong element of *malice* and *destructiveness* ran through the delinquency, for example, breaking and entering or burglaries would be accompanied by wanton vandalism.

- Negativism

  Much of the delinquent behaviour appears an inversion of respectable values.

- Short run hedonism

  The desire for instant, rather than delayed, gratification; immediate pleasure or reward of sorts.

- Versatility

  Gang activities were not highly specialised, rather they covered a wide spectrum of delinquency, ranging from theft or vandalism, to interpersonal violence and aggression.

- An element of *primary loyalty to the delinquent gang* existed. Other allegiances were subordinated to gang loyalty.

In summary these characteristics constitute an ideal type of delinquent sub-culture.

Four empirical assumptions underlie Cohen's theory:

- A large percentage of lower class youth do poorly at school.
- Poor school performance is related to delinquency.
- This poor school performance can largely be attributed to the conflict between the dominant middle class values embodied in the school and the values and structural position of the lower class youth.
- Lower class male delinquency is largely committed in a gang context as a means of developing positive self images, gaining status and nurturing anti-social values.

On the face of it, Cohen's theory appears a coherent explanation accounting for the facts of official crime. Downes and Rock (1988), however, argue that it is neatly tailored to account for the much lower rate of such delinquency among the middle class, since they are far more likely to attain success by the conventional route. The lower rates of delinquency amongst girls can be explained under this theory, in that they are taught to value marriage to an occupationally successful male rather than achieving success in career terms themselves. Moreover, it appears to explain the lower rates of crime in rural areas in that the pressures of school are less because of access to more traditional modes of occupation.

There have been many empirical doubts cast on Cohen's theory. Although class differences *are* important in relation to school performance it is not proved that such class differences give rise to the processes outlined by Cohen. Nor has the Freudian process of displacement been shown as providing an effective explanation. Neither does it appear that school failure is always interpreted in such a way as to necessitate a delinquent response. The reasons for a delinquent response as compared to the adaptive corner boy response are not brought out.

It remains significant for beginning to develop interactional processes and for highlighting the non-utilitarian features of much delinquency. Moreover, it points to the complexity of culture, in that while Cohen's theory appears similar to Merton's rebellion adaptation, this form of rebellion is a reaction against middle class values rather than the pursuit of material success. One weakness lies in its overreaching determinist ambitions.

Cloward and Ohlin

In *Delinquency and Opportunity: A Theory of Delinquent Gangs* (1960), Cloward and Ohlin appeared to integrate notions from Merton and Cohen, as well as ideas stemming from the Chicago ecologists, in particular the role of neighbourhood influences. Whereas Merton had assumed the universal goal of monetary success, and Cohen the universal striving for status, Cloward and Ohlin argued that these were separate aspirations or strivings, which could operate either together or independently. Thus some youths may strive for status in the form of membership of the middle class without seeking to improve their economic position; whilst others may seek to improve their economic position without aspiring to change their class position.

Cloward and Ohlin developed a four-fold typology of lower class youth:

- Youth who strive for both middle class status and monetary success.
- Youth who strive for middle class status but are not interested in monetary success.
- Youth who strive for monetary success but not middle class status.
- Youth who strive for neither middle class status nor monetary success.

According to Cohen's theory most delinquency will be committed by youths of either category (1) or (2) who are seeking to improve their status and actually aspiring for membership of the middle class. Cloward and Ohlin agree that when pressures towards delinquency arise with these youth they could be described by Cohen's theory, ie as reactions against middle class values the youth believes in but with which he has been unable to conform. However, they go on to argue, these youths do not commit the most serious delinquency. Instead, the serious delinquency comes from type (3) youths who desire material success, without any corresponding desire for middle class status or membership. These youths are orientated towards conspicuous consumption, fast cars, fancy clothes, flashy women, and do not see success in terms of a middle class life style. These youth experience the greatest conflict with middle class values, since they are frowned upon both for what they do not want, ie the middle class lifestyle and for what they do want, crass materialism. Type (4) youths, although they may incur criticism from middle class authorities for their lack of ambition are not normally involved in trouble; they tend to avoid middle class institutions as much as possible. Thus Cloward and Ohlin, like Cohen, followed Merton in looking at achievement values and aspirations, and the means of obtaining them. Like Merton, they argue that lower class delinquency results from a systematic exclusion of the lower classes from real access to the legitimate channels that lead to economic success in society. But since they place the original emergence of delinquent sub-cultures as arising out of an economic pursuit of monetary success, without any accompanying desire to adhere to middle class values, the school becomes an irrelevance. Thus the economic pursuit of monetary success is the prime source of embittered frustrations in the metropolitan slums. The sub-culture comes about because discontented lower class youth seek material success and status within their own community and employ illegitimate means to achieve these ends.

Cloward argues that not all those denied legitimate success can take advantage of criminal means of achieving success. Some persons are 'double failures' unable to find either legitimate or illegitimate means of success available to them:

> 'Note, for example, variations in the degree to which members of various classes are fully exposed to and thus acquire the values, education, and skills which facilitate upward mobility. It should not be startling, therefore, to find similar variations in the availability of illegitimate means.' (1960. 176)

In contrast to Cohen, Cloward and Ohlin suggest that most serious lower class delinquency, far from being purposeless, is the result of a goal orientated action by people who do rationally understand their economic position and act accordingly. Lower class delinquency comes out of blocked legitimate economic opportunities which America's conventional institutions are not providing. Moreover, the specific nature of the opportunities available is a factor in the characteristics of the delinquency. The character of particular neighbourhoods structure the opportunities for committing illegal acts, and the types of illegal acts. Cloward and Ohlin thus determine that the opportunity to commit illegal acts is not constant throughout societies; this theory is, therefore, sometimes called a theory of 'differential opportunity structure'. Both legal, and illegal, avenues for achieving economic success are unequally distributed throughout society. Cloward and Ohlin distinguish three types of delinquent sub-cultures:

- the criminal sub-culture or gang;
- the conflict sub-culture or gang;
- the retreatist sub-culture or gang.

Whether any one of these sub-cultures predominates is a factor dependent upon (a) the opportunities for integration in conventional values and behaviour systems; and (b) the impact of organised illegitimate values and behavioural systems.

The criminal sub-culture or gang

The criminal sub-culture emerges in conditions where there is a significant presence of organised adult criminal activity in the lower class neighbourhood. Adult criminals provide successful role models for juveniles further developing criminal skills within the neighbourhood. These neighbourhoods display a stable relationship between adult criminals and juveniles with patterns of accommodation and mutual interdependence; for example, networks of dealing in stolen items are provided. Local political and criminal justice officials also accommodate the criminal behaviour, whether by ignoring it, or by offering protection in return for personal gains, or community stability. We have therefore a 'collective delinquent solution':

> 'Interaction among those sharing the same problem [discrepancies between aspiration and opportunity] may provide encouragement for the withdrawal of sentiments in support of the established system of norms. Once freed of allegiance to the existing set of rules, such persons may devise ... delinquent means of achieving success. A collective delinquent solution to an adjustment problem is more likely to evolve by this process in a society in which the legitimacy of social rules can be questioned apart from their moral validity ... What seems expedient, rational, and efficient often becomes separable from what is traditional, sacred, and moral as a basis for the imputation of legitimacy. Under such conditions it is difficult for persons at different social positions to agree about the forms of conduct that are both expedient and morally right. Once this separation takes place, the supporting structure of the existing system of norms becomes highly vulnerable.' (1960: 108-9)

This relative community stability and set of cultural values which make delinquency and criminal activity acceptable, albeit illegal, also imposes limitations upon the type of delinquency found acceptable, and orientates gang behaviour towards theft rather than violence, since violence would prove more disruptive. Thus illegitimate behaviour must not be irrational, or out of control: 'there is no place in organised crime for the impulsive, unpredictable individual'.

The conflict sub-culture or gang

The conflict sub-culture emerges in the absence of either legitimate or illegitimate opportunities in neighbourhoods where no stable organised pattern of adult criminality has developed. In areas characterised by unstable and transient living conditions and lifestyles, adult role models, either criminal or conventional, do not develop. Juveniles experience a high level of frustration and discontent and resort to violence as a primary form of delinquent behaviour. This acute frustration is unstructured, and results in violence, partly because of the absence of stable structures of social controls; either those of the criminal sub-culture or conventionalist systems.

The retreatist sub-culture

The retreatist sub-culture bears similarities to Merton's retreatist adaptation, and is characteristic of youths unable to achieve either economic success or resort to violence but instead turn to drugs or alcohol and drop out. Not all double failures become members of the retreatist sub-culture, some scale down their desires and aspirations to become 'corner-boys', which particular path a youth will adopt depends on the personality of the youth, and also his peer group and particular circumstances. Some youths who fall into the retreatist sub-culture may well have been rejected by other gangs, because of their inability to handle gang life.

Cloward and Ohlin stress the role of neighbourhood; the criminal sub-culture relies upon the presence of relatively stable adult role models, or groups, who may be said to encourage criminal activity – whilst the conflict gang exists in areas without such stable patterns. An assumption of Cloward and Ohlin's theory is that much lower class gang behaviour is specialised, and that the specialisation is related to neighbourhood characteristics. A criticism of the frustration element has been made by Kornhauser (1978) writing from the control perspective and proposing a general criticism of all strain theories, who argued that the empirical research did not support the assumption of delinquency as being a factor of high aspirations and low expectations. Instead, she claimed, delinquency is more often associated with both low expectations and low aspirations, thus there would be no strain because there was little gap between what youths aspired to, and what they actually expected to achieve. Kornhauser claimed that the evidence suggested that most delinquents did not expect much from society, but they did not want much either.

Strain theories have been generally criticised for assuming a consensus of values in society. Edwin Lemert (1961), for example, criticised Merton's use of anomie theory for assuming that modern society had one dominant set of values.

Both Cohen and Cloward and Ohlin have additionally been criticised for placing too much emphasis upon gang delinquency at the expense of accounting for individual or small group delinquency.

Walter Miller

The work of Walter Miller proposed a much more autonomous notion of lower class culture, claiming that delinquency was an extension of a separate and relatively self-governing value system responsive to adult working class culture. In a famous article *Lower Class Culture As A Generating Milieu of Gang Delinquency* (1958) Miller argued that instead of being produced as a reaction to the dominant culture – an inversion of the ethics of the dominant society – lower class culture had its own established values or 'vocal concerns'. Rather than constituting a counter-culture, lower class delinquency is a direct expression of the dominant values or culture patterns of the lower class community. Thus lower class gangs were predominantly male and street orientated groups, and were an expression of a generic lower class cultural system. For Miller delinquency comes about from a clash of conduct norms or cultural understandings. Rather than being created as a reaction, sub-cultures are in direct conflict with dominant middle class values which may be inscribed in the laws. Miller is clear:

'... engaging in certain cultural practices which comprise essential elements of the total life pattern of lower-class culture automatically violates certain legal norms.' (1958: 68-69)

Miller recognised six focal concerns to lower class culture:

- Trouble

  Conflict with police, authority, state bureaucrats, and the issues around fighting or sexual activity for males, and the use of drugs.

- Toughness

  A concern with physical prowess and strength; the development of so-called masculine traits; with an associated lack of emotional display.

- Smartness

  A desire to outwit others through mental gymnastics and cunning; the ability to hustle.

- Excitement

  The pursuit of thrills experienced through alcohol, sex, gambling, going out on the town. Such excitement may be periodic, interspersed with periods of inactions or 'handing-out'.

- Fate

  The feeling that one's future is out of one's hands and that one's destiny is out of one's control.

- Autonomy

  A paradoxical position, reflecting, on the one hand, a strong desire to be free of external controls such as the boss; the wife; bureaucratic authorities, while on the other hand, a consistent pattern of seeking out nurturing situations, such as a steady job or comforting wife, can be discerned beneath this claim to interdependence.

Miller further claimed that many working class households were dominated by a strong mother figure, which drove many adolescent males from home in the search of male identity in street gangs.

'A significant proportion of lower-class males are reared in a predominantly female household and lack a consistently present male figure with whom to identify and from whom to learn the essential components of a "male" role. Since women serve as a primary object of identification during the pre-adolescent years, the almost obsessive lower-class concern with 'masculinity' probably resembles a type of compulsive reaction-formation.' (1958: 9)

Thus the gang resolves problems of identity by magnifying the pursuit of masculine traits and status.

This was a widespread idea in 1950s American sociology. The leading American sociologist of the 1950s and 1960s, Talcott Parsons, for example, asserted that the structure of the American family, and the sharp differentiation between occupational roles and kinship responsibilities of the father, make it very difficult for American boys to develop masculine traits and characteristics naturally. The requirements of occupational roles, which had become much more sophisticated, keep the father preoccupied with interests outside the home and leave the mother as the most significant person in the family. The relative absence of the father from the family, and the consequent weakening of his domestic status, make him an unfit model for identification, thus depriving American male children of the opportunity to develop skills, attitudes, mannerisms, and characteristics associated in American culture with the masculine image. Because of this faulty (non)identification with a masculine model, some youngsters join gangs. They overreact to their basic sense of masculine ineptitude by acting tough, by engaging in fights and other types of anti-social activity, which are the identifying mark of delinquent groups in America. The process was described by Parsons as follows:

'Our kinship situation, it has been noted, throws children of both sexes overwhelmingly upon the mother as the emotionally significant adult. In such a situation, "identification" in the sense that the adult becomes a 'role model' is the normal result. For a girl this is normal and natural, not only because she belongs to the same sex as the mother, but because the functions of housewife and mother are immediately before her eyes and are tangible and relatively easily understood by a child ... Thus the girl has a more favourable opportunity for emotional maturing through positive identification with an adult model, a fact which seems to have much to do with the well-known earlier maturity of girls. The boy, on the other hand, has a tendency to form a direct feminine identification, since his mother is the model most readily available and significant to him. But he is not destined to become an adult woman. Moreover he soon discovers that in certain vital respects women are considered inferior to men, that it would hence be shameful for him to grow up like a woman. Hence when boys emerge into what Freudians call the "latency period", their behaviour tends to be marked by a kind of "compulsive masculinity". They refuse to have anything to do with girls. "Sissy" becomes the worst of insults.

They get interested in athletics and physical prowess, in the things in which men have the most primitive and obvious advantage over women. Furthermore, they become allergic to all expression of tender emotion; they must be "tough". This universal pattern bears all the earmarks of a "reaction formation". It is so conspicuous, not because it is simple "masculine nature", but because it is a defence against a feminine identification.' (1954: 304-5)

Parsons remarks that the structure of the American family system, and the relative absence of a masculine model at home, results in 'a strong tendency for boyish behaviour to run in anti-social if not directly destructive directions, in striking contrast to that of pre-adolescent girls'. While Parsons does not himself claim that this lack of identification with a masculine figure is the cause of juvenile delinquency, the work of Miller and Cohen placed the problem of masculine identification as a causal factor.

In Miller's favour, there is some empirical support that a definite lower class culture emphasising particular lifestyles and values particular to the lower class has existed. A variant of this concept is Oscar Lewis's (1959) *culture of poverty thesis* which became influential in the 1960s. Wolfgang and Ferracuti in their study of violence (*The Sub-Culture of Violence*, 1967) specifically located a sub-culture of violence amongst young, urban males. Moreover, the concept of masculine consciousness being associated with crime is a recurring theme in all studies of lower class crime, from the work of the Chicago School onwards.

In criticism, many have argued against this identification of matriarchically-headed home situations of working class families. Empirical studies did not appear to show a predominance of female dominated households in the lower class. In recent decades we have seen the growth of one parent families most of which are headed by women. Yet as late as 1988 the US statistical abstract found that fewer than half of lower class families with children are headed by females alone with no male spouse present. Further the linkage between such households and delinquency is not simple; assertions for it are often highly anecdotal and simplify the complete processes at work.

In America, attempts to empirically test the theory concerning the role of the *matriarchical family*, became embroiled in the issue of race rather than social class. The culture of poverty thesis became imbued with racial connotations after the controversial report by Daniel Moynihan in 1965 (*The Negro Family*), in which he argued that the contemporary urban Black population was becoming divided into two sections: a stable middle class and a deteriorating lower class. This deteriorating lower class section of blacks was directly related to the presence of female-orientated households, which, it was argued, was traceable in American to the breakup of the black family structure during the period of slavery (in which no marriage between blacks was legally recognised). Female dominated households create a situation in which the lower class black family is subjected to a range of pathologies, including a high rate of delinquency.

The reaction to the Moynihan report is a reflection of the politically and culturally loaded nature of social science. On the one hand it appears liberating to deny that working class culture is nothing but an unconscious reaction to an inversion of middle class values, but the particular formulation of Moynihan's report was criticised for locating the causal responsibility for the conditions of black households not in the structures of contemporary white-dominated society, but within the contentious, but unalterable, legacy of history. In this way instead of a campaign against institutionalised racism, the causal factor for the failure of blacks to achieve middle class status could be located in conditions which are historically created, but contemporarily located in the black family; thus implying that there was little social programmes could achieve by way of improving the situation. Miller has suffered a similar structural criticism.

Culture and social structure: does working class culture, or a culture of poverty, determine social conditions, or social conditions determine culture?

In his 1969 work, Travis Hirschi was scathing towards the idea of a coherent and self-sustaining lower class culture:

> 'The issue is whether acceptance of (lower class) beliefs is rooted in culture or social structure, whether the feeling that one is powerless arises from objective powerlessness or is transmitted by one's culture, regardless of one's power in some objective sense.' (1969: 219)

Lower class beliefs were a factor of the objective conditions people found themselves in:

> 'The ease with which middle class children absorb 'lower-class' beliefs, and the ease with which they are discarded or ignored by lower-class children forces us to conclude that if 'lower-class' culture is 'many centuries old', it is only because powerlessness and deprivation are older. If they were to disappear, lower-class culture would quickly die. And there would be no one to mourne its passing.' (Ibid: 223)

This implies that one solution to crime is social integration. Crime is directly influenced by the offender having sets of definitions of the situation favourable to violations of the law, and such definitions 'often reflect the absence of stakes in conformity', therefore increasing the return on conformity, in other words playing the social games by the rules, should lower the production of social definitions (cultural factors) favourable to crime. Note: Social control theories such as Hirschi's, and strain theories, such as Merton's, are usually seen as mutually exclusive, but can we not read Hirschi's lack of stakes in conformity and hence commitment, and Merton's lack of legitimate opportunities, as pointing to a similar existential phenomenon? Namely, the absence of an internally felt direction to one's actions which points to achieving universally accepted desires? Hirschi calls this freedom; Merton stress. In the chapter on existentialism in the current text, it is proposed that this indicates certain macro-cultural conditions of modernity: namely the dicta to be self-directing and self-creating, the dicta to take control of one's situation, a driving force which can be interpreted in much the same ways as Merton's drive for monetary reward, and which imposes throughout the variety of social locations.

Let us clear up a common misunderstanding concerning culture in criminological writing. It has become common to criticise Merton for postulating a universal cultural driving force throughout society; specifically financial success. The distribution of crime is then a factor of the distribution of legitimate opportunities in the social structure, and given blocked legitimate opportunities; thus crime is a rational choice for some individuals given their location in social structure. It is sometimes asserted that Merton's theory is very specific and gives us one constant cultural drive in any particular society because of cultural uniformity (Bernard, 1987b). It seems to some, that if we allow a variety of cultural messages we discredit Merton. But our use of Merton's theory should not preclude a range of other cultural factors, instead it should alert us to the fact that we can sensibly refer to certain large scale, macro-cultural prescriptions. In our concern to trace theoretical criminology from modernity to post-modernism, our argument has asserted a range of these in the process of individualism modernity throws into place. The next chapter will argue that post-modernism denotes a process wherein certain prescriptions are being internationalised under the dicta of consumption and the significance of personal worth and status by possession of consumer goods.. Surely Merton is correct to warn us that we are never free from macro-cultural forces, we exist at the site of various sets of cultural messages? The fact that more of them are being created, and that they are getting complicated, does not reduce the strain of being modern – it may increase it.

Hirschi's (1969) comments on powerlessness and deprivation point criminology towards the investigation of the linkage between social structure, the cultural production of resentment and emotional states which may be conducive to criminal conduct. While this would appear essential for a general theory it is under-developed; in fact, strong factors in current conditions point in an opposite direction.

In Chapter Seventeen the discussion of the emerging underclass phenomenon notes the extent to which a culture of poverty argument is fundamental to the Right's blame of welfare for the creation of the underclass. From the first chapter we have noted the strong individualist orientation of contemporary Right criminology; social explanations are being sidestepped in favour of locating responsibility firmly on a self which has failed to both control and link itself into the supposed meritocratic structures of late-modernity. When social factors are indicated, they are factors located in close proximity to the individual self – faulty socialisation, the rise of one-parent families, the absence of responsibility in appropriate role models (specifically absent fathers) – all of which are not adequately located in wider forces. In other words it is argued that the moral fabric of individuals and their individual belief patterns, not the social and economic structure of society, that is taken to be at the root of current problems. The cultural beliefs of the poor and powerless are somehow their responsibility and the determining factor as to why they are poor and powerless (for a review see William Julius Wilson, 1994).

Bridging concepts: from social structural to individual or psychological states

By bridging concepts is meant ideas on the integration of macro factors (such as culture) with theory derived from clinical research findings at the level of the individual. In what way can the experiences of our past, our upbringing, our labelling processes (see the Chapter Fourteen), be incorporated into a model of the *self* without overwhelming it?

One method is to understand that *actions have an action rationale*; in other words, we must bring out the meaning of the behaviour for the participant. If you try to be faithful to the individual's perception of what he or she was about, you may find a disjunction between that view and the predictive generalisations of large scale theory which of necessity, to a certain extent at least, assumes, or takes for granted, certain motives of the actors. We may assume, for example, that a central cultural message in a modern society is that educational achievement makes possible occupational mobility, and that high school performances and going on to tertiary education opens the way to a higher ranking job, but individuals do not possess this image in equal degrees. Individuals have sets of everyday theories which make sense of their world and guide their actions; these are based on past experiences which are unique to some degree. This is so even when two or more individuals share various characteristics, and come from a similar location in social geography. It is often asserted in criminology that theories of strain, or relative deprivation, cannot be accepted as causal influences for crime because not all poor people commit crime, or not all of the unemployed commit crime (interestingly, it is less frequently heard that we should look at the experiences of those who do not commit crime to see why not!). This is to make a mistake arising from generalisation. Individuals vary in their socialisation in deprived or privileged conditions. Although we can have certain expectations as to behaviour according to our social classification (otherwise what does it mean to talk of class or other social forces?), we cannot predict from this expectation that any one individual will behave in a predetermined way.

When we say that an individual possesses an *action pack of knowledge* which forms a repertoire of norms and rules for his own behaviour, we build variation into our expectation. The action pack is clearly influenced by an individual's experience of participating in, or being excluded from, society's most coveted goods and titles – a person exists, not just as an individual but also as a member of social categories demarcated by race (ethnicity), class and gender. The action pack of knowledge has both a certain contextual specificity and a certain universality; the questions the individual poses him or herself are part of certain questions of what is deemed proper to do as a man, a woman, or otherwise. At any one time, the options culturally held out simply fit into a set of possibilities. How one learns social activities – what it means, for instance, to drink properly, how to become a successful ganja smoker, how to carry out everyday tasks properly – these add to the action pack of your everyday wisdom. Sociology even has a specific branch called ethnomethodology which analyses the intricate and complex layers of interaction and skills everyday existence calls upon; it points out the richness of those diverse sets of understanding and social skills which members of society draw upon to negotiate the interactions they engage in throughout a 'normal day'. No day is actually boring if one bores deeply enough into its layers!

Post-modernism intensifies ambiguity, ambivalency and increases the complexity and range of information available to everyday life. The post-modern city, such as London, reels with diverse communication technologies and units of cultural significance originally embedded in a (relatively) coherent structure (the sari, the food stalls, the three-piece suite, the veiled women), which now are random significations within diversity, plurality and interpreted (ideally) with tolerance. What were once significations of ethnic purity, become significations of ethnic diversity – conversely, we ask, are they thereby enjoyed or seen as insults? This depends on the audience, and the tolerance of the audiences sensibilities; a question of socialisation. Socialisation involves learning the predictability of the behaviour of others; the dialectics of the civilising process require a reciprocity of expectation. Trutz Trotha (1974) reviewed the situational cultural factors of inner-city life, highlighting normative ambiguity and inconsistency in the observation of conventional norms and sanctioning responses. Inner-city poor live in the midst of both serious and petty crime (including prostitution and drugs), varying police activity, welfare and social work officials, and various government bureaucracies. Many of the roles and effects of the police, social and welfare officials, as well as government bureaucracies, may appear as much part of the problems than as part of the solutions. All these factors render everyday life heavily upon the poor and reduce the predictability of behaviour and life in general; to survive, a 'hustling' orientation is one consequence. For Trotha the oppositions within Walter Miller's 'focal concerns' of the lower-class is a result of the reduced behavioural predictions, normative ambiguity, and inconsistency in sanctioning. Thus the belief that luck or fate largely determine the course of one's life chances is intensified by the structural conditions of deprivation and disadvantage that are necessarily beyond one's control. There is a growing body of writing indicating that arousal of emotion cannot be divorced from mediation through cultural definitions of the situation (Shott, 1979; Hochschild, 1979), although there is dispute as to the actual dynamics. However, we clearly need to move beyond micro-level analysis into addressing not only the social basis of emotion but also the social impact. Certain emotional states (or the readiness with which emotions are aroused) may prepare for action, while others inhibit. It may be that the social structural location of individuals may systematically prepare them for certain emotions and decrease the frequency of others; the development of resentment may be a case in point.

Is the idea of action pack compatible with, or antagonistic to, the idea that personality deficiencies cause people to commit crimes? Does it fit in with the relatively clear-cut ideas of seeking causal influences in the effects of unequal distribution of chances in society and widespread emotional reaction to it, particularly amongst the young, together with relative class bias in the labelling of criminal activity in society? Certainly, the individual's action pack can have common elements, and items particular to that individuals' specific experiences; it also varies across time and space, in other words elements are added by historical specificity.

Culture and crime: an extreme example?

The first issue of *The Guardian Weekly* of 1984, carried an article entitled 'A Murder in Namibia' relating to events on a farm, in Namibia, in 1983. A white farmer, van Rooyen, aged 24, had tortured and killed 18 year old Thomas Kasire, a new black worker on his farm. On account of the language he speaks and the area he comes from, Kasire was accused by his boss of being a supporter of the national liberation movement SWAPO (South Western African People's Organisation).

The white farmer kept Kasire chained by the neck in his farmyard for several days, tortured and abused him. Eventually, Kasire is killed as van Rooyen's drinking pals applaud and take pictures.

The article is accompanied by three pictures, one showing the murderer 'as he appeared in court', wearing a suit and tie. The other two pictures are from the 'scene' of the crime: a close-up of Kasire's head, bleeding, one ear half cut off, a heavy iron chain around his neck, with the white left arm of his torturer holding on to the chain, intruding from the left into the middle foreground of the picture. The third photograph has the caption: 'The victim is forced to pose with a clenched fist (SWAPO salute), while a friend of the murderer takes photos.' The murderer himself is in the picture, towering over the young black man whom he holds by the chain. He is wearing farm clothes and a cap (they could also be paramilitary gear) and he is facing the camera. The young black man looks as if he were held up on his feet chiefly by the chain the white man holds.

These pictures provided the damning evidence. Without them, the court would in all probability have acquitted van Rooyen, since the explanations given by him and his white friends would have outweighed the statements of any black witnesses. So safe were the whites in their dominant position within the apartheid system, that the whole event was photographed at van Rooyen's request. The act of photography and the kind of violence were linked. The pictures were not snapped by a journalist or observer by chance in the right place at the right time but were deliberately taken to record the power and imbalance in the social relationship. For Susanne Kappeler (1986) the events verge on pornography:

'The victim is forced to "pose"; the perpetrator of the torture positions himself in the other picture with reference to the camera. Another white man is behind the camera, framing the picture. The picture may remind us of those taken by fishermen and hunters posing with their catch, smiling into the camera. But the catch is a human being, a victim, and thus the picture also reminds us of some of the darkest photographic memories of the Vietnam war, those pictures which break the documentary mould and where a temporary victor briefly poses for the camera with his victim vanquished, acknowledging the presence of the camera, drawing it into complicity. The picture may also remind us, or some of us, of pornography, a woman in the place of the black man, the white men in their respective positions – in the picture, behind the camera – unchanged.' (1986: 6)

Culture is the necessary mediation for modernity: the mileau which helps position the moral (non)relationship between victim and offender. Post-modernist writers argue that the hegemony of culture in modernity has both given coherence and allowed domination: the celebration of post-modernism is of a hope that a radically differentiated culture – a culture of pluralism and diversity – will make domination impossible. Post-modernism will, in other words, lead to Durkheim's idea of moral individualism: the creation of a social individuality conscious of the interdependency plurality and differentiation requires. But whether this hope becomes a reality is an open question.

CHAPTER THIRTEEN

CULTURE AND CRIME IN THE POST-MODERN CONDITION

'Overweening ambition always exceeds the results obtained, great as they may be, since there is no warning to pause here. Nothing gives satisfaction and all this agitation is uninterruptedly maintained without appeasement. Above all, since this race of an unattainable goal can give no other pleasure but that of the race itself, if it is one, once it is interrupted the participants are left empty-handed. At the same time the struggle grows more violent and painful, both from being less controlled and because competition is greater. All classes contend among themselves because no established classification any longer exists. Effort grows, just when it becomes less productive.' (Emile Durkheim, *Suicide*: 257)

'The ultimate support for any social system is the acceptance by the population of a moral justification of authority ... The "new capitalism" of the twentieth century has lacked such moral groundings, and in periods of crisis it has either fallen back on the traditional value assertions, which have been increasingly incongruent with social reality, or it has been ideologically impotent.' (Daniel Bell, *The Cultural Contradictions of Capitalism*, 1979: 77)

The challenge of culture under post-modernism: democraticism or incoherence?

Durkheim asked how could moral individualism be achieved in modernity? While Weber pessimistically foresaw the necessity for bureaucratic modernity, Durkheim argued that durable social order came about in a more spontaneous or organic fashion. The previous chapter contained two radically contrasting roles for culture. One was the cultural prohibitions which allowed Indian people to starve rather than commit crime; the other was a horrific crime committed in Namibia – only it did not appear a crime to its perpetrator and immediate audience. The relationship between (non) perpetrator and (non) victim is always a moral relationship – a relationship mediated by culture, by sets of meanings, by sets of 'significations', messages, information, pieces of larger narratives – a relationship constituted by the resources we use to 'represent' the other.

For Durkheim the 'collective conscience' could not be simply manufactured; Weber's bureaucratic imagery inspired critics to warn of an impending Orwellian world of 1984, where control of cultural imagery dominates the social body; political rule achieved through the twin element of hegemony and repression. Durkheim, conversely, argued for a social consciousness which would express and reinforce the organic reality of *interdependency which expressed the continuation of social cooperation in modernity based around the complex division of labour and differentiation and pluralism of social spheres.*

Two points: (i) while it is possible for political leaders to have recourse to the rhetoric of popular purity (as we see in differing forms from Thatcher's appeal to Victorian values, Reagan's appeal to the moral majority, Islamic fundamentalism, a greater Serberia) – this is a pathological appeal in that it is premised upon the foundation of a moral and cultural homogeneity which can only be policed through repression (epitomised in ethnic cleansing); (ii) while it is possible to use state power to pacify and homogenise populations (for example Socialist Bureaucracy under Stalin or Apartheid), durable social order must retain some collective sentiment of naturalism or voluntarism; it cannot be superimposed through the agency of the state.

If social order is a social construction, if the traditional and custom bound forms of social solidarity must give way for modernity to gain in progressive power, and if state imposed regimentation is unstable, what is the ultimate guarantee of social solidarity? Durkheim, as in all things, argued for a balance, a mean between riding the roller-coaster of progress (with the prospect of anomie) and seeking stability (with the prospect of stagnation and fatalism). The culture of the society must encourage individuality without so loading the dice in favour of self-interest over the interests of others, that no social solidarity is possible; while a society that encourages self-denial at the expense of self-assertion would not know freedom – it would not be modern. Cultural understandings are both resources and weapons. Traditionally, culture reinforced rather static powers of social structure. What happens when culture becomes relatively autonomous? Or, when the social structure is radically differentiated? Is the cultural fluidity and rapid change of current conditions – a feature commentators have traced to the impact of mass communication and new technologies of transport and imagery – responsible for a post-modernisation of culture posing new challenges and opportunities for social order?[1] While a society or social location, that offers no hope for the future also offers no defences against social predation and crime, a society that changes with extreme rapidity and fluidity, may rob the population

---

1 The features referred to by the post-modernisation of culture are the increasing fragmentation and differentiation of culture, as a consequence of the pluralisation of life styles and the differentiation of social structure; the employment of irony, allegory, pastiche and montage as argumentative styles and as components of rhetoric; the erosion of traditional 'grand narratives' of legitimation in politics and society; the celebration of the idea of difference and heterogeneity (against sameness and standardisation) as minimal normative guidelines in politics and morality; the globalisation of post-modern culture with the emergence of global networks of communication through satellites; the emphasis on flexibility and self-consciousness in personality and life-style; the greater demands for reflexivity in personal and organisational development; a weakening of the idea of coherence as the goal of personality and the scientific picture; the decline of 'industrial society' and its replacement by complex 'post-fordist' highly technological and service orientated configurations; the decline of the demarcation between 'high' and 'low' culture epitomised in the rise in acceptability of Jazz and Blues music; the technological production of cultural forms (epitomised by the poster and the electronic guitar which leads on to Techno); the wider acceptance of drugs as enhancers and instigators of 'moods'; the growing acceptance of 'inter-disciplinary' studies (epitomised in the collapse of the line between literature and cultural studies); etc.

of normative expectations and undercut predictability of social and individual events, thus removing important constraints on individual behaviour, and ensuing that the activities of individuals lose their signification. If criminology has sought to provide information and some guidance to our views on crime and punishment in modernity, the cultural challenge of post-modernism entails that they may lose whatever meaning they have and become lost in normative stupidity. Two contrasting positions – at least – are possible, cultural incoherence, stupidity and indifference – we can call this the position of MacIntyre (1981) – or a radical democratic possibility in the freeing of cultural messages from a settled social structure – we can call this Richard Rorty's (1989) position. Rorty believes

> our time is the first epoch in human history in which large numbers of people have become able to separate the question 'Do you believe and desire what we believe and desire?' from the question 'Are you suffering?' In my jargon this is the ability to distinguish the question whether you and I have the same vocabulary from the question of whether you are in pain? (1989:1981)

Thus Rorty believes that post-modernism has made it possible to free 'questions about pain from questions about the point of human life'. While Rorty points us to a progressive and optimistic reading of post-modernism, we do not know the answer to the question whether post-modernism is a celebration of the greater democratisation in life-forms of the social body, or increasing noise and ungovernability. Thus, while cultural unity has been split by the process of modernity and the advent of post-modernism, the allure of a reactionary fundamentalisation of society and culture, a splitting of society into the insiders and the outsiders, the moralists and the criminals, becomes strong; whether this is achieved by the openness of a social apartheid and repressive policing, or the market. But there may be no fundamental contradiction between modernity and post-modernism; hence understanding modernity may offer resources to sustain human interaction in post-modernism.

Conceptualising modern identity

What does it mean to conceive of ourselves as modern? One of our beliefs is that we are cut off from traditional values and ways of life. We may rejoice, interpreting liberation from tradition as freedom, while others, with equal logic, may claim that the results are a loss of roots, a loss of core meaning to life. We live at a distance from what was taken for granted in earlier ages, and still taken for granted in many societies in the world. We do not follow traditions as if they provide for us the natural way of life. We do not define ourselves by the socially given as closely as we believe our ancestors did. We wish to create a place for ourselves separate from the social framework – the ideas of class, values, roles and institutions – that have structured our parents. We almost believe that we can distance ourselves from the framework itself, seeking authenticity in some other true form of self-sustainability.

Perhaps this can be summed up in one sentence: *We do not accept ourselves as limited to the status we were born with – that is mere contingency – this understanding is the cultural key to being modern.*

What does this mean? I shall restate this from the bottom up. When we are born, what we are born, to whom we are born, our location in social geography – all these are not predetermined, thus our life begins as a contingency. We all could have been something, someone else, *we could have been the other*: this is the perception of contingency only known to the late-modern.[2] Nothing in the history of the world predetermined that I should be born a white male, in New Zealand, to the particular set of parents, in their particular set of socio-economic circumstances. There is no natural order that prefigures our existence. I might just as easily have been born a black female in Kenya ... but I was not ... from the time that I am born I can begin from no other starting point than that and where I am. The pre-modern world fought against this existential awareness of contingency – it created the image of God's will, of fate, of destiny – but we moderns know of no such solace; even if we were to seek it. The burden of dealing with contingency is the cultural burden of being truly modern – it is the flipside of the demand to be free – it is an awareness which comes to bite upon us only after the search for fundamental ontological security by modern science has demonstrated the reality of process and not some ontological bedrock. This is an existential weight which science has created; the search for some structure in the cosmos which we humans can latch on to, some set of deterministic social laws which structure the way things operate and ought to be, has not just failed to uncover any, but has resulted in the realisation that the cosmos operates in an open-ended way. The place in the order of things one was born to in pre-modern life set limits and possibilities; being born into a particular status meant that certain things were expected of you, certain possibilities open to you (if born to the highest stratum the greatest possibilities were open to you). As Durkheim indicated, for early modernity a functional division of labour appeared to set limits upon what an individual expected in life; in times of disturbance this may be upset, and then there would be no bounds on ambition/desire because the sense of contingency overwhelmed the sense of the natural order. As modernity has developed, this ideology of the natural order of things, which provided a cultural corollary to the functional division of labour, has come unstuck. While we once may have accepted our fate to be born into this or that part of the functional structure, into this or that part of the operation of things, that now merely provides our context. It represents only the locality of our position, and neither the forms of life it holds out to us, or the possibilities it appears to naturally offer us, are accepted as the natural limits of our existential determination. The culture of modernity, precisely the culture of late-

---

2   In social and political theory this is the cultural underpinnings of the moral decision-making procedure of the 'original position', or 'veil of ignorance' utilised in John Rawls' massive *Theory of Justice* (1972). In other words, whatever the social structures of a society, the position/location of the 'other' might have been mine, and 'I', might, be the 'other'.

modernity, the culture that knows of the death of God and embraces contingency, holds *the self as the bearer of possibilities*. Everything becomes possible if only the self can transcend the constraints of his or her context – transform the limitations of locality – but how can this be done?

A tension boarding on an inbuilt schizophrenia is present in late modernity. Let us recap. The self becomes the focus of the modernising process in that the determinations of culture (the demand to become modern) works against the determinations of the social structure (your position at birth, your skin colour, your gender). The essence of that which you are, is not to be read from the location of your birth, but from the creative positioning of your future. Your future depends upon your actions, you are to be the maker of your life – the modern is the self-made man or woman – those who merely carry out the fate of their birth are pre-moderns wearing a false modernity; but it is structural conditions of modernity that allows such action.

Do we have the power to realise this demand to be modern? Listen to the American 'realist' sociologist C Wright Mills writing in 1959:

'The very framework of modern society confines [people] to projects not their own, but from every side, such changes now press upon the men and women of the mass society, who accordingly feel that they are without purpose in an epoch in which they are without power.' (1959: 3)

The reality of modern society imposes constraints: what then is the cultural message? Does contingency demand an imagery of self-control and self-creation in modernity to over-come the reality of social constraints? Consider Heller and Feher:

'... it is not only the individual's relation to his or her initial 'context' that becomes contingent; the context itself also becomes contingent. Put simply, from a modern point of view, particular social arrangements and institutions can just as well exist as not exist. The world into which people are born is no longer seen as having been decreed by fate but as an agglomerate of possibilities. One can shape the world as much as one can shape oneself. *At least in our imaginations,* there are no limits to the possibilities for our 'shaping the world'. We can take the destiny of the world into our own hands. Just as our future depends on us, so too does the future of the world. How we can transform possibilities into destinies is now the question.' (1988: 17, emphasis added)

We encounter a dilemma similar in structure to the classical strain theory of Merton (1938). Instead, however, of the cultural message being the accumulation of money, the message now is taking control of our destiny. Modernity gives us a series of expectations as to self-realisation and personal growth – we are to become other than what we have been through the choosing of identities, employment roles, and seizing opportunities – but actual human beings have not fully escaped being defined by their location in situations of enablement and restraint. Human beings will be disappointed – they wish to take control of their selves, they wish to realise their (future) self-potential, but are located in demeaning and restraining circumstances – a crisis demanding action develops.

The post-modern condition is the contingency of the normal

Consider the interaction: contingency, normalcy, everyday, modernity. Contingency may be a criminogenic factor – what does this claim amount to? How can such an abstract concept as contingency have enough bite to be an influence on crime?

The culture of contingency is both a determinate and recognisable set of understandings, and a variable set of interpretations by individuals. An individual accepts contingency, when, for example, he or she refuses to listen to any claim that it had to be like this; that there is a natural reward for this or that level of service; that this or that is your natural station in life; that this is the appropriate level of your horizon; that you ought only to desire to this level.

Contingency has a generality in that it is the realisation of the unnaturalness of modernity. Contingency is the cultural fate of the project to liberate human beings from their subjection to nature, from unchosen ties, and to resolve the contradictions inside themselves. Contingency is the counter-claim to the idea of the natural order, it upsets all claims for an order of things that is not wholly satisfactory, ie that is not holding itself out as striving for justice. Contingency recognises the impossibility of justice as a state of being that will last – contingency is the understanding of the fluidity of life – contingency is the understanding that while it is important to strive, while it is important to pursue justice, a stable state of justice will be unattainable. We will never know justice yet she is the goal.

Post-modernism has appeared to some as if it were a mood – a strange sort of melancholia at the end of a great project – wherein we ask what modernity has all been about, and we do not know the answer. Modernity subjected life itself to scientific examination; we were sceptical towards the old narratives – those that held out life as a gift of God – and asked science to tell us the answers. But science cannot; so we keep asking the questions ... with little hope of a scientific answer. Science can tell us the *how*, but leaves us with the *why* unanswered and returns to us the quest for meaning. Life ... what is it? what is its force, its flows, wherein does it reside? The moods of post-modernism are indices of the dialectics of everyday existence.

Its first movement represents the misery of everyday life, its tedious tasks and humiliations, its degradations which reflect most strongly on the lives of the working classes and underclass. The 'flying fucks' that the women of slavery had to endure, are the extreme of the reality of the lot of women in the owned portion of humankind; a bondage intensified by child bearing and child-rearing and the basic preoccupation with the bare necessities. Daily life weighs heaviest upon the poorest sections – the daily tasks of many are burdened by the absence of money; urgent negotiations with the utilities companies; the threat of gas or electricity or water being cut off; the tone of dismissal from a petty bureaucrat at the other end of the phone; the realm of numbers which do not meaningfully relate to experienced reality; an all-too-familiar knowledge of the intimate things beyond material reality (the connection with living death) – poor health, 'irrational' spontaneity, vitality; the constant recurrence of problems which appear petty to others; unending poverty; the endlessness of want; the non-choice of economy and abstinence, hardship, repressed desires, meanness and avarice; the beauty of the fantasy world; the endless mirage of popular music; music videos which cut scenes and transpose images to confuse all sense of (un)reality, leading one to escape into the other-than-real ...

Its second movement represents the power of everyday life, its flexibility, its surprises, the adaptation of the body to variations in time and space, the continuation of desire when its momentum is failing. The linkage of environment and the home; the unpredictable and unmeasurable tragedy forever lurking ready to surface. The renaissance of women, the phenomenon which has often appeared the crushed and overwhelmed object of history and society, but also the inevitable subject, and foundation of renewal; the creation by humans of sensitivity and hope from recurrent blows of a world of sensory pain; the everlasting journey of experience; the enjoining of satisfaction with (unexpressed) need; the success of work; the encountering of pleasure in beauty; the ability to create out of the material of everyday life from its solids and its spaces, and to change the terminologies, to develop character in the individual or the group; the reproduction and continuity of essential relations; the ability of the women of Bosnia to forgive those who have killed their fathers, and husbands, and raped their sisters ...

Everyday life is the battlefield where wars are waged between the sexes, generations, communities, ideologies; the struggle between those at home and those not, between the adapted and those not, the shapelessness of subjective experience and the chaos of the void; meditations between these terms and the aftermath of emptiness, where antagonisms are bred ...

How are we to understand this? Let us first look to Marx. Everyday life is produced; this production is not the mere making of products but includes a 'spiritual' production, that is, the creation of social things (such as the understanding of time and space) and the material production of things (cars, houses, wages). Above this, there is human production; the social self-production of 'human beings' in the process of historical self-development (which in turn entails the production of social relations). Finally, for Marxism, the term production entails re-production, not simply the biological but the perpetuation of the social structure and human relations, of technical instruments and the tools of industry; all those things which give structure to societies. Throughout this social reproduction lies the binding forces of ideology. What are ideologies? Ideologies are made of cultural understandings and interpretations (religious, philosophical, common-sensical) of the world plus illusion. Ideologies are the false yet the necessary – without which the system could not operate. Culture is also a praxis, or a means of distributing meanings in a society and thus directing the flow of the production; culture in the widest sense is an element in the means of production in that it stimulates, it drives, it provides the source of ideologically motivated actions and activities. The notion of production, thus understood, has its full significance as production by human beings of their own existence. For modern Marxism, modernity has become consumption driven; consumption is twinned with production and mediated by ideology, culture, institutions and organisations. There is a feedback between production and consumption; culture structures and gives life to desires, wants and satisfactions. Everyday life is the terrain of this feedback; it has a dual character, the residuum of all the specific and specialised activities and the product of society in general. It is a point of delicate balance and where imbalance always threatens. A revolution takes place only where the balance of everyday life cannot be sustained.

Modern social life is unnatural in a way not knowable to the past. Conversely, with country or village life the rhythm of nature still held its ideology, but with urbanity this is unable to be sustained. What factors have we identified which demand we uncover the extraordinariness of everyday life?

- man's disembeddedness or estrangement from nature, accompanied by a feeling of loss (loss both of nature and of the past);
- the substitution of signs and signals for symbols and symbolism;
- the dispersal of communities and the rise of individualism;
- the profane displacing (but not replacing) the sacred and the accursed;
- the advance of the division of labour and growth of specialisation, the growth of knowledge divided into disciplines;
- a growing complexity or post-modernism surrounding culture and the location of meaning to the normal; the condition for a global system of symbolic interaction and exchange – the growth of the spectacle as the significant mode of organisation of feeling in the 'semiotic society';
- anguish and a general sense of meaninglessness, a proliferation of signs and signifiers, which cannot make up for the general lack of significance.

As we have constantly emphasised, however, everyday life has, and still does, in considerable part, appear natural, unproblematic. The social science of modernity had a crucial role in this – the ideology of positivism, together with the functionalist approach of social science, conspired to render life naturalised. The former superstitions that used to pervade everyday life, and give irrational value to objects, receded before a greater more deep-rooted irrationality that was an extension of official rationality – nature was receding, since even the manual labourer had mostly lost contact with his material, yet a sort of general naturalisation of thoughts, reflections and social contacts took place. According to those who had the tasks of investigation, of articulation – sociologists – society was a functional formation. Everything had natural functions. This general framework was aided by the routine of observation made possible by positivism.

Positivism accepts the objectification of (social) reality. Thus, objects reflect abstract forms that appear to belong to them, social and moral forms appear as given in a society, so does the ritualised form of social relations. The rational is considered normal according to the norms of a society sufficiently self-conscious and organised for the misunderstanding to take root; and the normal becomes the customary, and the customary is taken for natural, which in turn is identified as the rational, thus establishing a circuit or blocking to critical awareness. The consequences of such apparent logic is convention understood as naturalism, naturalism understood as the rational – all contradictions are abolished, social reality is natural, social reality is rational, but this reality is narrative, knowledge is ideology.

But the contingency of the post-modern condition speaks to two paths. One, the intertextuality of all; the interconnectedness of all. Two, the contingency of all, it could have been other ... what then can justify an assertion that one set of cultural particulars are more *natural*, or more *just*, or simply *superior* to the other?

The criminology of modernity predominantly assumed a normal culture and a sub-culture; the normal was associated with the middle-class ethic of western industrialised society focused around achievement, stable families and economic exchange. While Lemert (1964) could criticise Merton for assuming the domination of one set of cultural values, one answer to crime implicitly taken has been to hope that all of society becomes middle class. In Wolfgang and Ferracuti's (1967) *The Subculture of Violence*, the middle class ethic was regarded as variable and rich enough to contain crime. The middle class ethic kept at bay the ironies and nihilism of a subculture of violence the working classes were prone to. What, however, is nihilism and why does it appear as a cultural phenomena so much today? Consider Helmut Thielick writing in 1969:

'A middle class life is stable because its forms have the power of myth. Those forms silently shape perceptions and expectations. Hunger, disease, ignorance, confusion, violence, and risk – for most of the human beings in history the stuff of existence are kept outside the hedges of the suburbs. It is no wonder that young people of the middle class can hardly understand the philosophy and literature of the humanities; they have little experience of what most historical peoples meant by "humanity".

What is remarkable is that the radical young have in the last few years seen through the illusions of scientific, technical, democratic stability. They have tasted nothingness. Their refusal to accept the most powerful fantasy of security ever attained by human beings is one of the great spiritual triumphs of history. Their lack of spiritual discipline, of a tradition of dealing with nothingness, makes their triumph fragile and dangerous.' (1969: 3-4)

The middle class ethic denoted a world that made sense; a world of functional forms – the criminology (and this is the criminology of the Chicago School and Merton) of the middle class, was the criminology which offered the public policy of social organisation, of creating the conditions for a controlled bureaucratic (semi)meritocracy. We were offered important messages that wages and rewards were determined on the basis of performance and desert – but in a world of various strategies of desert and value, in a world where it is only too apparent that those born into a certain social station have the greatest chance of going to the right schools, of attaining the advanced qualifications necessary for the higher paid occupations, how can a sense of community and objectivity be created? In other words, how can the cultural messages of the society and time, offer a sense of justice?

Contingency and the sense of justice

Certainly 'justice is relative to social meanings' (Walzer, 1983: 312). A classic notion of justice has been the giving to each what he or she is due. Thus justice is internal to the cultural sets of understanding of function and desert. If the social structure is static (a feature of the social orders Gellner (1994) has called 'segmentary' societies, and which Durkheim referred to as characterised by mechanical solidarity), then the social meanings are integrated and hierarchical – the sense of justice is a fixed and reassuring ideology (and to our modern minds supportive of inequality). Walzer, using the example of the Indian caste system, refers to a summary account of the hierarchy operating in the distribution of grain in an Indian village:

'Each villager participated in the division of the grain heap. There was no bargaining and no payment for specific services rendered. There was no accounting, yet each contributor to the life of the village had a claim on its produce, and the whole produce was easily and successfully divided among the villagers.' (Quoted in Walzer, 1983: 313)

While everybody had a claim, each persons claim varied according to his station in the order of things. The distribution was unequal, but perceived as just. We say that the villagers shared in a set of doctrines which supported the caste system; they did not distance themselves as individuals out of the totality of this universe of meanings. An individual could only perceive the distribution as unjust if he or she could distance him or herself from the circle of the meanings in which he or she was emersed.

A sense of separation and distance – which has been traced to many things, christianity, capitalism, science, to masculine modalities – is central to late-modernity. It is undeniable that our relations to ourselves are clearly affected by distance; by movement out of locality we are told that we are free, we should choose rewarding lifestyles, we should be authentic, we should be self-calculating, self motivating and we should view ourselves as an unfinished life project. What is self-development if the self is absolutely fixed? It is the achievement of our telos ... but in the contingency of the modern condition there is no telos. Perhaps the real message of Alisdair MacIntyre's (1981) analysis in *After Virtue*, was that outside of the conditions of the well-balanced community the process of self-development becomes more important than the image of what you are to be. In other words the goal of participating in a process of building ourselves, can be defined independently of any particular content the self possesses. The process of creating yourself, of acting, becomes more important than being 'good' (as laid down by some structure of virtue), or being a person of 'virtue'.

Is it too strained to apply the distinction Weber made between substantive and formal rationality to this process of self-creation in late-modernity? Do these messages of restructuring, redevelopment, retraining of the self, amount to a formal methodology of development of the self – the unification of ourselves, the striving for freedom to develop, the searching for new possibilities, the creation of individuality, all of these can be goals and processes – referred to without mentioning any concrete substance or content for our choices. Is it the case that the process of self-development itself can become the goal? And is this reflected in social development, where social progress may become an endless sea of change without any substantive goal to be reached?

If so, then we cannot satisfy the ambitions of self-creation and self-direction – we cannot make ourselves into that wherein we are happy for what we are substantively – the secret to satisfaction/happiness will have to be something other. Socially, there can not be a just society in the sense of a state of being, or organisation that is the end of the search – the image of the goal of the just society will have to be something else.[3]

3　Consider a central cultural message inscribed in the ethical philosophy of modernity, namely, utilitarianism, which tells us to treat social life as a question of calculation, of seeing others as units to be added up or subtracted. For the German philosopher Immanuel Kant it was never right to use another person as a means. However, he saw the whole cultural edifice of modernity as increasingly embracing an alternative view: the other is to be treated as the instrument of your own self-satisfaction. The individual was to be the centre of a system of calculation, a structure of rational choice ... the others were mere pawns in the game of self-gratification.

How am I made aware of the consequences of my actions? How do I assume responsibility for my actions? In unmediated form preforming our actions towards others become the expressions of our will – of our very humanity. But modern life is a radically mediated life; the other we come into contact with is not directly visible to us, is not revealed, but identified; we cannot have direct experience of the selves we encounter around us. We rely upon an array of things interposed between our 'self' and the reality of the 'other' – we rely upon representations of the other. This is the unavoidable sociality of role, status, of social distance; the combination of social distance and utilitarian thought in the conditions of modernity tells us to use the other as the instrument of our will. From Kant onwards we can understand crime as the deepest expression of the culture of utilitarianism. Psychic distance is perhaps proportionate to lack of knowledge as to the other. Our ignorance of our actions is partly a consequence of the chains of intermediaries between ourselves and our acts. The longer the chain of intermediaries the less one retains control over them. How are the others represented to the self? Consider pornography. What is pornography? Pornography is not sex, it is not eroticism, rather it is the representation of women as objects. It is the presentation of women as objects of use, abuse, humiliation and submission in such a way usually that we are told this is their real role.

We may call the situation of embeddment as a structure of coherent and intergrated cultural messages as narratives as *hard culture*, our position, in the contemporary West, is not embeddment in hard culture, rather it is disorientatory, pulsating, multivarious, a mixture of language bites, significators which float free from their structure of signification – pieces of larger narratives which have broken free.

Instead of intergration our locality is the post-modern city – and cultural melange supported by bureaucracy and communication technology. Within this terrain everyday life takes its forms and energy.

The melange of the late or post-modern

Late modern society is characterised by a fluidity in ideology and boundaries. The political ideologies of democracy, communism, socialism, liberalism, conservativism are blurring; the modern boundaries between states are collapsing (USSR, Yugoslavia, Rwanda), governments are losing control of their economies (the effect of internationalisation of capital) and cannot contain the internal integrity of the cultural imagery (satellite TV etc). The citizenship of a country does not overlap with a particular cultural imagery and goods, or necessarily constrain the style of the person. Traditional meanings of health, illness, the human body, reproduction, medicine, sexuality, the family, intimacy, love, education, work, leisure, science, religion, art, entertainment, the private and the public are being destroyed or rendered unstable. As these effects bite, nostalgia for the supposed certainties of the past lead to uncomplicated images of the past being represented in the medium of popular culture.

The late modern or post modern is characterised by the cultivation of consumption, consumer life styles which were established under capitalism, and which render the self as a matter of signification, as a matter of the style of presentation. The public self is an array of masks ranked by the prestige and exchange value of their appearance(s), located in a internationalised media-orientated mass culture in which the meaning of personal civility, personal pleasure and desire, is principly understood by values flowing from the technologies of representation (advertising, films, television, magazines). The past and present are intermingled (noisy, brightly coloured TV advertising is laced with the soft nostalgia of old black-and-white films (in 1994, as Clinton prepared to invade Haiti, a series of carefully staged black-and-white photographs were released to remind the public of Kennedy and the Cuban missile crisis of 1962), classical music (16th century religious music provides the score for advertisements promoting aftershave products). By the early 1980s Lyotard argued that cultural eclecticism had become the post-modern way of life, a new international cultural subject becomes the norm:

> '... the degree zero of contemporary culture: one listens to reggae, watches a western, eats McDonalds's food for lunch and local cuisine for dinner, wears Paris perfume in Tokyo and "retro" cloths in Hong Kong; knowledge is a matter for TV games.' (1984: 76)

Open the weekly guide to activities in London, *Time Out*, where do you want to go in London tonight? We could watch a play from Britain, US, Brazil, China; opera from Italy, France and Russia; ballet from Poland, and Japan; or we can watch a movie from almost everywhere (mostly US if you want to go the mainstream large cinemas but a large range of countries/languages if you go to the smaller or repertory cinemas). We can eat, well, lets start with Asian ... Japanese, Chinese, Korean, Malaysian ... anything ... Then go to a range of nightclubs ... All one needs is money ...

Surrounded by this pulsating melange a degree of confusion arises.

The skills of post-modern living: or how can we live in the absence of 'real' meaning?

Modernity set out the project of building the good society upon the firm foundation of secure knowledge, but knowledge has become temporary, a matter of experimental strength. Knowledge proliferates providing an immense number of studies or bites of information. Knowledge was meant to bring emancipation (consider Marx's argument that truth would mean escape from ideology) the end to victimisation, the end to humans doing cruelty to others.

The increase in information, the depiction in myriad forms of reality, makes it difficult to conceive of a *single* reality. We become drunk with images.

In *Fatal Strategies: crystal revenge*, Jean Baudrillard (1990) presents post-modernism as the disappearance of true meaning as we become surrounded by a pulsating ecstasy or communication of meanings. Modernity has produced the distorted intensification of certain elements of its forms, and we have moved into a social environment of play and localised enjoyment but melancholy, boredom and pessimism impact upon us when we consider making sense of the larger picture. Whereas modernity was seemingly based on a structure of binary oppositions – true/false, male/female, insider/outsider, white/black, sane/insane, normal/deviant – increasing differentiation has made confidence in each of these identities appear simplistic. Modernity itself has become bored with the attempt to reconcile them. Instead it has allowed their proliferation. We are locked into an indefinite process wherein each of these terms or oppositions no longer allude to some stable reality, but are merely a process of bids to signify, or to position, the unknowable. We are surrounded by images and information bites which look obscene if we believe they depict some natural reality. In our search for the real, for the authentic, we have become seduced by signs. It is no longer possible to make sense of the world in its totality, we are adrift in a sea of communication – reality is debauched by signs, it becomes a perversion of reality. Where are we? What is the meaning of our present times? How can we actually tell? We move inside a spectacular distortion of facts and representations – the triumph of simulation. How can talk of socialisation make sense? What are we going to socialise the next generation into if there is no stable social structure for them to find their place? As a young, black, solo mother put it in talking of rearing her son in New York:

'How can I give my child a sense of real being in the midst of all those signs?'
(Personal Communication)

A range of writers, such as Wilson and Herrnestein (1985) and Charles Murray (1985; 1990) imply that a cultural change has occurred which has resulted in a different appreciation of time amongst late-modern youth. The time-horizon has been shortened; instant, rather than delayed gratification has resulted in the pursuit of short-term goals at the expense of building up long term projects. This short-term time horizon is said to result in a willingness to disregard the normative structures which are supportive of longer term methodologies and projects. This change in time horizons is said to be a crucial part of the culture-of-poverty and, for Murray, is indicative of the development of an underclass (see Chapter Seventeen). Writers such as Murray however, distort if they imply that being anti-human is the conscious, although irrational, longer-term choice of increasing numbers of people in late-modernity and thus determines the criminogenic situation of the underclass – the question is rather how can one construct a strong humanity in the midst of the ocean of signs that present us only with reflections. And it would be easier to resist, to keep sane, to keep normal, if we believed that these were simply the signs imposed by 'those who have the power' (in sections of American Black narratives, for example, it has been seriously argued that AIDS and drugs may have been created by white elites to destroy black youth), but the meta-narratives of capitalism, socialism, racism and the secure power elites have become unstable. Late modernity is a world of signs and multi-layered processes ... without a dominating master key.

Put another way, late or post-modernity has become a systematic condition without a corollary centre of political and social action which serves as the touchstone of all others. We cannot believe in the one meta-narrative. As criminologists we move from the one perspective, such as that of David Garland in *Punishment and Welfare* (1985) to multiple perspectives as in *Punishment and Modern Society* (1990) which we understand as connected in an interactive development. Reality becomes interactional.

Addressed on another terrain, one cannot any more believe in a sociology of deviance or in the progressive typologising of positivism – for the ascription deviant is by the signification of censure and to believe in positivism's ability to tackle imminent finality is senseless reason.

What can social progress mean? Marxists used to believe that the world would be moved forward through a series of conflicts or dialectical struggles which would finally result in reconciliation, but why did we think reconciliation is the end of history? Is not late-modernity sworn to extremes. For Baudrillard it is clear that social diversity does not aim for equilibrium, but is merely pulsating radical antagonisms incapable of reconciliation or synthesis. While this is the principle of growth, it is also the principle of evil or the victory of unreason. The processes of the world do not proceed of their own accord to any utopia of triumphant harmony.

What tactics therefore are possible if we lose sight of positivism and functionalism? One (perhaps it was after all De Sade's) is to fight obscenity and crime not in terms of a dialectical opposition (ie to oppose crime by punishment) but by taking it on its own terms in search of limits (to offer films, TV shows which are only crimes, only full of the symbolism of violence so that we may be cleansed of violence in our passive selves). We seek the radical secret quality of truth by opposing the false with the even falser, not in opposing the ugly by the beautiful but looking for the uglier than ugly; by meeting the monstrous. We cannot oppose the visible to the hidden; we can only use more and more forms of visibility, but our search is always for that which is more hidden than hidden: the secret. We are committed to an ascent to extremes.

We have raised every trait to a superlative power in a spiral of increasing complexity and technical verbosity whereby we extend the true into the truer, the beautiful into the more beautiful in search of the more beautiful than beautiful, the realer than real. Ecstasy and inertia: we lie tired on our bed exhausted from the performance of the daily life, do we really want to perform at that restaurant date? Yes we shall go, but we place on the post-modern escutcheons of the (non)self our roles, our jewels, our designer clothing. We go to seduce, and this seduction is achieved not by some simple attraction (not by the presentation of the self, for that remains hidden, in private) but by the redoubled attraction of a sort of challenge – do we repeat the story – what is presented is not the (other) true self that was left on our bed with the discarded jeans, but a different true, one that has absorbed all the energy of the false ('I feel a con') a simulation. But the simulation is truer than the true, it has greater performability, a dazzling over performance, which works through the multiplication of the formal qualities of social skills.

We live in the age of the model and the effigy of the model assured by the variety of wigs – the wig means she can change style, he can change age. The body becomes the 'living display unit of the post-modern person'. (Lefebvre, 1984: 173) The model is truer than true, since she/it is the quintessential of the significant features of a situation producing a vertiginous sensation of truth. The super-model achieves in the domain of fashion the being of more beautiful than the beautiful. The fascinations which seduce in a process greater than any one value judgment. The superficial, the fragile, the total passion, the desire, the imagination ... Fashion is the ecstasy of the beautiful, a pure and empty form of an aesthetic which is spinning upon itself. The real becomes lost in the multiplicity of simulation. The same process occurs in all the sites of communications. On the television news real events follow each other in a dizzying, stereotypical, unreal and recurrent fashion that dulls sense, while providing an uninterrupted concatenation for the allotted time space. Real news has a duration of use and exchange value, a shelf life similar to the brand name of the jeans. Things have stopped being real. Our communication processes offer us a form of hyper-reality; they provide a cancer of information. The search for knowledge has taken revenge upon its human actors in excrescence. The construction process of knowledge and power is short-circuited by a monstrous overkill.

What are the sites of everyday life? While the greatest damage of crime may be in the unreported damages of white-collar crime (pollution, computer scams, government corruption, political mismanagement) quantitatively official crime is the activity in the main of youth – today adolescents are given or demand their own operational physical and electronic environment (TV, bedrooms, CD players, cars, street corners, clubs, schools, sports, hobbies, make-up, drugs) where they learn to understand, appropriate and value the symbols of happiness, eroticism, taste, power, meaning, pulsation, highs, and personal experience. What is at stake? The search for a locality, an experience which is uniquely one's own. An individuality which is learnt to be expressed through hair style, clothing, perfumes, aftershave lotions, make-up and jewellery which is put on in private and worn in public. For Lefebvre the pursuit of an authentic self becomes tied into the methodologies and roles of the market: consumption, wearing, display:

'... everybody is confronted in his daily life with the heart breaking choice between non-freedom or non-adaption.

Youthfulness with its operational environment ... enables adolescents to appropriate existing symbolisations, to consume symbols of happiness, eroticism, power and the cosmos by means of expressly elaborated metalanguages such as songs, newspapers articles, publicity – to which the consumption of real goods is added; thus a parallel everyday life is established. The adolescent expresses such a situation in his own way, stresses it and compensates for it in the trances and ecstasies (simulated or sincere) of dancing.' (1884: 171)

We can see in the combination of dance and drug – *ecstasy* in the *rave* scene – the perfection of the late-modern commodification and consumerisation of life (now ecstasy becomes available in a tablet form) and a music fits a drug perfectly, a music which is the production of technology (techno or jungle). Under the influence of the drug ecstasy, the brain patterns change to fit the music ... where is reality? What is substance, what is enchantment? What is the cause of this technically enhanced dizziness? What is so post-modern about ecstasy? Take a rave with large scale video screens. Ravers dance to techno or jungle (an even more technically enhanced techno music) while around them are screens where a simultaneous video is shown of the dance floor – they watch themselves while tripping on the drug which increases the feeling of fellow-feeling; feelings, emotions, have become hyper-real. The whole is an ecstasy of simulated communication and simulated empathy. The totality is a lived experience which owes its existence to a technology of music and drugs – to the creation of technologies of the real, and the manufacturing of the real and understandings of the real. The whole is real, while it is comprised of manufactured realities. And what is actually the supposed reality of the whole?

What is everyday life for those who cannot club everyday? Lefebvre asks how can one escape the orbit of a youthfulness which is a simulation of 'fulfilment, charm, happiness, completeness'?

'The inevitable outcome of such tuned-up, geared-down dizziness is a feeling of incalculable discomfort and unrest, a sense of frustration that cannot easily be distinguished from satiety, a craving for make-believe, compensations, and evasions into unreality.' (Ibid: 171)

In this loveless everyday life eroticism is a substitute for love', youth the measure of joy and freedom. The cult of eros and youth (love and death) turns sexuality into a commodified entity traded for the simulation of intimacy and love. But as ageing takes place the young woman finds the social structure is not yet totally open: patriarchy works its magic and in early adulthood women are usually once again placed within the male domain (faithful wives) who now become a team set to consume the late-modern cultural symbolism of adulthood (TV, VCR's, family cars, house, foreign holidays). The alternative: solo parenting ...

We have attunement to systematicity: consider two paths – One the pursuit of pure desire, the perfection of desire, can it be attained? Second the institutionalisation of romantic love via the modern marriage for love.

Can the first be satisfied? For Lefebvre desire can not be satisfied by the possession of the significants that it sought when desire was aroused.

> 'Desire refuses to be signified, because it creates its own signs as it arises – or simply does not arise; signs or symbols of desire can only provoke a parody of desire that is never more than a pretence of the real thing.' (1984: 172)

The commodification of desire, of all forms from the commodification of love into sexuality, or the commodification of feeling good into drugs, means that desire cannot of its nature be ever satisfied no matter how many commodities desire accumulates.

Location by consumption patterns

Late modernity offers equal access to the world of the image – as a viewer – and we demand equal access to the goods so (re)presented – as a participant. The late modern demand of citizenship is for access to an equal standard of consumption. For Turner:

> 'Equality of opportunity allows individuals to enter a race at the same point, but it does not guarantee equality of outcome; indeed it partly requires significant inequalities in terms of ultimate benefits. Social groups which experience major disadvantages will seek to achieve greater equality of conditions, which will compensate for differences in individual capacities. Employing the analogy of an athletic race, we can say that elderly participants within the games will seek some compensation (such as starting the race in advance of younger competitors).' (1988: 44)

Many commentators regard the races of late modernity as a return to status; modernity has turned cyclical. Whereas the utopia of modernity is self-definition, the self needs a language involving the recognition of others to understand him or herself. Socially, personal worth in early modernity may have escaped from the feudal hierarchies of status into a class structure defined in relation to the system of production (working class, middle class, upper class); late-modernity tends to make such definition of class increasingly redundant. Instead, consumption patterns and the achievement of *lifestyle* serve to locate new forms of stratification. While this may appear unorganised – it certainly will be more fluid and apparently chaotic than in early and middle modernity – the game will have rules. The overriding rule is *recognition,* or stratification, on the basis of consumption, and the presentation of (self)image this consumption makes possible. Purchasing consumer goods becomes an investment in a status claim, which may or may not pay off. The time period is short, a new item may be purchased and the old one taken to the opportunity shop or thrown out almost immediately. For Baudrillard (1988) in this late-modern consumer society, objects are not purchased for use, but so that they can function as signs. The brand name prominently displayed on the jacket matters. The previously important, utilitarian, characteristic as a garment for warmth, becomes a lesser function in their new role as signs, providing a reading as to quality of the product and the type of person weaning it. The status (the standing of the person) becomes visible through consumption:

> 'Within 'consumer society', the notion of status, as the criterion which defines social being, tends increasingly to simplify and to coincide with the notion of 'social standing'. Yet 'social standing' is also measured in relation to power, authority and responsibility. But in fact: There is no real responsibility without a Rolex watch! Advertising refers explicitly to the object as a necessary criterion: You will be judged on – An elegant woman is recognised by – etc. Undoubtedly objects have always constituted a system of recognition (reperage), but in conjunction, and often in addition to other systems (gestural, ritual, ceremonial, language, birth status, code of moral values, etc). What is specific to our society is that other systems of recognition (recognisance) are progressively withdrawing, primarily too the advantage of the code of 'social standing'.' (1988: 19).

In this analysis, the industrial system with its production of commodities for exchange, has been replaced with a system where the production of signs for communication is paramount. But a new stable system cannot be based on cybernetics, instead we are surrounded by simulations and indeterminacy; instability is inbuilt. It has become difficult to grasp the reality of one's social position; the supposed concrete reality of the modern social system based on ones' place in the system of production, ones' class location and the cultural signification of ones' locality, has imploded on itself leaving us lost in a vast sea of media messages, significations, referential objects pointing to a reference points of their own making; in short, to use Baudrillard's phrase, we live in a system of the hyper-reality of self-referential systems. Our cultural indices, our cultural signposts, are signs which point to other signs rather than to any certain reality.

Located amidst the swirl of late or post-modern culture the individual inhabits a circle of image, simulation, stimulation, desire and materiality: but can contemporary desire be satisfied?

Criminology has worked with rather basic models of desire. From Merton (1938) onwards, criminology saw the overriding goals of material success and crime as a response to the frustration of that desire. Perhaps Durkheim's original formulation was richer, it moved more towards the possibility of a desire which could never be satisfied, no matter what material goods were provided. The question for criminology is, has modernity unleashed insatiable desire(s) which cannot now be brought under control?

Desire, growth, materiality and the coherence of practical justice

A rather neglected criminological theory of crime, desire and culture is that of W I Thomas (1909, 1923). Thomas argued an inevitable contradiction arose between the desires and needs of individuals and the social order. The task of social control was to mediate and regulate the four central desires of an individual – for *security*, *new experiences*, *response*, and *recognition* – through a cultural moral code or 'definitions of situations'. This needs to be coherent to prevent social disorganisation. As American society was developing, the cultural surrounds were throwing up sets of competing definitions of behaviour, and issuing new demands for rights and freedoms. Thomas saw, in particular, greater opportunities for young women with new public settings of office, stores and factories. Young women were being subjected to conflicting and competing demands. In *The Unadjusted Girl*, Thomas argued that sexuality took on a new exchange value: '... sex is used as a condition of the realisation of other wishes. It is their capital' (1923: 98).

For women, located in the social disorganisation of the new city and conflicting cultural messages, sex became an item to be traded, and an instrument for materialising the desires for 'security, new experience, and response'.

The desires, Thomas acknowledges, are not desires for material things, but rather desires for existential phenomena for which material things are medium. In his studies for *The Gang*, Thrasher (1937) defined these wishes as 'lively energies' which helped make adolescent life free and wild. Gang members were not immoral – they actually had moral codes of their own – but their language for expressing, and the ways of achieving their desires, were deviant. The activities of the gangs were full of adventure and fun not rivalled in the playgrounds, or the more orderly portions of the city.

What offers both recognition and self-worth in the culture of contingency? For Hume the self as an embodied theatre makes sense of life through its biography, its memory and the criteria it holds as to value. The self has a project when it approaches the world as the site for activities which provide meaning – thus the self is dependent upon the cultural messages of the world to find its direction, to locate its desires for authenticity, fulfilment and meaning. Perhaps this is the message of control theory (both Durkheim, Thomas, Thrasher and Hirschi may be agreed on this), in that the narratives of civil society serve to constrain one by providing images of the good, and allocating value for your endeavours; these informal patterns constrain since they determine whether your actions are worthwhile or viewed as shameful by your peers and important others. Classical criminology is mostly read as setting up a formal system of criminal justice but this formal structure and the use of the utilitarian science of ethics to control the rational desire of the populace for pleasure and the avoidance of pain sat on top of assumptions concerning civil society for the middling masses. While the dangerous classes needed to the rationalised,

Bentham listed a whole host of social sanctions which the 'normal' person was constrained by in everyday life. We can call these factors determining the integrity of everyday actions. For those who would, or could, not be so controlled by rational calculation, Bentham indicated the Panopticon – imprisonment was the fate of the irrational. The divisions rational versus irrational, those able to appreciate the truths of political economy, versus those unable to, became the division of the prison walls. This was a feature endemic to utilitarianism (Morrison, 1995,b). The question is simple: can the culture of post-modernism operate to constrain crime? Or does its differentiation, pluralism, its hyper-reality, so distort bearings that cultural/social disorganisation result?

The return to neo-classicism, with the demands for fixed and severe punishment, coupled with the demand that individual responsibility must be strengthened, has been prompted in part by the confusion engendered by the apparently dramatic increases in crime when the West appears to be the lands of plenty. Modernity has given material abundance and technological progress, so why all the crime? Are we not surrounded by the instruments of happiness? And, as opposed to the images of classical utilitarianism, we are not being force fed the entities which will 'make us happy'; we have released the market to satisfy our individual preferences. Is it rather that we have so many items of happiness, so many consumerable entities, that we cannot carry them all, cannot enjoy them all? Or is it we can observe them all, but enjoy only a few?

And existential questions arise ... is this the home the early moderns thought they were constructing for us? Does material plenty, or the stimulation and material gratification of our desires, guarantee satisfaction? It is a cruel irony that improvements in the standard of living leave us more comfortable but not happier ... And by some strange inversion every granted wish may take us further from wholesomeness and inner peace.

This did not appear so to Thomas Hobbes, who set out a creed that remains a central part of the official consciousness of the industrial liberal-democratic world today. To Hobbes, happiness is a function of the goods we possess and the things we consume: it is a result of urges satisfied. In his best known work, *Leviathan*, he summarised the attainment of happiness in a classic definition:

'Continual success in obtaining those things which a man from time to time desires, that is to say, continually prospering, is what men call FELICITY.'

Taken in this light, the introduction of massive advertising and credit buying are the two greatest steps ever taken to promote the happiness of man. Advertisements create new desires, and consumer credit makes it possible for these cravings to be instantly gratified. The unbroken circle of new desires and satisfactions guaranteed, amounts to that 'continual prospering' which *men call felicity*. Continual success – ie happiness – is the share of the citizen who desires, purchases and consumes in proportion to the instalment payments he can meet. What is purchased need not be a fabricated object – it may be love; nor need the payment be a sum of money – it may be time to listen to a concerto, another person's troubles or the promise of security.

Is the legacy of Hobbes correct? Is happiness the satisfaction of desires on the basis of astuteness in trading? No, we simplify the problem if we read the process of desire and consumption so narrowly. As Nietzsche and others recognised, goods are not simply objects of materiality, but significations of status, or 'positional goods', ie goods denoting the relative status of the wearer/possessor.

How does this effect criminological theorising? Criminology not only operates with underdeveloped models of desire, but also largely restricts itself to narrow interpretations of strain theories; wherein crime is the result of frustration by the social structure of the needs which culture identifies for the individual. Today, even in the most contemporary of mainstream criminological theory, ideas of positionality and status are underdeveloped. Instead ideas of needs and greed predominate. For example, Braithwaite argues that both common crimes and white-collar crime have a common explanation:

'A general theory of both white-collar and common crime can be pursued by focusing on inequality as an explanatory variable. Powerlessness and poverty increase the chances that needs are so little satisfied that crime is an irresistible temptation to actors who have nothing to lose ... When needs are satisfied, further power and wealth enables crime motivated by greed. New types of criminal opportunities and new paths to immunity from accountability are constituted by concentrations of wealth and power. Inequality thus worsens both crimes of poverty motivated by *need* for goods for *use* and *crimes* of wealth motivated by *greed* enabled by goods for exchange. Furthermore, much crime, particularly violent crime, is motivated by the humiliation of the offender and the offender's perceived right to humiliate the victim. In egalitarian societies, it is argued, are more structurally humiliating. Dimensions of inequality relevant to the explanation of both white-collar and common crime are economic inequality, inequality in political power (slavery, totalitarianism), racism, ageism, and patriarchy' (1991: 40, emphasis is the original).

At stake, however, is not a simple greed for goods for exchange as mere wealth, but goods for status. Goods, commodities, become *readable*: possession of goods serves as signs of position and identity. Similarly, accumulation of goods signifies power, as indeed does the power derived from the humiliation of another in the perpetration of crime (power to humiliate, power to outwit).

Put another way, what is at stake is the creation of a meaningful location and signification of *being*. The modernism of Marx and Durkheim gave us a legacy of alienation and anomie, in which the frustration caused by systematic distancing of people from the goods which the culture held out as the source of value (labour reward for Marx, participation for Durkheim), resulted in the need for crime. But we are no longer in the fear of alienation but rather in the morass of communication. Weber told us of the fundamental need humans have for a meaningful cosmos (why else did they dream up God(s)?), and warned of fundamental human experiences being endangered by modernity, by the industrialisation and compartmentalisation which has occurred – the spread of machines mediates our contact with the world removing the experience of using the entirety of our bodies in the service of a task. Culture and bodies interact – we need to feel, to desire. Today, few of our normal tasks cause us to sweat; in the civilised world more sweat is due to worry than to work. Perhaps the only activities left that involve the whole body are sex, sport and dancing, and possibly in sublimated and distorted style, the taking of certain drugs. Our devotion to them reflects a need for, and joy in, total involvement; at stake is ecstasy. As Becker (1963) and others have pointed out, part of the problem with drugs that appears to upset moral entrepreneurs, is that they provide us with an artificial way to fulfil certain desires and cravings for bodily experiences. Consider Finestone's description of the meaning that heroin use had for the 'cool cats' who had created a cultural identity claiming superiority over the 'square' others:

> 'It was the ultimate "kick". No substance was more profoundly tabooed by conventional middle-class society. Regular heroin use provides a sense of maximal social differentiation from the "square". The cat was at last engaged, he felt, in an activity completely beyond the comprehension of the "square".' (1964: 285)

Perhaps what is being said in the discussion of late-modern culture, is that there is no one overriding criterion. There are various codes of success.

Consequently in a mobile late-modern society everyone is likely to feel somewhat insecure. Success in the framework of one set of values, is not success in the other. One reads a book encouraging consumption, and buys a book which offers another view, say *A River Sutra*. Personal enlightenment verses the accumulation of wealth.

Many of the codes, much of the criteria for success and security, from another perspective, appear illusions. But civil society does not collapse – in fact, in many respects, it is in rather good shape. Take a central theme of liberal civil society: tolerance (classically expressed by John Stuart Mill in *The Essay On Liberty* but by now fundamental). What are the conditions for one's tolerance? The early idea of tolerance as a strategy of accommodation while assimilation takes place, in other words, while difference is transformed into similarity, seems to have been replaced by tolerance as the foundational methodology of enabling a social solidarity to be established over difference. Late modern civil society flourishes on difference, on experimentation, and for most of this century it has been felt this lay at the root of Western economic success. While historically it does appear that tolerance was required to create and sustain modern economic prosperity, the advent of Japanese and Far Eastern success has presented us with new challenges. We may not need to be tolerant to be economically successful; particularly if we do not need the whole population to be involved as producers and full consumers.

Understanding the (non)reality of crime: the non–positivist sign

For Baudrillard it is becoming difficult to distinguish Disneyland from the real America – when we think of Disneyland we think it is fantasy, and thus believe there is a real America somewhere else. However, we err if we think Disneyland is false, Disneyland is America, it is real, except it is hyper-real. The new social order makes it difficult to accept the binary oppositions of the true-false, allowed-prohibited, science-metaphysics, black-white, woman-man – reality has become a spectacle, and the social world a cosmos of swirling world of signs.

No over-reaching theory of the social can be produced. Every perspective is but one perspective. Sociality is multiple ... pluralist ... the belief of criminology in 'subcultures', in others words, to priviledge the norm, and the other as thereby inferior, becomes the visualisation of merely different phenomena ... diverse aspects of the de-centred social cosmos. How can we identify the normal and the sub? That is not to say that we cannot do it, but that we have to develop a different methodology for post-modernism. One question re-occurs ... if God is dead how is it possible to commit a true crime? How is it possible, in other words, to really transgress? If post-modernity absorbs everything, and if there is no Super Other – for if there is no God then there is no Devil – how is it possible to do anything that really opposes this new social order? Nothing can be refused, everything is available for an appropriate sign, for an appropriate price (one among other systems of signification). How can one seduce if one is surrounded by sex?

> 'When desire is entirely on the side of demand; when it is operationalised without restrictions, it loses its imaginary and, therefore, its reality; it appears everywhere, but in generalised simulation. It is the ghost of desire that haunts the defunct reality of sex. Sex is everywhere, except in sexuality.' (Baudrillard, 1990: 5)

If reality is intertextuality, if deconstruction cannot draw us to some core of the natural ... how can we investigate crime? What is a crime if not a set of significants that have been used previously? Is that person taking cocaine really a criminal? Is that woman saying yes to the driver of that car really a prostitute? What is a prostitute? Is the corporation that gets information concerning the side effects of its drugs and neither passes on the information, or withdraws the drug from sale, really criminal? Does it have to be in breach of its duties for us to say it is a crime? By what criteria can legislation and censure proceed?

The cultural paradox of post-modernism: energy and exhaustion

Post-modernism ... the world of the hyper-real is the world of the hyper-active, a world that pulsates with an explosion of imagery and technological (re)development and (re)deployment. At the same time exhaustion overwhelms. One cannot portray it all as a totality. Who, or what, can take responsibility for a sociality which fluctuates and pulsates? Has not that grand attempt to portray the totality of the social in theory and practice, 'Marxism', collapsed? While its other rival to the West, Islam, although still growing, holds little for the believers in civil society to take heart from? So how then can a post-modernism be governed rationally? How can it be policed socially? If we can no longer believe in the coherence of the social, the answer looks simple: a formally rational framework of a rule of law and privatise the (non)social. The social has disappeared into hyper-reality ... how then can anyone take responsibility for it? Thus stands exhausted any appeal to a social responsibility read as accountability for societal fulfilment ... How can such an appeal escape from falling prey to the charge of being a mere expression of the interests of dominant groups or factions, if the idea of societal progress, as the realisation of universal aspects of human interdependence, no longer has meaning in the sea of images?

Thus we can hear the voices of 'personal responsibility'; the voices of 'self-control'. And the voices which call for the return of classicism ... And the voices which ask the market to determine our priorities and tell us to retreat to our private selves safe within our policed, segregated domains, parified from contact with the other.

CHAPTER FOURTEEN

LABELLING THEORY, AND THE WORK OF DAVID MATZA

'Our private sphere has ceased to be the stage where the drama of the subject at odds with his objects and with his image is played out: we no longer exist as playwrights or actors but as terminals of multiple networks.' (Baudrillard, 1988: 16)

'The lunatic was put into a coffin and laid in a vault in which was another coffin occupied by a man who at first pretended to be dead but who, soon after he was left alone with the lunatic, sat up, told the latter how pleased he was to have company in death, and finally got up, ate the food that was by him and told the astonished lunatic that he had already been dead a long time and therefore knew how the dead go about things. The lunatic was pacified by the assurance, likewise ate and drank and was cured.' (Hegel, 1971: para 408, p 139)

Introduction

Within American writings of the 1960s criminological positivism became attacked by an interactionist orientation called labelling theory, and the rise of a general anti-deterministic current within the philosophy of social science. This chapter will first consider how labelling theory changes the naturalist perspective of positivism into a concern with process, then discuss the work of David Matza, and suggest how we can read connections between the themes of Matza, and a philosophical position which represents some aspects of the modern human predicament and the culture of contingency, namely, existentialism.

Labelling theory: from mechanical naturalism into interactional process

At the core of the labelling orientation is the assumption of process: deviance and social control always involve processes of social definition and reaction. While the idea of social process had always been at the centre of the preoccupations of the Chicago School, labelling was to give it greater scope and implicitly introduce the idea of contingency. Howard Becker's famous definition emphasises the act of labelling:

'... social groups create deviance by making the rules whose infraction constitutes deviance, and by applying these rules to particular people and labelling them as outsiders. From this point of view deviance is not a quality of the act the person commits but rather a consequence of the application by others of rules and sanctions to an 'offender'. The deviant is one to whom that label has successfully been applied; deviant behaviour is behaviour that people so label.' (1963: 9)

The epistemological basis for labelling is pragmatic. Knowledge is humanly created and is true to the presumptions which are brought to bear, moreover these knowledge claims have totally empirical consequences. One's perception of the world is a vitally important factor in how one relates to the world, one's perceptions shape one's social world, they constitute it. As W L Thomas put it: 'if men define situations as real, they are real in their consequences'. To those who share the naturalist perspective Becker's remarks appear scandalous; the labelling school has often been misunderstood in the extent of its claims and its technical standing as a mode of explanation.

Labelling is a theory of process; deviance is not viewed as a static entity, but rather as a continuously shaped and reshaped outcome of dynamic processes of social interaction. Labelling theory came out of the traditions of the Chicago school and the general theme of process, which concentrates on deviant roles and the development of deviant self-conceptions, and has given rise to such concepts as 'career' and 'commitment'. In terms of its intellectual lineage, labelling is a development of the American sociological perspective of symbolic interactionism, and draws upon the image of the self which George Herbert Mead held, namely, that the self is a process and not a structure. Schemes that explain the self through an image of structure alone, ignore the reflexive process that Mead recognised as central to social interaction. For Mead, human action could not be viewed simply as a product of determining factors operating upon the individual, rather, he saw the human being as an active organism in its own right, facing, dealing with, and acting towards the objects he or she indicates. Social patterns are believed to reflect a continuous process of fitting developing lines of conduct to one another. As a consequence, we can expect interactions to produce outcomes which could not have been predicted using a Newtonian picture of determinant entities banging into each other like billiard balls. As the sociologist Norman Denzin (1969) puts it, interactionism alerts us to an emergent quality to the social situation that may not have existed before the parties came together.

We have been mapping the voyage of criminology through modernity into post-modernism. Post-modernist writers refer to an overburdened self – a self as the site of multiple exchanges of narratives and cultural messages. Denzin (1991) tells us that the post-modern self is a form of subjectivity hailed, or created, by specific sites of familial, group and ideological discourse. These include film, the media, television, biography, social science, and the speech situations of interaction with peers, friends, and enemies in everyday life.

The understanding of social psychology espoused by Herbert Mead

Mead argued for a social psychology which combined the actions we observers could note, with the mysterious subjective considerations an individual cannot really even communicate to others, 'those phenomena which are accessible to the individual alone':

'Social psychology is behaviourist in the sense of starting off with an observable activity - the dynamics of on-going social processes, and the social acts which are its component elements – to be studied and analysed scientifically. But it is not behaviouristic in the sense of ignoring the inner experience of the individual – the inner phase of that process of activity ... It simply works from the outside to the inside, in its endeavour to determine how such experience does arise in the process. The act, then ... is the fundamental datum in both social and individual psychology when behaviouristically conceived, and it has both an inner and an outer phase, an internal and external aspect ...' (1934: 7-8)

While human behaviour has easily observable overt features, the covert aspects are of crucial importance in determining human action. Behaviourist psychologists, such as Watson, condescendingly referred to 'mentalistic concepts', such as the study of consciousness, images and language, as shorthand statements which were to be reduced into more basic entities in the name of science. Mead, conversely, saw these as the foundational elements for an psychology true to the actors actual perceptions.

This raises the theme of process, and rejects what Albert Cohen (1965) has called the assumption of discontinuity in positivist criminology. When you place individuals in their full location in social life they are not discreet entities. A full explanation of human activity would include the social history and ramifications of the behaviour, rather than limit itself to the supposed basic characteristics of deviating acts or actors (as determined by examination of associations with standard sociological variables). For Albert Cohen, the positivist bias in American sociology had:

'... been toward formulating theory in terms of variables that describe initial states, on the one hand, and outcomes, on the other, rather than in terms of processes whereby acts and complex structures of action are built, elaborated, and transformed.' (1965: 9)

By contrast, Becker (1963) argued there were simultaneous and subsequential models of deviance. If all causes do not operate at the same time, we need a model which takes into account the fact that patterns of behaviour may or may not develop in relatively orderly sequences. This model, however, also needs to be aware of the possibility of ironical outcomes. Labelling theory questioned the static statistical comparisons that had tended, despite recognition of severe sampling problems, to dominate research into the 'causes' of deviating behaviour. Some American scholars, for example, Edwin Sutherland (1927), in his classic definition of criminology, had referred to knowledge of the processes of making laws, of breaking laws, and of reacting towards the breaking of laws. Sutherland saw these processes as constituting three aspects of a somewhat unified sequence of interactions, and concluded that this sequence of interactions is the object-matter of criminology. Setting out some over-riding unification process was, however, neglected.

The earliest statement of labelling comes in Frank Tannenbaum's textbook *Crime and the Community* (1938, first published 1923). Tannenbaum described a process in which some, but not all, of the individuals who engage in deviance are likely to be singled out for stigmatising treatment. Once a person has been publicly defined as a criminal, the person is likely to find the ratio of contacts he has with others defined as criminals, and those deemed law-abiding, changes dramatically. This change leads to the adoption of a criminal identity, and a criminal career becomes a natural progression. Tannenbaum calls this act of labelling 'the dramatisation of evil'.

> 'The first dramatisation of 'evil' which separates the child out of his group for specialised treatment plays a greater role in making the criminal than perhaps any other experience. It cannot be too often emphasised that for the child the whole situation has become different. He now lives in a different world. He has been tagged. A new and hitherto non-existent environment has been precipitated out for him:
>
> The process of making the criminal, therefore, is a process of tagging, defining, identifying, segregating, describing, emphasising, making conscious and self-conscious; it becomes a way of stimulating, suggesting, emphasising, and evoking the very traits that are complained of.' (1938: 19-20)

To its critics labelling is deterministic in that the person so labelled becomes the thing he is described as being – this criticism misses the elements of contingency and irony which are implicit to the theory. Labelling theory points to ironical outcomes. We think, that in defining some act as criminal, and some person as a criminal or deviant (or mentally ill) we are adopting an attitude which will lower the incidence of crime, or lead to treatment and cure. Unintended consequences, however, follow the act of labelling. The criminal conduct is actually continued, the illness worsens. It does not appear to matter whether the valuation is made by those who would punish, or by those who would reform. The harder they work to reform the evil, the greater the evil grows under their hands. The application of labels, whether criminality, deviance or illness brings out the behaviour that the label was supposed to control. To the labelling theorist the practical implications are clear: refuse to dramatise the evil.

The labelling process fits any type of socio-political order. As Edwin Lemert wrote in 1951:

> '... we start with the idea that persons and groups are differentiated in various ways, some of which result in social penalties, rejection, and segregation. These penalties and segregative reactions of society or the community are dynamic factors which increase, decrease and condition the form which the initial differentiation or deviation takes ...
>
> The deviant person is one whose role, status, function and self-definition are importantly shaped by how much deviation he engages in, by the degree of its social visibility, by the particular exposure he has to the societal reaction, and by the nature and strength of the societal reaction.' (1951: 22-23)

Lemert draws a distinction between primary and secondary deviation which seems to be an attempt to preserve a notion of natural deviancy that any group would label or define as 'deviance'. He argues we can distinguish between (i) a primary or initial act of deviation; and (ii) deviant roles, deviant identities, and broad situations involving deviance, as shaped by societal definitions and responses. As criticism of labelling theory mounted, it came to be seen as appropriate to explain the second part of the process rather than the initial primary deviancy.

In general, the labelling school asserts that deviant outcomes reflect complex processes of action and reaction, of response and counter-response – labelling theory points us to certain contingencies of social life. If there is no natural crime, then what constitutes crime in a given society could have been something else; the structure of definitions could have been organised in another way. Moreover, criminalisation is only one tactic for dealing with troublesome situations.

Deviance 'outcomes' encompass both individual consequences of societal reactions (as represented by the secondary deviant, defined by Lemert as 'a person whose life and identity are organised around the facts of deviance'), and situational consequences for society at large (for example, the economic consequences of labelling certain forms of deviating behaviour as criminal). At times the labelling perspective has seemed to be concerned only with the former type of outcome, that is, with the production of deviant identities, or characters in individuals, however, the labelling perspective placed on the agenda for discussion all aspects of the way in which the labels came to be thought up in the beginning; in other words, why criminalise?

The labelling perspective poses difficult methodological questions. On the one hand, the individual deviator (at least his personal and social characteristics) appears to matter less than under positivism, while, on the other hand, we are asked to focus on him more intensively, and question the meaning of his behaviour as it appears to him, to seek out the nature of his self-concept as shaped by social reactions, and so on. Normally this has been viewed as an issue of responsibility and freedom but it also provides an underdeveloped route to a contrast between the positivist approach to deviance and existentialism. Within criminology, positivism remains strong, but labelling-influenced strategies take us deeper into the individuals world. Under positivism, to the extent that the individual 'offender' remains an object of direct investigation, clearly the dominant, or favoured, mode of research is still statistical comparison of 'samples' of supposed deviants and non-deviant, aimed at unearthing the differentiating 'causal factors'. The labelling-influenced research methodology works with direct observation, in-depth interviews, and personal accounts, which can illuminate subjective meanings and the impact of situational contexts.

The most obvious advance that labelling theory accomplished was as a consequence of the implicit argument that 'deviant' is in large measure an ascribed status (reflecting not only the deviating individual activities but the responses of other people to them); which resulted in a shift of focus from the deviator himself to the reactors. As Kai Erikson puts it:

'Deviance is not a property inherent in certain forms of behaviour; it is a property conferred upon these forms by the audiences which directly or indirectly witness them. Sociologically then the critical variable is the social audience ... since it is the audience which eventually decides whether or not any given action will become a visible case of deviation.' (1962: 308)

What constitutes an 'audience'? There are both direct and indirect 'audiences' which react to either a given deviating individual, or a particular deviance problem/situation in a given society. Different levels of analysis come into play for each audience. One 'audience' is society at large, the complex of interwoven groups and interests from which emerge general reactions to (and therefore labelling of) various forms of behaviour. Another 'audience' comprises those individuals (including significant others) with whom a person has daily interaction, and by whom he or she is constantly 'labelled' in numerous ways, positive and negative, subtle and not so subtle. A third 'audience' includes official and organisational agents of control. They are among the most significant of the direct reactors or labellers, for they implement the broader and more diffuse societal definitions through organised structures and institutionalised procedures. It is on this third audience that the labelling approach especially focused, but this audience is only one of several important research targets suggested by a labelling orientation. The labelling orientation has brought to the fore the conflict, or political aspect in the processes of criminalisation, in a non-ideological manner, together with emphasising the close relation between deviance and social change. Becker appears to operate within a pluralist political model of law and society, and offers the concept of moral entrepreneurs operating within a set of social conflicts, to account for the increased pressure to classify certain activities (such as drug taking) illegal.

In addition to recognising that deviance is created by the responses of people to particular kinds of behaviour, by the labelling of that behaviour as deviant, we must also keep in mind that the rules created and maintained by such labelling are not universally agreed to. Instead, they are the object of conflict and disagreement, part of the political process of society. (Becker, 1963: 34)

This view of law as a political weapon, and of the use of law in areas where we were better off without it, upset the idea of consensus which served as the background for many American scholars. Given that a Marxist orientation was simply unacceptable (particularly in the 1950s and early 1960s in the era of the Cold War), it required a seemingly non-political theoretical orientation, in which rule-making was a major focal point of analysis (rather than a taken-for-granted natural process) before the conflict-political features of deviance problems could emerge to prominence. By the end of the 1960s, John Lofland could consider this element crucial in providing a basis for defining deviance:

'Deviance is the name of the conflict game in which individuals or loosely organised small groups with little power are strongly feared by a well-organised, sizable minority or majority who have a large amount of power.' (1969: 14)

The emphasis upon process demands a greater appreciation of the openness and contingencies of social life. Consider the practical consequences of the labelling approach on the work of sociology. It points to unpredictability and ironic results for social policies and individual labelling situations; it asks us to question the very basis of the naturalist underpinnings that a positivist sociology of deviance had relied upon. In terms of research it does not so much represent a striking departure from standard, acceptable research methods, as rather provided the impetus to revitalise and give renewed appreciation to some basic sociological methods that had fallen out of fashion, such as participant observation, and related techniques, which seek to enter into the mind-set of the person(s) concerned. Such techniques are particularly appropriate to efforts at capturing and depicting the nature and impact of the social processes on which the labelling perspective focuses. With participant observation, for example, the researcher gains knowledge by empathising with the role of his subjects. Putting himself, as far as possible, in the context of the observed, he re-creates in his own imagination and experiences the thoughts and feelings which are in the minds of those he studies. The observer attempts a symbolic interpretation of the 'experienced culture' of the subject under investigation to bring out the meaning of the social world as the subject actually experiences it.

Such efforts at deeper understanding have a substantial tradition in the sociology of deviance (specifically in the ethnographical wing of the Chicago school, see Beckers' introduction to the reissue of Clifford Shaw's *The Jack-Roller*, 1966), yet, before the influence of the labelling perspective, this tradition appeared likely to be overwhelmed by preferences for research geared to statistical comparison of 'matched samples' and so forth.

The concern with using a labelling-theory-influenced methodology has led into a concern with a concept of *the existential self* (that is, a self whose nature and structure is an open ended and contingent process) but using non-quantitative or qualitative approaches has gone hand in hand with renewed interest in developing a sociology geared to a general understanding of social phenomena. It was believed, following Weber's concern for *verstehen*, or understanding, that sociologists should once again concern themselves more directly with explanations that exhibit adequacy on the level of meaning, in addition to causal adequacy. Work such as Anthony Gidden's *Modernity and Self-Identity: self and society on the late-modern age* (1991) can, perhaps, be seen as the result of this orientation. Certainly the rather crass positivism we saw in earlier chapters, has been dramatically compromised by labelling and related approaches; this search for relevant meaning has sometimes led to quite radical critiques of quantification. An example is Jack Douglas' comments about official statistics on suicide (a deviation to which, because of its total and final nature, we might expect the labelling perspective to have only limited relevance, and which served as Durkheim's core case study):

> 'Sociologists who have used the official statistics on suicide have erred in not recognising that the imputation of the social category of 'suicide' is problematic,

not only for the theorists of suicide but for the individuals who must impute this category to concrete cases in fulfilment of their duties as officials ...

The imputation of the official category of the "cause of death" is very likely the outcome of a complex interaction process involving the physical scene, the sequence of events, the significant others of the deceased, various officials (such as doctors, police), and public and the official who must impute the category.' (1967: 189-190)

This renders much positivist theorising on the basis of official statistics very suspect; since the theory is built upon the foundations of the statistics, if the statistics are not correct the resultant theory is compromised. Qualitative techniques are necessary to get at the process aspects and meaning contexts of deviation-control situations.

In conclusion, the labelling approach not only contributes to the identification of aspects of the process, it causes us to face the whole issue of the relationship of language to the world. Its effects are potentially to destroy any simplistic positive theory. In reality it redefined the nature of criminological theory — but positivism fought back: (i) the effects of labelling theory were constrained by arguing it cannot be a full causal explanation of deviance; (ii) while it ushered in the era of multiple perspectives and a concern with overall synthesis, the difficulties involved in such an enterprise meant that late-modern criminology entered into an era of realist concerns. Labelling theory contributed to the de-legitimating of the positive enterprise, a new foundation was required, which realism (both right and left) allowed — or the issue was ignored.

David Matza: from hard to soft determinism

In the 1960s another attack on the positivist enterprise came in the over determination of hard determinism: put simply why were not more people committing crimes? From the control perspective came the argument that strain theories over-predicted delinquency. If the root cause of crime was to be found in slum life; criminal traditions; differential learning; lack of legitimate opportunity; and the emphasis upon property acquisition; how was it to be explained that most of the individuals living in such situations did not appear to indulge in persistent criminal or delinquent behaviour? The work of David Matza appeared to resolved these concerns with his replacement of 'hard determinism' by the concepts of 'drift' and 'soft determinism'.

Matza is interesting, not only for his actual work, but for the implicit direction he provided for criminology. Matza was specific. Since its conception, the positive approach had simply accepted the products of the criminal justice system, and of official statistics, ie offenders and offending rates, as the basis for its investigations. It neglected the process of constructing criminal laws, placing certain behaviour into the illicit category, and also the nature of going against the laws of a society, what Matza called infractions. Thus Matza specifically asked for an approach that included scope for metaphysics, rather than avoided it. As he put it in his 1964 work *Delinquency and Drift*:

'Positivism, blessed with the virtues and prestige of science, has little concern for the essence of phenomenon it wishes to study. That is metaphysics. Thus positive criminology could for close to a century display little concern for the essence of crime - infraction.' (1964: 5)

There were two strands to this.

- Contrary to the structure of carrying out criminology as it then was, Matza asked criminology to begin its theories with a notion of crime which saw it as an 'infraction', and to take seriously the empirical features which characterised infractions. For Matza an infraction entailed counteracting what had been socialised into a person as the moral code of the society; that the empirical features of crime were that it was often transient (rather than permanent), intermittent (rather than pervasive), characterised, not by commitment or compulsion, but looser factors and represented something which most delinquents simply grew out of with age.

- In a later 1969 work, Matza drew a contrast between *correction* and *appreciation* as differing stances to deviant phenomenon:

'The goal of ridding ourselves of the deviant phenomenon, however utopian, stands in sharp contrast to an appreciative perspective and may be referred to as correctional.' (1969: 15)

The correctional perspective experiences a 'loss of phenomenon' by 'reducing it to that which it is not'. The overriding concern with causation or etiology:

'... systematically interferes with the capacity to empathise and thus comprehend the subject of inquiry. Only through appreciation can the texture of social patterns and the nuances of human engagement with those patterns be understood and analysed.

The appreciative attitude is on the other hand a subjective view; it demands a commitment to render the phenomenon with fidelity, and without violating its integrity.

It delivers the analyst into the arms of the subject who renders the phenomenon, and commits him, though not without regrets or qualifications, to the subject's definition of the situation. This does not mean that the analyst always concurs with the subject's definition of the situation; rather that his aim is to comprehend and to illuminate the subject's view and to interpret the world as it appears to him.' (1969: 25)

It is not, of course, possible to escape to an innocent set of the subject's own definitions; as Foucault, among others, has cautioned us, the language of the interior by which we know our deeper selves comes from the outside. The act of self-description and of self-analysis of one's situation is necessarily conducted in the language of the 'other'. It is possible, however, to play with alternative sets of language games, to not obey the dictate to speak only in the language of the scientist, but be open to the potentiality of alternative forms of language games to inform and advance 'criminology'.

Conversely to these two themes Matza found:

'... positive criminology accounts for too much delinquency. Taken at their terms, delinquency theories seem to predict far more delinquency than actually occurs.' (1964: 21)

In the late 1950s and early 1960s Matza joined Sykes (1961) to criticise the total determinism of sub-cultural theory, arguing that even the most obvious 'criminals' or delinquents were not committed to an alternative set of cultural values, but were actually conventional in their beliefs. Why then were they not restrained by that powerful instrument of self-control in the modern West, namely conscience and feelings of guilt (as opposed to shame, which is engendered by considering what others feel about our actions) aroused in the psyche of an individual when that individual contemplated the performance of an anti-social action? Obviously this question, as well as being central to criminological theorising, has immense repercussions for the legitimation of punishment, since, in the rationalist tradition of punishment (building upon Judaic-Christian foundations) as exampled by Hegel, punishment is a communicative activity in which the offender is brought to appreciate the consequences of his or her actions and ideally, comes to agree with the rightness of punishment being inflicted upon him or her. In experiencing guilt the convict or offender comes to affirm the judgment of the court, and to approve of the actions taken against him or her, and thus comes closer to society. From all accounts, however, the operation of our criminal justice system fails to bring about this outcome. Partly the explanation may lie in the penal system and social attitudes, but Sykes and Matza highlighted the process whereby the offender, while not immune to feelings of guilt, has strong avoidance mechanisms which they termed *techniques of neutralisation*. These avoidance mechanisms enable a delinquent to avoid the morally problematic aspects of his or her activities. The delinquent, furthermore, does not see him- or herself as anti-social, rather he or she is motivated by various desires and images which are suppressed as *latent* in the dominant culture – these are termed *subterranean values*.

The delinquent does not live in some different or inverted world, where the norms and values were the opposite of those prevailing in conventional society. Instead, we are told, he or she shares the values of the larger society; however, the value structure of society is not a coherent, comprehensive system, but full of conflicts and various layers. Theories of delinquent subculture over-predicted crime and over-stressed the difference between 'delinquents' and 'non-delinquents'. Why then do individuals who accept the conventional morality and who are essentially integrated into society and respectful of its regulations violate its conventions? Sykes and Matza argued that while learning the conventional values of the society, individuals could also learn certain excuses or techniques of neutralisation, which, temporarily at least, neutralised conventional norms, and thus permitted violations in specific cases, and under certain circumstances, without necessarily rejecting the norms themselves.

Five distinct techniques are developed, all of which have some basis in society at large.

- *Denial of responsibility*

  The offender appropriates the language of the social scientist, or humane jurist, or social worker who sees him as a product of his environment; he presents himself as the helpless object of social forces (slum neighbourhood, bad parents, peer group pressure). This obviates guilt since guilt cannot be aroused as the deeds are not his own. We are familiar with this in the case of the soldier who views himself as part of the larger whole, regiment or army, without effective means to counter orders. Not only are thousands of his comrades doing the same thing but there are others giving the orders and directing the enterprise. Thus the deeds are not his own, but the product of orders, the product of the forces of the society, the country, or the military. Ultimately he can earnestly state: 'it wasn't really me that did it'.

- *Denial of injury*

  The delinquent argues that the behaviour complained of has not really caused any harm. Thus vandalism is only 'mischief'; car theft is 'borrowing'; stealing is 'getting paid', or 'getting my due'; and 'anyway, they could afford it'; gang fighting is a 'private quarrel'. Psychologically, the spatial distancing of modernity aids this; consider computer fraud, or, the soldier who can hide behind the remoteness of modern weaponry.

- *Denial of a victim*

  Like the soldier who is fighting the enemy, the delinquent is facing a victim who is also guilty. In other words 'they had it coming', so why should the offender care what happened? It is the victims who are the wrongdoers.

- *Appeal to higher loyalties*

  The delinquent presents himself as torn between two groups, the victims, and the smaller group to which he belongs and owes allegiance, demonstrates loyalty towards, and defends his belonging to. The needs of this smaller group – the army unit, the family, the gang, the country in the hour of need – serve to change the nature of the acts he would not otherwise normally do. What was regrettable, perhaps evil, because it was required by loyalty to this group, now becomes justified, perhaps even obligatory.

These four defences do not appear to be positive forces, they appear to be purely defensive measures. Summed up as avoidance mechanisms, they prevent the self-esteem of the offender being washed away while serving to present him as someone worthy of respect and appreciation. A fifth technique acts to deflect the shaming powers of the others who are in communication with the offender.

- *Condemnation of the condemners or rejection of the rejectors*

Here the delinquent shifts the focus of attention from his own deviant acts to the motives and behaviour of those who disapprove of his violations. This time, the other who is to be viewed as the enemy if guilt is to be avoided, is the whole class of those who disapprove of the behaviour in question. The captors are either hypocrites, actually deviants in disguise, or impelled by personal motives. This technique is not one of engaging in communication with the disapprovers, and of convincing them of the position of the offender, of persuasion, but of rejecting them. There is no need to counter the basis of the disapproval, instead the other is rejected as someone with whom no interaction need take place. The discrediting of the other removes both the need to interact in this fashion, and the basis by which the other could affect the self-image of the offender. The only communication which the offender could end up with is with himself.

The reaction of authorities usually misses the core of the delinquents motivations for infraction. While much of the authority has harmful consequences the motivation usually was not to cause harm. Instead, Sykes and Matza suggest that:

'... the delinquent has picked up and emphasised one part of the dominant value system, namely, the subterranean values that coexist with other, publicly proclaimed, values possessing a more respectable air.' (1961: 717)

These subterranean, or latent, values include a search for adventure, excitement, and thrills, and are said to exist side by side with such conformity inducing values as security, routinisation, and stability. Citing the work of Arthur Davis and Thorsten Veblen, Sykes and Matza argue that the delinquents are actually conforming to society, rather than transgressing it when they put the desire for 'big money' central to their value system. Overall, subterranean values make delinquency desirable, while the techniques of neutralisation allow this desire to take direction and become effectual.

Drift theory

In the 1960s Matza analysed the life patterns of juveniles, in terms of their not being any more committed to their delinquency than to conventional situations and enterprises. Their delinquency was a matter of drift, made more possible by a 'subterranean convergence' between their own techniques and certain ideologies of those authorities who represented the official moral order. The authorities had themselves often excused violations by blaming parents, citing provocation on the part of the victim, or accepting explanations defining the infraction as involving self-defence, or accidental actions, and, thus, aiding the norm neutralisation of the juveniles. Thus the controlling power of conventional norms could be weakened by the growing presence of a variety of qualifications, or an array of objections, excuses, and vacillations.

In *Delinquency and Drift* (1964) Matza specifically built an alternative picture of the delinquent under the dictates of soft, rather than hard, determinism. One consequence was to facilitate a conjoining of classical and positive assumptions. It is worth quoting at length.

Some men are freer than others. Most men, including delinquents, are neither wholly free not completely constrained but fall somewhere between. The general conditions underlying various positions along a continuum from freedom to constraint may be described. Viewed in this way, determinism loses none of its heuristic value. We may still act as if we were knowable, but we refrain at least temporarily from an image of the delinquent that is tailored to suit social science. The image of the delinquent that I wish to convey is one of drift; an actor neither compelled not committed to deeds nor freely choosing them; neither different in any simple or fundamental sense from the law abiding, nor the same; conforming to certain traditions in American life while partially unreceptive to other more conventional traditions; and finally, an actor whose motivational system may be explored along lines explicitly commended by classical criminology – his peculiar relation to legal institutions.

Matza's appreciation leads not to romanticism or heroics. We are dealing not with the sensational committed criminal of the media reports, nor with the heroic fighter against the status quo which Marxist accounts sometimes appeared to suggest. Instead, Matza stresses the mundaneness of delinquency, its pettiness, its transitoriness. He also puts central to his argument, the ambiguity of the moral order arguing that the contact and experiences of the juvenile with the correctional system is itself a criminogenic factor. Let us also consider the concept of human nature which is underlying this. It is much more open than the positivists viewed it. Note that neutralisation only makes delinquency possible, as Matza put it:

'Those who have been granted the potentiality for freedom through the loosening of social controls but who lack the position, capacity, or inclination to become agents in their own behalf I call drifters, and it is in this category that I place the juvenile delinquent.'

Matza did not consider delinquency as some natural or steady state, which overtakes an individual with the correct propensities once controls are relaxed, but, as something which is involved in processes. Two processes acted as triggering factors, namely the combination of 'preparation' and 'desperation'. *Preparation* was the process whereby a person discovered that a given infraction could be successfully accomplished by someone, that he had the ability to do it himself and, further, that the fear or apprehension connected with the event could be managed. But even if the person realised that a delinquent infraction could be managed, it might not occur unless he or she learned that it was possible, felt confident that he or she could do it, and was courageous, or stupid, enough to minimise the dangers. If these processes did not interact the possibility would not become a reality. *Desperation* came into play when the self experienced a form of fatalism, a feeling that the self was overwhelmed, and felt a consequential need to violate the rules of the system so as to reassert individuality. Matza did not ask us to consider this need for individuality as dangerous egoism. This need for individuality to assert itself we can see as one bridge between Matza's writings, and the existential posterings of philosophers such as Nietzsche, but first we shall consider other directions in which labelling and Matza took criminology.

Direction One: the irony of labelling and the reproduction of delinquency by state intervention

Labelling highlights the irony of state intervention and bureaucratic response. Labelling calls into question both the process of criminalisation, and the institutional response to law-breaking.

1. An example is the policy of criminalising the possession and use of certain drugs; and why the labelling of their users as criminals need not lead to desirable outcomes. The present drug-control regime in the US and Britain uses essentially a conservative, 'law and order' approach and in many ways operates expressly counter to the impetus of modernity (see Morrison, 1995a). Various commentators have pointed out a range of functions and outcomes to consider. Among them:

- Drugs are pleasurable and/or effective. For a drug to be useful it should be largely compatible with the chemical composition of the human body, and they provide a reward the very first time they are used. They therefore may well attract experimentation, especially among the disaffected. Other drugs, for example, cocaine, may enhance performance and the ability to handle stress.

- Normally, drugs give little indication of their addictive power at first. The casual user does not immediately feel threatened.

- Certain drugs may with time become intensely addictive, so that persons in their grip suffer without them. At this point drugs possess what economists call 'inelasticity of demand', meaning demand will continue irrespective of the price. This, naturally, attracts suppliers.

- Suppliers are also encouraged because, while addicts will pay extremely high prices for drugs, they are very inexpensive to produce and purify (disregarding the costs of avoiding arrest).

- Given the very high profit margins, this should attract competition among suppliers, while in an open (legal) market this would tend to drive prices down, in the closed underworld of illegal drug dealings the users may only have contact with one or two trusted suppliers. With such limits on competition, prices are driven still higher, attracting more suppliers.

- Law enforcement crackdowns reduce the number of suppliers; thus ironically increasing the profits of those who are left. This creates an incentive for others to move into the market.

- As time passes, the amount of the drug required for a given 'kick' increases; hence the user is driven to demand greater quantities. This further increases expenses beyond most users' capacity to meet by legitimate means. Hence the prohibiting of drugs produces, not only drug offences themselves (supply, possession), but also increases in theft, robbery, and other secondary offences.

- One of the few ways to obtain enough money to pay for one's habit is to become a pusher; hence users, as well as producers, become agents for the further spread of the problem.

- The supplying of drugs eventually becomes so lucrative that drug wars are fought between rival suppliers. This violence constitutes yet another form of crime escalation.

- Drug profits are so enormous that bribery and pay-offs among enforcement officials become possible, posing a major problem, thus adding even further to crime escalation.

- Most law enforcement catches the 'small fry,' the latter's new criminal record precludes certain occupations, often diminishing chances for legitimate income, once again increasing the volume of predatory crime.

- A small amount of a drug can produce great pharmacological effects, and small amounts of a drug are easily concealable. Hence, more and more taken-for-granted civil liberties are lost as authorities turn to increasingly desperate search measures. Finally,

- enforcement doesn't work, and it is clearly seen not to be working; this breeds despair and disrespect for law enforcement and civil society. But

- the rhetorical and institutional investment in the war on drugs is so high that the authorities cannot change course without acknowledging that an enormous mistake in strategy and overuse of the criminal law has occurred. Hence more resources are poured into the campaign, while research shows the counter-productive nature of the enterprise.

The search for a way out of this nightmare has led some social scientists to propose the legalisation of narcotic drugs. With a constant supply of cheap drugs, the unanticipated consequences of anti-drug laws are reduced or eliminated, specifically items 5 through to 13. But legalisation carries with it the risk of its own unanticipated consequences. Might it not become more fashionable to take drugs? Might not the new, legal producers attempt to promote their product? Unless taken at low levels, narcotics are generally bad for one's health; if usage increased under legalisation, might this have the unanticipated consequence of greatly increasing public health costs?

2. The 1960s saw a range of work, which adopted either or both an anti-bureaucratic and labelling approach, looked at various institutions, such as prisons and mental hospitals, which took their legitimacy from a treatment and rehabilitative ideology. Although institutionalisation had in the 18th and early 19th century been a rather mixed affair, by the turn of the 20th century specialised institutions, each dealing with a particular form of deviancy (mental

illness, crime, delinquency, orphanages), had become established. Historians, such as David Rothman (1980), analysed the ideology of treatment which argued a case by case approach was required, with specific problems being referred and confined in specific institutions under the supervision and programmes of specialised treatment personnel in terms of the 'institutional interests' behind such developments. These institutions lay at the end of the positivist technicalisation of deviancy, that progressive rationalisation of the world Weber had foreseen. In Weber's analysis the world becomes 'disenchanted' through reducing social life to the dominant idea of the application of technical methods to the solution of social problems. This becomes a world view, which relegates aesthetic, religious and customary thought to the status of the non-rational; conversely, *labelling became a weapon of the disenchanted with dis-enchantment*. Franz Kafka's fictional work *The Trial* had emphasised the nightmarish qualities of an uncaring, unfeeling bureaucracy, and sociologists now showed that actual institutions had a virtually total power to intervene in individuals' sense of self, to shape and dominate personal identity; to determine the future liberty of the incarcerated subject. Soon an 'anti-psychiatry' movement associated with Laing, Cooper, Szasz (1961) and Goffman (1968, first published 1961), was joined by the critical accounts of Foucault (1965) and his followers (for example, Donzelot who saw the techniques spread into the wider realms of the welfare society (1979)), while Scull (1961) could simply argue for decarceration for those institutionalised under *The Myth of Mental Illness*. At much the same time Ken Kesey added the popular fictional account of *One Flew Over the Cuckoo's Nest* (1962), which was turned into a highly successful film.

For Goffman contingency is the overriding factor in determining the reality of mental illness. In other words people who end up in mental hospitals are not naturally ill, but rather adjudged ill, and institutionalised as a result of a series of interactions and powers. Total institutions lay at the end of the knowledge-power-bureaucracy spiral. At stake was the very underpinnings of faith in the enlightenment path of knowledge and professionalism; in the hands of revisionists, the project of modernity looked suddenly very different:

> '... professionalism did not emerge, in the nineteenth and early twentieth centuries, in response to clearly defined social needs. Instead, the new professions themselves invented many of the needs they claimed to satisfy. They played on public fears of disorder and disease, adopted a deliberately mystifying jargon, ridiculed popular traditions of self help as backward and unscientific, misleadingly legitimated themselves in terms of the mantle of science, and generally created or intensified demands for their own services. The most important case for the utility of the helping-healing-human service professionals rested, not on their technical or scientific superiority and efficacy, but on their ability to control clients.' (Holzner, B. and Marx, H. 1979: 351)

Professionalism, it was argued, actually created many of the needs and disorders that it claimed the right to treat. Institutions created their own client groups. As Goffman put it: 'A crime must be uncovered that fits the punishment, and the character of the inmate must be reconstituted to fit the crime.' (1968: 334)

Additionally, labelling theory stimulates research into the process by which the label is produced. It argues that if we are to punish, we must consider the totality of the labelling enterprise. Moreover, labelling has strong effects in the foundations of jurisprudence. In the hands of Becker, and the resurgence of Marxist inspired writings, the legal order was freed from the structural-functional idea that it was the positivist expression of popular morality and was enforced fairly and equally. The ideal of legal-rational authority was now seen as it always was intended by Weber; as an ideal type rather than the expression of the functionality of the actual social body. It may have been what legitimated the institutions and government, but it only partially represented social reality.

Direction Two: the power of collective representation: from Matza to Foucault?

The irony of the labelling outcome is so extreme for Matza that he is led into asking is Leviathan aware of the outcome, and if so, is Leviathan implicated? In other words, does this creation of delinquency have a function in the perpetuation of Leviathan's power? This notion, or direction, is implicit, rather than further developed in Matza, but bears a striking resemblance to the work of Michel Foucault. Consider the final two paragraphs of *Becoming Deviant*:

'Even at the conclusion of the signification process – imprisonment and parole – the process of becoming deviant remains open. Reconsideration continues; remission remains an observable actuality. Nonetheless, signification implies a closure or finality, at least in the minds of conventional members of society and empowered officials, though not in the lives of deviant persons. The finished product of signification is the collective representation of concentrated evil, or deviation, and pervasive good, or conformity. Guided by its imagery and eternally beguiled by the illusion that man has discovered the secret of correction, agents of signification complete the symbolic representation of a deviant person by claiming to cure or fix him. In that manner every contingency is covered. Apprehended again, the subject continues to be a thief; or, with his way of life changed, he may be known as one who used to be a thief but has reformed. The benevolence of society and the wisdom of the state – the positive sides of the collective representation – are affirmed.

In its avid concern for public order and safety, implemented through police force and penal policy, Leviathan is vindicated. By pursuing evil and producing the appearance of good, the state reveals its abiding method – the perpetuation of its good name in the face of its own propensities for violence, conquest, and destruction. Guarded by a collective representation in which theft and violence reside in a dangerous class, morally elevated by its correctional quest, the state achieves the legitimacy of pacific intention and the appearance of legality – even if it goes to war and massively perpetrates activities it has allegedly banned from the world. But, that, the reader may say, is a different matter altogether. So says

Leviathan – and that is the final point of the collective representation. (1969: 196-7)

But who, or what controls 'collective representation'? Does 'self-interest' override social interest? A host of questions one raised as to the signification of the images of deviancy and crime which the discourse of our society perpetrates. From Durkheim onwards we have been made aware of the scapegoating effect of labelling; we have even had essays produced on the conditions for successful degradation and scapegoating! (Garfinkel, 1956). Society has appeared to need its images of the 'dangerous classes' so that the power to punish can be mobilised. But once activated, crime control threatened to even extend itself (cf Christie, 1993; Gordon, 1991).

Certain measures add to the original problem. Take imprisonment – in the US and Britain record use is being made of imprisonment and the US is resorting to capital punishment – yet as punishment levels have increased, and rituals aimed at deterrence have intensified, crimes involving drugs and violence have increased in the key areas. Imprisonment may create more crime through the negative labelling effects, the disruption of social bonds, and the disruption of future employment possibilities. But the failure of imprisonment does not affect the reliance upon imprisonment. What is going on? Are we seduced by the image?

The importance of the sign: the construction of hyper-reality

In our discussion of late-modern or post-modern culture we have stressed the degree to which reality has become representational; whereas Bentham believed that the public would visit the prisons, would see for themselves the reality of punishment, the images of punishment now come to the citizen via media technologies. The American Presidential election between Bush and Dukais was clearly influenced by advertisements concerning the crimes a convicted violent offender committed on weekend leave from prison. The legacy of the labelling perspective on the ontology or the 'reality' of crime is only part of our cultural melage of representation. The world can come into your TV room; the fashions and customs of the ethnically diverse world can be located in your dresser; knowledge of how to mix and match located in your fashion magazine or weekly fashion slot on TV (while multiple channels ensure that it is always time for that slot). Your walls display African masks, posters of Venice, rugs from Iran, the creations of Miro re-represented into a consumerable item suitable to take from that art exhibition the magazine had said was unmissable. When, after seeing multiple representations of the *Sunflowers* by Van Gogh in friends' flats and a hundred books, you 'actually' see it in the National Gallery, you understand with a sense of shock that you didn't realise it 'really' looked like that (not real, somehow, the colours a little garish). You prefer the poster, or the book, or, better, the memory of the poster.

We are wrapped in a new language of the visual or video image. This language displaces, rather than replaces, the earlier forms of literacy based on orality and the printed media. It creates a new set of media logics and media formats – even in newspapers the colour photograph assumes dramatic centrality, while magazines become a collection of photo spreads. A new relationship of the person to the 'real' is entailed through these new technologies of the 'real'. It is possible to be surrounded by images (photographs, video reels) of the other place (Bosnia, a victim, an offender). These disrupt the old narrative modality of recounting what lies over there, what that person is like, since now one can see 'what it is really like', one can 'look at his image'. But this is a new form of narrative and a new epistemological technique – the commitment is to the image, to the sign. The individual whose photograph is represented is turned into a cultural object; an object which produces cultural knowledge and cultural texts via the new information formats. Social cultural practices do not evolve 'freely'. The proliferation of images and distribution of roles, stigma, and values, is dependent upon, and supported by, technological changes and social and political organisations. We are presented with images of the Women protestors at Greenham Common, with scenes of the 'riot' – but who chose those scenes? Who, or what, guarantees epistemological adequacy? Why that image and not another? Riots look dramatically different when the photographs (or video footage) presented are shot from behind the police lines, or from behind the protestors (rioters). In the hands of the powerful they become weapons for (re)presenting the reality of a situation; or aid in the expansion of an authoritarian, technological and administrative attitude to the ordering of the social body.

What was more real: the reality of the disturbance/riot/uprising or the images? The images certainly have more effect – they are disseminated further, they are believed more than the biased accounts of those who in 'reality' were there (who must have been biased, why else would they have been there?), but who didn't see what you saw, did not see the truth of the photograph, an image 'which doesn't lie'. The image both accentuates and simulates reality, it increases its power ... therefore *meaningful reality becomes hyper-reality.*

It is little wonder that the most fashionable cultural tool of the so-called post-modernist radical left is *deconstruction*. Deconstruction is a de-centering and anti-foundational process of attacking cultural artifacts, books, articles, photographs; destroying their claim to represent truth, to present the unpresentable as if it were successfully packaged in this newspaper, or that TV news slot. Epistemological warfare is waged ... but what is the result? Deconstruction opens up the labelling process to contingency, and demonstrates the multiplicity of readings of (non)reality ... but what are we left with? Does it encourage the void which appears to be the ever present result of through-going searches for absolute foundations in late-modernity? Deconstruction without a pragmatic reconstruction (which itself could be meat to the grill of further deconstruction) simply leaves the confusion at an intensified level, allowing the appeal to the man of common sense to win the day. The issue surely is to disentangle the representation of collective forms of social solidarity from a simultaneous hostile opposition to (an)*other* group.

Responding to the tension of the new cultural subject: containing the diversity of late-modernity by the recourse to common sense

The contemporary post-modern social structure threatens to get out of order – the result: an appeal to law and order strategies, combined with the inate feeling of right and wrong which every upright citizen is deemed to possess. In both America and Britain, the late 1970s saw the rise to power of conservatives and the radical right, with a corresponding coupling of the rhetoric of law and order and the rights of the individual against the collective interest (privatisation). Labelling was sidestepped in favour of a new realism. In the rhetoric of the right the subject of real normalcy was defined as personifying the values of religion, hard work, health and self-reliance. This ideology attempted to reinstate the certainties of the ordinary, normal, commonplace individual who understood his position in the order of things, and realised that the disappearance of certainties was the fault of those fashionable, leftish intellectuals who spouted their nonsense of relativism, pluralism and contingency. Thus a central core and foundation could be asserted for debates on crime, abortion, child abuse, sex education, gay rights, AIDS, family violence, drug and alcohol abuse, the war on drugs, homelessness, the general social health and the overall climate of moral hygiene in British and American society. A new, rather repressive and reactionary politics emerged in the 1980s, the immediate legacy of which was carried into the 1990s. The demise of social certainties was blamed on the permissiveness of the 1960s and the democratic socialism of the 1970s. The new certainties demanded a 'just say no' approach to drugs, a romantic nostalgia for the past, a vigorous popularism and the rise in popularity of mass produced (ie media influenced) religion. The new conservativism was not confined to the British Conservative party, or the American Republic party, with so-called socialist governments, such as those in Greece, New Zealand, and Islamic regimes also using these sets of devices. In Britain and US the new right sought to dominate the core of legitimate popular culture through a hegemony on discourse on the family, the body, sexuality, desire and a patriotic individuality that made the military a symbol of national virility (the Falklands, the collapse of the USSR, the Gulf War).

The appeal was to common sense and ordinary human values: a return to basic standards, or 'back to basics'. With crime it was time to stop explaining (identified with providing excuses) and return to formula of punishment according to offences. Ordinary people understood the difference between right and wrong, understood the need for extensive policing with increased police powers, for surveillance, the necessity to build more prisons – the prison became a new containment point and an employment area for the old working class. A set of ideological, religious, political and juridical polemics emphasised crisis and the need to be patriotic while defining out of the social frame the underclass, welfare recipients, the homeless, the drug addict, the sexually promiscuous as morally unworthy persons who were in difficult straits (out of work, addicted to drugs, with AIDS) because they chose to be.

Direction Three: positivism fights back asking for a reconciliation with process: seeing criminality as a thought process

Positivist psychology had searched for the criminal personality as if some stable entity could be located. In 1976, a psychiatrist Samuel Yochelson, and a clinical psychologist Stanton Samenow, published the first of their three volumes of a great positivist enterprise mapping *The Criminal Personality* which saw criminality as a problematic thought process (1976, 1985, 1986). As Samenow explained the point of this enterprise in a related publication:

'I shall expose the myths about why criminals commit crimes, and I shall draw a picture for you of the personality of the criminal just as the police artist draws a picture of his face from a description. I shall describe how criminals think, how they defend their crimes to others, and how they exploit programs that are developed to help them.' (1984: 5)

This paragraph contains many of the flawed assumptions of the positivist enterprise. They assume that there is a specific set of characteristics creating a criminal personality, and that this could be gauged from investigating those imprisoned – they do not even use a control group. They developed a series of conceptualisations from interviews they conducted with approximately 250 offenders (all but three of whom were male), who had been adjudged not guilty by reason of insanity, and remanded to the custody of officials at St Elizabeth's Hospital in Washington, DC. In a dozen or so cases, Yochelson and Samenow logged as many as 5,000 interview hours per subject. These in-depth qualitative discussions with known offenders provided a great deal of information about the thinking and behaviour of the subjects.

Their analysis focuses upon both the content and process of the thought patterns of their subjects. They developed a system of 52 'errors of criminal thinking' that, supposedly, form the criminal personality, including:

* superoptimism;
* criminal pride and perfectionism;
* a very self-serving attitude toward school, work, other people, and society in general;
* chronic lying;
* great energy;
* manipulativeness;
* an inflexibly high self-image.

We can see, however, that their work was entirely within a correctional outlook. The whole aim of the study appears to be to find a new methodology for treating the criminal personality, seen now, not as some static cerebral structure, but as a distorted process of cognition. The traditional psychological approach had tended towards the view that Gaylin had proposed, namely:

> '... psychiatrically speaking nothing is wrong – only sick. If an act is not a choice but merely the inevitable product of a series of past experiences, a man can be no more guilty of a crime than he is guilty of an abscess.' (1982: 253)

But how can one engage in moral debate with someone who is mentally ill? Instead therapy was all that could be legitimately carried out – even though both critics and the prisoners perceived of this as a tyrannical form of punishment. Yochelson and Samenow attempt to prove a positivist psychology in which moral condemnation and exhortation can take place. Four assumptions serve as the foundation of the approach of Yochelson and Samenow:

- man can will;
- man can choose;
- deterrents exist that are capable of correcting a criminal's erroneous thinking; and
- constructing a 'moral inventory' of one's daily thoughts is an essential step in the correction process.

Yochelson and Samenow's work has been criticised as poorly operationalised; difficult to evaluate empirically (Hagan, 1986); being dismissive of the role of environmental factors in the etiology of criminal conduct despite evidence to the contrary; and for resting almost entirely on the case study approach and so lacking in generalisability (Meir, 1983). Additionally, in taking an a theoretical approach to the question of crime, they become lost in the provision of a wealth of descriptive information; their ideas lose a certain degree of applicability by not being tied to a coherent theoretical framework. However, they do point us in the direction of process and cognitive reasoning. A recent investigation by Michael L Benson (1985), based on interviewing a sample of 80 white collar offenders, arrived at the conclusion that these individuals employed a variety of rationalisations, and cognitive distortions in an effort to assuage guilt feelings, minimise the seriousness of their rule-breaking behaviour, and retain a view of themselves as 'good people'. These findings were obtained using a sample of predominately caucasian, middle-class, white collar criminals, and were quite consistent with the patterns Yochelson and Samenow witnessed in a group of predominately black, lower class, person-oriented offenders.

This also highlights further issues (eg choice, thought, and personal responsibility), which serve to place more subjectivity upon the individual holding out the image that the individual is free to choose his path in life; that thinking is the primary vehicle through which this choice is expressed. And, therefore, for change to take place, the offender must assume greater responsibility for his or her actions.

How can the individual take responsibility for his or her life choices in the contexts of contingencies not of their making? The process outlook destroys the naturalism and essentialism of positivism. The features that characterise the process of activity which constitutes offending, are the same processes of life which constitute success. The determined actor was a misnomer. For positivism the actor only acted in such a way wherein his choice was determined by his own nature. He chooses by way of a natural tendency. Any feeling of free will is the mere ratification of a choice which appears to have been made by him, but which is actually made by something which transcends him – his naturalism.

The problem encountering soft determinism is the existentialist problem of reconciling freedom and necessity. Let us remember the classical or Kantian resolution of the dilemma. Kant's solution left us with two spheres of freedom and necessity: it is our animal instinctual side which is subject to the laws of the universe, our human side is subject to the laws of morality. The question which constantly eludes analysis becomes 'where does the control and responsibility of this human freedom reside?'

Direction Four: does the act of labelling invite irrational responses? The games of law, desire and death

We have so far neglected one of the great theoretical perspectives of modernity: *psychoanalytic* theory. Whatever one thinks of Freudian theory, or that of his French interpreter Lacan, or other variations (and this body of theory has many detractors, including Karl Popper who believed it was a pseudo theory and virtual nonsense), psychoanalytical perspectives are challenging and stimulating. They speak to a counter tradition to that criminology usually engages in, namely the irrational, or subconscious. Analytical discourse, the dictate of post-enlightenment focus, has destroyed the interrelated beingness of things. By contrast psycho-analytic theory returns us to a circle of *desire, prohibition, obligation, guilt, desire.*

Psychoanalytical theory has several approaches to crime. In particular:

- crime may be a result of psychic imbalance, with a turmoil of desires in the subconscious which are virtually out of control;

- crime may be a form of neurosis, which finds latent expression, rather than breaking out into recognisable symptoms. But the most interesting claim is that

- the existence of law creates crime. This occurs in two methodologies:

    (i)   law creates a prohibition which in turn creates the desire to transgress; or

    (ii) law provides an opportunity to offend, and thus be punished. The offender may actually desire punishment. The offender offends out of some suppressed turmoil, and sense of guilt, which the subconscious wants a response to.

Conventional criminology used Freudian perspective, which derived out of the treatment of individual patients. It usually toned down the radicalism of Freud's original writings. It talked instead of the denial of normal or healthy desires in neglected faulty upbringing, and usually presupposed that a healthy normalcy constituted modernity. The aim of the therapist was to repair the damage caused by faulty childrearing practices. For example, Abrahamsen asserted:

'Every element that prevents children developing in a healthy way, both physically and emotionally, tends to bring about a pattern of emotional disturbances which is always at the root of anti-social or criminal behaviour. Such behaviour when found in youngsters, is called juvenile delinquency ...

The psychopathology of the juvenile delinquent and of the emotionally disturbed non-delinquent is manifold because each youngster goes through the same psychological development, although each one experiences it differently. Both may be said to be fixated at one or more stages of their development.' (1960: 56 and 74)

In general, all psychoanalytical perspectives refer to human activity as motivated by latent, rather than openly instrumental, reasons. The vital meanings for activity are not those on the surface, which positivist approaches may discuss, but meanings which lurk in the subconscious, and are below the apparent rational intentions of the individual. These unconscious meanings are essentially symbolic and libidinal. The language of psychoanalytic theory involves ideas of pleasure and fear intermixed; play, dream, myth, scene, symbol, fantasy, representations, desire, the death wish, the castration complex, penis envy, phallocentricity, the dialectic of the sensuous and the rule bound, the fantasy of the mother and father, the symbolic authority of the law, the domination of sovereignty, the dialectic of love and law. It is a gigantic forest for the uninitiated.

Freud generally warns that our drives, our desires are always in conflict with one another, our faculties are in a state of continual warfare, and our satisfactions are fleeting and tainted by guilt. We desire success, but plunge into guilt as soon as we achieve it.

What are the foundations of the contradiction which lie within the human spirit/body? For Freud it is our basic sexual nature; modernity demands the suppression of sexuality in the name of the civilising process. For others, it lies in the difficulty we have in actually articulating into language the range of desires we experience. No matter how hard we attempt to express our desires, we cannot bring them to fulfilment in the language-bound methods of communication we are committed to. In both cases tension is created which demands action: delinquency and crime are consequences.

Many have said that there is little in Freud that is not found in Nietzsche. Freud simply substituted sexuality for the will to power which Nietzsche argued was the basic driving force of humanity. Writing in the 1990s, it is somewhat hard to fathom the hatred Freud had of sexual prohibitions, since – compared to the 1940s and 1950s – late-modernity has granted increasing sexual freedom. Indeed, from a Nietzschean perspective, liberal modernity has found it easier to grant sexual freedom than the enjoyment of power.

In the Freudian perspective there is no utilitarian calculation that is innocent of the libidinal. Classical criminology drew upon the picture Hobbes painted, whereby the naturally aggressive drives of man are civilised in their rational subordination to a powerful sovereign whose power is symbolised in the organisation of his commands in law. But Freudian theory argues that the state can never be absolved from these aggressive drives. The state is never fully rational. Beneath the apparently rational, knowledge-bound discourse of the modern criminal trial and the penal apparatus, lies a mass of conflicting desires, pleasures, inversions, scars, needs and victimisations.

The rationality of the criminal process can never hope to do justice to the harms of the body resulting from crime. While in policing and judging an unbridgeable gap is created between articulate reason and mute force, between material practice and the significations of ritual and discourse. A criminal justice system committed to reason and calculation – committed to system efficiency – cannot face up to the realm of the unconscious. The criminology of the surface (positivism), and the criminology of rational calculation, cannot come to terms with the inarticulate irrational.

Civilisation, the projects of modernity, the rule of law, are in a perpetual state of tension. Modernity involves the conjoining of our basic narcissism and our primary aggressiveness to projects of constructivism. Modernity may placate our conflicts; insofar as it offers the image of the building of cities, of the domination of nature, of the struggle to achieve a collective goal, then the death wish which lurks within our aggressivity is tricked into the task of establishing social order in the name of the future life, the future pleasure. The early modern organisation of classical criminology amounts to a challenge to the self but the legislation and coercion of classicism was complemented by the hegemony of a social project. In this hegemony the legitimation of the social is partly the identification of one's own desires as represented in the social. Freud warns that a society must ensure that the majority believe that the projects of the society are reflecting their desires.

But a civilisation always experiences difficulties. The social order entails a renunciation of instinctual gratification – the more civilised we become, the more we lose close contact with our body in the tasks of rational calculation and technological advancement, the greater the brutality and suppressed aggression which lurks within. The more we embrace technological power, the greater the possibility of self-hatred.

What if we slacken and reject the discourse of the project of modernity? If we renounce modernity in favour of the privatisation of the collective? How will the conflicting drives be harnessed to cooperative activity? In *The Future of an Illusion*, Freud warned that no society can survive for long if its minorities are not drawn into believing that they are participating in the culture and structures of the society. If they do not believe that they either are, or will be at some stage in the future, integrated then we cannot expect cultural prohibitions to be internalised among the oppressed. Political power would cease to be hegemonic. Are we seeing this process with the increase in white collar crime and in the creation of an underclass? The political authorities do not appear to want to take seriously white collar crime, seeking instead to create hegemony by intensifying the criminalisation of the underclass. But can the political powers be certain that the energies of an underclass will be taken in by the seductions of market induced pleasures, which they can not hope to legitimately achieve; in the rave scene; in the drugs the underclass are given by the lucrative drug trade; by sexual conquest? Can the powerful be certain that the crimes of the underclass will continue to be largely committed by members of the underclass on their peer group?

The overuse of law: law's ability to create crime

As modernity developed, the civilising process (to use Elias's phraseology) sought to replace the coercion of law apparent in the power of the sovereign by the hegemony of the social project. As we will argue in Chapter Seventeen, we would expect the splitting of late-modern societies into a superclass, seduced by the market, and an underclass, constrained by the coercion of the law, to face extreme challenges to law and order. Perhaps post-modernity could survive if we destroyed many of the present criminal laws, and launched radical programmes of localisation and community education. If is clear from Freudian theory that the existence of law creates a desire to transgress it, and that coercive policing, of its nature, arouses resistance. How is this? Freudianism returns us to the symbolism of our first experiences.

The first experiences of the child, of birth or food, are linked to the mother. The mother is the supplier of warmth, of nutrition (breast feeding), of pleasure ... she is the only locus of existence, the focus of the void, the significant of the good ... she is the Good. The child wants to bond with the good, to know the good for eternity. What is stopping it? For Freud it is the Father - the father is the original site of prohibition, since the father possesses the mother which the child wants. The child's want of the mother is successfully labelled as incest. This is the original law (it would, of course, amount to the appropriation of the property of the father), in response the child wants to kill the father. We can note that structural anthropology locates the whole development of civilisation upon the strength of this original prohibition – since he cannot rely upon his mother and sisters for sex and breeding, the male has to look outwards for sexual partners, and for the production of children. Hence he must either steal the women of other men, or trade for them. The prohibition against incest becomes the functional basis for economy – the spreading outwards of the trading universe of the male.

The original desire for the mother is subjected to a prohibition, we are under an obligation to refrain – but this does not destroy desire, it merely subjects it to the power of guilt. Desire, prohibition, guilt ... prohibition, guilt desire ... once in motion the circle moves in various ways. Prohibition causes desire, causes guilt, desire interacts with guilt.

The desire to transgress is placed by Freud at the centre of culture. The murder of the father is the foundational form of crime; it is the original desire which has been criminalised.

In the hands of the French psychoanalytic writer Lacan we deconstruct the desire to possess the mother which Freud saw as foundational – this is actually only the signification of something deeper. The mother was the provider of that which gave life – hence it is not the mother which is desired, but the life which the mother signifies – put another way, the mother is the site which prevents death. It is death which is feared, death which must be kept at bay – we do this through prohibition. The role of prohibition, the role of law is to keep death within bounds. To stave off death as long as possible. (Note: we are now into the realms of classical liberal political theory, from Hobbes onwards through classical criminology.) We create social order to stand as the bastion of life against death – but, in so doing we encourage the instinct to transgress – the death instinct. Law will, and must, be transgressed. What is the relation of the self to the law? Is the self that commits crime merely the self that lacks self-control against the power of desire? No, it cannot be reduced to such a simplistic arrangement. Instead self, desire, other, death, command, obedience are only visible through a series of reflections which feed off each other; they cannot exist separately, they are constituted in interaction.

For liberals, to create a law means, by definition, that we have the freedom to transgress it – it is upon this rock that guilt can be established. For psychoanalytic theory the law creates desire – enacting a law which specifies that an activity is to be refrained from amplifies whatever desire there is to perpetrate that activity. It is in the nature of taboos to intensify the longings they forbid; to excite the very concupiscence they frown upon.

An example: the prohibition on certain kinds of drugs. In our discussion of labelling theory we noted the ironic consequences of this policy in the creation of a vast illegal market with huge profits. The question here is would legalising these drugs result in a decrease or increase in their use? We cannot be certain. The evidence from the decriminalisation of soft drugs in Holland, seems to indicate, that for native Dutch people, usage of soft drugs has decreased since decriminalisation. Are there a range of activities in which different avenues of education and (self)control could replace legal prohibition?

Certainly we should be aware that we overuse the criminal law. it is only one of several possible ways of handling troublesome situations and perhaps the most disruptive of social relations. But is there any alternative in late-modern societies – can we be moderns without the law?

Direction Five: the latent power of existentialism within criminology

The philosophy of existentialism is underdeveloped within criminology theory, but it is only a short step from Matza, the culture of contingency, and our understanding of the division of the self within late-modernity. The radical philosophy of existentialism is the expression of the late-modern experience, it starts with the realisation of the death of God, and, accordingly, the necessity for us to make ourselves constantly anew. It is to this perspective that we now turn.

CHAPTER FIFTEEN

CRIME AND THE EXISTENTIALIST DILEMMA

'... throughout the modern era, the quest of the individual is for his self, for a fixed and unambiguous point of reference. He needs such a fixed point more and more urgently in view of the unprecedented expansion of theoretical and practical perspectives and the complication of life, and the related fact that he can no longer find it anywhere outside himself. All relations with others are thus ultimately mere stations along the road by which the ego arrives at its self. This is true whether the ego feels itself to be basically identical to these others because it still needs this supporting conviction as it stands alone upon itself and its own powers, or whether it is strong enough to bear the loneliness of its own quality, the multitude being there only so that each individual can use the others as a measure of his incompatibility and the individuality of his world.' (George Simmel, 1971: 219-23)

'[For the criminal] thinking about crime is exciting. Committing the crime is exciting. Even getting caught is exciting. Trying to figure out a way to beat the rap is exciting.' (Samenow, *Inside The Criminal Mind* 1984)

Combating the vertigo of freedom: the existentialist reconciliation in sincerity and authenticity

Existentialist philosophy[1] takes seriously the fact of God's death and will not find any solace in positivism and functionalism. For the French philosopher Jean–Paul Sartre:

'The existentialist, on the contrary, finds it extremely embarrassing that God does not exist, for there disappears with Him all possibility of finding values in an intelligible heaven. There can no longer be any good *a prior*, since there is no infinite and perfect consciousness to think it. It is nowhere written that "the good" exists, that one must be honest and not lie, since we are now upon the plane where there are only men. Dostoevsky once wrote "If God does not exist, everything would be permitted"; and that, for existentialism is the starting point. Everything is indeed permitted if God does not exist, and man is in consequence forlorn, for he cannot find anything to depend upon either within or outside himself. He discovers forthwith, that he is without excuse.' (Quoted in Kaufmann, 1957: 294-5)

Without God man must invent his own values; he must freely choose his destiny and his social meaning. In the existentialist orientation the vertigo of

---

1   'It is, of course, contentious to write such a term. Existentialism is *not* a system: Existentialism is of its nature irreducible to a clear cut social philosophy. However, existentialism is *not* nihilist. Exactly the opposite – the void of existentialism is not to be filled by ideology, rather the onus is placed upon the individual to avoid mistaking the temporary social "truth" of the groups with actual, or ideal, truth. The individual must have recourse to his/her own understanding of the requirements of being fully human.

freedom is ever present; modernity breeds perpetual anxiety. The German theorist Heidegger identified this as the essential human characteristic:

'Being-free for one's ownmost potentiality-for-Being, and therewith for the possibility of authenticity and inauthenticity, is shown with a primordial, elemental concreteness, in anxiety.' (1962: 236)

It is not the environment which prevents freedom, but the refusal of being true to oneself. The freedom to act is replaced by the ideas of spontaneous, or sincere action which seeks to cope with the ambiguous concept of freedom. We bear responsibility for our actions in the sense that we must think contemporaneously to our actions. As moral-cultural creatures, mankind have an obligation (which can be incurred or rejected) to remain attentive to the forms which experience (our actions and their results) directly assumes. Existentialism demands we avoid becoming dulled to the intensity of our life through familiarity, schematised through intellectual or moral laziness, or standardised through desire for conformity or habitual action. A free act is a significant act.

Put in another form: whereas negative freedom sees one as free when one is released from something, positive freedom is an active conception. Positive freedom is the freedom to do something. In the existentialist perspective we are free when we have a clear and distinct idea of the causes of our own states, physical and mental; thus we can take responsibility for our actions even when they are in circumstances certainly not of our choosing.

My free actions are those actions of which I am the author. This is as much a prescriptive standard for authenticity in modernity as a description. Kierkegaard asks us to look on our lives as aesthetic projects, we must live so that our essential spirit can recreate itself. He understands life as a process of affirmation and reaffirmation, particularly centred around the life of the spirit; the spirit alone can repeat itself, that is, renew itself in its permanence. Ethics are the process of reaffirmation, duty and fidelity to the spirit of the activities of the self; this is the true domain of choice and self-committal. In working out one's dilemmas, we should obey not the dictates of what is universally required (as in some categorical imperative), but what is personally required in terms of being faithful to the values which man has set for the type of person he most wishes to become. This links freedom and necessity into our life seen as a project; an enterprise of self-discovery and creation by becoming. We constantly go beyond that self; this moving beyond our present self is the finest action of our self. The acts most essentially mine are the actions of which I am the author: freedom is a kind of superior necessity – the determination of the self by the self. In the positivist guise the self must act out the script written by its position in the natural order of things in obedience to the essentialism of that which he or she is; the self performs the actions which correspond to the exact typology of the kind of rapist he is, of the exact type of criminal that he or she is. But the essence of existentialist human nature is the absence of an essence. For Sartre the central doctrine is that 'existence precedes essence, or, if you prefer, that subjectivity must be the starting point' ([1947] in Kaufmann, 1957: 289):

'If man, as the existentialist conceives of him, is indefinable, it is because at first he is nothing. Only afterward will he be something, and he himself will have made what he will be. Thus, there is no human nature, since there is no God to conceive it. Not only is man what he conceives himself to be, but he is also only what he wills himself to be after this thrust towards existence.' (1965: 35-36)

Man is condemned to be free. This does not mean that we are alone in a world that does not impose upon us through our past and the context of our dilemmas, no, we inhabit a world full of pressures, but even within the chaos and multiplicity of forces impinging upon us, we can manoeuvre enough so as to shape the key elements of our course of action. The imperative of existential action is simple: we must remain contemporary with our actions, seeking no refuge in a past of efficient causes, or a future of retrospective justifications. To hide behind the techniques of neutralisation, which Sykes and Matza uncover, is to discard the burden of being human. When we avoid the essentialism of the naturalist premise, when we move beyond positivism, freedom is not a thing nor an attribute of a thing, otherwise we would merely possess it or not possess it (thus we can see the need for positivism to differentiate and typologise individuals into types, and so delineate the types of freedom each individual possesses). Existential freedom resides in the (non-positivist) ontology of the human being, his processural nature imbedded in the ambiguity and ultimate mystery of being. The organic, which is rooted and ordered in time, is only a factor of reality. For existentialism *action* is the focal site of human reality. The meaning we humans give to action is the unveiling of human reality. By our acts – and the labels we apply to our acts – we give ourselves meaning, we determine our reality. But to understand ourselves we must keep ourselves some distance from our action: we must see both the implications and the requiredness of a situation and the consequences of our determinations. To hide either through reliance upon some *organicism*, or some retrospective justification, or some immersion, is to escape into inauthenticity. For existentialism, our actions express ourselves, not some conjunction of pre-existing forces, not some set of contingently embodied activity.

Existentialism has a tension: it not only recognises experience as being something immediate but stresses it ought to be immediate. It argues that any attempt to stuff Kantian style rationality or positivist materiality into human experience is immoral; such attempts deny freedom. Yet total immersion in immediacy loses meaning, loses authenticity.

The optimistic ethos of criminological existentialism

The heading requires explanation. There is no officially defined criminological existentialism: there should be.

Existentialist perspectives are an underdeveloped resource in criminology. One full length book Katz (1988), uses what can be called a harsh existentialist account, as does David Jones (1986) in his final chapter which offers an outline reading based on the Nietzschean "Will be power", while Sagarin and Kelly (1981) offer a reading of existentialism to encourage personal responsibility in the face of the bureaucratic which dominates modernity. Sagarin and Kelly interpret the message of existentialism ethos as addressed to "those who have embraced bureaucratic manipulations," and those who "shun responsibilities not out of selfishness but because they are confused about the limits of responsibilities, duty, obligation, and rights, (1981:38). Various liberating or optimistic features flow from the existentialist perspective.

- The individual is entrusted with his/her own individual decision-making he/she should not surrender his/her sense of personal responsibility or initiative to any social group

- "Truth" is not a given entity that can be possessed in its entirety. While the search for truth is the goal, all people are too limited in time and circumstances to ever possess objective truth. All positions are perspectives – they have various consequences, various effects and various genealogies – they must be accepted as an act of will, not as something imported from outside.

- Existentialism stands opposed to all arguments of social or natural necessity – the social world was our creation – mankind can change it.

- Existentialism turns against the numerical, the quantitative in favour of the unique. In the numerical – for example classical 19th century utilitarianism – Nietzsche and Kierkegaard argue the differences between the members of a class, the distinctness of the human, can be ignored. Whenever an individual human being can be treated as if he/she was a number, dehumanisation is the result; herd, or crowd, morality operates. The existentialist can only oppose.

Frankl, the Existential psychologist, tells of this incident about the operation of the concept of law within a concentration camp:

'It had been a bad day. On parade, an announcement had been made about the many actions that would, from then on, be regarded as sabotage and therefore punishable by immediate death by hanging. Among these were crimes such as cutting small strips from our old blankets (in order to improvise ankle supports) and very minor "thefts." A few days previously a semi-starved prisoner had broken into the potato store to steal a few pounds of potatoes. The theft had been discovered and some prisoners had recognized the "burglar." When the camp authorities heard about it they ordered that the guilty man be given up to them or the whole camp would starve for a day. Naturally the 2,500 men preferred to fast.'(Viktor Frankl, 1959:102).

The harsh end of criminological existentialism

Existentialism seeks out the meaning of things as they are in their full empirical actuality – thus in understanding the human personality the emotions should be analysed, not ignored as 'accidental' or inconsequential, therefore such emotions as fear and dread, boredom and passion are at the core of activity not peripheral; the results of this centrality to analysis are not always to our liking

In a justly famous section, *Of the Pale Criminal* from *Thus Spoke Zarathustra*, Nietzsche relates how the acts we call crime often involve the offender doing an action in which he 'judged himself' and gave himself a 'supreme moment'. Those who staff the criminal justice agencies tend to ignore the meaning of the event and action for the person committing it; they translate the living phenomenon into a language removed from the heat and passion of the event:

'But the thought is one thing, the deed is another, and another yet is the image of the deed. The wheel of causality does not roll between them.

An image made this pale man pale. He was equal to his deed when he did it: but he could not endure its image after it was done.

Now for evermore he saw himself as the perpetrator of one deed. I call this madness: in him the exception has become the rule.

The chalk-line charmed the hen; the blow he struck charmed his simple mind – I call this madness after the deed.

Listen, you judges! There is another madness as well; and it comes before the deed. Ah, you have not crept deep enough into his soul!

Thus says the scarlet judge: "Why did this criminal murder? He wanted to steal." But I tell you: his soul wanted blood not booty: he thirsted for the joy of the knife!

But his simple mind did not understand this madness and it persuaded him otherwise. What is the good of blood? it said. Will you not at least commit a theft too? Take a revenge?

And he harkened to his simple mind: its words lay like lead upon him – then he robbed as he murdered. He did not want to be ashamed of his madness.

And now again the lead of his guilt lies upon him, and again his simple mind is so numb, so paralysed, so heavy.'

In committing the crime a private set of desires and interpretations were at play; a private reality the public language, the language of criminology, will not acknowledge. Who is this man asks Nietzsche? His reply denies essentialism and evokes the contemporary descriptions of the left realists of the offender involved with double victimisation:

'A knot of savage serpents that are seldom at peace among themselves – thus they go forth alone to seek prey in the world.

Behold this poor body! This poor soul interpreted to itself what this body suffered and desired – it interpreted it as lust for murder and greed for the joy of the knife.

The evil which is now evil overtakes him who now becomes sick: he wants to do harm with that which harms him.'

The legacy of Nietzsche demands we get into the rhythm of a self which makes a 'positive' action in defying the forest of signs surrounding the civilising process and resorts to the love of blood, which seeks and experiences the dizziness of the void. The harsh end of existentialism would point us towards reading crime in the light of looking for a self which defies the civilising process. Sometimes the results are upsetting: Connolly (1989) finds that pornography is the revenge of civilised bodies. We are unaccustomed to accepting evil as fully human (I shall leave evil undefined). Lombroso did not accept that it was human to enjoy 'excessive idleness, love of orgies, and the irresistible craving for evil for its own sake, the desire not only to extinguish life in the victim, but to mutilate the corpse, tear its flesh, and drink its blood'. Lombroso looked away and saw only a reversion to the non-human, the atavistic being who was an evolutionary throwback.

Nietzsche wants us to see the positive side of the criminal action as it appeared to the subjectivity of the actor. We may not wish to do so: (i) we may desire to side with the victim; (ii) we may wish to speak a scientific language which is cleansed of the metaphysics of evil; (iii) we may have learnt from the false romanticism of the 'radical' criminologist of the late 1960s and 1970s who appeared to see the criminal as a politically motivated fighter against the system. Of course the criminal is not directly interested in his act to create a more just society – but he may be attempting to achieve an act, a leap into action which gives power to his being.

Sartre claimed that we had to work through the human setting and the human subjectivity inherent in every statement and action – all human activities are meaningful. Existentialism seeks to preserve the freedom of the individual self from the domination of the administered world, the Weberian universe of bureaucratic rationality and knowledge which sets out categories of law-like generalisations. But how are we to understand the phenomenology of the criminal act? What was criminology doing to the actuality of crime? For Nietzsche it appears the logos of crime (criminology) was transforming the being of the criminal into a thing, into a piece of reality which a discourse of science could speak about and uncover the predictive elements (the hope of a technical science) and so control. But this turns the criminal from an agent into a mere vessel for other forces. Both the categorial moral laws of the Kantian position, and the naturalism of Lombroso, turned away from the existential dilemma of the person; both of these eliminated his individual significance and made the person a space through which something else (the moral law, flows of determinism) passed.

Early modernity and the crime of passion

It was not such a long time earlier than Nietzsche's writings that public punishment often provided a festive occasion. Nietzsche complained of the systematic levelling of the world: perhaps the crime of passion, regarded as quintessentially French, serves as an example. Joelle Guillais argues that:

'... nowadays, perpetrators of crimes of passion are relegated to the category of "insane" and fade into the dreariness of everyday poverty. They are regarded as failures, undeserving of any special attention unless they have committed sacrilegious acts, such as cutting up and eating the flesh of their beloved one. In the last century, lawyers presented them as decent individuals and "gently" rebuked them. In the eyes of the law, they had one excuse: their passion, which affected their will power. [They] made an impression on a public thirsting after powerful emotions and bloody thrills. This very real violence fuelled their imagination. Everyone regarded the defendant who was about to be judged not simply as a mentally sick person, but as a true criminal, and they enthusiastically waited outside the courtroom to see this man who was said to look just like any other. The public, ever eager for something out of the ordinary, something sensational, perceived the criminal act with a great deal of genuine emotion, for its theatricality exacerbated the tragedy of life.' (1990: 229-230)

Guillais interprets crimes of passion, even of the working class, as continuing certain higher loyalties such as the concept of honour or defence of pride:

'A crime of passion was in itself an honourable act, since it was an act of revenge capable of making amends for the departure of one's partner, for adultery, or for a rejected marriage proposal; all these insults implied the loss of social dignity within one's circle.' (1990: 24)

A crime of passion was also a defence of power. Guillais highlights the fact that the notion of sexual honour was equally grounded in symbols of woman's purity and a stake in the property/power relationship of patriarchal society. What is the meaning of violence in these situations? A synonym of force and power, an accepted part of the male make-up. Suffering an affront to one's honour without hitting back is thereby thought to be tantamount to admitting to a lack of virility. Virility is signified in physical strength, courage, and an ability to take one's drink. Thus alcohol is not a causal agent for crime as the temperance movement argued, merely a trigger mechanism. Crimes of passion of the working class occur in localities of great poverty, where violence, both verbal and physical are commonplace. How is the stability of individuals in conditions continually verging on the critical and chaotic rightly to be assumed? Many men, facing these conditions, welcomed the punishment of death or penal servitude:

'... bowed too often by adversity; they wanted to break the endless chain of failure and misfortune which bound them like a curse. In an explosion of revolt and confused hatred, they exposed themselves to death through death. This meaningless act raised them out of anonymity by allowing them at last to be heard.' (1990: 38)

But then these acts are not meaningless but full of the richness of tragedy. Are we honestly to state their acts were a mere lack of self-control? How can the self be brought under control when one's heart is torn, when one's pocket is empty, when emotional tension and economic poverty cry out one's abysmal failure to direct the situation? In this situation crisis and confusion both act as consequence and cause. Drift has given way to desperation; desperation to the determination to act. Whatever the resultant act, it serves to take control of the moment.

Note that, whereas 19th century writers emphasised the horror of the deed, modern criminology has rendered it mundane. Positive criminology turned to the study of the offender and found what? The pitiful, the weak, the mundane. Nietzsche predicted it:

'A criminal is frequently not equal to his deed: he makes it smaller and slanders it.

The lawyers defending a criminal are rarely artists enough to turn the beautiful terribleness of his deed to his advantage.'

(Epigrams 109 and 110, *Beyond Good and Evil*)

Modern criminology cannot speak of the existential love of crime as a powerful determination by a self grasping for control. It cannot speak of the love of debasement, of the seduction in imposing humiliation on another, of the rage of the pre-modern self scourged when forced to accept a modernism he or she does not understand, with little resources of self-esteem and self-worth to face alienation, humiliation and the battles of the post-modern condition.

In some circumstances the offender is taking revenge against the civilising processes of modernity. This notion of the offender as a rebel against modernity has little to do with the idea of the Marxist rebel in class conflict. Our picture of revenge and rebellion is of acts inarticulately aimed against discipline into the established order of things. For those on the fringes of organised mainstream society it is not just a case of being pushed around, of being dominated, but of being disciplined into docility. Against normalcy their resources of resistance were more a question of skiving off work, of cohabiting, of spending their wages on drink, of wandering from job to job, thereby opposing the structure of mainstream moral values and calling into question the Leviathan of state power over civil society. By contrast, the violence so openly expressed in the crime of passion reveals the play of power, and the will to escape. No wonder that many have been prepared to read of these crimes and these offenders as of characters in a rich tapestry. A tapestry which offers a reflection on the tragedy of the human condition and the deepness of the mystery of morality; a mystery so deep that the word evil positions itself as the gateway into its dialectics.

Modern criminology has turned away from this celebration of the depth of the morality of everyday life. It has denied these festivals of cruelty, these phenomenologies of the blood and the knife which point to the openness of human character. It is almost impossible to read accounts of the great crimes in criminology textbooks. Where are the accounts of the Holocaust, where are the accounts of Stalin's atrocities, of slavery, of government sanctioned torture? When the numbers who have died as a result of the crimes of government make the numbers who die as a result of street crimes pale into insignificance, why (and how) does criminology continue to concentrate upon the terrain of everyday street crime? Is it because to face up to these other events would reveal the normalcy of the criminal? Would taking seriously the enormous extent of the crimes of the powerful render problematic the labelling of the powerless as anti-social and criminal? Moreover, what is the effect of the treatment by criminology of the crimes of the everyday? While criminology seemingly concentrates upon the crimes of everyday life (so-called street crime and crimes of civil society) it turns these into statistical regularities and matters of generalisations. The horror of the everyday is repressed. To a limited extent this horror features in the tabloid press, but criminology must work to civilise, to explain, to render transparent and thereby safe, a modern self which contains in its mysterious depths the beingness of evil. Modern criminology has worked to reassure us that the 'normal' person was not evil – crime was a result of deviancy or pathology. Is this why the image of the psychopath reoccurs so often? Does it not shuffle off unpredictability and unsociality into the guise of some other-than-us and thus compartmentalise the image of danger, the image of the unknowable, and dare we say it, of evil? How do we deny the ever-present (potentially) evil to the *beingness* of our selves?

Tactic one: the beast within who can overtake us when we are weak or asleep

The pre-modern world knew of possession by spirits. A spirit would enter into the body of the person taking over his or her actions. For the ancient Greeks many of their worst (and sometimes best) actions were when they listened to the suggestions of the Gods; St Joan listened to her voices. In this way of understanding our actions are not our own, we are vehicles of the others intentions. In fun (as generations of *Werewolf* films tell us) or in philosophy, we attribute to some other entity the origin of these actions. Of course, this offends the existentialist, who demands that we take full responsibility for ourselves, but we all know of the other.

Who has not experienced a fantasy of revenge or of rampant sexuality? Of domination? What is the status of these fantasies, in which we throw off the bonds of restraint, in which we become all powerful (or submissive). Those times which, as Plato said:

> '... bestir themselves in dreams, when the gentler part of the soul slumbers, and the control of reason is withdrawn. Then the Wild Beast in us, full-fed with meat and drink, becomes rampant and shakes off sleep to go in quest of what will gratify its own instincts. As you know, it will cast off all shame and prudence at such moments and strike at nothing. In fantasy it will not shrink from intercourse with a mother or anyone else, man, god or brute, or from forbidden food or any deed of blood. It will go to any lengths of shamelessness and folly.' (Republic 9 571c, quoted in Midgley, 1979: 37)

What are we to make of this wild beast? Is it the uncivilised self? That which is in us and lurks whenever the bonds of control loosen? Or are these fantasies actually escape valves? Are they places where the beingness of evil resides so that it does not come into the social (daylight) reality of late modernity?

Tactic two: the psychopath

One interpretation of Nietzsche's *will to power* is to see in it a straightforward domination of other people, even delight in tormenting them. We like to argue that this is 'certainly clearer, but false, except of psychopaths' (Midgley: 1979: 8).

Midgley reads Nietzsche as equating this fascination with power as a sign of strength but, she argues, it can equally be a sign of weakness. Two points arise: first, the notion of the psychopath may deflect our understanding that desires for violence and cruelty are part, albeit repressed, of being human, instead making such desires a symptom of not being truly human. Second, we may wish to develop the idea that the infliction of pain – the desire to dominate – is a consequence of a feeling of loss of power. That it is a consequence of the existential perception of weakness, or of impaired masculinity, and thus we witness the transformation of humiliation into rage, and, finally, the humiliation of the objectified other.

Recognising the existential sensuality of crime

Texts which argue that the existential sensuality of crime be recognised are very much a minor tradition in criminology.[2] One recent and well received study by Jack Katz (1988) dwells on the sensuality of crime and has done much to point the way towards an existential tradition in criminology. Although he does not explicitly use the existentialist paradigm, in *Seductions of Crime: Moral and Sensual Attractions of Doing Evil* Katz is concerned to write in the appreciative mode and to gain a grip inside the actors perceptions. Nonetheless, he is at pains to point out that he is attempting empathy not sympathy. He, as indeed am I in presenting the sometimes upsetting accounts which follow, is endeavouring to draw attention to the lived attractions of crime, not to condone them.

Katz argues that social science has failed to convey what it:

'... means, feels, sounds, tastes, or looks like to commit a particular crime. Readers of research on homicide and assault do not hear the slaps and curses, see the pushes and shoves, or feel the humiliation and rage that may build toward the attack, sometimes persisting after the victim's death.' (1988: 3)

Lost in theories stressing the instrumentality of crime and criminality as one or other form of pathology, we do not understand that for adolescents shoplifting or vandalism offers a thrilling experience. We fail to see what exactly are the attractions of the commitment to gang-membership. We neither feel the reality of 'cold-blooded, senseless murders', nor understand the human dynamics which are at play in the actuality of the event. Few people have recognised the

---

2   It is actually difficult to find secondary source material which conveys the lived experience of committing crime. In the following discussion extracts are taken from several texts which do provide accounts in the actors own words and from fieldwork the author has carried out on Social Services Juvenile Justice teams where young people were interviewed and asked to describe their experiences.

distinctive attractions of robbery – apart, and it is a big apart, from the tradition of symbolic interactionism. But this tradition often appears as an appendage to the dominant approaches which draw their foundation from the material of statistical regularity. The appreciative wing of the Chicago school laid down the challenge of explaining the qualities of deviant experience. But largely this has not become incorporated into the mainstream. There are some exceptions. The world of the football hooligan has been sampled and conveyed. Allen and Greenberger (1978) point to the aesthetic element of vandalism where vandals enjoy the visual, auditory, and tactile sensations stemming from their creative conversion of material things. Instead of focusing on the background of crime Katz seeks to understand the foreground, the emergence of distinctive sensual dynamics. The range of sensual dynamics runs from enticements that may draw a person into shoplifting to furies that can compel him to murder. Bizarre things happen: during the My Lai massacre, after having killed all those who were in the village, the American soldiers began to eat lunch. Two young girls who were away returned, the marines who had killed their parents and brothers and sisters offered to share their own lunch with them – the furies had passed. (Kelman and Hamilton, 1989)

Katz suggests a way in which we can explain the weakness of criminology. Criminology has focused too much on the materiality of crime and neglected what Matza told us was central: infraction, ie the moral nature of the interaction. Katz suggests that central to all the experiences are:

> '... *moral emotions*: humiliation, righteousness, arrogance, ridicule, cynicism, defilement, and vengeance. In each, the attraction that proves to be most fundamentally compelling is that of overcoming a personal challenge to moral – not to material – existence.' (1988: 9)

For example, the impassioned killer in the act of killing may be escaping a situation which he sees as inexorably humiliating. Not able to see how he can move with self-respect from the current situation, he moves out of the mundane and leaps into a course of action which embodies 'through the practice of "righteous" slaughter, some eternal universal form of good'.

Some earlier writings had focused on this theme. Luckenbill (1977) argued that some crime is motivated by the desire to preserve individual or collective honour. Thus, trying to maintain one's sense of self, when insulted by another, can lead to homicide. In their study of Chicano Gang violence Horowitz and Schwartz (1974) argued gang violence was often triggered by the desire to defend the gang's collective honour and thereby protect the self-esteem of its members. Klemke (1978) found that equal numbers in his sample of adolescent shoplifters stole for expressive reasons, such as the pursuit of excitement, as for instrumental reasons (ie a desire for the goods taken). This may take on the form of a game. Richards, Berk, and Foster (1979) depicted middle class delinquency as a form of play, wherein the delinquency fulfils needs similar to those catered for by other forms of leisure: namely, adding interest to the daily routine, providing entertainment, learning new techniques and skills and learning social rules. In lower class areas 'joy riding' offers a good time, risk, status among peers, prestige in dare-taking and learning the skills of driving.

At the other extreme shoplifting is turned into a thrilling melodrama about the self – apart from the goods taken, the getting away with it is a demonstration of personal competence. The very fact of infraction adds to the excitement. Parker found this challenge is especially apparent in some white collar crimes, for example those involving computers:

> 'A general characteristic of computer programmers is their fascination with challenges and desire to accept them. In fact, they face the great challenge of making computer systems do their bidding day in and day out. Telling a programmer that a computer system is safe from penetration is like waving a red flag in front of a bull. The challenge of an unauthorised act often overshadows the question of morality.' (1976: 47-48)

Status may lead to a redefinition of self. Katz argued that in building a series of robberies the individual redefines himself as a 'badman', creating a personal style. Lejeune (1977) found that his sample of casual robbers stole to buy drugs and clothing not only for the status the goods offered, but also, to enhance their standing among peers, and to create a more exciting life.

For Katz the acts can be explained only through a theory of *moral self-transcendence*. He argues that we have lost touch with the lived reality of evil, with the fascination with evil that we, as moral creatures, have always had. Has criminology in becoming scientific lost touch with humanity?

The existentialist message is roughly as follows: in setting out a positivism which analyses the conditions of existence, we are in danger of forgetting that the offender is an existential phenomenon. Our theorising becomes a process of analytical reductionism which does not explain the existential reality of life. By developing a criminology that talks the dry language of modernist control, strain, learning, genetics or constitutionalism, we neglect the essentially moral struggle that individuals wage with anomie, with alienation, with inadequacy, with powerlessness, with the desire to possess, with the need to create themselves. Thus we weaken our ability to grasp the reality of crime, both for the petty inadequate street offender and for the apparently powerful corporate executive. What does crime look like if we are to believe that crime is seductive? That the existential beingness of the commission of crime takes up the body and exposes it to rushes of excitement and adrenalin or to the mystical attractions of being possessed by a dream?

The sensuality of stealing

One rather habitual offender who specialised in house breaking, seemed clear that the sensuality of the experience might only be compared to sexual intercourse:

> 'I begin to feel giddy and restless ... I feel as if I have to do something. This feeling becomes gradually more marked until I feel compelled to enter a house

and steal. While stealing I become quite excited, involuntary begin to pant, perspire and breath rapidly as if I had run a race; this increases in intensity and then I feel as if I have to go to the closet and empty my bowels. After its all over I feel exhausted and relieved.' (Quoted in Hibbert, 1963: 221)

A large amount of burglary is accompanied by the offender urinating or defecating while on the premises. There is the symbolism of sacrilege but it is also because the body is aroused. As another offender put it:

'Stealing is a passion that burns like love ... and when I feel the blood seething in my brain and fingers, I think I should be capable of robbing myself, if that were possible.' (Quoted in Hibbert, 1963: 221)

A juvenile who was on a supervised session of a Social Services Team, and who had a history of shoplifting, described his experiences as follows:

'Once I'd got over the initial fear it was a trip I needed when things got bad. I would feel better from the time I knew I was going to take a go ... The planning ... well ... it wasn't really planning, more a sense of building up anticipation ... then the walk to the store. I always wore special clothing ... walked slow ... *I was more than me* ...' (Morrison: Fieldnotes)

For this adolescence the ritual of shoplifting offered the opportunity to be possessed by a self-image greater than his mundane normalcy. While the actual event may only take a short time the psychological preparation was a girding of the loins as for a contest, and knowing the risks involved (he had been caught on more than one occasion) his body took on the chemical stimulation of danger during the event:

'When I begin to walk for the door ... I don't know .. but I can never breath ... I'm holding my breath ... As I walk through the door its almost suffocating, I know that's the total danger time ... when I'm ten or so yards down the road I take a deep breath, my head spins ... It's a total rush ...,' (Morrison: Field-notes)

Lejeune (1977) saw in casual robbery 'adventurous deviance', all the more pleasurable because of the risk of apprehension, although the individuals involved worked to keep the risk to a 'manageable level'. For another adolescent, the act of shoplifting was an existential question of being and not-being, of presence and transcendence:

'They think they are watching you all the time. They aren't ... I'm invisible ... I'm there but I'm not there ...

They think the camera sees everything ... But I can see the light ... I'm only being watched when the red light is on ... When I see there is no light sometimes I look right at the camera when I take something.' (Morrison: Field-notes)

This is a dare: control me if you can. It is showdown time.

When asked if he was daring the camera, the respondent replied, 'I'm stuffing them ... stupid gits ...' When asked, 'Who are they?' he replied, 'all of them ... the whole fucking lot ...'.

One young man related the time he had lost the ability to carry through the theft. He had gone to a major bookstore, even though he had little interest in books:

'I slipped a book, real expensive, into my coat and then walked around the shop. That part was good ... I was playing at being at home. But it wasn't really my scene. When I went down the stairs to leave the guards were by the door. Normally I would have walked through ... I was sure that I hadn't been seen, but I didn't feel right. It [the book] wasn't worth it ... I went around the shop for awhile ... then I put it back on the shelf ...' (Morrison: Field-notes)

When asked if he meant it was not worth enough money, he replied, 'No ... I mean it wasn't worth it ... It wasn't me ... It wasn't the sort ...'. In other words a relation of appropriate desire hadn't been established with the object, the metaphysics were wrong. In fact the bookshop appeared too middle class, which was part of the reason for choosing it in the first place, but the quality of the experience was affected both by the object and the foreign terrain. The environment that the event takes place in has to fit the style of the person's image for the event, otherwise things are apt to go wrong. The act of shoplifting appears sensually highly gratifying when it is the coming together of the inner self with an object worthy of desire in a setting that serves as a theatre of style.

In Katz's work the reports of students who had shoplifted for a sneaky thrill were analysed. Although there was often no long term history of shoplifting, the experience had given moments that lived in the consciousness. One student, who had stolen a necklace, related:

'Once outside the door I thought Wow! I pulled it off, I faced danger and I pulled it off. I was smiling so much and I felt at that moment like there was nothing I couldn't do.' (quoted, 1988: 64)

The feeling was similar to that a serial sexual killer identified as he related why his memory was so good for those particular events:

'I have a shabby memory on things I don't want to remember, and things that are shocking or very vivid, I don't forget. I trip on those for years.' (Ressler, *et al* 1993: 164)

The significance associated with the offending pattern may be consciously desired: the identity of what Katz termed the *badass* formed. Here the person develops himself through his engagement in tough situations. His focus is not on physical destruction, or moral self-justification, but on the transcendent appeal of being mean. The badass wants to attain public testimony to his badass status. When asked about recent proposals by the Home Secretary which would make community penalties more demeaning, more rigid, and supposedly tougher, one youth on supervision was clear:

'... doesn't he [the Home Secretary] know what he's doing? Putting out that these things [community measures for young offenders] are getting tougher will not stop anything.. It just raises the stakes ... [If we] get it tougher here, we'll give it tougher there ...'

Another youth, who was listening in, was specific:

'They are thick ... we can't be frightened ... not by fear ... the excitements' the trip ...' (Morrison: Field-notes)

These youths saw the reported moves to tougher sanctions as an inducement into battle. Who did the Home Secretary think he was? The Sheriff of Tombstone? It was a compliment to be thought of as so serious that newer, tougher measures, had to be taken. It would be an achievement if they came to pass.

This idea of crime as the enhancement of power is something greater than mere excitement. While a variety of writers have noted that excitement and relief from boredom are motives to petty crime (Thrasher, 1927, 1963; Mayo, 1969; Belson, 1975; Csikszentmihalyi and Lawson, 1978), the idea of the will or drive to power expresses another positive element in the activity. Moreover, it may not matter if one is caught ... the very fact of succeeding in the act has meant that you have leapt over the hurdles of your immediate context. John Wilkes Booth was upset that his behaviour when shooting the President of the US (President Lincoln) in Ford's Theatre in Washington was not reported in courageous enough light:

I struck him boldly and not as the papers say; I walked with a firm step through thousands of his friends; was stopped but pushed on.' (Quoted in Hibbert, 1963: 241)

For Al Capone (the Chicago gangster) the conditions are tough, he does not, however, back away from the tasks but meets them head on:

'I'm a businessman ... Hell, it is a business. I'm thirty-two years of age and I've lived a thousand ... I can't change conditions. I just meet them without backing up.' (Quoted in Hibbert, 1963: 247)

And the badass is he who has transcended the mediocrity of the masses. As James Spenser, a convict who having served time in Dartmoor went on to America so that he might be taken for a first timer if caught again, explained his feelings after his first successful buy with his new illicit earnings:

'I took the Buick out by myself and drove around for a while ... I looked at the men and women walking alone on the sidewalk and I felt a high contempt for them all – poor fish! Working themselves to death for starvation money! "Hell", I said to myself. "They've got no guts. They just work and work and work. And when they have sweated for four months, they'll have earned less than what I have in four hours" ... If I have a creed at all, I think Darwin summed it up for me in his "survival of the fittest".' (Quoted in Hibbert, 1963: 249)

The dream world becomes the reality. Thomas Wainwright referred to his crimes as 'speculations'; when asked how he could have poisoned his young woman victim, he replied 'I don't know, unless it was because she had such thick legs'. Time becomes nonlinear, when asked if he had any remorse about the men he had killed, one American gangster replied: 'Why the hell should I? They are dead ain't they?'

In the dream world revenge, humiliation, fantasy and reality become intermixed: the body of one's victims may remind one of the power one has.

As one serial sexual killer recounted the events after a double killing:

> 'I drive up to my apartment with two murdered girls in my car. The trunk is a mess, with one body stabbed to death. The other [body] is on the back seat. The landlord is [at my apartment] with two friends I [drove] right up and they kept on talking and I thought, wow, would they freak out if I just got out and opened my trunk and back seat and just threw bodies out in front of them ... I took the heads up to my room. I could sit there looking at the heads on an overstuffed chair, tripping on them on my bed, looking at them [when] one of them somehow becomes unsettled, comes rolling down the chair, very grisly. Tumbling down the chair, rolls across the cushion and hits the rug, bonk. The neighbour downstairs hates my guts. I'm always making noise late at night. He gets a broom and whacks on the ceiling "Buddy," I say, "I'm sorry for that, dropped my head, sorry." That helped bring me out of the depressions. I would trip on that.' (Ressler, et al, 1993: 53)

Here the killer has exercised control over his environment, he has remained unaffected by events which would shock and disturb the ordinary person. He is tempted to announce his deeds to his landlord, to demonstrate how well his self-consciousness is organised, how he displays the power of non-affectedness – how well he has controlled the situation.

Street elites: aristocrat verses rabble

Katz suggests that for many gang members and street offenders, violence transforms the mundaneness of their association into glorious combat. Violence committed in the name of the gang gives out the image of sovereignty; it establishes the claim of elite status in an aura of dread. Violence is one means of conjuring up this feeling of dread. Katz quotes Robby Wideman:

> 'Straight people don't understand. I mean, they think dudes is after the things straight people got. It ain't that at all. People in the life ain't looking for no home and grass in the yard and shit like that. We the show people. The glamour people. Come onto the street with the finest car, the finest woman, the finest vines. Hear people talking about you. Hear the bar go quiet when you walk in the door. Throw down a yard and tell everybody to drink up ... *You make something out of nothing.*' (1988: 315, emphasis added)

You make something out of nothing! In committing his crimes is Wildeman following Nietzsche's call to authenticity, obeying the cultural message embedded as one of the deepest themes of modernity? Listen again to the words of Nietzsche:

> 'Every human being is a unique wonder; they (the artists) dare to show us the human being as he is, down to the last muscle, himself and himself alone – even more, that in this rigorous consistency of his uniqueness he is beautiful and worth contemplating, as novel and incredible as every work of nature, and by no means dull. When a great thinker despises men, it is their laziness that he despises: for it is on account of this that they have the appearance of factory products and seem indifferent and unworthy of companionship or instruction. The human being who does not wish to belong to the mass must merely follow his conscience which shouts at him: "Be yourself! What you are at present doing, thinking, and desiring, that is not really you".' (Quoted in Kaufmann, 1957: 101-2)

Rape and sexual homicide

The legal category of rape covers an array of situational interactions. The sensual dynamic of a rape, or of murder, may vary greatly; positivist attempts to uncover the structure of the personality of the rapist have inevitably resulted in varying typologies. One basic dilemma lies in the respective roles played by (i) the pursuit of power, or (ii) sexuality. Traditionally, studies have varied in the extent to which they see rape as a sexual crime (ie engaged in purely for sexual gratification) or primarily power based (ie engaged in for the feeling of power achieved by the rapist in getting the victim to do something he or she did not want to do, and the resultant humiliation the victim experiences). Groft (1979) claimed the most common type of rapist was the 'power rapist' who wanted to possess his victim sexually rather than harm her to demonstrate mastery and control; the next most common was the 'anger rapist', who discharged contempt and hostility towards all women through the act of rape; least common was the 'sadistic rapist', who eroticised aggression toward the victim, deriving gratification from her anguish and suffering.

In the FBI report on *Sexual Homicide* the following extract relates an interaction where the researchers identified resistance of the victim precipitated her being killed to preserve a fantasy centred around control and domination:

> 'We were upstairs and I was taking my clothes off. That's when she started back downstairs. As a matter of fact, that's the only time I hit her. I caught her at the stairs ... She wanted to know why I hit her. I just told her to be quiet. She was complaining about what time she would get home and she said her parents would worry. She consented to sex ... then I remember nothing else except waking up and her dead in the bed.' (Ressler, *et al* 1993: 51)

Consent? Men often argue that the problem of consent does not arise in the sex industry, because women enter voluntarily into prostitution and are paid money to have their bodies sexually entered, filmed and put on display, or perform before the cameras in the construction of pornography. Conversely, Catherine MacKinnon has argued: 'never mind that consent in sex ... is supposed to mean freedom of desire expressed, not compensation for services rendered.' (1987: 11) The particular offender's action pack of practical wisdom cannot see that consent through fear is no consent – she, ought, after all to submit – men ought to be able to control their environment, this is a moral injunctive. This woman ought to obey the wishes of that which is more powerful, more central; he has the right to impose this order of things and defend it against usurpers. The crimes of passion touched upon earlier also illustrate this. Katz relates an incident where a man killed a neighbour who was his good friend, and whom he suspected to be having an affair with his wife. The grand jury refused to bring charges against the killer, therefore this was never officially labelled as homicide, even though there was detailed evidence given by the wife that the killing occurred when her husband discovered the victim and herself engaging in sexual activities in a parked car outside her home. (Katz: 1988: 13-14) The jury understood the moral challenge and the moral right of reaction.

The narratives of knowledge and control infuse the culture of modernity creating a mind set wherein the world is a complex set of objects to observe and control. Cultural messages help constitute an individual: our existential freedom is not some asocial detachment but *pragmatic existentialism*. *If the offender is he who wages war on the civilising and disciplining tendencies of modernity, his are the actions of neither a benign nor generous Don Quixote.* Our interest in the existentialist perspective is that it rescues the offender from his location in a set of determinist forces, but we ignore the reality of social geography if in placing the offender central we deny his or her location as the interlocutor of a plurality of social and cultural forces. Following Althusser (1971: 171), we may accept cultural messages help constitute the individual as a concrete subject who has been 'hailed by' or called to an ideological site where his subjectivity may be enacted.

The subject comes to a situation with a history and a set of social skills to negotiate situations. In the following sections data is utilised which comes from an in-depth study appearing in the Cambridge Studies in Criminology namely, *Understanding Sexual Attacks* (West et al, 1978). This study drew upon accounts of histories, circumstances and motives which a small group of extremely aggressive offenders in prison related while undergoing psychotherapy for grade 'A' sexual crimes. The offenders lives were characterised by unhappy childhoods, broken homes, aggressive tendencies, numerous indications of psychological instability, a variety of anti-social behaviour, relationships with women had been mostly disastrous, and those who had undertaken marriages had generally failed to maintain them. Many of the offenders were poorly educated and had drifted about the country from job to job, many of them had committed sexual offences after imbibing large quantities of alcohol or drugs or both. The victims range from under 14 years of age to elderly married women, but mostly consisted of females in their late teens or twenties. The majority of those who raped used violence to beat the victim(s) into submission, and two thirds made use of some weapon or gun. As opposed to rape in general the majority (four-fifths) of the offenders did not know their victims before they attacked them, and, except in only three circumstances where the offenders and victims had been drinking together beforehand, was there any suggestion that the girls had in any way led to or encouraged a sexual advance. The group discussion sessions involved slow and searching explorations of the details and situation of some extremely serious crimes. What was at stake? Reflexivity.

In recounting the adversities of early life, the researchers indicate how one theme which predominated was the notion of troubled masculinity. All the offenders seem to share to some extent feelings of inadequacy, confusion, anxiety or discontent about their ability to fill the social and sexual requirements of the masculine role. The common home background picture was of defective parental attitudes and emotional turmoil in the home during upbringing. The homes had been places of sometimes open emotional turmoil and unpredictable events.

In the discussions we can see a process of investigating *social individuality*, and uncovering extreme states of existential denial and anxiety – who am 'I' and what sort of person am 'I' The states of remorse engendered sometimes border on feelings of having carried out injunctions to be a man, but instead of the process of socialisation having constructed, or deposited, a phenomenon of mind and identity as a structured entity inside the body of the person, an underdeveloped reflexivity and confusing series of messages and interpretations arise rather than any self-conscious calculation. At play are a whole series of emotional states and definitions of belonging and not-belonging.

From the existential perspective these men were not often free: they were unable to account for themselves to themselves. They appeared to experience a fear of being summoned before some place of judgment and found inadequate, a feeling which adds a huge weight to the quality of everyday life, a question of feeling inadequately in control where an observer might conclude that the person had adequate control. At stake is an intersection between the *self* and *control*.

We are not simply repeating our refrain that the free individual of the West is the product of the social forces of modernity, or simply that even those who some psychologists have labelled psychopaths (defined by being too self-contained and unable to understand the relationships with others), cannot be seen in any atomist form of human identity (see Taylor, 1985, for a general critique of the separatist, individualist, or atomist, view of human identity). Rather, that the existentialist points us to the problem that if *genuine freedom* is a matter of executing one's own actions, and living a life that is one's own, then a factor is the ability to know what one's position is and how one's actions relate to it, and accept our responsibility for our actions. The problem for the existentialist is to develop a scientific picture of human action; not human behaviour. *The confident existential self-judge is the person who had say, 'Yes I alone did it, and in doing it, it became my act, I brought it into existence'.*

The dialectic of self-awareness and self-control

Gottfredson and Hirschi (1990) locate the principal blame for low rates of self-control in defective socialisation. From the existential perspective, the role of socialisation is to equip the self with a sense of belonging to an identity, and a sense of inner self which can serve as a partially unifying, although changing resource, to map out a evolving pattern of intentionality to shape our lives. Without this resource, a sense of self (including variable amounts of self-esteem and self-worth), albeit however much this is simply taken for granted, the person is continually threatened by a sense of being formless, meaningless, lost, disintegrated, confused and shattered; life becomes constricted, tyrannised by anxiety, dread, and panic. A secure sense of self, one so secure that we can take it for granted, enables freedom of growth, joyful experimentation, self-development and creative activity. Let us redefine the experiences of family and early socialisation in terms of providing the self-to-be with resources to become. This may be practicable (time spent reading with young children directly influences later reading abilities, and probably IQ scores), or as influences on predictability (in particular, erratic home discipline confuses), or in observing directional and purposeful activity (again clearly influenced by not being able to understand the reasons for constraint, or the purposes of punishment; children who cannot observe adults engaged in employment), and the mediating of experiences which appear threatening to the child. The initial sense of self is the gradual process of separation from the others, the learning to negotiate some direction in one's daily life, and a growing sense of the world. Self-reflection is an ability which has to be constructed out of the experiences of adolescence; self-degradation may become a form of threat to the self; self-integrity, a factor of the ability of the environment to provide a suitable terrain for projects of the self. The later, adult self, is a factor of all *those little choices that add up to the creation of the (non)secure existential self.* In Matza's (1964, 1969) analysis people often drift into their deviant status. There is not an occasion of one clear cut choice or rational calculation to disobey the rules – they appear committed to the conventional order by feelings of pride invested in conformity, and by a sense of shame or guilt at the thought of having done wrong which they sidestep through techniques of neutralisation – rather, it is a process of direction(less) in which *gradually, a whole series of little choices add up.*

The existential self is affected by (i) *the grounding of home experiences and the security and place to develop a self the home provided.* The experiences of the home are important for a well-developed sense of ontological security; the home creates the conditions for emotionality; (ii) *the cultural surrounds which imparts the resources of basic values, these basic values change human behaviour into activities.* For Durkheim, when we act according to our basic values, we do not experience this as any constraint, because these values are part of us; (iii) *the range of basic emotions experienced; emotions orientate or guide the will in choosing to act, and then in choosing what actions to take.* Emotions are not a subjective, individual and socially separated experience, emotions arise in and influence the outcome of social relations. Emotions are stimulated by cultural interpretation, and enjoyed or down-played in social interaction.

The events which constituted these offences were social actions embodying relations; actions mediated through culture and emotions

The offenders' narratives of their actions are filled with accounts of their situations, cultural significations of women and emotions; emotions gave a readiness for action and the emotions experienced reflect the situation and the interpretation of cultural messages; the actions involve the body, acts of physical strength, acts of interpersonal domination, sexual penetration, and, occasionally, the act of killing another. In the following extract, the offenders' account relates a mixture of hate and attraction towards women, in which the victim becomes an object for power and domination; the particular set of behaviour is not best seen as any response to a particular sexual expression, of a set of instrumental behaviour, but as a social relation among the men and between them and the victim. As the deed develops, as power becomes unleashed, the harder it is for the situation to be controlled, and it begins to control the offender:

'We went out intentionally looking for girls. Each time we were drunk. It was towards the end of the month, I believe, that we grabbed our first victim. She was walking along the street with a carrier bag. We drove slowly by and asked if she wanted a lift. She said "No". I told Derek to slow up and that I was going to grab the bitch. When she was about even with the car, I rushed her, grabbing her by the throat and telling her to shut up or I would kill her. At that moment I felt like an animal, strong and sure of myself. I dragged her onto the front seat, while she let out a few screams. I remember her dropping her purse and the carrier bag before I got her into the car. She was wearing a sweater and ordinary socks and high boots and she kept repeating "You won't kill me will you?" After a few minutes she quietened down and we drove out. On the way, I kept telling her to be quiet or else my buddy, who had a gun, would kill her.

I then told her I would help her to escape. As soon as the car stopped I would open the door for her to run for her life, while I fought to hold Derek back. I had no intention of letting her go, and I got a laugh, deep down, that she believed me. When we finally did stop on a farm road she began to run a few yards. I let out a laugh and went running after her. When I finally did catch her, I dragged her roughly back to the car, asking her if she really thought I was such a fool as to let her get away. We made her get into the back seat, and I was already sexually aroused for the degrading raping of her. I wanted her to take everything off by herself, making her feel ashamed and abused. We were on each side of her in the back seat, and Derek started telling her to strip, giving her a few slaps, but she didn't move. Suddenly I grabbed her by the throat and started shaking her, feeling powerful and not wanting to stop. I said to her something like "Listen you bitch, you start stripping now or I'll kill you. Who do you think you are?" I felt so strong, and in a way maybe I would have killed her, but she kept croaking "all right, all right", and Derek kept calling my name to make me let up. After I let her go, I told her to get into the front seat to let me have first shot at her.

She slowly disrobed and I attempted to have intercourse, but due to the cramped space and my state of drunkenness, I kept getting an erection and then losing it. Finally, in rage and frustration, I got out and let Derek have a go. I waited only a few minutes and became insanely jealous and selfish and told him now it was my time again. This time I dragged her out of the car, both of us naked, and attempted intercourse on the cold ground, but it was just like in the car. Finally, she got on top of me and got the head of my penis into her. She kept rocking back and forth as my penis got stronger. I didn't like her on top of me, so I slowly rolled her over onto her back, trying to keep my erection hard inside her. She was very tight and finally I started to pump away. She kept repeating, 'You won't come inside me, will you'? I kept telling her I wouldn't, but the sexual feeling, the tightness of her, and her pleading words, drove me wild and I let myself go inside her, knowing all the time I would. We made her get dressed, drove her back, let her out, and made off.' (West, *et al.* 1978: 115-6)

The rape may be an act of revenge against another woman who had caused his masculinity to be brought into question; who had humiliated the offender in some way. The victim becomes the object which rights the scale:

'I was quite stoned and hallucinating somewhat, but I was aware of my purpose and that the woman I was following was not Nancy [the girl who had deceived him]. But I recall some flashes that left me wondering about that a few times. I used the gun that I had stolen. I had her take her clothes off and I made her walk ahead of me on the street for a few minutes. In one of the more severe hallucinatory periods, when I had a flash for two or three seconds and suddenly saw the face of Nancy, I took a shot at her. The girl thought it was intentional and almost became hysterical. I got her onto a lawn beside a house and my clothes came off. I made her do a number of sexual acts and then I committed the rape. I ran off as soon as I had my clothes on again. I had distinct feelings of satisfaction at her reactions to being made to walk naked in the street and to carrying out the sex acts, all obviously embarrassing and humiliating for her, to the point of being aghast by it all. That was the primary concern of mine, the purpose it was to serve. The rape was secondary. In fact, it took me some time and a lot of trying to maintain an erection and reach a climax.' (West, *et al* 1978: 117)

In another case the victim was a girl who had been flirting with, and sexually teasing, the offender without allowing him to have full sex. The victim became the focus for the powerlessness and frustrations felt by the offender. As he recounts the narrative, the offender went looking for her with rape on his mind but events took over:

'I drove past the place where she lived and stopped under some trees. By now I had it in my mind that I would like to rape her. I shut the car off and walked up to her door and knocked. She came to the door and let me in. She was wearing pyjamas. I told her my car wouldn't start. There was something said then about me being so drunk. I asked her if she would give me a hand. She said sure, and went into the bathroom and changed. We walked down to the car. There was a tyre lever in the car and I got this out, telling her I was going to use it to tighten up the battery posts. I asked her to look for a flashlight which was somewhere under the front seat. She bent over and started looking around. I lifted the lever and stopped. My mind was racing away on me. I could see part of her backside above her low cut hipsters. It was like being on a high diving board and afraid to dive, but there's no stopping once you start. As she went to stand up, I hit her. She slumped down without making a sound. I bundled her into the car and drove off.

I thought to myself that I would have intercourse with her and I parked the car. I had started to masturbate as we drove along. I had some trouble with an erection, but when I got into a position it only took a few seconds. I don't know if I realised that I was having intercourse with an unconscious woman or not. Then she started to move her arms. At this point my mind started racing again. I thought that she would tell what happened and I would be caught. I thought to myself what would a man do who was raping and killing a woman. I pretended to myself

I was angry and I hit her on the head a few times. I think I even swore at her, and I beat her on the stomach and breasts with my fists. I listened to her heart and she was dead ...'

[He drove on and dumped the body over the side of a wharf into the water.] 'I was exhausted and started to come down. I prayed, hoping there was a heaven and that she would go there. I then drove home. I set the alarm for early in the morning. I fell asleep and started to dream I was in a coffin and the boards were rotten and water was dripping in and I couldn't move. I woke up. It was only an hour since I had gone to bed. I went into the bathroom and began to throw up. I was so sick I couldn't breathe and I thought I was going to die. I went back to bed and woke up again at 7.30. I had to go and look at my car. I was sort of hoping it had all been a nightmare. There was blood in the car, and then I was sure it was all real.' (West *et al*, 1978: 118)

While events may take place when the offender has been drinking or taking drugs, the effect of the drug cannot be viewed as causal. It merely triggers off a disregard for the environment, the offender becomes in this respect more powerful and feels able to control the environment:

'It was about midnight and I had sobered up just a little. While parking the car outside a restaurant I saw this good-looking blonde parking her car and I gave up my spot to let her in. Inside the restaurant she was sitting alone, so I asked if I could join her and she said sure. She was wearing a vivid coloured mini-skirt and was very good looking. When she left I suddenly had the urge to molest and rape her. I followed her in the car. I pulled up behind when she stopped outside her place and made a mad dash. Just as she opened her driver's door, I was there and told her I wanted to talk to her. She didn't want to come into my car, I had to choke her and drag her and threaten her to get in. Even then I had to slam the door on her legs and feet several times, till she couldn't stand the pain, to make her bring her legs inside so that I could close the door. I drove off out of town, knowing the cops would soon be following, but I wanted to satisfy my craving ...

I got her into the back seat and made her have a drink of the whisky I still had with me, I got her laying across the seat completely naked and I entered her with no trouble at all. Just as I started to feel good I noticed some headlights approaching. I felt it was the police, but I didn't care. I was still going to get my sex release, so I went at it again and she started to moan as if she were enjoying it. I kept on and finally ejaculated while the cops were banging on the windows. I was pulled out by the hair with my jeans around my knees. I knew I would be in for a rough time.'

[After the arrest his mood was very different.] 'I had terrible headaches and nightmares of dying. I thought of hanging, but didn't have the courage. Finally, I swallowed a dose of lavatory cleanser ...' (West *et al*, 1978: 120)

Thus the process of objectification may break-down and the reality of the victim as a person brought home:

'It was a late hour and I was drunk. I grabbed one girl right on the main street, but she screamed and ran away. This was about 1.30 am. I caught a bus with the intention of going home. After I got off the bus, I still didn't have any intentions

371

of getting a girl. As I was on my way home, right on the main road, I noticed a young girl in a phone booth. At that point the urge came to me to rape her. It didn't matter to me what she looked like or what she was wearing, the uncontrollable urge to rape her was there, and I didn't think about where I was or what would end up happening to me. I crossed the street and walked by her once, and then came back to the phone booth. I told her that I had a gun and that she was to come with me. She then hung up the phone and told me I was bluffing, so I grabbed her and tried to pull her out of the booth. She started screaming and scratched me on the face. Then I hit her a couple of times. Then, at that point, she said okay. We walked over to a large truck in a parking lot and got into the back of it. I then had intercourse with her. When I had done and got dressed we sat and talked for ten to fifteen minutes. Then I decided to drive her home. I am not sure why I wanted to drive her home instead of just running off. I told her I was sorry for doing it, and maybe I wanted to try to make it up to her in some way.' (West *et al*, 1978: 119)

Another rapist planned to kill his victim, and was driving her to a deserted spot, when she related how she was extremely depressed because her parents were dying of cancer. The offender thought of his brother who also was dying of cancer and empathised. He understood that she 'already had it tough' and dropped her off at a restaurant. In another incident the victim drew the offender into her reality of pain and humiliation:

'I was drinking with a friend one evening. After we had a few rounds he left to go elsewhere and I sat there for a few more rounds, as I was really beginning to enjoy myself. Not long after he left, I began to feel angry and bitter as I had done before. I then decided to try my car out to see if the garage had fixed it properly as I felt that they had not done it in the way that they should have. Once I started driving again I thought of picking up girls. I stopped and picked up three girls who were thumbing a ride. There was very little conversation between us. I think perhaps that they were scared of my driving. I let them off without any sort of incident happening. I then saw three more girls hitch-hiking. I stopped and gave them a ride out of town. When at first I began to threaten, they refused to do anything, but after I drove past the point where they wanted to get off, they started to undress. I suppose they felt at this time they had no choice, I should say that the two of them got undressed, the third one became hysterical and started to cry. The others asked me to leave her alone, if they would do what I wanted to do. I agreed to this and never bothered this one girl at all.

The other two disrobed, while I drove the car. When we were parked off on a side road, I began to fondle one girl, and then said to get in the back of the car. When we got into the back, I started to fondle the second girl. I got her to lay back and was now in the process of starting to have sexual contact with her, when she began to cry. This caused me to think of other things other than sexual pleasure, and I immediately stopped my actions. It was then that my conscience took over and I realised just what I was attempting to do and how wrong it was. I proceeded to drive the girls home. I felt really scared, not only for what I had done or tried to do, but for what I had become, an animal in my own eyes. I dropped the girls off and went home. By the time I got home the fears inside me had really sobered me up to the point of being almost completely sober.' (West *et al*, 1978: 121)

In another incident the rage appears to be against women in general, a rage against the very being of femininity. West relates an incident which took place after an all-night drinking session The offender saw a woman walking along the street early in the morning on her way to work, followed her and seized her with great violence:

'He pushed one hand into her mouth to stop her screams, causing her to choke helplessly, and pulling several teeth out in the process. With the other hand he tore at her genitals, ramming several fingers into her vagina. He wanted to get his whole hand up to claw at her. Had he succeeded in doing so, he might have caused even worse damage, as it was, she sustained internal injuries and was in hospital for three days. At one point during the attack, when he was in the "sixty nine" position, he bit savagely into her labia. The accompanying fantasy, which flashed back into his mind again and again in the months that followed, was the satisfaction of destroying the victim's femininity. It was the attack on her genitals that mattered, the remembrance of nearly choking her to death gave him no satisfaction.' (West et al, 1978: 116-117)

The offender recounted subsequent periods of depression and horror at his own thoughts and actions. When he was caught, he put up no legal defence but felt like being shut away and desired punishment.

Moral transcendence

Katz argues that one reason that homicide is concentrated among the lower class is that many killings are a desperate attempt to rescue respectability; when there is a convergent disrespect in a person's occupational and intimate life the necessity to defend challenges to one's self-esteem, no matter how crazy or dysfunctional they appear to others, is all the more pressing.

The closer we actually look at crime, at the performance of crime, at the living event, the more 'the moral emotions' become vividly relevant. This perspective stresses the righteousness of the criminal, his desire for freedom. As Paul Tillich a theological existentialist described the desire and existential reality of transcendence:

'Man, in so far as he sets and pursues purposes, is free. He transcends the given situation, leaving the real for the sake of the possible. He is not bound to the situation in which he finds himself, and it is just this self-transcendence that is the first and basic quality of freedom. Therefore, no historical situation determines any other historical situation completely. The transaction from one situation to another is in part determined by man's centred action, by his freedom. According to the polarity of freedom and destiny, such self-transcendence is not absolute; it comes out of the totality of elements of past and present, but within these limits it is able to produce something qualitatively new.' (1963: 303)

The actor has seized the moment; he has turned the trap of his position into an occasion for transcendence. He has chosen to leap into activity; he has set in motion a new course of events – he has exercised his freedom.

Can this perspective be combined with positivism? In *Sexual Homicide: Patterns and Motives*, a study by the FBI's behavioural Science Unit on sexual killers based upon reading of records and interviews with 36 convinced and incarcerated sexual murderers. Multiple problems existed in family structure, substance abuse was a major problem; psychiatric disorders; for some a mix of psychiatric disturbance and aggressive acts was present when the offender was a child; half of the sample had family members with criminal histories; several had problems in accepting the sexual activities of their parents for example, observing the mother drinking and bringing home men for sex; there was instability of home structure with only one-third of the men growing up in the one location thus there was minimal involvement with a local community thus reducing the child's chances of developing positive, stable, relationships outside the family that might compensate for family instability; in over half the cases the paternal father had left the home before the boy was 12 and many complained of a lack of feeling that a father figure that cared for them was present; over 40% lived outside the home by the age of 18; for two-thirds the dominant figure during childhood and adolescence was the mother and the men reported little involvement with a father figure. The researchers suggest it was not absence on the whole which accounted for the boy's sense of non-involvement with his father but rather the lack of ability on behalf of the father to project a positive self-image of himself to his son and express positive regard for the boy; this set the stage for an empty existence. The dominant impression conveyed by the men was of a poor emotional quality to their family relationships, at the extreme this amounted to hatred of the boy by the father, with the sample including attempts by at least one father to kill the boy. Another common theme was sexual problems in childhood, for example witnessing disturbing sex or sexual violence, sexual abuse (just under half reported being sexually abused under the age of 12 (for example: 'I slept [sexually] with my mother as a young child', 'I was sexually abused by father from the age 14'). The individuals typically constructed a world of fantasy amid imagery at odds with their 'reality'; some of the men preferred sex only with dead women. The interviewers suspected that of the 16 offenders who did not report an age for first consenting sex, most never experienced consenting 'normal' sex. The authors accept some of Yochelson and Samenow's argument that criminal behaviour is a result of the way specific individuals think, but stress background features which have caused these individuals to think in the ways that they do and which sets up a criminal career. Fantasies are both reactions to events and the experiencing of powerlessness in 'real life', and sites where the men become strong. As one offender related:

> 'My early adolescent deviant fantasies are importantly different than those following my return from Vietnam. I was only the victim in those of adolescence; the deviant fantasy expressions of rage and anger did not have the external objects, women and society, until after Vietnam.' (Quoted, Ressler et al, 1993: 31)

The authors suggest a conceptual framework for understanding sexual homicide with five interacting components: (1) the offender's social environment, (2) child and adolescent formative events, (3) patterned responses to these events, (4) resultant actions toward others, and (5) the killer's reactions, via a mental 'feedback filter', to his murderous acts.

If these accounts appear extreme consider that everyday childrearing practices are a question of importing social capital, social resources by which to play the games of late-modern life. These extreme cases are the end points of a continuum. Jeff is one example. His background:

'Jeff (a pseudonym) was the youngest of three children, having an older adopted brother and natural sister. The parents separated and divorced when Jeff was seven years old, with both parents remarrying shortly thereafter. Jeff continued to live with his mother even though the second marriage dissolved. He completed age-level work until his senior year in high school when he was involuntarily withdrawn from school because of excessive absenteeism and lack of progress. He was of average intelligence and had aspired to attend college. He was athletically inclined and played league baseball. He was outgoing, often attending social events, and had a close circle of friends, both male and female. He saw himself as a leader, not a follower. At birth, it is reported that he was an Rh baby and required a complete blood transfusion. He has reportedly suffered no major health problems.

Jeff was sent out of state to a psychiatric residential facility following his first felony of rape and burglary at age fourteen. During his 19 month stay he received psychotherapy, and the discharge recommendation was that he live at home, attend public school, and continue psychotherapy on a weekly outpatient basis, with his mother actively involved in his treatment. He readily admitted to the use of alcohol and drugs of all types from his early teen years. He worked sporadically throughout his high school years as part of a program in which he attended school in the morning and worked in the afternoon.' (Ressler et al 1993: 124)

His record consisted of a gradual escalation of criminal behaviour from petty larceny at 12 and charges of disrupting school, through burglary and rape, into a series of sexual homicides.

If Gottfredson and Hirschi (1990) stress the mundaneness of crime and depict criminality as a lack of self-control, what do they make of accounts which are full of domination; which are full of careful planning and calculations; which display the offender playing with his victims, who if they submitted were given no additional orders but if they resisted were severely beaten then killed? Note the 'moral transcendence' in the following account:

'She faints and falls down on the floor. I pat her face. She wakes up, has a real frightened look on her face and she starts to scream. I stick the gun to her head and tell her if she screams I'm going to blow her head off. She asks what I want and I tell her I want money and to rape her. She balked on that and said, 'No white man doing that to me.' I'm thinking, she's one of those prejudiced types. I backhanded her. She whimpered. I told her to take off her clothes. She refuses.

I cocked the trigger back and she started hurrying up. And this time I'm feeling good because I'm domineering over her and forcing her to do something and I'm thinking this prejudiced bitch is going to do what I want her to do.' (1993: 129).

In concentrating upon the generalisations of positivism we blind ourselves to the existential reality of the event. In the mundaneness of everyday life the individual turns, presents a display, struts, asking the audience to understand and engage with the symbols of evil – a symbolism fully understood by the young men who are linked in the groups we often call gangs. What appears random and senseless becomes understandable as a closely choreographed set of moves. Muggings, stick-ups, robberies, contain an array of 'games' or tricks that turn victims into fools before their pockets are turned out. Positivism turned against the pre-modern discourse of good and evil, but crime is part of the refusal to play the modern game. Crime can show us glimpses of the 'other' of modernity

Katz has called this a process of moral transcendence – the theory of this text is slightly different it is, rather, the attempt to gain control of the self and the environment. Listen again to the voice of the criminal, Charles Manson reflecting on his state of mind before the Tate/LaBianca murders:

'All I could focus on was, "What the fuck is happening here? One by one this fucked-up society is stripping my love from me. I'll show them!" They made animals out of us – I'll unleash these animals – I'll give them so much fucking fear the people will be afraid to come out of their houses!" These thoughts might sound like pure insanity, but every abuse, every rejection in my entire life flashed before me – hatred, fury, insanity – I felt all of these things.' (1986: 199)

If that is too extreme, then listen to a young man on Supervision from a Social Services Juvenile Justice Team after persistent 'joy-riding' (taking cars without permission and driving them recklessly):

'Why do I do it ... because I'm bored ... everything is boring ... life is a drag ...' (Morrison: Field-notes)

Now listen to Adorno, one of the great critics of existentialism and the jargon of authenticity:

'The weaker the individual becomes, from a societal perspective, the less can he become calmly aware of his own impotence. He has to puff himself up into selfness, in this way the futility of this selfness sets itself up as what is authentic, as Being.' (1973: 293)

Adorno argues that the drive to authenticity, self-control and self-sustainability desocietalises human subjectivity. The self becomes viewed as something which is meant to be complete 'in-itself', but this turns 'a bad empirical reality into a transcendence'. The individual 'who can no longer rely on any firm possession, holds onto himself in his extreme abstractness as the last, the supposedly unloseable possession' (1973: 116).[3] The (a)moral transcendence will be the worst form of existentialist authenticity.[4] An individual may experience life as futile but creates a mythology which turns impotence and isolation into strength. In his notebooks for *The Idiot* written in the late 19th century, Dostoevsky described the increasing weight given to the idea of the self and the pursuit of self-control as functions of pride not morality. If society was to build up the idea of a self-contained human self, responsible for controlling his or her actions by and for him or herself, society would create a an uncontrollable *idiot*. Self-domination, self-control is therefore a crucial aspect of the causal mechanism of crime – crime is the pursuit of self-control in the face of the perceived chaos 'out there' – but it is a self-control Dostoevsky rightly called 'idotism'.

In *The Possessed*, Dostoevsky presented insanity, murder, arson and suicide as consequences of individuals perceiving a loss of coherence in the surrounding social structure. It was not impending doom, but the impossibility of being sure there was a connecting thread, that was terrifying. As a consequence individuals began to appreciate the experience of crisis and chaos for their own sake and for the physical/psychological effect. Dostoevsky describes a group of young people who find that a man has committed suicide in a hotel. It is suggested that each one in turn goes in and observes the scene. As one of the group expresses it: 'Everything's so boring, one can't be squeamish over one's amusements, so long as they're interesting' (1936: 332).

For Katz the lived phenomenology of much crime is an investment of style into an otherwise tedious existence. His perspective highlights in the careers of persistent robbers men for whom gambling and other vices are a way of life, who are 'wise' in the cynical sense of the term, and who take pride in a defiant reputation as 'bad'. In the lived sensuality behind events of cold-blooded 'senseless' murder, we witness:

> '... the power that may still be created in the modern world through the sensualities of defilement, spiritual chaos, and the apprehension of vengeance.
>
> Running across these experiences of criminality is a process juxtaposed in one manner or another against humiliation. In committing a righteous slaughter, the impassioned assailant takes humiliation and turns it into rage; through laying

---

3 Adorno correctly points to one feature of the discourse of authenticity which stems from the economic conditions of late modernity: namely, the intensification in the process of defining self-worth by property. Whereas the identity of the early modern may lie in the ability to control property, the late-modern must invest in himself, must see himself as property. C.B. MacPherson (1962) has analysed how deeply embedded this idea was – ie possessive individualism – the liberal philosophy of early modernity. The existential ground of freedom in early modernity was material possession. Today the ability to key into the system is the grounds; thus the individual as a site of *capital* is the systematic foundation for existential security.

4 In choosing the criminal act for his *supreme moment* of power, of being, the offender betrays his claim to uniqness; he loses himself in the cultural flows of frustration or consumer desire. In the crime, the experience may be authentic, but the choice is based on non-authentic values.

claim to a moral status of transcendent significance, he tries to burn humiliation up. The badass, with searing purposiveness, tries to scare humiliation off; as one ex-punk explained to me, after years of adolescent anxiety about the ugliness of his complexion and the stupidity of his every word, he found a wonderful calm in making "them" anxious about his perceptions and understandings. Young vandals and shoplifters innovate games with the risks of humiliation, running along the edge of shame for its exciting reverberations. Fashions as street elites, young men square off against the increasingly humiliating social restrictions of childhood by mythologising differences with other groups of young men who might be their mirror image. Against the historical background of a collective insistence on the moral non-existence of their people, "bad-niggers" exploit ethnically unique possibilities for celebrating assertive conduct as "bad".' (1988: 312-313)

But what has criminology acknowledged? Most theories, such as Merton's, have concentrated upon explaining motivation in a generalisable form; but have they contributed to the exorcism of evil from crime? Have these theories robbed crime of the desire for power, of the lust, of the desire to humiliate, of the love of the knife, of those things which Nietzsche warned that the criminal was about when he did the act but could not acknowledge the reality afterwards? Have we developed a sentimental criminology in the name of positivism?

Symbolic displacement

And so we fall into a trap. Because we ignore the sensuality of crime, we believe that law and order politics can lower crime. We oppose the interactionism of crime with the claims of rational deterrence. But how can adding to the thrill of crime, since the game takes on an even greater risk (and even greater buzz of adrenaline), reduce crime? We turn from the study of crime to study the offender but do not study him in his interaction; we do not listen to the words of crime, taste the fear and blood of crime, and so we reduce the possibility of a logos true to crime down to one which touches only the epidemiology of the pale criminal.

But you may ask are you not almost glorifying in irrationality? And suppose we were to accept the logic of your position is it possible? Can we encounter power? Can we share in the adrenaline of violence? In the kicks of blood, of the knife, and, perhaps it is wrong to do so – is it not bordering upon pornography? What purpose would it serve?

Truth is one purpose. Criminology has increasingly subjected its desire for knowledge and wisdom to short-term research contracts providing managerial information for the social control bureaucracy. Yet the late-modern context displays a division of discourse – criminology talks a distanced, 'rationalised' logos while we are surrounded by a popular culture that portrays (non)crime as a festival of violence. Surrounding us is an international mass culture with the icons of *Rambo*, *RoboCop*, *Mangum*, etc. What is the function of all of this violence, all of this killing, all of this sex, that we are surrounded by? Perhaps the reproduction of violence, of lust, of rampant sexuality keeps the others quiet. A century ago Henry David Thoreaux wrote that the majority of people live their lives in quiet desperation: if their will to power was stimulated how could the social order hold? So there must be a process of transposition: a mass of films which usually only actually titillate (compare the superficiality of *Bitter Moon* to the ending of *Last Tango in Paris*) provide this function (*Rambo, Superman, Blade Runner, Wild at Heart, Blue Velvet* ...). Inside the experience of watching these movies we are protected voyeurs of our darkest hearts desires – let loose – in hyper-reality. In the midst of all of this violence, what is the meaning of pain? Where is the reality of victimisation, of the civilised use of (personal) power?

Without contextualising or positioning it, contemporary criminology, in the guise of Gottfredson and Hirschi (1990) understand the central feature of late-modernity – the rock upon which this secular castle is built – the self. Self-restraint will give the self coherence, render it predictable, render it suitable for order. Modernity will take the pre-modern self cushioned by custom, tradition and shame, positioned in the rigidity of mechanical solidarity, and convert it through the festival of violent penology, through the celebration of an obvious power, into something else. Into us.

We, the moderns, the successfully organised, civilized selves, the selves who speak reasoned logos, men of intellect who once handed over our swords to Hobbes' sovereign and were then civilized through reasoned discourse, and disciplined through routinization when we forgot the lines. We are told that living together in peace, the balance between the needs of society and those of the individual, will, for modernity, be achieved by controlling passion through self-love and using reason, the modern disciplines, to understand ourselves. But there is a risk: living together in civilized peace seems to require the concealment from one another of our raging, insatiable passions. The harmony of modern life will be an extension of the peace within the self. But post-modernism seeks not equilibrium, but radical plurality and dynamic transformation – the fate of the self is insecure in a context where:

'... reality no longer has the time to take on the appearance of reality; it captures every dream even before it takes on the appearance of a dream.' (Baudrillard, 1983: 152)

The accounts we have encountered in this chapter do not speak of peace. We have entered the sort of world Peter Greenaway presents in *The Cook, The Thief, His Wife, and Her Lover*, a world of violence, chaos, power and control, a world of multiple realities, of fantasies, of over-determinations, but criminology texts do not talk about this. Why? because they offer logos – reasoned speech – and so criminology cannot talk about the existentialism of crime. It destroys crime, packages it up for symbolic consumption – it washes the blood from crime and renders it into materialism, into innovation, into a loss of self-control – and renders itself at a distance from the very subject it is meant to know. Thus we risk increasing crime, for our passions may not be constrained – sterilised – we may need words and forms of analysis which understand the reality of passionate action.

Conclusion: the message of existentialism?

Existentialism stresses the difficulty of being modern. As Sartre reads the plight of the main character in Kafka's *The Trial* we face a world which demands that we control our destiny while from all around us chaotic forces impose. We are condemned to act – all actions are against something and for something else – the characteristic feature of human reality is similar to being perpetually in court. To be free is to have one's freedom perpetually on trial (Sartre, 1956: 478).

What are we to make of this? What happens when one reads most texts that call themselves criminological? We do not read much of the current existential concerns of living and dying in the post-modern moment, of making do, being free, bad faith, lies, deceptions, connecting dreams to realities, living lives that are more real than the hyper-real. We do not read of the reality of drugs, of AIDS, of confused identities, of the constant search for something to hang a sense of wholeness on, of being subjected to a host of conflicting and overlapping messages, of desperately searching for events or things that can provide a sense of status. While the conservative criminology talks of the rational calculator, or the person of low self-control, we do not read of the frustrated individual who wishes to be authentic, who wishes to feel normal, but constantly feels 'that the world is full of crap', or 'the forces surrounding me are too big to understand'. These concerns do not involve indifference, or the waning of humanity represented in a depthless superficiality. The emotions of modernism – anxiety, alienation, self-destruction, radical isolation, anomie, private revolt, madness, hysteria, and neurosis, are not able to be subsumed into self-control. These emotions are reflected in the increased incidence of alcoholism and drug addiction, homeless isolation, the alienation of ethnic minorities, and self-destruction. To these emotional forms of being are now added anger and fear; fear of the unknown and the inability to control it, anger at the disenfranchised by those on the right; anger in the underclass towards those in power. Is anger and fear, coupled with existential anxiety, the only uniting forces in a society which understands that MacIntyre was right? That nothing gives full legitimacy to our bureaucratic rulers? Modernity promised more than it delivered. Today is powerlessness all-pervasive? The post-modern moment senses that this world, out there and in here, is out of control. It is not the Big Brother 1984 world of Weber and of George Orwell that we now fear since the media is not speaking with one voice (contrast contemporary American talk-back radio which is full of macho male angst with TV which is full of politically correct panel discussions). Some of the ceaseless flow of images and commentary on everyday life attempts to make this world appear controllable, but other images show it clearly is not. Emotions are stimulated and simulated, stress kept under control by valium and coke, tensions and fears controllable by alcohol and hashish, heroin and ecstasy produce an anxious euphoria. Euphoria promises to blot out the fears, in return for a moment of peace. But in this hyper-strange world the only safe place is with the fantasies inside one's head, or a general theory which does not include the social. Here, where reality no longer crowds in closure occurs, and a meaninglessness so well understood is experienced as 'a walking nihilism'. How can we have this meaninglessness?

In contrast to Gottfredson and Hirschi, we followed Katz into the sensuality of crime. We looked not for the mundaneness of crime but its extraordinariness – the criminal is caught in a net of contingencies, and must fight to make something of himself – the criminal is in danger of not possessing a self – hence the leap into crime is the desperate attempt to exert control over his (non)self. To the existentialist the criminal has made the wrong choice – as Tillich puts it:

> 'One must ask: what is this self that affirms itself? Radical existentialism answers: what it makes of itself. This is all it can say, because anything more would restrict the absolute freedom of the self. The self cut off from participation in its world, is an empty shell, a mere possibility. It must act because it lives, but it must redo every action because acting involves him who acts in that upon which he acts. It gives content and for this reason it restricts his freedom to make of himself what he wants. In classical theology, both Catholic and Protestant, only God has this prerogative: He is à sè (from himself) or absolute freedom. Nothing is in him which is not by him. Existentialism, on the basis of the message that God is dead, gives man the divine 'a–se–ity'. Nothing shall be in man which is not by man. But man is finite, he is given to himself as what he is. He has received his being and with it the structure of his being, including the structure of finite freedom. And finite freedom is not aseity. Man can affirm himself only if he affirms not an empty shell, a mere possibility, but the structure of being in which he finds himself before action and (non)action. Finite freedom has a definite structure, and if the self tries to trespass on this structure it ends in the loss of itself. The nonparticipating hero in Sartre's *The Age of Reason* is caught in a net of contingencies, coming partly from the subconscious levels of his own, partly from the environment from which he cannot withdraw. The assuredly empty self is filled with contents which enslave it just because it does not know or accept them as contents. This is true too of the cynic, as was said before. He cannot escape the forces of his self which may drive him into complete loss of the freedom that he wants to present.' (*The Courage To Be*, 1952: 151-152)

He has made himself into a criminal – he has became a subject of the crim-o-logos, he has fallen into the circle of the label; he has failed to understand himself (to place himself in a position where he could look at himself, and say, 'yes, that is me'). Instead he will become the object of the knowledges of normalcy, the disciplines of psychology which will open out his soul and strip bare his *motivation*; he desires to step out of the circle, but chooses the *means* of *criminality*. By the opportunity that was presented, the denial of the control of the other, through the criminal act he has taken control of the self, but this self is *now to be controlled and penalised by the power of others*.[5]

---

5   What else could he or she have done? Controlled or mitigated scepticism; we can call this the refusal of Hume. Scepticism towards the narratives of everyday life; the narratives which enforce consumption, which stress a (returned) style. A scepticism which enables the individual to work on the central thrust of becoming a modern within a modern *civil society*.
Our domain?
- the strength of information and knowledge;
- the impact of the communication and transportation technologies (the mass media);
- the increased flow of information, imagery and cultural interaction does not make the late or post-modern society more transparent or at ease with itself, but more complex, chaotic;
- the search for freedom
- division, segregation, ... a chaos within which exits the possibilities for emancipation, for choice, for authencity

However this is an emancipation available only to rhe *truly modern*.

The truly modern individual is the ideal of modernity: he who exercises self-control, motivation. and flexibility. He who can be sure of himself and confident of his worth; but who – in our conditions – can be truly that? Are we not located in a social terrain stratified by gender, class and race?

CHAPTER SIXTEEN

MODERNITY, GENDER AND CRIME: FROM THE BIOLOGICAL PARADIGM INTO FEMINIST INTERPRETATIONS

'There's not a woman on earth who would ever have had cause to complain of my services if I'd been sure of being able to kill her afterwards.' (The Marquis de Sade quoted in *Time Out*, March 1994)

'Sometimes I wake up and all I can think of is getting myself a penis ... A real big one. I'd like to strap it on under my pin-striped suit and then go off to the office. That bulge under my suit ... Then I'd feel safe ...' (A 30 year old woman lawyer discussing conditions in the professional work-place of the 1990s personal communication)

'... women don't know what they want ... I fell for this one right ... I really tried to be the 'new man' ... considerate, listening like ... the soft touch ... treated her fine and didn't screw around. You know what? ... She went and left me for a right bastard ... all macho.. lied to her all the time and screwed plenty of others as well ... I took it for a few months and then saw him in a pub. Knocked him up proper ... That's why I'm here ... He went to the police ... assault they said! Fuck women ... fuck being nice ...' (Morrison, Field Notes: Transcript of interview with Young Offender supervised by a Social Services Team)

Do women exist?

Do women exist? This is a rather obvious preliminary point for a discussion of criminology and women. Perhaps it is not clear, it shall be rephrased.

'Have women existed in modernity independently of male fears and fantasies?'

Certainly women exist in male dreams and nightmares: the narratives warn that women seduce, dispossessed of a penis they cannot know pleasure except through male energy, hence they constantly wish to seduce the male from his reasoned pursuit of sensibility, from the progressive tasks of modernity. In *Politics and the Arts*, Rousseau warns that 'never has a people perished from an excess of wine; all perish from the disorder of women'. While wine just render men stupid the 'disorder of women' contains a host of vices which can bring all government to an end (1968: 109). In *Civilisation and its Discontents*, Freud warns that women are hostile to and stand in opposition to civilisation (1961: Ch 4). Woman cannot achieve the sublimation of the passions which the task of civilisation requires. In the 18th century, Hegel criticised the actions of Antigione in the classical Greek drama for opposing the right of the state with her own subjectivity; Hegel warned that the community created an enemy for itself within its own gates with women. Specifically, when women hold the reins of political power the state is at once in jeopardy. (1949: 496)

Thus, the wise men warned: women must be kept separate from the creative sites of modernity. Women are the negative of the dominant male: the empty space of patriarchy's other, constitute by factors opposing the progressive. Women are the body which the mind disowns yet needs (materialism), the purity which contrasts to the necessarily active role of construction (the virgin), the nature which serves as the fertility for culture (maternalism, menstruation), the night that comes after day offering rest (the non-thinking) and sensuality (the whore), the bringer of madness to reason (the site of hysteria).

Woman has been the 'other' of the criminal; absent in the official criminal statistics she is the overlooked (especially in traditional criminological theories where she is hardly discussed), or the one that is regarded with suspicion. This absence is explained by the extremes of passivity (women don't commit crime because crime is a tough reality which woman have no power to engage), or total power (behind every criminal is a manipulative woman: the man goes to prison, the woman just spends his 'take'). But raising the question of the treatment by criminology of gender offers an entry into the core concerns of the status of women and the project of modernity. Who, or what, determines the position of women in the construction project? Can women exist independently of the male gaze, independently of the way in which men have interpreted the biological constitution of (non)women: a constitution which defined and limited her ontology, her naturalness, her possibilities? How are women to become modern? What resources, intellectual, personal and structural are required? What are the contours of a fully modern woman? What would a modern woman's body look like if it did not have to conform to the specifications of the male gaze? What would the norms and expectations of a woman's everyday life be if they were not prefigured by male power? What is the difference between the gaze of masculinity and that of femininity? Would the liberated woman be man's equal in committing crime?

Women in the construction of modernity

The first period of criminology was part of the construction process of liberal-philosophical modernity. In this movement from status to contract, criminology offered a discourse of control and administration. The utopian aspect of this early phase of the project of a liberal society focused on the idea of human autonomy and rational development, which was philosophically universal and without boundaries in principle. Kant's ideal of a global society, inclusive of all individuals in an egalitarian form, was the philosophical dream of the Kantian (1957) project of perpetual peace.

The process was realised to be socially dangerous; the building project was to be a controlled project – it required the participation of those who were fully rational, those who had a stake in the social body, who did not allow their labour or their bodies to be used by others. The empirical foundations of the good society could not be articulated in philosophy, and were incompletely elaborated in practice. The very notion of the contractual basis for liberal social structure provided an incoherent intellectual means of setting boundaries, which were otherwise provided by the setting of identities and assumptions drawn from observing activity. Thus, in early modernity, as in ancient Athens, the law of property prefigured and structured the living law of political participation. Possession of property was a correlate of participation: ownership of land conferred the right to participate in the political life of the (city)state or polis. Property helped constitute the identity of the insider, of the citizen, set against the notion of the outsider, the other, the subject. In a very real sense the other (the woman, the slave) were property, were possession, were objects of a domination that was both power and responsibility; they were things to be contained and the responsibility of the participant. Early modernity laid out the foundations of a social formation which lived up to the universalism and individualism explicit in the philosophy of the liberal project only in a very restricted sense. The development of late-modernity, a development characterised and enabled by the progressive splitting of social life into spheres with their own criteria of success (economics, politics, ethics, art) meant property could become the correlative for wealth alone, and thereby political participation could be freed from the necessity of property. What was previously property (slaves, women) could become included (and could themselves order property).

Boundary setting: modernity and the otherness of women

The conception of a humanity divided between the normal and the deviant, the familiar and the other, involves a whole set of self-authenticating devices which include, among others, the ideas of the rational and the insane, the orthodox and the heretical, the male and the female. We have characterised modernity as a construction project organised around the ideas of calculation, reason, knowledge and the analytical approach to problem solving. The modern was to be free from the entanglements of custom, tradition and status; a freedom to be rational, calculating ... scientific. In her overview of western philosophy, Genevieve Lloyd highlights an idea of women's inferior capacity to reason that stretched back to the ancient Greeks, where Philo demarcated the male, who was 'active, rational, incorporal and more akin to mind and thought', from the female, who, being closer to nature, was 'material, passive, corporal and sense-perceptive' (1983: 491). Women have been viewed as entangled in a circle of sense and materiality caused by their inescapable nearness to nature. While it tied women to a reproductive and nesting role, nature gave males a freedom which enabled the intellect to develop the capacity for abstract thought; the roles of social life reflected this. As Hegel put it in the *Philosophy of Right* (Law):

'Women regulate their actions not by demands of universality but by arbitary inclinations and opinions. Women are educated – who knows how? – as it were by breathing in ideas, by living rather than acquiring knowledge. The status of manhood, on the other hand, is attained only by the stress of thought and much technical exertion.' (Quoted in Lloyd, 1983: 511)

It fell to males to lay out the structure of progress; thus modernity continued a process of gendering reality.

To say that reality has been genderised is not to claim that these ideas refer to some fixed or natural ontology, but rather that they are a set of attitudes generating or governing a relationship between a lived reality and some area of problematic existence. The attitudes which defined who the subject of modernity was and was to be, also defined the woman as too natural, too tradition bound, incapable of being a fully fledged emancipated modern – the woman was the other of the man, to inhabit a domestic space, a space protected by the domination of the masculine.

Who was the true bearer of modernisation? Read the masses of writings on crime and social control – what does one find? Throughout these writings true humanity appears identified with membership of a specific social class – citizen and bourgeois. The question may now arise: if women are to become insiders – as they have been doing for the last half a century or more – on what terms is their incorporation? Who is it that will define the nature of modern women? For, if the nature of the (non)modern woman has been previously defined by men, with what resources of language and material can the nature of the modern woman be defined (created)?

What has criminology said about all of this?

If positive criminology sought to uncover the constitutional condition of the offender, women were noticeable by their absence. There have always been vastly fewer women offenders (persons subject to the formal mechanisms and labelling processes of social control) than men. For much of criminology, this did not seem like a problem, theories were created based on explaining what was, in retrospect, male crime rates; theories were not expressly gendered theories, but purported to be theories of 'crime' and 'criminality'. Recent revisionism has asked criminology to become reflexive on this issue.

Much of criminology is concerned with the nuts and bolts of social control and the maintenance of social groupings. The new criminological literature on gender and crime is a part of the developing genre of sociological literature which explores gender divisions, and the gender aspects of social institutions as diverse as the family, education, political attitudes and participation, and crime.

Sociologists like to distinguish between: *Sex*, by which we mean a term that refers to the biological characteristics of males and females; and *gender*, a term that refers to those traits which are associated with men and women under the terms the masculine and the feminine, but which are not biologically derived and have a social rather than physical basis.

Statistical discrepancy in the commission of crime between men and women

Most scholars agree that males commit more offences than females and their offences are more serious than those of females. As Nagel and Hagan put it:

'The relation between gender and criminality is strong and is likely to remain so. Woman have traditionally been much less likely than men to commit violent crimes and that pattern persists today ... While the relative increase in women's property crime involvements is significant, female participation even in these crimes remains far less than that of men.' (1983: 91)

Males account for the vast majority of those arrested for crimes involving force or fraud, and the victim and self-report studies support the picture. Regardless of age or type of crime male involvement is substantially higher than female. The official picture for 1992 in England and Wales was as follows.

Individuals found guilty or cautioned for indictable offences per 100,000 people in the population

AGE	MEN	WOMEN
10	583	121
11	1,229	342
12	2,397	838
13	3,999	1,638
14	5,225	2,299
15	6,466	2,316
16	7,220	2,087
17	8,249	1,899
18	8,256	1,612
19	7,376	1,333
20	6,525	1,198
21–24	4,736	905
25–29	3,146	655
30–39	1,588	380
40–49	778	193
50–59	406	112
60	126	34
TOTAL	2,029	442

Source: Criminal Statistics England & Wales 1992, HMSO.

How the crime figures break down:

Indictable offences (tried in Crown Court)

	MEN	WOMEN
violence against the person	39,800	3,800
sexual offences	4,900	100
burglary	43,000	1,200
robbery	4,800	300
theft/handling stolen goods	103,900	24,000
fraud and forgery	15,600	4,400
criminal damage	9,000	800
drug offences	20,600	2,100
other (excl. motoring offences)	33,100	2,900
motoring offences	10,300	400
TOTAL	285,000	40,000

Summary offences (tried in magistrates' courts)

	MEN	WOMEN
offences (excl. motoring)	322,500	149,200
motoring offences	653,300	69,800
TOTAL	975,800	219,000
ALL OFFENCES TOTAL	**1,260,800**	**259,000**

Understanding the official statistics and criminal involvement

The gender difference in officially recorded crime has been described as so sustained and so marked as to be perhaps the most significant feature in recorded crime (with age the next). For England and Wales in 1992, 541,100 people were found guilty or cautioned for indictable offences: 81% were men, 19% were women. Men committed 10,300 indictable motoring offences; women 400. In 1992, for sexual offences, the male-to-female ratio was 49:1, for burglary 36:1. Even in the areas where women were most represented (theft, handling stolen goods, fraud and forgery) men outnumber women by four to one.

As a consequence the criminalisation and penal involvement rate of men and women is substantially different; a much higher per centage of males than women are convicted or cautioned. Women offenders also have fewer previous convictions than men and a higher proportion of women convicted are in fact first time offenders.

Several writers have denied the truth of differential involvement in crime

One approach has been to deny that women are substantially less involved; the most famous example of this is the work of Otto Pollak (1950) in *The Criminality of Women*. Pollak's tactic was to doubt whether the official statistics were in any way an accurate reflection of reality for three major reasons.

- Female crime was masked by its relative invisibility, and since crimes of women remain under-reported to a greater extent than do crimes of men, the official sex differentials, as stated in the official statistics, are mythical. He concluded that men and women commit about the same number of crimes, but that women's crimes – illegal abortion, prostitution, and shoplifting – were infrequently reported. Furthermore, men are more often criminalised than women, as, for example, certain offences in England and Wales can only be committed by men by definition, such as rape. We can note, however, that newer definitions of rape tend to be sex-neutral.

- Women are more prominent than men in the hidden figure. Pollak saw women as inherently deceitful and cunning and so more able to conceal crimes. His reasoning is interesting and obviously suspect: he argues certain natural features of women's existence cause them to become inherently deceitful. Specifically, women and not men can fake organisms, women learn to conceal their menstruation, and women withhold the truth of sexuality from their children. Pollak calls upon the support of a number of female authors to reinforce this. However, the issue of the male gaze (the strength of the ideology of the masculine-feminine divide) is not addressed – if the dominant ideology holds out certain things as natural, even women sociologists may perceive social reality in this way. As 'evidence' concerning offences he points to the large dark figure in abortion, theft and child abuse. Undoubtably, Pollak is picking his offences; moreover, the assumption that the unreported figures of male crime are low is not plausible. There are clearly large unreported figures in certain male dominated offences – such as domestic violence and rape. A linked view is that women instigate rather than perpetrate criminal acts and remain in the background because of this. In the late 19th century, Lombroso and others had depicted women criminals either as biologically underdeveloped, or especially manipulative. Influencing every criminal man there was some woman who, while remaining unseen, had helped to write the most startling pages in the annals of crime.

- There was a 'chivalry' factor at work among members of the general public and criminal justice personnel. Pollak argues that victims tend not to report female offenders to the police, and that consequently, female offenders are more likely to remain in the dark figure.

Because most criminologists neglected the study of women offenders, Pollack's portrait of the hidden female offender gained a certain credibility and was almost the only authoritative view available in the 1950s. Well respected texts of the 1960s, such as Walter Reckless' *The Crime Problem* (1967), seemed to accept his line relatively uncritically. Both Pollak's evidential base and his arguments have been re-examined, and it is clear that in comparison with men, females commit very few crimes, particularly serious ones. Consequently, both Greenwood (1981), and Box (1983), felt able to conclusively state that it is images such as Pollak's of the 'masked female offender' which have been turned into mythology.

Victim surveys and self-report tests support the official statistics

Victimisation surveys provide a view of public willingness to report female suspects to the police. Surveying victimisation data throughout the 1970s, Hindelang (1971, 1979, and with Gottfredson and Garofalo, 1978) argued almost one-half of 'traditional crime' involving male offenders, and only one-third involving female offenders were reported to the police. However, while women contributed far less than men to serious crime, the most serious crimes committed by female offenders were slightly more likely to be reported to the police. Box (1983: 169) argues that ironically women may be over-reported and over-represented in the official statistics, because of the vast amount of unreported corporate crime, governmental and social control agency crime, or organised crime – areas of crime that women have very little opportunity to be involved with.

Most large scale comparison of the official statistics and victim surveys (such as Smith and Visher, 1980) find an overwhelming similarity in both sets of data. In general, the self-report and victimisation studies show a similar picture concerning sex and violence in crime as those derived from official data for the same types of crime (Box, 1983: 167-69). Frances Heidensohn argues that if there is an understatement in official statistics it is of the crimes done to women.

> 'There is little or no evidence of a vast shadowy underworld of female crime hidden in our midst like the sewers below the city streets. As we have become increasingly aware in modern times, quite the opposite is true. There is a great deal of crime which is carefully hidden from the police, from families, friends and neighbours. Much of this takes the form of domestic violence, the abuse of children both physically and sexually, incest and marital rape. The overwhelming majority of such cases involve men, usually fathers and husbands injuring or abusing their wives and children.' (1989: 87)

Has there been leniency or chivalry by officials within the Criminal Justice System in their dealings with women?

There have been a number of more or less sophisticated, statistically-based, quantitative studies, designed to test whether chivalrous judges and prosecution attorneys treat women offenders more leniently than men. Often these studies treat women as a single category and do not differentiate for class, race or education. (For a review up until the early 1980's see Box, 1983.)

Some have been unable to reach a firm conclusion (Parisi, 1982; Gelsthorpe, 1989), some have found preferential treatment (Steffensmeier and Steffensmeier, 1980), others that they are treated more harshly (Smart, 1977; Chesney-Lind, 1973, 1978; Dominelli, 1984), others argue that there are no disparities or that previous disparities are receding (Kempinen, 1983; Douglas, 1987), or that for serious crimes there is a difference but not for lesser offences (Zingraff and Thomson, 1984).

Farrington and Morris (1983) found that the lighter sentences passed on women offenders are accounted for by basic legal considerations, such as the nature of their offences and previous convictions. Similar findings explained the greater proportion of females cautioned by the police.

However, domestic circumstances – in particular marital status – were important additional factors. Heidensohn (1985) found support for the view that women are doubly punished when their rule breaking is compounded by perceived role-breaking. For Carlen (1985) imprisonment for women is more easily justified for those regarded to have failed as mothers. In the US, Nagel (1981) found that divorced or separated women were more likely to receive severe sentences.

Eaton (1986) argued that young females are far more likely to be institutionalised than boys, because they are perceived to need protection. This supposed protection is often given to young females who have not committed any serious delinquent act, but are simply ungovernable, or unmanageable as far as their parents or teachers are concerned. In exercising this parental concern, juvenile magistrates are often transformed into stern parental surrogates, who lock up their naughty daughters for behaving in ways that seek attention. It has been a relatively common argument that the juvenile court has used its discretionary power in the service of traditional sex-roles. The court appears to be less concerned with the protection of female offenders, than the protection of the sexual status quo (Datesman and Scarpitti, 1980)

The Steffensmeiers' (1980) argued that women who commit serious crimes will be less severely sanctioned than men, since (i) judges do not want to separate a mother from her children, because they view social reproduction as an important female job; and (ii) judges, both in private and in public, have difficulty conceptualising serious female crime, and prefer to believe that she didn't really do it, or wasn't capable, or did it for love.

This line of argument argues that the dominant ideology of femininity creates an image where women are not generally believed to be criminal. Hence a criminal act is more likely to be viewed as irrational, or an emotional response to a passing situation, and the woman is not really dangerous. The natural state of women is believed to be rather passive and non-aggressive.

Box (1983) concludes that when the reality of chivalry and leniency is dissected it reveals a series of beliefs which may tend to deflate the contribution women make to serious crime. Conversely, when women do commit minor offences, they are more readily seen as in need of a treatment response, and often put away for their own protection; this contributes to the criminality of women through labelling and the opening of deviant pathways.

Box notes that victimisation surveys provide an interesting window on the public willingness to report females to the police. Hindelang (1979) found that the most serious crimes committed by women were slightly more likely to be reported to the police than male offender crimes and, if 'chivalry' did exist, then it was a female virtue as females reported female offenders less than did males. Studies on the reporting of shoplifters either by customers to store detectives, or by store detectives to the police, and a study of traffic citations, were unable to locate any evidence supporting the view that women were favourably treated. The offence rather than the gender seemed to be the major determinant of social response. The general conclusion appears to be that when the offence revealed 'inappropriate role behaviour' the penal outcome tended to be harsher, thus supporting the view that it acts to protect 'traditional women' by punishing those who are unconventional.

The findings of the British work of Farrington and Morris were virtually replicated in the US by Nagel and Hagan (1983), who concluded that women were more likely to be released without bail, but that when bail was set there was no difference by sex in the amount at which it was set. Sex was not found to make a difference in the decision to prosecute a defendant, nor were there differences in the use of plea bargaining, or in the likelihood of being convicted. In sentencing they found a small but consistent leniency towards female defendants, even when variables such as prior criminal record and the nature of the offence were taken into account.

Other commentators have called for the studies to exercise a greater level of differentiation in their analysis. For example, you may have to take into account the tactical and symbolic interactions of the trial and demeanour of the defendant. Women who exhibit behaviour that is socially defined as appropriate for women are most likely to be treated leniently; older white women, who are apologetic and submissive, are better placed than women who are young, black, and hostile towards the authorities. Kruttschnitt (1982) argues that women who are economically dependent on their husbands may be treated more leniently than economically independent women, perhaps because judges think the courts need not exercise so much formal social control over women who are controlled by the men on whom they are economically dependent. Daly (1989) found the court making decisions in light of effects on the children and family, rather than on the woman herself.

British feminist scholars have tried to respond with more sensitive analyses to catch effects which the methodologies using statistical correlations may not show up.

This, more theoretically inclined, type of analysis takes as its focus not a simple male-female distinction, but how different categories of women are treated in the criminal justice system. From Smart (1976) onwards, the argument is that it is not women, *per se*, that are treated differently but women as they display their gender roles, ie as successful, or otherwise, wives, mothers, or rebels. Hudson (1987: 119-21) argues that women who display the appropriate signs of the middle-class feminine woman are likely to be treated more leniently than those who are working-class, black, unmarried or in any other way perceived as obviously deviant. In an earlier work she had argued that this process doubly caught young women displaying deviant signs:

'If something can be seen as a 'phase', as normal, albeit undesirable, youthful behaviour, then the expectation is that increasing maturity will bring about its end; but if a form of behaviour is regarded as gender-inappropriate then there are fears that a girl is seriously disturbed, that she is not following the pattern of normal social and emotional development, and the behaviour comes to be judged not by its own seriousness in terms of consequences, social harm done, degree of delinquent motivation, or any other common-sense notion of seriousness, but it comes to be overblown as predictor of future, more serious trouble. Adolescence is, after all, the status a teenage is moving out of, so that adolescent failings can be tolerated; but femininity is what a girl is supposed to be acquiring, so that any signs that she is rejecting rather than embracing the culturally-defined femininity are treated (by those whose professional vocabulary enables them to read the signs and offer such interpretations) as necessitating intervention and urgent resocialisation.' (Hudson, 1984: 43-4)

The agents of the criminal justice system have their own action pack for interaction: the social constructions of sexuality, behaviour and gender inform, therefore, the construction of the normal and deviant, defining who is properly a criminal woman (see Worrall, 1990). These perceptions constitute signposts in the process of girls 'growing up good' in western societies (Maureen Cain, 1989).

The contemporary feminist position is trying to move beyond the leniency-verse-severe treatment dichotomy and pose the issue as one of the constructive features of criminal justice as it relates to the constitution of the modern subject. In other words, how can criminological theory face the issues of how law helps in the social construction of the gender division of masculine and feminine?

A necessary task in this is the destruction of mythologies. Carlen describes her own interpretation of feminism in this area:

'... because they have collectively contributed to a demolition of certain sexist myths concerning women's lawbreaking and have called into question the more discriminatory and oppressive forms of the social control and regulation of women, I shall ... use feminist very loosely to refer to all of those who, in writing of women lawbreakers, have been concerned to remedy the wrongs done to *women* criminals by criminologists, police, courts, and prisons.' (1990: 107; her emphasis)

A key example of this new type of analysis is the work of Eaton (1986) which places the creation of social inquiry reports, pleas of mitigation, and the assumptions of magistrates, within the broader context of social relations and ideologies. The courts relate to both male and female defendants in the context of the defendants' families; but this builds upon the sexual inequality of the family; thus, the operation of the 'law' reinforces the sexually stratified social order.

This type of analysis engages in critique and demonstrates the mythological basis of much decision making; it is carried to its logical conclusion in the latest form of demolition of sexist mythologies, namely deconstruction. An example is Alison Young's analysis of how the women protestors who camped around the American necular war-head base of Greenham Common were portrayed in the media (*Femineity in Dissent*, 1990). The media focused upon reports of the woman's bodily activity in the various incidents at the camp. At work was a form of policing; a surveillance, dressage and disciplining. The Greenham women are presented as in need of policing through the press invoking an image of a social body which has unhygenic parts which require control by the police, moral reformers and by hygenists. The press reports of their dirtiness, their unsanitary habits, their morally defective values, in reality are replies to the women transgressing the 'lines of gender, territoriality, sexuality, familiarity' and 'the symbolic content of the dominant discourse'. Would men have been so portrayed? What could be seen as rational protest was rendered into another example of the hysterisation of women's bodies. Any critical impact that the women's action could have gathered was dissipated through recognising them as in need of censure for unfeminine activity. Young is not asserting that this was a conscious action by the media. Instead we are concerned with a 'culturally unconscious level of a wish to condemn, a recourse to gendered notions of reason/unreason, men/women, legitimate protest/hysteria'. (1990: 83-5)

Deconstruction can bring out the unconscious levels of demarcation and of subordination and domination. But we might ask does not deconstruction need to lead onto work which proposes, which aims to map out new territories, new forms of gender and interactional policies for criminal justice?

What type of crime do women commit? And should we expect their crime to increase?

Recorded statistics tell us little about the quality of crime, legal labels conceal a wide variety of activities and so it is difficult to tell from them whether a woman's crime is less serious than a man's. There have been some displays of common sense over the years; apparently, women steal fewer items of aftershave than men! Several studies found that the incidents committed by men differ from that of women. Victims of women were most often related or the woman's friends or those with whom she has an affectionate relationship, and the majority of women are convicted for attacks on their friends and neighbours for incidents which arose out of domestic or romantic disputes.

The most common offence attributed to women is shoplifting. In 1985 nearly 50% of the women sentenced for indictable offences in magistrates' courts were shoplifters, compared with 10% of men. But research suggests that women are over-represented in the shoplifting offences.

In an observation of shoplifting in selected stores, Buckle and Farrington (1984) found that men are twice as likely as women to shoplift; out of 503 shoppers observed, nine shoplifted – four men and five women. As a percentage of those observed it was 2.8% men and 1.4% women. Are women more prominent in shoplifting statistics because detectives and sales persons expect women to shoplift and, because of preconceived notions of 'menopausal' or 'kleptomaniacs', observe women far more closely? This obviously increases a woman's chance of detection.

Campbell's (1981) self-report studies support this view; in response to the question have you taken anything from a shop when the shop was open?' 12% of girls and 28% of boys responded positively.

How did criminology traditionally account for this? One immediate suspicion was the high shoplifting figures for women were simply a consequence of *opportunity*. If modernity largely confined women to a domestic sphere then the opportunities for crime would have been largely located in that arena. The major activity which has been apportioned as being women's is the taking care of the home and shopping; therefore where they were allowed, they committed crime. Thus, as the realm of women's activities have recently expanded, it has become almost an article of faith in certain quarters that the crime rate of women will increase, and perhaps approximate with men, when they achieve 'liberation'. The liberated woman will be man's equal in crime.

Why have there been so few theories on crime which are gender specific?

Heindesohn (1989) proposes a number of reasons for the failure to examine the obvious issue of gender involvement in crime:

- the study of crime was dominated by men, as Oakley (1982) had pointed out, it was no accident that we talk of the founding fathers of sociology;
- commentators tended to equate gender wholly with sex and then only discuss masculinity, leaving women as an assumed afterthought;
- male power predominated in academia and this was widespread and pervasive;
- women's low and unspectacular crime rates, were harder to find and study because they were so rare;
- female offenders fear the stigma and loss of reputation associated with their offences more than their male counterparts and this makes them elusive as subjects;
- one of the critical reasons for avoiding gender in the study of crime was the crucial nature of gender for theory. In practice most theories of crime are

based on assumptions about gender, and those assumptions are asserted rather than explained and explored only in relation to masculinity.

There has been an increase in the study of women and crime in recent years. Campbell (1981; 1984) published two major studies of delinquent girls in gangs which overturned a number of stereotypes about girls and their involvement in gangs where violence was used. Shackladysmith (1970) depicted colourfully the life of female gang leaders. Eleanor Miller (1986) provided a vivid portrait of the life and work of a group of women street hustlers in Wisconsin.

Studies have also been compiled on the prison and penal policy. Women's experience of imprisonment has been put on the agenda. The results are not conclusive. Lucia Zendner (1991), studied the role and practice of women's imprisonment in Victorian society, and suggested that women prisoners were not punished as severely as men (and some preferred prison to the destitution and prostitution they were forced into on the outside). While others, for example, Dobash, Dobash and Guttridge (1986), argue that the regimes of women's prisons were more repressive.

The Offical Statistics have been analysed to reveal both a reflection of gender relations and a gendered set of priorities concerning policing. There are offences committed mainly by men against women and children in which they use their power or force in the defence of traditional gender roles. This includes, wife beating, rape, sexual assaults, sexual abuse, harassment. Many so-called sex linked crimes are power, not sexually based. As Dobash and Dobash argue, differential responsibility and marriage give the husband both the perceived right, and the obligation, to control his wife's behaviour; these provide both motives and justifications for beating her.

Moreover, numerous studies have shown how violent crimes against women are grossly under-reported (eg see Morris, 1987: 160-192) – official agencies are traditionally very reluctant to protect women from male violence. The police are reluctant to intervene in cases of domestic violence and it was only recently that marital rape became recognised in the UK. Stanko (1984, 1990) relates that the dominate attitude in the police has been that we are even better off if they 'kiss and make up' rather than if the police put him in jail. Heidensohn (1989) argues that women face a double jeopardy: they are not protected against domestic violence by the police and court system, but when they step beyond the normal image of the feminine they face stigmatisation and labelling.

Criminological explanations were not set out as 'arguments explaining why men commit more crime then women'

We must first acknowledge how the advent of feminist orientations has changed the way in which this issue has been conceived. Feminist criminology is a diverse body of writings taking the critical view that the understanding of the criminality of women and the role of gender in constituting deviance in general have all been ill served by both traditional and new criminologists. In her 1982 review of theoretical criminology Leonard was scathing:

Theoretical criminology was constructed by men, about men. It is simply not up to the analytical task of explaining female patterns of crime. Although some theories work better than others, they all illustrate what social scientists are slowly recognising within criminology and outside the field; that our theories are not the general explanations of human behaviour they claim to be, but are rather particular understandings of male behaviour. (1982: 1-2)

In Britain the emergence of feminist criminology is generally assigned to the publication of Carol Smart's *Women Crime and Criminology* (1976). Criminology was taken to task for largely reflecting an uncritical attitude towards sexual stereotypes of women and girls, largely confirming the ideologically determined inferior status of women both in the normal, conforming world and in the world of crime and delinquency.

She notes that the neglect of female criminality by the predominantly male criminological profession had several undesirable consequences:

- the arrested development of the subject, leaving research in female deviance to be thrown back to the earliest stages of criminological evolution;

- policies and attitudes towards female criminality were male dominated, and there was an assumption that women were irrational, compulsive and slightly neurotic. Not only were issues where women were the victims not taken seriously (incest, domestic violence, the handling of rape), but there was no provision for speaking of women's experiences. Adolescent girls faced a higher risk of institutionalisation than boys for non-criminal forms of sexual deviance. Regimes in Holloway Prison confirmed the biological view, with therapy but no vocational training for women;

- notions about women's 'nature' had lent prominence to 'sexual deviance' as the focus of inquiry appropriate to the study of female criminality. Thus prostitution was more studied than rape. Cohen (1950) had assumed that female delinquency consists of sexual delinquency or of involvement in situations that are likely to spill over into overt sexuality. Gouldner (1977) states that criminologists have portrayed the female deviant as a woman on her back, rather than a women fighting back.

Another prominent feminist writer, Heindensohn (1968, 1985), argued that the feminist critique of the study of crime had from its inception two main aspects: (i) women were largely invisible in the literature on crime, and (ii) when they did appear it was to be portrayed in ways which disturbed and marginalised their experience. These two factors led to (iii) the avoidance of gender, as an issue, so that the crimes of male criminality were presented as the crimes of all criminalities. Feminist criminology began then, very much as a critique of mainstream criminology. It has developed three other forms:

- Arguments to change the dominant notions of criminal justice practice; in particular pressure groups pushed for higher sentences for rape, the use of new defences, for example arguments over the provocation defence, and the handling of women victims;

- Strategies changing the perception of victimisation, for example, the campaigns over rape, incest, and domestic violence;

- The provision of general critiques of the forms and structuring of legal ideology and the political forms of power in our societies, in particular, the argument that political philosophy has been clearly masculine and phallocentric.

One impact has been for writers to accept that masculinity is at least as much of a problem to be analysed and explained as femininity. In fact, it is logically an even greater problem, since it is masculinity which is associated with crime and delinquency, whereas femininity is linked to conformity. Masculinity has been under-researched and under-discussed; in part because men are used to treating themselves as the 'norm', and the central category, with women as a sub-category. But if masculinity is no longer seen as the general and universal condition of the human species, as a 'norm' upon which modernity is to be built, the 'norm' from which femininity is a deviation, then we need to analyse the basis for the very concepts of masculinity and femininity and the behavioural traits usually associated with them. The traditional way of grounding gender differences has been to resort to biology.

Biological and psychological explanations: a critique

Biological determinism constituted a strong theory of criminality of both sexes in the 19th and 20th centuries. Lombroso (with Ferro, W, 1985) argued women were 'atavistically nearer to her origin than the male', and that her lesser involvement in crime was due to her 'piety, maternity, want of passion, sexual coldness, weakness and an undeveloped intelligence' (1895: 105, and 151). While modern explanations have shifted towards theories with a more sociological basis, biological determinism continued to dominate theory and practice in explaining women's crime. Morris (1987: 57-63) highlights the tendency of male criminology to explain female crime as a consequence of disturbed sexuality; it was as if a rational woman offender could not be accepted

In his review of the literature, Klien (1973) claimed that the path from biology to the present was surprisingly straight. Several writers had referred to the relative stability of the rates of crime involvement of man and women over a variety of times and places as evidence of biological differences. Women's lower rate of criminal behaviour has been attributed to their affiliative nature, their physique and lack of assertiveness, all of which were claimed to have a biological base.

In their huge text Wilson and Herrnstein ultimately relied upon a bio-social foundation: 'the best guess centres on the difference in aggression and perhaps other primary drives that flow into the definition of sex roles' (1985: 124).

It is not surprising that women's crime is often viewed as biologically based since biology is commonly assumed to determine women's lives generally. In Freud's view (1925), anatomy is destiny. But Biologists have pointed out that neither chromosomes nor hormones determine what is defined as masculine and feminine behaviour or attitude. Sex is not gender.

The effect of aggression and biology?

Maccomby and Jacklin (1974) believe the difference between men and women's aggression has a biological foundation. They claim four points:

- There is evidence that men are more aggressive than women in all human societies. By contrast, social anthropologists, from Margaret Mead (1935) onwards, have demonstrated the qualities that we think of as naturally masculine and feminine, have been relative to some extent to time and place, and that in some cultures both sexes have been aggressive or both sexes gentle.

- Differences in aggression are found early in life, when there is no evidence of differential socialisation which have been brought to bear by adults. Others, for example, Caplan (1975) argue socialisation starts from birth.

- Aggression is related to levels of sex hormones and can be affected by experimental administration of these hormones. The level of testosterone is argued as an explanation for violence in men. By contrast, Powers argues that both men and women have male and female hormones in varying amounts, and even in one sex the variation is great. Hormone levels also vary in each person in moments of stress on different days and at different times of life. Boys and girls have very similar hormone patterns before puberty yet differences in aggression appear before them;

- Similar differences in aggression exist in all human primates. But Powers argues there are wide variations among primates in all aspects of behaviour including aggression.

Therefore each of Maccomby and Jacklin's arguments can be countered (see the discussion in Wilson and Herrnstein 1985: 117-19), but a belief in the biological basis for differences in aggression remains strong. Indeed Wilson and Herrnstein conclude their discussion by saying that while aggression is often situationally controlled, and the forms which it takes are shaped by learning, the durability, universality and generality of the relative aggressiveness of males cannot plausibly be blamed entirely on arbitrary sex roles. However, their discussion raises the image of a range of primary and secondary reinforcers, and there are a large range of interacting factors in any criminal event.

Sex role socialisation

Many writers have agreed that sex role socialisation is linked to criminality in such a way that it accounts for the much lower rate of female crime. Carol Smart began her 1976 analysis using a mixture of socialisation and role theory:

'Girls are generally more closely supervised than boys, and are taught to be passive and domesticated while boys are allowed greater freedom and are encouraged to be aggressive, ambitious and outward going ... both socialisation and the later development of consciousness and self-perception does vary considerably between the sexes. As a result of this girls are usually expected to be non-violent and so are not allowed to learn how to fight or use weapons. Girls themselves tend to shrink from violence, and look for protection rather than learn the skills of self-defence, hence few women have the necessary technical ability or strength to engage in crimes of violence, armed robberies or gang fights.' (1976: 66)

Differential socialisation prepares the growing child for different pathways in life. Writing in 1976, Scutt presented a picture, perhaps now under stress, whereby girls are encouraged to be passive and gentle and they are taught not to fight with each other and their brothers. During childhood they are constantly reminded of the role expected to be adopted in the future; ever-present is a mother who represents the adult they will become. This is different for boys since their father is away from home, at work, every day.

Both Smart and Scutt, however, are clear that role and socialisation theory can only provide partial answers; consideration must be given to other factors. Many writers draw upon an image of criminal activity that presents it as closely tied to masculine behavioural traits. Boys are encouraged to be independent, self-sufficient, brave and daring, able to take risks and to go for what they want. By contrast, there is little in their upbringing to teach them to care, or to show that they care. Boys are toughened against caring and attachment to enable mobility. For Oakley the demonstration of physical strength, aggressiveness, achievement, legal or illegal, are facets of the ideal male personality and also factors of criminal behaviour. To become a proper man, the boy must lessen personal attachments and sentiment, must be stalwart and brave, loyal to his mates and show little pity or empathy for outsiders whose loss may be his gain. It is the man who is being prepared for the job, the most vital thing in his life, the task of bringing home the money and supporting the family – is crime a form of breadwinning when the others are not available or appear too much of a burden? Is that not part of the theory of differential opportunity? For John McVicar (a former offender who served time for crimes of violence, now a sociologist) strength and physical courage are vital factors by which young men build their self-esteem – the same qualities which sustain many forms of criminal activity and loose groupings. McVicar is clear that crime is not an attractive career for a women. She has not been trained either physically or mentally to hold her own in the criminal fraternity.

According to this image, criminality thus varies directly in proportion with the socialisation into features of the masculine role. But are we taking about the intensification of masculine traits or a defective socialisation? Is the person who commits crime the extra-masculine, or one who has received a distorted socialisation?

This has looked a promising line of inquiry, but there are two sets of methodological difficulties with this view:

- What are the variables, and how would the forms of proper socialisation and poor sex role socialisation be measured? Once this was agreed defective socialisation and male/female delinquency would have to be documented by measuring both variables and then discussing their inter-relationship.

- It assumes the subjective meaning of criminal activity to the offender can be inferred merely by knowing their sex. Many writers appear to have made such crass assumptions. Cohen (1955) portrayed girls as committing crimes because they are preoccupied with boys, and boys were seen as committing crimes because they are preoccupied with aggressive and competitive pursuit of occupational and worldly success.

Certain studies have attempted to identify gender differences and relate them to differing rates of involvement in delinquency/crime.

Shover et al, (1979) interfaced control theory, masculinity theory and the differential delinquency of boys and girls. As a result of an upbringing in which girls are touched, handled, and talked to more than boys, and in which conformity and dependency are actively encouraged, girls are orientated towards finding self-affirmation in love and acceptance of others, while boys are rewarded for independent, objective achievements. The authors conceptualised gender roles as identifiable behavioural expectations which people hold for themselves, expectations about such matters as appropriate conduct or plans for the future. They predicted positive relationships between traditional feminine expectations and belief in the validity of rules and law and negative relationships between traditional masculine role expectations and the latter. The results were consistent with the view, that for both boys and girls the more traditionally feminine their expectations, the greater their respect for the law and attachment to conventional others (such as teachers and mothers), the less severe was their involvement in property offences.

Thornton and James (1979) required respondents to state how far they perceived themselves to possess the stereotypical masculine traits of aggression, independence, objectivity and dominance, competitiveness and self-confidence. They conclude that the findings showed little effect of masculine traits on delinquency behaviour and that a movement towards masculine attitudes did not appear to increase a persons propensity to engage in various forms of delinquency.

These studies attempt to integrate control theory and differential socialisation. The original formulation of the control theory stems from Hirsch

(1969) who observed that adults attempt to overcome the problem of preventing their young committing deviance by seducing them with affection and trapping them with possessions and myths. People are introduced to conformity by becoming attached to adults, by becoming committed to future conventionalities of activity and by coming to believe in the moral superiority of conventional legal standards. To the extent that adolescents are bonded in this way they remain insulated from the temptations of deviance.

The theory sets out a mechanism for how adolescents get involved in delinquency in the first place. It asserts that the more they are attached to parents and teachers, the less they are likely to be involved with delinquent peers, their values, the temptations that they offer, because they do not want to upset those whom they love or fear. Also they can more easily resist the temptations, as being properly socialised conventional adults, they do not perceive delinquency as fun or advantageous.

The relevance of these ideas to explaining the small contribution of females, to official rates of crime has been clear to a number of researchers, who show that the social location of women contains more of those factors which act as constraints on delinquent behaviour.

Hagan, Simpson and Gills (1979) conclude that women are over-socialised – more specifically – over-controlled. Hagan draws upon the classical sociology of Weber and recent work on the sociology of law by Donald Black. Weber's (1947) analysis specifies that the distinction between a public realm of production (populated by males), and a domestic realm of consumption (the realm of women and the family) is fundamental to capitalism, while Black (1976) specifies an inverse relation between the state and family-based systems of social control. The stratification of work and domestic arrangements, into public and private spheres, makes women the instruments of informal social controls. Females are more closely supervised than men and the burden of that job falls on mothers; therefore women find themselves encapsulated in the nuclear family and less free to explore the temptations of the world beyond.

Hagan (1987) developed this theory into a structural theory of opportunity, control and socialisation. The answer to the different rates lay:

'... in the social organisation of the world of work, the stratification system, and the different means to control men and women.' (1987: 268)

Structurally women are more restricted in their entry into the world of work, men are more commonly ascribed to the public arena (ie, the world of work/production) and women to the private sphere (ie, the home). One consequence of this restriction of women is to make them less available for the public ascription of criminal and delinquent statuses. Hagan is clear that 'both crime and work are sexually stratified'. This is backed up by Auld et al's (1986) analysis of drug dealing which argued the reasons for girls not becoming involved in heavy drug dealing were economic as well as cultural; a product of the males' wish to dominate this irregular economy. Historically, the development of a complex division of labour required by industrialisation and large scale trade and commerce, developed a differentiation between informal and formal agencies of social control – a decline of influence of local groupings, such as kinship groups, and the prominence of state sponsored system of segregative control – to cover the arena of work and public spaces. Private spaces, the domain of the family and largely the terrain of women, remained subjected to informal systems of control. The new forms of work, and the experience of social life in public spaces, required and brought into being a new form of social control, namely, 'crime control', operationalised in modern forms of criminal justice. In the main, men have been the daily objects of this control, since they were the subjects moving most readily into the new and more public areas of work. For Hagan:

'... the result was to subject men increasingly to the formal control of the emerging criminal justice system, while leaving women to the informal social control of the family ... two well established statistical regularities – the exclusion of women from the 'race' for stratification outcomes and less crime among women – have as a common source patterns of informal social controls involving women, which are established and perpetuated within the family.' (1987: 268-9)

Hagan's concept of informal social controls extends beyond the family to include activities of peer and work groups – importantly it includes the pressures which go to create femininity rather than masculinity. Additionally, Hagan argues, females are not only the objects, more often than males, of informal social control, but also the instruments. Specifically, mothers exercise control over children while daughters, more than sons, are the objects of this control. Analysers of child-rearing practices have, until recently, been united in saying that 'women are the primary socialisers'. In the construction of gender roles for the children certain 'requirements' of each role are instilled in the developing child. As Udry sees it:

'... by age three, the boy will begin to perceive that some new requirements go with being male. Males are not supposed to be passive, compliant, and dependent but on the contrary, are expected to be aggressive, independent, and self-assertive.' (1974: 53)

Hagan believes the family, and the controls exercised therein and outside, help constitute the social complex of power-structure wherein gender relations are established, maintained, perpetuated, and otherwise reproduced. The traditional family of organised modernity is that of the patriarchal family – the ideal type of which is a husband who is employed in a position of authority over others, and a wife who is not employed outside of the home – this family will tend to reproduce daughters who focus their futures around domestic labour and consumption, contrasted with sons, who are prepared for participation in direct production. A specific type of social-psychology will be encouraged in each. The relationship to control lies in the fact that aggressiveness, independence, and assertiveness connote freedom (or the absence of control) more than restriction.

In this relationship 'criminal and delinquent behaviour are recognised as pleasurable, if not liberating. Crime and delinquency can be fun.' (1987: 271) Thus women define risk-taking less positively than men; women define involvement in crime and delinquency less positively than men; women are therefore less likely to be involved in criminal and delinquent behaviour than men. Women are systematically 'over-socialised'; women are kept in a restricted world *vis à vis* the world of work and public space 'through a socialisation sequence that moves from mother to daughter in a cycle that is self-renewing'. While some commentators argue (i) there is a new breed of violent, aggressive women offenders; or (ii) behavioural differences between the genders are diminishing; or (iii) as the opportunities for womens participation in the world of work increase they will become more frequently the subject of the agents of formal social control, and therefore patterns of crime will become more alike, Hagan points to the increasing 'double burden' women face. Participation in some new kinds of work do not relieve them of responsibilities for child-care; alternatively, the relief of some upper class women is at the expense of employing underclass home help; thus the home-based concentration continues and male and female rates of criminality are likely to remain quite different for some time to come.

There have been attempts to integrate structural theories, differential socialisation, differential association and opportunity theories. Johnson (1974) found that the low rate of delinquency amongst women was, at least in part, a reflection of their social location – they were more controlled and supervised by their parents, more willing to accept conventional values, and less influenced by or involved with delinquent peers. Female friends are more home than street centred, and play a protective role; consequently female peer groups reinforce dependence, compliance and passivity by thus keeping down the frequency of female encouragement into delinquency. For Ronald Akers (1977) control theory should be integrated with social learning. Socialisation leads to a choice of social bonding and friendship networks which create constraints diminishing the opportunity to commit delinquency. It is not just the presence or absence of opportunity but:

> '... a person will participate in deviant activity ... to the extent that it has been differentially reinforced over conforming behaviour and defined as more desirable than, or at least as justified as, conforming alternatives'. (1977: 58)

Although people may have a motive to deviate they may be unable to do so simply because they had no opportunity. Opportunity theories highlight the sexism of crime in that the attitudes and beliefs of established criminals see women as emotional, unreliable etc. 'Organised crime isn't an equal opportunity employer.' Several commentators have argued that men who inhabit the world of crime, prefer to walk with, and associate with, and do business with, other men. They see their crimes as too hard and dangerous for women; when women are recruited, it is a sexual and supportive role they play.

Is there an increase in female crime? Does the liberation of women necessitate that they become as criminal as men?

It is argued that if the social position of women changes in such a way that they come to share the same privileges and resources as men – if they become more powerful – then it follows that there should be a convergence between the sexes in the frequency and pattern of crimes they commit. Therefore does emancipation mean that females will commit more serious crimes?

In the 1930s, Bishop (1931) was warning that the fight for emancipation had been mostly won but was it worth it? The cost of victory was the savage taste of disappointment:

'... women of this country were never in a more unhappy state than they are today ... many more women have become criminally minded during the past years than ever before.' (1931: 3-4)

By 1950 Pollak could almost rejoice, in telling us that voices:

'... ever since the 1870s, have predicted that the progressing social equalisation ... would lead to an increase in the volume of female crime.' (1950: 58)

Radzinowicz and King (1977: 14-15) argued when women took over some of the traditional male roles in Germany during the Second World War, female crime rates rose to almost equal those for males. The rates dropped back to the pre-war levels when the women returned to their traditional female roles. Clifford (1976: 125-132) argued in Japan the rates of female crime have increased as women entered the labour market, married later and became more like men in the roles they played.

In a book entitled *Sisters in Crime*, Freda Alder (1975) stated that female criminologists had seen the darker side of the women's movement in recent years. She asserted: 'Women are indeed committing more crimes than ever before. Those crimes involve a greater degree of violence.' (1975: 3) Certainly, the number of women subject to custodial punishment is increasing, for example, between 1970 and 1980 the average daily population of women in custody almost doubled from around 800 to 1,500. (HMSO Criminal Statistics 1981) Mostly variations of opportunity theory were put forward in explanation: for Simon (1975) it was simply to be expected as a function of both expanded consciousness, as well as occupational opportunities that women's participation role and involvement in crime would change and increase.

However, this portrayal of changing female crime does not enjoy consensus amongst all writers. Some deny any positive relationship between female emancipation and crime, while others assert that contemporary women are committing more masculine crimes, more violent crimes, and more serious crimes. Steffensmeier claimed:

'The new female criminal is more a social invention then an empirical reality and that the proposed relationship between the women's movement and crime is, indeed, tenuous and even vacuous. Women are still typically non-violent, petty property offenders.' (1980, quoted in Box, 1983: 192)

Adler's *Sisters In Crime* presumes that crime has been a male activity and that the modern woman desires to become like a man – why?

Adler had presented a picture of new independent women who now took on traditional masculine qualities of assertion, aggression and independence in their deviant roles, as well as in their new involvement in business. Thus she claimed the new prostitute was better educated, better accepted, and more independent of men; women were more inclined to use illicit drugs and to pursue sources of supply into illicit channels; and they are becoming as eager as men to reach out for thrills rather than just relief. Hence Adler's view is of the new woman who wants both the joys and pleasures of modernity as well as bearing the burden: the crimes of the new woman will be crimes of desire and not crimes of desperation or relief. Yet Adler's analysis seems to fall into the trap which MacKinnon argued women may find in their quest to be modern. Specifically that 'women can't fuck their way to freedom' (1987). For MacKinnon it is not the women's movement that has told women to become as men, but the ideology of control and domination central to capitalist modernity.

MacKinnon (1982, 1987) builds upon a Marxist perspective in which understanding power, domination, alienation and the pursuit of a true future state of social relations are clear themes. She suffers, in turn, from many of the same faults that have befallen earlier marxist analysis, namely, she appears to assume a truth for her theory that transcends the others, she claims the possibility of a true essence of women which we are unable to presently consider, and insists on the totality of male domination throughout the social order.

For MacKinnon the first site of domination lies in the male appropriation of women's pre-social natural sexuality, an appropriation which constitutes woman as the object of male desire. Thus women's sexuality in society is structured into an objectification of the male gaze rather than a consequence of natural or true forms. Gender formations are structured on the basis of this; ultimately the power which constitutes the structure of gender relations and the domination of women by men is the power of visualising and defining the nature of women's sexuality and thus gender (1982: 515). Out of this difference, out of the structure of interaction in the mode of activity of sexuality, comes a domination through difference:

'Difference is the velvet glove on the iron fist of domination. The problem then is not that differences are not valued; the problem is that they are defined by power. This is as true when difference is affirmed as when it is denied, when its substance is applauded or disparaged, when women are punished or protected in its name.' (1987 :219)

As with Marx we cannot look at the behaviour of the oppressed, of the hungry, as the behaviour of natural man, for MacKinnon we cannot look at any of the behaviour of women under contemporary conditions as the truth of their gender. Women's subordinate set of gender roles does not correspond to any extra-social natural division but has its 'truth' only as a creation of social processes:

> 'Gender is what gender means. It has no basis in anything other than the social reality its hegemony constructs. The process that gives sexuality its male supremacist meaning is therefore the process through which gender inequality becomes socially real.' (1987: 149)

We cannot trust the present perceptions of women, of femaleness, since these have the meaning and the form which has been given and been allowed, by the male dominated processes of social reality. As a consequence:

- Women cannot trust the state – even the supposed neutral liberal rule-of-law state is the embodiment of the male gaze.

The secret of this domination, the key to its success, is the hegemonic belief that the structure of the liberal rule of law state actually prevents domination. By creating such an image of impartiality the rule of law is blind to the fact that it operates to reinforce structural inequalities which pre-exist the appeal to law and which inhere also in the jurisprudence of the law. For if the subjects of the law come to the law as citizens, as the rights bearing creatures of modernity, the subject of the women as rights-bearer is male-identified and male constructed. To claim the protection of the law is to claim the protection of something already established in the male point of view – to enforce the abstract law is to enforce that which has been constructed in the male view. The liberal rule of law state is the rule of men under the guise of the rule of law – its power intensified through the hegemony of subterfuge.

- Not only is the state not to be trusted but the very notion of equality is suspect – instead one must ask 'equality as what?' If women want to claim equal rights are they not claiming only the right to be viewed as men under the gaze of the male state?

MacKinnon's (1989) argument is at the level of hegemonic understandings, the social inequality which existed in the traditional patriarchical social order has not been destroyed by the legal rights offered by liberalism. The equal protection of the law would be just if women were actually equal before the law – if the liberties of the social body were evenly distributed – but they are not. Women are thus in a terrible bind: to become fully functioning moderns they renounce the restraints which kept them in the position of subjugated women, but this means their identity will be constituted in the gaze of men. In desiring to be modern will they become as men?

What is the empirical evidence in criminology?

Alder's analysis was flawed in its primary example of the 'black sister'. Adler assumed that the structural role of black women in the US had condemned them to be stronger, more aggressive and, hence, more liberated that their white counterparts. The fact, she argued, of their higher crime rate was thus a prediction of things to come generally. But black women are more easily seen as extremely vulnerable, as doubly victimised (by racism and patriarchism), as facing serious demands. Their crime may be a tactic of survival rather than freedom.

Those studies which try to prove a causal connection between emancipation and female crime by merely documenting the historical overlap between these two social events are fatally flawed. The methodological question, analytically as well as philosophically, is 'what is female liberation?'

Steffenmeiser tried to analyse the matter concerning crimes of violence, but concluded that female crimes of violence against the person have increased absolutely but not relatively to the male rate, whereas female property offences have increased faster than the male rate. He was sceptical:

> 'The new female criminal is more a social invention than an empirical reality and that the proposed relationship between the women's movement and crime is indeed tenuous and even nonexistent. Women are still typically, non-violent, petty property offenders.' (1978: 580)

Fox and Hartnagel (1979) in Canada, asked how could one measure the time period of liberation? They suggested the rate of labour force participation, educational involvement, fertility and 'being single' as indicators of female emancipation and correlated these against female criminal convictions; their conclusion was one of increase in rates of criminal convictions.

Smart (1979), Box (1983), Box and Hale (1983), and Carlan (1987), point to other factors which may provide a common explanation embracing the increase in male crime rates, specifically, the growing economic marginalisation of large groups of women. Let us be under no illusion: the liberation of the new woman may be of the upper and middle class and occur at the expense of the double bind of the marginalised (perhaps the icon of this is the career women in the US who can only be the new successful woman because she can employ various home help at very low wages who are other women ... particularly members of ethnic minorities).

There may also be a change of ideology whereby the other members of the public expect new tough women. Traditionally, statistics show higher rates of violence among men than women and it is commonly believed that men are more aggressive than women. However research and self report studies reveal a different result. For example, Campbell (1986) asked a sample of schoolgirls about their experience of fighting – all admitted to having been involved in a fight but only a few had been involved with interaction with the police over it. The majority of them rejected the statement 'I think fighting is only for the boys'.

Box and Hale (1983) concluded that the liberation movement *per se* had no direct effect, either on crimes of violence, or property offences; most of the increase in female convictions for violence seemed to be explained by changes in social labelling practices; that is, the public being more willing to report female offenders, the police to prosecute, and judges to convict. In this sense female liberation, may have had an indirect effect, as the behaviour of the public, police and justice personnel is influenced by their image of female crime and, if this has changed recently – because of portrayal in the media and publicised link between liberation and violent aggressive crimes – then what is believed as real, becomes real in its consequences. The relative increase in female conviction rates for violent offences is then a self fulfilling prophecy, rather than a reflection of any real change in female propensity to crime.

Who are the women who are taken into prison? A class-sensitive analysis tends to see them as marginalised (a sizable portion of women in British prisons are ethnic minorities many of whom were arrested for petty drug trafficking). The major factor accounting for the increase in property crime seems to be economic marginalisation. As women become economically worse off, largely through unemployment, and inadequate compensatory levels of welfare benefits, so they are less able and willing to resist the temptation to engage in property offences as a way of helping to shelter financial difficulties. Critics, such as Carlan, argue that we should look to increasing female marginalisation, brought on by the changing structure of British industry, and a government (headed for a considerable time by a woman) determined to restore the family with a full time, non-working mother, to find the causes for the reduction in the sex differentials of property offences.

The problematising of masculinity in post-modernism

To some extent this is a feature or consequence of the incorporation of women into the mainstream of late-modernity; how has this occurred? Early modernity involved the philosophical conception of equality and universality, at the same time as a social structural categorisation and differentiation operated at the level of class and gender within the western nation state, and ethnicity aided in separating out the 'other'. Two processes are at work to allow participation in late-modernity: (i) increased participation in the public sphere; (ii) changing forms of gender relations in the domestic sphere. Both processes are clearly influenced by technological changes with different patterns of 'skill' required in newer forms of production. The structures which we publicly proclaim, the so-called constitution of the society, are dependent upon the networks underlying them and which make them possible. The core of the domestic relation has been the conjugal one, in which men control women by virtue of being their spouses. This control is direct in that men had the right of disposition over the labour, the bodies and the children of women, a right existent in fact and law. In the early 19th century the combination of the right of men to freely direct the labour of conjugal partners as if they were chattels, and the severe constraints of the form and consequences of biological reproduction (little birth control, a high death rate in pregnancy and childbirth), positioned women in the most marginal and worst paying employment. Participation of women in the public sphere was extremely limited. Employment was as domestics (domestic servants, governesses, home teachers), participation in non-domestic production was either unskilled in factories or womanised (eg as a midwife, nurses), mostly under the direction of men (textiles, clothing, food, doctors).

The 20th century saw the breakdown of formal barriers to woman's participation. This involved the removal of legal barriers on female participation in the public sphere (voting, representation, equal pay for equal work, gender discrimination outlawed), and a greater freedom in domestic gender relations (specifically, divorce became easier, abortion became decriminalised, attempts were made to control domestic violence). Technological developments removed several so-called natural connections, for example, the advent of cheap and effective birth control (condoms, the pill) as well as advances in medicine destroyed the traditional linkage between sexuality, reproduction and death (about a fifth of all child-births in the 19th century resulted in death). While Giddens (1992) demonstrates that changes in the technology of birth control affect sexuality – creating what he terms a 'plastic sexuality', able to be a site of pleasure and meaning of and for itself – in turn enabling a democratisation of the domestic relations, the advent of post-industrialisation, and the rise in new technologies, have rendered obsolete the connection between physical power and labour. Even the women's movement can be seen as directly a factor of technological changes (Huber, 1976).

Feminists argue that partriarchy is maintained today through social arrangements indirectly securing men's interests, giving men market advantages before and above women, and hegemony in personal relations between the sexes. Male control is achieved through the process of social reproduction. There is still control of the means of material subsistence by men in families which is used to constrain women within domestic roles; the cultural representations of gender and role models emphasises a set of idealisations which are functionally and hierarchically differentiated; men practise covert forms of discrimination in public contexts; the incorporation of women into the systems of production and service industries has been into segmented labour markets with separate career structures. As MacKinnon and others have stressed, the specification of the job is usually as the male has previously done it, hence, if it is to be available to a woman, the woman must do it as the male does it; thus female careers have largely been structured in terms of male characteristics, without arrangements for interruptions for childbirth, and without provision for day-care facilities for children.

While men maintain a privileged position the socio-cultural movements of late modernity, however, in particular the feminist movement, are on such a scale as to constitute a social revolution: 'Feminism was, and has remained, the greatest and most decisive social revolution of modernity.' (Heller and Feher, 1988: 144) A social revolution is a process from within, a cultural transformation. Experiences which give rise and foundational support to a female culture, hitherto marginalised, cannot be contained within segregated bounds. The feminist claim to set out a right to articulate perspectives covering half of the world population compromises not just the language of modernity, but that of all other cultures. The culture of the anti-modern (as in fundamentalist religions are often not the neglect of the equality of feminine, but the denial of the feminine as human relegating it to the status of the merely natural).

Lengermann and Wallace summarised these developments as they impacted upon the US:

'A widely ranging increase in female participation in the labour force, to a rate of over 50% in 1980 and an estimated level of about 60% in 1990.

A movement of women into traditionally male occupations at both working and middle class levels. Much female labour force participation is in service sector/caring occupations but this is principally in the public arena rather than the domestic arena. (Internal labour market segmentation between managers and secretaries is the most resistant form of occupational segmentation.)

Women's increasing participation in formal political structures, through holding representative offices.

An overall increase in the extent of educational participation and attainment by women although some fields of higher education (science and engineering) remain resolutely masculine.

A trend towards reduced family size indicating an increased level of control by women over their own procreative capacities and reduced domestic chores.

A redistribution of domestic duties in the family. One form of this redistribution is the increasingly prevalent single-parent family in which a single adult carries out all domestic duties. Another is redistribution between the genders in dual-income households, although the redistribution of housework towards men is very limited.

Legislation affecting access to employment, relative rates of pay, and increased opportunity for men in divorce and child custody cases.

The removal of explicitly sexist content in educational materials, governmental and legislative documents, and the mass media.

The development of male liberation and masculine consciousness raising groups.' (1985: 195-231)

This has been interpreted by some commentators to amount to a crisis of masculinity:

'... many men feel themselves to be involved in some kind of change having to do with gender, with sexual identity, with what it is to be a man. The 'androgyny' literature of the late 1970s spoke to this in one way, the literature about the importance of fathering another... It seems clear enough that there have been recent changes in the constitution of masculinity in advanced capitalist countries, of at least two kinds: a deepening of tensions around relationships with women, and the crisis of a form of heterosexual masculinity that is increasingly felt to be obsolete.' (Carrigan et al 1985: 598)

Does this amount to a crisis in the hegemony of masculinity?

Are these changes social or structural in character or are there also changes in the differentiation of cultural meanings? In other words is the binary opposition masculine-feminine still rigid or is there a development of androgyny? Is there a coming together of masculine and feminine 'personality types' into an androgynous type? Or are masculine and feminine types or ideals of thought becoming freed from gender, ie from the relationship with a body, and available for anyone to use (identify with)?

The criminological fear is that the new woman will incorporate the worst of both worlds. Epitomised in recent films such as *Fatal Attraction* and *The Last Seduction,* she will use both the power of masculinity and the sexual power of the body, seduction means she will vivaciously possess the phallus. Is there a sea change? Or a series of sites of crisis, located in ex-working-class locations precipitated by unemployment, retraining which is into 'women's employment (computer operators, office administrators), failed marriages, sexual inadequacy, the rise of the gay movement, wayward teenage children?

We have indicated the post-modernist argument that consumption power, rather than location in the relations of production, determines status, therefore it should not matter whether you earn your money as a keyboard operator or a miner, the more the money and the style of goods purchased, the higher the status. It is not the body but the suit, or the Rolex, or the BMW. However, we are not supposing such totalisations. The crisis of masculinity may be part of the breakdown of the security of an opposition based on domination-submission, an opposition which is breached in the process of individualisation (in which gender is only one characteristic of the person) and emancipation. Gender identity is only one aspect of the tools of self-belief and self-expression, the advent of late- or post-modernisation opens up the possibilities of a playful choice ... but may also doom to a deep existential crisis those who do not have the resources, both personal and financial, to play the game. The progressive politics of personal relationships can turn into the resentment of the dispossessed – masculine rage. Domestic violence, used in the past as an assertion of the right to control, may be an expression of the desperate need to regain control of a self which is no longer in the terrain that it once was.

Questioning the post-modernist turn

Many feminists seem to welcome post-modernism. If there is doubt as to the permanence of structure, if the naturalist premise is finally bankrupt, if we see social identities as cultural products, then surely women will find the space to (re)constitute themselves freely?

But the sceptics ask, with what? What discursive resources can you be sure of if everything is deconstructable? Why should feminist positions be somehow privileged? Nancy Hartsock is suspicious of the timing of the post-modern condition and reads in it a conservative destabilising effect of woman's powers of articulation:

'Why is it, exactly at the moment when so many of us who have been silenced begin to demand the right to name ourselves, to act as subjects rather than as objects of history, that just then the concept of subjecthood becomes problematic? Just when we are forming our own theories about the world, uncertainty emerges about whether the world can be adequately theorised? Just when we are talking about the changes we want, ideas of progress and the possibility of 'meaningfully' organised human society become suspect?' (1987: 196)

Counter to this the role of a new range of theorising must work on three levels:

- The epistemological task of countering the appeals to common sense and tradition which are espoused to climb out of the void made more visible by the post-modern condition and deconstruction. We need work on the intellectual foundations of a new order of gender and participation, a new sensitivity to pleasure and pain.

- The practical tasks of (i) deconstructing the myths of past practices and images which constrain both women and men, as well as (ii) engage in a practical politics of policing priorities, refuge centres, victim support and so forth.

- To continue the process of modernist construction – to create new images of interaction and equality.

Can a criminological theory of rational conformity, which does not reduce femininity to passivity or over-control, be developed?

Let us first ask what is the fear of the new woman who is as a man? To what extent is it a fear of the possibility of the feminine? How does the feminine contrast with the legacy of De Sade; who is regarded as the father figure of modern pornography?

The Sadian heritage is simple. Down play at all times the role of women and their connection with birth and their capacity as mothers. As De Sade has her father inform Eugenie when demanding she wreak revenge upon her mother:

'Be unafraid, Eugenie, and adopt these same sentiments; they are natural: uniquely formed of our sires' blood, we owe absolutely nothing to our mothers. What, furthermore, did they do but co-operate in the act which our fathers, on the contrary, solicited? Thus, it was the father who desired our birth, whereas the mother merely consented thereto.' (De Sade, 1966: 207)

To become free women must reject the role of mother, must sow up the very bodily passages through which they came into the world. The loss of the mother is the first step in becoming autonomous.

Some modern writers have joined in this. Ascher (1979: 2 discussed in Brodribb, 1992) points out how De Beauvoir used the spirit of De Sade to argue that women would find authenticity in crime, in murder. The act of crime would be the source of genuine transcendence, woman would join in the acts of separateness, and other-than-joined-to-others, that males took for granted. Women would turn away from the experiences of immanence and the bloody and the dirty biological reality of their labouring and giving birth. They would cleanse their minds of the reality of morning sickness, or the weight of the pregnancy, of the linkage to another, of their necessity to place another before themselves. Such facility prevents the attainment of a self-directioness that promotes power.

> 'One becomes self-directive when one comes to regard the universe as one's own to control, to consider oneself to blame for its faults and to glory in its progress, to regard the entire earth as territory for one's domination.' (De Beauvoir, 1974: 793)

The safety of the reproductive function was interpreted by males as requiring women to keep to the camp. The male became the warrior and hunter, involved in a dance with the kill and the chance of death. For De Beauvoir:

> '... he proved dramatically that life is not the supreme value for man, but on the contrary that it should be made to serve ends more importantly than itself. The worst curse that was laid upon woman was that she should be excluded from these warlike forays. For it is not in giving life but in risking life that man is raised above the animal; that is why superiority has been accorded in humanity not to the sex that brings forth but to that which kills.' (1974: 72)

In return, Ascher argues, women have often thanked him. They have provided encouragement to kill and an appreciative audience. Sometimes they have asked the male to kill, at other times they have participated vicariously in male violence: never have women universally asked for a system of female values to be placed in opposition to male values.

Rational conformity?

Are there female values which can serve as a basis for a theory of rational conformity? Do women have a greater stake in general conformity, perhaps related to their collective experience of relative powerlessness?

In the work of the psychologist Carol Gilligan (1982), the conception of self and world revealed is one of relationship rather than domination. On the basis of comparing in-depth interviews between men and women, concerning moral dilemmas and views on life, Gilligan claims to find women's identity is defined in the context of relationships and judged by a standard of responsibility and care. One of her subjects describes being alone or unconnected as 'like the sound of one hand clapping ... there is something lacking' (1982: 160). In contrast, male self-descriptions, while speaking of attachments, were characterised by adjectives of separation:

> '[I]nvolvement with others [was] tied to a qualification of identity rather than to its realisation. Instead of attachment, individual achievement rivets male

imagination, and great ideas or distinctive activity defines the standard of self-assessment and success.' (Ibid: 163)

Gilligan claims that women *reason in a different voice being directed by an ethic of care and responsibility, as opposed to rational reasoning and separateness*. Are these poles total? What is the growth of a person and what is maturity? For Gilligan true maturity for both sexes would be to move away from the absolutes with which they are associated. That is, men must move away from the absolutes of rights, truth and fairness, to a realisation of differences between other and self, and a recognition that multiple truths exist. Similarly, women must move away from the absolute of care, and recognise a claim for equality and rights that transforms their understanding of relationships and their definition of care.

The American feminist Robin West argues that male legal theorists exhibit a specific form of reasoning, because they experience the world firstly and fundamentally as separate, autonomous individuals. The foundation of all traditional and critical masculine jurisprudence is a 'separation' thesis. By contrast, women:

> '... are not essentially, necessarily, inevitably, always, and forever separate from other human beings ... [but] ... are in some sense 'connected' to life and to other human beings during at least four recurrent and critical material experiences: the experience of pregnancy itself; the invasive and 'connecting' experience of heterosexual penetration, which may lead to pregnancy; the monthly experience of menstruation, which represents the potential for pregnancy; and the post-pregnancy experience of breast-feeding.' (West, 1988: 2-3)

Women reason out of a 'connectedness' which men cannot experience. This other experience of women provides the basis of an alternative to legal theory which through the presuppositions of the separation thesis has become 'essentially and irrevocably masculine'. (Ibid: 2)

Can we read a form of consciousness to women different from men which affects their rational calculation? In other words is there a rational reason for conformity? Consider again Adler's thesis that liberation was causing women to be more criminal. Her argument was backed up by the official criminal statistics on the sex ratio of black offenders in the US. Adler argued that this ratio was much smaller than for white offenders, in other words, there was a greater involvement of black woman in crime, since for Adler in a 'grimly sardonic sense the black female has been liberated for over a century'. Adler interpreted the position of black women in America, where they had often been the sole breadwinner in a family as one which had made them independent. 'Aggressiveness, toughness, and a certain street-wise self sufficiency were just a few of the characteristics necessary for the black woman to shepherd her beleaguered flock of children, siblings, and consorts through the wastelands of educational, social, financial and cultural deprivations.' (1975: 140-142) Adler's thesis was problematic. She assumes that woman's liberation has given women an intense competitive instinct; the liberated woman is more assertive, more aggressive, in short, more masculine. She also presumes that the woman's liberation movement has opened up structural opportunities for women to offend, since women now occupy many more roles in the workplace. Adler assumed that crime is a male activity, both appealing and prestigious. And she presumed that women would want to emulate men. She appears blind to any of the writings by black women expressing the subjectivity of their position.

By contrast, Ngaire Naffine combines the work of Carol Gilligan with insights gained from control theory, to construct an idea of a non-masculine woman demonstrating a high commitment to conventional relationships and conformity. For Ngaire Naffine:

'... the type of conforming woman who exemplifies the ethic of care may indeed be a stout character. She may believe in the equality of the sexes, she may be strong and assertive, but she may nevertheless take seriously her social duties. What appeared to Adler to be an obvious reaction to independence, women testing the criminal waters, becomes an irrational act to the woman who is conscious of her place in a network of social responsibilities.' (1987: 132)

Is it too bizarre to suggest that the early experiences and socialisation of girls, results not so much in passivity, but in a responsibility, partly based on an understanding that the collective experience of historical powerlessness helps constitute? What is the reality of the conforming woman? She may be a housewife and mother, who also juggles paid employment, and spends time looking after an ailing parent. This 'ideal type' woman may be entirely involved and engrossed in conventional life. She may be literally run off her feet. She may be subjected to a multiplicity of demands and expectations; but she may also be actively concerned about the effect of her behaviour on her loved ones, particularly her dependant children. Her experiences, both vicariously, and actually, in child birth and the nurturing of children, may provide her with a powerful attachment to the conventional order, since she knows only too well – in her vulnerability – of the consequences of the breakdown of the order. The injunction to responsibility, to be an upright citizen, is strong. This 'ideal type' is not suggesting an over-socialised, or over-controlled, person. Instead of passivity, unthinking compliance, or weak dependency, we have the rational understanding of social bonding. The law abiding woman is actually a powerful female persona. For Naffine:

'Law abiding women are not vapid, biddable creatures, clinging helplessly to conventional society. Instead, they are, to use Hirschi's description of conforming men, responsible, hard working, engrossed in conventional activities and people, and perfectly rational in their calculation not to place all this at risk by engaging in crime.' (1987:131)

What then of the future? It lies to be constructed. Is the future a mixture of the feminine and masculine? And what of our guiding metaphors of the building project? If modernist constructionism founded on the rigidity of suppressing the other (the woman, the black) lies undercut, then perhaps we should dream of a building founded on the mystery of difference and otherness. Undoubtably, it would not be a tower.

CHAPTER SEVENTEEN

CONTEMPORARY SOCIAL STRATIFICATION AND THE DEVELOPMENT OF THE UNDERCLASS

'At the end of the eighteenth century, people dreamed of a society without crime. And then the dream evaporated. Crime was too useful for them to dream of anything as crazy – or ultimately as dangerous – as a society without crime. No crime means no police. What makes the presence and control of the police tolerable for the population, if not fear of the criminal? This institution of the police, which is so recent and so oppressive, is only justified by that fear. If we accept the presence in our midst of these uniformed men, who have the exclusive right to carry arms, who demand our papers, who come and prowl on our doorsteps, how would any of this be possible if there were no criminals? And if there weren't articles every day in the newspapers telling us how numerous and dangerous our criminals are?' (Michel Foucault, 1980: 7)

The arrival of the underclass

By the late 1970s conservative American writings were identifying a problematic stratum of American society which was claimed to be a product of a misguided welfare system that had 'created a new caste of Americans – perhaps as much as one-tenth of this nation – a caste of people free from basic wants but almost totally dependant upon the state, with little hope of breaking free' (Anderson, 1979: 56).

The term first entered public prominence at the hands of Ken Auletta, a New York journalist, in 1982. He argued that while most people officially classified as poor in America, overcome poverty after a generation or two, a sizeable number (perhaps 9 million) do not assimilate. Auletta mixed together a range of 'losers' into a loose category of an underclass which constituted 'both America's peril and shame' (1982: xvi -xviii). The reviews were mixed, for example, Fox:

'The underclass, or synonyms for it, has a long history as a useful abstraction. The word caricatures a segment of humanity and provides a license to exempt them ... from the same standards and opportunities as the rest of us ... Auletta speaks for numerous relatively prosperous Americans who seem to need an underclass. Racists and conservatives need one to explain the inadequacies of affirmative action. Advocates of social scientism – of variations on the venerable theme of a culture of poverty – need one to explain the genealogy of intergenerational misery ... proponents of an underclass have wanted us to believe that American society was endangered by unassimilable creatures who suffered defects in both their heredity and their environment.' (1982: 62)

An ambiguity as to who comprises the 'underclass' has continued in the more scholarly literature which took up this term. Whilst in the US it has come to refer predominately to the black inner-city population concentrated in areas of extreme deprivation and virtual social apartheid the term 'underclass' has more universally become popularised as a loose categorisation containing those individuals who commit most of the traditional street crime and provide the cause of contemporary urban riots; most frequently in analysis in the US (Glasgow, 1981; Auletta, 1982; Murray 1984; Lemann, 1986; Wilson, 1987; Katz, 1989; the media coverage of the Los Angeles riots of 1992), and applied to Britain (Murray, 1990, 1994; and from the left: Dahrendorf 1985, 1987; Pahl 1988; Fields, 1989; Saunders 1990; Mann, 1990, but note arguments for rejecting the term in Macnicol 1987, 1990; Gallie, 1988; Dean and Taylor-Gooby, 1992) and applied in Japan (Schoenberger, 1990), while trends in underclass development have been argued in New Zealand and Australia.

Although the term has entered into widespread use there is debate as to whether it is so value laden as to be unusable.[1] As two writers critical of the term have stated:

> 'Perhaps the really dangerous class is not the underclass but those who have propagated the underclass concept ... Because it is so ill-defined and sloppy the underclass can mean whatever the user intends it to mean.' (Bagguley and Mann, 1992: 118)

Three reasonably coherent conceptual schemes, each with specific political and social flavours have, however, developed:

- a tradition which looks for discernable features either of the constitution of the members (such as low IQ) or immediate culture (a culture of poverty tradition);

- a social structural argument cast in terms of social and spatial processes of post-industrialisation or post-modernism which links the development of the underclass to changes in employment opportunity and skills level; and

- a class and power analysis which sees the underclass as partially, at least, cased by conservative retrenchment of welfare provisions in a time of economic recession and a change in attitudes of the well-off working class to the less fortunate.

---

1   A note on sociological definition: the traditional definition of class stemming from the work of Marx and Weber has been by differential location in the system of production. Using this perspective Runciman argues:

> 'The term must be understood to stand not for a group or category of workers systematically disadvantaged within the labour market ... but for those members of British society whose roles place them more or less permanently at the economic level where benefits are paid by the state to those unable to participate in the labour market at all.' (1990: 388)

Thus 'underclass' denotes those neither engaged in, nor able to participate in gainful productive work (officially at least, as Murray and others argue some may be engaged in the so-called grey or black economy). Newer forms of identifying social stratification attempt differentiation in terms of consumption cleavages, or life chances. These methods have little difficulty in applying the term 'underclass' to the very poor, irrespective of whether they are in the labour market and enjoy a minimal set of consumption opportunities, social prestige, and life chances.

1 The radical right's tradition of constitutional or cultural features aided by mistaken social policy as explaining the emergence of the underclass

Perhaps most vocal of the contributions to the underclass debate is the set of conservative, or radical right, anti-welfare writings which have been loosely based upon the culture of poverty tradition and a recently renewed interest in constitutional factors. In the US this revitalises discussions held in the 1960s on race, the causes and implications of urban poverty that resulted from the Moynihan report (which had found black families trapped in a 'tangle of pathology'), and on Oscar Lewis's writings on the culture of poverty. The rediscovery of urban poverty and inner city decline by radical right philosophy in the late 1970s and 1980s was, however, rooted in both a social and political context (Charles Atherton, 1989). It provided (i) a critique of the cost that middle class taxpayers were bearing in financing social welfare measures; (ii) a claim that welfare states are both ineffectual and counterproductive and, (iii) as Charles Murray (1984) argued in *Losing Ground*, a radical abolitionist stance in which the entire federal welfare system, Aid to Families with Dependent Children (AFDC), Medicaid, Food Stamps, and unemployment insurance should be abolished because it is counter-productive and inimical to the social good. Welfare undermines the sources of social solidarity. Berger and Neuhaus (1977) argued that the provision of welfare is deemed to destroy 'mediating structures' or 'those institutions standing between the individual in his private life and the large institutions of public life'. Government had marginalised religion, taken traditional responsibilities from neighbourhoods, the family no longer had control over the education of their children, and voluntary social service had been destroyed by professional bureaucracy. Public policy should change to defend, rather than undercut such structures (1977: 2-6) In the US, Murray has been the most prominent and clear cut writer from the right on the underclass, consistently arguing that it is the task of small-scale voluntary associations to build communities, and that 'much of what central government must do first of all is to leave people alone' (1988: 297).

Radical right advocates argue that the relatively high tax rates of advanced welfare states also reduce profit margins and thus impede entrepreneurial incentives to invest and produce. Eventually, the demand of welfare recipients for more benefits outstrips the capacity of a market economy to provide these benefits without losing its competitive edge. As a *Times* reporter claimed:

'At its present levels, the welfare apparatus has simply become too expensive for most governments, and their taxpayers. Across Europe, social security systems are grappling with fiscal crisis, in part because ponderous, costly bureaucracies have mushroomed to administer a vast array of programs that sometimes neglect the essential to serve up what is merely desirable. Bloated beyond its architects' intent, welfarism is threatening bankruptcy in some countries.' (Painton and Malkin, 1981: 32)

In *Losing Ground*, Murray (1984) identified the underclass by a type of behaviour among sections of the poor; specifically welfare dependency and petty crime. This behaviour was not some perverse irrationality, but a rational reaction to the changed environment provided in advanced welfare states; individuals simply reacted to the unintended incentives provided by the social policy of welfare to those remaining poor. As Murray put it:

'A government's social policy helps set the rules of the game, the stakes, the risks, the pay offs, the trade offs, and the strategies for making a living, raising a family, having fun, defining what 'winning' and 'success' mean .... The most compelling explanation for the marked shift in the fortunes of the poor is that they continued to respond, as they always had, to the world as they found it, but that we – meaning the not-poor and un-disadvantaged – had changed the rules of their world ... The first effect of the new rules was to make it profitable for the poor to behave in the short term in ways which were destructive in the long term. Their second effect was to mask these long term losses to subsidise irretrievable mistakes.' (1984: 9)

Although some commentators claim it is relatively easy to demonstrate that writings of the right on the underclass neglect the long and contested history of this concept (Macnicol, 1987). Murray's work deliberately harps back in its analysis to the grand tradition of interested observers who reject the specific language of social theory in order to convey the human reality of social processes. Murray locates himself within the images and warnings which Alexis de Tocqueville had given in his *Memoir on Pauperism* written in 1835 after a visit to England (Drescher, 1968). De Tocqueville had described England as the 'eden of modern civilisation' finding a multitude of sights to make 'the tourists heart leap'. Paradoxically he argued that 'one-sixth of the inhabitants of this flourishing Kingdom live at the expense of public charity'. Furthermore, while England displayed a greater concern for the problem of poverty than any other country in Europe, the relative wealth of England actually caused a perception of poverty where the poor were actually relatively well-off.

Moreover, whilst it was a 'moving and elevating sight to observe England continually examining itself, probing its wounds, and undertaking to cure them', its effort to use the surplus of its wealthy to relieve the misery of the poor was doomed to create unfortunate effects. By ignoring a basic fact of human nature – that man had a 'natural passion for idleness' – guaranteeing the population a means of subsistence as a legal right relieved the poor of the obligation to work. Furthermore, the fact of receiving poor relief via a public institution, and as a result of legal categorisation, had the effect of publicly acknowledging the individual recipient's inferiority. This right, as opposed to private charity, publicised and legalised the inferiority of whole groups. It amounted to institutional degradation. By comparison individual charity was both more efficient and more humane: 'it devotes itself to the greatest miseries, it seeks out misfortune without publicity and it silently and spontaneously repairs the damage'. Public measures were only suitable for certain categories, such as the relief of infants and the aged, the sick and the insane, or as a spontaneous, temporary measure in times of disaster. Granting a legal right, however was a recipe for future doom.

In carrying on this tradition, much of the appeal of the radical right's analysis is the fact that their writing deliberately engages and draws upon 'common sense' perceptions of the current state of society; as his critics point out Murray's definition of underclass seems to be based upon 'innuendos, assertions and anecdotes.' (Walker, 1990)

But these small-scale human narratives demonstrate to Murray that underclass refers, not to a degree, but rather a type of poverty which 'normal' citizens can understand and react to.

> 'I grew up knowing what the underclass was; we just didn't call it that in those days. In the small Iowa town where I lived, I was taught by my middle class parents that there were two kinds of poor people. One class of poor people was never even called "poor". I came to understand that they simply lived on low incomes, as my own parents had done when they were young. There was another set of poor people, just a handful of them. These poor people didn't just lack money. They were defined by their behaviour. Their homes were littered and unkept. The men in the family were unable to hold a job for more than a few weeks at a time. Drunkenness was common. The children grew up ill-schooled and ill-behaved and contributed a disproportionate share of the local juvenile delinquents. British observers of the 19th century knew these people. To Henry Mayhew ... they were the "dishonest poor".' (1990: 1)

Here again, we are consciously returned to notions of the 'undeserving poor' of Victorian writers, which is an image which finds easy support in letters and journalistic accounts in the popular press (Murray's article first appeared in the *Sunday Times* magazine 26 November 1989, and the *Sunday Times* has subsequently run special features on the underclass. See the coverage of the Los Angeles Riots, May, 1992; and 'Wedded to Welfare' 11 July 1993, as well as articles contributed by Murray on his return to Britain in May 1994).

In his first analysis of the UK, Murray (1990) claimed a small, but growing, underclass by quoting rates of illegitimacy, violent crime and the drop-out rate from the labour force. Such analysis can in part be dismissed as a product of the ecological fallacy whereby the attributes of a shared space are believed to imply shared attributes among individuals occupying that space. Moreover, Murray's methodology is scientifically suspect. His use of illegitimacy, for example, as a criterion for measuring the underclass has come under considerable criticism. Illegitimacy is defined as a child being without two parents and legally without a father from birth and is more concentrated amongst the lower social classes than the rest of society. For Murray a jointly registered birth signals a stable relationship. The decline of joint registration is concentrated in the lower social classes and points to a growing number of children being raised in one parent families; predominantly without a father present. This Murray claims is a predictive factor of future crime. Even if economic circumstances are similar,

Murray argues, the children of single mothers do much worse than those of two parent families and will develop a reliance upon welfare. Others are not so convinced. In responding to his article, Joan Brown criticised Murray's use of misleading statistics. She states that single mothers tend to spend shorter periods on benefit than divorced or widowed mothers and often marry and introduce a new father into households quicker than other groups, thus escaping welfare. Habitual criminals are, in Murray's terms, classic members of the underclass. They are invariably young because: 'As males get older, they tend to become more civilised.' This is a key empirical fact which other writers of the right in American criminology (specifically, Gottfredson and Hirschi, 1990) also rely upon. Murray states that while the number of young male teenagers has decreased in the 1980s, violent crime has increased – the implication is clear, violence is principally concentrated in a subsection of youth and adults, a section which escapes the civilising tendencies of proper socialisation and which is increasing and actually being encouraged by misguided welfare provisions.

While aware of increasing unemployment Murray argues that Britain's unemployment figures include an unknown but probably considerable number of people who manage to qualify for benefit, even if, in reality, very few job opportunities would tempt them back to work. To his critics the social pathologies of the members of Murray's underclass are based upon pure speculation or personal prejudices: while he claims he does not wish to attribute blame the implications of his work appear to be that the underclass are to blame for their responses to welfare and the rest of society need no longer feel any responsibility towards the poor (Walker, 1990).

Whilst Murray is keen to find common ground in any opponent who will use the notion of underclass, he disputes writers, such as Frank Fields, claims that inequality has increased during the last decade under the free market economics of Thatcher and Reagan. He claims that the relevant policies have changed very little under Thatcher declaring 'let us think instead in more common-sense terms'. For Murray the root cause of the underclass is that social policy has altered how young people make sense of the world. For example, the social stigma and severe economic hardships which single parent mothers faced before the 1960s have, according to Murray, been swept away. Young women want to have babies (partly to enjoy the unquestioned love of another) and the benefit system allows them to do so without dire consequences. Moreover, solo parents are now in a better position to find housing since they will move onto the priority list for Local Authority accommodation. It must, however, surely be accepted that for a single mother on benefit, economic hardship is not a thing of the past, and there still remains for many a social stigma attached to illegitimacy.

Murray goes on to postulate that crime has become safer through (i) low clear-up rates, (ii) the decreasing likelihood, even if caught, of being convicted, (iii) less severe penalties coupled with a reluctance by courts to impose prison sentences. The implications for criminology are clear: 'Swiftness, certainty, consistency and comparative severity of penalties' are needed.

For Murray all these social problems interconnect with one another. In order to tackle the issue of the rise in violent crime, other social issues need to be addressed. Murray suggests a radical decentralisation and localisation of social control operations. He argues for the need for self-government by local communities with control over criminal justice, education, housing and benefit systems. They should be free to create their own values and those who do not hold to these localised community values should be allowed to move out of that particular area. In our discussion of the city, however, while we have recognised the need for localisation we have stressed that so much of the reality of the city is determined by outside economic factors. Locality has also been shown in the past to be harsh and unjust: punishing and excluding those judged deviant. Murray's solution may well replace the tyranny of the welfare state by a far fiercer tyranny of various unfettered corporate or neighbourhood welfare states.

To those who claim radical left intellectual status, such as Bagguley and Mann, 'the underclass is the ideology of the upper class' (1991: 125). For these writers, the concept of the underclass is part of a fundamentally ideological socio-political conception of contemporary social processes, and a vital rhetorical device for an attack upon welfare. The readings of the radical right distort the complexity of contemporary social structure in the name of popular individualism.

The three ideologies of (a) economic individualism, (b) cultural traditionalism, and (c) authoritarian populism are at the centre of the radical right's world view. The central ingredients of the case against the welfare state are the issues of responsibility, efficiency, freedom, and prosperity. The movement contends that the welfare state is a governmental institution, managed by a liberal or socialist elite, which has weakened traditional values of hard work, responsibility and sobriety, created a large and inefficient bureaucratic state welfare apparatus, intruded excessively into the private lives of citizens, diminished choice and individual preferences, and harmed economic productivity and growth.

The radical right's critique of the welfare state is decidedly populist and sectarian. Government welfare programmes are blamed for a breakdown in mutual obligations between and within groups, a lack of attention to efficiencies in the way programmes are operated and benefits awarded, the induced dependency of beneficiaries on programmes, and the growth of the welfare industry and its special interest groups, particularly professional associations. Radical right thinkers believe that the welfare state erodes individual responsibility and initiative. Rather than alleviate destitution, welfare state programmes induce dependency and the proliferation of a culture of poverty. By fostering 'dependence' on welfare, beneficiaries of the social services need not work hard, save, or act in a responsible manner. The radical right sees the underclass in terms of crime and ungovernability, of promiscuous self-indulgence, of a culture in which rational self-control is lacking, and explains its arrival as a consequence of the unconditional social programmes offered by the welfare state which do not obligate beneficiaries to behave conventionally in order to receive benefits. To the right, the underclass is the ironical result of the projects of modernity designed to attain social solidarity in modern western industrial states (Murray, 1984, 1989, 1994).

This attack is also linked to wider assaults on the welfare state seen as economically detrimental to a market economy since it uses up taxes, monies needed by the private sector for capitalisation. At the same time as the right talk of the underclass development, supply-side economic discourse justifies for the well off, middle and employed working class, substantial reductions in their direct payment tax obligations (although indirect taxation may well increase squeezing the less well off the hardest) which cuts the amount of transfer payments members of the 'underclass' are entitled to.

Radical right advocates argue that the present level of tax transfer payments reduce profit margins and entrepreneurial incentives. Welfare demands become self-perpetuating destroying the possibility of a competitive edge to welfare states. The operation of a welfare state, moreover, demands an increasing intrusion of the state into private life, and becomes, in effect a harbinger of totalitarianism: paternalistic and anti-libertarian. This argument maintains that any state which has the power to shift resources from one group to another exercises a form of economic tyranny. Instead of the social-democratic-liberal approach which emphasises the rights of the poor, the radical right focuses on the rights of those coerced into subsidising the poor. The welfare state has, furthermore, in their view, lost sight of basic social values (for America – see Gilder, 1981). According to these critics, the welfare state has failed to reinforce the work ethic; the goal of self-sufficiency, self-support, and self-initiative; the importance of intact families (Mead, 1985); the fiscal responsibility of parent to child; and the notion of reciprocity – the belief that recipients have a social obligation to perform in return for receiving assistance. The new right's solution, therefore, is to replace dysfunctional (liberal) values with functional (conservative) values: delayed gratification, work and saving; commitment to family and to the next generation; education and training; self-improvement and self-control; and the rejection of crime, drugs, and casual sex (Institute for Cultural Conservatism, 1987: 83).

The radical right believes that the family is the basis of correct socialisation and the focus of welfare functions. These functions can only be preserved if the family is defended and strengthened as the basic institution in Western society. In the US the Institute for Cultural Conservatism (1987) laid out a programme for defending family life. Firstly, the traditional nuclear family must be restored and one parent, the mother, should remain in the home permanently to raise children. Secondly, the incidence of divorce, out-of-wedlock pregnancy, abortion, and pre-marital sex must be reduced; these as part of a crisis in moral standards are identified as a major cause of social decline in the western industrial nations. Thirdly, it is necessary to reinstate certain values on which stable families depend, including responsibilities to and for offspring, disapproval of extra-marital sex, and reverence for life, both before and after birth. The legal system can play an important role by defending the legal control of parents and in presuming the reasonableness of parental action. Legislative, administrative and judicial actions which work to undermine the traditional family, must be avoided, and economic conditions developed to enable stable nuclear families to be self-sufficient. In short the government should not be indifferent to the form of family existence, but rather actively support and recreate the traditional form of the immediate, nuclear family. If a particular nuclear family is unable to be self-sufficient, members of the extended family, friends and neighbours should be the preferred sources of assistance. Often such support is 'informal', a classic example being the American custom of community barn raising. The supposed advantage of such activities is that they reinforce existing social ties and make assistance a highly personal affair. Whereas, however, to the needy, immediately known to neighbours, support is prudently offered, to the non-conformist or one who is foreign, the stranger, there is little rationale for providing aid.

The radical right's image of the future of civil society

Murray (1994) later argued a radical split was developing in Britain between 'new Victorians':

- educated and working in professional occupations;
- incomes above the level at which considerations of tax or benefit changes determine whether they have children;
- less mesmerised by careers than in the past; more concerned about children and community;
- free sexual expression less of a priority;
- revived interest in religion and spiritual matters;
- renewed concern for concepts such as fidelity, courage, loyalty, self-restraint and moderation;
- less inclined to divorce.

  The new Victorians were opposed by a 'new rabble':

- low-skilled working class, poorly educated;
- single-parent families are the norm;
- largely dependent on welfare and the black economy;
- high levels of criminality, child neglect and abuse, and drug use;
- impervious to social welfare policies designed to change their behaviour;
- will not enter legitimate labour force when times are good, and will recruit more working class people when times are bad;
- children attend school irregularly and pose discipline problems;
- large and lucrative market for violent and pornographic films, television and music.

For Murray, given current welfare conditions: 'In the low skilled, working class, marriage makes no sense'. However, widespread illegitimacy is bad for children and catastrophic for social organisation. Its increase ensures a deterioration of lower-class culture because the next generation will know no other way to live. Young males are:

' "essentially barbarians" who are civilised by marriage. That image has become all too literal in the american inner city, where male teenage behaviour is often a caricature of the barbarian male: retaliate against anyone who shows you the slightest disrespect ("disses" you). Sleep with and impregnate as many girls as possible. Regard violence as a sign of strength. To worry about tomorrow is weakness. To die young is glorious. What makes these attitudes so disturbing is not that they describe behaviour, but that inner-city boys articulate them as principles. They are explicitly the code they live by.' (1994: 12)

Murray is clear: 'under the scenario I have painted, British Civility is doomed.' Better employment prospects will not stem the changes, the only solution is to phase out benefits for unmarried women altogether:

'The welfare of society requires that women actively avoid getting pregnant if they have no husband, and that women once again demand marriage from a man who would have them bear a child. The only way the active avoidance and the demands are going to occur is if the childbearing entails economic penalties for a single women ... Babies need fathers. Society needs fathers ... The stake is the survival of free institutions and a civil society.' (Ibid: 13)

It is only through marriage that members of the underclass could learn the responsibilities which fully socialise them into the civilised state. Without responsible fathers as role models, personal responsibility cannot be properly learnt.

2 The social democratic thesis of the underclass as a consequence of post-industrialisation

This position concerns the role of structural changes, in particular economic changes with regard to lowering employment opportunities, and the lack of interventionist government policy to cope with this. From this perspective, the underclass is a recent phenomenon which is caused by transformation into a post-industrial society, and made worse by a lack of both understanding and coherent government policies to deal with these transformations.

In the US it is associated with the work of William Wilson, predominately in his *The Truly Disadvantaged* (1987). To Wilson the main cause for the formation of the underclass was fundamental changes in the economy, which resulted in prolonged joblessness in certain segments of the lower class, particularly the black population. These economic changes had a spatial structuring effect on the city resultant from a diminishing of the traditional manufacturing sector, the development of higher skilled employment opportunities, and the shift of employment from the inner cities to the suburbs. Blacks living in the inner city were disproportionately affected by the contraction of unskilled, blue-collar work, and lived too far from the suburbs to compete for the jobs being created there. The middle class, black residents who could compete for the new jobs left the inner city neighbourhoods, thus removing an important social buffer which in the past had prevented black unemployment from leading to an underclass. With the removal of the black, middle class, social institutions such as the church, schools, stores and recreational facilities found it difficult to survive, and with the disappearance of basic role models went the idea 'that education is meaningful, that steady employment is a viable alternative to welfare, and that family stability is the norm, not the exception' (1987: 56). With the movement out of the inner city of the black, middle classes, the social milieu became progressively more demoralising, with chronic joblessness, welfare dependency, female-headed families, crime and drugs becoming accepted as 'a way of life'; as this way of life becomes established an underclass is created (Ibid: 57).

Wilson's account is distinguished from the culture of poverty accounts, in that, while he does not deny the real effects of a set of cultural attitudes he, nevertheless, does not claim individuals come to constitute an underclass because of their prior possession of dysfunctional values, such as laziness or an inability to delay gratification. These traits are, rather, the result of the personal effects of economic dislocation and social isolation. Social isolation is structurally determined; it does, however, create localised perceptions and beliefs, local narratives which are criminogenic. But Wilson denies that these attitudes lead the underclass to be self-perpetuating as conservative theorists appear to claim. If proper policies and real opportunities are created these attitudes can be turned around:

'... unlike the concept of the culture of poverty, social isolation does not postulate that ghetto-specific practices become internalised, take on a life of their own, and therefore continue to influence behaviour even if opportunities for mobility improve. Rather, it suggests that reducing structural inequality would not only decrease the frequency of these practices; it would also make their transmission by precept less efficient ' (Wilson, 1990: 186)

While both Wilson (1987, 1990, 1991) and Kasarda (1990) argue a new 'disorganised' ghetto of an underclass has superceded the relatively organised poor areas, in his 1991 Presidential Address to the American Sociological Association, Wilson argued that the term underclass was so overladen with moral overtones that the phrase 'ghetto poor' should be preferred. This group is largely the result of a mismatch between the social location of labour and demand, and effective social policies can have a huge impact. For Wilson, racially constructed divisions or class are not so important in the contemporary labour market which is skills driven; the social structure will take up candidates of any race if they possess the skills. Racial and structural disadvantage, however, may be responsible for de-skilling or hampering the attainment of skills which the labour market requires. Radical policies of retraining and employment placement could begin the ascent out of ghettoisation.

The task, however, is huge. Hacker (1987 following points drawn from Feldman 1993: 247-50) provided a dramatic summary of the scale of the social changes and reality of social isolation and impacted deprivation. By the mid 1980s:

- More than 60% of black infants are born out of wedlock. Almost as many black families are headed by women. A majority of black children live with their mothers (in absent-father households). These figures are three to five times those for white Americans and three times those for blacks of only one generation earlier. In previous generations most black households had been headed by two parents.

- There are huge black/white differences in youthful sexual activity, pregnancies and births, even when education and income are controlled: 75% of black females begin sexual activity before 18 as compared to 50% of whites. There is also a difference in the use of contraception (significantly less among sexually active black girls than their white counterparts). As a result 40% of black girls have become pregnant by the age of 18, as against 20% of whites. This 2:1 disparity becomes 4:1 for births to unmarried girls aged 15-19. By 18, one in every four unmarried black women is a mother, and this increases to 40% by the early 20s. Almost all unmarried black (and white) mothers aged 15-19 keep and raise their babies. The reasons are diverse but religious prohibitions may play a large part. If young, black, American women used abortion to a similar extent to their Japanese or Russian counterparts, the teenage birth ratio would be considerably lower. The outcome of all this is that over half of all black women who have had families have never been married. The relative proportion for white women is only one-seventh.

- The fastest growing group is the three-generation household (a mother, often teenaged, with one or more children, sharing a small crowded apartment with her own mother, a grandparent in her thirties). The extended family, which provides a wider base of support, is less evident than in the past. Between 1970 and 1987 black, multi-generational households increased threefold. Most of these young mothers dropped out of school to bear and care for their babies. Fathers, often equally young, drop by from time to time.

- All of the above applies to over one half of young, black, women, half of whom in turn had no wish for early and unmarried motherhood. The behaviour of young, black men is a key factor. Only 39% of black men aged 25-34 are married and live with their wives as compared with 62% of whites. (And at least 20% of this age group is missed by census takers, implying a lack of settled jobs, even settled addresses. Of those black men the census reaches, less than half have full-time jobs.)

- In 1986, approximately the same number of white and black single mothers were below the poverty line (about 1.3 million in each case). But blacks form only 12% of the population. And there are differences between the two impoverished groups: whereas of the white mothers, 46% had only one child, 71% of the blacks had two or more. And twice as many white as black mothers received support payments (from fathers).

- Overall, white and black poverty groups seem two distinct populations. More than two-thirds of families among the black poor are headed by women, as against one third of whites. And lower-income whites are more likely than not to be elderly couples and to live in non-metropolitan areas.

- In 1954, over 75% of black men had full-time jobs. By 1986, this was true of only 40%. Many jobs formerly held by black men are now the province of black women. More black women are employed than are black men, and more finish school – they hold two-thirds of all the professional-level jobs occupied by blacks (the comparable figure among whites is 48%). If black women can avoid early motherhood, they are much more likely than black men to finish high school with the literacy and good diction employers expect.

For black males raised in segregated neighbourhoods, as many are, prowess in the streets counts for more than anything else, and there is a disdain for jobs that pay only 'chump change', They see themselves as native-born Americans: parking cars and washing-up in restaurants are thought suitable for immigrant Hispanics and Asians – not for blacks.

- The respective graphs for family income (in 1986) differ markedly: black families form a pyramid with a majority receiving under $20,000; that for whites is more like a Greek cross, with families on $35,000 outnumbering those on less than $20,000. Although only 10% of white families had less than $10,000 per year, this was true for 30% of blacks. Moreover, this poorest group tended to consist of single mothers among blacks, but elderly couples among whites.

- The majority of blacks still live in all black neighbourhoods as opposed to integrated ones (over 90% in Chicago, 75% in New York). Even the newest minority groups are less segregated. In one poll only 12% of blacks preferred segregation, as against 86% whose preference was for a more equal mix. In response to black entry into a formerly all white area, whites stay and new ones even enter as long as the black population is below 8% of the total. But when it reaches 20%, at least one-quarter of the whites leave and no new ones enter. This phenomenon of white flight leaves the neighbourhood all black or nearly so. Equally important is the departure of better-off blacks to new locations. Those left behind lack role models of steady employment and family stability.

The conservative reaction to these statistics is to blame the state for providing policies which aid such a social transformation, instead we should return the task of socialisation (and hence the fight against criminality) to stable families. Gottfredson and Hirschi hinted that the high crime rate of the black, American citizens could largely flow from faulty child rearing practices. Given that their theory argues the origins of criminality of low self-control are found in the first six or eight years of life, during which time the child remains under the control and supervision of the family or a familial institution,they provide the central image of 'responsible adults committed to the training and welfare of the child' (1990: 273). In looking for an explanation the criminologist 'should focus on differential child-rearing practices and abandon the fruitless effort to ascribe such differences to culture or strain' (Ibid: 153). Thus we are led away from a truly general theory of crime into a localisation of the self – the politics of individualism lead us away from the need for the attempt to provide a social structural theory on underclass development. We cannot doubt that the concentration of contemporary black child-rearing (ie since the 1960s) in the underclass phenomenon implies a sharply reduced capacity for effective child-training; our related factors do not relate to ethnicity as such, but to their location in a social stratification with both relative and absolute deprivation, as well as geographical segregation. Teenage parenthood is most pronounced in segregated settings, in which schools, housing and acquaintances are almost entirely within one's own race. The American underclass is a separated condition:

> 'Being black and poor is a very different condition from being white and poor ... white youths across the country from inner Boston to rural Arkansas commit crimes, drop out of school and become parents in their teens ... in most cases, however, those who do so are not typical of their areas or neighbourhoods, which tend to be solidly working-class.. few white districts are predominantly poor in the way so many black sectors are ... It is social and cultural isolation – a climate whites never really know – which more than any other single force encourages the early siring and bearing of children without thought for the future.' (Hacker, 1987: 33)

While the conditions of such obvious social apartheid do not exist in Britain a somewhat similar warning of dire future conditions, unless concerted social policy is not effectual, is found in the works of Ralf Dahrendorf (1985, 1987) and Frank Fields (1989).

For Dahrendorf, instead of the 'immiseration' of the working class and their greater and greater exploitation which Marx predicted, divisive class conflict was transformed into progressive activity via the 'institutionalisation of the class conflict' which centred around the meaning of citizenship. The development of 19th and 20th century western societies witness a change in the political status of individuals from subjects to citizens. Citizenship has come to mean the possession of legal rights, choice, participation, a decent income and mobility (both geographically and socially). In advancing industrial societies both the opportunities and the social risks involved in mobility have expanded to an unheard-of measure. The expansion of opportunities changes the picture of social existence for much of the working class, and for many of them it leads to entry into a newly enlarged middle class.

Via the process of the institutionalisation or democratisation of the class struggle, social changes developed which gave rise to a new correlation of citizenship and social class. The result is the emergence of a large category of democratic citizens, who may describe themselves as middle class, and who benefit from the system. Thus a category of two-thirds, possibly three-quarters, of all citizens of modern free societies have a common interest in the maintenance of political institutions which guarantee economic growth and social peace. Their divergent interests are relatively minor and, when subjected to a class analysis, in large part the majority is one class with all the internal distinctions and differences which have always been characteristic of classes – it is the majority class.

Those who are left out are implicated in the crisis of the welfare state or, as Dahrendorf calls it, 'the social state'. Drawing on Frank Fields analysis of 'groups in poverty', Dahrendorf sees these as the unemployed, the old, the low paid, single-parent families, sick and disabled people, single women with aged dependents, and poor people in institutions. They have little in common except that most are dependent upon transfer payments. They are the most vulnerable to curbs in public expenditure and public transportation, or to rises in value added taxes and the cost of housing. They are those least able to defend themselves as the state reduces its benefits.

Dahrendorf recognises a new boundary 'between the majority class and those who are being defined out of the edifice of citizenship' (Ibid: 98).

Economically the situation is different from any previous class relationship in that this new class is not in a relationship of exploitation with a superior class, it does not constitute a reserve pool of labour. The Marxist class analysis proposed classes which are locked into each other, and thus are needed for the long term survival of each other. The concomitant result was, that when economic recovery took place, it would without question bring large numbers of the unemployed back into the labour force. Conversely:

> '... today, this is no longer the case. The majority class can live perfectly well, including new cars every three or four years, holidays in Spain, annual real increases in wages and salaries, and relaxed debates about where the cuts in social expenditure should fall, without unemployment ever falling much below 10 per cent. There are those who are in and those who are out, and those who are out are not needed.' (Ibid: 102)

The tradition, which Dahrendorf writes owes much of its recent sociological weight to the analysis of T H Marshall (1977) on *citizenship* and *social class*, began in the 1950s. In effect Marshall claimed that the welfare state developed as the solution of the tension between capitalism and democracy. Marshall positioned the modernist development of post-war Britain in a narrative of class and citizen rights developments. Whereas traditional and pre-industrial societies sustained clearly differentiated structures, modern industrial societies required a freer social structure to facilitate a free market. To maintain the allegiance of the population equal and common legal rights had to be granted similar to those contained in the American Bill of Rights. These freedoms from arbitrary state power distinguished citizens from subjects. While early liberalism sustained a universe of what philosophers call negative freedoms, in its 19th century form it developed a normative theory of individual freedom which lead to actual social practices. Positive freedoms, for example, the winning of adult suffrage, brought another set of demands, namely that such suffrage has real effect and political institutions function openly. Marshall interpreted the process of change embodied in the legislation passed in Britain in the period 1944-1948, as creating a whole set of social rights and obligations. These acts sought to give citizens the right to a basic standard of education, health, food and shelter, adding positive freedoms to the philosophical and political freedoms won earlier. The crucial consideration is that these freedoms are interdependent. The capacity to benefit from the absence of arbitrary state power depends upon citizens possessing reasonably good basic living standards. These rights or entitlements, if and when they can be fulfilled, however, carry obligations to participate in the democracy, to obey the law and to contribute to the common purse. The arguments of the radical right in recent times appear to play down the interdependence between the different aspects of freedom. This has resulted in the 1980s in the attempt to downgrade or deny the validity of social rights and positive freedoms, and insist instead that legal and political rights are fundamental.

In *Losing Out*, Fields (1989) argues that four forces have brought about the underclass in the UK: unemployment; the widening of class differences; the exclusion of the poorest from rising living standards; and a change in public attitude towards those who have not succeeded.

For, perhaps, 40 years following the Second World War, full employment brought about a greater degree of equality in income distribution. Conditions changed during recent years, so that while for those employed this state of affairs has continued, those out of work have suffered downward mobility. As a consequence increasing class divisions have broken up the sense of 'common citizenship, whereby each of us feels we belong to the same society' (1989: 3). The poor have not gained from the rising standards of living of the rest of society for benefit levels have merely been protected from rising prices. The individualist ideology of the Thatcher years has resulted in a change in attitudes towards those on the bottom rung of society. The solidarity of the working class has, according to Fields, been replaced by a 'drawbridge' mentality whereby those working class people who have benefited during the last decade do not wish others to follow their success. Fields sees the difficulties of the Labour Party in finding a 'coalition of voters with common interests' as a reflection of this phenomenon (Ibid: 4).

The long-term unemployed, single-parent families and elderly pensioners live under a 'subtle form of political, social and economic apartheid' (Ibid: 4). Fields, however, warns of oversimplification; not all of the members of these three groups can be said to be members of an underclass. How these factors affect an individual depends upon his psychological make-up and his surrounding environment. By comparison, the American underclass situation is clearly linked to a form of social apartheid. A CBS/New York Times poll taken at the time of the 1992 riots in Los Angles found that less than half of the respondents reported having spent an evening in the previous three to four months with a friend of another race. Neighbourhoods are highly segregated by race and ethnic background, and although the highest level of intergroup contact is in the workplace this rarely takes place on the basis of equality (Barbanel, 1989).

3 The class thesis that the underclass is partly a creation of a redistribution of wealth from the poor to the rich in the 1980s

The more Marxist British analysis of Kirk Mann (1992) places the underclass in terms of a specific position in the social division of welfare; a class conflict over resources; the requirements for a reserve army of labour; and spatial processes of marginalisation which has seen a transference of wealth from the less well off to the richer sections. The images of the undeserving, wasters and loafers, are ideologically effective in creating a distance between sections of the working class and thus preventing comprehensive programmes for social change (Bagguley and Mann, 1992).

In the US, Mike Davis writes of the 1980s as characterised by a process of 'overconsumption' located within 'an increasing political subsidisation of a sub-bourgeois, mass layer of managers, professionals, new entrepreneurs and retainers'. In the tax and welfare cuts of the first Reagan administration, low-income families lost around $23 billion in income and federal benefits, while high income families gained more than $35 billion. A split-level economy has developed obvious to even magazines such as *The Economist* and *Business Week*: 'with the masses of the working poor huddled around their K-Marts and Taiwanese imports at one end, while at the other there is a (relatively) 'vast market for luxury products and services, from travel and designer clothes, to posh restaurants, home computers and fancy sports cars' (Davis: *Prisoners of the American Dream*, 1986: quoted in Callinicos, 1989: 162).

While it is tempting to adopt a theory of pluralism as characterising contemporary social relations, the class specific nature of economic policies adopted throughout the 1980s should not be avoided. The language of disinflation, increasing productivity and rationalisation should not blind analysis to the real effects resulting from increasing unemployment, the reduction in the security of employment, the reduction of employment benefits and working conditions.

Undoubtedly, welfare provision has decreased dramatically in the US. In New York City, for example, the actual value of welfare payments declined by about one-third between 1978 and 1988; as the rules changed the number of recipients declined by about 6% between 1970 and 1982, and by about 10%

from 1983 to 1988. (Fainstein, *et al* 1992: 140) During the same period assistance for larger households declined substantially.

Avoiding responsibility by reference to global recession

In Britain the underclass concept arrived later; it was fashionable for a time to talk of the working class as becoming middle-class (the embourgeoisement of the working class) and the victory of the Conservative Party in 1979 as evidence of the absolute and relative decline of the working class (Offe, 1985). This belief lay behind a new political party of the middle ground forming in the early 1980s. The Social Democratic Party was founded to cater for a new middle class, which it seemed, was to occupy a vast middle ground stratified only by skills and the ability to be flexible. As Raphael Samuel described it, this salaried middle class:

> '... distinguishes itself more by its spending than its saving. The Sunday colour supplements give it both a fantasy life and a set of cultural cues. Much of its claim to culture rests on the conspicuous display of good tastes, whether in the form of kitchenware, "continental" food, or weekend sailing and cottages. New forms of sociability, like parties and "affairs" have broken down the sexual apartheid which kept women and men in rigidly separate spheres.
>
> Class hardly enters into the new middle class conception of themselves. Many of them work in an institutional world of fine gradations but no clear lines of antagonism.
>
> The new middle class have a different emotional economy than that of their pre-war predecessors. They go in for instant rather than delayed gratification, making a positive virtue of their expenditure, and treating the self-indulgent as an ostentatious display of good taste. Sensual pleasures, so far from being outlawed, are the very field on which social claims are established and sexual identities are confirmed. Food, in particular, a postwar bourgeois passion ... has emerged as a crucial marker of class.' (1982, quoted in Callinicos, 1989:162-3)

Membership of this class was seen to have its own ideology: your worth no longer depended on birth or accumulated capital but on education, social skills and adaptability: high learning curves were the new requirement. The key example was the ability to handle the computer, to learn skills for software and hardware which would become obsolete before you had actually fully managed them. A new form of social solidarity was expected to come into play.

But the SDP's appeal was obscure; embourgeoisement did not result in an expansion of reasonability and tolerance but rather a splitting apart – fear of the new rabble and a 'go for it' mentality – in a desocialisation of the social which was epitomised in the rhetoric of privatisation which went beyond mere economic configurations into the perception of sociality itself. The failure of the appeal of the SDP illustrated that the new middle class was by no means a coherent body but was identified as a class only through a strained idea of position within the means of production. Fortunes varied: managerial employment in the private spheres, in the Service Businesses of Banking and

Insurance, denoted large bonuses and quick money, while employment in the Public Services of Health and Education saw retrenchment. By the mid-1990s fortunes had been made and lost, while the Public services continued to decline.

Throughout the western world during the late 1970s and 1980s the myth of recession loomed large. In Britain disastrous economic decisions by the Conservative government in the budgets of 1981 and 1982 greatly reduced demand and radically cut government spending at a time when Keynesian economics required a logic of increased spending – the Neo-Chicagoan economic 'experiment' (the neo-classical approach) destroyed nearly 20% of Britain's manufacturing base in a few years – the subsequent reinflation of the late 1980s which resulted in a false boom could only suck in imports and perpetuate a boom and bust cycle. Unemployment soared, although it appeared to be kept in check by altered methods of calculating the figures and North Sea Oil revenues financed a growing Social Security budget rather than investment.

But there was no world recession. Economies boomed in the Far East and China, Brazil and latterly in India. As Paul Kellogg (1987) points out, at the same time as the politicians of the West cried out the need to wage war on welfare, and lower the regulatory protections on working conditions, economies in the developing world were expanding their industrial and manufacturing bases sometimes by multiples; employment in manufacturing in South Korea, for example, showed a growth of 2,500% between 1956 and 1982, in Brazil between 1970 and 1982 by 212%. Between 1977 and 1982 the industrial working class in the 36 leading industrial countries increased in numbers from 173 to 183 million, including the year 1982 which was widely regarded as the worst recession in the post-Second World War period seeing millions of redundancies in the west.

If the reality of world 'recession' is largely the consequences of shifting growth patterns (this would be even more obvious if Purchasing Power Parity provided the method for calculating GDP rather than the present methodology where all internal GDP figures are translated into the equivalent in American dollars, presently building a four bedroom house in New Delhi counts less than a studio flat in central London) the growth of the fabled service industries was also largely mythical. The growth in part time employment took large numbers off the unemployed lists, but offered low wages and minimal or no protection. Part-time labour intensified the stratification of labour by class, gender and race.[2]

As welfare cuts took hold women with children were occupying a range of part-time employment. The gains of the well publicised, professional woman usually required at least one home help working for minimum wages, often drawn from the ethnic minorities.

The underclass concept denotes the reality of a new social dialectics:

---

2   A standing joke of the 1980s went as follows: 'Q: What do you say to a black man who has got a job in Regan's America? ... A: I'll have a big Mac and medium fries.'

overconsumption versus deprivation; freedom and existential angst for the super-class versus ghettoisation for the emerging underclass. The growth of Yuppie culture verses the inevitable resentment of the have-nots who saw their position being worsened at the same time as they were made the object of scorn – singled out as the cause (due to 'their reluctance to work', and, 'demands for a high minimum wage') for economic decline.

The underclass and criminology

While we must be aware of the rhetorical weight of the term 'underclass', we can agree with other overviews of the debate (for example, Jencks and Peterson, 1991) that point to a set of processes through which a substantial category of persons exist, and are being recreated, that are well outside the mainstream in terms of their participation in everyday work and responsibilities. Exhibiting high rates of deprivation, involvement in crime and drug abuse, this social phenomenon provides fertile ground for many of the traditional themes of criminological theory to analyse, for example, family socialisation, neighbourhood development, peer group involvement, cultural imagery and success measures. While this is the traditional grist for criminological concerns there is a more abstract range of concerns which can be discerned by placing the underclass concept in the context of post-modernism.

The underclass and post-modernism

Much of the underclass debate has focused upon the political implications of the various writings and the empirical adequacy of the concept. The debate as to empirical adequacy is inconclusive, indeed it is almost impossible to satisfy. In large part this is because of the openness or unboundedness of the concept of the underclass. As Hughes (1989) points out in American studies which argue for a more complex situation than the paradigm of moral individualism, the empirical data employed has failed to withstand 'culture-of-poverty' interpretations while the level of generalisation involved has equally failed to recognise the spatial reality of 'the isolated deprivation of the "impacted ghetto" '. To conduct a properly scientific study, Hughes argues, economic geography needs to reconstitute the phenomena in terms specific to its tools and terrain. But the very unboundedness, or sloppiness, of the underclass concept may indicate that what is actually at stake with its acceptance is a more non-scientific or metaphysical phenomena. In short, rather than a creature of empirical social science, the underclass concept may only make sense when viewed as part of an intellectual struggle defining the true nature of modern humanity. Three themes predominate: (i) the underclass as an entity of narratives on social progress; (ii) the underclass and the metaphysics of contingency; (iii) the underclass and the dialectics of social participation and control.

Narratives of modernity and social progress

The enlightenment made it possible to conceive of society as an artifact which could be transformed and developed by human endeavour. Thus, until recently, both liberal and conservative accounts could explain the development of social welfare as a humanitarian and progressive creation of modern, advanced, societies. According to these narratives, even the current American system of welfare (and certain other related ideologies) can be traced back to Elizabethan Poor Law (Friedman, 1968). The right builds its understanding of the underclass on a reading of the 'growth of welfare' narrative. It accepts the liberal, whig, narrative of the creation of modern welfare as providing progress out of the poor laws but with a difference.

Historically, images of the poor have been divided into the 'worthy' or 'deserving' (for instance, orphans, or the handicapped without family) and the 'unworthy' or 'undeserving'. Around the beginning of the 19th century a new doctrine emerged that related poor relief to the threat of over-population; Thomas Malthus attacked the English Poor Law, and was, for a time, successful in having it revoked. He proceeded from the position that people were 'inert, sluggish, and averse from labour unless compelled by necessity', and noted that the then extant Poor Law provided for family allowances based on the number of children. In the Malthusian view, this practically encouraged the poor to be prolific. In addition, the scientific 'laws' of classical economics emerged, uniformly pointing to the negative consequences of 'encouraging sloth' by aiding the poor.

All of this came to a head in Britain in 1834; the Poor Law was amended to become the New Poor Law, which established the workhouse as the principal means of assisting the poor. The workhouse was deliberately designed to be as unpleasant as possible, so as to remove any possibility that people would be encouraged by charity to abandon their work. Those on public assistance were stigmatised severely by, as a contemporary put it:

> '... imprisoning (them) in workhouses, compelling them to wear special garb, separating them from their families, cutting them off from communication with the poor outside, and, when they died, permitting their bodies to be disposed of for dissection.' (Quoted, Hirschman, 1989)

What the whig accounts lay stress upon is not the issue of absolute poverty, but rather the development of a sensitivity towards poverty when social wealth was flourishing. This issue 'poverty amid plenty' received publicity with Robert Hunter's book *Poverty* in 1904 (Coll, 1969). But conservative voices, such as that of the sociologist William Graham Sumner, were already issuing warnings in terms similar to those of the right in the 1980s:

> 'The humanitarians, philanthropists, and reformers ... in their eagerness to recommend the less fortunate classes to pity and consideration forget all about the rights of other classes ... When I have read certain of these discussions I have

thought that it must be quite disreputable to be respectable, quite dishonest to own property, quite unjust to go one's way and earn one's own living, and that the only admirable person was the good-for-nothing. The man who by his own effort raises himself above poverty appears, in these discussions, to be of no account. The man who has done nothing to raise himself above poverty finds that the social doctors flock about him, bringing the capital which they have collected from other classes.' (*What Social Classes Owe to each Other*, 1900; Quoted in Messner, 1966)

In the whig accounts the experience of the Great Depression of the 1930s stimulated dramatic action by federal governments in the US and Canada which laid the foundation for the modern welfare state which was further improved as societies grow in economic and social strength. However, in the late 1970s and throughout the 1980s the liberal narrative of welfare growth, while accepted as the historical picture was subjected to withering attack by the new right as counter-productive.

It hardly needs saying that the whig account of humanitarian progress has been undercut from the left as well. Piven and Cloward (1971) have pointed out the cyclical nature of poor relief in modern societies. They advance considerable evidence for the thesis that only when times are economically harsh – and large numbers of vocal, articulate persons are unemployed – does relief even begin to approach adequacy. In prosperous times, conditions of welfare are tightened and provisions are made even less generous.

Much of the critical perspective of the centre and left against the right's use of the underclass notion, although correctly claiming that the underclass is a concept which only makes sense when it is viewed as coming out of a narrative tradition, misses the point. The point is not that the controversy which the term arouses lessens our ability to do methodologically correct social science; nor is it that the underclass notion is so loaded that anyone who uses it soon slides into a culture-of-poverty framework – these are important issues – but writers who try to take these seriously and evade the term neglect the very moral power which the underclass notion brings. To Wilson (1991) the moral issue is how to avoid falling into a 'blame the victim' position, while continuing to stress the explanatory and empirical issues involved in the combination of marginality in the labour market and the fact that their economic position is uniquely reinforced by their social milieu. A different form of moral issue is at stake when we see the underclass as a post-modern phenomenon; as a consequence of the failure of modernity to deliver the implicitly (and often explicitly) promised just society.

The underclass, the end of modernity and the existential metaphysics of contingency

What makes the underclass phenomenon different from the desperate status of the poor in the 18th and 19th centuries? Or even the poor of the inner cities in the earlier parts of this century? Some differences are clearly observable:

'Although the black ghetto neighbourhoods of the mid-twentieth century were typically very poor, they did not have the high rates of joblessness, welfare dependency, teenage pregnancies, out of wedlock births, female-headed households, drug abuse, and violent crime which now characterise so many black ghettos today.' (Boxill, 1991: 579)

Other differences are harder empirically to discern. However, the existential position of everyday life in the 1990s, with mass communication, club and street fashion, the pleasure drive, and the cultural measures to be authentic and modern, cannot be ignored in analysis. Moreover, when the *Economist* placed a photograph of two African-American children on its cover under the caption 'America's Wasted Blacks', its message was simple:

'The slums in America's great cities are shameful. They are a damning indictment of the richest country in the world ... The nation now has a quarter of a century's worth of anti-poverty experiments to draw upon ... Poverty persists despite these efforts.' *(Economist,* 5 April 1991).

The point is that it very much matters that the underclass arrived after the modern war on poverty. The mood of much of the writings is post-modernist, in the sense that there is pessimism as to the project of modernity. In particular, there is a refusal by the right to accept that any public programmes can work any longer. Paul Goldberger, the architecture critic for the *New York Times,* sees this reflected in the social geography of life in New York city:

'Human anguish is surely more visible on the streets of New York than ever before. But the illness that affects the cityscape is not only a matter of human suffering. In a broader sense, the city is only rarely these days a place of hope or promise or glory. It is not merely that it is harsh and dirty, for New York has always been harsh and dirty. It is that it has become so indifferent to the very idea of the public realm, to the notion that the city is a collective, a shared place, a place that is in the most literal sense common.' (Goldber, 1989: quoted in Fainstein, *et al* 1992: 138-9)

Moreover, common to many accounts of the underclass (Field, Mann, Murray, Dahrendorf) is the implicit acceptance that the underclass is a direct result of previous government policy; whether due to the creation of the welfare state, the failure to develop post-industrial strategies, or rejecting social justice in favour of free-market, supply side economic theories. The implicit message given to the members of the underclass is that there is nothing natural in their position, it is rather a creation of society; their life and their suffering is a contingency. The message at the same time as they are made the scapegoat for economic decline is: 'You could just as well have been born the son or daughter of a white wealthy individual'. The individuals who comprise the underclass are faced with the post-modern condition in a number of ways in which an awareness of contingency or radical unnaturalness is dominant:

- in the structural position in relation to work in a post-fordist (post-industrial) era where employment has been exported out to other nations willing to allow what Mike Davis has called 'bloody Taylorism' (for example the absence of fire escapes which ensured that the fire in a toy factory in Thailand in 1993 killed more than 250);

- in the anti-traditionalist and anti-naturalist foundational ontologies, that is the argument wherein their position is shown as simply the result of 'frozen politics' and past social decisions;

- the problematic nature of individual identity; specifically, while the answer to the question 'who am I and how am I to behave?' could traditionally have been answered in terms of the narratives of everyday life (ie narratives told externally to the self), those narratives which specified the individual's gender, work, place, family, class, and past, modernity has turned into temporal guides rather than truths; placed the burden of identity onto an abstract self to create continually anew (ie self-reflexive). Thus identity becomes a burden as much as a refuge, providing only the weakest of ontological security and little protection against the demands of consumerism and the dialectics of angst-desire.

The dialectics of social class, participation and social control

The underclass is, therefore, a new phenomenon distinguishable from any other group of 'poor' or 'surplus labour' in modernity. In contrast to the members of early modern poor groups, or even dangerous classes, there is no recourse to narrative notions of progress (such as Marxism, or the reformist idealism of a Comte) to tell these groups that 'your time will come'. Moreover, the desperation of the underclass condition is most pronounced when viewed 'against the narratives of modernity' and, in particular, takes on a threatening aspect because of the nature of the balances which sustain civil society in late modernity. Civil society comprises, in part, a system in which various features act to manage conflict aided by processes of participation which guide the interaction of social and self-control. Namely:

- the institutionalisation of the class conflict via the introduction of legitimate working class organisations (trade unions, political parties of the moderate left) which have specific institutional methodologies for attaining class related ends;

- the incorporation of 'oppressed groups' (women, ethnic minorities, homosexuals) via institutional recognition of their social participation in their abstract (legal-rational) forms (ie bearers of 'rights' and subjects of anti-discrimination legislation);

- the civilising of modern society via the monopolisation of violence and taxation in the hands of the state (the police/military complex) and the rational self-control of the population. As we have seen in the analysis of Norbert Elias, the civilising of the individual and the civilising of the state are thus co-dependent.

- the provision of economic resources by means of transfer payments and insurance contributions to sections of the population marginalised from employment participation;

- general cultural significants of status and self-worth become connected with market production and consumption power. Transfer payments enable a basic subsistence level of consumption and rhetorically serve to relocate recipiants back into consumption opportunities at a later time (for example, when they are re-employed).

The underclass phenomenon threatens these processes in various ways, namely:

- institutionalised features of class conflict, such as trade unions and political parties, do not cover their situation. The dialectics of apathy/irrelevance result;

- oppressed groups become marginalised or the features of incorporation become distorted, for example, the feminisation of work may allow black women some employment opportunities while condemning black males to unemployment. Such work is likely to have low levels of job security or opportunities for self-esteem;

- resistance by the underclass tempts the police complex into coercive responses thus revealing the structure of coercion behind the civilisation of the state;

- the reality of non-employment, and the devastation of the family, changes socialisation processes which may reverse the civilising process; an incompatibility of social messages (via the mass communications network) complicate and place conflicting demands upon the process of creating an authentic individual identity; and differential opportunities for self-creation and expression may result in emotions of resentment and revenge and the desire for domination;

- legitimacy becomes increasingly a problem, since modernity undercuts previous legitimation systems but the post-modern anti-naturalism, anti-foundationist metaphysics cannot provide (even in systems theory) any suitable legitimation process for the underclass to accept. Thus, contingency impacts as a criminogenic factor (for why should the present rules of the game be played with, that is, lawful conduct be regarded as a necessity for underclass life, if the arrangements have no legitimacy or naturalness?). The experience of deep inequalities, bereft of the security of naturalness and cast in the light of contingency, create not alienation (for what is there to be alienated from?) but resentment. This question of the emotionality of the post-modern condition provides the material for other discussions, but here we may accept Nietzsche's warning that the emotion of the repressed in the post-modern condition cannot be seen within the rationality of meaningful dialectical engagement, but rather as the absence of meaningfulness. The rage of the deprived is vengeance on anything which links to the excesses of the advantaged. How can there be a way to make people content, or reconcile them either to the advantages of others, or the disadvantages of themselves, when the narratives of legitimacy have become subjected to the trope of irony, and one's position in the seemingly arbitrary and chaotic array of life chances, sacrifices, rewards and benefits, understood as just that, arbitrary and contingent?

Against this there has recently been a desperate attempt to reinstate a functionalist and positivist account of the underclass. Charles Murray and Richard Herrnstein (1994) in *The Bell Curve* draw connections between ethnic IQ scores and the underclass. In effect the social-structural segregation of the underclass is turned into a cognitive underclass. Their picture is of a society in which IQ and social skills determine one's position within the social stratification; a meritocracy which is currently distorted by positive discrimination and attempted social engineering. Positive knowledge declares stable IQ differences between mongoloids 110, caucasoid 100 and negroid (American blacks) 90. Thus we would expect more blacks to be in the underclass, naturally. Instead of aspiring they should tone down their aspirations and realise they can be happy playing football (this was Wilson and Herrnstein's preferred solution in Crime and Human Nature (1985)). Smarter people get more rewards in the economic sphere; they deserve more, but there are other realms.

Critics of *The Bell Curve* have argued along four lines: (i) declaring a stark and intractable gap between intellectual abilities of black and white Americans is a political act; (ii) the data relied upon is extremely suspect; (iii) the logic of their argument points to even more detailed subdivisions (among white, among racially mixed) which they do not engage in; (iv) the conclusions of the book – that no social policies can affect IQ – do not follow from the analysis. Since if large amounts of IQ differences are environmental, the policy differences could partly remedy this.

Conclusion

The concept of underclass has aroused considerable controversy, and proved difficult to empirically pin down into a settled set of circumstances. Whilst it has had little impact upon criminological writings considerable potential exists. Its potential is not to be seen in purely positivistic terms of adequacy to data, but in seeing the very unboundedness of the concept as a product of its moral overtones. The concept of the underclass is both a social scientific term, which may inadequately reference a complex set of social processes, and a moral term, denoting a structure of marginalisation, and non-participation, in the processes and achievements of late or post-modernity. While it does not appear to have been properly analysed within criminology and incorporated into criminological paradigms, we should not forget that social responses are occurring. There may be some appreciation (ie discourse which seeks to articulate the experience of the members of the underclass and communicate this to us superclass members), but there is also target hardening, differential policing and the use of the criminal justice system to contain members of the underclass. The underclass has become material for an expanding prison industry (Christie, 1993; Morrison, 1995b). Accepting the underclass as a usable concept has implications for the rest of criminological and sociological explanation. The underclass will serve symbolically as the focus for superclass fear (we can see this in terms of the current 'wars' on drugs which tend to become wars on underclass members who trade or use drugs) and reinforce the current moves to abandon all 'social projects' in favour of economic projects, and the primacy of economic discourse for discussion of social issues. The victory of economic discourse flies in the face of the apparent failure of economics to deliver on its promises. In Britain, the fact that economic discourse has operated as the master discourse since the late 1970s has not resulted in a vibrant economy, or the betterment of the less well off (as trickle down economics promised), but rather social polarisation and economic stagnation. Its only victory is to successfully render social issues as 'externalities', not able to be included in the primary parameters of discussion.

However, if we use a backdrop of modernity, we can draw a link between the development of self-control and the monopolisation of violence into the hands of the nation states (where it resides in the police and military). The ability of urban civil society in modernity to become free from the constraints of religion, status, and cast hierarchies, and the ability of individuals to become socially and thus creatively mobile, has depended upon the 'pacification' of civil society. Economic well being as well as the symbolic value of believing in a just society require strategies of incorporation rather than exclusion and containment. Neglecting the social processes that may be creating the underclass risks much of the gains of modernity itself. Here criminological theorising demonstrates itself as providing a reading of general social forms, but, more than that, the discourse of the underclass may serve for a post-modern criminology to retrace the steps to the beginnings of modern social theory, that is to moral social theory.

Postscript: A note on the Los Angeles Riots of 1992

The riots of Los Angeles were the first post-modern riots. They concerned the possibility of allocating blame when reality was questioned. The world appeared shocked when a jury, comprised mostly of whites, acquitted four Los Angeles policemen filmed beating a black motorist, Rodney King, after he had been seen racing through a red light, and led police on an eight mile chase reaching speeds of 110 miles per hour. Within hours of the acquittal Los Angeles was witnessing the worst riots in US history. The *Daily Telegraph* of 4 May 1992 reported 46 dead (mainly young black and hispanic males); 2,116 injured; 9,400 people arrested; 5,273 buildings destroyed or heavily damaged by fire; and more than $600 million worth of damage. In an effort to contain the riots President Bush mobilised 6,000 national guards and dispatched 1,000 federal law officers;

special weapons teams; riot police from the border patrol, the prison service and the FBI in support. While a brigade of 2,500 infantrymen with armoured personal carriers, and 1,500 marines assembled around the city.

Socially the 1980s had seen a decline in the relative standing of California – wages had declined especially amongst the poor. Nationally, between 1973 and 1990 the average yearly income of black, high school graduates decreased in real terms by 44%. Latino earnings fell by 35% (*The Guardian*, 2 May).

The prosecution occurred against a background of persistent charges of police malpractice, and complaints that the police were more interested in staging media-covered round-ups of suspected gang members in black neighbourhoods than dealing with the real policing problems of those areas. The violence and abuse of civil liberties involved in the raids tied in with media hype of the war on drugs and gangs, but the effect was to encourage black animosity to the police, since many blacks and Latinos saw these clean ups as attempts to appease white residents. In 1990 more than $11 million had been paid out in law suits against the police. Many of the complaints however, came to nothing when brought before a police review board dominated by officials from the police hierarchy. Most of the complaints were not able to provide sufficient evidence to support criminal charges against officers of the law. The Rodney King case was welcomed because it seemed to have cast-iron evidence – the brutality long alleged against the police was in this instance captured live on video tape. When either five-second flashes or nearly two minutes of grainy video tape, in which Mr King was struck 56 times with night-sticks and repeatedly kicked, was shown on television, it elicited outrage from all sectors of the public including the Oval office. Tom Bradley, the black mayor of Los Angeles, was plain speaking: 'This is something we cannot and will not tolerate.'

The officers involved protested their innocence claiming they acted in self-defence. In the prosecution that followed the defence attorneys were determined to move the case out of the Los Angeles area. They succeeded in having it set in Simi Valley, a small rural community 100 miles north-west of Los Angeles; Simi Valley has a black population of 2%, while Los Angeles county has 10.5%. Perhaps, more importantly, the 100,000 residents of Simi Valley had virtually no experience of the kind of urban violence that is routine in Los Angeles, and little exposure to its racial tensions; there were the objects of community policing rather than the military policing of south central Los Angeles. The jury consisting of six men and six women, comprised 10 whites, an Hispanic and an Asian.

In court the defence tried to reduce the horror of the video-tape to a less emotional level. It was helped by the fact that the victim had previous convictions for robbery and was on parole after serving a sentence for an armed robbery. The prosecution did not call King. Darryl Mounger, the lawyer for one of the defendant police officers, claimed: 'If he had got in the box, we would have showed that he had used make-up to exaggerate his wounds, puffed out his cheeks to make his face look more bruised, and lied in his statements to the press. We all agreed that the beating was terrible and brutal, but the jury had to find they did something unlawful and wrong.'

Although the television had screened at most two minutes of film, the actual film lasts nearly seven minutes. It opens with Mr King standing by his car, lurching towards the police. Defence lawyers argued that this showed he was uncooperative and potentially dangerous. As it turned out, he was drunk.

At one point, after being beaten, King tries to rise from the ground, the lawyers isolated these frames of the film, contending that he was controlling the action by acting aggressively and not staying motionless on the ground.

In the US, the standard procedure for a motorist stopped by the police is to emerge from a stopped car with hands up. It is vital, even for a simple speeding offence, to show police that you are unarmed, especially after a wild drive through streets used as a night-time hunting ground by armed street gangs. This must be taken as the context for the pent-up rage by the Los Angeles Police Officers towards a black man following an eight-mile chase at speeds of up to 110 mph. Nevertheless, even the husband and wife police team that initiated the high-speed pursuit, testified that the actions of at least one of their fellow officers were inexcusable.

The prosecution may have made a mistake in not calling Mr King, who, in the jurors eyes, remained always a vague and shadowy video image. From their perspective there were sensible reasons. If called he would have had to answer why, after the car chase, he did not immediately surrender, as did his two black companions, who were unhurt. He would also have been seen to be a large man, and questioned about his past, which included a spell in prison. Prosecutors say he did not testify because he had only a vague recollection of the incident. Tactically, by keeping him off the stand, it was easier to cast him in the role of an entirely innocent and victimised citizen.

The video film became the focus of defence attention. The opening of the film shows Mr King stumbling towards the officers, falling when hit by an electronic stun gun, and then getting up to charge one officer, who, by all accounts, was the most aggressive man on the police team. A juror interviewed by the Los Angeles Times said: 'I know the film was horrible, but there's a lot more to it than the film, and a lot more to it than the small pieces that were shown on TV. The film does not show all of the things that went on before.' The juror said that if Mr King had submitted to the orders of the officers as they tried to arrest him, the beating would never have happened. 'He refused to get out of the car. His two companions got out and complied with all the orders and he just continued to fight. So the police department had no alternative. He was obviously a dangerous person, of massive size and threatening actions ... The police used everything they had at their availability.'

By cutting and isolating images on the video, the defence neutralised the frenzy of violence captured therein and managed to dehumanise Mr King. In addition, some of his injuries, they claimed, seemed to have been caused when he hit the ground; in particular, had the break of the bones in his face occurred when he fell for the first time on to the pavement? When defence lawyers reviewed the flurry of blows, they repeatedly stopped, or slowed the tape to show that police were either missing their victim, or retreating, in possible fear, from the man.

The prosecution produced evidence that showed conflicting testimony from the different police officers involved and even got some policemen to testify that excessive force had been used. The defence argued that the police action was appropriate in dealing with a dangerous man. The jurors spent a week meticulously examining the evidence. 'It was not a snap decision by any stretch of the imagination', said one. 'He was just not as damaged as you'd expect after seeing the small clip of video on television.' Only one member of the jury seemed torn with doubt about the verdict. The woman rang a chat show in tears, saying she had argued for conviction of the accused because 'they could not take away what my eyes saw.' However, she eventually agreed to acquit three of the four accused on all charges and find the fourth guilty of only a minor charge.

One of the jurors explained why the video was not enough to convict the policemen. 'When I first saw the video, I was appalled. But after you sat through the trial with all the evidence, the witnesses, everything that was said – the video too – you had to see what was going on. Had Rodney King gotten out of his vehicle, as he was ordered to do, and complied with the policemen's orders, nothing would have happened to him.'

The pictures of Mr King lurching towards the officers were interpreted by another juror as extremely threatening: 'The cops were afraid he was going to run or even attack them. He had not been searched, so they didn't know if he had a weapon. He kept going for his pants, so they thought he might be reaching for a gun.'

One of the accused said he was certain Mr King was on PCP; a drug that is claimed to make an addict almost uncontrollable. Mr King, in fact, was not taking the drug. But, as the defence said, the issue was a matter of perception – the question was what were the thought processes of the police officers? As one Prosecutor complained after the verdict: 'They continually emphasised the size of King, his erratic behaviour and the fact that everything was happening so quickly. In effect, they were telling the jury: "Don't believe what you see on the video tape – believe instead the evidence of the officers. They are not lying – the camera is".'

Mr King's abnormal behaviour, and unsteady gait, was referred to as being 'animal-like' and 'inhuman'. Combined with rarely referring to Mr King in court by name, this tactic appears to have persuaded the jury to believe that the police honestly thought they were dealing with some sort of monster. As a prosecution lawyer put it: 'Their strategy worked in part because the jury was ready to believe the police officers' version of what happened, and, in part, because they presented their case very well. The defence lawyers virtually achieved the impossible, and made 12 people disbelieve the evidence of the own eyes' (Mr Correio).

Three of the officers said they believed Mr King was under the influence of the drug PCP and that they were only using 'managed and controlled force', as set out in police regulations, to subdue him. The fourth took a different tack acknowledging that the incident had 'got out of control', and insisting that he stepped in to try to stop the violence. Although he appeared on video to be stamping on Mr King, he was, he said, merely trying to hold him down with his foot to prevent further violence.

In the face of this defence deconstruction of the filmed 'reality', 'common sense' came to the jurors – yes, the police could be taken to have believed that King was on some miracle drug giving him (a large black) almost superhuman strength. Instead of the filmed reality of police brutality and oppression, Mr King was a menacing, superhuman beast who had a ring of armed police fearing for their lives.

The trial and subsequent riot was a site where various images and narratives of behaviour intersected. For Henry Louis Gates: 'That jury was more afraid of the potential of being mugged by some hypothetical black male than it was of the abuse of the Constitution, of civil rights.' For Jim Sleeper: 'We're at the dividing line now, where perception becomes reality, where the prophecy becomes self-fulfilling. The fact that the looters are out there doing the rioting only confirms what people have decided: this is what the cops are there to protect us from.' (*Time*, 11 May 1992: 35)

In a Washington Post-ABC News survey 68% said the verdict was wrong, the break down was 64% of whites and 92% of blacks. Asked whether the *King* case demonstrated that blacks were discriminated against in the judicial system, 78% of blacks agreed against only 25% of whites (*The Independent*, 4 May).

Perceptions of the fairness and reasons for the verdict varied by race. Bradely, the black Mayor of Los Angeles speaking immediately after the verdict stated plainly: 'The system has failed us. The jury's verdict will never blind what the world saw, what we saw.' While for Maxine Walters, the Congresswoman for South Central Los Angeles: 'There is no logic to this. It is pure racism.' The riots are the natural reaction to outrage and despair over 'an incomprehensible decision' (both quotes, *The Times*, 1 May).

As the riot progressed Bradely obviously became unable to appreciate, let alone control, events. It was clear that, although he was black, he was middle class and unable to communicate with the rioters. For their part the comments of many of the individuals involved in the disturbances demonstrated how foreign the political leaders of the state appeared. The attitude to Pete Wilson, the white Republican Governor of California, was contemptuous: 'He's a joke. He already cut our welfare – now he wants to starve us to death' (The Guardian, 2 May):

'For some the resulting riot was a consequence of the system's bias being clearly exposed. The Rev Bennie Newton, who saved a Hispanic motorist from a mob by throwing himself over the unconscious body, said the violence was "brought on by frustration, disillusionment, bitterness, anger – and most of all betrayal."' (*The Independent,* 2 May 1992)

As reporters tried to speak to participants, resentment became the common emotion apparent in the statements of the residents as well as looters. 'None of this would happen if they gave us proper justice – look around, you see foreigners who come here and take jobs and business opportunities from people born in the USA. Me, I'd like to start a business too, I'd like to go to college and be a lawyer, but because I'm black, no one will lend me the money, no way.' Frustration mixed with resentment: 'This is not just us taking apart our community – everybody is pissed off. We have tried to be peaceful but that didn't work.' Another: 'We are taking this all the way to Beverly Hills.' Reports were full of colourful language: many of the rioters were said to have 'hissed venom at the rich' (quotes in *The Daily Telegraph,* 2 May, 1992)

To *The Sunday Times,* resentment explained some of the logic of the attacks and destruction of buildings, for example, the torching of a video shop owned by a Korean. The blacks were seen to resent:

'... the more ambitious Korean immigrants who have worked hard and managed to prosper. The resentment has been fuelled by American Asians moving into black areas to open their shops and who do not live in the ghetto or share the poverty of the ghetto. Tensions between blacks and Koreans flared after a woman store owner was given a probation sentence the year earlier for shooting dead a black teenage girl who allegedly stole a can of drink from her shop. A hit song by the rap star Ice Cube warns Korean merchants to treat black customers with respect or 'we'll burn your store right down to a crisp'. Koreans in turn, make no secret of their belief that blacks are lazy and criminally inclined.' (*The Sunday Times,* 3 May 1992)

The riot was in part a bizarre carnival. As one participant shouted while loading a shopping trolley:

'Hey man, lets party. Take it. It's free. It's ours. Take the whole shop, man. Let's kill.' (*The Sunday Times,* 3 May 1992)

But style was important: 'LA Gear isn't really cool. Tonight I'm going back to get me some Nikes' (25 year old, black looter who had taken 20 pairs of shoes).

Visualising reality

The riots were screened world-wide. They were also screened to the participants. One could look outside the window, or at the TV screen. On the second night of the riots the decision was made by one of the leading television channels to stop the almost constant coverage and screen the final episode of *The*

Cosby Show. It raised a debate: was it a stroke of common sense in the midst of overreaction, an attempt to show that the riots were an abberation of normalacy? Or was it insensitive and evidence of the vast gulf between media portrayal (of successful black, middle class life) and social reality (the black underclass)?

What was happening? What was the message? While the black and Hispanic underclass having inhabited a locality unemployment, drug-addiction, and with extreme gang-warfare were witnessing and participating in the riots, while more than 9,000 were being arrested, the cultural fantasy system underpinning the American Dream worked through the portrayal of the leading middle class, black, professional family. What greater contrast and questioning of the reality of the communication network could there be than this (obscenity?)?; while the inhabitants of a world of alcohol and drug abuse, domestic violence, drug addiction, illness, homelessness, elderly helplessness, apathy, chronic unemployment screamed their resentment ('what else can we do until they build schools in this area instead of prisons?'), while the existentialist freedom of the criminal event operated, each could connect up to the hyper-reality of the American Dream.

The riot as an indicator of the post-modern future?

For Jessie Jackson the events were symptomatic of the absence of any public project to build American cities into a social space: 'We need a plan. There is a plan to rebuild eastern Europe, there is a plan to help Russia, but we have no plan to rebuild the cities of America' (*The Guardian*, 2 May 1992). For many, it was simply the future, arrived early. The signification that modernity was over.

CHAPTER EIGHTEEN

BUILDING CRIMINOLOGICAL THEORY IN POST-MODERNISM

'Inherently inferior organisms are, for the most part, those which succumb to the adversities or temptations of their social environment and fall into anti-social behaviour... it is impossible to improve and correct environment to a point at which these flawed and degenerate human beings will be able to succeed in honest social competition.' (Hooton, *Crime and the Man*, 1939: 388)

'The dismantling of the Welfare State is essentially a process of "putting moral responsibility where it belongs" – that is, among the private concerns of individuals. It spells a hard time for moral responsibility; not only in its immediate effects on the poor and unfortunate who need a society of responsible people most, but also (and perhaps, in the long run, primarily) in its lasting effects on the (potentially) moral selves. It recasts "being for Others", that cornerstone of all morality, as a matter of accounts and calculation, of value for money, of gains and costs, of luxury one can or cannot permit. The process is self-propelling and self-accelerating: the new perspective leads inevitably to relentless deterioration of collective services (the quality of the public health service, of public education, of whatever is left of public housing or transport), which prompts those who can to buy themselves out from collective provisions – an act which turns out to mean, sooner or later, buying themselves out of collective responsibility.' (Bauman, *Postmodern Ethics*, 1993: 244)

This text has presented a narrative of criminology's theoretical development through modernity to post-modernism; the story has not been simple, and there are, undoubtedly, competing versions. What, however, cannot be doubted is the complexity and ambiguity of our contemporary social context. How shall we face this ambiguity? To some social observers post-modernism denotes a crisis of confidence which threatens to undercut the tremendous advances of modernity. We inhabit the future the philosophers of the enlightenment dreamed of; yet feel we can no longer dream of a truly modern social solidarity. Certain commentators even blame the very idea of a normative social project itself for the new tensions threatening our sociality. Murray (1988) and others argue our problems of social order are attitudinal; a matter of the failure of individuals themselves to assume moral responsibility and enter into social interactions which do not rely upon force or fraud. Murray demands we do not deny that even the worst-off in modern western societies enjoy a standard of living beyond the dreams of their Victorian counterparts; if, therefore, the problems are of relations between people, late- or post-modern social problems do not require the state to take responsibility. We must rather seize back the moral task from the state. At present 'we' do not take sufficient trouble over the variety of social interactions and networks a healthy, spontaneous, social solidarity would require; the decline of family life is one symptom. To the writers of the right, in the name of a social construction project, modernity has stripped the self of moral responsibility: 'functions that people as individuals and as communities are *able* to carry out on their own should be left to them to do as individuals and communities.' (1988: 272)

But what of social distance in late-modernity? What of the chains of mediation which obscure the morality of the social; which make it easier for the individual to act in an inhuman manner; and easy for the state to forget the reality of social interdependence? Not only does the scale of problems involved in the growth of the underclass and globalisation (including the globalisation of organised crime and multi-national corporations) make this argument to leave individuals, and the groups they form, alone to get on with their lives appear naive, but it poses the question: in whom, or what, has responsibility for articulating, and taking responsibility for, the increased range of social suffering the destruction of a public normative project might well involve.

Articulating private concerns has often been the domain of the novelist and poet while the novelist or poet has no other public responsibility than to write, great writing offers social solidarity: it confers upon the reader some insight and interweaves strands of the human condition. But the distinction between private and public concerns is problematic a disciplinary discourse such as criminology has a public responsibility – one of seeking to articulate perspectives and truths of the human condition in such a way as to make problems, issues and consequences become more apparent. Harold Pepinsky and Richard Quinney (1991: ix) argue for a new form of 'peace-making criminology', which seeks 'to alleviate suffering and thereby reduce crime'. Suffering is partially the flipside of doing, the consequence of (non)action. It is clearly visible in the conditions of the underclass; in sexual and personal victimisation located in the imbalances of personal power throughout society; in the imbalance of power existing between consumers and large corporations which withhold information concerning their products, or maintain faulty products; in drug companies which charge inflated prices for cheaply produced drugs while failing to invest in forms of medical research which may show their products to be of dubious efficacy; it particularly operates in the philosophical and economic suffering created when a substantial section live in relative poverty while a few assume huge wealth. Suffering is part of the essence of crime – the victimisations which the rational logos of criminology has not sufficiently conveyed. Criminology has supported the power to legislate and organise: while social order in modernity responded to the power to legislate and organise – dissembedding humans from their location in custom and status into categories of human objects recognisable and relatable according to their functionally specific traits – the catch cry of post-modernism might be that *social order is problematic.* The great enterprises of legislating for the common good or of mapping social space, of engaging in a positivistic criminological enterprise locating the identities of the normal and the deviant, the sane and the insane, the criminal and the upright citizen, have been undercut. Social space cannot be located and mapped with certainty – it cannot be easily ordered – ambivalence and confusion have caught out the projects of founding the human construction of modernity. Has criminology therefore no right to exist? Is all the action merely a mirage – a frenzy of professionals who no longer have a coherent project to work within. At least one contemporary criminologist, Colin Summner (1994), thinks that the mainstream sociological version has died. His *Sociology of Deviance* text is subtitled: *An Obituary*. Perhaps, however, what has died is the form of theorising developed around the categories of structural progress and the nation state, which saw social problems as internal to societies, and power as the instrument of the state. Increasingly, instead of the nation state providing the framework, both analysis moving upwards from the minute to those of the truly global interact; analyses of global boundaries and of macro-sociological processes – such as modernity and post-modernism – which seek to address issues of the human condition are required. Theories of the socially specific must be in dialogue with general theorising. Yet we should be aware of the countervailing forces which we have noted throughout this text, and the analysis of Lyotard can serve as a final reminder.

Lyotard and the death of modern social theory

The French writer Jean-François Lyotard is credited with the classic text of post-modernism, *The Postmodern Condition* (1984). On the surface, a report on the impact of computer technology on the field of knowledge, *The Postmodern Condition* is a critique of modernist science which raises a host of questions concerning our conduct of, and expectations for, science under post-modernism. In particular, Lyotard is concerned with the legitimation of knowledge through narratives – or everyday and scientific language games – and how this affects the social bond. There are three stages to his critique:

- Modernity was underpinned by a faith in certain grand narratives – particularly those of progress, self-advancement and emancipation – which linked with narratives given by father figures of social theory – such as Marx, Durkheim and Weber – concerning the ability of truth and science (such as positivism) to provide foundations for the structuring of society and identify the direction for progressive social development (such as the dialectical advancement of humanity). These narratives can no longer serve as anchoring points in the post-modern condition; we have developed an incredulity towards meta-narratives.

- Modernity became dominated by two methodologies for conceiving of society as a totality:

  (a)   structural functionalism, or the idea that society forms an organic functioning whole with each entity able to be placed within the overall picture (the traditional picture of criminological theorising); or

  (b)   critical theory in the legacy of Marx, which rests on the principles of class struggle and advancement through opposition. This, however, turned out to be as functionalist as the first model and has failed. As a result:

- While capitalism has succeeded, we face a crisis of legitimation which is most apparent in the status of scientific knowledge; this crisis of legitimation threatens to engulf modern society – it defines the post-modern condition. While legitimation is problematic the market dominates; even truth becomes a matter of saleability – knowledge has been turned into a commodity. The Industrial Revolution demonstrated that without technology there could not be modern wealth, and wealth enabled technological development. As a result of this wealth-technology-wealth-technology spiral, ultimately science became a commodity. Investment was required for a new technical apparatus, more effective technical apparatuses gave greater profit, which enabled greater investment. In this process 'a portion of the sale is recycled into a research fund dedicated to further improvement. It is at this precise moment that science becomes a force of production, in other words a moment in the circulation of capital' (1984: 45). Science cannot be seen as a pure enterprise dedicated to the pursuit of truth; it becomes a productive activity, judged by its ability to generate money. This performative criteria replaces the enlightenment drive for truth.

Research in universities is increasingly a question of 'soft money', or piecemeal research contracts. Grants from corporations and government departments finance research and thus direct the production of information, of knowledge bytes; pragmatic considerations, tied to quite specific requirements, dominate. We can no longer think of society as a normative, construction project; it becomes a collection of localised language games interacting within a market context. It becomes impossible to paint a picture of the whole, without falling into one or other of the discredited traditions. Lyotard tells us not to worry since 'we have paid a high enough price for the nostalgia of the whole' (Ibid: 82). Instead, we should do battle with the narratives, deconstruct and help articulate the unpresentable, and allow subdued voices to come to the surface. We should embrace the demise of modernity with joy, conduct life as one great party, enjoy diversity, wonder at complexity, and marvel at how intelligent we are. Except – as we criminologists realise only too well – not all are invited to the party.

Lyotard asks us to be seduced by the rhetoric of a new pure modernity; the performability of language games shall be their only criterion of inclusivity or exclusivity – this is the image of the perfect meritocracy – of course, the criteria of demarcation becomes skill and performability; a new form of knowledge-power relationship. Reflexivity catches even Lyotard: while he relates the decline of the meta-narratives, his own text is itself a meta-narrative of the rise and decline of meta-narratives.

Does post-modernism imply the impossibility of constructing a general theory, or even of integrating different theories?

The normative utopia of modernity sought for an organised social structure constructed by man's co-operative efforts. Modernity (re)constructed social order out of a reflexive (non)understanding of the void underlying human existence: to structure means to counter-balance randomness, to ensure predictability. The tools were knowledge and power. A strong society needed to control those who betrayed it: punishment was just in that it was not a defence of the illusions of metaphysics, or arbitrary political judgment, but part of the body of knowledge of society and man's place within it. The well adjusted citizen – the socialised individual – was to be one who understood what the society stood for, understood the necessity for rules for the social game, and played by the rules. The desire for individual advancement resulted in an increase in performability and skills in the practices which the rules delineated – the desire of the individual to better him or herself enriched the society. Social theory kept randomness, kept contingency, under control by claiming to uncover structure, rather than engage in practices of destruction and construction. And to a large extent this ideology has worked, but we now realise, with Unger (1976), that social theory is in a sense both metaphysical and political. It takes stands on issues of human nature and human knowledge for which no 'scientific' elucidation is, or may ever be, available. We can no longer deny that the development and fate of social theory is inseparable from the fate of society.

> 'The progress of theory depends upon political events. The doctrines theory embraces are ideals as well as descriptions: the choices theory must make are choices among conceptions of what society ought to be as among views of what it is. These choices are neither arbitrary nor capable of logical or empirical proof. They build upon speculative conceptions of the requirements of social order and of the demands of human nature, conceptions that are informed by historical knowledge but which cannot pretend to follow necessarily from it.' (Roberto Unger, 1976: 267)

Classical criminology aided the construction of early modernity, laying out a structure for legitimating the legislative drive and the use of crime as a central conception of management linked with the growing centralising political power of the nation state; criminology then became part of the positive project, the great enterprise of creating knowledge capable of legitimating organised, bureaucratic modernity; it developed various positive strategies, ranging from consensual functionalism to critical functionalism. For much of this century, within traditional criminology, the idea of law reflecting social consensus kept the proponents of critical theory largely at bay (beyond the walls of the liberal-capitalist–urban complex), and the intimate connection between labour and capital gave rise to a 'fordist' style of urban life, easily understandable as a functionalist/positivist complex. The beginnings of post-modernism, perhaps identified first with a concern with the multi-functional properties of language, may be seen with labelling theory, which, highlighted the concepts of process and censuring as identifying the deviant. While bureaucracy could use critical theory as a body of ideas which it could use as a metaphysical enemy, or raid, as appropriate, labelling theory demonstrated the plurality and contingency of the very bureaucracy that supposedly provided welfare and security. At the same time, social structural changes of a global nature made control of economies and cultural imagery difficult; the divorce between labour and capital, captured by the label of post-industrial society, robbed society of its innermost social relationship – it seemed impossible to believe any more in simplistic consensus. But, in reply, simplistic theories appeared to gain ground. The solution to increasing complexity, diversity, and plurality, became for many a retreat into common sense or managerialism; into denying the need to theorise totality, while taking comfort in easier, more apparent entities or geographies.

There is, possibly to be expected, a large amount of sense in common sense criminology: common sense involves making it more difficult for crime to occur to you by target hardening and listening to opportunity theory; this amounts to privatising social space by walling off the expensive estates; by concentrating crime among the underclass; by giving more resources to the police at the expense of education or child rearing centres; by investing in greater technologies of surveillance and tracking the easily identifiable criminals; by building more prisons as drug rehabilitation clinics are closed; above all, perhaps, by rejecting diversity in favour of working and living with people who look and feel like oneself – of controlling the plurality of post-modernism by a neo-tribalism. Theoretically, in the face of epistemological diversity, realism became the name of the game. Contemporary criminology is largely realist in working for the contracts available or concentrating on the crimes which confront the senses: street crime and the obvious offender. Conflict theory, or left idealism – as it came to be termed – was relegated, probably with some justification, to the realm of idealist utopia; while left realism, in America in the guise of writers such as Mike Davis and Elliot Currie, and in Britain Jock Young and others, sought a foundation in the real concerns of working class people. In most works grand theorising became only a mirage; it became fashionable to comment that if one wanted to do criminology one should have a general theory, but, after some nebulous comments concerning the development of a short-term time horizon as characterising our contemporary times (Wilson and Herrnstein 1985), or 'our commitment to liberty, our general prosperity, our child-rearing methods, our popular values' (Wilson: 1985 251), or self-control (Gottfredson and Hirschi: 1990), the writers invariably returned to measures concerning the control of individuals committing the most obvious crimes. Additionally, the state no longer needed sociology or criminology to determine techniques of control; those citizens who were in were seduced, and played their ever moving roles as consumers; those who were out were becoming the grist of the repressive mill, and we already knew their characteristics, so what had criminology to offer? And where criminology could potentially matter – in the study of global tendencies, in the uncovering of real social harms – who would pay? The state no longer had any interest in 'true' general theories.

But why should attempts at general social theory cease to be coherent simply because things have become vastly more complex? Why should the project of knowledge and power be surrendered to the market and we accept the dictum of localised individuality?

First consider some of the plurality of theoretical perspectives that modernist criminology has left us. True to David Hume's dictum that the key to social theory was understanding human nature, criminological theories differ according to their conceptions of human nature social order. Eleven structures of criminological theory can be presented as follows.

Eleven structures of criminological theory Table 2

Theory	View of Human Nature	View of Social Order	Concept of Normal Development	Cause of Deviance	Reforming Deviant
Differential Association	Man is a social being who must learn from others	Plurality of values and cultural groupings, one dominates	Modelling behaviour on appropriate role models and social learning	Association with delinquents and criminals	Associating with non-criminals
Strain Theory	Man is social being who tends towards the good	Relative consensus on values; dominant cultural goals	Pursuit of socially sanctioned goals and institutional means	Disjuncture between goals and available means	Increased opportunity for everyone
Social Control	Negative: man is naturally asocial and egoistic	Consensus on values and social institutions	Creation of bonding mechanisms – seduction by 'normal' means	Weak/broken bond to conventional social order	Increasing attachment to the conventional social order; increasing stake in conformity
Labelling	Man is a social animal who reacts to significations	Plurality of social values and political positions	Attributions and symbolic interactionalism	Negative labelling experiences	Refusing to dramatise deviance – changes in criminal justice system's approach to deviance
Development of Self Theories	Humans are motivated by growth	Society is a meritocracy where personal investment achieves growth	Defining one's self relative to society's norms and images of success	Implementation of a self-image consistent with crime – low self-control	Challenging old beliefs about self and developing a new self-identity
Psycho-analytic Theory	Libidinal	Social structure is based on suppression and repression of desires, fantasies are driven unto the subconscious	Gratification of instinctual drives within the limits established by society	Inadequate resolution of early conflicts resulting in either guilt or weak super-ego development; desire to transgress law; desire for punishment	Developing greater insight into the unconscious determinants of behaviour – repealing surplus criminal law
Pathological Stimulation Seeking	Man is naturally a social being, but the deviant has abnormal faculties and conditioning	Consensual structure allows for normal pleasures	Achieving an optimal level of sensory stimulation	Drive for increased levels of stimulation coupled with negative family experiences	Finding socially appropriate outlets for stimulation seeking tendencies
Rational Choice Theory	Hedonistic	Society is a series of social games laid out by law with rules known to all	Maximising pleasure/gains and minimising pain/costs	The cost benefit ratio for crime exceeds the cost. benefit ratio for non-crime	Increase the cost of crime and certainty of detection and/or increase the benefit of non-crime
Existentialism	Man is an open vessel to be determined by context and experience	Appears absurd – out of control – nihilism threatens	Taking control of life course; will to power	A world of tensions and conflicting pulls, inability to direct life plan	Self-knowledge and awareness of contingency, taking responsibility for one's life
Social Deprivation, Underclass	Varies as a result of conditioning, once socialised difficult to change	Various	Trapped in a subculture, a culture of poverty or structural disadvantage	Excluded from normal channels of participation, resentment, or badly socialised	Various – range from radical programmes of employment creation to reduction of welfare provisions
Marxist/Left Idealist	Man is a social being, naturally cooperative but dependent upon social structure	Structured by oppositions and class conflict, laws protect system interests and aid dominant social class	Develop cooperative and harmonious relations; in capitalism lean to commodify oneself and trade oneself	Experience of alienation and distorted growth under capitalism, the self is forced into relations of domination and market exchange determines worth	Radical social restructuring; destroy the tension between life world and social structure

Each theoretical structure appears to maintain purity and logical coherence at the expense of empirical exposure. Apart from existentialism – which may be an exception – each obeys the dicta of modernity: build a citadel, develop firm foundations and construct a coherent framework upon this. Are they mutually exclusive or can they be integrated? Gottfredson and Hirschi (1990) maintain that integration is difficult, since theories construct world-views of their own; instead we must build a coherent theory on its own terms.

For Gottfredson and Hirschi a general theory should

- attend to the everyday reality of crime;
- keep faith with the insights of classical criminology; and
- keep faith with the positivist project. These authors resolve the traditional clash between classical criminology and positivism by claiming classical criminology is a control theory of *crime*, whereas positivism sought to explain *criminality*.

The scope for a general theory was reduced, however, since to the authors

- crime was a mundane event of everyday life, and the entity to be explained (crime) was as reflected in the criminal statistics. Thus complex and corporate crimes, the crimes of the powerful, the whole extraordinariness of much of crime were simply overlooked;
- classicism became an explanation of offence explanations. There was no discussion of the reflexivity of classical criminology, ie the issue of social justice was ignored; while
- positivism became the search for offender explanations, resolved by the notion of differential self-control as a result of varying socialisation practices.

Gottfredson and Hirschi's theory is a limited, rather than a general theory of crime. Not only does it have no discussion on the nature of social order, or the legitimacy of law, it offers little feel for the historical contingency of the self and the contemporary context. While we are offered an image of criminality as caused by faulty socialisation, we are not offered any definition of the role of socialisation. Daily life is left at an unproblematic level instead of presenting it inside macro-sociological processes: conversely for us, daily life consists in sets of rules, resources, identities, activities, purposes, localities, capabilities, (un)certainties, (mis)understandings, projects, legitimations and moralities which are the result of a series of historical contingencies. Thus criminality is not some natural identity, but the (sometimes temporary, sometimes developmental) result of processes.

The construction of secure identities is inherently part of the process of constructing social order. The complexity of late-modern social order in post-modernism renders the idea of a safe and 'unproblematic', natural, personal identity an anachronism. In response to post-modernism, the late-modern western state denies responsibility for its space. To a large extent it can do little other; but in its rhetoric, it denies that space is social, it denies that the self is always constructed socially and acts socially. Instead we witness the privatisation of social space. Such privatisation can enable individuals personally to utilise resources in a more efficient way, or offer new opportunities for voluntary cooperation, but this appears to occur at the expense of social tensions and solidarity which require that the reality of interdependency is acknowledged. Only a truly sociological imagination can aid in our understanding and guide projects. Without this how can we have any faith that the privatisation of the social networks internal to the nation state will mean the growth of extra-national bodies, and the increasing self-awareness and reflexivity and control exercised by the self over the self's projects and life plans? On the contrary, in contemporary Britain and the US, we witness a rhetoric which decries international agreements, and denies any basic necessity or responsibility for interfacing and mediating the range of social processes which constitute individuality. The voices of the right claim that only by leaving the underclass to their own devices can a sense of personal responsibility be (re)created. Gottfredson and Hirschi demonstrate the impossibility of positivistically locating the criminal, while privatising the very concept of criminality – what greater example of privatisation can we find than the argument that the solution to crime lies in self-control, and that self-control is the result of the processes of socialisation of familial institutions without any contextualising of this process?

If post-modernism comes out of modernity, then who are we? Where are we? How do we make sense of criminological 'reality'?

Who are we? We are the result of the contingencies of our history and the construction process of modernity. We are the product of an over-determination of social forces. The ideal of personal identity in modernity is the modern self, independent of gender, class, and race, creating a selfhood as a personal project. The ultimate aim for the social project is a socially differentiated order with multiple roles and aspirations, dreams and desires, but in which people are located and interact on the basis of their desires, preferences, aspirations, needs ... without exploitation, oppression, victimisation, without the need to subject the other to crime ... yet gender, class and race do matter.

Gender, race, and class-social geography help constitute the (non) modern identity. Contingency means that any diagram of the structures of criminological theory – suitable for post-modernism – cannot be one which presupposes a firm foundation; instead variable patterns of constitutionalism must be visualised. A start has been made by Martens (1993, himself drawing upon an earlier article by K Sandquist and reproduced in Bottoms, 1994).

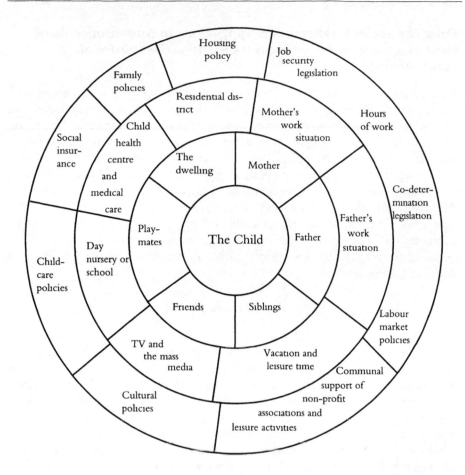

If we are to be faithful to the project of positivism, then we are concerned to understand the offender and the creation of his or her constitution; the advance this type of diagram offers is that we can see the interaction of local and wider policies. Each ring is itself mobile; the components impact upon each other. For example, the qualities of the dwelling, and the residential district, provide opportunities and stresses for both mother and father. The personalities of the family interact with social structures over time; ideologies, cultural messages, notions of the self, flow through various of these structures and the political and cultural surrounds impact in a variety of ways. Dannefer (1984: 100) suggests the failure of most traditional theories of the self and socialisation, is their 'ontogenetic' approach which down-plays the 'profoundly interactive nature of self-society relations', and the variability of social environments.

The diagram cannot be static in time, it must allow for modernity itself. The constitution of modern individuals requires an historically specific social ecology and social control.

How can social arrangements appear just in post-modernism? How can social order be legitimate under the culture of contingency?

Traditionally, social arrangements attain legitimacy when they appear to reflect a natural order. Weber's typology distinguishes the static nature of legitimacy based on tradition and custom (the Indian caste type) to that of legitimacy based on rational discussion, agreement and formalised procedure (legal-rational). Sociology has aided in legitimising modern social arrangements through reinforcing the conception of modern society as freeing itself from the remnants of the pre-modern feudal system and becoming the reflection of a structural-functional complex. Social theory which stresses meritocracy, jurisprudence which holds out law as rational, coherent and well principled, aids legitimacy by sustaining the imagery of a functioning system working for modern aims. This is rendered problematic by post-modernism. Late-modern legitimacy works in a different fashion:

Self-control and disciplinisation

A crucial aspect of social control is socialisation. Socialisation is the incorporation of mechanisms of predictability and repetitive behaviour in the actor without obvious recourse to the coercion of the state; modern actions are deemed rational actions, that is a specific form of social action in which actors can explain their actions by reason defined by the pursuit of an understandable goal or as fitting the norms (rules) of behaviour. Instead of social control as represented by socialisation into the fixed pattern of beliefs of a *mechanical solidarity*, the social control of *organic solidarity* was a dialectic, or interaction, of self and socialising context, with self and social control being two aspects of the same process. This process has intensified, and while it denotes the social creation of the autonomous self for late-modernity, it occurs in the problematic conditions of post-modernism.

Hegemony

A Marxist term which implies that control in today's democratic societies is exercised by the elites' hegemony on the production of meaning. The critical impact of post-modernism's picture of the irrationality of many legitimacy strategies is constrained, since the possible subversive role of the media and discourses of disruption is defused by structuring (non) communication so that the messages would not radically disrupt the hegemonic ideology of society. The idea of hegemony was used in the 1950s and 1960s to sensitise us to the processes of:

*   the centralisation of the responsible media, eg the corporatisation of newspapers, television;

- the marginalising and rendering non-sensical the messages of the dissent media;
- the standardisation of the public with prefabricated, standard motives for important action, eg consumption;
- multiplicity of non-important messages, eg style, fashion, personal scandals.

Hegemony is more complex in post-modernism; it is a process which is almost a mirage of itself. It exists in post-modernism as a consequence of the increasing diversity of knowledge bytes and perspectives; while such diversity means it is difficult to give an overriding substantive justification to policy which ensures consensus, it is also difficult to sustain a critique which stops policy.

Late-modern political and social decision-making remains the rule of experts

Late-modern democracy depends upon apathy. A full discussion of social issues in the culture of contingency and the over-supply of information would be difficult to steer into consensus. Hence while we keep a facade of discussion, involvement and political influence needs to be confined to the reasonable and rational; the 'others' are distanced and rendered unable to perceive the worth of involvement. Privatising social space looks like it returns power to localities, it looks like it empowers individuals at the expense of bureaucracies – which both anarchists and libertarians claim oppress – but amounts to a de-socialising of space which threatens to unleash multiple sites of oppression, small scale and ubiquitous.

Under post-modernism substantive legitimacy is not crucially important: the appearance of legitimacy resides in procedure

One aim for knowledge in modernity was to make society visible to itself – to enable reflexivity. It is the ideal of the open society, or the transparent society, where knowledge reflects reality. Conversely the post-modern perception of knowledge holds knowledge, scientific truths, to be a matter of procedure – what we defend as truth is a result of the best effort(s) we can make in the search for it, but it is always limited to our efforts and procedures, hence it is never absolute. Thus decisions made by experts are human, and not linked to some extra-human scientific guarantee. Decisions made by experts are always a result of holding some factors relevant and others irrelevant. If the criteria of relevance changes, the outcome of the decision changes – the legitimacy of the decision, the justice of the distribution of costs and benefits, becomes a result of the criteria of relevancy; and this is ultimately a question of drawing boundaries. In other words it is deeply political. It is a matter of saying we hold these factors to be relevant and these not to be – but this is not how rational-legal legitimacy is presented: it is presented as if it had to be this way, as if this outcome follows naturally. What then is the present law in post-modernism founded upon? Classical criminology founded it upon certain narratives of social development, and utilitarianism as the revealed ethics of nature, what can post-modernism found law upon? Answer: it does not need foundations since it can create it own legitimacy in procedural correctness. This, properly understood, is Weber's point: modern legal-rational authority does not need substantive legitimation, only formal legitimation. Thus we can make any activity or omission a crime – crime still exists where there is no legitimate social purpose to such legislation. The objectivism of this naturalist paradigm is a mirage – a rhetoric which obscures reality. It is because of this very non-availability of some natural objectivism that law becomes increasingly important. Law does not need foundations – law can become autopoietic – hence law provides a strong post-modern foundation; it is pure pragmatism. How do we resolve the crisis of pure rationality? We engage in practical rationality, ie we act. We legislate. We can continue to do so. The crisis engendered by post-modernism can be countered by legislation (including de-legislation ie decriminalisation) and policing.

This de-legitimising of legitimacy requires a psychological frame. Easton (1965) adopted a system's approach to political authority arguing that a political system will appear legitimate if (a) it reflects the ethnic and cultural identity of the nation, and (b) it meets the needs and interests of the population. Both of these factors may become more difficult in post-modernism, resulting in the state losing faith in its ability to manage many of the 'progressive' tasks it adopted in modernity, and the populace losing faith in the rational, political structure. The 'rational' political system will be followed as long as the social goods are provided which meet the needs and interests of the populace.

Social justice, positionality and the emotions of post-modernism

Positionality – social geography – is a crucial factor in drawing up the discourses of justice and social theory. The practical reality of justice has usually been the justice of the victors. Criminology has neglected the vast crimes which the victors have not labelled. Common to both the later Marx and Nietzsche, was the argument that a great deal of what we call the philosophy of social justice, or the sociology of structural functionalism, is the ascription of the labels 'just', 'natural' or 'functional' to arrangements that are phenomena of power which victimise, neglect, marginalise and discipline others. As left realism points out, we err when we attribute the phenomena of the criminal act to the offender alone, for the self is located in social networks. Conversely, right realism uses an idea of 'reactive attitudes'. Reactive attitudes are emotional states aroused when we observe the actions of others or groups of others, whom we consider are agents acting within the same moral framework that we inhabit, and capable of diverse activity; we get angry when they commit crime because we treat them as fellow moral creatures. When harm is caused by accident our anger decreases, since we realise no moral blame is attributable – Right realism claims positivism appears to run counter to these moral reactions, since it sometimes argues the offender is not responsible for his or her actions (cf the Kantian argument of Strawson, 1974, on how deeply embedded these moral reactions are). Right realists assert it is correct to get angry over crime. In their analyses, crime is not simply a social problem, it is a matter calling for the expression of anger and we rightly ask for revenge; to act otherwise would be to deny our involvement in moral communities.

But this anger is not the only emotion which gains ground in post-modernism. Resentment, as defined by Denzin (1984: 224-8) is the self-poisoning form of self-hatred which arises from the systematic repression of certain emotions, including envy, pride, anger, and the desire for revenge and self-conquest. Denzin believes it to be the predominant post-modernist emotion. It moulds all of the above emotional states into a pervasive view of the world. This emotion, which builds on revenge, hatred, malice and joy at another's misfortune, reflects an underlying self-hatred and lack of self-worth. It develops an emotional mood systematically produced by those social structures, including the social democracies, which espouse the equality of rights for all, while permitting wide gaps between expectations and what is in fact achievable. These social structures 'engender resentment on the part of the young, the elderly, women, the handicapped, the sexually and morally stigmatised, and members of racial and ethnic minorities' (Denzin, 1984: 226). Resentment is greatest when self, or group, injury is experienced as destiny and beyond one's control. When powerlessness and hopelessness are great, resentment increases. In such moments the other is transformed into an object deserving of revenge and violence.

Denzin argues that the cultural logics of late capitalism amplify and increase resentment. The continual circulation of commodified fantasies stressing erotic beauty, wealth, masculinity, achievement, happiness, successful love relationships, and joyous, free selfhood make it clear that for many these states can never be attained. Existential anxiety, fear, and hatred feed on these conditions; violence towards self and others is thereby produced. The impact is particularly acute in the US; for over half of the African American population an overwhelming part of life in post-modernism consists of these conditions (West, 1988: 277).

In the Nietzschean analysis, resentment flows from two sources:

- rage against the human condition with the inevitability of death for us all: we can calls this *existential resentment*. Whilst pre-modern religious structures offered solace in the after-life, in modern conditions we can find no transcendental purpose for suffering and death; and

- from the institutional arrangements which impose victimisation, suffering and injury on some for the benefit of others. We can call this *civic resentment*. The culture of contingency magnifies both sources of resentment setting up a fund of emotionality which can prove destructive.

How can a form of social justice be constructed that copes with the culture of contingency?

To quote the spirit of Weber again: human beings need a meaningful cosmos. If an individual becomes radically uncertain as to his or her identity, inaction and social paralysis results. What is the result if a nation has no means of ensuring that the existential feeling of inclusivity is achieved? The appeal of the new common sense of new right realism is to simple certainties and an uncomplicated cosmos. Herrenstein and Murray (1994), for example, attempt to placate both forms of resentment among the black underclass: by arguing that lower I.Q. is the reason for their greater burden of suffering in everyday life, the authors try to down-play contingency, provide a naturalism to legitimise disparity, and sooth the existential crisis. For Murray the members of the underclass should simply change their aspirations to more realistic levels: they should, in other words, deny their modernity. The utopia of modern organisational 'social or positive' justice, lay in the expectation that modernity could ultimately show us who or what everyone – women, men, blacks, homosexuals, jews, criminals, the mentally ill – actually or 'really' are. When we knew the basic truths of the human condition the just society could be created and stabilised. But the world discovered by science has not become a place of stable identities and essential objects whose secrets are known for all time, but rather a set of techno-objects, of experimental results, of commodities and images. Counterpoised to this unstable world is the nostalgia for the world of familiar, solid, unitary, stable and 'authoritative' reality. Can a justice which is fluid and a question of procedure be argued for? An argument that while we can not have a stable state of justice we can act justly? Lyotard (1985), without a touch of irony, calls this *Just Gaming*.

Is a post-modern justice a question of mobility, of striving for the just even though one realises that no one particular social arrangement is just? Is the just arrangement that result which is to be accepted if it is the best that we can achieve, given the conditions?

Without a continuing narrative of modernity, *Just Gaming* becomes just gaming

This image of a Just Gaming depends upon building upon the projects of the enlightenment, but the voices of both the right and far left cry out that modernity lies exhausted ... empowerment, it is said, is a question of more money in one's pocket. Without the dream of the social, what is to be the reality of everyday life, what are we to do? We simply game. We seduce, we offer, we accept, we take, we play, we game – the social becomes a site of games connected only by the market and those who have the skills enjoy everyday life – for the others, a quiet (and sometimes not-so-quiet) terrorism awaits. Skills are differentially distributed and rewarded: and a special set of skills are required to negotiate the post-modern condition.

Institutions also game: the central tactic of defending white collar crime is simple – make it appear so complicated that no one can follow it and thereby allocate responsibility. Commentators of post-modernism, such as Baudrillard (1990), remind us that we increasingly live in a world of symbols where they have their own exchange value, not only different from their use value, but contradictory to it. Thus when in order to assess criminal liability, the American Government asked the multinational Exxon for a general report on all its activities throughout the world, the response was 12 volumes of 1,000 pages each, which would take any prosecution team years of work to read, yet alone analyse. The request for information delivers us into the impossibility of useful information. Exxon game with the request for information and thus the old structure of knowledge mirroring nature, and thereby apportioning liability, is incapable of fruition.

Gaming is different for the underclass. Harrison's *Inside the Inner City* (1985) paints a grim picture of a bleak world of immediate existence for those who live on benefits. In the charity Campaign Against Poverty's *Decade of Despair* a basic rate pensioner writes:

> 'When you are poor, you have to be extra good at managing, extra good at self-discipline, extra good at economising, extra good at managing without and extra good at dealing with constant crisis, stress and frustration. Few of us are extra good. The rich aren't.' (Quoted Fainstein, *et al*, 1992: 146)

Is post-modernism the collapse of any drive towards social individuality; are we mere modular components?

Lefebvre (1984), in his Marxist influenced analysis of everyday life, claimed the failure of modernity lay in the alienation we experience as we understand our powerlessness to influence the world in which we live; our search for moral guidelines for our conduct and belief finds meaninglessness; our search for commonality founders upon our experience of isolation from others and estrangement from ourselves. Modern society must have meaning beyond the games of consumption to offer coherence and   as John Stuart Mill earlier – Lefebvre offers it in the production of autonomous, thinking, feeling individuals able to experience their own desires and develop their own life-styles. This is a utopia which links desires of both right and left. Critics, however, ask; 'has the modern project of individual autonomy been subordinated and subsumed by the market-defined and market-orientated freedom of consumer choice?' (Bauman, 1987: 189). Post-modernism, moreover, does not mean the end of bureaucracy; there is a new form of organised structuring. Ernest Gellner (1994) presents the image of *modular man*. Modular man is a similar idea to that of modular furniture:

> 'The point about such furniture is that it comes in bits which are agglutinative: you can buy one bit which will function on its own, but when your needs,

income or space available augment, you can buy another. It will fit in with the one acquired previously, and the whole thing will still have a coherence, aesthetically and technically. You can combine and recombine the bits at will.' (1994: 97)

With traditional furniture you buy the complete unit in one go. Endeavouring to combine one piece of modular furniture with traditional furniture is risky and usually results in an eclectic, incoherent mess. Traditional man fits a particular social structure; he is like a piece of furniture vividly marked by a given style. He simply does not blend with men of a different cultural mould. Throughout history men have not been modular, rather they have inhabited a segmentary society in which their actions make sense and have subjective meaning only as part of the totality. Modernity created in the West a civil society with tolerance, diversity, opportunity, chance, unexpected events, contingency and the preparedness to perform a variety of tasks. Civil society exists with a social order forged through links both effective and flexible, specific and instrumental. Modular man:

'... is highly variable, not to say volatile in his activities. He is modular because he is capable of performing highly diverse tasks in the same general cultural idiom, if necessary reading up manuals of specific jobs in the general standard style of the culture in question.' (Ibid: 102)

Modular man games: he attends an employment interview and convinces the panel that he can do the job. He may lie in over-stating his experience – seduce the panel with his performability – but the seduction is also a promise to perform further. He has asserted that he is capable of an amazing, indeed bewildering, diversity of tasks. For Gellner:

'It is his emergence or reproduction which is the crucial problem of Civil Society.' (Ibid: 102)

This idea of the modular man is a variation of the capabilities expected of our late-modern self – modernity has (ideally) a form of selfhood which developed the sense of inwardness; it is an interiorised self; a self with a developed memory (the key to identity for Hume); a self which has learned to plan today for its future (the rational self of Weber; a self of delayed gratification); a self which has learned to relate to the world as a terrain of commodities, and to treat itself as a commodity worth investing in (the drive to education, to gain degrees etc); a self which has learned to organise itself as an agent of self-interest; a self which has learned to read its soul as an object of knowledge and freedom; a self which has learned to monitor its impulses, its desires so they can be directed and redirected into purposes which cohere with each other fitting into the structures and games of the social; a self which has learned the interiority of the rules of the social, to abide by the norms; a self whose increased interiority and coherence enables it to develop a sense of guilt (as opposed to shame), and renders it capable of being held responsible for actions which are now viewed as pertaining, and for all practical purposes (for the practical rationality of Kantian judgment – the courtroom) as originating, with itself (his actions, his crimes) and subjected to his control (his criminality).

But this is also a self that has learned to judge its success by its ability to use the market and to attain the commodities the market exchanges. The late-modern self is a consuming self, a self which returns to the status driven emblems of the pre-modern, but while the pre-modern self fitted into his or her emblems by the status location of his or her birth, the culture of contingency makes the status of the late-modern self, the accumulation of the emblems of status, a matter of personal choice. So this self, located in post-modernism, claims he or she provides style to his or her life; claims that in accumulating and using commodities before they can become a bind, that he or she is free. But in turning the individual's needs for personal autonomy, self-definition, authentic life and personal development into the systemic process of the need to possess, and consume market-offered goods, the self may prove weak to the very task of self-definition and personal autonomy that appear the goal. Surrender to the market and to the image of the self-regulating system, is the failure of the enlightenment project, and in the self amounts to a resistance to becoming truly modern. The (all-too) social self thus renders itself susceptible to mental illness, crime, drug-taking, delinquency and the emotionality of resentment.

The ideal late-modern self fits a variety of late-modern games; our modular man possesses social capital: is criminality a function of social capital?

To game successfully one needs capital. Post-modernism creates and demands new forms of capital. Today, capital is not just money, it is also a range of individual factors – such as IQ and personality traits and social skills such as tolerance levels, the ability to handle stress in a non-violent way, the ability to articulate and communicate ideas and experiences. The aim of criminological positivism has been to locate the roots of the perceived behavioural consistency of delinquents and adult offenders in a stable tendency (criminality) towards offending and other forms of troublesome behaviour. If one assumes that 'there exists a single syndrome made up of a broad variety of antisocial behaviours arising in childhood and continuing into adulthood' (Robins and Ratcliff, 1980: 248), then finding its foundation solves the issue of criminality. Critics of Gottfredson and Hirschi's thesis of self-control, for example, Nagin and Paternoster (1991), identify an assumption of population heterogeneity in an underlying propensity to crime established early in life and which remains stable over time. The varying forms of labelled 'anti-social behaviour', especially drug-taking, reckless behaviour causing accidents (particularly while driving), are read as expressions of the same underlying trait or propensity. But, as labelling theory highlighted, continuity may be for a variety of reasons, and embedded in a range of processes in which individual traits or propensities are only one factor; this is most clear when we place the processes which labelling theory alerts us to within an awareness of social structures, structural disadvantages and diminished life chances. Additionally, it may be that early delinquent behaviour indirectly affects later criminal offending by reducing the range of informal links and informal social controls. For Gottfredson and Hirschi (1990), the connection between early delinquency and adult crime is the underlying propensity. Similarly, Herrenstein and Murray (1994) hold that as individuals sort themselves out in their life courses, where they end in the various niches of the social structure is a result of underlying propensities or traits (personality, IQ, self-control). Other features, such as the experience of unemployment or location in social geography, are regarded as spurious and largely consequent upon the individual-level differences which are either inherited or caused by family-school processes at an early age (see, for example, Gottfredson and Hirschi, 1990: 154-168).

Much of the empirical work of traditional criminology gains in depth when we re-analyse it allowing for the changing requirements of socialisation and the development of late-modernity. In *Crime in the Making: pathways and turning points through life*, Sampson and Laub (1993) use the concept of 'social capital' to develop a theory of informal social control based on a re-analysis of data created by the longitudinal studies involving 1,000 individuals carried out by the Gluecks in the 1940s and 1950s. They concluded that the causes of crime within the Glueck's study lay 'in structural disadvantage, weakened informal social bonds to family, school, and work, and the disruption of social relations between individuals and institutions that provide social capital' (1993: 255).

Family and social structural factors interact: although many studies indicate that low income, unemployment and under-employment increase the risk of family disruption (for example, Currie, 1985; Wilson, 1987; Sampson 1987) the tendency in previous criminology (for example, Burt (1925), and the Gluecks, 1940, 1968) was to see social context and family factors as somehow separate. This demarcation was mirrored in the public-private distinction embedded in political philosophy and legal thought. While a more thoroughgoing interactive approach must be accepted we can also see that a tendency towards staticity was inbuilt in previous theorising. For example, for much of this century, the notion of the appropriate social role was the idea through which sociology linked social structure and individual constitutionality; successful socialisation in large part was learning the social personality, the expectations and norms, appropriate for this or that role prescribed for you by your place in the social structure. In post-modernism the relatively well established foundations of viewing society, self, and community constructed within the context of industrialism have been radically shaken, if not toppled completely. Under the relative consensus existing in the 1940s, 1950s and 1960s and still harboured after today, socialisation and childrearing practices emphasised concepts of belonging, and saw the development of the self as a process enabled and restrained by location in relatively coherent and integrative practices. Positivist criminology subjected to analysis those individuals appearing to fail to integrate into the structure of normalcy. Such analysis must change in a post-modernism which downgrades notions of social order based on foundations and functional coherence, in favour of a more process-based, fluid and action-orientated model. When we acknowledge that social processes involve both individual characteristics such as personality traits and IQ tolerance levels, and social structural factors such as family disruptions, poverty, underclass in interaction, a considerable range of variables converge, interact and constitute each other.

Neither, in searching for explanations for crime in individual traits, can personality forms and self-control be separated out from the life course and the changing patterns of daily life, since the various forms of crime are structured by social opportunities to commit or refrain from crime, differential reactions by concerned agencies/individuals and the criminal justice system, the constraints imposed by ageing and the networks of social ties which change, weaken, or intensify feelings of belonging and bonding to significant others. Processes of informal social control vary in their effects across different parts of social geography and from childhood to adulthood. The important institutions of informal and formal social control vary across the life span and in individual locations. We have noted, for example, that women have been more the object of informal social control centred on the family and home than men, who have been more the subjects and objects of formal control. Such informal control need not be seen as imposed from outside but may consist in large part of internalised expectations and attitudes. The previous discussion of the ethics of responsibility alerts us to the idea of informal social control as also being the acceptance of responsibility, of the social ties of love and nurturing, which may serve to defy the utilitarian demands to commit crime. Across the life span, individuals vary in their contact with, and experience of, family, school, peer groups, neighbourhood environment, contact time with concerned 'others', institutions of higher education or vocational training, employment, love affairs and understanding of the other sex and other racial groups. They vary, additionally, in their contact with welfare and juvenile justice system officials, police and the adult criminal justice system. While a central feature of the social control perspective is that of crime resulting from the weakening of individuals' bonds to society and near groups (family, school), as such bonds decrease the tendency is to require the formal social control network to increase surveillance, demand conformity and incarcerate those offending; yet social control from a constructivist perspective is the ability of a social group to create itself, regulate itself according to desired principles, norms and values and to make the norms and rules effective through socialisation. The dream of the classical criminologist is to achieve such a coherent and rationally structured whole – that is a social justice; post-modernism renders the whole complex and ambiguous. *The weakness of neo-classicism is to return to justice without the social.*

Faced with the absence of a coherent and well structured modernity, life in post-modernism can be a grand adventure. Surrounded by a multiplicity of images, in a terrain devoid of the ultimate markers of certainty, armed with the injunction to create oneself, both the late-modern individual and the late-modern society are engaged in a journey into the unknown. If individual and social happiness is the goal, the search for happiness occurs in a condition where the boundaries of the possible and the imaginable constantly recede. This is an adventure only partially possible to a very small number of the elites of past generations. Late-modernity declares that it is now open to us all, rather it is imposed on vast numbers who may not have the resources to benefit, who may not be able to play, who lack the resources to make oneself and to voyage within post-modernism – *economic*, *human* and *social* capital. We traditionally acknowledge that those who do not have enough economic capital have lesser life chances, we now understand that the conditions of post-modernism demand more and greater sophistication in social skills and technical ability – we can call this *human capital*; we can see that personality, flexibility, tolerance, and self-esteem are also required, and these come for individuals from their relationships with others. The quality and effects of these relationships we can call *social capital*. Thus social capital is the result of investments in personal relationships, the experiencing of being loved, valued, appreciated, desired, supported, tutored, trusted, relied upon, and the myriad other forms of deep human interaction and dependency; qualities most clearly visible in the total dependency of the new born child, and, when appropriately mediated, characterises all forms of social life thereafter.

The three forms of capital – economic, human and social – interact. One aspect of social capital is the experiencing of love and human resources, for example, time and attention, as a child. Individuals vary in the amount of attention they receive as (potential) individuals. No two children are treated exactly the same. Currently, many parents, for example, spend more time reading to their baby daughters then they do to their sons. Since school performance is highly focused around literacy (reading/writings skills), they are, albeit unwittingly, devoting more social capital towards constructing daughters who will preform better at school than sons. Socio-economic disadvantage, or a shortage of economic capital (associated, for example, with parents who must work extremely long hours and cannot afford a child-minder), means a reduction in the amount of social capital invested in the child. We would expect, therefore, poverty and disadvantage to have strong indirect effects on crime, irrespective of direct effects. Social relations between individuals – child and parent(s), teacher-student, friends, employer-employee – at any stage in the life course, are a form of social investment or social capital. Social capital derived from strong social relations (or strong social bonds), is first experienced as a child within the family, and thereafter apparent, in differing forms, as an adolescent at school, among peer groups and 'significant others', among colleagues and employers at work, and among fellow members of sporting teams. These experiences, if positive, augment the self, strengthening the psychological resources individuals can draw upon as they move through life and strongly supporting their sense of self-worth, self-esteem and self-confidence.

Social capital is a factor in the construction of social solidarity. Durkheim's message of social solidarity in organic conditions was of the variety of such relations and the expectation that if they were experienced with an appreciation of interdependence, then individuals would value such interaction and understand the interconnectedness of modernity. Interdependent social bonds flow from the increasing division of labour, complexity of tasks and life networks; the experiencing of interdependent social bonds increases social capital and requires personal investment in social relations and institutions (as well as social values: the maintenance of deep social relations with individuals of a range of ethnic and social groups amounts to a practical adherence to the principles of tolerance and multi-ethnicity). Social capital can be affected by social policy since social capital, for example, social ties embedded in work and family institutions, flows from experiences and relations between people in socio-economic situations and is affected by social stratification, ideologies and gender concepts. It can be directly affected by criminal justice policies of incarceration and punitive control which serve to undermine the various forms of informal social control; thus criminal justice can cause crime.

A final end-word? Beyond post-modernist doubts?

Where are we? Where do we go? What is the nature of this journey? As long as we keep asking these questions we are moderns – obsessed with the task of understanding (our)selves and contexts – obsessed with the task of building an immanence, a place to reside, and giving ourselves a presence to grace it.

To make the work the place for a modern, rational, autonomous self, man killed the transcendental presence of the God(s) that previously set the contours of the natural. We were to fill the world with the structures and forms of new buildings, bounded by the phenomena of the true nature and society. Firm contours, firm knowledges, secure societies; criminology took on a task, that of giving advice to the powerful concerning social control and understanding crime. We have traced its journey through modernity into post-modernism; among the themes it played with were the twin demands of liberty and discipline – of sociology and moral theory – of empiricism and normative theory. Universal values stand off against the claims of parochial localities; communal desire humanises the abstractness and distance of the universalistic concept.

Because its knowledges were twined with power, criminology has mainly been the discourse of the socially powerful – it has not been helped by the narrowness of its concerns with official crime. Modernity was ruthless in its construction process; it was founded in part on what we now call crimes against humanity – on slavery, on the extinction of indigenous populations, on broken treaties, on extortion – but because it moved under the narratives of progress these events were called part of the civilising process. While the crime of genocide has never been prosecuted, the concept of crimes against humanity was created by the victors after a world war, and we now consider no conduct of humans an immunity beyond law: beyond crime.

What are the limits of our discourse? If criminology were to remove itself from official power all and everything becomes talked about. Today, the voices of law and order, of the anger of the super-class, calls upon criminology to provide more and better information for social control. Social order is under stress world wide: Pessimistic commentators claim a new empire of fortress Europe, North America, Malaysia, Singapore, Japan, Australia and certain other countries seems certain to face a new barbarism outside its walls. Within its walls our cities begin to radically divide – the underclass threatens. When we look around we seem surrounded by crime while it becomes difficult to tell the important from the unimportant. Modernity destroyed to create – power ensued – but no settled structure ensued. Structures we now understand as meditations, as techo-rods, as blends of knowledge and power, as hybrids – nowhere do we build using pure materials, pure humanity, pure selves, pure natural forces. Thus the late-modern world takes on the appearance of hyper-reality; its forms the creation of a world where the attribution of value gets even more difficult to ascribe, where we are surrounded by signs, perspectives; where nothing is pure essence and everything is other-than-essential.

Now, in that process we call post-modernism, we search for commonality, for social solidarity. Modernity set in train the very processes that created the modern self, and now offers only the warning that the self must control itself. But the self needs guidance, needs the touch of the transcendent. Must it be condemned to dream and to dreams alone? In the *Gay Science* Nietzsche warned of our fate: we would know we were dreaming, but go on dreaming. Currently we fool ourselves that deconstruction, demystification, so strips the Emperor of his clothing that the world will simply right itself. Another dream ...

The dialectic of life is of the mind, the body and our dreams. At one point, as Christ lay dying, previous narratives told of the violence and vulnerability which underlies the human spirit – christians, henceforth, knew of the transubstantiation of the body and blood of Christ. The foundation of divine purpose... but we now know we are of the flesh and blood of mortality. Humanity is its own secret; its own foundation. We cannot dream of other than us ... we are mystery enough. Perhaps Brian Patten recognised this in his poem *A Drop of Unclouded Blood* wherein he thought:

'of these cities floating fragile
across the earth's crust
and of how they are in need
of a drop of magic blood
a drop of unclouded blood.'

Patten dreamed of purity, of an essence for:

'children adrift in their temporary world

beneath their dreaming is a drop of blood

refusing the sun's heat

a drop of blood more pure than any other blood.'

This search for purity is not a refusal of hope, or progress, nor reaction, for this blood reflects the dialectic of the particular and the universal.

'I need to sever all connection with the habits

that make the heart

love only certain things

I need a drop of magic blood for that

a drop of unclouded blood.'

Blood comes in many forms – the spilling of human blood pre-dates the concept of crime modernity constructed – but it takes new meanings in post-modernism. If the Los Angeles riots were the first post-modern urban riots, then the conflict in Ex-Yugoslavia is the first post-modern war. Racked by multiple perspectives and competing interest domains, its tragedy is the destruction of the hope for democratic plurality; the turning away from the building of a vibrant society of interaction and individuality; from constructing identities whether Bosnian-Serb, Bosnian-Muslim, or Bosnian-Croat, that are modern. The international community, faced with the prospect of making a stand on a normative orientation to post-modernism, has lost itself in double dealing and cynical hypocrisy; the words crime and criminal become used and abused. I am told of a Serbian soldier who was tenth in line to gang-rape a Bosnian-Moslem woman. As the person who was eighth penetrated the beaten, unconscious, mutilated, semen-soaked body, this soldier could take it no longer, and placing his rifle against her prostrate head, he blew out her brains. The Bosnian-Serb authorities, apparently, thought him a perfect scapegoat, he was to be charged with rape and murder, and proposed for the War Crimes Tribunal – but others spoke of the 'reality', and no action took place. Another unreported crime, another action to be forgotten; another event criminology finds difficult to talk about. Was he a criminal, or was he just a man who had belatedly found his humanity? Are the real criminals those powers that stood by allowing this conflict to continue? And what is the role of those who said the truth was too difficult to ascertain?

We talk, we analyse, we argue; we lose our selves in our doubts – but we also suffer, kill, love, despair. Our need is for discourses which move between the forms and structures of the big and the small, of the powerful and the victims; for a criminology which mirrors self-doubt, not as a reason for despair, but as the grounding for continual (re)construction. Doubt is essential to creation; self doubt, ambivalence as to the human condition is the foundation. The fact that we doubt all is not grounds for inaction, but evidence of the actions of moderns searching for a better humanity, conscious of contingency and their social fragility; conscious, that is, of their modernity and the very fragility and imcompleteness of its constitution.

BIBLIOGRAPHY

Abrahamsen, D (1944) *Crime and the Human Mind*, New York:
Columbia University Press

Adler, F (1975) *Sisters in Crime: The Rise of the New Female Criminal*,
New York: McGraw Hill

Adorno, T (1973) *The Jargon of Authenticity*, Evanston, Ill: Northwestern
University Press

Akers, Ronald (1977) *Deviant Behaviour: A Social Learning Approach*,
Belmont, Calif: Wadsworth

Allen, V and and Greenberger, D (1978) 'An Aesthetic Theory
of vandalism', *Crime and Delinquency*, 24

Allsop, JF and Feldman, MP (1975) 'Extraversion, neuroticism
and psychoticism and anti-social behaviour in school girls', *Social
Behaviour and Personality*, 2

Althusser, Louis (1971) *Lenin and Philosophy*, New York: Monthly
Review Press

Amdur, RL (1989) 'Testing casual models of delinquency:
A methodological critique', *Criminal Justice and Behaviour*, 16

Anderson, M (1979), *Welfare, Palo Alto*: Hoover Institute Press

Arblaster, Anthony (1984) *The Rise and Decline of Western
Liberalism*, Oxford: Basil Blackwell

Arendt, H (1964) *Eichmann in Jerusalem: A Report on the Banality of Evil*,
New York: Viking Press

Ascher, C (1979) 'On Encountering the I and the We in Simone de
Beauvoir's Memoirs', in *The Second Sex - Thirty Years Later*, New York:
New York Institute for the Humanities

Atkinson, JM (1971) 'Societal Reaction to Suicide', in S Cohen (ed),
Images of Deviance, Harmondsworth: Penguin Books

Auld, J, Dorn, N and South, N (1986) 'Irregular work, Irregular
Pleasures: Herion in the 1980's', in Roger Matthews and Jock Young
(eds), *Confronting Crime*, London: Sage

Auletta, K (1982) *The Underclass*, New York: Random House

Austin, J (1832) *The Province of Jurisprudence Determined and the Uses of the Study
of Jurisprudence*, London: Wiedenfeld and Nicolson
- (1873) *Lectures on Jurisprudence or the Philosophy of Positive Law*
4th ed (1885, 5th edn), edited by R Campbell, London: John Murray

Austin, RL (1977) 'Commitment, neutralization and delinquency', in
TN Ferdinand (ed) *Juvenile delinquency: little brother grows up*, Beverly
Hills, CA: Sage

Barbanel, J (1989) 'How despair is engulfing a generation in New York', *New York Times*, April 2

Bachman JG & O'Malley, PM (1978) Youth in transition, Volume VI: *Adolescence to adulthood: Change and stability in the lives of young men*, Ann Arbor: University of Michigan Press

Bacon, Francis *Collected Works*, Vol 3

Bacon, R and Eltis, W (1978) *Britain's Economic Problem: Too Few Producers*, London: Macmillan

Bagguley, P and Mann, K (1992) 'Idle Thieving Bastards? Scholarly Representations of the 'Underclass'', *Work, Employment & Society*, Vol 6, No1

Bahr SJ (1979) 'Family determinants and effects of deviance', in WR Burr, R Hill, FINye & IL Reiss (eds), *Contemporary theories about the family: research-based theories*, Vol1, New York: Free Press

Barnes, Harry E, and Teeters, Negley K (1951) *New Horizons in Criminology*, 2d ed New York: Prentice-Hall, Inc

Bartol, CR (1980) *Criminal Behaviour: A Psychosocial Approach*, Englewood Cliffs, NJ: Prentice-Hall

Baudrillard, Jean (1981) *For a Critique of the Political Economy of the Sign*, St Louis: Telos Press
- (1988) *Selected Writings*, Stanford, Cal: Stanford University Press
- (1990) *Fatal Strategies: crystal revenge*, New York: Semiotext(e)/Pluto Press

Bauman, Zygmunt (1987) *Legislators and Interpreters*, Cambridge: Polity Press
- (1989) *Modernity and the Holocaust*, Cambridge: Polity Press
- (1991) *Modernity and Ambivalence*, Cambridge: Polity Press
- (1993) *Postmodern Ethics*, Oxford: Blackwell

Baxter, James K (1980) *Collected Poems*, Wellington/Oxford: Oxford University Press

Beccaria, Cesare ([1764] 1963) *On Crimes and Punishments*, Henry Paolucci trans Indianapolis: Bobbs-Merrill Also
- ([1764] 1986) *On Crimes and Punishments*, David Young trans Indianapolis: Hackett Publishing

Becker, Howard (1963) *The Outsiders: Studies in the Sociology of Deviance*, New York: Free Press

Beirne, Piers (1993) *Inventing Criminology: essays on the rise of 'Homo Criminalis'*, Albany: State University of New York Press

Bell, D (1979) *The Cultural Contradictions of Capitalism*, New York

Belson, William (1975) *Juvenile Theft: The causal Factors*, London: Harper & Row

Benedict, Ruth (1946) *The Chrysanthemum and the Sword: Patterns of Japanese Culture*, Boston: Houghton Mifflin

Benson, ML (1985) 'Denying the guilty mind: Accounting for involvement in a white-collar crime', *Criminology*, 23

Bentham, J (1982) *A Fragment of Government and an Introduction to the Principles of Morals and Legislation*, J Barns and H Hart, (eds) London
- ([1791] 1843) 'Panopticon or Inspection House', in the *Collected Works of Jeremy Bentham*, J Bowring (ed), London

Berger, P, Berger, B, and Kellner, H (1974) *The Homeless Mind*, New York: Vintage Books

Berman, M (1983) *All That is Solid Melts into Air*, London: Verso

Bernard TJ (1987) 'Structure and control: Reconsidering Hirschi's concept of commitment', *Justice Quarterly*, 4
- (1987) 'Testing Structural Strain Theories', *Journal of Research in Crime and Delinquency*, 24

Berns, Walter (1979) *Capital Punishment*, London: Basic Books

Bernstein, Richard, J (1986) 'Rethinking the Social and the Political', in *Philosophical profiles: Essays in a Pragmatic Mode*, Oxford: Polity Press/Basil Blackwell

Bishop, C (1931) *Women and Crime*, London: Chatto and Windus

Black, Donald (1976) *The Behaviour of Law*, New York: Academic Press
- (1984) 'Crime as Social Control', in Toward a General Theory of Social Control: Vol 2: *Selected Problems*, Donald Black, ed, London: Academic Press, INC

Blackstone, William ([1765-9] 1973) *Commentaries on the Laws of England*, G Jones (ed), London

Blumenberg, Hans (1983) *The Legitimacy of the Modern Age*, Cambridge, Mass: MIT Press

Bock, KE (1980) *Human Nature and History: a response to sociobiology*, New York: Columbia University Press

Bonger, Willem (1936) *An Introduction to Criminology*, London: Methuen

Bottoms, Anthony, E (1994) 'Environmental Criminology', in Mike Maguire, Rod Morgan, and Robert Reiner (eds), *The Oxford Handbook of Criminology*, Oxford: Clarendon Press

Bowlby, J (1944) 'Forty-four juvenile thieves', *International Journal of Psychoanalysis* 25: 1-57
- (1946) *Forty-Four Juvenile Thieves: Their Characters and Home-Life*, London: Baillière, Tindall, & Cox

- (1951) *Maternal Care and Mental Health*, Geneva:
World Health Organisation
- (1979) *The Making and Breaking of Affectional Bonds*, London: Tavistock

Bowlby, J and Salter-Ainsworth, MD (1965) *Child Care and the Growth
of Love*, Harmondsworth: Penguin

Bowlby, J, Ainsworth, MD, Boston, M, and Rosenbluth, D (1956)
'The effects of mother-child separation: a follow-up study', *British
Journal of Medical Psychology* 29
- (1982) 'Physical appearance and criminality',
Current Psychological Reviews 2: 269-81

Box S (1971) *Deviance, Reality and Society*, London: Holt, Rinehart & Winston
- (1983) *Power, Crime and Mystification*, London: Tavistock

Box S and C Hale (1983) 'Liberation and Female Criminality in England
and Wales', *British Journal of Criminology* 23

Boxill, Bernard, R (1991) 'Wilson on the truly Disadvantaged', *Ethics*, Vol 101

Braithwaite, J (1981) 'The myth of social class and criminality
reconsidered', *American Sociological Review*, 46
- (1989) *Crime, Shame, and Reintegration*, Cambridge: Cambridge
University Press
- (1991) 'Poverty, Power, White-Collar Crime and the Paradoxs
of Criminological Theory', *Australian and New Zealand Journal
of Criminology*, January
- (1992) 'Reducing the Crime Problem: a not so dismal criminology',
Australian and New Zealand Journal of Criminology, 25

Brennan, T and Huizinga, D (1975) *Theory validation and aggregate national
data* (Integration Report of the Office of Youth Opportunity Research,
Boulder, Co: Behavioural Research Institute

Brenner, H (1971) *Time Series Analysis of Relationships Between Selected Economic
and Social Indicators*, vol 1: Texts and Appendices, Washington,
DC: US Government Printing Office

Brodribb, Somer (1992) *Nothing Mat[t]ers: a feminist critique of postmodernism*,
Melbourne: Spinifex

Buckle, A, and Farrington, D (1984) 'An Observational Study of Shoplifting',
British Journal of Criminology, 24

Burgess A (1962) *The Clockwork Orange*, London: Heinemann

Burt, C (1925) *The Young Delinquent*, London: University of London Press

Cain, Maureen (1989) *Growing up Good: Policing the Behaviour of
Girls in Europe*, London: Sage

Callinicos, Alex (1989) *Against Postmodernism: a Marxist Critique*, Polity Press

Campbell A (1981) *Girl Delinquents*, Oxford: Basil Blackwell
- (1984) *The Girls in The Gang*, Oxford: Basil Blackwell

Caplan, P (1975) 'Sex Differences in anti-social behaviour: does research methodology produce or abolish them?', *Human Development*, 18

Carby, H (1987) "On the threshold of woman's era': lynching, empire and sexuality in black feminist theory', in H Gates (ed), *Figures in Black*, Oxford: Oxford University Press

Carlen, P (1983) *Women's Imprisonment*, London: Routledge and Kegan Paul
- (1985) *Criminal Women*, Oxford: Polity Press
- (1990) 'Women, crime, feminism and realism', *Social Justice*, 17 (4)

Carlen, P and Worrall, A (eds) (1987) *Gender, Crime and Justice*, Milton Keynes: Open University Press

Carrigan, Tim Connell, Bob and Lee, Lohn (1985) 'Toward a New Sociology of Masculinity', *Theory and Society*, 14(5)

Cernkovich, S (1978) 'Evaluating two models of delinquency causation', *Criminology*, 16

Cernkovich, S, and Giordano, P (1979) 'Delinquency, opportunity, and gender', *Journal of Criminal Law and Criminology*, 70

Chadda, Parminder (1992) 'Southall', in *The Popular Front of Contemporary Poetry Anthology*, London: Apples and Snakes

Chambers, I (1986) *Popular Culture: the metropolitan experience*, London
- (1987) 'Maps of the metropolis: a possible guide to the present', *Cultural Studies*, 1, 1-22

Chapman, JR (1980) *Economic Realities and the Female Offender*, Lexington, Mass: Lexington Books

Chesney-Lind, M (1973) 'Judicial Enforcement of the female sex role', *Issues in Criminology*, 8
- (1978) 'Chivalry Re-examined: Women and the Criminal Justice System', in LH Bowker (ed) *Women, Crime and the Criminal Justice System*, Lexington, Mass: Lexington Books

Christiansen, KO (1977) 'A preliminary study of criminality among twins', in S Mednick and KO Christiansen (eds) *Biosocial Bases of Criminal Behaviour*, New York: Gardner Press

Christie, Nils (1977) 'Conflicts as Property', *British Journal of Criminology*, 17
- (1981) *Limits to Pain*, Oxford: Martin Robertson
- (1993) *Crime Control as Industry: Towards Gulags, Western Style?*, London: Routledge

Cicourel, Aaron, V (1968) *The Social Organisation of Juvenile Justice*,
New York: Wiley

Clarke, A and Clarke, A (eds) (1976) *Early Experience: Myth and Evidence*,
London: Open Books

Cleckley, H (1964) *The Mask of Sanity* (4th edn), St Louis, Mo: CV Mosby
- (1976) *The Mask of Sanity* (5th edn), St Louis, Mo: CV Mosby

Clifford, W (1976) *Crime Control in Japan*, Lexington, Mass:
DC Heath

Clinard, M (1968) *Sociology of Deviant Behaviour*, New York: Rinehart
and Winston

Clinard, MB, & Abbott, DJ (1973) *Crime in developing countries:
A comparative perspective*: New York: Wiley

Cloward, Richard A and Ohlin, Lloyd E (1960) *Delinquency and Opportunity:
A Theory of Delinquent Gangs*, Glencoe, III: Free Press

Cohen, Albert K (1955) *Delinquent Boys: The Culture of the Gang*,
New York: Free Press
- (1965) 'The Sociology of the Deviant Act: Anomie Theory and
Beyond,' *American Sociology Review*, 30

Coll, Blanche D (1969) *Perspectives in Public Welfare: A History*,
Washington: DC: United States Department of Health, Education,
and Welfare

Collins, H (1982) *Marxism and Law*, Oxford: Clarendon Press

Colman, Alice (1985) *Utopia on Trial: Vision and reality in Planned
Housing*, London: Hilary Shipman
- (1988) 'Design Disadvantage and Design Improvement', *The Criminologist*
- (1989) 'Disposition and Situation: Two sides of the Same Crime', in DJ
Evans and DT Herbert, eds, *The Geography of Crime*, London: Routledge

Colvin, M, & Pauly, J (1983) 'A critique of criminology: Toward an
integrated structural Marxist theory of delinquent production',
American Journal of Sociology, 89

Comte, Auguste (1974) The Positive Philosophy, New York: AMS Press Inc

Committee on Mentally Abnormal Offenders Report (Butler
Report) London: HMSO, 1975

Connolly, W (1988) *Political Theory and Modernity*, Oxford: Basil Blackwell

Cortes, JB and Gatti, FM (1972) *Delinquency and Crime:
A Biopsychological Approach*, New York: Seminar Press

Cotterrell, Roger (1989) *The Politics of Jurisprudence: a critical introduction
to legal philosophy*, London: Butterworths

Cressey, DR (1960) 'Epidemiology and individual conduct: A
case for criminology', *Pacific Sociological Review*, 3

Csikszentmihalyi, M and Lawson, R (1978) 'Intrinsic Rewards in School Crime', *Crime and Delinquency* 24

Curran, DJ (1984) 'The myth of the 'new' female delinquent', *Crime and Delinquency*, 30

Currie, E (1985) *Confronting Crime*, New York: Pantheon

Danneter, Dale (1984) 'Adult Development and Social Theory: A Paradigmatic Reappraisal', *American Sociological Review*, 49

Dalgaard, OS and Kringlen, E (1976) 'A Norwegian twin study of criminality', *British Journal of Criminology* 16

Daly, K (1989) 'Rethinking Judicial Paternalism: Gender, Work-Family Relations and Sentencing', *Gender and Society*, 3

Datesman, S K, and Scarpitti, F R (1980) (eds) *Women, Crime and Criminal Justice*, New York: Oxford University Press

David, O, Hoffman, S, Sverd, J, Clark, J, and Voeller, K (1976) 'Lead and hyperactivity Behaviour response to Chelation: a pilot study', *American Journal of Psychiatry* 133

Davis, Mike (1990) *City of Quartz: excavating the future in Los Angeles*, London/New York: Verso

Dahrendorf, Ralf (1979) *Life Chances*, London: Weidenfeld and Nicolson
- (1985) *Law and Order*, London: Stevens & Sons
- (1987) 'The erosion of citizenship and its consequences for us all', *New Statesman*, 12 June

De Beauvoir, Simone (1974) *The Second Sex*, New York: Basic Books

Dean, H and Taylor-Gooby, P (1992) *Dependency Culture: the explosion of a myth*, London: Harvester Wheatsheaf

Denzin, Norman K (1969) 'Symbolic Interactionism and Ethnomethodology: A Proposed Synthesis,' *American Sociological Review*, 34
- (1991) *Images of Postmodern Society: Social Theory and Contemporary Cinema*, Newbury Park, CA: Sage

Dobash, R P, Dobash, RE, and Gutteridge, S (1986) *The Imprisonment of Women*, London: Basil Blackwell

Dolan, B and Coid, J (1993) *Psychopathic and Antisocial Personality Disorders: research and treatment issues*, London: Gaskell

Dominelli, L (1984) 'Differential Justice: domestic labour, community service and female offenders', *Probation Journal*, 31

Donzelot, J (1979) *The Policing of Families*, New York: Pantheon

Dostoyevsky, F (1936) *The Possessed*, New York: Modern Library

Douglas, Jack (1967) *The Social Meanings of Suicide*, Princton: Princton University Press

Downes, David and Rock, Paul (1988) *Understanding Deviance: A Guide to the Sociology of Crime and Rule Breaking*, 2nd ed Oxford: Oxford University Press

Drescher, S (1968) *Tocqueville and Beaumont on Social Reform*, New York

Dugdale, R (1910) *The Jukes*, New York: Putnam

Dupaquier, J (ed) (1983) *Malthus Past and Present*, London: Academic Press

Durkheim, Emile (1951, 1966 [1897]) *Suicide: A Study in Sociology*, John A Spaulding and George Simpson (trans), *Glencoe*, III: Free Press
    - (1965) *The Rules of the Sociological Method*, Solovay, S and Mueller, J (trans), Catlin, E (ed) New York: The Free Press
    - (1933) *The Division of Labour in Society*, New York: Macmillan

Dworkin, Ronald (1986) *Law's Empire*, London: Fontana Press

Eagleton, Terry (1990) *The Ideology of the Aesthetic*, Oxford: Basil Backwell

Easton, D (1965) *A Systems analysis of political life*, New York: Wiley

Eaton, M (1986) *Justice for Women? Family, Court and Social Control, Milton Keynes*: Open University Press

Edell, Abraham (1955) *Ethical Judgement: The Use of Science in Ethics*, New York: The Free Press

Elias, N (1978 [1939]) *The Civilizing Process*, vol 1: The History of Manners, Oxford: Basil Blackwell
    - (1991) *The Society of Individuals*, Oxford: Blackwell

Elliott, DS, Ageton, SS, and Canter, R (1979) 'An integrated theoretical perspective on delinquent behaviour', *Journal of Research in Crime and Delinquency*, 16

Elliott, DS, & Voss, H (1974) *Delinquency and dropout*, Lexington, MA: DC Heath

Engels, F ([1845] 1958) *The Condition of the Working Class in England*, WO Henderson and WH Chaloner (Trans and ed), New York: Macmillian
    - (1973 [1884]) *The Origin of the Family, Private Property and the State*, New York: International Publishers

Erikson, Kai T (1962) 'Notes on the Sociology of Deviance', *Social Problems*, 9

Erlanger, HS (1980) 'The allocation of status within occupations: The case of the legal profession', *Social Forces*, 58

Estabrook, A (1916) *The Jukes in 1915*, Washington, DC: Carnegie Institute of Washington

Eysenck, HJ (1964) *Crime and Personality*, London: Routledge & Keegan Paul
    - (1970) *Crime and Personality* (2nd edn), London: Granada
    - (1973) *The Inequality of Man*, London: Temple Smith
    - (1977) *Crime and Personality* (3rd edn), London: Routledge & Kegan Paul

Eysenck, HJ and Eysenck, SBG (1968) 'A factorial study of psychoticism as a dimension of personality', *Multivariate Behavioural Research* (special issue): 15–31

Eysenck, SBG, Eysenck, HJ, and Barrett, P (1985) 'A revised version of the psychoticism scale', *Personality and Individual Differences* 6

Eysenck, SBG and McGurk, BJ (1980) 'Impulsiveness and venturesomeness in a detention centre population', *Psychological Reports* 47

Fainstein, S, Gordon, I, and Harloe, M (eds) (1992) *Divided Cities: New York and London in The Contemporary World*, Oxford: Basil Blackwell

Farnworth, M, and Leiber, MJ (1989) 'Strain theory revisited: Economic goals, educational means, and delinquency', *American Sociological Review*, 54

Farrington, DP (1982) 'Longitudinal analyses of criminal violence', in ME Wolfgang & NA Weiner (eds), *Criminal violence*, Beverly Hills, CA: Sage

Farrington, DP and AM Morris (1983) 'Sex, Sentencing and Reconviction', *British Journal of Criminology*, 23

Farrington, DP, Ohlin, LE, and Wilson, JQ, (1986) *Understanding and Controlling Crime: Toward a New Research Strategy, New York*: Springer-Verlag

Feldman, MP (1977) *Criminal Behaviour: A Psychological Analysis*, Chichester: Wiley
  – (1983) 'Lay Theories of delinquency', *European Journal of Social Psychology* 13
  – (1993) *The Psychology of Crime*, Cambridge: Cambridge University Press

Ferri, E (1913) *The Positive School of Criminology*, Chicago
  – (1917) *Criminal Sociology*, J Kelly and J Lisle (trans) Boston: Little, Brown

Fields, F (1989) *Losing Out: the emergence of Britain's Underclass*, Basil Blackwell: Oxford

Finestone, H (1964) 'Cats, kicks and colour', in Becker, HS (ed) *The Other Side*, New York: Free Press

Finnis, J (1980) *Natural Law and Natural Rights*, Oxford: Oxford University Press

Fischer, John (1945) 'India's Insoluble Hunger', *Harper's Magazine*, 190

Foucault, Michel (1963) *Naissance de la clinique*, Paris: PUF English Translation, *The Birth of the Clinic*, New York: Pantheon 1973
  – (1965) *Madness and Civilization*, New York: Pantheon
  – (1975) *Surveiller et punir*, Paris: Gallimard English translation
  – (1978) *Discipline and Punish*, New York: Pantheon
  – (1978) *The History of Sexuality*, vol 1, An Introduction, trans New York: Robert Heurl
  – (1979) 'On Governmentality', I & C, 6
  – (1980) *Power/Knowledge: Selected Interviews and Other Writings 1972-1977*, Gordon, C (ed), New York: Pantheon Books

Fox, D (1982) 'Review of Auletta, The Underclass', *Social Policy*, 13 (2)

Fox, J and Hartnagel, T F (1979) 'Changing Social Roles and Female Crime in Canada', *Review Canadian Sociology and Anthropology*, 16

Frankl, Viktor E (1959) *From Death Campt to Existentialism, a Psychiatrist's Path to a New Therapy*, Ilse Lash (trans), Boston: Beacon Press

Freud, S (1925) 'Some psychical consequences of the anatomical distinction between the sexes', in *The Standard Edition of the Complete Psychological Works of Sigmund Freud*, vol 19, London: Hograth Press
- ([1930] 1961) 'Civilization and Its Discontents', in *The Standard Edition of the Complete Psychological Works*, J Strahey (trans), vol 21 London: Hogarth Press

Friday, PC and Hage, J (1976) 'Youth Crime in Postindustrial Societies: An Integrated Perspective', *Criminology*, 14

Friedman, Lawrence M (1968) *Government and Slum Housing: A Century of Frustration*, Chicago: Rand McNally

Friedman, M (1962) *Capitalism and Freedom*, London: University of Chicago Press

Fromm, E (1941) *Escape from freedom*, New York: Rinehart

Galasgow, D (1981) *The Black Underclass*, New York: Vintage Books

Galbraith, John, K (1992) *The Culture of Contentment*, London: Penguin

Garfinkel, Harold (1956) 'Conditions of Successful Degradation Ceremonies', *American Journal of Sociology*, 61

Garland, David (1985) *Punishment and Welfare*, Aldershot: Gower
- (1990) *Punishment and Modern Society*, Oxford: Clarendon Press

Garolafo, R (1914) *Criminology*, R Millar (trans) Boston, reprinted Montclair, 1968

Gath, D (1972) 'High intelligence and delinquency - a review', *British Journal of Criminology*, 12

Gatrell, VAC (1994) *The Hanging Tree: execution and the English People 1770-1868*, Oxford: Oxford University Press

Gaylin, W (1982) *The Killing of Bonnie Garland*, New York: Simon and Schuster

Gaylord, Mark S and Galliher, John F (1988) *The Criminology of Edwin Sutherland*, New Jersey: Transaction Books

Geertz, C (1980) *Negara: The theatre state in nineteenth-century Bali* Princeton, NJ: Princton University Press

Gellner, Ernest (1994) *Conditions of Liberty: Civil Society and Its Rivals*, London: Hamish hamilton

Gelsthorpe, L (1989) *Sexism and the Female Offender*, Aldershort: Gower

Giddens, Anthony (1989) *Sociology: a brief but critical introduction*, London: Macmillian

- (1990) *The Consequences of Modernity*, Cambridge: Polity Press
- (1991) *Modernity and Self-Identity: self and society in the late modern age*, Cambridge: Polity Press
- (1992) *The Transformation of Intimacy: Sexuality, Love and Eroticism in Modern Societies*, Cambridge: Polity Press

Gilder, G (1981) *Wealth and Poverty*, London: Buchan and Enright

Gilligan, C (1982) *In a Different Voice: Psychological Theory and Women's Development*, Cambridge: Harvard University Press

Giordano, PC and SA Cernkovich (1979) 'On Complicating the Relationship between Liberation and Delinquency', *Social Problems*, 26

Glueck, S, and Glueck, ET (1940) *Juvenile Delinquents Grown Up*, New York: Commonwealth Fund
- (1960) *Unraveling Juvenile Delinquency*, Cambridge, Mass: Harvard University Press
- (1956) *Physique and Delinquency*, New York: Harper and Row
- (1959) *Predicting Delinquency and Crime*, Cambridge Mass: Harvard University Press
- (1968) *Delinquents and nondelinquents in perspective*, Cambridge MA: Harvard University Press

Goddard, HH (1914) *Feeble-Mindedness Its causes and Consequences*, New york: Macmillan
- (1921) *Juvenile Delinquency*, New York: Dodd, Mead

Goffman, E (1968) *Asylums*, New York: Anchor
- (1969) *Where the Action Is: Three Essays*, London: Allen Lane

Goldberger, P (1989) 'Why design can't transform cities', *New York Times*, June 23

Goldstein, AG, Chance, JE, and Gilbert, B (1984) 'Facial stereotypes of good guys and bad guys: a replication and extension', *Bulletin of the Psychonomic Society* 22

Gordon, Diana (1991) *The Justice Juggernaut: fighting street crime, controlling citizens*, New Brunswick: Rutgers University Press

Goring, C (1913) *The English Convict*, London: Darling and Son

Gottfredson, Micheal and Hirschi, Travis (eds) (1987) *Positive Criminology*, New Park, CA: Sage
- (1990) *A General Theory of Crime*, Stanford, CA: Stanford University Press

Gould, SJ (1981) *The Mismeasure of Man*, Harmondsworth: Penguin

Gould, GC (1976) *Women and Philosophy: Toward a Theory of Liberation*, New York: GP Putnam's

Graef, Roger (1992) *Living Dangerously: Young Offenders in Their Own Words*, London: HarperCollins

Greenwood, V (1981) 'The Myth of female Crime', in A Morris and L Gelsthorpe (eds), *Women and Crime*, Cambridge: Cambridge Institute of Criminology

Groth, A Nicholas (1979) *Men Who Rape: The Psychology of the Offender*, New York: Plenum Press

Grygier, T, Chesley, J, and Tuters, EW (1970) 'Parental deprivation: a study of delinquent children', *British Journal of Criminology* 9

Gunn, J, Robertson, G, Dell, S, and Way, C (1978) *Psychiatric Aspects of Imprisonment*, London: Academic Press

Guttmacher, M (1973) *The Mind of the Murderer*, New York: Arno Press

Habermas, J (1976) *Legitimation Crisis* London: Heinemann
- (1979) *Communication and the Evolution of Society*, London: Heinemann
- (1985) *Modernity - an incomplete project*, in H Foster (ed), Postmodern Culture, London: Pluto
- (1987) *The Philosophical Discourse of Modernity*, Cambridge: Polity Press

Hacker, AC (1987) 'American apartheid', *The New York Review*, Dec 3

Hagan, FE (1986) *Introduction to criminology: Theories, methods, and criminal behaviour*, Chicago: Nelson-Hall

Hagan, John (1987) *Modern Criminology: crime, criminal behaviour and its control*, New York: McGraw-Hill

Hagan, J, Simpson, J an Gillis, A 'The Sexual stratification of social control: a gender-based perspective on crime and delinquency', *British Journal of Sociology*, 30

Hall Williams, JE (1982) *Criminology and Criminal Justice*, London: Butterworths

Hamilton, JR (1985) 'The special hospitals', in L Gostin (ed) Secure Provision: *A Review of Special Services for the Mentally Ill and Mentally Handicapped in England and Wales*, London: Tavistock

Harris, Anthony (1977) 'Sex and Theories of Deviance: Towards a Functional Theory of Deviant Type-Scripts' *American Sociology Review*, 42

Harrison, P (1985) *Inside the inner city*, Harmondsworth: Penguin

Hartsock, Nancy (1987) 'Rethinking modernism: minority vs majority theories', *Cultural Critique*, 7

Hart HLA (1955) 'Are There Any Natural Rights?' in *Philosophy Review*, 64
- (1961) *The Concept of Law*, Oxford: Clarendon Press

Harvey, David (1990) *The Condition of Postmodernity: an inquiry into the origins of Cultural Change*, Cambridge Mass: Basil Blackwell

Hawley,C and Buckley, RE (1974) 'Food dyes and hyperkinetic children', *Academy Therapy* 10: 27-32

Hay, D (1975) 'Property, Authority and the Criminal Law', in D Hay, P Linebaugh, EP Thompson, et al, *Albion's Fatal Tree*, London: Allen Lane

Hayman, R (1978) *De Sade: A Critical Biography*, London: Constable

Hayashi, S (1967) 'A study of juvenile delinquency in twins', in H Mitsuda (ed) *Clinical Genetics in Psychiatry*, Tokyo: Igaku Shoin

Hegel, GWF (1949) *The Phenomenology of Mind*, JB Gailie (trans), London: Allen & Unwin
- (1952) *The Philosophy of Right*, TM Knox (trans), London:
- (1971) *Encyclopedia of the Philosophical Sciences: Part III*, trans by W Wallace, with Zusatze, trans by AV Miller, Oxford: Clarendon Press

Heidegger, Martin (1962) *Being and Time*, John Macquarrie and Edward Robinson (trans), New York: Harper & Brothers

Heidensohn, Frances (1968) 'The Deviance of Women: A Critique and an Enquiry', *British Journal of Sociology*, 19
- (1985) *Women and Crime*, London: MacMillian
- (1989) *Crime and Society*, London: MacMillan Education

Heller, Agnes and Feher, Ferenc (1988) *The Postmodern Political Condition*, Cambridge: Polity Press

Hepburn, JR (1976) 'Criminology: Testing alternative models of delinquent causation', *Journal of Criminal Law and Criminology*, 67

Herbers, John (1981) 'Fear of Crime Leads in Survey of Reasons to Leave Big Cities', *The New York Times*, May 16

Herrenstein, RJ and Murray, Charles A (1994) *The Bell Curve: Intelligence and Class Structure in American Life*, New York: Free Press

Hibbert, C (1963) *The Roots of Evil: A Social History of Crime and Punishment*, London: Weidenfeld & Nicolson

Hill, D and Pond, DA (1952) 'Reflections on a hundred capital cases submitted to electroencephalography', *Journal of Mental Science*, 98

Hindelang, MJ (1971) 'Age, Sex, and the Versatility of delinquent Involvements', *Social Problems*, 18
- (1973) 'Causes of delinquency: A partial replication and extension', *Social Problems*, 20
- (1979) 'Sex Differences in Criminal Activity', *Social Problems*, 27

Hindelang, M J, Gottfredson, Micheal R and Garofalo, James (1978) *Victims of Personal Crime*, Cambridge, Mass: Ballinger

Hindelang, MJ, Hirschi, T, and Weiss, JG (1981) *Measuring delinquency*, Beverly Hills, CA: Sage

Hindelang, MJ and Weiss, JG (1972) 'Personality and self-reported delinquency: an application of cluster analysis', *Criminology* 10

Hirschi, T (1969) *Causes of Delinquency*, Berkeley, Calif: University of California Press

Hirschi, T and Hindelang, MJ (1977) 'Intelligence and delinquency: a revisionist review', *American Sociological Review* 42
- (1987) 'Lay explanations of delinquency: global or offence-specific?', *British Journal of Social Psychology* 26

Hirschman, Albert O (1989) 'Reactionary Rhetoric', *Atlantic Monthly*, 263

Hobbes, Thomas ([1642] 1949) *De Cive*, or *The Citizen*, ed S Lamprecht, New York
- ([1650] 1889) The Elements of Law, F Tonnies (ed), London
- ([1651] 1950) *Leviathan,* or the *Matter, Forme and power of a Common-wealth Ecclesiastical and Civil*, New York/London: Everyman's Library (Also Penguin ed)

Hochschild, A R (1983) *The Managed Heart: Commercialization of Human Feeling*, Berkeley: University of California Press

Holzner, Burkhart, and Marx, John H (1979) *Knowledge Application: The Knowledge System in Society*, Boston: Allyn & Bacon

Hooton, EA (1939a) *The American Criminal: An Anthropological Study*, Cambridge, MA: Harvard University Press
- (1939b) *Crime and the Man*, Cambridge, Mass: Harvard University Press

Horowitz, Ruth and Schwartz, Gary (1974) 'Honor, Normative Ambiguity and Gang Violence', *American Sociological Review* 39

Howarth, E (1986) 'What does Eysenck's psychoticism scale really measure?', *British Journal of Psychology* 77

Howells, K (1983) 'Social constructing and violent behaviour in mentally abnormal offenders', in J Hinton (ed) *Dangerousness: Problems of Assessment and Prediction*, London: Allen and Unwin

Huber, Joan (1976) 'Toward a Socio-Technological Theory of the Women's Movement', *Social Problems*, 23

Hudson, B (1984) 'Femininity and Adolescence', in A McRobbie and M Nava (eds) *Gender and Generation*, London: Macmillan
- (1987) *Justice Through Punishment: A Critique of the Justice Model of Corrections*, London: Macmillan

Hughes, Mark, A (1989) 'Misspeaking truth to power: a geographical perspective on the 'underclass' fallacy', *Economic Geography*

Hulsman, L (1986) 'Critical Criminology and the Concept of Crime', *Contemporary Crises* 10/1

Hume, David ([1739] 1978) *A Treatise on Human Nature*, Oxford: Oxford University Press

Hurwitz, S and Christiansen, KO (1983) *Criminology*, London: Allen & Unwin

Ingold, Tim (1986) *Evolution and Social Life*, Cambridge:
   Cambridge University Press

Institute for Cultural Conservatism (1987) *Cultural Conservatism: Toward a New
   National Agenda* Washington, DC

Jackson, Bruce (1969) *A Thief's Primer*, New York: Macmillan

Jacobs, J (1962) *The Death and Life of Great American Cities*,
   Harmondsworth: Penguin Books

Jacoby, Susan (1985) *Wild Justice: the evolution of revenge*, London: Collins

Jager, Bernd (1975) *Theorizing, Journeying, Dwelling, Duquesne Studies in
   Phenomenological Psychology*, Volume 11, Giorgi, C Fisher, E Murray (eds),
   Pittsburg: Duquesne University Press

James, J and Thornton, W (1980) 'Women's liberation and the
   female delinquent', *Journal of Research in Crime and Delinquency*, 17

Jameson, F (1984) 'Postmodernism, or the cultural logic of late capitalism',
   New Left Review, 146

Jencks, C (1984) *The language of post-modern architecture*, London

Jensen, GF (1972) 'Parents, peers, and delinquent action: A test of
   the differential association perspective', *American Journal of Sociology*, 78

Jensen, GF, and Eve, R (1976) 'Sex differences in delinquency', *Criminology*, 13

Johnson, RE (1979) *Juvenile delinquency and its origin*, Cambridge:
   Cambridge University Press

Jones, David (1986) *History of Criminology: A Philosophical Perspective*,
   New York: Greenwood Press

Jones Gareth (ed), (1973) *The Sovereignty of Law: Selections from Blackstone's
   Commentaries on the Laws of England*, London: Blackstones

Jordon, W (1982) 'First impressions: initial English confrontations
   with Africans', in C Husband (ed), 'Race', in Britain, London: Hutchinson

Kant, Immanuel (1957) *The Metaphysics of Morals*, Cambridge:
   Cambridge University Press
   - ([1795] 1957) *Perpetual Peace*, Indianapolis: Bobbs–Merrill
   - (1929) *The Critique of Pure Reason*, Hampsire: Macmillan

Kappeler, Susanne (1986) *The Pornography of Representation*, Cambridge:
   Polity Press

Katz, Jack (1988) *Seductions of Crime: Moral and Sensual Attractions of Doing
   Evil*, New York: Basic Books

Katz, Leo (1987) *Bad Acts and Guilty Minds: Conundrums of the Criminal Law*,
   Chicago/London: University of Chicago Press

Katz, M (1989) *The Undeserving Poor: From the War on Poverty to the War
   on Welfare*, New York: Pantheon Books

Kaufmann, Walter (1957) *Existentialism from Dostoevsky to Sartre*, New York: Meridian Books

Kelman, Herbert C, and Hamilton, V Lee (1989) *Crimes of Obedience*, New Haven/London: Yale University Press

Kelsen, Hans (1967) *The Pure Theory of Law*, M Knight trans Berkeley: University of California Press

Kitsuse, JI and Dietrick, EDC (1959) 'Delinquent boys: A critique', *American Sociological Review*, 24

Klein, D (1973) 'The Etiology of Female Crime: A Review of the Literature', *Issues in Criminology*, 8

Klemke, Lloyd W (1978) 'Does Apprehension for Shoplifting Amplify or Terminate Shoplifting Activity?', *Law and Society Review* 12

Kohlberg, Lawrence (1981) *The Philosophy of Moral Development*, San Francisco: Harper & Row

Kornhauser, R (1978) *Social Sources of Delinquency*, Chicago: University of Chicago Press

Kotlowitz, Alex (1991) *There Are No Children Here: The Story of Two Boys Growing Up in the Other America*, New York: Doubleday

Kranz, H (1936) *Lebensschicksale kriminellen zwillinge*, Berlin: Julius Springer

Krier, R (1987) 'Tradition-modernity-modernism: some necessary explanations', *Architectural Design Profil*, 65

Krige, J (1980) *Science, Revolution and Discontinuity*, Hassock, Sussex: Harvester Press

Kruttschnitt, C (1982) 'Women, Crime, and Dependency: An application of the theory of law', *Criminology* 19
– (1982) 'Respectable women and the law', *The Sociological Quarterly*, 23

Lange, J (1929) *Verbrechen als Sochicksal (Crime as Destiny)*, Leipzig: Verlag

Laqueur, T (1987) 'Orgasm, generation, and the politics of reproductive biology', in C Gallagher, and T Laqueur (eds), *The Making of the Modern Body Sexuality and Society in the Nineteenth Century*, Berkeley, CA: University of California Press

Lea, John, and Young, Jock (1984) *What is to be done about Law and Order?* London: Penguin (Rev ed London: Pluto, 1993)

Lefebvre, Henri (1984) *Everyday Life in the Modern World*, New Jersey: Transaction

Lefort, Claud (1988) 'Reversibility: Political Freedom and the Freedom of the Individual', In *Democracy and Political Theory*, Cambridge: Polity Press

Legras, AM (1932) *Psychese en criminaliteit bij twellingen*, Utrecht: Keminken Zoon NV

Lemann, N (1986) 'The Origins of the Underclass', *Atlantic Monthly*, June – July

Lemert, Edwin M (1951) *Social Pathology*, New York: McGraw-Hill
- (1964) 'Social Structure, Social Control, and Deviation', in *Anomie and Deviant Behaviour*, Marshall Clinard (ed) New York: Fee Press
- (1972) *Human deviance, social problems and social control* (2nd ed), Englewood Cliffs, NJ: Prentice-Hall

Lengermann, Patricia M and Wallace, Ruth A (1985) *Gender in America* Englewood Cliffs, NJ: Prentice-Hall

Leonard, E B (1982) *Women Crime and Society: a critique of Criminology Theory*, London: Longman

Levinas, Emmanuel (1988) *The Provocation of Levinas Rethinking the Other*, R Bernasconi, and D Wood (ed), London: Routledge

Levi-Strauss, C (1966) *The Savage Mind*, London: Weidenfeld & Nicolson
- (1978) *Myth and Meaning*, London: Routledge & Kegan Paul

Lewis, Oscar (1959) *Five Families: Mexican Case Studies in the Culture of Poverty*, New York: Basic Books

Lindblom, Charles, E (1990) *Inquiry and Change The Troubled Attempt to Understand and Shape Society*, New Haven: Yale University Press

Linquist, CA, Smusz, TD, and Doerner, W (1985) 'Causes of conformity: An application of control theory to adult misdemeanant probationers', *International Journal of Offender Therapy and Comparative Criminology*, 29

Liska, AE (1971) 'Aspirations, expectations, and delinquency: Stress and additive models', *Sociological Quarterly*, 12

Little, A (1965) 'Parental deprivation, separation and crime: a test on adolescent recidivists', *British Journal of Criminology* 5

Lloyd, Genevieve, (1984) *The Man of reason: 'Male' and Female' in Western Philosophy*, London: Methuen

Lofland, John (1969) *Deviance and Identity*, Englewood Cliffs, NJ: Prentice-Hall

Lombroso, C (1911) *Crime: Its Causes and Remedies*, Boston: Little Brown

Lombroso, C and W Ferrero (1985) *The Female Offender*, London: Fisher Unwin

Loomis, SD, Bohnert, PJ, and Huncke, S (1967) 'Predictions of EEG abnormalities in adolescent delinquents', *Archives of General Psychiatry* 17

Luckenbill, David F (1977) 'Criminal Homicide as Situated Transaction', *Social Problems* 25

Luhmann, Niklas (1986) *Love as Passion*, Cambridge: Polity Press

Lyons, David (1984) *Ethics and the Rule of Law*, London

Lyotard, Jean-François (1984) *The Postmodern Condition: A Report on Knowledge*, Manchester: Manchester University Press

Lyotard, Jean-François and Thebaud, Jean-Loup, (1985) *Just Gaming*,
  Minneapolis: University of Minnesota Press

Maccoby, E E , and Kacklin, CN (1974) *The Psychology of Sex Differences*,
  Stanford: Stanford University Press

MacIntyre, A (1962) 'A Mistake about causality in social science', in Plaslett
  and WG Runciman eds, *Philosophy, Politics, and Society*, Second
  Series, Oxford: Blackwell
  - (1981, 2nd ed 1985) *After Virtue: a study in moral theory*, London:
  Duckworth
  - (1988) *Whose Justice? Which Rationality?*, London: Duckworth

MacKinnon, CA (1983) 'Feminism, Marxism, Method, and the State:
  Towards Feminist Jurisprudence', *Signs*, 8
  - (1987) *Feminism Unmodified: Discourses on Life and Law*, Cambridge
  Mass: Harvard University Press
  - (1989) *Toward a Feminist theory of the State*, Cambridge, Mass:
  Harvard University Press

Macnicol, J (1987) 'In pursuit of the underclass', *Journal of Social Policy*, 16,
  293-318
  - (1990) 'Nightmare on easy street', *The Times Higher Education Supplement*,
  29 June, 15

MacPherson, CB (1962) *The Political Theory of Possessive Individualism*,
  Oxford: Oxford University Press

Mannheim, Hermann (1965) *Comparative Criminology*, 2 vols,
  London: Routledge and Kegan Paul

Manson, C (with N Emmons) (1986) *Manson: In his own words*,
  New York: Grove Press

Marshall, TH (1977) *Class, Citzenship and Social Development*, Chicago
  and London: University of Chicago Press

Martens, P L (1993) 'An Ecological Model of Socialisation in Explaining
  Offending', in DP Farrington, RJ Sampson, and P-O H Wikstrom,
  eds *Integrating Individual and Ecological Aspects of Crime, Stockholm:
  National Council for Crime Prevention*

Marx, Karl (1964) *The economic and political manuscripts of 1844*, trans
  M Milligan, (ed) DJ Struik, New York: International Publishers
  - (1975) 'Preface to A Contribution to a Critique of Political Economy',
  in *Earl Writings*, Q Hoare, ed R Livingstone and G Brown trans New York:
  Random House

Marx, Karl and Engles, F (1978) *The Marx-Engels Reader*, Robert C Tucker,
  ed 2nd ed New York: Norton

Matseuda, RL (1982) 'Testing control theory and differential association:
A casual modelling approach', *American Sociological Review*, 47

Matza, D (1964) *Delinquency and Drift*, New York: Wiley
- (1969) *Becoming Deviant*, Englewod Cliffs, NJ: Prentice Hall

Mawson, AR and Jacobs, KJ (1978) 'Corn consumption, tryptophan, and
cross-national homicide rates', *Journal of Orthomolecular Psychiatry* 7

Maxwell, Nicholas (1984) *From Knowledge to Wisdom*, Oxford: Basil Blackwell

Mayhew, H (1862) *London Labour and the London Poor*, London: Griffin Bohn

Mayo, Patricia E (1969) *The Making of a Criminal: A Comparative Study of Two
Delinquency Areas*, London: Weidenfeld and Nicolson

McBride, WL, 1972 'Noncoercive Society: Some doubts, Leninist and
Contemporary', in Pennock and Chapman, *Coercion*, Chicago:
Aldine-Atherton (NOMOS XV)

McCandless, BR, Persons, WS III, and Roberts, A (1972) 'Perceived
opportunity, delinquency, race, and body build among delinquent
youth', *Journal of Consulting and Clinical Psychology*, 38

McCord, W and McCord, J (1964) *The Psychopath: An Essay on the Criminal
Mind*, New York: Van Nostrand Reinhold

McEwan, AW and Knowles, C (1984) 'Delinquent personality types and the
situational contexts of their crimes', *Personality and Individual Differences* 5

McGurk, BJ (1978) 'Personality types among normal homicides',
British Journal of Criminology 19

McGurk, BJ and McDougall, C (1981) 'A new approach to Eysenck's theory of
criminality', *Personality and Individual Differences* 2

McGurk, BJ and McGurk, RE (1979) 'Personality types among prisoners and
prison officers - an investigation of Megargee's theory of control', *British
Journal of Criminology* 19

McKenzie, RD (1925) 'The Ecological Approach to the Study of the Human
Community', in Park, RE, et al, *The City*, Chicago: University of Chicago
Press

Mead, George Herbert (1934) *Mind, Self, and Society*, Chicago:
University of Chicago Press

Mead, L (1986) *Beyond Entitlement: The Social Obligations of Citizenship*
New York: Free Press

Mead, M (1935) *Sex and Temperament in Three Primitive Societies*,
New York: William Morrow

Mednick, SA Gabrielli, WF, and Hutchings, B (1983) 'Genetic influences in
criminal behaviour: evidence from an adoption cohort', in KT VanDusen
and SA Mednick (eds) *Prospective Studies of Crime and Delinquency*,
The Hague: Kluwer-Nijhoff Publishing

Meier, RF (1983) 'United States of America', in EH Johnson (ed), *International handbook of contemporary developments in criminology: General issues and the Americas*, Westport, CT: Greenwood Press

Merton, Robert (1938) 'Social Structure and 'Anomie'', *American Sociological Review*, 3
- (1957) *Social Theory and Social Structure*, New York: Free Press of Glencoe
- (1968) *Social Theory and Social Structure*, (enlarged ed) New York: The Free Press

Messner, H ed (1966) *Poverty in the Affluent Society*, New York: Harper & Row

Messner, SF (1982) 'Poverty, inequality, and the urban homicide rate: Some unexpected findings', *Criminology*, 20
- (1984) 'The 'dark figure' and composite indexes of crime: Some empirical exploration of alternative data sources', *Journal of Criminal Justice*, 12

Michalowski, Raymond (1981) *Order, Law and Crime: Introduction to Critical Criminology*, Glenview, Il: Scott, Foresman

Midgley, Mary (1979) *Beast and Man: the roots of human nature*, London: Methuen

Milgram, S (1970) 'The Experience of Living in Cities: A Psychological Analysis', *Science* 167

Mill, John Stuart (1970) 'On the Subjection of Women', in *Essays on Sex Equality*, John Stuart Mill and Harriet Taylor Mill, Chicago: Chicago University Press
- (1962) 'On Liberty' , in Mill *Utilitarianism*, London: Fontana

Miller, Eleanor (1986) *Street Women*, Philadelphia: Temple University Press

Miller, WB (1958) 'Lower Class Culture as a generating milieu of gang delinquency', *Journal of Social Issues*, 14

Mills, C Wright (1959) *The Power Elite*, New York: Oxford University Press

Montagu, MF Ashley (1941) 'The Biologist Looks at Crime', *Annals of the American Academy of Social and Political Science*, September

Morgan, Patricia (1975) *Child Care: Sense and Fable*, London: Temple Smith
- (1978) *Delinquent Fantasies*, London: Temple Smith

Moriyama, T (1993) 'Crime, Criminal Justice and Social Control: Why Do We Enjoy a Low Crime rate?', paper presented to the British Criminology Conference, Cardiff

Morris, Alison (1987) *Women, Crime and Criminal Justice*, Oxford: Basil Blackwell

Morris, Terence, (1957) *The Criminal Area: A Study in Social Ecology*, London: Routledge and Kegan Paul

Morrison, W Douglas (1895) 'Introduction', in Caesar Lombroso, *The Female Offender*, London: T Fisher Unwin

Morrison, WJ (1994) 'Criminology, Modernity and the 'Truth' of the Human Condition: Reflections on the Melancholy of Postmodernism', in Nelken, D (ed) *The Futures of Criminology*, London: Sage
- (1995a) 'Modernity, knowledge, and the criminalisation of drug usage', in I Loveland (ed) *The Limits of Criminalisation*, London: Sweet and Maxwell
- (1995b) 'Modernity, imprisonment and social solidarity: notes on a bad relationship', in Roger Mathews (ed) *Prisons 2000*, London: Routledge

Moyer, KE (1976) *The Psychobiology of Aggression*, New York: Harper & Row

Mukherjee, SK and RW Fitzgerald (1981) 'The Myth of Rising Female Crime', in Mukherjee and Scutt (eds) *Women and Crime*

Mukherjee, SK and JA Scutt (eds) (1981) *Women and Crime*, Sydney: Australian Institute of Criminology with Allen & Unwin

Mullings, Beverly (1991) *The Colour of Money: the impact of housing investment decision making on black housing outcomes in London*, London: The Runnymede Trust

Murray, C (1984) *Losing Ground*, New York: Basic Books
- (1988) *In Pursuit of Happiness and Good Government*, New York: Simon and Schuster
- (1990) 'The British Underclass', *The Public Interest*, 99
- (1994) 'The New Victorians and The New Rabble', *The Sunday Times*, 29 May

Nagel, I (1981) 'Sex Differences in the Processing of Criminal Defendants', in Morris, A and Gelsthorpe, L (eds), *Women and Crime*, Cambridge: Institute of Criminology

Nagel, I and Hagan, J (1983) 'Gender and Crime: Offense Patterns and Criminal Court Sanctions' In *Crime and Justice: An Annual Review of Research*, Vol 4, M Tonry and N Morris eds Chicago: University of Chicago Press

Nagin, D and Paternoster, R (1991) 'On the Relationship of Past and Future Participation in Delinquency', *Criminology*, 29

Naffine, Ngaire (1987) *Female Crime: The Construction of Women in Criminology*, Sydney: Allen & Unwin

Newman, O (1972) *Defensible Space: Crime Prevention Through Urban Design*, New York: Macmillan

Nietzsche, Friedrich (1888) The AntiChrist, in (1968) *The Portable Nietsche* Walter Kaufmann (trans and ed), New York: Viking Press
- (1966) *Basic Writings of Nietzsche*, Walter Kaufmann (trans), New York: Random House
- (1886) Beyond Good and Evil, in *Basic Writings of Nietzsche*

- ([1888] 1969) Ecce Homo, Walther Kaufman (Trans and ed)
New York: Vintage
- (1882) *The Gay Science*, Walter Kaufmann, trans New York:
Random House
- ([1887] 1969) *The Genealogy of Morals*, Walther kaufmann and R J
Hollingdale (trans), New York: Vintage Books
- (1878) Human All Too Human, in *Basic Writings of Nietzsche*
- ([1886-88] 1968) *The Will to Power*, Walter Kaufmann and RJ
Hollingdale (trans and eds), New York: Random House

Oakley, A (1981) *Subject Women*, Oxford: Martin Robertson

O'Brien, Mary (1981) *Politics of Reproduction*, Boston: Routledge & Kegan Paul

Offe, Claus (1985) *Disorganised Capitalism*, Cambridge: Polity Press

Offord, DR (1982) 'Family backgrounds of male and female offenders',
in J Gunn and DP Farrington (eds), *Abnormal Offenders, Delinquency,
and the Criminal Justice System*, Chichester: Wiley

Orcutt, JD (1987) 'Differential association and marijuana use: A closer
look at Sutherland (with a little help from Becker)', *Criminology*, 25

Packer, H (1968) *The Limits of the Criminal Sanction*, Stanford:
Stanford University Press

Pahl, RE (1988) 'Some remarks on informal work, social polarization and the
social structure', *International Journal of Urban and Regional Research*, 12, 247- 67

Parisi, N (1982) 'Are Females Treated Differently? A Review of the Theories
and Evidence on Sentencing and Parole Decisions', in NH Rafter and EA
Stanko (1982) *Judge, Lawyer, Victim, Thief: Women, Gender Roles and Criminal
Justice*, Northwestern University Press

Park, Robert E (1952) *Human Communities*, Glencoe: The Free Press
- ([1916] 1969) 'The City: Suggestions for the Investigation of Human
Behaviour in the Urban Environment', in *Classic Essays on the Culture of
Cities*, Richard Sennett (ed), New York: Appleton-Century-Crofts

Parker, Donn B (1976) *Crime by Computer*, New York: Scribner's

Parsons, Talcott, (1954) *Essays in Sociological Theory*, rev ed Glencoe, Ill:
Free Press

Patten, Brian (1992) *Love Poems*, London: Flamingo/HarperCollins

Paul, GL (1969) 'Outcome of systematic desensitization II: Controlled
investigation of individual treatment, technique variations and
current status', in CM Franks (ed) *Behaviour therapy: Appraisal and
status*, New York: McGraw-Hill

Pearce and Tombs, (1989), 'Realism and Corporate Crime', in *Issues in
Realist Criminology*, London: Sage

Peckham, M (1962) *Beyond the Tragic Vision: the Quest for Identity in the Nineteenth Century*, Cambridge: Cambridge University Press

Pepinsky, Harold, and Quinney, Richard (eds) (1991) *Criminology as Peacemaking*, Bloomington: Indiana University Press

Pfohl, S (1977) 'The 'discovery of child-abuse'', *Social Problems*, 24: 310-214
- (1981) 'Labelling Criminals', in *Law and Deviance*, Laurence Ross (ed), London: Sage

Phares, EJ (1984) *Introduction to Personality*, Columbus, Ohio: Charles E Merrill

Piaget, Jean(1965) *The Moral Judgement of the Child*, New York: The Free Press

Pick, Daniel (1989) *Faces of Degeneration: A European Disorder*, c 1848-1918, Cambridge: Cambridge University Press

Piven, FF and Cloward, RA (1971) *Regulating the Poor: The Functions of Public Welfare*, New York: Vintage
- (1982) *The New Class War*, New York: Pantheon

Podolsky, E (1955) 'The Chemical Brew of Criminal Behaviour', *Journal of Criminal Law*, 45

Polk, K, Adler, C, Bazemore G, Blake, G, Cordray, S, Coventry, G, Galvin, J, and Temple, M (1981) *Becoming adult: An analysis of maturational development from age 16 to 30 of a cohort of young men* (Final report of the Marion County Youth Study), Eugene, Or: University of Oregon

Pollak, O (1950) *The Criminality of Women*, New York: AS Barnes

Poole, ED, and Regoli, RM (1979) 'Parental support, delinquent friends, and delinquency: A test of interactional effects', *Journal of Criminal Law and Criminology*, 70

Popper, Karl (1968) *The Logic of Scientific Discovery*, London: Hutchinson First published 1959 Expanded version of *Logicik der Forschung*, 1934

Pound, R (1930), *Criminal Justice in America*, Dacapo Paperback, Brown University, 1957 [1930]

Quay, HC (1987) 'Intelligence', in HC Quay (ed), *Handbook of Juvenile Delinquency*, New York: Wiley

Quinney, Richard (1974) *Critique of Legal Order*, Boston: Little, Brown

Quinney, Richard, and Wildeman, John (1977) *The Problem of Crime: A Critical Introduction to Criminology*, New York: Harper and Row

Rada, RT (1978) 'Classification of the rapist', in RT Rada (ed) *Clinical Aspects of the Rapist*, New York: Grune and Stratton

Radzinowicz, Sir Leon (1948) *A History of English Criminal Law and its Administration from 1750*, Vol 1, London: Stevens & Sons
- (1966) *Ideology and Crime*, London: Heinemann

Radzinowicz, Sir Leon and Hood, Roger (1986) *The Emergence of Penal Policy in Victorian and Edwardian England* (Vol 5 of *A History of English Criminal Law and its Administration from 1750*), London: Stevens & Sons

Radzinowicz, Sir Leon, and King, Joan (1977) *The Growth of Crime: The International Experience*, New York: Basic Book

Raine, A and Venables, PH (1981) 'Classical conditioning and socialization - a biosocial interaction', *Personality and Individual Differences* 2

Rankin, J (1977) 'Investigating the interrelations among social control variables and conformity', *Journal of Criminal Law and Criminology*, 67

Rawls, John (1972) *A Theory of Justice*, Cambridge, Mass: Harvard University Press

Reckless, Walter, C (1967) *The Crime Problem* (Fourth ed), New York: Meredith Publishing Company

Rees, L (1973) 'Constitutional factors and abnormal behaviour', in HJ Eysenck (ed) *Handbook of Abnormal Psychology*, London: Pitman Medical

Reiss, AJ and Rhodes, AL (1961) 'The distribution of juvenile delinquency in the social class structure', *American Sociological Review*, 26
- (1964) 'An empirical test of differential association theory', *Journal of Research in Crime and Delinquency*, 1

Ressler, RK, Burgess, AW, and Douglas, JE (1993) *Sexual Homicide: Patterns and Motives*, London: Simon & Schuster

Richards, P, Berk, R, and Foster, B (1979) *Crime as Play: Delinquency in a Middle Class Suburb*, Cambridge, Mass: Ballinger

Rime, B, Bonvy, H, and Rouillon, F (1978) 'Psychopathy and nonverbal behaviour in an interpersonal situation', *Journal of Abnormal Psychology*, 87

Robins, L (1966) *Deviant Children Grown Up*, Baltimore, Md: Williams & Wilkins

Robins, LN West, PA & Herjanic, BL (1975) 'Arrests and delinquency in two generations: A study of black urban families and their children', *Journal of Child Psychology and Psychiatry*, 16

Robins, LH and Ratcliff, KS (1980) 'Childhood Conduct Disorders and Later Arrest', in *The Social Consequences of Psychiatric Illness*, Lee N Robins et al, (eds) New York: Brunner/Mazel

Robinson, Sophia, M, (1936) *Can Delinquency Be Measured?*, New York: Columbia University Press

Rogers, CR (1951) *Client-centered therapy*, Boston: Houghton Miffin

Rorty, Richard (1979) *Philosophy and the Mirror of Nature*, Princeton, New Jersey: Princeton University Press
- (1989) *Contingency, Irony and Solidarity*, Cambridge: Cambridge University Press

Rosanoff, AJ, Handy, LM, and Plesset, I (1941) 'The etiology of child behaviour difficulties, juvenile delinquency and adult criminality with special reference to their occurrence in twins', *Psychiatric Monographs* (California) No 1, Sacramento Department of Institutions

Rose, Nikolas (1990) *Governing the Soul: the shaping of the private self*, London: Routledge

Rosenbaum, JL (1987) 'Social control, gender, and delinquency: An analysis of drug, property and violent offenders', *Justice Quarterly*, 4

Roshier Bob (1989) *Controlling Crime: The Classical Perspective in Criminology*, Open University Press: Milton Keynes

Rossi, A (1982) *Architecture and The City*, Cambridge, Mass: Basil Blackwell

Rothman, David J (1980) *Conscience and Convenience: The Asylum and Its Alternatives in Progressive America*, Boston: Little, Brown

Rousseau, J-J (1968) *Politics and the Arts: A Letter to M D'Alembert on the Theatre*, ABloom, (trans) Ithaca NY: Cornell University Press

Rowe, C and Koetter, F (nd) *Collage City*, Cambridge, Mass

Runciman, W (1990) 'How many classes are there in contemporary British society?', *Sociology* 24 (3)

Rusche, George and Kirchheimer, Otto ([1939] 1968) *Punishment and Social Structure*, New York: Columbia University Press

Rutter, M (1972) *Maternal Deprivation Reassessed*, Harmondsworth: Penguin
- (1981) *Maternal Deprivation Reassessed* (2nd edn), Harmondsworth: Penguin

Sade, Marquis de ([1797]1968) *Juliette*, A Wainhouse trans New York: Grove Press

Sagarin, E, and Kelly, RJ (1981) 'Morality, Responsibility and the Law: An Existential Account', in H Laurence Ross (ed) *Law and Deviance*, London: Sage

Saint-Simon, Henri Comte (1952) *Selected Writings*, FMH Markham (ed), Oxford: Basil Blackwell

Samenow, Stanton, E (1984) *Inside the Criminal Mind*, New York: Times Books

Sampson, Robert, J (1987) 'Urban Black Violence: The Effect of Male Joblessness and Family Disruption', *American Journal of Sociology*, 93

Sampson, Robert J and Laub, John H (1993) *Crime in the Making: pathways and turning points through life*, Cambridge, Mass: Harvard University Press

Santos (1977) 'The Law of the Oppressed: A Construction and Reproduction of Legality in Pasargada', in *Law & Society Review*, Vol 12

Sartre, Jean-Paul (1956) *Being and Nothingness*, Hazel Barnes, trans New York: Philosophical Library

- (1965) *The Philosophy of Existentialism*, New York: Philosophical Library

Saunders, P (1990) *Social Class and Stratification*, London: Routledge

Schoenberger, K (1990) 'In Japan's Worst Slum, Angry Underclass Feels a Nation's Prejudice', *Los Angeles Times*, 30 October

Schoenthaler, S and Doraz, W (1983) 'Types of offenses which can be reduced in an institutional setting using nutritional intervention', *International Journal of Biosocial Research* 4

Schur, EM (1971) *Labelling deviant behaviour: Its sociological implications*, New York: Harper & Row

Schwendinger, Herman, and Schwendinger, Julia (1970) 'Defenders of Order or Guardians of Human Rights?', *Issues in Criminology*, 5

Scott, A (1988) *Metropolis: From the division of labour to urban form*, Berkeley, CA: University of California Press

Scull, AT (1976) 'Madness and Segregative Controls: The Rise of the Insane Aslum', *Social Problems*, 24
    - (1977) *Decarceration: Community Treatment and the Deviant - A Radical View*, Englewood Cliffs, NJ: Prentice-Hall

- (1979) *Museums of Madness: The Social Organisation of Insanity in Nineteenth-Century England*, London: Allen Lane

Scutt (1976) 'Role conditioning theory: an explanation for disparity in male and female criminality', *The Australian and New Zealand Journal of Criminology*, Vol 9

Selin, Thorsten (1938) *Culture, Conflict and Crime*, New York: The Social Science Research Council, Bulletin No 41

Sellin, Thorsten (1977) 'Beccaria's Substitute for the Death Penalty', in SF Landau and L Sebba (eds), *Criminology in Perspective*, Massachusetts: Lexington Books

Sharpe, S (1976) *Just Like a Girl - How girls learn to be women*, Harmondsworth: Penguin

Shavit, Y, and Rattner, A (1988) 'Age, crime, and the early life course', *American Journal of Sociology*, 93

Shaw, Clifford R, with Frederick M Zorbaugh, Henry D McKay, and Leonard S Cottrell (1929) *Delinquency Areas: A Study of the Geographic Distribution of School Truants, Juvenile Delinquents, and Adult Offenders in Chicago*, Chicago: University of Chicago Press

Shaw, Clifford R, and McKay, Henry, D (1931) *Social Factors in Juvenile Delinquency*, Washington, DC: Government Printing Office

- (1942) *Juvenile Delinquency and Urban Areas*, Chicago: University of Chicago Press

Shaw, Clifford R (1966, reissue) *The Jack-Roller*, Chicago: Phoenix

Sheldon, WH (with the collaboration of SS Stevens and WB Tucker) (1940) *The Varieties of Human Physique*, New York: Harper
- (with the collaboration of SS Stevens) (1942) *The Varieties of Temperament*, New York: Harper
- (with the collaboration of EM Hartl and E McDermott) (1949) *Varieties of Delinquent Youth*, New York: Harper

Shils, E (1981) *Tradition*, Chicago: University of Chicago Press

Short, JF (ed) (1968) *Gang Delinquency and Delinquent Subcultures*, New York: Harper & Row
- (1953) *Science and Human Behaviour*, New York: Macmillan

Shott, S (1979) 'Emotion and social life: a symbolic interactionist analysis', *American Journal of Sociology*, 84 (6)

Shover, NS Norland J James, and W Thornton (1979) 'Gender Roles and Delinquency', *Social Forces*, 58

Silverman, IJ and S Dinitz (1974) 'Compulsive Masculinity and Delinquency: An Empirical Investigation', *Criminology*, 11

Simmel, Georg ([1903] 1969) 'The Metropolis and Mental Life', in *Classic Essays on the Culture of Cities*, Richard Sennett (ed) New York: Appleton-Century-Crofts

Simmel, Georg (1971) *On Individuality and Social Forms*, Donald N Levine (ed), Chicago: University of Chicago Press

Simon, RJ (1975) *Women and Crime*, Lexington, Mass: Lexington Books

Singer (1973) *Democracy and Obedience*, Oxford: Oxford University Press

Sinha, M (1987) 'Gender and imperialism: colonial policy and the ideology of moral imperialism in late nineteenth century Bengal', in M Kimmel (ed), *Changing Men New Directions in Research on Men and Masculinity*, Newbury Park, CA: Sage

Skinner, Quentin (1978) *The Foundations of Modern Political Thought*, Cambridge: Cambridge University Press

Sluckin, W, Herbert, M, and Sluckin, A (1983) *Maternal Bonding*, Oxford: Blackwell

Smart, C (1976) *Women, Crime and Criminology, A Feminist Critique*, London: Routledge
- (1979) 'The New Female Criminal: Reality or Myth?', *British Journal of Criminology*, 19
- (1990) 'Feminist approaches to criminology', in L Gelsthorpe and A Morris (eds) *Feminist Perspectives in Criminology*, Milton Keynes: Open University Press

Smith, DR, Smith, WR & Noma, E (1984) 'Delinquent careers-lines: A conceptual link between theory and juvenile offenses', *Sociological Quarterly*, 25

Smith, D and Visher, C A (1980) 'Sex and Involvement in Deviance/Crime: A Quantitative Review of the Empirical Literature', *American Sociological Review*, 45

Smith, T (1990) 'The Obligation to Obey the Law: A New Theory and an Old Problem', *Osgoode Hall Law Journal*, vol 28 no: 4

Soper (1985) 'The Obligation to Obey the Law', in Gravison R (ed), *Issues in Contemporary Legal Philosophy - the Influence of HLA Hart*, Oxford: Oxford University Press

Spector, M (1981) 'Beyond Crime: Seven Methods to Control Troublesome Rascals', in *Law and Deviance*, Laurence Ross (ed), London: Sage

Spierenburg, Pieter (1984) *The Spectacle of Suffering: Executions and the evolution of repression: from a preindustrial metropolis to the european experience*, Cambridge: Cambridge University Press

Spiro, Melford E (1968) 'Culture and personality' in *International Encyclopedia of the Social Sciences*, 17 vols New York: MacMillan and Free Press

Stack, S (1983) 'Homicide and property crime: The relationships to anomie', *Aggressive Behaviour*, 9

Stanko, E (1984) *Intimate Intrusions*, London: Routledge and Kegan Paul
- (1990) *Everyday Violence*, London: Pandora

Staples, R (1982) *Black Masculinity: The Black Male's Role in American Society*, San Franciso: Black Scholar Press

Steffensmeier, DJ (1978) 'Crime and the Contemporary Woman: An Analysis of Changing Levels of Female Property Crime, 1960-1975', *Social Forces* 57
- (1981) 'Assessing the impact of the women's movement on sex-based differences
in the handling of adult criminal defendants', *Crime and Delinquency*, 26
- (1982) 'Trends in Female Crime: It's Still a Man's World', in BR Price and NJ Sokoloff (eds) *The Criminal Justice System and Women*, New York: Clark Broadman

Steffensmeier, D and RH Steffensmeier (1980) 'Trends in Female Delinquency: An Examination of Arrest, Juvenile Court, Self Report and Field Data', *Criminology* 18

Strauss, Leo (1953) *Natural Right and History*, Chicago/London: The University of Chicago Press

Strawson, PF (1974) *Freedom and Resentment*, London: Methuen

Sumner, Colin (1994) *The Sociology of Deviance: An Obituary*, Buckingham: Open University Press

Sumner, Graham (1906) *Folkways*, Boston: Ginnand Co

Sutherland, E (1924) *Criminology*, Philadelphia: JB Lippincott
 - (1926) 'The Biological and Sociological Processes', *Papers and Proceedings of the Twentieth Annual Meeting of the American Sociological Society*, 20
 - (1937) *The professional thief*, Chicago: University of Chicago Press
 - (1949) *White Collar Crime*, New York: Holt, Rinehart and Winston Inc

Suttles, G (1968) *The Social Order of the Slum*, Chicago: University of Chicago Press

Sykes, GM and Matza, David (1961) 'Delinquency and Subterranean Values', *American Sociological Review*, 26

Szasz, T (1961) *The Myth of Mental Illness*, New York: Harper and Row

Tannenbaum, Frank (1938) *Crime and the Community*, New York: Ginn

Tappan, PW (1947) 'Who is the criminal?', *American Sociological Review*, 12
 - (1960) *Crime, Justice and Correction*, London: McGraw-Hill

Taylor, Charles (1985) 'Atomism', in C Taylor, *Philosophy and the Human Sciences*, Cambridge: Cambridge University Press

Taylor, Ian (1994) 'The Political Economy of Crime', in Mike Maguire, Rod Morgan and Robert Reiner (eds) *The Oxford Handbook of Criminology*, Oxford: Oxford University Press

Taylor, Ian, Walton, Paul, and Young, Jock (1973) *The New Criminology: for a Social Theory of Deviance*, London: Routledge and Kegan Paul

Taylor, L (1984) *Born to Crime: the genetic causes of criminal behaviour*, London: Greenwood Press

Thielicke, Helmut (1969) *Nihilism: Its origin and nature - with a Christian Answer*, New York: Schoken

Thomas, WI (1907) *Sex and Society*, Boston: Little, Brown
 - (1923) *The Unadjusted Girl*, Boston: Little, Brown

Thomas, WI, and Znaniecki, Florian (1958) *The Polish Peasant in Europe and America: Behaviour Problems and Programs*, New York: Alfred A Knopf

Thompson, WE, Mitchell, J, and Dodder, R (1984) 'An empirical test of Hirschi's control theory of delinquency', *Deviant Behaviour*, 5

Thornberry, TP, Moore, M, and Christensen, RL (1985) 'The effect of dropping out of high school on subsequent criminal behaviour', *Criminology*, 23

Thornton, WE and J James (1979) 'Masculinity and Delinquency Revisited', *British Journal of Criminology*, 19

Thrasher, Fredrick M (1927, 1963) *The Gang: a Study of 1,313 Gangs in Chicago*, Chicago: University of Chicago Press

Tierney, K (1982) 'The battered women movement and the creation of the wife beating problem' *Social Problems*, 29

Tillich, Paul (1963) *Systematic Theology*, Vol III Chicago: The University of Chicago Press

Title, CR, Burke, MJ and Jackson, EF (1986) 'Modelling Sutherland's theory of differential association: Toward an empirical clarification', *Social Forces*, 65

Tittle, CR, Villemez, WJm & Smith, DA (1978) 'The myth of social class and criminality: An empirical assessment of the empirical evidence', *American Sociological Review*, 43

Tonnies, Ferdinand ([1877] 1955) *Community and Association (Gemeinschaft und Gesellschaft)*, CP Loomis (trans) London

Tonore (1981) 'Must we Obey? Necessity as a Ground of Obligation' *BA Law Review*, vol 67

Trotha, Trutz (1974) *Jugendliche Bandendelinquenz*, Stuttgart: Verlag

Udry, JR, (1974) *The Social Context of Marriage*, Philadelphia, Lippincott, Uhlman, Thomas and Darlene Walker

Unger, Roberto (1976) *Law in Modern Society*, New York: Basic Books
  – (1987) *Social Theory: Its Situation and Its Task: a critical introduction to Politics, a Work in Constructive Social Theory*, Cambridge: Cambridge University Press

Vold, George B (1958) *Theoretical Criminology*, New York: Oxford University Press

Vold, George B and Bernard, Thomas J (1978) *Theoretical Criminology*, (2nd ed) (1986) New York: Oxford University Press

Voltaire, FMA De (1901) *Works*, Vols 1 – 42, New York: ER Dumont

Voss, HL (1964) 'Differential association and delinquent behaviour', *Social Problems*, 12

Wagner, Peter (1994) *A Sociology of Modernity: Liberty and Discipline*, Routledge: London/New York

Walker, A, (1990) 'A Poor Idea of Poverty', *The Times Higher Education Supplement*, 17 August, 16

Walker, Nigel (1977) *Behaviour and Misbehaviour: explanations and non-explanations*, Oxford: Basil Blackwell

Walter, Glenn G (1990) *The Criminal Lifestyle: patterns of serious criminal conduct*, Newbury Park, CA: Sage

Walvin, J (1982) 'Black caricature: the roots of racialism' in C Husband (ed), *'Race', in Britain*, London: Hutchinson

- (1982) *A Child's World: A social history of English Childhood 1800-1914*, Harmondsworth: Penguin

Walzer, M (1983) *Spheres of Justice: a defence of Pluralism and Equality*, Oxford: Basil Blackwell

Warren, MQ (1983) 'Applications of interpersonal-maturity theory of offender populations', in WS Laufer and JM Day (eds), *Personality theory, moral development, and criminal behaviour*, Lexington, MA: Lexington Books

Webber, Storme (1992) 'To be a woman in New York City' in *The Popular Front of Contemporary Poetry Anthology*, London: Apples and Snakes

Weber, Max (1947) *The Theory of Social and Economic Organisations*, trans, by Talcot Parsons and A Henderson, New York: Free press
- (1984) 'Legitimacy, Politics and the State', in W Connolly ed *Legitimacy and The State*, Oxford: Basil Blackwell

West, DJ (1982) *Delinquency: Its Roots, Careers, and Prospects*, Cambridge Mass: Harvard University Press

West, DJ and Farrington, DP (1973) *Who Becomes Delinquent?*, London: Heinemann Educational
- (1977) *The Delinquent Way of Life*, London: Heinemann

West, DJ, Roy, C and Florence L Nicholas (1978) *Understanding Sexual Attacks*, London: Heinemann

West, R (1988) 'Jurisprudence and Gender', *University of Chicago Law Review*, 55

Whyte, W F (1943) *Street Corner Society*, Chicago: University of Chicago Press

Wiatrowski, MD, Griswold,DB and Roberts, MK (1981) 'Social control theory and delinquency', *American Sociological Review*, 46

Widom, CS (1976) 'Interpersonal conflict and cooperation in psychopaths', *Journal of Abnormal Psychology*, 85

Wiles, Paul (1971) 'Criminal Statistics and Sociological Explanations of Crime', in *Crime and Delinquency in Britain*, W Carson & Paul Wiles (eds), London: Martin Robertson

Wille, W (1974) *Citizens who commit murder*, St Louis: Warren Green

Williams, Katherine (1994) *A Textbook on Criminology*, London: Blackstone Press

Wilson, James Q (1975, rev ed 1983) *Thinking About Crime*, New York: Basic Books

Wilson, James Q and Herrnstein, Richard J (1985) *Crime & Human Nature: the definitive study of the causes of crime*, New York: Simon & Schuster

Wilson, W J (1987) *The truly Disadvantaged: The Inner City, the Underclass, and Public Policy*, Chicago: University of Chicago Press

- (1990) 'The Underclass: issues, perspectives and public policy', *Annals* (AAPSS), 501 (January)
- (1991) 'Studying Inner-City Social Dislocations: the Challenge of Public Agenda Research', *American Sociological Review*, Vol 56
- (1994) 'Citzenship and the Inner-City Ghetto Poor', In Bart van Steenbergen (ed) *The Condition of Citizenship*, London: Sage

Wolfgang, Marvin (1960) 'Cesare Lombrosso', In H Mannheim, (ed), *Pioneers in Criminology*, London: Stevens

Wolfgang, Marvin and Ferracuti, Franco (1967) *The Subculture of Violence: towards an integrated theory in criminology*, London: Social Science Paperbacks

Wolfgang, Marvin Savitz, L, and Johnston, N (eds) (1970) *The Sociology of Crime and Delinquency*, New York: Wiley

Wootton, B (1959) *Social Science and Social Pathology*, London: Allen and Unwin
- (1963) *Crime and The Criminal Law*, Hamlyn Lecture Series, London: Stevens and Sons

Worral, A (1990) *Offending Women: Female Lawbreakers and the Criminal Justice System*, London: Routledge

Yochelson, S, and Samenow, SE (1976) *The criminal personality: VolI A profile for change*, New York: Jason Aronson
- (1985) *The criminal personality: Vol II The change process* (reved), New York: Jason Aronson
- (1986) *The criminal personality: Vol III The drug user*, New York: Jason Aronson

Yoshimasu, S (1961) 'The criminological significance of the family in the light of the studies of criminal twins', *Acta Criminologiae et Medicinae Legalis Japanica* 27

Young, Allison (1990) *Femininity in Dissent*, London: Routledge

Young, Jock (1986) 'The failure of Criminology: the need for radical realism', in R Matthews and J Young (eds) *Confronting Crime*, London: Sage
- (1987) 'The Tasks of a Realist Criminology', *Contemporary Crises*, 11
- (1992) 'Ten points of realism', in Young, Jock and Matthews, Roger (1992) *Rethinking Criminology: the realist debate*, London: Sage

Zedner, L (1991) *Women, Crime and Custody in Victorian England*, Oxford: Clarendon Press

Zukin, S (1992) 'The City as a landscape of power: London and New York as global financial capitals', in L Budd and S Whimister (eds), *Global Finance and urban living: the case of London*, London: Routledge

INDEX

Index

Index

Lightning Source UK Ltd.
Milton Keynes UK
UKOW040704300312

189875UK00001B/53/A